"Novakovic provides a welcome and long-anticipated contribution to the Baylor Handbook on the Greek New Testament series. Tackling the deceptive simplicity of John's language, Novakovic deftly untangles John's subtlety and takes up grammatical questions too often overlooked in commentaries or dismissed by those too focused on John's 'elementary Greek.' Her insights not only guide readers just beginning to learn more about Greek syntax but also engage seasoned scholars by offering detailed interpretations with ranging interpretive and theological possibilities."

—**Alicia Myers**, *Associate Professor of New Testament & Greek, Divinity School, Campbell University*

"Because grammar and syntax are the foundations for interpretation, this handbook is a valuable resource for serious students of the Gospel of John. In the introduction Novakovic briefly summarizes distinctive characteristics of the Gospel's vocabulary and style, repetition and variation, tenses and verbal aspect, and word order. The translation provides a fresh, literal rendering of the Greek text, which is itself often a guide to interpretation. While this is not a commentary, the annotations on well-known cruxes of interpretation are remarkably insightful. These are volumes you will want to keep on your desk!"

—**R. Alan Culpepper**, *Dean and Professor of New Testament Emeritus, McAfee School of Theology, Mercer University*

"The aim of this series is to supplement standard New Testament commentaries with an 'accessible and succinct' guide to the dynamics of the Greek text, and in these volumes Lidija Novakovic does this for the Fourth Gospel with precision, care, and clarity. Her methodological assumptions are crafted with considered sensitivity to scholarly discussion on Johannine style. Her glossary furnishes a ready means for entering the kind of discourse required by syntactical and text-critical issues. Her analysis, itself, while comprehensive, is consciously pitched to the problems most challenging for interpretation."

—**Michael A. Daise**, *Walter G. Mason Professor, College of William & Mary*

BHGNT

Baylor Handbook on the Greek New Testament
Lidija Novakovic
General Editor

OTHER BOOKS IN THIS SERIES

John 11–21	Lidija Novakovic
Matthew 1–14	Wesley G. Olmstead
Matthew 15–28	Wesley G. Olmstead
Mark 1–8	Rodney J. Decker
Mark 9–16	Rodney J. Decker
Luke	Martin M. Culy, Mikeal C. Parsons, and Joshua J. Stigall
Acts	Martin M. Culy and Mikeal C. Parsons
1 Corinthians 1–9	Timothy A. Brookins and Bruce W. Longenecker
1 Corinthians 10–16	Timothy A. Brookins and Bruce W. Longenecker
2 Corinthians	Fredrick J. Long
Galatians	David A. deSilva
Ephesians	William J. Larkin
Colossians and Philemon	Constantine R. Campbell
The Pastoral Letters	Larry J. Perkins
James	A. K. M. Adam
1 Peter	Mark Dubis
2 Peter and Jude	Peter H. Davids
1, 2, 3 John	Martin M. Culy
Revelation	David L. Mathewson

JOHN 1–10

A Handbook on the Greek Text

Lidija Novakovic

BAYLOR UNIVERSITY PRESS

© 2020 by Baylor University Press
Waco, Texas 76798

All Rights Reserved. No part of this publication may be reproduced, stored in a retrieval system, or transmitted, in any form or by any means, electronic, mechanical, photocopying, recording, or otherwise, without the prior permission in writing of Baylor University Press.

Typesetting by Scribe Inc.
Cover Design by Pamela Poll

The Library of Congress has cataloged this book under the
ISBN978- 1-4813-0575-4.

CONTENTS

Series Introduction	ix
Preface	xv
Abbreviations	xvii
Introduction	xxi
John 1:1-5	1
John 1:6-8	6
John 1:9-13	7
John 1:14-18	12
John 1:19-28	19
John 1:29-34	28
John 1:35-42	35
John 1:43-51	43
John 2:1-11	51
John 2:12-17	60
John 2:18-22	65
John 2:23-25	70
John 3:1-12	72
John 3:13-21	83
John 3:22-30	93

John 3:31-36	100
John 4:1-3	105
John 4:4-26	107
John 4:27-30	126
John 4:31-38	129
John 4:39-42	135
John 4:43-45	137
John 4:46-54	139
John 5:1-18	146
John 5:19-29	160
John 5:30-47	169
John 6:1-15	181
John 6:16-21	190
John 6:22-24	194
John 6:25-29	197
John 6:30-35	201
John 6:36-40	206
John 6:41-51	210
John 6:52-58	217
John 6:59-71	223
John 7:1-9	232
John 7:10-13	237
John 7:14-24	240
John 7:25-31	248
John 7:32-36	253
John 7:37-39	257
John 7:40-44	260

John 7:45-52	263
John 7:53-8:11	268
John 8:12-20	275
John 8:21-30	282
John 8:31-36	291
John 8:37-47	294
John 8:48-59	305
John 9:1-7	314
John 9:8-12	319
John 9:13-23	323
John 9:24-34	332
John 9:35-41	340
John 10:1-6	345
John 10:7-10	350
John 10:11-13	353
John 10:14-18	356
John 10:19-21	360
John 10:22-30	361
John 10:31-39	367
John 10:40-42	375
Glossary	377
Works Cited	387
Author Index	397
Grammar Index	402

SERIES INTRODUCTION

The Baylor Handbook on the Greek New Testament (BHGNT) is designed to guide new readers and seasoned scholars alike through the intricacies of the Greek text. Each handbook provides a verse-by-verse treatment of the biblical text. Unlike traditional commentaries, however, the BHGNT makes no attempt to expound on the theological meaning or significance of the document under consideration. Instead, the handbooks serve as supplements to commentary proper. Readers of traditional commentaries are sometimes dismayed by the fact that even those that are labeled "exegetical" or "critical" frequently have little to say about the mechanics of the Greek text and all too often completely ignore the more perplexing grammatical issues. In contrast, the BHGNT offers an accessible and comprehensive, though not exhaustive, treatment of the Greek New Testament, with particular attention given to the grammar of the text. In order to make the handbooks more user friendly, authors have only selectively interacted with secondary literature. Where there is significant debate on an issue, the handbooks provide a representative sample of scholars espousing each position; when authors adopt a less known stance on the text, they generally list any other scholars who have embraced that position.

The BHGNT, however, is more than a reliable guide to the Greek text of the New Testament. Each author brings unique strengths to the task of preparing the handbook, such as textual criticism, lexical semantics, discourse analysis, or other areas. As a result, students and scholars alike will at times be introduced to ways of looking at the Greek language that they have not encountered before. This feature makes the handbooks valuable not only for intermediate and advanced Greek courses, but also for students and scholars who no longer have the luxury of increasing their Greek proficiency within a classroom context. While handbook authors do not consider modern linguistic theory to be a panacea for all questions exegetical, the BHGNT does aim both to help move linguistic insights into the mainstream of New Testament reference works and, at the same time, to help weed out some of the myths about the Greek language that continue to appear in both scholarly and popular treatments of the New Testament.

Using the Baylor Handbook on the Greek New Testament

Each handbook consists of the following features. The introduction draws readers' attention to some of the distinctive characteristics of the New Testament document under consideration and treats some of the broader issues relating to the text as a whole in a more thorough fashion. In the handbook proper, the biblical text is divided into sections, each of which is introduced with a translation that illustrates how the insights gleaned from the analysis that follows may be expressed in modern English. Following the translation is the heart of the handbook, an extensive analysis of the Greek text. Here, the Greek text of each verse is followed by comments on grammatical, lexical, and text-critical issues. Every verb is parsed for the sake of pedagogical expediency, while nouns are parsed only when the form is unusual or requires additional explanation. Handbook authors may also make use of other features, such as passage overviews between the translation and notes.

Each page of the handbook includes a header to help readers quickly locate comments on a particular passage. Terminology used in the comments that is potentially unfamiliar is included in a glossary in the back of the handbook and/or cross-referenced with the first occurrence of the expression, where an explanation may be found. This is followed by a bibliography of works cited, providing helpful guidance in identifying resources for further research on the Greek text. Each volume concludes with a grammar index and an author index. The list of grammatical phenomena occurring in the biblical text provides a valuable resource for students of Greek wanting to study a particular construction more carefully or Greek instructors needing to develop illustrations, exercises, or exams.

The handbooks assume that users will possess a minimal level of competence with Greek morphology and syntax. Series authors generally utilize traditional labels such as those found in Daniel Wallace's *Greek Grammar beyond the Basics*. Labels that are drawn from the broader field of modern linguistics are explained at their first occurrence and included in the glossary. Common labels that users may be unfamiliar with are also included in the glossary.

The primary exception to the broad adoption of traditional syntactic labels relates to verb tenses. Most New Testament Greek grammars describe the tense system as being formally fairly simple (only six tenses) but functionally complex. The aorist tense, it is frequently said, can function in a wide variety of ways that are associated with labels such as "ingressive," "gnomic," "constative," "epistolary," "proleptic," and so forth. Similar functional complexity is posited for the other tenses. Positing such functions, however, typically stems not from a careful analysis of Greek syntax but rather from grappling with the challenges of translating Greek verbs into English. When we carefully examine the Greek verb tenses, we find that the tense forms do not themselves denote semantic features such as ingressive, iterative, or conative; at best they may allow for ingressive, iterative, or conative translations. In addition, the tense labels have frequently led to exegetical claims that go beyond the syntax. For this reason, handbook authors do not generally utilize these labels but seek to express nuances typically associated with them in the translation.

Avoidance of traditional tense labels is based on the insights gained from the discussions about verbal aspect theory over the past three decades, which distinguish *Aktionsart* (kind of action) from aspect (subjective portrayal of an action). Many contributors to the BHGNT series agree with the basic premise of verbal aspect theory that tense forms do not grammaticalize time and adopt a three-aspect paradigm that differentiates between perfective aspect, imperfective aspect, and stative aspect. Some authors also concur with Stanley Porter's (1989; 1994) claim about different levels of semantic density or markedness, i.e., the concept of the perfective aspect as the least marked (background), the imperfective aspect as more marked (foreground), and the stative aspect as the most marked aspect (frontground). There is, however, still significant scholarly disagreement concerning the nature of verbal aspects and their semantic functions. Constantine Campbell (2008), for example, identifies the Greek perfect not with stative aspect, like Porter and others, but with imperfective aspect with heightened remoteness, which he describes as a dynamic action in progress. Steven Runge (2014), conversely, challenges the foundational idea of Porter's verbal aspect theory that Greek tense forms do not have temporal references and argues for a mixed time-aspect system. Handbook authors are encouraged to interact with these and other discussions about verbal aspect and incorporate their insights in the analysis of the Greek text.

Deponency

Although series authors will vary in the theoretical approaches they bring to the text, the BHGNT has adopted the same general approach on one important issue: deponency. Traditionally, the label "deponent" has been applied to verbs with middle, passive, or middle/passive morphology that are thought to be "active" in meaning. Introductory grammars tend to put a significant number of middle verbs in the New Testament in this category, despite the fact that some of the standard reference grammars have questioned the validity of the label. Archibald Robertson (332), for example, argues that the label "should not be used at all."

In recent years, a number of scholars have taken up Robertson's quiet call to abandon this label. Carl Conrad's posts on the B-Greek Internet discussion list (beginning in 1997) and his subsequent formalization of those concerns in unpublished papers available on his website have helped flesh out the concerns raised by earlier scholars. In his essay, "New Observations on Voice in the Ancient Greek Verb," Conrad argues that the Greek voice system is not built upon trichotomy (active, middle, and passive) but upon a bipolar basis (active and middle/passive). He further claims that the verbs that have been traditionally termed "deponent" are by their nature subject focused, like the forms that are regarded as genuine middle, and suggests that "both term and concept of 'Deponency' should be eliminated forever from formal categories and thinking about ancient Greek voice" (11). Similar conclusions are reached by Jonathan Pennington (60–64), who helpfully summarizes the rationale for dispensing with the label, maintaining that widespread use of the term "deponent" stems from two key factors: (1) the tendency to analyze Greek syntax through reference to English translation—if a workable translation of a middle form appears "active" in English, we conclude that the verb must be active in meaning even though it is middle in form; and (2) the imposition of Latin categories on Greek grammar. Pennington concludes, "Most if not all verbs that are considered 'deponent' are in fact truly middle in meaning" (61).

The questions that have been raised regarding deponency as a syntactic category, then, are not simply issues that interest a few Greek scholars and linguists without much bearing on how one understands the text. Rather, the notion of deponency has, at least in some cases, effectively obscured the semantic significance of the middle voice, leading to imprecise readings of the text (see also Bakker; Taylor). It is not only middle-voice verbs, however, that are the focus of attention in this debate. Conrad, Pennington, and others also maintain that deponency is an invalid category for passive verbs that have traditionally been placed in this category. To account for putative passive deponent verbs, these scholars have turned to the evolution of voice morphology in the Greek language. They draw attention to the fact that middle morphology was being replaced by passive morphology (the θη morpheme) during the Koine period (see esp. Conrad, 3, 5–6; cf. Pennington, 68; Taylor, 175; Caragounis, 153). Consequently, in the Common Era we find "an increasing number of passive forms without a distinctive passive idea . . . replacing older middle forms" (Pennington, 68). This diachronic argument leads Conrad (5) to conclude that the θη morpheme should be treated as a middle/passive rather than a passive morpheme. Such arguments have a sound linguistic foundation and raise serious questions about the legitimacy of the notion "passive deponent."

Should, then, the label "deponent" be abandoned altogether? While more research needs to be done to account for middle/passive morphology in Koine Greek fully, the arguments are both compelling and exegetically significant. Consequently, users of the BHGNT will discover that verbs that are typically labeled "deponent," including some with θη morphology, tend to be listed as "middle" or "middle/passive."

In recognizing that so-called deponent verbs should be viewed as true middles, users of the BHGNT should not fall into the trap of concluding that the middle form emphasizes the subject's involvement in the action of the verb. At times, the middle voice appears simply to be a morphological flag indicating that the verb is intransitive. More frequently, the middle morphology tends to be driven by the "middle" semantics of the verb itself. In other words, the middle voice is sometimes used with the verb not in order to place a focus on the subject's involvement in the action, but precisely because the sense of the lexical form itself involves subject focus.

It is the hope of Baylor University Press, the series editors, and each of the authors that these handbooks will help advance our understanding of the Greek New Testament, be used to equip further pastors and other church leaders for the work of ministry, and fan into flame a love for the Greek New Testament among a new generation of students and scholars.

Martin M. Culy
Founding Series Editor

Lidija Novakovic
Series Editor

PREFACE

I would like to thank Carey Newman, director of Baylor University Press, who in 2015 invited me to serve as editor of the BHGNT series, which gave me the opportunity to refine my editorial skills before I undertook the task of writing one of the handbooks myself. I am also grateful to the Baylor Arts & Sciences Research Leave Committee for awarding me a research leave in the spring of 2018, which allowed me to complete the greater part of this project. Special thanks are due to my graduate assistants Jeremiah Bailey, who did the initial parsing of most of the verbs, and Daniel Glover, who helped with proofreading. Above all, I am indebted to John Genter, who not only proofread the entire manuscript but also prepared the abbreviations list and the glossary. I also wish to thank my husband, Ivo Novakovic, and my children, Andreja and Matthew. I could not have finished this project, which required countless hours of painstaking work, without their continuous support.

I wish to dedicate this handbook to the memory of Claus Meister, my first Greek teacher at the Baptist Theological Seminary, Rüschlikon, whose ingenious explanations of grammatical intricacies instilled in me a deep love for the Greek language. It was his textbook with selected readings that gave me a chance to read my first sentence in Greek: Ἐν ἀρχῇ ἦν ὁ λόγος, καὶ ὁ λόγος ἦν πρὸς τὸν θεόν, καὶ θεὸς ἦν ὁ λόγος (John 1:1).

ABBREVIATIONS

1st	first person
2nd	second person
2 Pet	2 Peter
3rd	third person
acc	accusative
act	active
aor	aorist
ASV	American Standard Version
BCE	Before the Common Era
BDAG	Danker, *A Greek-English Lexicon of the New Testament*, 2000
BDB	Brown, Driver, Briggs, *A Hebrew and English Lexicon of the Old Testament*
BDF	Blass, Debrunner, Funk, *A Greek Grammar of the New Testament*
CEB	Common English Bible
ch.	chapter
cf.	compare (*confer*)
CJB	Complete Jewish Bible
dat	dative
DBY	The Darby Bible
e.g.	for example (*exempli gratia*)
ESV	English Standard Version

et al.	and others (*et alii*)
fem	feminine
FG	Fourth Gospel
fut	future
gen	genitive
GNT	Good News Translation
GW	God's Word
HCSB	Holman Christian Standard Bible
HP	historical present
i.e.	that is (*id est*)
impf	imperfect
impv	imperative
ind	indicative
inf	infinitive
JB	Jerusalem Bible
J.W.	*Bellum judaicum* (*Jewish War*)
KJV	King James Version
LEB	The Lexham English Bible
lit.	literally
LN	Louw and Nida, *Greek-English Lexicon*
LSJ	Liddell, Scott, Jones, *A Greek-English Lexicon*
LXX	Septuagint
masc	masculine
MHT	Moulton, Howard, Turner, *A Grammar of New Testament Greek*, 4 vols.
mid	middle
MSG	The Message
MSS/mss	manuscripts
MT	Masoretic Text
n.	note
NA^{28}	Nestle-Aland, *Novum Testamentum Graece*, 28th ed.
NAB	New American Bible

NASB	New American Standard Bible
NCV	New Century Version
NEB	New English Bible
NET	New English Translation
neut	neuter
NIV	New International Version
NKJV	New King James Version
NLT	New Living Translation
nom	nominative
NRSV	New Revised Standard Version
NT	New Testament
NWT	New World Translation
opt	optative
OT	Old Testament
pace	with deference to
pass	passive
pl	plural
plprf	pluperfect
PN	predicate nominative
PP	prepositional phrase
pres	present
prf	perfect
ptc	participle
REB	Revised English Bible
RHE	Douay-Rheims Catholic Bible (English translation of the Vulgate)
RSV	Revised Standard Version
SBLGNT	The SBL Greek New Testament
sg	singular
subj	subjunctive
TCNT	Twentieth Century New Testament
TDNT	Kittel, *Theological Dictionary of the New Testament*, 10 vols.

TSKS	article-substantive-καί-substantive (relating to Granville Sharp's rule)
UBS⁵	The United Bible Societies' Greek New Testament, 5th ed.
v./vv.	verse/verses
voc	vocative
WBT	Webster Bible
WYC	Wycliffe Bible

INTRODUCTION

The Gospel of John, habitually called the Fourth Gospel because of its placement in the New Testament canon, is sometimes described as "a book in which a child can wade and an elephant can swim" (Barackman, 63). Indeed, the profound theology of the Fourth Gospel is expressed through one of the most accessible Greek texts. Consisting of twenty-one chapters, 879 verses, and 15,635 words, the Gospel of John employs only 1,011 different words. Compared with 1,345 different words used by Mark, 1,691 different words used by Matthew, and 2,055 different words used by Luke, John's vocabulary is quite limited. Barrett rightly notes, however, that "[i]n spite of the small vocabulary the reader never receives the impression of an ill-equipped writer at a loss for the right word" (7). The syntax of John's sentences is also less complicated than that of the Synoptic Gospels. Individual clauses are typically linked by καί (parataxis) rather than by subordinating conjunctions and participles, or they are laid side by side without the use of any coordinating conjunctions (asyndeton).

Yet the apparent simplicity of John's language and syntax could be deceptive. As I methodically worked through the text of the Fourth Gospel, I encountered numerous convoluted constructions that are only sporadically explained in standard grammars and commentaries. The purpose of this handbook is to help students, pastors, and interested scholars better understand the grammar and syntax of the Greek text of John's Gospel. I wish to emphasize that this is not a commentary but a prequel or a supplement to a commentary. The questions of authorship, sociohistorical context, compositional history, structure, and theology of the Fourth Gospel are not addressed here. Rather, I seek to explain the syntactical role of individual words, phrases, and clauses in the canonical version of the Gospel of John. I have also provided comments on major text-critical issues in the Greek text, using the critical apparatus in the 28th edition of Nestle-Aland, *Novum Testamentum Graece*. My translations correspond to my grammatical explanations, seeking to approximate the syntax—even when it is cumbersome or runs counter to the default English word order—and function of the Greek text as much as possible for educational purposes. I have used square brackets in the translations to indicate that the English words within them do not have equivalents in the Greek text.

John's Style

In addition to the use of parataxis and asyndeton mentioned above, one of the distinguishing characteristics of the style of the Fourth Gospel is the numerous repetitions of words, phrases, or clauses. For example, the prepositional phrases μετὰ τοῦτο (2:12; 11:7, 11; 19:28) and μετὰ ταῦτα (3:22; 5:1, 14; 6:1; 7:1; 13:7; 21:1) are routinely used to indicate a transition to a new scene or to a new section. The formulaic clause ἀμὴν λέγω ὑμῖν/σοι introduces Jesus' declarations twenty-five times (1:51; 3:3, 5, 11; 5:19, 24, 25; 6:26, 32, 47, 53; 8:34, 51, 58; 10:1, 7; 12:24; 13:16, 20, 21, 38; 14:12; 16:20, 23; 21:18). The ἐγώ εἰμι saying is repeatedly used as an absolute statement (6:20; 8:24, 28, 58; 13:19; 18:5, 6, 8) or is followed by a predicate that metaphorically describes what Jesus is: "the bread of life" (6:35, 48, 51), "the light of the world" (8:12; 9:5), "the door for the sheep" (10:7, 9), "the good shepherd" (10:11, 14), "the resurrection and the life" (11:25), "the way, the truth, and the life" (14:6), and "the true vineyard" (15:1, 5). The evangelist sometimes repeats entire clauses verbatim: ἔμπροσθέν μου γέγονεν, ὅτι πρῶτός μου ἦ (1:15 and 1:30), κἀγὼ οὐκ ᾔδειν αὐτόν (1:31 and 1:33), Ἐγώ εἰμι ὁ ἄρτος τῆς ζωῆς (6:35 and 6:48), ἐγὼ ἐν τῷ πατρὶ καὶ ὁ πατὴρ ἐν ἐμοί (14:10 and 14:11), οὐκ ἔστιν δοῦλος μείζων τοῦ κυρίου αὐτοῦ (13:16 and 15:20), ἐν τῷ ὀνόματί σου ᾧ δέδωκάς μοι (17:11 and 17:12), οὐκ εἰσὶν ἐκ τοῦ κόσμου καθὼς ἐγὼ οὐκ εἰμὶ ἐκ τοῦ κόσμου (17:14 and 17:16), Ἦν δὲ Σίμων Πέτρος ἑστὼς καὶ θερμαινόμενος (18:18 and 18:25), μὴ καὶ σὺ ἐκ τῶν μαθητῶν αὐτοῦ εἶ (18:17 and 18:25), σημαίνων ποίῳ θανάτῳ ἤμελλεν ἀποθνῄσκειν (12:33 and 18:32), ἦραν τὸν κύριον ἐκ τοῦ μνημείου καὶ οὐκ οἴδαμεν ποῦ ἔθηκαν αὐτόν (20:2 and 20:13), and γύναι, τί κλαίεις (20:13 and 20:15). There is a growing recognition among Johannine scholars that "to speak about repetition and variation is to speak about the style of John's Gospel. Style in the last analysis consists of the eternal repetition and variation of an otherwise limited vocabulary" (Van Belle, 31). In his study of the relationship between repetition and functionality in the Fourth Gospel, van der Watt concludes that "repetition and variation are *inter alia* functionally employed to develop a particular concept, reminding the implied reader of a concept in relation to others, linking different contexts together aiming at developing the relationship between the concepts mentioned in those contexts" (2009, 108).

Other distinguishing markers of John's peculiar style include his frequent use of οὖν as a transitional particle rather than as an inferential conjunction and of ἐκεῖνος as a third-person personal pronoun rather than as a demonstrative pronoun. The prepositional phrase ἐκ + genitive is used in place of the partitive genitive fifty-two times. The subordinate conjunction ἵνα introduces not only purpose clauses but also epexegetical clauses (eighteen times). The Fourth Evangelist is also fond of various point/counterpoint sets, such as οὐκ/μὴ ... ἀλλά (thirty times) and οὐκ/οὐδεὶς ... εἰ μή (eight times). He also likes to use words or phrases that are open to two interpretations (double entendre), such as κατέλαβεν (1:5), ὁ ζῆλος (2:17), ἄνωθεν (3:3, 7), ὕδωρ ζῶν (4:10), δοξάζω (7:39; 12:16, 23; 13:31, 32; 17:1), ὑπάγω (8:21), κεκοίμηται (11:11), and ἀναστήσεται (11:23).

John's limited vocabulary and distinctive literary style, especially the use of parataxis, asyndeton, and the epexegetical ἵνα clauses, are usually explained by presuming some Semitic influence on the Greek text, although most scholars today reject the idea, proposed by Burney and Torrey in the early twentieth century, that the Fourth Gospel is a Greek translation of a lost Aramaic original. The most evident influence is the appearance of various Aramaic words that are transliterated and then translated into Greek, such as ῥαββί, ὃ λέγεται μεθερμηνευόμενον διδάσκαλε (1:38; cf. 20:16), τὸν Μεσσίαν, ὅ ἐστιν μεθερμηνευόμενον χριστός (1:41; cf. 4:25), Κηφᾶς, ὃ ἑρμηνεύεται Πέτρος (1:42), or Θωμᾶς ὁ λεγόμενος Δίδυμος (11:16; 21:2), as well as the frequent use of the pleonastic clause καὶ εἶπαν/εἶπεν αὐτῷ/αὐτῇ/αὐτοῖς (thirty times).

Verbal Aspect

This handbook incorporates major insights of verbal aspect theory advanced by McKay, Porter, Fanning, and Campbell. It presumes that a speaker or writer grammaticalizes a view of a particular situation by selecting a particular verb form in the verbal system: the aorist tense if the situation is viewed as a complete event without regard for its progress (perfective aspect), the present or imperfect tense if the situation is viewed as in progress without regard for its beginning and end (imperfective aspect), and the perfect or pluperfect tense if a writer depicts a state of affairs that exists with no reference to any progress (stative aspect). Although I do not agree with Campbell's view that the perfect tense grammaticalizes imperfective aspect, I find his suggestion that the distinguishing semantic quality of the perfect tense is heightened proximity with intensive implicature (2007, 195–201) applicable to some contexts (e.g., the intensive rendering of ἕστηκεν in 1:26 or πεπιστεύκαμεν in 6:69).

Regarding the contentious question of whether Greek tenses carry any temporal references, I side with scholars who think that in the indicative mood Greek verbs do encode time. I am not persuaded by Porter's (1989, 75–83) test of contrastive substitution, i.e., the reasoning that if different tense forms could be used in the same context or, conversely, if the identical tense form could be used in different temporal contexts, we must conclude that Greek verbs do not grammaticalize time (Porter 1993, 32; for a critique of Porter's argument, see Runge 2014, 154–73). To expect that a verb tense must always have the same temporal reference is to create an absolute category into which no language could fit. Runge rightly points out that "[e]ven a highly time-oriented verbal system like English does not grammaticalize uncancelable, absolute temporal references" (167). Another observation that supports the idea that in the indicative mood Greek verbs encode time is the existence of two tense forms (the present and the imperfect) that convey imperfective aspect and two tense forms (the perfect and the pluperfect) that convey stative aspect. In a recent article that examines cross-linguistic evidence for polysemous past tenses, Fresch concludes that "there is substantial reason to regard +PFV [perfective aspect] and +PAST [past-temporal reference] as semantic components of the aorist indicative," though he adds that, "in a perfective past verb form, such as the aorist, perfective aspect will typically be the dominant component and the past-temporal reference will be secondary" (410).

Although my analysis of the Fourth Gospel is informed by the above understanding of the semantics of Greek verbs, my task in this handbook is pragmatic: to interpret aspect and the temporal dimension of verbs as they are used in specific passages. Since I do not understand temporal information grammaticalized by the indicative mood absolutely, I have paid attention to various contextual features and asked how they inform the meaning and function of individual verbs.

The aorist indicative is the default tense form in the Fourth Gospel (used 836 times), which is not surprising given its narrative genre. It is primarily used to portray the events that constitute the main story line. The imperfect tense occurs 289 times. Its less frequent use in the narrative, however, is not a sufficient reason to regard it as a tense that carries more prominence than the aorist, as Porter (1989, 92–93) claims.

The primary function of the imperfect is "to provide background details about events, persons and other features of the mainline narrative. These expressions, which are generally short and often parenthetic, typically appear anywhere inside the body of the episode" (du Toit, 222). Levinsohn (2000, 174) claims that the imperfective aspect of the imperfect makes it especially suitable to convey the information that is of less importance than the information conveyed through the aorist in the main storyline. This does not mean, however, that every imperfect verb is less prominent than the aorist. The particular function of the imperfect depends on a correlation between its imperfective aspect and the specific background information it conveys. For example, the likely effect of using the imperfect ἔλεγεν in 8:31 is foregrounding because it does not describe an event that can be viewed as being in progress (cf. Levinsohn 2000, 175; 2016, 169–70).

The perfect indicative plays an important role in the Fourth Gospel because it allows the evangelist to emphasize the ongoing relevance of God's and Jesus' acts in relation to each other and to believers. Of 206 perfect indicatives in John, 198 (96 percent) occur within indirect discourse. In most of these occurrences, the semantic weight of the perfect tense corresponds to its prominence in the text or, to use Porter's term, the perfect tense is frontgrounded (1989, 92–93). Frey is therefore right to conclude that "the use of the perfect here results from an authorial choice of the linguistic expression. It characterizes the Johannine style and expresses, beyond this, the constitutive relatedness of the post-Easter community to the enduringly valid word and work of Christ and his connection back to the initiative of the Father, who sent and authorized him" (2018, 81). The perfect tense is particularly prominent in connection with specific lexemes such as δίδωμι, ἀποστέλλω, ὁράω, and λαλέω. The perfect tense of δίδωμι conveys the idea "that what the Father 'has given' to the Son . . . is definitively in his hand," of ἀποστέλλω that "the sending of Jesus . . . is regarded not only as an act of the past but as the enduring foundation of the sending of the disciples," of ὁράω "that what the Son 'has seen' . . . stays enduringly before his eyes," and of λαλέω that what Jesus "'has spoken' . . . is enduringly valid revelation" (81).

The distribution of the historical presents in the Fourth Gospel is uneven, occurring mostly in chapters 1, 4, 13, 20, and 21. One of its main functions is to indicate structural or thematic prominence, i.e., to help the readers/hearers discern the themes to which they should pay attention. The use of the historical present with the verbs of speaking, which is by far the most frequent use of the historical present in John's

Gospel (119 forms of λέγω out of 164 historical presents), however, is not to mark the action of speaking for prominence. Rather, as Runge explains, "attention is drawn prospectively to the speech that the quotative frame introduces" (2010, 137 n. 45).

Word Order

I have frequently called attention to word order that differs from the default order of a Greek clause in which the finite verb is placed in the initial position (Levinsohn 2000, 38). When other elements of a clause are placed before the verb, i.e., when they are "fronted," they receive more prominence, but the pragmatic effect of such a departure from the standard word order could be varied. I have adopted Runge's view that "[p]lacing nonfocal information in [the] clause-initial position has the effect of establishing an explicit frame of reference for the clause that follows. It does not result in emphasis. By definition, emphasis refers to taking what was already most important in a clause and placing it ... at the beginning of the clause" (2010, 224). Similarly, when the verb is placed at the end of a clause, the most likely pragmatic effect is that the verb becomes the focal point of a clause. My comments on the specific functions of clausal elements that depart from the default word order are generally informed by the *Lexham Discourse Greek New Testament*.

I have also adopted Runge's suggestion that various cleft constructions should be interpreted linguistically as dislocations. I have identified forty-four left-dislocations, "where the new entity is dislocated to the beginning of the clause and then resumed in the main clause through the use of a pronominal trace" (2010, 289), and eleven right-dislocations, which entail "referring to a participant in the midst of a clause using a pronoun or generic phrase and then adding more information about the same participant at the end of the clause" (317), in the Fourth Gospel. The categories of left- and right-dislocations allow us to understand various detachment constructions, which are typical for John's syntax, not as cumbersome structures due to the evangelist's limited linguistic skills but as convenient rhetorical devices that are frequently more effective in introducing new entities, especially when they are complex, than the more conventional methods. To approximate the structure of the Greek sentence in the translation without sacrificing clarity, I have frequently used the em dash (—) to indicate the end of the left-dislocation and the beginning of the main clause.

A HANDBOOK ON THE GREEK TEXT OF
JOHN 1-10

John 1:1-5

¹In the beginning the Word [already] was, and the Word was in fellowship with God, and the Word was God. ²He was in the beginning with God. ³All things came into being through him, and without him not even one thing came into being that has come into being. ⁴In him was life, and that life was the light of human beings. ⁵And the light shines in the darkness, and the darkness did not apprehend it.

1:1 Ἐν ἀρχῇ ἦν ὁ λόγος, καὶ ὁ λόγος ἦν πρὸς τὸν θεόν, καὶ θεὸς ἦν ὁ λόγος.

Ἐν ἀρχῇ. Temporal. The article is often omitted in prepositional phrases that designate time (BDF §255.3; Robertson, 791). Since this PP is most likely an allusion to ἐν ἀρχῇ in LXX Gen 1:1, the anarthrous ἀρχῇ is definite ("in [the] beginning"; cf. Porter 1994, 105), referring to the beginning of the creation (see 1:3). In this clause, Ἐν ἀρχῇ is fronted as a temporal frame, which establishes an explicit frame of reference for the first declaration about ὁ λόγος, the main topic of the prologue (Runge 2010, 210-11).

ἦν. Impf act ind 3rd sg εἰμί. Because Greek does not distinguish between the imperfect and the aorist verb forms of εἰμί, ἦν is "aspectually vague" (Porter 1989, 443). The combination of the stative ἦν and the temporal PP Ἐν ἀρχῇ referring to "a point of time at the beginning of a duration" suggests the Word's preexistence: "before the world was created, the Word (already) existed" (LN 67.65).

ὁ λόγος. Nominative subject of ἦν. According to the method for determining the subjects in clauses in which two nouns are linked with an equative verb devised by McGaughy (36–54), if one substantive is articular and another anarthrous, as here, the noun that has the article is the subject, and the anarthrous substantive is the predicate nominative.

καί. Coordinating conjunction.

ὁ λόγος. Nominative subject of ἦν. Fronted as a topical frame. According to Runge, "The two primary uses of topical frames are: to highlight the introduction of a new participant or topic, or to draw attention to a change in topics" (2010, 210). In this clause (καὶ ὁ λόγος ἦν πρὸς τὸν θεόν), ὁ λόγος, which is introduced in the previous clause (Ἐν ἀρχῇ ἦν ὁ λόγος), is placed in a fronted frame of reference to highlight its status as the main topic of the prologue (211).

ἦν. Impf act ind 3rd sg εἰμί.

πρὸς τὸν θεόν. Association (LN 89.112). In this PP, the force of πρός, a preposition of motion, is overridden by the stative verb εἰμί (Wallace 1996, 359). Porter, however, rightly notes that the usual translation ("with God") "does not do full justice to this use of the preposition to mean face-to-face presence" (1994, 173). If one understands πρός + accusative as an equivalent to παρά + dative after εἶναι, then the PP denotes position, that is, punctiliar rest (cf. Mark 6:3//Matt 13:56; Mark 9:19//Luke 9:41; 1 John 1:2; cf. Harris 2012, 191), which could be translated in the local sense, such as "in God's presence" (REB; Brown, 1:3) or "by the side of God" (Cassirer). But if one agrees with Robertson that "[t]he accusative with πρός is not indeed exactly what the locative would be, especially with persons" (625), then the PP conveys the relationship between ὁ λόγος and ὁ θεός, implying "a certain reciprocity of fellowship" (Harris 2012, 192). To express this dynamic sense of πρός, I have adopted Harris' (190) translation of this phrase: "in fellowship with God."

καί. Coordinating conjunction.

θεός. Predicate nominative. Fronted for emphasis. According to Colwell's rule, "[d]efinite predicate nouns which precede the verb usually lack the article" (20). Consequently, "a predicate nominative which precedes the verb cannot be translated as an indefinite or a 'qualitative' noun solely because of the absence of the article; if the context suggests that the predicate is definite, it should be translated as a definite noun" (20). Colwell's rule, however, cannot establish the definiteness of predicate nominative (Porter 1994, 109). It establishes only that the definiteness of a preverbal anarthrous predicate nominative cannot be excluded a priori, i.e., it establishes what cannot be claimed rather than what can be claimed. For example, Colwell's rule shows that θεὸς ἦν ὁ λόγος cannot be translated "the Word was divine" (Goodspeed; Moffatt) or "the Word was a god" (NWT) simply on the basis of the absence of the article before θεός, but it does not show that θεὸς ἦν ὁ λόγος is equivalent to ὁ λόγος ἦν ὁ θεός (Wallace 1996, 257). In subsequent publications, Harner and Dixon have argued that the anarthrous preverbal predicate nominatives are usually qualitative, rather than definite or indefinite. Wallace summarizes the insights of Colwell, Harner, and Dixon into a general rule: "An anarthrous preverbal PN [predicate nominative] is normally qualitative, sometimes definite, and only rarely indefinite" (262). Thus, the arguments for the definitiveness of θεός in 1:1 are usually based on a misunderstanding of Colwell's rule (267–68). Wallace's (269) own proposal that "[t]he most likely candidate for θεός is qualitative," expressing the divine essence of the Word while distinguishing him from the person of the Father, seems to me quite plausible because it is consistent with Jesus' claims in the FG that he and the Father are one (10:30; 17:11, 21, 22) yet distinct from one another. If so, θεὸς ἦν ὁ λόγος is not a convertible proposition that presumes complete interchangeability between the subject and the predicate nominative comparable to a mathematical equation. Rather, "a subset proposition is envisioned here. The λόγος belongs to the larger category known as θεός" (45) because, as Louw and Nida rightly point out, "[o]ne can ... translate 'the Word was God' but not 'God was the Word'" (LN 58.67). Robertson (767–68) remarks that a statement "ὁ θεὸς ἦν ὁ λόγος (convertible terms) would have been Sabellianism."

ἦν. Impf act ind 3rd sg εἰμί.

ὁ λόγος. Nominative subject of ἦν.

1:2 οὗτος ἦν ἐν ἀρχῇ πρὸς τὸν θεόν.

οὗτος. Nominative subject of ἦν. Fronted as a topical frame. οὗτος refers to ὁ λόγος from the previous verse. The demonstrative pronoun functions as a third-person singular personal pronoun with a simple anaphoric force (Wallace 1996, 328–29).

ἦν. Impf act ind 3rd sg εἰμί.

ἐν ἀρχῇ. Temporal (see 1:1).

πρὸς τὸν θεόν. Association (see 1:1).

1:3 πάντα δι' αὐτοῦ ἐγένετο, καὶ χωρὶς αὐτοῦ ἐγένετο οὐδὲ ἕν. ὃ γέγονεν

πάντα. Nominative subject of ἐγένετο. Fronted as a topical frame.

δι' αὐτοῦ. Secondary (intermediate) agency. This formulation suggests that the primary (ultimate) agent of creation is God (Wallace 1996, 434).

ἐγένετο. Aor mid ind 3rd sg γίνομαι. This is the first aorist in the FG, which is juxtaposed to four imperfects of εἰμί in the previous two verses. "While this aorist refers to the 'act' of creation, the imperfect points back to its 'background' or, in other words, to a state 'before' creation" (Frey 2018, 80).

καί. Coordinating conjunction.

χωρὶς αὐτοῦ. Separation. Fronted as a topical frame. χωρίς ("without," "apart from") is an improper preposition. The main distinction between improper and proper prepositions is that the former cannot be prefixed to verb forms. When they are used in prepositional phrases, as here, improper prepositions function in the same way as proper prepositions (Porter 1994, 140).

ἐγένετο. Aor mid ind 3rd sg γίνομαι.

οὐδέ. A combination of the negative particle οὐ and the postpositive conjunction δέ (LN 69.7). It negates ἕν. οὐδὲ ἕν is equivalent to οὐδέν (attested in 𝔓66 ℵ* D f¹ Cl[exThd]), but it is more emphatic (Robertson, 750–51).

ἕν. Nominative subject of ἐγένετο.

ὅ. Nominative subject of γέγονεν. The relative pronoun ὅ introduces a relative clause whose function depends on the punctuation of the Greek text, which is absent in the oldest manuscripts of the FG (𝔓66.75 ℵ* A B). NA²⁸/UBS⁵ and SBLGNT have the full stop after ἕν, indicating that the headless relative clause, in its entirety, should be seen as the subject of the sentence that continues in v. 4a: ὃ γέγονεν ἐν αὐτῷ ζωὴ ἦν ("what has come into being in him was life" [NRSV]). If the full stop is put after γέγονεν, however, the relative clause is not headless but modifies ἕν, resulting in a somewhat smoother syntax and translation ("and without him was not any thing made that was made" [ESV; KJV; cf. LEB; NIV]). While the punctuation of the text remains an open question, I am more persuaded by Metzger's arguments (167–68) in his dissenting opinion from the UBS committee's decision, which favors taking ὃ γέγονεν with the preceding sentence, such as "John's fondness for beginning a sentence or clause with ἐν and a demonstrative pronoun (cf. 13.35; 15.8; 16.26; 1 Jn 2.3, 4, 5; 3.10, 16, 19, 24; 4.2, etc.)" and "Johannine doctrine (cf. 5.26, 39; 6.53)."

γέγονεν. Prf act ind 3rd sg γίνομαι. The verb form marks a shift from the acts of creation, conveyed through the repeated use of the aorist ἐγένετο, to the state of creation, expressed through the perfect-tense γέγονεν (Porter 1989, 261).

1:4 ἐν αὐτῷ ζωὴ ἦν, καὶ ἡ ζωὴ ἦν τὸ φῶς τῶν ἀνθρώπων·

ἐν αὐτῷ. Locative. Fronted as a topical frame.

ζωή. Nominative subject of ἦν. Fronted for emphasis.

ἦν. Impf act ind 3rd sg εἰμί. The present-tense variant ἐστιν is attested by ℵ D it vg^mss et al., but this is most likely the result of an effort to solve the difficulty created by taking ὃ γέγονεν from v. 3 as the subject of ἦν. Moreover, the imperfect is required by the presence of the second ἦν in the clause that follows (Metzger, 168).

καί. Coordinating conjunction.

ἡ ζωή. Nominative subject of ἦν. Fronted as a topical frame. The article is anaphoric. When both substantives linked by an equative verb are articular, the one mentioned first is the subject (Porter 1994, 109; Wallace 1996, 44).

ἦν. Impf act ind 3rd sg εἰμί.

τὸ φῶς. Predicate nominative.

τῶν ἀνθρώπων. Objective genitive qualifying φῶς.

1:5 καὶ τὸ φῶς ἐν τῇ σκοτίᾳ φαίνει, καὶ ἡ σκοτία αὐτὸ οὐ κατέλαβεν.

καί. Coordinating conjunction.

τὸ φῶς. Nominative subject of φαίνει. Fronted as a topical frame.

ἐν τῇ σκοτίᾳ. Locative.

φαίνει. Pres act ind 3rd sg φαίνω. The verb stands in final, emphatic position.

καί. Coordinating conjunction. This is usually regarded as an adversative καί (Harris 2015, 24), but the adversative sense is not a special function of καί but an observation about the semantic relationship of two clauses joined by καί (Moule, 178). As Runge (2010, 23–27) explains, the basic function of καί is to join two items (individual words, phrases, or clauses) of equal status. "The labels *adversative* and *connective* may be helpful in determining an English translation, but they cause confusion when it comes to understanding the function of καί in Greek" (23).

ἡ σκοτία. Nominative subject of κατέλαβεν. Fronted as a topical frame.

αὐτό. Accusative direct object of κατέλαβεν.

οὐ. Negative particle normally used with indicative verbs.

κατέλαβεν. Aor act ind 3rd sg καταλαμβάνω. The verb stands in final, emphatic position. In this context, καταλαμβάνω could mean either "to overcome, to gain control of" (LN 37.19) or, in a figurative extension of the verb's meaning, "to come to understand something which was not understood or perceived previously" (LN 32.18). A third option is that this is a deliberate double entendre typical for the FG (32.18; Moule, 197).

John 1:6-8

⁶There appeared a man sent from God (his name was John). ⁷He came for a testimony, to testify concerning the light, that all might believe through him. ⁸He was not the light, but [he came] to testify concerning the light.

1:6 Ἐγένετο ἄνθρωπος, ἀπεσταλμένος παρὰ θεοῦ, ὄνομα αὐτῷ Ἰωάννης·

Ἐγένετο. Aor mid ind 3rd sg γίνομαι. The verb γίνομαι functions as "a marker of new information, either concerning participants in an episode or concerning the episode itself" (LN 91.5).

ἄνθρωπος. Nominative subject of Ἐγένετο.

ἀπεσταλμένος. Prf pass ptc masc nom sg ἀποστέλλω (attributive). The participle modifies ἄνθρωπος, standing in the fourth attributive position (noun-attributive participle) (Wallace 1996, 310–11, 618).

παρὰ θεοῦ. Primary (personal) agency. παρά + genitive is sometimes used instead of ὑπό + genitive to express the primary agency of a passive verb (Wallace 1996, 433).

ὄνομα. Parenthetic nominative, which functions as the subject of a verbless explanatory clause within another clause.

αὐτῷ. Dative of possession ("the name [belonging] to him").

Ἰωάννης. Predicate nominative in a verbless clause. Lit. "the name [belonging] to him [was] John" = "his name was John."

1:7 οὗτος ἦλθεν εἰς μαρτυρίαν ἵνα μαρτυρήσῃ περὶ τοῦ φωτός, ἵνα πάντες πιστεύσωσιν δι' αὐτοῦ.

οὗτος. Nominative subject of ἦλθεν. οὗτος refers to Ἰωάννης from the previous verse. This demonstrative pronoun is not needed to identify the subject of the verb because John was already introduced in v. 6. Runge (2010, 375) explains that it is used here "to clarify the current center of attention, identifying which participant is thematically central." The use of the near-demonstrative indicates John's thematic significance as a witness to the light.

ἦλθεν. Aor act ind 3rd sg ἔρχομαι

εἰς μαρτυρίαν. Purpose.

ἵνα. Introduces a purpose clause.

μαρτυρήσῃ. Aor act subj 3rd sg μαρτυρέω. Subjunctive with ἵνα.

περὶ τοῦ φωτός. Reference.
ἵνα. Introduces a purpose clause.
πάντες. Nominative subject of πιστεύσωσιν.
πιστεύσωσιν. Aor act subj 3rd pl πιστεύω. Subjunctive with ἵνα.
δι' αὐτοῦ. Intermediate agency. The pronoun refers to John.

1:8 οὐκ ἦν ἐκεῖνος τὸ φῶς, ἀλλ' ἵνα μαρτυρήσῃ περὶ τοῦ φωτός.

οὐκ . . . ἀλλ'. A point/counterpoint set ("not this . . . but that") that negates the incorrect assertion ("he was the light") and replaces it with the correct one ("he came to testify about the light"). Heckert emphasizes that ἀλλά as a "global marker of contrast . . . introduces a correction of the expectation created by the first conjunct; an incorrect expectation is cancelled and a proper expectation is put in its place" (23). Runge adds that ἀλλά "does more than just indicate contrast. This holds true even if the preceding element is positive rather than negative. It provides a corrective to whatever it stands in contrast with" (2010, 93).

ἦν. Impf act ind 3rd sg εἰμί.
ἐκεῖνος. Nominative subject of ἦν. The demonstrative pronoun refers to Ἰωάννης from 1:6. The switch from the near-demonstrative οὗτος in 1:7 to the far-demonstrative ἐκεῖνος in this verse signals a shift in perspective. John's thematic significance (see 1:7 on οὗτος) now becomes athematic because the center of attention changes to the light about which John came to testify (Runge 2010, 375).

τὸ φῶς. Predicate nominative.
ἵνα. Introduces a purpose clause. The ἵνα clause is elliptical, presuming an introduction, such as ἀπεσταλμένος ἦν ("he was sent to . . .") or ἦλθεν ("he came to . . .").
μαρτυρήσῃ. Aor act subj 3rd sg μαρτυρέω. Subjunctive with ἵνα.
περὶ τοῦ φωτός. Reference.

John 1:9-13

⁹The true light, which enlightens every person, was coming into the world. ¹⁰He was in the world, and the world came into being through him, but the world did not know him. ¹¹To his own he came, but his own people did not receive him. ¹²But all those who received him—to them he gave authority to become children of God, to those who believe in his name, ¹³who were born, not from blood or from the physical desire or from the will of man, but from God.

1:9 Ἦν τὸ φῶς τὸ ἀληθινόν, ὃ φωτίζει πάντα ἄνθρωπον, ἐρχόμενον εἰς τὸν κόσμον.

Ἦν. Impf act ind 3rd sg εἰμί. The subject of the verb could be (1) τὸ φῶς that John testified about from the previous verse ("he/that was the true light . . ."), or (2) τὸ φῶς τὸ ἀληθινόν in this verse ("the true light was . . .").

τὸ φῶς τὸ ἀληθινόν. Predicate nominative if τὸ φῶς from v. 8 is the subject of Ἦν (see the first option above) or nominative subject of Ἦν (see the second option above). The adjective ἀληθινόν stands in the second attributive position (article-noun-article-adjective) (Wallace 1996, 306–7; Porter 1994, 117).

ὅ. Nominative subject of φωτίζει. The antecedent of the relative pronoun is τὸ φῶς τὸ ἀληθινόν.

φωτίζει. Pres act ind 3rd sg φωτίζω.

πάντα ἄνθρωπον. Accusative direct object of φωτίζει. The pronominal adjective πάντα is used distributively ("every human being"). In this construction, the noun does not need the article to be definite (Wallace 1996, 253).

ἐρχόμενον. Pres mid ptc neut nom sg (or pres mid ptc masc acc sg) ἔρχομαι. If the participle is neuter nominative singular, it agrees with τὸ φῶς. In that case it could function in three principal ways. (1) It could be attributive, modifying τὸ φῶς τὸ ἀληθινόν ("the true light that was coming into the world, which enlightens every person"). (2) It could be causal ("he was the true light, which enlightens every person, because he came into the world" [if τὸ φῶς τὸ ἀληθινόν is the predicate nominative], or "the true light, which enlightens every person, was in existence because he came into the world" [if τὸ φῶς τὸ ἀληθινόν is the subject]). (3) It could form an imperfect periphrastic construction with Ἦν. This option works only if τὸ φῶς τὸ ἀληθινόν is the subject of the sentence ("the true light, which enlightens every person, was coming into the world"). In my translation above, I have preferred the third alternative. If the participle is masculine accusative singular, it agrees with ἄνθρωπον. In that case it could function only attributively ("which enlightens every person who comes into the world"). Contextual factors, however, do not favor this interpretation because the next clause in v. 10, ἐν τῷ κόσμῳ ἦν, clearly refers to τὸ φῶς/ὁ λόγος.

εἰς τὸν κόσμον. Locative.

1:10 ἐν τῷ κόσμῳ ἦν, καὶ ὁ κόσμος δι' αὐτοῦ ἐγένετο, καὶ ὁ κόσμος αὐτὸν οὐκ ἔγνω.

ἐν τῷ κόσμῳ. Locative. Note the difference between εἰς τὸν κόσμον + a verb of motion (ἐρχόμενον) in v. 9 and ἐν τῷ κόσμῳ + a stative verb (ἦν) here. Fronted for emphasis. With a few exceptions (11:9; 17:5, 24; 21:25), in the FG ὁ κόσμος refers not to the totality of creation but to the world of human affairs. The Fourth Evangelist typically portrays the world as being unreceptive and antagonistic to Jesus and his followers: the world does not know him (1:10) and the Father (17:25); the world hates Jesus (7:7; 15:18) and his disciples (15:18-19; 17:14); neither Jesus (8:23) nor his disciples belong to this world (15:19; 17:14), in which they face persecution (16:33); the world cannot receive the Spirit of truth (14:17); Jesus came for the judgment of this world (12:31; 16:11); and Jesus' kingdom is not of this world (18:36). Yet the world is also the object of God's love (3:16) and the Son's saving mission (3:16-17; 8:26; 10:36; 12:47; 16:28; 17:13, 18; 18:20, 37), Jesus takes away the sin of the world (1:29), he gives life to the world (6:33), Jesus is "the Savior of the world" (4:42) and the "light of the world" (8:12; 9:5; 12:46), Jesus sends his disciples into the world (17:18), and his ultimate purpose is that the world may believe that the Father sent him (17:21).

ἦν. Impf act ind 3rd sg εἰμί. The implied subject of the verb is τὸ φῶς τὸ ἀληθινόν.

καὶ. Coordinating conjunction.

ὁ κόσμος. Nominative subject of ἐγένετο. Fronted as a topical frame.

δι' αὐτοῦ. Secondary (intermediate) agency (see 1:3).

ἐγένετο. Aor mid ind 3rd sg γίνομαι.

καὶ. Coordinating conjunction. This is not a special case of the so-called adversative καί (Haubeck and von Siebenthal, 523; Harris 2015, 30) but an observation about the semantic relationship of the clauses joined by καί, whose primary function is coordination (see 1:5).

ὁ κόσμος. Nominative subject of ἔγνω. Fronted as a topical frame.

αὐτὸν. Accusative direct object of ἔγνω. The use of the masculine singular αὐτὸν, rather than the neuter singular αὐτό in agreement with the implied grammatical subject of the clause τὸ φῶς, indicates that the author of the FG describes τὸ φῶς in personal terms or refers to the ultimate subject of the prologue ὁ λόγος (v. 1).

οὐκ. Negative particle normally used with indicative verbs.

ἔγνω. Aor act ind 3rd sg γινώσκω. The verb stands in final, emphatic position. γινώσκω occurs fifty-seven times in the FG, in comparison with sixty occurrences in all the Synoptics together.

1:11 εἰς τὰ ἴδια ἦλθεν, καὶ οἱ ἴδιοι αὐτὸν οὐ παρέλαβον.

εἰς τὰ ἴδια. Locative. Fronted for emphasis. BDAG (467.4.b) suggests that the neuter substantival adjective τὰ ἴδια ("one's own") may refer to one's home or to one's own property or possessions (cf. Luke 18:28). Acccording to Louw and Nida, τὰ ἴδια can be understood "in the sense of 'his own nation'" (LN 57 n. 5).

ἦλθεν. Aor act ind 3rd sg ἔρχομαι.

καὶ. Coordinating conjunction. This is not a special case of the so-called adversative καί (Harris 2015, 30) but an observation about the semantic relationship of the clauses joined by καί, whose primary function is coordination (see 1:5).

οἱ ἴδιοι. Nominative subject of παρέλαβον. Fronted as a topical frame. The masculine substantival adjective refers "persons who in some sense belong to a so-called 'reference person'—'his own people'" (LN 10.12).

αὐτὸν. Accusative direct object of παρέλαβον.

οὐ. Negative particle normally used with indicative verbs.

παρέλαβον. Aor act ind 3rd pl παραλαμβάνω. The verb stands in final, emphatic position.

1:12 ὅσοι δὲ ἔλαβον αὐτόν, ἔδωκεν αὐτοῖς ἐξουσίαν τέκνα θεοῦ γενέσθαι, τοῖς πιστεύουσιν εἰς τὸ ὄνομα αὐτοῦ,

ὅσοι. Introduces a pendent clause in a left-dislocation (Runge 2010, 287–313), resumed by αὐτοῖς. The clause ὅσοι δὲ ἔλαβον αὐτόν functions as the "the logical (not grammatical) subject at the beginning of the sentence, followed by a sentence in which that subject is taken up by a pronoun in the case required by the syntax" (Zerwick §25). Runge emphasizes that this construction serves to introduce a new entity into the discourse. Within the pendent clause, ὅσοι is the nominative subject of ἔλαβον. This correlative pronoun ("as many as") can be translated as "all who" even when it is not preceded by πάντες (BDAG, 729.2).

δὲ. Marker of narrative development.

ἔλαβον. Aor act ind 3rd pl λαμβάνω. ἔλαβον probably has the same meaning as the compound παρέλαβον in v. 11 due to "the survival in NT Greek of a classical idiom by which the preposition in a compound is omitted, without weakening the sense, when the verb is repeated" (MHT 1:115).

αὐτόν. Accusative direct object of ἔλαβον.

ἔδωκεν. Aor act ind 3rd sg δίδωμι.

αὐτοῖς. Dative indirect object of ἔδωκεν, resuming the pendent clause in left-dislocation, ὅσοι δὲ ἔλαβον αὐτόν. αὐτοῖς is placed in an unmarked position (following the verb), which occurs relatively infrequently in the FG (here and in 7:38; 15:2; 17:2). Much more common are left-dislocations that have the resumptive pronoun in a marked position (at the beginning of the clause).

ἐξουσίαν. Accusative direct object of ἔδωκεν. Robertson (794) notes that in Greek "[n]o vital difference was felt between articular and anarthrous abstract nouns."

τέκνα. Predicate accusative.

θεοῦ. Genitive of relationship qualifying τέκνα.

γενέσθαι. Aor mid inf γίνομαι (epexegetical to ἐξουσίαν).

τοῖς πιστεύουσιν. Pres act ptc masc dat pl πιστεύω (substantival). Dative in apposition to αὐτοῖς. The appositional information receives emphasis through right-dislocation (Runge 2010, 317–36). πιστεύω means "to entrust oneself to an entity in complete confidence, *believe (in), trust*, w[ith] implication of total commitment to the one who is trusted" (BDAG, 817.2). The imperfective aspect of the present participle portrays believing as an unfolding process, without regard to its beginning or end.

εἰς τὸ ὄνομα. Goal of actions or feelings directed toward someone (BDAG, 290.4.c.β). πιστεύειν εἰς + accusative ("trust or believe in someone") is a distinctively Johannine phrase: from forty-five NT occurrences, thirty-six are found in the FG (1:12; 2:11, 23; 3:16, 18 [2x], 36; 4:39; 6:29, 35, 40; 7:5, 31, 38, 39, 48; 8:30; 9:35, 36; 10:42; 11:25, 26, 45, 48; 12:11, 36, 37, 42, 44 [3x], 46; 14:1, 12; 16:9; 17:20). In this PP, ὄνομα is a synecdoche for the whole person. Elsewhere in the FG, the expression πιστεύειν εἰς τὸ ὄνομα occurs in 2:23 and 3:18.

αὐτοῦ. Possessive genitive qualifying ὄνομα.

1:13 οἳ οὐκ ἐξ αἱμάτων οὐδὲ ἐκ θελήματος σαρκὸς οὐδὲ ἐκ θελήματος ἀνδρὸς ἀλλ' ἐκ θεοῦ ἐγεννήθησαν.

οἵ. Nominative subject of ἐγεννήθησαν. The antecedent of the relative pronoun is ὅσοι/τοῖς πιστεύουσιν from the previous verse. The relative pronoun is used here in its usual sense, to describe, clarify, or restrict the meaning of the noun (Wallace 1996, 336–37).

οὐκ...οὐδὲ...οὐδὲ...ἀλλ'. A compound point/counterpoint set that negates three prepositional phrases that ascribe the origin of the children of God to physical birth and replaces them by the claim that they are born of God.

ἐξ αἱμάτων. Source/origin ("from blood"), means ("by blood"), or cause/reason ("as a result of blood"). BDAG (296.3.a) notes that "in expr[essions] which have to do w[ith] begetting and birth ... ἐκ introduces the role of the male." ἐξ αἱμάτων could be a reference to blood as the means of procreation as, for example, in Wis 7:2 and Philo, *Opif.* 132, but the plural ("bloods") is peculiar and cannot be easily explained.

ἐκ θελήματος. Source/origin ("from the desire of the flesh"), means ("by the desire of the flesh"), or cause/reason ("as a result of the desire of the flesh"). σαρκὸς θελήμα is an idiom for "desire for sexual gratification" (LN 25.29).

σαρκὸς. Attributive genitive qualifying θελήματος ("fleshly desire, physical desire").

ἐκ θελήματος. Source/origin ("from the will of man"), means ("by the will of man"), or cause/reason ("as a result of the will of man").

ἀνδρὸς. Subjective genitive qualifying θελήματος.

ἐκ θεοῦ. Source ("from God") or agency ("by God").

ἐγεννήθησαν. Aor pass ind 3rd pl γεννάω.

John 1:14-18

¹⁴And the Word became flesh and dwelt among us, and we have seen his glory, such glory as of the only Son from the Father, full of grace and truth. ¹⁵John testified concerning him and cried out, "This was the one of whom I said, 'He who comes after me ranks higher than me because he was before me.'" ¹⁶For from his fullness we all received, namely, grace upon grace. ¹⁷For the law was given through Moses; grace and truth came through Jesus Christ. ¹⁸No one has ever seen God. The only One, God, who is in the bosom of the Father, that one has made him fully known.

1:14 Καὶ ὁ λόγος σὰρξ ἐγένετο καὶ ἐσκήνωσεν ἐν ἡμῖν, καὶ ἐθεασάμεθα τὴν δόξαν αὐτοῦ, δόξαν ὡς μονογενοῦς παρὰ πατρός, πλήρης χάριτος καὶ ἀληθείας.

Καὶ. Coordinating conjunction.

ὁ λόγος. Nominative subject of ἐγένετο. The article marks the subject of the clause (see 1:1). Fronted as a topical frame.

σὰρξ. Predicate nominative. This is an example of qualitative predicate nominative because "[t]he idea is not that the Word became 'the flesh,' nor 'a flesh,' but simply 'flesh.' That is, the Word partook of humanity" (Wallace 1996, 264). ὁ λόγος and σὰρξ are not convertible terms. Rather, ὁ λόγος belongs to a larger category of entities characterized as σὰρξ, i.e., "humans as physical beings" (LN 9.11). For a discussion of Colwell's rule, see 1:1 on θεὸς.

ἐγένετο. Aor mid ind 3rd sg γίνομαι. The verb means "to come to acquire or experience a state—'to become'" (LN 13.48). Note the difference between ὁ λόγος σὰρξ ἐγένετο (the Word's incarnation) and Ἐν ἀρχῇ ἦν ὁ λόγος (the Word's preexistence).

καὶ. Coordinating conjunction.

ἐσκήνωσεν. Aor act ind 3rd sg σκηνόω. The verb σκηνόω, a cognate of σκῆνος ("a temporary abode as opposed to a permanent structure" [BDAG, 929]), means to "to take up residence, to come to reside, to come to dwell" (LN 85.75).

ἐν ἡμῖν. Locative. BDAG (929) suggests that this PP may be "an expression of continuity with God's 'tenting' in Israel" (cf. Exod 25:8; 29:46; Zech 2:14), but the scope of ἡμῖν could also be humanity in general (Brown, 1:13; Barrett, 165–66). The latter view is supported by the parallels about wisdom's temporary dwelling among humans, such as Bar 3:37; Sir 24:8, 11-12; and 1 En. 42.1-2.

καὶ. Coordinating conjunction.

ἐθεασάμεθα. Aor mid ind 1st pl θεάομαι. There is a shift in meaning between ἡμῖν and the implied subject of ἐθεασάμεθα ("we"), which is now more narrowly conceived, referring to "the apostolic witnesses, as in the Prologue of I John" (Brown, 1:13).

τὴν δόξαν. Accusative direct object of ἐθεασάμεθα.

αὐτοῦ. Possessive genitive qualifying δόξαν.

δόξαν. Accusative in apposition to τὴν δόξαν.

ὡς. Comparative particle.

μονογενοῦς. Possessive genitive qualifying δόξαν ("such glory as belonging to the only son from the Father"). The nominal phrases τὴν δόξαν αὐτοῦ and δόξαν . . . μονογενοῦς are parallel. The adjective μονογενής ("pert[aining] to being the only one of its kind or class, *unique [in kind]*" [BDAG, 658.2]) is used as a substantive. The PP that follows (παρὰ πατρός) restricts this meaning to familial relationships, referring "to the only child of one's parents" (TDNT 4:738). The application of this term to Isaac in Josephus, *Ant.* 1.222 (Ἴσακον δὲ ὁ πατὴρ Ἀβραμος ὑπερηγάπα μονογενῆ ὄντα καὶ ἐπὶ γήρως οὐδῷ κατὰ δωρεὰν αὐτῷ τοῦ θεοῦ γενόμενον ["Now Isaac was passionately beloved of his father Abraham, being his only son and born to him on the threshold of old age through the bounty of God"]) shows that, contrary to the popular opinion, μονογενής does not mean "the only begotten" (because Isaac was not Abraham's only biological child) but "the one-of-a-kind" (because Isaac was a child born to Abraham in his old age as a result of God's promise).

παρὰ πατρός. Source. The PP qualifies μονογενοῦς. According to Harris, it is equivalent to τοῦ ἐξελθόντος παρὰ πατρός ("who came from the Father") and "alludes to the Son's mission, not to his eternal generation" (2015, 35).

πλήρης. Since the adjective πλήρης ("filled, full") is indeclinable when followed by the genitive (MHT 3:315; BDF 137.1), it can be regarded either as nominative singular modifying ὁ λόγος or as genitive singular modifying μονογενοῦς. Although πλήρης could also modify τὴν δόξαν, this is less likely because, as Bultmann observes, "it is the Revealer who is being described" (73 n. 2).

χάριτος καὶ ἀληθείας. Genitive complements of πλήρης. The combination of these two nouns also occurs in 1:18 (ἡ χάρις καὶ ἡ ἀλήθεια).

1:15 Ἰωάννης μαρτυρεῖ περὶ αὐτοῦ καὶ κέκραγεν λέγων· οὗτος ἦν ὃν εἶπον· ὁ ὀπίσω μου ἐρχόμενος ἔμπροσθέν μου γέγονεν, ὅτι πρῶτός μου ἦν.

Ἰωάννης. Nominative subject of μαρτυρεῖ.

μαρτυρεῖ. Pres act ind 3rd sg μαρτυρέω. This is the first occurrence of the historical present in the FG. The distribution of the historical presents in John is uneven (they mostly occur in chapters 1, 4, 13, 20, and 21) and cannot therefore be used to argue for a stylistic unity of the FG (O'Rourke, 587–88; for a different view, see Leung, 711–12). A historical present is usually defined as "a present tense that is used instead of a past tense, when that past tense would not only have been perfectly acceptable, but the semantics of the past tense are still understood to obtain in spite of the present tense form in the text" (Robar, 329). Robar argues that the historical present "functions on a completely *different level* from tense and aspect ... functioning such that tense and aspect are not applicable" (332; cf. Wallace 1996, 527, who says that "[t]he aspectual value of the historical present is normally, if not always, reduced to zero"). One of its main functions is to indicate structural or thematic prominence, i.e., to help the readers/hearers discern the themes to which they should pay attention. The use of the historical present with the verbs of speaking, which is by far the most frequent use of the historical present in the FG (119 forms of λέγω out of 164 historical presents in John), however, is not to mark the action of speaking for prominence. Rather, as Runge explains, "attention is drawn prospectively to the speech that the quotative frame introduces" (2010, 137 n. 45). Runge's observation is consistent with Callow's conclusion that, in the FG, the historical present "does not draw attention to the event which the HP verb itself refers to, as those events, in themselves, are not particularly important—to go, to say, to gather together, to see, etc. . . . [I]t has a cataphoric function; that is, it points on beyond itself into the narrative, it draws attention to what is following" (2). In this verse, the historical present calls attention to John's subsequent testimony and marks it as thematically prominent (Leung, 718–19). Another important function of the historical present in the FG is, as Frey explains, its "*'present-making' effect* for the readers. By having past events and conversations appear present rhetorically and, beyond this, by having the extended discourses be 'quoted' directly, the readers are fictively situated in the present of the activity of Jesus. In the speech act of the reading of the Gospel, Jesus' words become present. In this way the *temporal distance* between the past time of the earthly activity of Jesus and the time of the later community is bridged" (2018, 82).

περὶ αὐτοῦ. Reference.

καὶ. Coordinating conjunction.

κέκραγεν. Prf act ind 3rd sg κράζω. The perfect tense (stative aspect) describes the action concurrent with the plot of the narrative "which in no way can be explained as indicating a state of the subject . . . as the result of a completed action" (Porter 2015, 213). The verb form gives prominence to John's announcement of the one who comes after him.

λέγων. Pres act ptc masc nom sg λέγω (pleonastic).

οὗτος. Nominative subject of ἦν. Fronted for emphasis.

ἦν. Impf act ind 3rd sg εἰμί.

ὅν. Accusative of respect.

εἶπον. Aor act ind 1st sg λέγω. εἶπον introduces a new direct speech within the existing direct discourse.

ὁ . . . ἐρχόμενος. Pres mid ptc masc nom sg ἔρχομαι (substantival). Nominative subject of γέγονεν. Fronted as a topical frame.

ὀπίσω μου. Temporal. ὀπίσω is an improper preposition (see 1:3 on χωρὶς αὐτοῦ). The PP, placed between the article and the participle, functions as an attributive modifier of ἐρχόμενος. In the FG, substantival ἐρχόμενος frequently occurs with embedded prepositional or adverbial phrases: ὁ ὀπίσω μου ἐρχόμενος (here and in 1:27), ὁ ἄνωθεν ἐρχόμενος (3:31), ὁ ἐκ τοῦ οὐρανοῦ ἐρχόμενος (3:31), ὁ εἰς τὸν κόσμον ἐρχόμενος (11:27).

ἔμπροσθέν μου. Advantage. ἔμπροσθέν is an adverb of place ("in front, ahead" [BDAG, 325.1.a]) that here functions not as a preposition denoting time (because in such a case the following clause would be tautological; cf. Harris 2012, 259) but as a preposition denoting rank (BDAG, 325.1.b.ζ). ἔμπροσθέν τινος γίνεσθαι means "to rank higher than someone." ἔμπροσθέν, which has an acute accent on the antepenult, acquired an additional accent, the acute, on the ultima from the enclitic μου (Smyth §183; Carson 1985, 48).

γέγονεν. Prf act ind 3rd sg γίνομαι. The stative aspect of the perfect tense, combined with the PP ἔμπροσθέν μου, conveys the idea of superiority rather than the idea of temporal priority.

ὅτι. Introduces a causal clause.

πρῶτός. Predicate adjective. The superlative πρῶτος ("first, earliest") is used here for the comparative πρότερος ("earlier"; cf. BDF §62). πρῶτός, which has a circumflex accent on the penult, acquired an additional accent, the acute, on the ultima from the enclitic μου (Smyth §183; Carson 1985, 48).

μου. Genitive of comparison.

ἦν. Impf act ind 3rd sg εἰμί.

1:16 ὅτι ἐκ τοῦ πληρώματος αὐτοῦ ἡμεῖς πάντες ἐλάβομεν καὶ χάριν ἀντὶ χάριτος·

ὅτι. Introduces a causal clause. If the ὅτι clause belongs to John's speech, it provides an explanation of his declaration of Jesus' priority: "He existed before me *because* of his fullness we have all [even I] had a share" (Brown, 1:15). Most interpreters and English translations, however, rightly regard v. 15 as a parenthetical statement that interrupts the flow of thought between vv. 14 and 16, both of which are formulated as first-person plural declarations. If, then, v. 16 is related to v. 14, the ὅτι clause explains that the "we" group—the apostolic witnesses—could see the glory of the incarnated Word full of grace and truth because they all received grace upon grace from his fullness.

ἐκ τοῦ πληρώματος. Source. This is the only occurrence of the term πλήρωμα ("fullness") in the FG.

αὐτοῦ. Possessive genitive qualifying πληρώματος.

ἡμεῖς πάντες. Nominative subject of ἐλάβομεν.

ἐλάβομεν. Aor act ind 1st pl λαμβάνω.

καὶ. This is usually regarded as an epexegetical καί ("that is to say . . ." [BDF §442.9]) or an explicative καί that connects one word-group with another word-group "for the purpose of explaining what goes before" (BDAG, 495.1.c).

χάριν. Accusative direct object of ἐλάβομεν.

ἀντὶ χάριτος. Substitution. This PP describes Christian life as a continuous exchange of one grace for another. "As the days come and go a new supply takes the place of the grace already bestowed as wave follows wave upon the shore" (Robertson, 574).

1:17 ὅτι ὁ νόμος διὰ Μωϋσέως ἐδόθη, ἡ χάρις καὶ ἡ ἀλήθεια διὰ Ἰησοῦ Χριστοῦ ἐγένετο.

ὅτι. Introduces a causal clause that explains the phrase χάριν ἀντὶ χάριτος. The ὅτι clause, which portrays the giving of the law through Moses as God's gift, offers an example of grace that God gave to his people. The next clause (ἡ χάρις καὶ ἡ ἀλήθεια διὰ Ἰησοῦ Χριστοῦ ἐγένετο), however, offers an example of surpassing grace through Jesus Christ—a superior gift of God's love—that replaced the previous gift of grace through Moses.

ὁ νόμος. Nominative subject of ἐδόθη. Fronted as a topical frame.

διὰ Μωϋσέως. Secondary (intermediate) agency. The unexpressed primary (ultimate) agent is God.

ἐδόθη. Aor pass ind 3rd sg δίδωμι.

ἡ χάρις καὶ ἡ ἀλήθεια. Nominative subjects of ἐγένετο. Fronted as a topical frame. The apparent incongruity between two subjects and the verb in the singular disappears if two nouns are regarded as forming one conceptual unit (Harris 2015, 37). The clause introduced by these nouns is connected to the previous one by asyndeton. As Runge explains, "[T]he use of asyndeton indicates that the writer did not feel the need to specify any kind of relationship between the clauses. The relation might be causative, it might be contrary to expectation, or it might simply be continuity" (2010, 20). It is therefore an overstatement to say with Harris (2015, 37) that "[b]y means of the asyndeton in v. 17b . . . a contrast is drawn between the two parts of the verse" (see Keener, 1:422, for a more balanced view). Asyndeton is the default unmarked means of connecting sentences in the FG (Levinsohn 2000, 82; Poythress, 324; Buth 1992, 154).

διὰ Ἰησοῦ Χριστοῦ. Secondary (intermediate) agency. The unexpressed primary (ultimate) agent is God. For a combination of γίνομαι and διά + genitive, see 1:3, 10. In the designation Ἰησοῦ Χριστοῦ, Χριστοῦ functions as a part of the name for Jesus; for a titular use of this term, see 1:20.

ἐγένετο. Aor mid ind 3rd sg γίνομαι.

1:18 Θεὸν οὐδεὶς ἑώρακεν πώποτε· μονογενὴς θεὸς ὁ ὢν εἰς τὸν κόλπον τοῦ πατρὸς ἐκεῖνος ἐξηγήσατο.

    Θεόν. Accusative direct object of ἑώρακεν. Fronted as a topical frame.
    οὐδείς. Nominative subject of ἑώρακεν.
    ἑώρακεν. Prf act ind 3rd sg ὁράω.
    πώποτε. Indefinite adverb of time.

μονογενὴς θεὸς. In this construction, μονογενὴς, which occurred for the first time in 1:14, can be understood either as a noun or as an adjective. If μονογενὴς is a noun, it functions as the nominative subject of ἐξηγήσατο in a left-dislocation, resumed by ἐκεῖνος, and θεὸς as the nominative in apposition to μονογενὴς. Many English translations reflect this understanding, either accentuating the unique nature of the subject or taking it as an equivalent to μονογενὴς υἱός: "the only one, himself God" (NET); "the one and only, God" (LEB); "the one and only Son, who is himself God" (NIV); "God, the only Son" (NRSV switches the subject and the apposition). If μονογενὴς is an adjective, it modifies θεὸς, standing in the first (anarthrous) attributive position (adjective-noun) (Wallace 1996, 309). On this reading, θεὸς is the nominative subject of ἐξηγήσατο in a left-dislocation, resumed by ἐκεῖνος. This understanding is also reflected in some English translations: "the only God" (ESV), "the only begotten God" (NASB). My translation presumes that μονογενὴς is a noun and θεὸς an apposition to it.

The manuscript tradition reveals that ancient scribes struggled with this construction in much the same way as do modern interpreters. There are three major textual variants:

(1) ὁ μονογενὴς θεὸς ($\mathfrak{P}^{75}$ ℵ¹ 33 Cl^{pt} Cl^{exThd pt} Or^{pt})
(2) ὁ μονογενὴς υἱός (A C³ K Γ Δ Θ Ψ $f^{1.13}$ 565 579 𝔐 et al.)
(3) μονογενὴς θεὸς ($\mathfrak{P}^{66}$ ℵ* B C* L sy^{p.hmg} Or^{pt} Did)

The external support is strongest for reading (3). This is also the more difficult reading, while ὁ μονογενὴς υἱός probably represents scribal assimilation to John 3:16 (τὸν υἱὸν τὸν μονογενῆ), 18 (τοῦ μονογενοῦς υἱοῦ τοῦ θεοῦ), and 1 John 4:9 (τὸν υἱὸν αὐτοῦ τὸν μονογενῆ) (Metzger, 169). The reading (3) also best explains the rise of other variants.

ὁ ὢν. Pres act ptc masc nom sg εἰμί (attributive). The participle modifies μονογενὴς, standing in the third attributive position (noun-article-attributive participle) (Wallace 1996, 307, 618). The imperfective aspect of the present tense portrays the Son's intimate relationship with the Father as a process without regard for its beginning or end. Thus, the claims about the temporal meaning of ὢν, such as that this participle describes the Son's permanent presence with the Father after his resurrection (McHugh, 49, 73) or that it stands for the imperfect tense referring to the Son's communion with the Father before the incarnation (Harris 2015, 38), cannot be derived from the verb form or the syntax of the clause.

εἰς τὸν κόλπον. Locative. κόλπος ("the region of the body extending from the breast to the legs, especially when a person is in a seated position") denotes here "an association of intimacy and affection" (LN 8.39). In this PP εἰς is used instead of ἐν, which is a common occurrence in Koine Greek (BDF §205). Thus, as Wallace remarks, "[o]ne cannot press the idea of motion here, as though the meaning is 'who was into the bosom of the Father.' . . . This is not to say that the relationship of Son to Father was not dynamic or energetic, just that this text affirms only their intimate relationship" (1996, 360). John 13:23 uses the idiom ἀνάκειμαι ἐν τῷ κόλπῳ to describe the Beloved Disciple's place of honor at the right side of Jesus at the last supper. In Luke 16:22, εἰς τὸν κόλπον Ἀβραάμ functions as a figure of speech for a blessed afterlife in Abraham's presence (Culy, Parsons, and Stigall, 532).

τοῦ πατρὸς. Possessive genitive qualifying κόλπον.

ἐκεῖνος. Nominative subject of ἐξηγήσατο, resuming either μονογενὴς or θεὸς, depending on how one defines the subject of the verb in a left-dislocation (see μονογενὴς θεὸς above). The demonstrative pronoun is used here to encapsulate all three characterizations of Jesus Christ in the first part of the clause.

ἐξηγήσατο. Aor mid ind 3rd sg ἐξηγέομαι. The verb stands in final, emphatic position. The implied direct object of ἐξηγήσατο is God the Father. "In keeping with its economic nature, Greek regularly implies an object that was already mentioned in the preceding context, rather than restating it" (Wallace 1996, 409 n. 5). ἐξηγέομαι means "to make something fully known by careful explanation or by clear revelation" (LN 28.41).

John 1:19-28

[19]And the testimony of John is this, when the Jews sent to him priests and Levites from Jerusalem so that they might ask him, "Who are you?" [20]And he confessed and did not deny, but confessed, "I am not the Messiah." [21]And they asked him, "What then? Are you Elijah?" And he said, "I am not." "Are you the prophet?" And he replied, "No." [22]Then they said to him, "Who are you? Tell us, so that we can give an answer to those who sent us. What do you say concerning yourself?" [23]He said, "I am the voice of one crying in the wilderness, 'Make straight the way of the Lord,'" just as Isaiah, the prophet, said. [24]Now, some had been sent from the Pharisees. [25]They asked him and said to him, "Why then are you baptizing if you are neither the Messiah, nor Elijah, nor the prophet?" [26]John replied to them, saying, "I baptize with water. Among you stands one whom you do not know, [27]the one who is coming after me, of whom I am not worthy to untie the strap of his sandal." [28]These things took place in Bethany across the Jordan, where John was baptizing.

1:19 Καὶ αὕτη ἐστὶν ἡ μαρτυρία τοῦ Ἰωάννου, ὅτε ἀπέστειλαν [πρὸς αὐτὸν] οἱ Ἰουδαῖοι ἐξ Ἱεροσολύμων ἱερεῖς καὶ Λευίτας ἵνα ἐρωτήσωσιν αὐτόν· σὺ τίς εἶ;

Καὶ. Coordinating conjunction.

αὕτη. Predicate nominative. Fronted for emphasis. The demonstrative pronoun agrees with the nominative subject ἡ μαρτυρία. Its force is cataphoric, i.e., it points to John's proclamation about the Messiah in the following verses. In equative clauses, cataphoric demonstratives typically function as predicates (Culy 2004, 11).

ἐστὶν. Pres act ind 3rd sg εἰμί.

ἡ μαρτυρία. Nominative subject of ἐστὶν (see 1:7).

τοῦ Ἰωάννου. Subjective genitive qualifying μαρτυρία.

ὅτε. Introduces a temporal clause.

ἀπέστειλαν. Aor act ind 3rd pl ἀποστέλλω.

[πρὸς αὐτὸν]. Locative (motion toward). This PP is absent in 𝔓[66*.75] ℵ C³ K L Wˢ f¹ 𝔐 et al. and present in B C* 33 892ᶜ it syᶜ·ᵖ et al. Functionally, it is redundant with the αὐτόν that occurs later in the verse, but it is difficult to decide whether it was deleted because of this redundancy or added later for clarity (Metzger, 170).

οἱ Ἰουδαῖοι. Nominative subject of ἀπέστειλαν. The noun Ἰουδαῖοι occurs sixty-seven times in the FG, in comparison with only sixteen occurrences in the Synoptics. In this context, the noun refers to the religious authorities in Jerusalem, not to the Jewish people in general.

ἐξ Ἱεροσολύμων. Source.

ἱερεῖς καὶ Λευίτας. Accusative direct objects of ἀπέστειλαν. This is the only reference to priests and Levites in the FG. Levites—a lower-level priestly class whose main function was assisting in the temple worship and acting as temple police (m. Tamid 7:4; m. Mid. 1:1)—are mentioned elsewhere in the NT only in Luke 10:32 and Acts 4:36.

ἵνα. Introduces a purpose clause.

ἐρωτήσωσιν. Aor act subj 3rd pl ἐρωτάω. Subjunctive with ἵνα.

αὐτόν. Accusative direct object of αὐτόν.

σὺ. Nominative subject of εἶ. Fronted as a topical frame.

τίς. Interrogative pronoun functioning as the predicate nominative of εἶ. Fronted for emphasis.

εἶ. Pres act ind 2nd sg εἰμί.

1:20 καὶ ὡμολόγησεν καὶ οὐκ ἠρνήσατο, καὶ ὡμολόγησεν ὅτι ἐγὼ οὐκ εἰμὶ ὁ χριστός.

καὶ. Coordinating conjunction.

ὡμολόγησεν. Aor act ind 3rd sg ὁμολογέω. BDAG (708.3b) suggests that in this context ὁμολογέω ("to concede that something is factual or true, grant, admit, confess") has judicial connotation because John is replying to interrogation by the authorities.

καί. Coordinating conjunction.

οὐκ. Negative particle normally used with indicative verbs.

ἠρνήσατο. Aor mid ind 3rd sg ἀρνέομαι. The verbs οὐκ ἠρνήσατο and ὡμολόγησεν create what Runge (2010, 145) calls a "redundant quotative frame" because the speech has already been introduced by ὡμολόγησεν at the beginning of the verse. "The redundant verbs in the quotative frame have the effect of interrupting the flow of the discourse as a means of building suspense, postponing the disclosure of the Baptist's answer" (156).

καί. Coordinating conjunction.

ὡμολόγησεν. Aor act ind 3rd sg ὁμολογέω.

ὅτι. ὅτι-*recitativum* that introduces the clausal complement (direct discourse) of ὡμολόγησεν.

ἐγώ. Nominative subject of εἰμί. The personal pronoun is emphatic because it is not required by the verb form, which already grammaticalizes a first-person singular subject.

οὐκ. Negative particle normally used with indicative verbs.

εἰμί. Pres act ind 1st sg εἰμί.

ὁ χριστός. Predicate nominative. The term χριστός is a Greek translation of the Hebrew term מָשִׁיחַ ("Anointed One"). Its earliest occurrence as a *terminus technicus* for the future deliverer of Israel ("the Messiah") is in Pss. Sol. 17:32; 18:5, 7. In this verse, the article indicates that χριστός is used as a title.

1:21 καὶ ἠρώτησαν αὐτόν· τί οὖν; σὺ Ἠλίας εἶ; καὶ λέγει· οὐκ εἰμί. ὁ προφήτης εἶ σύ; καὶ ἀπεκρίθη· οὔ.

καί. Coordinating conjunction.

ἠρώτησαν. Aor act ind 3rd pl ἐρωτάω.

αὐτόν. Accusative direct object of ἠρώτησαν.

τί οὖν σὺ Ἠλίας εἶ. These five words are transmitted in several variants:

(1) τί οὖν Ἠλίας εἶ σύ (A C³ K Γ Δ Θ 0234 $f^{1.13}$ 565 579 700 892 1241 1424 𝔐 lat syʰ)
(2) τί οὖν Ἠλίας εἶ (ℵ L a)
(3) σὺ οὖν τί Ἠλίας εἶ (B)
(4) Ἠλίας εἶ σύ (b r¹ co)
(5) τί οὖν σὺ Ἠλίας εἶ (τίς 𝔓⁶⁶) (𝔓⁷⁵ C* Ψ 33 [e] ff² l Or)

The age and diversity of manuscript gives strongest support for reading (5), which is adopted in NA²⁸/UBS⁵ and SBLGNT (Metzger, 170).

τί οὖν. Conversational formula: "What then?" (MHT 3:304).

τί. Interrogative particle used in an elliptical expression.

οὖν. Postpositive inferential conjunction.

σύ. Nominative subject of εἶ. Fronted as a topical frame.

Ἠλίας. Predicate nominative. Fronted for emphasis.

εἶ. Pres act ind 2nd sg εἰμί.

καί. Coordinating conjunction.

λέγει. Pres act ind 3rd sg λέγω. The historical present calls attention to the reply John gives to his interlocutors (see 1:15 on μαρτυρεῖ).

οὐκ. Negative particle normally used with indicative verbs.

εἰμί. Pres act ind 1st sg εἰμί.

ὁ προφήτης. Predicate nominative. Fronted for emphasis. The article is anaphoric in a broad sense, referring to the prophetic figure known to the audience (see 6:14; 7:40), such as the prophet like Moses mentioned in Deut 18:15 (Wallace 1996, 218, 222; Harris 2015, 42).

εἶ. Pres act ind 2nd sg εἰμί.

σύ. Nominative subject of εἶ. The personal pronoun is emphatic (see above).

καί. Coordinating conjunction.

ἀπεκρίθη. Aor mid ind 3rd sg ἀποκρίνομαι. On the voice, see "Deponency" in the Series Introduction.

οὔ. When the negative particle is accented, as here, it means "no." John's denials become progressively briefer: ἐγὼ οὐκ εἰμὶ ὁ χριστός (1:20), οὐκ εἰμί (1:21b), οὔ (1:21c).

1:22 εἶπαν οὖν αὐτῷ· τίς εἶ; ἵνα ἀπόκρισιν δῶμεν τοῖς πέμψασιν ἡμᾶς· τί λέγεις περὶ σεαυτοῦ;

εἶπαν. Aor act ind 3rd pl λέγω.

οὖν. Postpositive inferential conjunction and/or transitional particle (see 1:22 and 11:6). In the FG, the inferential and transitional uses of οὖν are frequently overlapping. In many cases, the transitional function of οὖν is more chronological than logical (Wallace 1996, 674).

αὐτῷ. Dative indirect object of εἶπαν.

τίς. Interrogative pronoun functioning as the predicate nominative of εἶ.

εἶ. Pres act ind 2nd sg εἰμί.

ἵνα. Introduces either a purpose clause or an imperatival clause. If the ἵνα clause expresses purpose, the construction is elliptical, requiring an introduction, such as the imperative εἰπέ ("[Tell us,] so that we can give an answer to those who sent us"). This is an example of brachylogy—"the omission, for the sake of brevity, of an element which is not necessary for the grammatical structure but for the thought. The abbreviated form of a train of thought is conventional in the ἵνα clauses which are put ahead of the main clauses and state the purpose of the subsequent clause" (BDF §483). In this verse, the ἵνα clause states the purpose of the questions that precede ("Who are you?") and follow it ("What do you say concerning yourself?"). If the ἵνα clause is imperatival ("Let us have an answer for those who sent us" [NRSV]; "Give us an answer to take back to those who sent us" [NIV]), it does not require a hypothetical introduction but functions like an independent clause with the force of a command (Wallace 1996, 476–77; BDF §388). Moule, however, explains that this is an extension of the final (a.k.a. purpose) ἵνα clause in "the well-known idiom whereby it becomes practically *imperative* in sense" (144). This means, then, that the two possible classifications of the ἵνα clause in this verse are closely related to each other.

ἀπόκρισιν. Accusative direct object of δῶμεν. Fronted for emphasis.

δῶμεν. Aor act subj 1st pl δίδωμι. Subjunctive with ἵνα.

τοῖς πέμψασιν. Aor act ptc masc dat pl πέμπω (substantival). Dative indirect object of δῶμεν.

ἡμᾶς. Accusative direct object of πέμψασιν.

τί. Accusative direct object of λέγεις.

λέγεις. Pres act ind 2nd sing λέγω.

περὶ σεαυτοῦ. Reference.

1:23 ἔφη· ἐγὼ φωνὴ βοῶντος ἐν τῇ ἐρήμῳ· εὐθύνατε τὴν ὁδὸν κυρίου, καθὼς εἶπεν Ἡσαΐας ὁ προφήτης.

ἔφη. Aor/impf act ind 3rd sg φημί. This verse is connected to the previous one by asyndeton (BDF §462.1).

ἐγώ. Nominative subject of an implied εἰμί in a verbless clause. The personal pronoun may convey contrast to John's previous denials, but the "subject focus" is on the positive formulation of John's identity (Wallace 1996, 322).

φωνὴ βοῶντος ἐν τῇ ἐρήμῳ· εὐθύνατε τὴν ὁδὸν κυρίου. A quotation of LXX Isa 40:3a (φωνὴ βοῶντος ἐν τῇ ἐρήμῳ ἑτοιμάσατε τὴν ὁδὸν κυρίου). The only difference is the replacement of ἑτοιμάσατε with εὐθύνατε (Menken, 190–205). The synoptic version of LXX Isa 40:3 (Mark 1:3//Matt 3:3//Luke 3:4) preserves ἑτοιμάσατε from the quoted text, but it also includes the next clause (εὐθείας ποιεῖτε τὰς τρίβους αὐτοῦ), which is here omitted.

φωνή. Predicate nominative.

βοῶντος. Pres act ptc masc gen sg βοάω (substantival). Possessive genitive qualifying φωνή.

ἐν τῇ ἐρήμῳ. Locative.

εὐθύνατε. Aor act impv 2nd pl εὐθύνω. The verb means "to make something straight" (LN 79.89).

τὴν ὁδόν. Accusative direct object of εὐθύνατε.

κυρίου. Possessive genitive.

καθὼς εἶπεν Ἠσαΐας ὁ προφήτης. The OT introductory formula, which here follows the quotation. In all other instances in the FG in which καθώς serves in this role (6:31; 7:38; 12:14), the introductory formula precedes the quotation. It is not clear whether this clause functions as a part of the direct speech of John (ESV; LEB; NET) or as the narrator's comment on it (NRSV; NIV).

καθώς. Introduces a comparative clause.

εἶπεν. Aor act ind 3rd sg λέγω.

Ἠσαΐας. Nominative subject of εἶπεν.

ὁ προφήτης. Nominative in apposition to Ἠσαΐας.

1:24 Καὶ ἀπεσταλμένοι ἦσαν ἐκ τῶν Φαρισαίων.

Καί. Coordinating conjunction.

ἀπεσταλμένοι. Prf pass ptc masc nom pl ἀποστέλλω (pluperfect periphrastic). Fronted as a topical frame. In some manuscripts, οἱ is added before ἀπεσταλμένοι (ℵ² Aᶜ C³ K N Wˢ Γ Δ Θ 0234 *f*¹·¹³ 33 565 1241 1424 𝔐 et al.), turning the participle into a substantive that serves as the subject of ἦσαν. The shorter reading, however, is to be preferred because it has better external support (𝔓⁶⁶·⁷⁵ ℵ* A* B C* L T Ψ 086 co Or) and represents the *lectio difficilior*.

ἦσαν. Impf act ind 3rd pl εἰμί. The implied subject of the verb is perhaps τινές (Haubeck and von Siebenthal, 525; Harris 2015, 43). For similar constructions in which τινές is implied, see 7:40; 16:7; for the constructions in which τινές is expressed, see 7:25, 44; 9:16; 11:37; 11:46; 12:20. On this reading, the verse introduces a new group of interlocutors that came along with the priests and Levites mentioned in 1:19 (cf. CJB; NIV). Alternatively, the implied subject of the verb could be the same group of characters—priests and Levites—who interrogated John up to this point. Many English translations that use the pronoun "they" (NRSV; NET; ESV; LEB; NASB) assume this interpretation.

ἐκ τῶν Φαρισαίων. Replaces the partitive genitive (if τινές is implied) or functions as an instrumental PP (if the implied τινές refers to a group sent by the Pharisees or if the implied subject of ἦσαν is the priests and Levites from v. 19).

1:25 καὶ ἠρώτησαν αὐτὸν καὶ εἶπαν αὐτῷ· τί οὖν βαπτίζεις εἰ σὺ οὐκ εἶ ὁ χριστὸς οὐδὲ Ἠλίας οὐδὲ ὁ προφήτης;

καὶ. Coordinating conjunction.
ἠρώτησαν. Aor act ind 3rd pl ἐρωτάω.
αὐτὸν. Accusative direct object of ἠρώτησαν.
καὶ εἶπαν αὐτῷ. Pleonastic clause under Semitic influence. In Hebrew, the verb of speaking is frequently followed by וַיֹּאמֶר, which the LXX translates with καὶ εἶπεν. While the Synoptic Gospels typically betray this influence through the use of pleonastic participles, the Fourth Evangelist prefers paratactic constructions with pleonastic finite forms of λέγω (BDF §420.1–2; MHT 3:156). Runge calls such clauses "redundant quotative frames" and argues that they typically serve "to accentuate a discontinuity or transition in the dialogue, thereby directing attention to the speech that follows" (2010, 150).
καὶ. Coordinating conjunction.
εἶπαν. Aor act ind 3rd pl λέγω.
αὐτῷ. Dative indirect object of εἶπαν.
τί. Adverbial use of the interrogative pronoun ("why?"). It marks the beginning of the apodosis of a first-class condition, which is placed before the protasis.
οὖν. Postpositive inferential conjunction and/or transitional particle (see 1:22 and 11:6).
βαπτίζεις. Pres act ind 2nd sg βαπτίζω. The imperfective aspect of the present tense portrays John's baptizing, which is mentioned for the first time in the FG, as an unfolding activity.
εἰ. Introduces the protasis of a first-class condition.
σὺ. Nominative subject of εἶ. Fronted as a topical frame.
οὐκ . . . οὐδὲ . . . οὐδὲ. Three negative particles ("not/neither . . . nor . . . nor") that negate three predicate nominatives. οὐδὲ is a combination of οὐ and the marker of narrative development δέ.
εἶ. Pres act ind 2nd sg εἰμί.
ὁ χριστὸς. Predicate nominative (see 1:20).
Ἠλίας. Predicate nominative (see 1:21).
ὁ προφήτης. Predicate nominative (see 1:21).

1:26 ἀπεκρίθη αὐτοῖς ὁ Ἰωάννης λέγων· ἐγὼ βαπτίζω ἐν ὕδατι· μέσος ὑμῶν ἕστηκεν ὃν ὑμεῖς οὐκ οἴδατε,

ἀπεκρίθη. Aor mid ind 3rd sg ἀποκρίνομαι. On the voice, see "Deponency" in the Series Introduction. This verse is connected to the previous one by asyndeton.

αὐτοῖς. Dative indirect object of ἀπεκρίθη.

ὁ Ἰωάννης. Nominative subject of ἀπεκρίθη.

λέγων. Pres act ptc masc nom sg λέγω (pleonastic).

ἐγώ. Nominative subject of βαπτίζω. Fronted as a topical frame.

βαπτίζω. Pres act ind 1st sg βαπτίζω.

ἐν ὕδατι. Instrumental/means ("with water") or locative ("in water").

μέσος ὑμῶν. Locative adverbial expression. Nominative adjective μέσος is used here to indicate "a position within a group, without focus on mediate position, *among*" (BDAG, 635.2.a); cf. Luke 22:55. The adjective μέσος agrees with the unexpressed subject of ἕστηκεν. This clause is connected to the preceding one by asyndeton.

ἕστηκεν. Prf act ind 3rd sg ἵστημι. The perfect tense of this stative verb describes the present state of the subject (standing) without any reference to its beginning. Campbell, who holds that the distinguishing semantic quality of the perfect tense is heightened proximity with intensive implicature (2007, 195–201), suggests that the intensive rendering of ἕστηκεν and οἴδατε in this verse "captures the pointed nature of John's claim: the one of whom he speaks is actually *among* them, yet he is not known" (203). Metzger, who also recognizes the intensive character of ἕστηκεν, argues that it expresses a "special force ... which was unappreciated by several Greek witnesses (B L f¹ Origen Cyril) as well by a variety of Latin, Syriac, and Coptic witnesses ..., all of which preferred the more syntactically appropriate present tense" στήκει (Metzger, 170–71).

ὅν. The relative pronoun introduces a headless relative clause that, in its entirety (ὃν ὑμεῖς οὐκ οἴδατε), serves as the subject of ἕστηκεν. Within its clause, ὅν is the accusative direct object of οἴδατε.

ὑμεῖς. Nominative subject of οἴδατε. Spelled out and fronted for emphasis.

οὐκ. Negative particle normally used with indicative verbs.

οἴδατε. Prf act ind 2nd pl οἶδα. The verb stands in final, emphatic position. This is the first occurrence of οἶδα in the FG. The perfect tense has the present meaning, describing "the enduring result rather than the completed act" (Smyth §1946) without any reference to how this knowledge (or lack thereof) emerged. Campbell argues that this verb cannot be used as a support for the stative aspect of the perfect tense because "οἶδα is *already* stative simply because of its lexical meaning, and irrespective of its expression as a perfect indicative" (2007, 188).

1:27 ὁ ὀπίσω μου ἐρχόμενος, οὗ οὐκ εἰμὶ [ἐγὼ] ἄξιος ἵνα λύσω αὐτοῦ τὸν ἱμάντα τοῦ ὑποδήματος.

ὁ ... ἐρχόμενος. Pres mid ptc masc nom sg ἔρχομαι (substantival). Nominative in apposition to the subject of ἕστηκεν from v. 26.

ὀπίσω μου. Temporal. ὀπίσω is an improper preposition (see 1:3 on χωρὶς αὐτοῦ). The PP, placed between the article and the participle, functions as an attributive modifier of ἐρχόμενος (see 1:15 on ὀπίσω μου).

οὗ. Genitive complement of ἄξιος ("of whom I am not worthy"). Alternatively, the relative pronoun could be regarded as a possessive genitive modifying ὑποδήματος, in which case αὐτοῦ is redundant (Harris 2015, 44; MHT 2:435). While such a redundancy could perhaps be explained as a Semitism, it still results in an awkward Greek syntax, not to mention the difficulty in explaining the distance between the head noun and its genitive modifier.

οὐκ. Negative particle normally used with indicative verbs.

εἰμί. Pres act ind 1st sg εἰμί.

[ἐγὼ]. Nominative subject of εἰμὶ. The personal pronoun is missing in $\mathfrak{P}^{66*.75.120}$ ℵ C L f^{13} 33 565 et al. Its presence is not required by the syntax so that, if original, it has emphatic function.

ἄξιος. Predicate adjective.

ἵνα. Introduces an epexegetical clause that clarifies the adjective ἄξιος; i.e., it explains what specifically John is not worthy of. An epexegetical ἵνα clause is equivalent to an epexegetical infinitive in classical Greek (Wallace 1996, 476; BDF §379; Caragounis 2004, 219). Thus, ἄξιος ἵνα λύσω αὐτοῦ τὸν ἱμάντα τοῦ ὑποδήματος = ἄξιος λῦσαι αὐτοῦ τὸν ἱμάντα τοῦ ὑποδήματος (cf. ἱκανὸς ... λῦσαι τὸν ἱμάντα τῶν ὑποδημάτων αὐτοῦ in Mark 1:7//Luke 3:16).

λύσω. Aor act subj 1st sg λύω. Subjunctive with ἵνα.

αὐτοῦ. Possessive genitive qualifying τοῦ ὑποδήματος ("his sandals"). The preposed pronoun is thematically salient (Levinsohn 2000, 64).

τὸν ἱμάντα. Accusative direct object of λύσω.

τοῦ ὑποδήματος. Partitive genitive qualifying ἱμάντα.

1:28 ταῦτα ἐν Βηθανίᾳ ἐγένετο πέραν τοῦ Ἰορδάνου, ὅπου ἦν ὁ Ἰωάννης βαπτίζων.

ταῦτα. Nominative subject of ἐγένετο. Fronted as a topical frame. This verse is connected to the previous one by asyndeton.

ἐν Βηθανίᾳ. Locative.

ἐγένετο. Aor mid ind 3rd sg γίνομαι. Neuter plural subjects typically take singular verbs, which is one of the most striking syntactical peculiarities of Greek (BDF §133).

πέραν τοῦ Ἰορδάνου. Locative. πέραν is an improper preposition (see 1:3 on χωρὶς αὐτοῦ) which, in this context, answers the question, "Where?" (BDAG, 796.b.β).

ὅπου. Particle denoting place. Caragounis (2004, 193) notes that in the NT "the relative pronoun is sometimes substituted for by a local adverb," as here (ὅπου = ἐν ᾗ).

ἦν. Impf act ind 3rd sg εἰμί.

ὁ Ἰωάννης. Nominative subject of ἦν.

βαπτίζων. Pres act ptc masc nom sg βαπτίζω. The participle can either be a part of the imperfect periphrastic structure ("where John was baptizing") or function adverbially indicating manner, i.e., way of life ("where John was, [and was] baptizing" [Zerwick, 126; cf. BDF §353.1]).

John 1:29-34

[29]On the next day, John saw Jesus coming toward him and said, "Here is the Lamb of God who takes away the sin of the world! [30]This is the one about whom I said, 'After me comes a man who ranks higher than me because he was before me.' [31]And I did not know him, but in order that he could be revealed to Israel—because of this I came baptizing with water." [32]John also testified, saying, "I have seen the Spirit descending like a dove out of the sky, and it remained on him. [33]And I did not know him, but the one who sent me to baptize with water, that one said to me, 'Upon whomever you see the Spirit descending and remaining upon him—this is the one who baptizes with the Holy Spirit.' [34]And I have seen and testify that this is the Son of God."

1:29 Τῇ ἐπαύριον βλέπει τὸν Ἰησοῦν ἐρχόμενον πρὸς αὐτὸν καὶ λέγει· ἴδε ὁ ἀμνὸς τοῦ θεοῦ ὁ αἴρων τὴν ἁμαρτίαν τοῦ κόσμου.

Τῇ ἐπαύριον. The article functions as a nominalizer, changing the adverb ἐπαύριον ("tomorrow") into the dative of time. In the NT, ἐπαύριον occurs only with the feminine dative article (e.g., Matt 27:62; Mark 11:12; John 1:29, 35, 43; 6:22; 12:12; Acts 10:9, 23, 24; 14:20; 20:7), which indicates that ἡμέρᾳ should be supplied: "on the next day" (BDAG, 360). This verse is connected to the previous one by asyndeton.

βλέπει. Pres act ind 3rd sg βλέπω. Both verbs in this verse are the historical presents, marking a transition to Jesus' first appearance in the narrative (Battle, 128) and drawing attention to John's proclamation of Jesus' identity (see 1:15 on μαρτυρεῖ).

τὸν Ἰησοῦν. Accusative direct object of βλέπει.

ἐρχόμενον. Pres mid ptc masc acc sg ἔρχομαι (predicative). The participle stands in the second predicate position (article-noun-participle) (Wallace 1996, 308, 617–19), functioning as the accusative complement to τὸν Ἰησοῦν in a double accusative object-complement construction (Culy 2009, 87–88).

πρὸς αὐτόν. Locative (motion toward). αὐτόν stands for ἑαυτόν.

καί. Coordinating conjunction.

λέγει. Pres act ind 3rd sg λέγω. The historical present gives thematic prominence to John's proclamation that follows (see 1:15 on μαρτυρεῖ).

ἴδε. An interjection (originally aor act impv 2nd sg ὁράω) that is "used when more than one pers[on] is addressed, and when that which is to be observed is in the nom[inative]" (BDAG, 466). This interjection is here used "to indicate a place or individual" and can be translated "here is" (466.3).

ὁ ἀμνός. Nominative of exclamation. Wallace notes that "[t]his use of the nominative is actually a subcategory of the nominative for vocative" (1996, 60), but unlike the latter it is not used in direct address. The article may be monadic ("one of a kind") if the genitive τοῦ θεοῦ is regarded as a part of the fixed formula (223–24).

τοῦ θεοῦ. Possessive genitive qualifying ἀμνός.

ὁ αἴρων. Pres act ptc masc nom sg αἴρω (attributive). The participle modifies ὁ ἀμνός, standing in the second attributive position (article-noun-article-attributive participle) (Wallace 1996, 306–7, 618).

τὴν ἁμαρτίαν. Accusative direct object of αἴρων. Brown (1:56) calls attention to a difference between the plural in 1 John 3:5 (ἵνα τὰς ἁμαρτίας ἄρῃ), which refers to sinful acts, and the singular here, which refers to a sinful condition.

τοῦ κόσμου. Possessive genitive qualifying ἁμαρτίαν ("the world's sin") or subjective genitive ("the sin committed by the world"). On the portrayal of the world in the FG, see 1:10 on ἐν τῷ κόσμῳ.

1:30 οὗτός ἐστιν ὑπὲρ οὗ ἐγὼ εἶπον· ὀπίσω μου ἔρχεται ἀνὴρ ὃς ἔμπροσθέν μου γέγονεν, ὅτι πρῶτός μου ἦν.

οὗτός ἐστιν ὑπὲρ οὗ ἐγὼ εἶπον. This clause is an expanded version of οὗτος ἦν ὃν εἶπον in 1:15. The change from the imperfect to the present tense is appropriate to the new context in which John spoke about Jesus who was no longer absent but present. In this way, as Frey emphasizes, the Baptist, who is "a figure of the distant past for the Johannine readers," becomes himself "a present witness to Christ" (2018, 80–81).

οὗτός. Nominative subject of ἐστιν. Fronted for emphasis. The anaphoric demonstrative refers to Jesus, who was mentioned in 1:29, and conveys the spatial proximity between the speaker and the referent. οὗτός, which has a circumflex accent on the penult, acquired an additional accent, the acute, on the ultima from the enclitic ἐστιν (Smyth §183; Carson 1985, 48).

ἐστιν. Pres act ind 3rd sg εἰμί. On the present tense, see οὗτός ἐστιν ὑπὲρ οὗ ἐγὼ εἶπον above.

ὑπὲρ οὗ. Reference/respect. ὑπὲρ οὗ is equvalent to περὶ οὗ (Harris 2012, 209–10).

ἐγώ. Nominative subject of εἶπον. Fronted as a topical frame.

εἶπον. Aor act ind 1st sg λέγω. εἶπον introduces a new direct speech within the existing direct discourse.

ὀπίσω μου ἔρχεται ἀνήρ. This finite clause is a paraphrase of the participial expression ὁ ὀπίσω μου ἐρχόμενος in 1:15.

ὀπίσω μου. Temporal (see 1:15, 21). Fronted as a temporal frame.

ἔρχεται. Pres mid ind 3rd sg ἔρχομαι. The present tense is here used for an action that is extended into the future.

ἀνήρ. Nominative subject of ἔρχεται.

ὅς. Nominative subject of γέγονεν.

ἔμπροσθέν μου γέγονεν, ὅτι πρῶτός μου ἦν. A verbatim repetition of ἔμπροσθέν μου γέγονεν, ὅτι πρῶτός μου ἦν in 1:15.

ἔμπροσθέν μου. Advantage (see 1:15). Fronted for emphasis. ἔμπροσθέν, which has an acute accent on the antepenult, acquired an additional accent, the acute, on the ultima from the enclitic μου (Smyth §183; Carson 1985, 48).

γέγονεν. Prf act ind 3rd sg γίνομαι. As in 1:15, the stative aspect of the perfect tense, combined with the PP ἔμπροσθέν μου, conveys the idea of superiority rather than the idea of temporal priority.

ὅτι. Introduces a causal clause (see 1:15).

πρῶτός. Predicate adjective. The superlative πρῶτος ("first, earliest") stands for the comparative πρότερος ("earlier"); see 1:15. πρῶτός, which has a circumflex accent on the penult, acquired an additional accent, the acute, on the ultima from the enclitic μου (Smyth §183; Carson 1985, 48).

μου. Genitive of comparison (see 1:15).

ἦν. Impf act ind 3rd sg εἰμί (see 1:15).

1:31 κἀγὼ οὐκ ᾔδειν αὐτόν, ἀλλ' ἵνα φανερωθῇ τῷ Ἰσραὴλ διὰ τοῦτο ἦλθον ἐγὼ ἐν ὕδατι βαπτίζων.

κἀγώ. Formed by crasis from καὶ ἐγώ. καί is a coordinating conjunction, but it could also be adverbial: ascensive ("even I") or adjunctive ("I also"). ἐγώ is the nominative subject of ᾔδειν. Fronted as a topical frame.

οὐκ . . . ἀλλ'. A point/counterpoint set ("not this . . . but that") that negates the incorrect assertion (John knew who Jesus was) and replaces it with the correct assertion (the purpose of John's baptizing activity was that Jesus might be revealed to Israel). On the function of ἀλλά in a point/counterpoint set, see 1:8.

ᾔδειν. Plprf act ind 1st sg οἶδα. This is the second occurrence of οἶδα in the FG, and it is again used with the negative particle. In the FG, every occurrence of the pluperfect within direct discourse is a pluperfect of οἶδα (1:31, 33; 4:10; 8:19 [2x]; 11:42). The pluperfect tense has the imperfect meaning, describing the state of knowing in the past without any reference to how this knowledge was gained or, as here, what prevented acquisition of knowledge (see 1:26 on οἴδατε).

αὐτόν. Accusative direct object of ᾔδειν.

ἵνα. Introduces a purpose clause that is in a left-dislocation, resumed by διὰ τοῦτο.

φανερωθῇ. Aor pass subj 3rd sg φανερόω. Subjunctive with ἵνα.

τῷ Ἰσραήλ. Dative indirect object of φανερωθῇ.

διὰ τοῦτο. Causal. The antecedent of the neuter near-demonstrative pronoun is the ἵνα clause that precedes it. In this context, the PP διὰ τοῦτο functions as a connective. According to Runge, "In the absence of a full morphological conjunction, διὰ τοῦτο plays the same functional role of indicating how the independent clause that follows is to be related to what precedes. The preposition διά contributes to a causal sense in most cases. . . . The demonstrative pronoun τοῦτο reiterates a proposition from the receding context. Thus, the clause introduced by διὰ τοῦτο is constrained to have a causal relation with the preceding discourse" (2010, 48).

ἦλθον. Aor act ind 1st sg ἔρχομαι.

ἐγώ. Nominative subject of ἦλθον.

ἐν ὕδατι. Instrumental/means ("with water") or locative ("in water"). Fronted for emphasis (compare the unemphatic position of this PP in 1:26).

βαπτίζων. Pres act ptc masc nom sg βαπτίζω (purpose or manner). Runge argues that adverbial participles that follow the main verb, as here, "have a somewhat different effect from those that precede it, in that they elaborate the action of the main verb, often providing more specific explanation of what is meant by the main action. . . . Rather than offering a distinct action in its own right, the participle relegates its action to supporting the main action" (2010, 262–63). Although the post-main-verb participles are typically more important than the pre-main-verb participles in relation to the main verb, they do not provide the foreground information because, as Buth rightly emphasizes, "they are ranked with lower prominence than the main head verbs because they are participles" (2016, 282 n. 9).

1:32 Καὶ ἐμαρτύρησεν Ἰωάννης λέγων ὅτι τεθέαμαι τὸ πνεῦμα καταβαῖνον ὡς περιστερὰν ἐξ οὐρανοῦ καὶ ἔμεινεν ἐπ' αὐτόν.

Καὶ. Adverbial (adjunctive) or connective, linking two clauses.

ἐμαρτύρησεν. Aor act ind 3rd sg μαρτυρέω.

Ἰωάννης. Nominative subject of ἐμαρτύρησεν.

λέγων. Pres act ptc masc nom sg λέγω (pleonastic).

ὅτι. ὅτι-*recitativum* that introduces the clausal complement (direct discourse) of λέγων.

τεθέαμαι. Prf mid 1st sg θεάομαι. The contextual markers indicate that the perfect tense describes an event that occurred in the past, most likely Jesus' baptism, but the stative aspect of the verb form gives prominence to John's recollection of that event in the present (see 1:34).

τὸ πνεῦμα. Accusative direct object of τεθέαμαι.

καταβαῖνον. Pres act ptc neut acc sg καταβαίνω (predicative). The participle stands in the second predicate position (see 1:29 on ἐρχόμενον), functioning as the accusative complement to τὸ πνεῦμα in a double accusative object-complement construction. καταβαίνω ("to move down, to come down, to go down, to descend" [LN 15.107]) denotes movement downward.

ὡς. Comparative particle, introducing an elliptical clause that presumes the repetition of the main verb (see below).

περιστερὰν. Accusative direct object of a first-person singular verb form of an implied θεάομαι: "as [I would see] a dove." The formulation τὸ πνεῦμα καταβαῖνον ὡς περιστερὰν is similar to τὸ πνεῦμα ὡς περιστερὰν καταβαῖνον in Mark 1:10, but John's placement of καταβαῖνον before the comparative particle ὡς probably indicates that the evangelist describes the manner in which the Spirit descended, rather than the form in which the Spirit appeared (Newman and Nida, 38).

ἐξ οὐρανοῦ. Locative. The placement of the PP after περιστερὰν indicates that it refers to a dove. The translation "out of the sky" is therefore more appropriate than "from heaven," adopted by most English versions because, as Michaels (114) perceptively notes, "[w]hile the Spirit comes from heaven, doves do not, and John is using the language of appearance" (Brown, 1:55).

καί. Coordinating conjunction.
ἔμεινεν. Aor act ind 3rd sg μένω.
ἐπ' αὐτόν. Locative.

1:33 κἀγὼ οὐκ ᾔδειν αὐτόν, ἀλλ' ὁ πέμψας με βαπτίζειν ἐν ὕδατι ἐκεῖνός μοι εἶπεν· ἐφ' ὃν ἂν ἴδῃς τὸ πνεῦμα καταβαῖνον καὶ μένον ἐπ' αὐτόν, οὗτός ἐστιν ὁ βαπτίζων ἐν πνεύματι ἁγίῳ.

κἀγὼ οὐκ ᾔδειν αὐτόν. This clause is the verbatim repetition of κἀγὼ οὐκ ᾔδειν αὐτόν in 1:31.

κἀγώ. Formed by crasis from καὶ ἐγώ. καί is a coordinating conjunction, but it could also be adverbial: ascensive ("even I") or adjunctive ("I also"). ἐγώ is the nominative subject of ᾔδειν. Fronted as a topical frame.

οὐκ ... ἀλλ'. A point/counterpoint set ("not this ... but that") that negates the first, incorrect, assertion (John knew who Jesus was) and replaces it with the second, correct, assertion (John recognized Jesus through the descent of the Spirit, which was announced beforehand). On the function of ἀλλά in a point/counterpoint set, see 1:8.

ᾔδειν. Plprf act ind 1st sg οἶδα. In the FG, every occurrence of the pluperfect within direct discourse is a pluperfect of οἶδα (1:31, 33; 4:10; 8:19 [2x]; 11:42). The pluperfect tense has the imperfect meaning, describing the state of knowing in the past without any reference to how this knowledge was gained or, as here, what prevented acquisition of knowledge (see 1:26 on οἴδατε).

αὐτόν. Accusative direct object of ᾔδειν.

ὁ πέμψας. Aor act ptc masc nom sg πέμπω (substantival). Nominative subject of εἶπεν in a left-dislocation, resumed by ἐκεῖνός. Left-dislocations "have the effect of either announcing or shifting the topic of the clause that follows. This attracts more attention to the topic than it would have otherwise received with one of the more conventional methods" (Runge 2010, 290). The left-dislocation of ὁ πέμψας brings God into more pronounced focus than if John had simply said, "The one who sent me to baptize with water said to me."

με. Accusative direct object of πέμψας.
βαπτίζειν. Pres act inf βαπτίζω (purpose).
ἐν ὕδατι. Instrumental/means ("with water") or locative ("in water").
ἐκεῖνός. Nominative subject of εἶπεν, resuming ὁ πέμψας. The anaphoric demonstrative reinforces what is already made prominent through the left-dislocation of ὁ πέμψας. ἐκεῖνός, which has a circumflex

accent on the penult, acquired an additional accent, the acute, on the ultima from the enclitic μοι (Smyth §183; Carson 1985, 48).

μοι. Dative indirect object of εἶπεν.

εἶπεν. Aor act ind 3rd sg λέγω. εἶπεν introduces a new direct speech within the existing direct discourse.

ἐφ' ὃν ἂν ἴδῃς τὸ πνεῦμα καταβαῖνον καὶ μένον ἐπ' αὐτόν. A headless relative clause in a left-dislocation, resumed by οὗτός, which in its entirety functions as a subject of ἐστιν.

ἐφ' ὃν ἄν. Locative. The particle ἄν marks the relative pronoun ὅν, indicating that "the element of contingency is not that of time but of person" (Wallace 1996, 478).

ἴδῃς. Aor act subj 2nd sg ὁράω. Subjunctive with ἄν in an indefinite relative clause.

τὸ πνεῦμα. Accusative direct object of ἴδῃς (see 1:32).

καταβαῖνον καὶ μένον. The participles stand in the second predicate position (see 1:29 on ἐρχόμενον), functioning as the accusative complements to τὸ πνεῦμα in a double accusative object-complement construction (see 1:32).

καταβαῖνον. Pres act ptc neut acc sg καταβαίνω (predicative).

μένον. Pres act ptc neut acc sg μένω (predicative).

ἐπ' αὐτόν. Locative. The PP with the personal pronoun is pleonastic after ἐφ' ὅν (BDF §297; Zerwick §201).

οὗτός. Nominative subject of ἐστιν, resuming the headless relative clause ἐφ' ὃν ἂν ἴδῃς τὸ πνεῦμα καταβαῖνον καὶ μένον ἐπ' αὐτόν. Fronted for emphasis. οὗτός, which has a circumflex accent on the penult, acquired an additional accent, the acute, on the ultima from the enclitic ἐστιν (Smyth §183; Carson 1985, 48).

ἐστιν. Pres act ind 3rd sg εἰμί.

ὁ βαπτίζων. Pres act ptc masc nom sg βαπτίζω (substantival). Predicate nominative.

ἐν πνεύματι ἁγίῳ. Instrumental/means.

1:34 κἀγὼ ἑώρακα καὶ μεμαρτύρηκα ὅτι οὗτός ἐστιν ὁ υἱὸς τοῦ θεοῦ.

κἀγώ. Formed by crasis from καὶ ἐγώ. καί is a coordinating conjunction, but it could also be adverbial: ascensive ("even I") or adjunctive ("I also"). ἐγώ is the nominative subject of ἑώρακα. Fronted as a topical frame.

ἑώρακα. Prf act ind 1st sg ὁράω. ἑώρακα, like τεθέαμαι in 1:32, refers to an event in the past, but the stative aspect of the verb form gives prominence to the recollection of that event in the present.

καί. Coordinating conjunction.

μεμαρτύρηκα. Prf act ind 1st sg μαρτυρέω. μεμαρτύρηκα, along with the previous perfect-tense verb ἑώρακα, serves as a climactic conclusion of John's testimony, drawing attention to his confession of Jesus' divine identity. The stative aspect of μεμαρτύρηκα is more pronounced than that of ἑώρακα, focusing on John's state of witness bearing rather than evoking the event that prompted his testimony.

ὅτι. Introduces the clausal complement (indirect discourse) of μεμαρτύρηκα.

οὗτός. Nominative subject of ἐστιν. Fronted for emphasis. The anaphoric demonstrative refers to Jesus, who was mentioned in 1:29, and conveys the spatial proximity between the speaker and the referent. οὗτός, which has a circumflex accent on the penult, acquired an additional accent, the acute, on the ultima from the enclitic ἐστιν (Smyth §183; Carson 1985, 48).

ἐστιν. Pres act ind 3rd sg εἰμί.

ὁ υἱὸς. Predicate nominative. The variant ὁ ἐκλεκτός is attested by 𝔓^{5vid} ℵ* b e ff^{2*} sy$^{s.c}$ et al. Although the external evidence for this reading is not very strong, some English translations (REB; NET) prefer it, presuming, as Barrett argues, that "it is much easier to understand the change of ἐκλεκτός to υἱός than the reverse" (178). This argument proved decisive for SBLGNT, which adopts the reading ὁ ἐκλεκτός, while NA^{28}/UBS^5 prefer ὁ υἱός on the basis of age and diversity of the manuscript tradition (𝔓$^{66.75}$ A B C L $f^{1.13}$ 33 892 et al.) and the consistency of this reading with the terminology of the FG (Metzger, 172).

τοῦ θεοῦ. Genitive of relationship qualifying υἱὸς.

John 1:35-42

^{35}On the next day, again John was standing with two of his disciples, ^{36}and, when he looked at Jesus walking by, he said, "Here is the Lamb of God!" ^{37}And the two disciples heard him speaking, and they followed Jesus. ^{38}When Jesus turned and saw them following, he said to them, "What are you looking for?" They said to him, "Rabbi" (which means, when translated, Teacher), "where are you staying?" ^{39}He said to them, "Come and you will see." So they came and saw where he was staying, and they stayed with him that day. It was about the tenth hour. ^{40}Andrew, the brother of Simon Peter, was one of the two who had heard John and followed him. ^{41}He first found his own brother, Simon, and said to him, "We have found the Messiah" (which is translated "Anointed"). ^{42}He brought him to Jesus. When Jesus looked at him, he said, "You are Simon, the son of John. You will be called Cephas" (which is translated "Rock").

1:35 Τῇ ἐπαύριον πάλιν εἱστήκει ὁ Ἰωάννης καὶ ἐκ τῶν μαθητῶν αὐτοῦ δύο

Τῇ ἐπαύριον. The article functions as a nominalizer, changing the adverb ἐπαύριον ("tomorrow") into the dative of time (see 1:29). Fronted as a temporal frame. This verse is connected to the previous one by asyndeton.

πάλιν. Adverb "pert[aining] to repetition in the same (or similar) manner" (BDAG, 752.2).

εἱστήκει. Plprf act ind 3rd sg ἵστημι. The pluperfect has an imperfect meaning (Robertson, 94).

ὁ Ἰωάννης καὶ . . . δύο. Compound nominative subject of εἱστήκει. When the verb precedes its two (or more) subjects, it is in the singular, agreeing with the first (BDF §135). The singular verb with multiple subjects can also be used to highlight one of them. According to Wallace, "The *first*-named subject is the one being stressed in such instances" (1996, 401). This explanation makes good sense here because it is John, and not two of his disciples, who calls Jesus the Lamb of God in the next verse.

ἐκ τῶν μαθητῶν. Replaces the partitive genitive.

αὐτοῦ. Genitive of relationship qualifying μαθητῶν.

1:36 καὶ ἐμβλέψας τῷ Ἰησοῦ περιπατοῦντι λέγει· ἴδε ὁ ἀμνὸς τοῦ θεοῦ.

καὶ. Coordinating conjunction.

ἐμβλέψας. Aor act ptc masc nom sg ἐμβλέπω (temporal). ἐμβλέπω ("to look straight at, to look directly at") is similar in meaning to βλέπω (LN 24.9), except that it calls attention to a particular object of one's vision. The participle ἐμβλέψας, which precedes the finite verb λέγει, provides the background information for John's declaration of Jesus' identity (Levinsohn 2000, 183; Runge 2010, 249–62). "Despite the various claims about the function of adverbial participles (e.g., manner, time, cause, purpose), the ones that precede the main clause share a unified function. The use of the participle represents the choice not to use a finite verb. Since the participle is dependent upon the main verb to supply the information that it does not encode on its own (e.g., mood), the participle does not obtain the same status as a finite verb. This means that the participle plays a supporting role to the main verb, and the role differs depending upon the placement of the participle with respect to the main verb. Those that precede the main verb have the effect of backgrounding the action of the participle, indicating that it is less important than the main verbal action" (249; cf. Buth 2016, 277–78, 281 n. 9). Since the participles that precede the main verb usually express the notion of completion, "so that the sequence normally was: the completion of the action denoted by the participle, then the action of the finite verb, the idea of relative past time became associated to a certain degree with the aorist participle" (BDF §339).

τῷ Ἰησοῦ. Dative direct object of ἐμβλέψας.

περιπατοῦντι. Pres act ptc masc dat sg περιπατέω (predicative). The participle modifies τῷ Ἰησοῦ, standing in the second predicate position (see 1:29 on ἐρχόμενον). This function is equivalent to the function of ἐρχόμενον in 1:29, which serves as a complement to τὸν Ἰησοῦν (the accusative direct object of βλέπει) in a double accusative construction. Since here the author uses ἐμβλέπω—a compound of βλέπει and the prefixed preposition ἐν—both the direct object of the verb (τῷ Ἰησοῦ) and its participial complement (περιπατοῦντι) are in the dative. We might call this structure a "double dative construction" in analogy to a "double accusative construction." This participle, therefore, should not be regarded as temporal (*pace* Haubeck and von Siebenthal, 526; Harris 2015, 48; cf. REB; ESV; KJV; LEB). As Culy (2003) has shown, temporal and other adverbial participles are always in nominative, agreeing with the subject of the verb, except when they modify a genitive subject (genitive absolute) or an infinitive whose semantic subject is in accusative.

λέγει. Pres act ind 3rd sg λέγω. The historical present gives thematic prominence to John's exclamation that follows (see 1:15 on μαρτυρεῖ).

ἴδε. An interjection (originally aor act impv 2nd sg ὁράω) that is "used when more than one pers[on] is addressed, and when that which is to be observed is in the nom[inative]" (BDAG, 466). This interjection is here used "to indicate a place or individual" and can be translated "here is" (BDAG, 466.3).

ὁ ἀμνὸς. Nominative of exclamation (see 1:29).

τοῦ θεοῦ. Possessive genitive qualifying ἀμνὸς.

1:37 καὶ ἤκουσαν οἱ δύο μαθηταὶ αὐτοῦ λαλοῦντος καὶ ἠκολούθησαν τῷ Ἰησοῦ.

καὶ. Coordinating conjunction.

ἤκουσαν. Aor act ind 3rd pl ἀκούω.

οἱ δύο μαθηταὶ. Nominative subject of ἤκουσαν. The article is anaphoric, referring to ἐκ τῶν μαθητῶν αὐτοῦ δύο in 1:35.

αὐτοῦ. Genitive direct object of ἤκουσαν.

λαλοῦντος. Pres act ptc masc gen sg λαλέω (predicative). The participle modifies αὐτοῦ. The combination αὐτοῦ λαλοῦντος is equivalent to a double accusative object-complement construction; the direct object (αὐτοῦ) and its complement (λαλοῦντος) are genitives because this case is required by the governing verb ἤκουσαν.

καὶ. Coordinating conjunction.

ἠκολούθησαν. Aor act ind 3rd pl ἀκολουθέω.

τῷ Ἰησοῦ. Dative direct object of ἠκολούθησαν.

1:38 στραφεὶς δὲ ὁ Ἰησοῦς καὶ θεασάμενος αὐτοὺς ἀκολουθοῦντας λέγει αὐτοῖς· τί ζητεῖτε; οἱ δὲ εἶπαν αὐτῷ· ῥαββί, ὃ λέγεται μεθερμηνευόμενον διδάσκαλε, ποῦ μένεις;

στραφεὶς. Aor pass ptc masc nom sg στρέφω (temporal). On participles that precede the main verb, see ἐμβλέψας in 1:36.

δὲ. Marker of narrative development.

ὁ Ἰησοῦς. Nominative subject of λέγει.

καὶ. Coordinating conjunction.

θεασάμενος. Aor mid ptc masc nom sg θεάομαι (temporal).

αὐτοὺς. Accusative direct object of θεασάμενος.

ἀκολουθοῦντας. Pres act ptc masc acc pl ἀκολουθέω (predicative). The participle functions as the accusative complement to αὐτοὺς in a double accusative object-complement construction.

λέγει. Pres act ind 3rd sg λέγω. The historical present grants prominence to Jesus' question that follows (see 1:15 on μαρτυρεῖ).

αὐτοῖς. Dative indirect object of λέγει.

τί. Accusative direct object of ζητεῖτε.

ζητεῖτε. Pres act ind 2nd pl ζητέω.

οἱ δὲ. A construction that is frequently used in narrative literature to indicate the change of the speaker in a dialogue. The nominative article stands in place of a third-person personal pronoun and functions as the subject of εἶπαν. Its force is anaphoric, referring to the two disciples whom Jesus saw. Fronted as a topical frame.

εἶπαν. Aor act ind 3rd pl λέγω.

αὐτῷ. Dative indirect object of εἶπαν.

ῥαββί. Vocative of direct address.

ὃ λέγεται μεθερμηνευόμενον διδάσκαλε. Parenthetical clause that interrupts the plot of the narrative. The purpose of this editorial gloss is to explain the meaning of the transliterated Hebrew term ῥαββί to the readers/hearers who are not familiar with it. For similar parenthetical comments, see 1:41, 42; 19:17; 20:16.

ὅ. Nominative subject of λέγεται. The antecedent of the relative pronoun is ῥαββί. ὅ is neuter rather than masculine because in explanatory phrases the neuter is used without much regard to the gender of the word that the phrase explains (Robertson, 411; BDF §132.2).

λέγεται. Pres pass ind 3rd sg λέγω. Lit. "which is called" = "which means."

μεθερμηνευόμενον. Pres pass ptc neut nom sg μεθερμηνεύω (temporal). The participle provides the temporal frame ("when translated") of the main clause ὃ λέγεται . . . διδάσκαλε ("which means 'Teacher'").

διδάσκαλε. Vocative of direct address.

ποῦ. Interrogative adverb of place.

μένεις. Pres act ind 2nd sg μένω.

1:39 λέγει αὐτοῖς· ἔρχεσθε καὶ ὄψεσθε. ἦλθαν οὖν καὶ εἶδαν ποῦ μένει καὶ παρ' αὐτῷ ἔμειναν τὴν ἡμέραν ἐκείνην· ὥρα ἦν ὡς δεκάτη.

λέγει. Pres act ind 3rd sg λέγω. The historical present again grants prominence to Jesus' words (see 1:15 on μαρτυρεῖ). This verse is connected to the previous one by asyndeton.

αὐτοῖς. Dative indirect object of λέγει.

ἔρχεσθε. Pres mid impv 2nd pl ἔρχομαι. Wallace (1996, 489) calls the imperative that is followed by καί + the future indicative a "conditional imperative" because it conveys the idea that "if X, then Y will happen." Thus, "come and you will see" means "if you come—and I want you to—you will see" (Wallace 1996, 490). This interpretation presumes that the future indicative is "prospective or looking toward the future" (Porter 1994, 44). If, however, its force is imperatival, then the imperative that precedes it cannot be regarded as conditional (see below on ὄψεσθε).

καί. Coordinating conjunction.

ὄψεσθε. Fut mid ind 2nd pl ὁράω. Regardless of whether one prefers Porter's view that "[r]ather than temporal values, *the future form grammaticalizes the semantic (meaning) feature of expectation*" (1994, 44) or Fanning's view that the future tense "tells the *temporal relation* of the verbal action to some reference-point, usually the time of speaking: the action is presented as *subsequent* (i.e. yet to take place)" (122), there is a general agreement that the future is a non-aspectual tense form whose specific function depends on the context. If ὄψεσθε here describes something that the speaker expects to happen in the future, the force of the imperative that precedes it is conditional, so that ἔρχεσθε καὶ ὄψεσθε means "come and (then) you will see." If, however, ὄψεσθε itself has imperatival force, ἔρχεσθε καὶ ὄψεσθε means "come and see (for yourself)."

ἦλθαν. Aor act ind 3rd pl ἔρχομαι. ἦλθαν is an alternative spelling for ἦλθον.

οὖν. Postpositive inferential conjunction and/or transitional particle (see 1:22 and 11:6).

καί. Coordinating conjunction.

εἶδαν. Aor act ind 3rd pl ὁράω. εἶδαν is an alternative spelling for εἶδον.

ποῦ. Interrogative adverb of place.

μένει. Pres act ind 3rd sg μένω. Unlike English, which requires adjusting the tense of the verb(s) in indirect discourse if the introductory verb is in the past tense, the tense of the Greek verb in the original utterance is retained in indirect discourse (see the direct question in v. 38).

καί. Coordinating conjunction.

παρ' αὐτῷ. Association. Fronted as a spatial frame.

ἔμειναν. Aor act ind 3rd pl μένω.

τὴν ἡμέραν ἐκείνην. Accusative indicating extent of time.

ὥρα. Nominative subject of ἦν. Fronted as a topical frame. This clause is connected to the previous one by asyndeton.

ἦν. Impf act ind 3rd sg εἰμί. This imperfect provides background information about the time when two of John's disciples joined Jesus. Du Toit argues that one of the major functions of the imperfect in the FG is "to provide background details about events, persons and other features of the mainline narrative. These expressions, which are generally short and often parenthetic, typically appear anywhere inside the body of the episode" (222). Since such explanatory comments are typically conveyed through the voice of the narrator, Culpepper (18) rightly calls the narrator in the FG "the whispering wizard of the imperfect tense."

ὡς. Particle used with numerals to denote an estimate ("about, approximately").

δεκάτη. Predicate adjective. δεκάτη (from δέκατος) is an ordinal number meaning "tenth"; "the tenth hour of a day" = 4 p.m. based on a customary reckoning of the twelve-hour day from sunrise (6 a.m.) to sunset (6 p.m.).

1:40 Ἦν Ἀνδρέας ὁ ἀδελφὸς Σίμωνος Πέτρου εἷς ἐκ τῶν δύο τῶν ἀκουσάντων παρὰ Ἰωάννου καὶ ἀκολουθησάντων αὐτῷ·

Ἦν. Impf act ind 3rd sg εἰμί. This verse is connected to the previous one by asyndeton.

Ἀνδρέας. Nominative subject of Ἦν.

ὁ ἀδελφὸς. Nominative in apposition to Ἀνδρέας.

Σίμωνος Πέτρου. Genitive of relationship qualifying ἀδελφὸς.

εἷς. Predicate nominative.

ἐκ τῶν δύο τῶν ἀκουσάντων . . . καὶ ἀκολουθησάντων. Replaces the partitive genitive. Two adjectival participles (ἀκουσάντων . . . καὶ ἀκολουθησάντων) modify δύο, standing in the second attributive position (see 1:29 on ὁ αἴρων).

ἀκουσάντων. Aor act ptc masc gen pl ἀκούω (attributive).

παρὰ Ἰωάννου. Source.

ἀκολουθησάντων. Aor act ptc masc gen pl ἀκολουθέω (attributive).

αὐτῷ. Dative direct object of ἀκολουθησάντων. The antecedent is not the closest noun in the clause (John) but Jesus; see 1:37 (ἠκολούθησαν τῷ Ἰησοῦ) and 1:38 (ὁ Ἰησοῦς . . . θεασάμενος αὐτοὺς ἀκολουθοῦντας).

1:41 εὑρίσκει οὗτος πρῶτον τὸν ἀδελφὸν τὸν ἴδιον Σίμωνα καὶ λέγει αὐτῷ· εὑρήκαμεν τὸν Μεσσίαν, ὅ ἐστιν μεθερμηνευόμενον χριστός.

εὑρίσκει. Pres act ind 3rd sg εὑρίσκω. Two historical presents, εὑρίσκει and λέγει, mark the appearance of a new character (Simon) in the narrative and give thematic prominence to the testimony that he receives (see 1:15 on μαρτυρεῖ; see 1:43 and 1:45. This verse is connected to the previous one by asyndeton.

οὗτος. Nominative subject of εὑρίσκει. The demonstrative pronoun refers to Ἀνδρέας from the previous verse, functioning as a third-person personal pronoun with a simple anaphoric force (Wallace 1996, 328–29).

πρῶτον. This word is transmitted in three variants: πρῶτον (𝔓$^{66.75}$ ℵ^2 A B Θ Ψ 083 $f^{1.13}$ 892 lat sy$^{p.h}$ Epiph), πρῶτος (ℵ* K L W^s Γ Δ 565 579 700 1241 𝔐), and πρωΐ (b e [j] r^1 sy^s). The reading πρῶτον is adverbial accusative, suggesting that "the first thing that Andrew did after having been called was to find his brother" (Metzger, 172). The reading πρῶτος ("first") suggests that Andrew was the first of Jesus' disciples who brought his own brother (or, more generally, another convert) to Jesus. The reading πρωΐ ("early in the morning") is the least ambiguous of the three, but it is poorly attested. The first variant (πρῶτον) has the best textual support in terms of the age and diversity of the manuscripts (172).

τὸν ἀδελφὸν τὸν ἴδιον. Accusative direct object of εὑρίσκει. The adjective ἴδιον ("one's own") stands in the second attributive position (see 1:9 on τὸ φῶς τὸ ἀληθινόν).

Σίμωνα. Accusative in apposition to τὸν ἀδελφὸν.

καὶ. Coordinating conjunction.

λέγει. Pres act ind 3rd sg λέγω. Historical present (see εὑρίσκει above).

αὐτῷ. Dative indirect object of λέγει.

εὑρήκαμεν. Prf act ind 1st pl εὑρίσκω. The verb describes an action that occurred in the past, but the emphasis falls on its present significance.

τὸν Μεσσίαν. Accusative direct object of εὑρήκαμεν. Μεσσίας is the Greek transliteration of the Aramaic term מְשִׁיחָא (Hebrew מָשִׁיחַ), which in the NT occurs only here and in 4:25. The articular noun indicates that it is used as a title ("the Anointed One").

ὅ ἐστιν μεθερμηνευόμενον χριστός. Parenthetical editorial comment that interrupts the plot of the narrative to explain the meaning of the transliterated Aramaic term Μεσσίαν to the readers/hearers who are not familiar with it. For similar parenthetical comments, see 1:38, 42; 19:17; 20:16.

ὅ. Nominative subject of ἐστιν. On the neuter gender of the relative pronoun, see 1:38.

ἐστιν. Pres act ind 3rd sg εἰμί.

μεθερμηνευόμενον. Pres pass ptc neut nom sg μεθερμηνεύω (present periphrastic).

χριστός. Nominative complement to ὅ in a double nominative subject-complement construction. Such constructions are common in passive clauses that are derived from the (real or hypothetical) active clauses that employ double accusative object-complement constructions. When an active clause is transformed into a passive formulation, its accusative direct object becomes the nominative subject, and its accusative complement becomes the nominative complement (Culy 2009).

1:42 ἤγαγεν αὐτὸν πρὸς τὸν Ἰησοῦν. ἐμβλέψας αὐτῷ ὁ Ἰησοῦς εἶπεν· σὺ εἶ Σίμων ὁ υἱὸς Ἰωάννου, σὺ κληθήσῃ Κηφᾶς, ὃ ἑρμηνεύεται Πέτρος.

ἤγαγεν. Aor act ind 3rd sg ἄγω. This verse is connected to the previous one by asyndeton.

αὐτόν. Accusative direct object of ἤγαγεν.

πρὸς τὸν Ἰησοῦν. Locative (motion toward).

ἐμβλέψας. Aor act ptc masc nom sg ἐμβλέπω (temporal). On participles that precede the main verb, see ἐμβλέψας in 1:36.

αὐτῷ. Dative direct object of ἐμβλέψας.

ὁ Ἰησοῦς. Nominative subject of εἶπεν.

εἶπεν. Aor act ind 3rd sg λέγω.

σύ. Nominative subject of εἶ. Turner thinks that this personal pronoun is "without much emphasis" (MHT 3:37). Fronted as a topical frame.

εἶ. Pres act ind 2nd sg εἰμί.
Σίμων. Predicate nominative.
ὁ υἱὸς. Nominative in apposition to Σίμων.
Ἰωάννου. Genitive of relationship qualifying υἱὸς.
σὺ. Nominative subject of κληθήσῃ. Fronted as a topical frame.
κληθήσῃ. Fut pass ind 2nd sg καλέω.
Κηφᾶς. Nominative complement to σὺ in a double nominative subject-complement construction (see 1:41 on χριστός). John is the only evangelist who uses the Greek transliteration of Peter's Aramaic nickname כֵּיפָא ("rock"), but Κηφᾶς frequently occurs in the letters of Paul (1 Cor 1:12; 3:22; 9:5; 15:5; Gal 1:18; 2:9, 11, 14).
ὃ ἑρμηνεύεται Πέτρος. Parenthetical editorial comment that interrupts the plot of the narrative to explain the meaning of the Greek transliteration of the Aramaic Κηφᾶς. For similar parenthetical comments, see 1:38, 41; 19:17; 20:16.
ὃ. Nominative subject of ἑρμηνεύεται. On the neuter gender of the relative pronoun, see 1:38.
ἑρμηνεύεται. Pres pass ind 3rd sg ἑρμηνεύω.
Πέτρος. Nominative complement to ὃ in a double nominative subject-complement construction (see 1:41 on χριστός). Although the feminine term πέτρα represents the accurate Greek rendering of the Aramaic term כֵּיפָא, the masculine form Πέτρος is used here because the term is applied to a man.

John 1:43-51

⁴³On the next day, he decided to go forth to Galilee, and he found Philip. And Jesus said to him, "Follow me." ⁴⁴Now Philip was from Bethsaida, the town of Andrew and Peter. ⁴⁵Philip found Nathanael and said to him, "We have found the one about whom Moses wrote in the law and also the prophets, Jesus, the son of Joseph, the one who is from Nazareth." ⁴⁶And Nathanael said to him, "Can anything good come from Nazareth?" Philip said to him, "Come and see." ⁴⁷Jesus saw Nathanael coming toward him and said concerning him, "Here is a real Israelite in whom there is no deceit!" ⁴⁸Nathanael said to him, "From where do you know me?" Jesus answered and said to him, "Before Philip called you, I saw you when you were under the fig tree." ⁴⁹Nathanael replied to him, "Rabbi, you are the Son of God. You are the King of Israel." ⁵⁰Jesus answered and said to him, "Do you believe because I told you that I saw you under the fig tree? You will see greater things than these." ⁵¹And he said to him, "Truly, truly I say to you all, you will see heaven opened and the angels of God ascending and descending upon the Son of Man."

1:43 Τῇ ἐπαύριον ἠθέλησεν ἐξελθεῖν εἰς τὴν Γαλιλαίαν καὶ εὑρίσκει Φίλιππον. καὶ λέγει αὐτῷ ὁ Ἰησοῦς· ἀκολούθει μοι.

Τῇ ἐπαύριον. The article functions as a nominalizer, changing the adverb ἐπαύριον ("tomorrow") into the dative of time (see 1:29). Fronted as a temporal frame. This verse is connected to the previous one by asyndeton.

ἠθέλησεν. Aor act ind 3rd sg θέλω. The implied subject of the verb is Jesus. The augmented verb forms of θέλω always have ἠ- instead of ἐ- (BDF §66.3). In this context, θέλω means "to have someth[ing] in mind for oneself, of purpose, resolve" (BDAG, 448.2).

ἐξελθεῖν. Aor act inf ἐξέρχομαι (complementary).

εἰς τὴν Γαλιλαίαν. Locative.

καί. Coordinating conjunction.

εὑρίσκει. Pres act ind 3rd sg εὑρίσκω. Two historical presents, εὑρίσκει and λέγει, mark the appearance of a new character (Philip) in the narrative and give thematic prominence to Jesus' call to follow him (see 1:15 on μαρτυρεῖ); see 1:41 and 1:45.

Φίλιππον. Accusative direct object of εὑρίσκει.

καί. Coordinating conjunction.

λέγει. Pres act ind 3rd sg λέγω. Historical present (see εὑρίσκει above).

αὐτῷ. Dative indirect object of λέγει.

ὁ Ἰησοῦς. Nominative subject of λέγει.

ἀκολούθει. Pres act impv 2nd sg ἀκολουθέω. The imperfective aspect of the present tense portrays the following of Jesus as an unfolding process.

μοι. Dative direct object of ἀκολούθει.

1:44 ἦν δὲ ὁ Φίλιππος ἀπὸ Βηθσαϊδά, ἐκ τῆς πόλεως Ἀνδρέου καὶ Πέτρου.

ἦν. Impf act ind 3rd sg εἰμί. This imperfect is used to provide background information about Philip's origin (du Toit, 224). On the function of the imperfect in the FG, see 1:39 on ἦν.

δέ. Marker of narrative development.

ὁ Φίλιππος. Nominative subject of ἦν.

ἀπὸ Βηθσαϊδά. Source. The preposition ἀπό is used here "to indicate someone's local origin" (BDAG, 105.3.b).

ἐκ τῆς πόλεως. Source. The preposition ἐκ serves as a marker denoting the city of origin (BDAG, 296.3.b).

Ἀνδρέου καὶ Πέτρου. Possessive genitive broadly defined qualifying πόλεως ("the town of Andrew and Peter" = "the town where Andrew and Peter lived").

1:45 εὑρίσκει Φίλιππος τὸν Ναθαναὴλ καὶ λέγει αὐτῷ· ὃν ἔγραψεν Μωϋσῆς ἐν τῷ νόμῳ καὶ οἱ προφῆται εὑρήκαμεν, Ἰησοῦν υἱὸν τοῦ Ἰωσὴφ τὸν ἀπὸ Ναζαρέτ.

εὑρίσκει. Pres act ind 3rd sg εὑρίσκω. The verb stands in final, emphatic position. Two historical presents, εὑρίσκει and λέγει, mark the appearance of a new character (Nathanael) in the narrative and give thematic prominence to the testimony he receives (see 1:15 on μαρτυρεῖ); see 1:41 and 1:43. This verse is connected to the previous one by asyndeton.

Φίλιππος. Nominative subject of εὑρίσκει.

τὸν Ναθαναὴλ. Accusative direct object of εὑρίσκει. Since Ναθαναὴλ is indeclinable, the article is added to indicate its case.

καὶ. Coordinating conjunction.

λέγει. Pres act ind 3rd sg λέγω. Historical present (see εὑρίσκει above).

αὐτῷ. Dative indirect object of λέγει.

ὅν. The relative pronoun introduces a headless relative clause that, in its entirety (ὃν ἔγραψεν Μωϋσῆς ἐν τῷ νόμῳ καὶ οἱ προφῆται), serves as the direct object of εὑρήκαμεν. Within its clause, which is fronted as a topical frame, ὅν is the accusative of respect ("concerning whom," "about whom").

ἔγραψεν. Aor act ind 3rd sg γράφω.

Μωϋσῆς . . . καὶ οἱ προφῆται. Compound nominative subject of ἔγραψεν. When the verb precedes its two (or more) subjects, as here, it is in the singular, agreeing with the first (BDF §135). The verb in the singular may also indicate that the author wanted to lay emphasis on the first-named subject (Wallace 1996, 401). Indeed, Moses is mentioned in the FG three times more often (1:17, 45; 3:14; 5:45, 46; 6:32; 7:19, 22; 8:5; 9:28, 29) than the prophets (1:45; 6:45; 8:52, 53).

ἐν τῷ νόμῳ. Locative (BDAG, 326.1.a).

εὑρήκαμεν. Prf act ind 1st pl εὑρίσκω. The verb describes an action that occurred in the past, but the emphasis falls on its present significance (see 1:41).

Ἰησοῦν. Accusative in apposition to the direct object of εὑρήκαμεν expressed through the relative clause ὃν ἔγραψεν Μωϋσῆς ἐν τῷ νόμῳ καὶ οἱ προφῆται. The appositional expression Ἰησοῦν υἱὸν τοῦ Ἰωσὴφ τὸν ἀπὸ Ναζαρέτ provides specific information about "the one about whom Moses wrote in the law and also the prophets," which is delayed to the end of the clause by dislocation. Runge calls such a construction "right-dislocation" because it "entails referring to a participant in the midst of a clause using a pronoun or generic noun phrase and then adding more information about the same participant at the end of the clause" (2010, 317).

υἱόν. Accusative in apposition to Ἰησοῦν.

τοῦ Ἰωσὴφ. Genitive of relationship qualifying υἱόν. Since Ἰωσήφ is indeclinable, the article is added to indicate its case.

τὸν ἀπὸ Ναζαρέτ. The article functions as a nominalizer, changing the PP ἀπὸ Ναζαρέτ into another apposition to Ἰησοῦν.

ἀπὸ Ναζαρέτ. Source. The preposition ἀπό is used here "to indicate someone's local origin" (BDAG, 105.3.b). ἀπό started to replace ἐκ in this sense in Koine Greek (BDF §209.3).

1:46 καὶ εἶπεν αὐτῷ Ναθαναήλ· ἐκ Ναζαρὲτ δύναταί τι ἀγαθὸν εἶναι; λέγει αὐτῷ [ὁ] Φίλιππος· ἔρχου καὶ ἴδε.

καί. Coordinating conjunction.

εἶπεν. Aor act ind 3rd sg λέγω.

αὐτῷ. Dative indirect object of εἶπεν.

Ναθαναήλ. Nominative subject of εἶπεν.

ἐκ Ναζαρέτ. Source. When the preposition ἐκ is used with the stative verb εἰμί, as here, it retains its transitive force, so that "to *be from* Nazareth" corresponds to "to *come from* Nazareth" (Wallace 1996, 359). Fronted as a spatial frame.

δύναταί. Pres mid ind 3rd sg δύναμαι.

τι ἀγαθόν. Nominative subject of δύναταί. The neuter form ("any good thing") highlights the absurdity of the idea that the Messiah could come from a place as Nazareth.

εἶναι. Pres act inf εἰμί (complementary).

λέγει. Pres act ind 3rd sg λέγω. The historical present gives prominence to Philip's reply to Nathanael (see 1:15 on μαρτυρεῖ).

αὐτῷ. Dative indirect object of λέγει.

[ὁ] Φίλιππος. Nominative subject of λέγει. Scribal evidence for ὁ ($\mathfrak{P}^{66c.75vid}$ B L 33 579 *l*2211) and against ὁ ($\mathfrak{P}^{66*}$ ℵ A K W^s Γ Δ Θ Ψ $f^{1.13}$ 565 700 892 1241 1424 𝔐) was probably caused by the presence of the article with this proper noun in 1:44 and its absence in 1:43, 45, 48; 6:5.

ἔρχου καὶ ἴδε. Wallace (1996, 489, 491) regards ἔρχου as a type of conditional imperative ("if *X*, then *Y* will happen") because the trailing imperative (ἴδε) "function[s] semantically like a *future indicative*":

"Come and see" = "If you come, you *will* see" (491). The identical clause is found in 11:34.

ἔρχου. Pres mid impv 2nd sg ἔρχομαι.
καὶ. Coordinating conjunction.
ἴδε. Aor act impv 2nd sg ὁράω.

1:47 Εἶδεν ὁ Ἰησοῦς τὸν Ναθαναὴλ ἐρχόμενον πρὸς αὐτὸν καὶ λέγει περὶ αὐτοῦ· ἴδε ἀληθῶς Ἰσραηλίτης ἐν ᾧ δόλος οὐκ ἔστιν.

Εἶδεν. Aor act ind 3rd sg ὁράω. This verse is connected to the previous one by asyndeton.
ὁ Ἰησοῦς. Nominative subject of Εἶδεν.
τὸν Ναθαναὴλ. Accusative direct object of Εἶδεν.
ἐρχόμενον. Pres mid ptc masc acc sg ἔρχομαι (predicative). The participle stands in the second predicate position (see 1:29 on ἐρχόμενον), functioning as the accusative complement to τὸν Ναθαναὴλ in a double accusative object-complement construction.
πρὸς αὐτόν. Spatial (movement toward).
καὶ. Coordinating conjunction.
λέγει. Pres act ind 3rd sg λέγω. The historical present calls attention to Jesus' words about Nathanael (see 1:15 on μαρτυρεῖ).
περὶ αὐτοῦ. Reference.
ἴδε. An interjection (originally aor act impv 2nd sg ὁράω) that is "used when more than one pers[on] is addressed, and when that which is to be observed is in the nom[inative]" (BDAG, 466). This interjection is here used "to indicate a place or individual" and can be translated "here is" (BDAG, 466.3).
ἀληθῶς Ἰσραηλίτης. Nominative of exclamation (see 1:29 on ὁ ἀμνός). Fronted for emphasis. ἀληθῶς is an adverb ("truly, really"), which is used here as an adjective: lit. "really an Israelite" = "a real Israelite" (BDAG, 44.b).
ἐν ᾧ. Locative. The antecedent of the relative pronoun is ἀληθῶς Ἰσραηλίτης, i.e., Nathanael.
δόλος. Nominative subject of ἔστιν. Fronted for emphasis. δόλος refers to "taking advantage through craft and underhanded methods" and means "deceit, cunning, treachery" (BDAG, 256).
οὐκ. Negative particle normally used with indicative verbs.
ἔστιν. Pres act ind 3rd sg εἰμί. The enclitic ἐστιν is accented ἔστιν when it comes at the beginning of a sentence, when it expresses existence, or when it follows ἀλλ', εἰ, καί, οὐκ, ὅτι, or τοῦτ'. The last two conditions are fulfilled here.

1:48 λέγει αὐτῷ Ναθαναήλ· πόθεν με γινώσκεις; ἀπεκρίθη Ἰησοῦς καὶ εἶπεν αὐτῷ· πρὸ τοῦ σε Φίλιππον φωνῆσαι ὄντα ὑπὸ τὴν συκῆν εἶδόν σε.

λέγει. Pres act ind 3rd sg λέγω. The historical present gives prominence to Nathanael's reply to Jesus (see 1:15 on μαρτυρεῖ). This verse is connected to the previous one by asyndeton.

αὐτῷ. Dative indirect object of λέγει.

Ναθαναήλ. Nominative subject of λέγει.

πόθεν. Interrogative adverb of place.

με. Accusative direct object of γινώσκεις.

γινώσκεις. Pres act ind 2nd sg γινώσκω.

ἀπεκρίθη. Aor mid ind 3rd sg ἀποκρίνομαι. On the voice, see "Deponency" in the Series Introduction.

Ἰησοῦς. Nominative subject of ἀπεκρίθη.

καὶ εἶπεν αὐτῷ. Pleonastic clause under Semitic influence, which functions as a redundant quotative frame (see 1:25 on καὶ εἶπαν αὐτῷ).

καὶ. Coordinating conjunction.

εἶπεν. Aor act ind 3rd sg λέγω.

αὐτῷ. Dative indirect object of εἶπεν.

πρὸ τοῦ. Used with the infinitive to denote time (see φωνῆσαι below).

σε. Accusative direct object of φωνῆσαι.

Φίλιππον. Accusative subject of the infinitive φωνῆσαι.

φωνῆσαι. Aor act inf φωνέω. Used with πρὸ τοῦ to denote subsequent time. The infinitival clause is fronted as a temporal frame.

ὄντα. Pres act ptc masc acc sg εἰμί (predicative). The participle functions as the accusative complement to the subsequent σε in a double accusative object-complement construction. It should not be regarded as temporal (*pace* Haubeck and von Siebenthal, 528; Harris 2015, 54) because temporal and other adverbial participles are always nominative, agreeing with the subject of the verb, except when they modify a genitive subject (genitive absolute) or an infinitive whose semantic subject is in the accusative, which is not the case here (Culy 2003). Since, however, expressing such a construction in English is awkward (lit. "I saw you being under the fig tree"), most English translations either omit the verb "to be" altogether ("I saw you under the fig tree" [NRSV; REB; CEB]) or use a temporal clause to describe Nathanael's condition when Jesus saw him ("when you were under the fig tree, I saw you" [ESV; LEB; NASB; NET]; "I saw you while you were still under the fig tree" [NIV]).

ὑπὸ τὴν συκῆν. Locative.

εἶδόν. Aor act ind 1st sg ὁράω. εἶδόν, which has a circumflex accent on the penult, acquired an additional accent, the acute, on the ultima from the enclitic σε (Smyth §183; Carson 1985, 48).

σε. Accusative direct object of εἶδόν.

1:49 ἀπεκρίθη αὐτῷ Ναθαναήλ· ῥαββί, σὺ εἶ ὁ υἱὸς τοῦ θεοῦ, σὺ βασιλεὺς εἶ τοῦ Ἰσραήλ.

ἀπεκρίθη. Aor mid ind 3rd sg ἀποκρίνομαι. On the voice, see "Deponency" in the Series Introduction. This verse is connected to the previous one by asyndeton.

αὐτῷ. Dative indirect object of ἀπεκρίθη.

Ναθαναήλ. Nominative subject of ἀπεκρίθη.

ῥαββί. Vocative of direct address; see 1:38, where the author explains the meaning of this term to his readers/hearers.

σύ. Nominative subject of εἶ. Fronted for emphasis.

εἶ. Pres act ind 2nd sg εἰμί.

ὁ υἱός. Predicate nominative.

τοῦ θεοῦ. Genitive of relationship qualifying υἱός.

σύ. Nominative subject of εἶ. Fronted as a topical frame.

βασιλεύς. Predicate nominative. Fronted for emphasis. Contextual considerations, such as the structural parallel between the assertion σὺ εἶ ὁ υἱὸς τοῦ θεοῦ, in which the predicate noun that follows the verb is articular, and the assertion σὺ βασιλεὺς εἶ τοῦ Ἰσραήλ, in which the predicate noun that precedes the verb is anarthrous, indicate that βασιλεύς is also definite. Colwell (13) says that his study of these two declarative statements was instrumental in developing the principle about preverbal predicate nouns, which is now known as Colwell's rule (see 1:1 on θεός).

εἶ. Pres act ind 2nd sg εἰμί.

τοῦ Ἰσραήλ. Genitive of subordination qualifying βασιλεύς.

1:50 ἀπεκρίθη Ἰησοῦς καὶ εἶπεν αὐτῷ· ὅτι εἶπόν σοι ὅτι εἶδόν σε ὑποκάτω τῆς συκῆς, πιστεύεις; μείζω τούτων ὄψῃ.

ἀπεκρίθη. Aor mid ind 3rd sg ἀποκρίνομαι. On the voice, see "Deponency" in the Series Introduction. This verse is connected to the previous one by asyndeton.

Ἰησοῦς. Nominative subject of ἀπεκρίθη.

καὶ εἶπεν αὐτῷ. Pleonastic clause under Semitic influence, which functions as a redundant quotative frame (see 1:25 on καὶ εἶπαν αὐτῷ).

καί. Coordinating conjunction.

εἶπεν. Aor act ind 3rd sg λέγω.

αὐτῷ. Dative indirect object of εἶπεν.

ὅτι. Introduces a causal clause. The placement of the ὅτι clause before the main clause gives it prominence and creates a specific frame of reference for Jesus' question that follows.

εἶπόν. Aor act ind 1st sg λέγω. εἶπόν, which has a circumflex accent on the penult, acquired an additional accent, the acute, on the ultima from the enclitic σοι (Smyth §183; Carson 1985, 48).

σοι. Dative indirect object of εἶπόν.

ὅτι. Introduces the clausal complement (indirect discourse) of εἶπόν.

εἶδόν. Aor act ind 1st sg ὁράω. εἶδόν, which has a circumflex accent on the penult, acquired an additional accent, the acute, on the ultima from the enclitic σε (Smyth §183; Carson 1985, 48).

σε. Accusative direct object of εἶπόν.

ὑποκάτω τῆς συκῆς. Locative. ὑποκάτω is an improper preposition (see 1:3 on χωρὶς αὐτοῦ). ὑποκάτω + gen has the same meaning as ὑπό + acc (see 1:48).

πιστεύεις. Pres act ind 2nd sg πιστεύω.

μείζω. Accusative direct object of ὄψῃ. μείζω (= μείζονα) is acc neut pl comparative adjective from μέγας.

τούτων. Genitive of comparison.

ὄψῃ. Fut mid ind 2nd sg ὁράω.

1:51 καὶ λέγει αὐτῷ· ἀμὴν ἀμὴν λέγω ὑμῖν, ὄψεσθε τὸν οὐρανὸν ἀνεῳγότα καὶ τοὺς ἀγγέλους τοῦ θεοῦ ἀναβαίνοντας καὶ καταβαίνοντας ἐπὶ τὸν υἱὸν τοῦ ἀνθρώπου.

καὶ. Coordinating conjunction.

λέγει. Pres act ind 3rd sg λέγω. The historical present highlights Jesus' solemn declaration with the double ἀμὴν that introduces his promise to Nathanael (see 1:15 on μαρτυρεῖ). It is also noteworthy that it is used mid-speech, adding extra prominence to the pronouncement that follows. Elsewhere in the NT, the historical present of λέγω is used mid-speech only in Mark 4:13; John 21:16, 17 (Runge 2010, 159 n. 38).

αὐτῷ. Dative indirect object of λέγει.

ἀμὴν ἀμὴν λέγω ὑμῖν. Jesus' solemn declaration that functions rhetorically as a metacomment (see Runge 2010, 101–24). A metacomment is "an abstracted statement about what is about to be said" that interrupts the speech to prepare the audience for something that the speaker considers of great importance (101, 106–7). In the FG, the clause ἀμὴν ἀμὴν λέγω ὑμῖν/σοι is used for this purpose twenty-five times (1:51; 3:3,

5, 11; 5:19, 24, 25; 6:26, 32, 47, 53; 8:34, 51, 58; 10:1, 7; 12:24; 13:16, 20, 21, 38; 14:12; 16:20, 23; 21:18]).

ἀμὴν ἀμὴν. Asseverative particles that mark the beginning of Jesus' solemn declaration (BDAG, 53.1.b). In the NT, the double ἀμήν occurs only in the FG, but it is also found in 1QS 1.20; 2.10, 18.

λέγω. Pres act ind 1st sg λέγω.

ὑμῖν. Dative indirect object of λέγω. Note the sudden switch to the plural form of the personal pronoun.

ὄψεσθε. Fut mid ind 2nd pl ὁράω.

τὸν οὐρανὸν. Accusative direct object of ὄψεσθε.

ἀνεῳγότα. Prf act ptc masc acc sg ἀνοίγω (predicative). The participle stands in the second predicate position (see 1:29 on ἐρχόμενον), functioning as the accusative complement to τὸν οὐρανὸν in a double accusative object-complement construction. The stative aspect of the perfect participle puts emphasis on the state of heaven ("standing open") without any reference to a prior event that initiated it.

καὶ. Coordinating conjunction.

τοὺς ἀγγέλους. Accusative direct object of ὄψεσθε.

τοῦ θεοῦ. Possessive genitive qualifying ἀγγέλους.

ἀναβαίνοντας. Pres act ptc masc acc pl ἀναβαίνω (predicative). The participle stands in the second predicate position (see 1:29 on ἐρχόμενον), functioning as the accusative complement to τοὺς ἀγγέλους in a double accusative object-complement construction.

καὶ. Coordinating conjunction, linking two participles with the same function.

καταβαίνοντας. Pres act ptc masc acc pl καταβαίνω (predicative). The participle stands in the second predicate position (see 1:29 on ἐρχόμενον), functioning as the accusative complement to τοὺς ἀγγέλους in a double accusative object-complement construction.

ἐπὶ τὸν υἱὸν. Locative.

τοῦ ἀνθρώπου. Genitive of relationship qualifying υἱὸν. The presence of the articles with the head noun (τὸν υἱὸν) and the genitive noun (τοῦ ἀνθρώπου) illustrates Apollonius' canon, which states that the head noun and genitive noun mimic each other with regard to articularity (Wallace 1996, 239).

John 2:1-11

¹And on the third day there was a wedding at Cana in Galilee, and the mother of Jesus was there. ²Jesus was also invited, together with his disciples, to the wedding. ³When the wine ran out, the mother of Jesus said to him, "They have no wine." ⁴And Jesus said to her, "Woman, what

concern is that to you and me? My hour has not yet come." ⁵His mother said to the servants, "Whatever he says to you, do it." ⁶Now six stone water jars were set there for the Jewish rites of purification, each holding twenty or thirty gallons. ⁷Jesus said to them, "Fill the jars with water." And they filled them to the brim. ⁸And he said to them, "Draw [it] out now and take [it] to the master of the feast." So they took [it]. ⁹When the master of the feast tasted the water which had become wine and did not know where it was from, though the servants who had drawn the water knew, the master of the feast called the bridegroom ¹⁰and said to him, "Every person serves the good wine first, and when they become drunk, the inferior. You have kept the good wine until now." ¹¹Jesus did this as the beginning of his signs in Cana in Galilee and revealed his glory, and his disciples believed in him.

2:1 Καὶ τῇ ἡμέρᾳ τῇ τρίτῃ γάμος ἐγένετο ἐν Κανὰ τῆς Γαλιλαίας, καὶ ἦν ἡ μήτηρ τοῦ Ἰησοῦ ἐκεῖ·

Καὶ. Coordinating conjunction.

τῇ ἡμέρᾳ τῇ τρίτῃ. Dative of time. Fronted as a temporal frame.

γάμος. Nominative subject of ἐγένετο. Fronted for emphasis. "The first mention of the substantive is usually anarthrous because it is merely being introduced" (Wallace 1996, 217). The subsequent mention of γάμος in 2:2 has the anaphoric article.

ἐγένετο. Aor mid ind 3rd sg γίνομαι.

ἐν Κανὰ. Locative.

τῆς Γαλιλαίας. Partitive genitive qualifying Κανὰ. Galilee denotes the territory within which Cana lies (MHT 3:210).

καὶ. Coordinating conjunction.

ἦν. Impf act ind 3rd sg εἰμί.

ἡ μήτηρ. Nominative subject of ἦν.

τοῦ Ἰησοῦ. Genitive of relationship qualifying μήτηρ.

ἐκεῖ. Predicate adverb of place. Predicate adverbs function as predicates of equative verbs, such as εἰμί and γίνομαι (MHT 3:226; BDF §434.1).

2:2 ἐκλήθη δὲ καὶ ὁ Ἰησοῦς καὶ οἱ μαθηταὶ αὐτοῦ εἰς τὸν γάμον.

ἐκλήθη. Aor pass ind 3rd sg καλέω. In this context, καλέω means "to request the presence at a social gathering, *invite*" (BDAG, 503.2).

δὲ. Marker of narrative development.

καὶ. Adverbial use (adjunctive). Some English translations presume that καὶ . . . καὶ form the "both . . . and" construction (KJV; NASB). It is, however, more likely that the first καί functions adverbially and the second καί as a conjunction linking two nominatives that form a compound subject of the verb.

ὁ Ἰησοῦς καὶ οἱ μαθηταί. Compound nominative subject of ἐκλήθη. When the verb precedes its two (or more) subjects, as here, it is in the singular, agreeing with the first (BDF §135). The verb in the singular could also indicate that the author regarded the first-named subject as being more important of the two; i.e., "Jesus was invited to the wedding and his disciples tagged along" (Wallace 1996, 401).

αὐτοῦ. Genitive of relationship qualifying μαθηταί.

εἰς τὸν γάμον. Locative. With καλέω, the preposition εἰς marks the event to which the guests have been invited. The article is anaphoric (see 2:1).

2:3 καὶ ὑστερήσαντος οἴνου λέγει ἡ μήτηρ τοῦ Ἰησοῦ πρὸς αὐτόν· οἶνον οὐκ ἔχουσιν.

καί. Coordinating conjunction.

ὑστερήσαντος. Aor act ptc masc gen sg ὑστερέω (genitive absolute, temporal or causal). In this context, ὑστερέω means "to be in short supply, *fail, give out, lack*" (BDAG, 1043.2).

οἴνου. Genitive subject of ὑστερήσαντος.

λέγει. Pres act ind 3rd sg λέγω. This and all subsequent verbs of speaking in 2:3-10 are historical presents. As thematic markers, they call attention to the dialogue between the characters (see 1:15 on μαρτυρεῖ). Fanning (234), however, suggests that their multiple occurrences in this episode are mechanical rather than purposeful.

ἡ μήτηρ. Nominative subject of λέγει.

τοῦ Ἰησοῦ. Genitive of relationship qualifying μήτηρ.

πρὸς αὐτόν. Locative (motion toward). The PP functions like an indirect object of λέγει.

οἶνον. Accusative direct object of ἔχουσιν.

οὐκ. Negative particle normally used with indicative verbs.

ἔχουσιν. Pres act ind 3rd pl ἔχω. The verb stands in final, emphatic position. The subject of ἔχουσιν is not specified.

2:4 [καὶ] λέγει αὐτῇ ὁ Ἰησοῦς· τί ἐμοὶ καὶ σοί, γύναι; οὔπω ἥκει ἡ ὥρα μου.

[καί]. Coordinating conjunction. It is printed within square brackets because the external evidence for ($\mathfrak{P}^{66}$ ℵ^{2a} A B K L W^s Δ Θ 0127 f^{13} 33

892 et al.) and against ($\mathfrak{P}^{75}$ $\aleph^{*.2b}$ Γ Ψ f^1 565 579 $\mathfrak{M}$ et al.) its inclusion is evenly balanced.

λέγει. Pres act ind 3rd sg λέγω. Historical present (see 2:3).

αὐτῇ. Dative indirect object of λέγει.

ὁ Ἰησοῦς. Nominative subject of λέγει.

τί ἐμοὶ καὶ σοί. An idiom (lit. "What to me and to you?") that can be rendered "What have I to do with you?" "What have we in common?" "Leave me alone!" "Never mind!" (BDAG, 275; cf. BDF §299.3; Smyth §1479). Although an equivalent idiom exists in Hebrew (מַה־לִּי וָלָךְ), τί ἐμοὶ καὶ σοί is probably not a Semitism because it is also found in extra-biblical Greek (Smyth §1479). In the NT, it occurs here and in Mark 5:7//Luke 8:28. The version with ἡμῖν instead of ἐμοί is found in Matt 8:29 and Mark 1:24//Luke 4:34. The idiom is used either as "a warning to refrain from interference" or to express "disengagement and aloofness while refusing a request," as here (Harris 2015, 57).

τί. Nominative subject of an implied ἐστίν in a verbless clause.

ἐμοὶ ... σοί. Datives of interest (Smyth §1479), but they could also be regarded as datives of possession conveying the idea "What do we have in common?" (Wallace 1996, 150–51).

γύναι. Vocative of direct address. Jesus addresses his mother with the same term that he uses to address the Samaritan woman (4:21) and Mary Magdalene (20:15). Although this term does not imply disrespect (cf. Luke 22:57; 1 Cor 7:16), "it makes Jesus' mother a stranger," as Michaels (145) perceptively notes. Runge calls such usage of vocative "thematic address" that "amounts to thematically motivated name calling" (2010, 349), which accomplishes a certain rhetorical effect "when the expression used is different from the default or expected referring expression" (354), as here.

οὔπω. Adverb of time ("not yet"). Fronted for emphasis.

ἥκει. Pres act ind 3rd sg ἥκω.

ἡ ὥρα. Nominative subject of ἥκει. On the arrival of Jesus' hour, see ἡ ὥρα in 12:23.

μου. Genitive of purpose qualifying ὥρα ("the hour destined for me").

2:5 λέγει ἡ μήτηρ αὐτοῦ τοῖς διακόνοις· ὅ τι ἂν λέγῃ ὑμῖν ποιήσατε.

λέγει. Pres act ind 3rd sg λέγω. Historical present (see 2:3). This verse is connected to the previous one by asyndeton.

ἡ μήτηρ. Nominative subject of λέγει.

αὐτοῦ. Genitive of relationship qualifying μήτηρ.

τοῖς διακόνοις. Dative indirect object of λέγει.

ὅ τι ἄν. Accusative direct object of λέγῃ. ὅ τι is the neuter singular form of the indefinite relative pronoun ὅστις (printed as two words to distinguish it from ὅτι; cf. MHT 2:179), whose indefiniteness is heightened with the marker of contingency ἄν. The indefinite relative clause ὅ τι ἄν λέγῃ ὑμῖν is fronted as a topical frame.

λέγῃ. Pres act subj 3rd sg λέγω. Subjunctive with ἄν.
ὑμῖν. Dative indirect object of λέγῃ.
ποιήσατε. Aor act impv 2nd pl ποιέω.

2:6 ἦσαν δὲ ἐκεῖ λίθιναι ὑδρίαι ἓξ κατὰ τὸν καθαρισμὸν τῶν Ἰουδαίων κείμεναι, χωροῦσαι ἀνὰ μετρητὰς δύο ἢ τρεῖς.

ἦσαν. Impf act ind 3rd pl εἰμί.
δὲ. Marker of narrative development.
ἐκεῖ. Adverb of place.
λίθιναι ὑδρίαι. Nominative subject of ἦσαν. λίθιναι ("made of stone") modifies ὑδρίαι ("water jars"), standing in the first (anarthrous) attributive position (adjective-noun) (Wallace 1996, 309–10).
ἓξ. Cardinal number ("six").
κατὰ τὸν καθαρισμὸν. Purpose.
τῶν Ἰουδαίων. Subjective genitive ("the rites of purification practiced by the Jews") or attributive genitive qualifying καθαρισμὸν ("Jewish rites of purification"). In this construction, the term Ἰουδαίων does not refer to a specific group of characters in the FG but to Jewish religious customs in a more general sense (Tolmie, 379).
κείμεναι. Pres mid ptc fem nom pl κεῖμαι, serving as prf pass ptc fem nom pl τίθημι (imperfect periphrastic). Although ἦσαν and κείμεναι are separated by ten intervening words, they probably form a periphrastic structure, which Robertson (906) calls "a periphrastic past perfect in sense" (Zerwick §362). If ἦσαν and κείμεναι are independent, κείμεναι can be regarded as a predicate participle standing in the second (anarthrous) predicate position vis-à-vis ὑδρίαι (noun-predicate participle), which is common in equative clauses (Wallace 1996, 311, 618–19).
χωροῦσαι. Pres act ptc fem nom pl χωρέω (attributive). The participle modifies ὑδρίαι, standing in the fourth attributive position (see 1:6 on ἀπεσταλμένος). χωρέω means "to have room for, to be space for, to contain" (LN 80.4).
ἀνὰ μετρητὰς. Distributive. With numbers the preposition ἀνά means "each, apiece" (BDAG, 58.3). μετρητὰς (accusative plural of μετρητής) is a NT *hapax legomenon* that denotes an ancient liquid measure amounting to about ten gallons, or forty liters (LN 81.22; BDAG, 643).
δύο. Cardinal number ("two"), agreeing with μετρητὰς.

ἤ. Marker of an alternative/disjunctive particle (BDAG, 432.1).
τρεῖς. Cardinal number ("three"), agreeing with μετρητὰς.

2:7 λέγει αὐτοῖς ὁ Ἰησοῦς· γεμίσατε τὰς ὑδρίας ὕδατος. καὶ ἐγέμισαν αὐτὰς ἕως ἄνω.

λέγει. Pres act ind 3rd sg λέγω. Historical present (see 2:3). This verse is connected to the previous one by asyndeton.
αὐτοῖς. Dative indirect object of λέγει. The pronoun refers to the servants mentioned in v. 5.
ὁ Ἰησοῦς. Nominate subject of λέγει.
γεμίσατε. Aor act impv 2nd pl γεμίζω. The verb means "to put someth[ing] into an object to the extent of its capacity, *fill*" (BDAG, 191); the object of filling is in the accusative and the substance with which it is filled is in the genitive.
τὰς ὑδρίας. Accusative direct object of γεμίσατε.
ὕδατος. Genitive complement of γεμίσατε.
καὶ. Coordinating conjunction.
ἐγέμισαν. Aor act ind 3rd pl γεμίζω.
αὐτὰς. Accusative direct object of ἐγέμισαν.
ἕως ἄνω. Locative. ἕως functions here as a preposition of place ("until, as far as"). ἄνω ("above, up") is an adverb, which in this PP indicates the upper level of filling ("to the brim").

2:8 καὶ λέγει αὐτοῖς· ἀντλήσατε νῦν καὶ φέρετε τῷ ἀρχιτρικλίνῳ· οἱ δὲ ἤνεγκαν.

καὶ. Coordinating conjunction.
λέγει. Pres act ind 3rd sg λέγω. Historical present (see 2:3).
αὐτοῖς. Dative indirect object of λέγει.
ἀντλήσατε. Aor act impv 2nd pl ἀντλέω. The verb means "to draw a liquid, normally water, from a container or well" (LN 47.1).
νῦν. Adverb of time.
καὶ. Coordinating conjunction.
φέρετε. Pres act impv 2nd pl φέρω. All imperatives of φέρω in the NT are in the present tense (Matt 14:18; Mark 9:19//Matt 17:17; Mark 11:2; 12:15; Luke 15:22-23; John 2:8; 20:27) except for ἐνέγκατε in John 21:10 (BDF §336.3). Fanning, however, notes that "the nine present imperatives occur in utterances which seem to call for aorist [= perfective] aspect: they involve specific commands, and many have a goal or destination stated, which in the indicative mood tends to produce aorist usage (viewing the whole act of 'bringing' or leading in summary)"

(347). In this verse, the use of the aorist indicative of φέρω in the clause that describes the execution of Jesus' command (οἱ δὲ ἤνεγκαν) provides corroborating evidence that there are no aspectual differences between the present imperative φέρετε and the aorist imperative ἀντλήσατε.

τῷ ἀρχιτρικλίνῳ. Dative indirect object of φέρετε. ἀρχιτρίκλινος is "the head servant in charge of all those who served at meals or feasts" (LN 46.7).

οἱ δὲ. A construction that marks the continuation of the narrative (BDF §251). The nominative article stands in place of a third-person personal pronoun and functions as the subject of ἤνεγκαν. Its force is anaphoric, referring to the servants to whom Jesus gave orders. Fronted as a topical frame.

ἤνεγκαν. Aor act ind 3rd pl φέρω.

2:9 ὡς δὲ ἐγεύσατο ὁ ἀρχιτρίκλινος τὸ ὕδωρ οἶνον γεγενημένον καὶ οὐκ ᾔδει πόθεν ἐστίν, οἱ δὲ διάκονοι ᾔδεισαν οἱ ἠντληκότες τὸ ὕδωρ, φωνεῖ τὸν νυμφίον ὁ ἀρχιτρίκλινος

ὡς. Temporal conjunction (BDAG, 1105.8.a; BDF §455.2), introducing a clause that is fronted as a temporal frame.

δὲ. Marker of narrative development.

ἐγεύσατο. Aor mid ind 3rd sg γεύομαι.

ὁ ἀρχιτρίκλινος. Nominative subject of ἐγεύσατο.

τὸ ὕδωρ. Accusative direct object of ἐγεύσατο.

οἶνον. Predicate accusative. οἶνον stands in a predicate relationship to τὸ ὕδωρ, with which it is connected by γεγενημένον.

γεγενημένον. Prf pass ptc neut acc sg γίνομαι (attributive). Although the noun that the participle modifies (τὸ ὕδωρ) is articular, the participle itself is anarthrous. Despite this structural anomaly, however, the relationship of the participle to the noun is best conceived as adjectival (Wallace 1996, 191). The participle describes an action that occurred before the action of the main verb, but its stative aspect puts less weight on the turning of the water into wine and more on the water that has now become wine.

καὶ. Coordinating conjunction.

οὐκ. Negative particle normally used with indicative verbs.

ᾔδει. Plprf act ind 3rd sg οἶδα. The pluperfect of οἶδα is rendered by the imperfect. This pluperfect has a supplemental function (Campbell 2007, 219).

πόθεν. Interrogative adverb of place. It introduces an indirect question.

ἐστίν. Pres act ind 3rd sg εἰμί. The present tense is retained from the (hypothetical) direct question (see 1:39 on μένει).

οἱ ... διάκονοι. Nominative subject of ᾔδεισαν. Fronted as a topical frame.

δέ. Marker of narrative development.

ᾔδεισαν. Plprf act ind 3rd pl οἶδα. The pluperfect of οἶδα is rendered by the imperfect. This pluperfect also has a supplemental function (see ᾔδει above).

οἱ ἠντληκότες. Prf act ptc masc nom pl ἀντλέω (attributive). The participle modifies οἱ ... διάκονοι, standing in the second attributive position (see 1:29 on ὁ αἴρων). The perfect participle gives prominence to the state of the servants, emphasizing the contrast between the steward and the servants (Porter 1989, 276).

τὸ ὕδωρ. Accusative direct object of ἠντληκότες.

φωνεῖ. Pres act ind 3rd sg φωνέω. The historical present is here used to introduce the bridegroom to an existing scene; on this function of the nonspeech historical presents in the FG, see 6:19 on θεωροῦσιν.

τὸν νυμφίον. Accusative direct object of φωνεῖ.

ὁ ἀρχιτρίκλινος. Nominative subject of φωνεῖ.

2:10 καὶ λέγει αὐτῷ· πᾶς ἄνθρωπος πρῶτον τὸν καλὸν οἶνον τίθησιν καὶ ὅταν μεθυσθῶσιν τὸν ἐλάσσω· σὺ τετήρηκας τὸν καλὸν οἶνον ἕως ἄρτι.

καί. Coordinating conjunction.

λέγει. Pres act ind 3rd sg λέγω. Historical present (see 2:3).

αὐτῷ. Dative indirect object of λέγει.

πᾶς ἄνθρωπος. Nominative subject of τίθησιν. Fronted as a topical frame.

πρῶτον. Adverbial accusative.

τὸν καλὸν οἶνον. Accusative direct object of τίθησιν. Fronted for emphasis. The adjective καλὸν stands in the first attributive position (article-adjective-noun) (Wallace 1996, 306).

τίθησιν. Pres act ind 3rd sg τίθημι.

καί. Coordinating conjunction.

ὅταν. Introduces an indefinite temporal clause, which is fronted as a temporal frame.

μεθυσθῶσιν. Aor pass subj 3rd pl μεθύσκω. Subjunctive with ὅταν. μεθύσκω occurs in the NT only in the passive voice, which means "to become intoxicated" or "to be drunk" (BDAG, 625). The subject of the verb is not specified, but presumably it refers to the guests.

τὸν ἐλάσσω. Accusative direct object of τίθησιν. ἔλασσον is used as a comparative of μικρός.

σύ. Nominative subject of τετήρηκας. The personal pronoun is selective and contrastive, specifying one individual ("you") among all humanity who behaves contrary to social conventions (Porter 1994, 129; Harris 2015, 60).

τετήρηκας. Prf act ind 2nd sg τηρέω. The stative aspect of the perfect tense gives prominence to the surprising behavior of the bridegroom. Campbell rightly notes that "it is highly unlikely that there is any reference to the entrance of the state in view here; the bridegroom is not pictured as having *begun* to keep the good wine, but as having kept it" (2007, 191).

τὸν καλὸν οἶνον. Accusative direct object of τετήρηκας.

ἕως ἄρτι. Temporal. ἕως functions here as a preposition of time ("until"), and the adverb ἄρτι as a substantive (Robertson, 548). ἕως ἄρτι = "until now" (BDAG, 423.1.b.γ).

2:11 Ταύτην ἐποίησεν ἀρχὴν τῶν σημείων ὁ Ἰησοῦς ἐν Κανὰ τῆς Γαλιλαίας καὶ ἐφανέρωσεν τὴν δόξαν αὐτοῦ, καὶ ἐπίστευσαν εἰς αὐτὸν οἱ μαθηταὶ αὐτοῦ.

Ταύτην. Accusative direct object of ἐποίησεν in a double accusative object-complement construction. Fronted for emphasis. Ταύτην does not function as an attributive modifier of ἀρχὴν because "[t]he article is used with substantives (adjectives) when combined with οὗτος and ἐκεῖνος" (BDF §292; cf. Robertson, 701–2), which is not the case here. Wallace emphasizes that "[i]f [the demonstratives] are related to an anarthrous noun, they function independently, as pronouns" (1996, 241) and criticizes the translations such as ASV ("this beginning of his signs Jesus did") that "miss this basic rule of Greek grammar" (242). It seems that some ancient scribes also missed this grammatical point and added the definite article to ἀρχὴν to indicate that Ταύτην has an attributive function: ταύτην ἐποίησεν τὴν ἀρχὴν (ℵ*(*).1* K W^s Γ Δ *f*^{13} 700 892 𝔐 sy^h) or ταύτην τὴν ἀρχὴν ἐποίησεν (1241 1424).

ἐποίησεν. Aor act ind 3rd sg ποιέω.

ἀρχὴν. Accusative complement to Ταύτην in a double accusative object-complement construction (Wallace 1996, 187).

τῶν σημείων. Partitive genitive qualifying ἀρχὴν. Since this is the first mention of this noun in the FG, the article cannot be anaphoric, but it might be possessive ("his signs" [NRSV; ASV; ESV]) because the context indicates that these signs are done exclusively by Jesus. The use of the term σημεῖα for Jesus' miracles is one of the distinctive features of the FG (see 2:23; 3:2; 4:48, 54; 6:2, 14, 26; 7:31; 9:16; 11:47; 12:18, 37; 20:30; cf. Barrett, 75–78; Keener, 1:272–79; Thompson, 65–68).

ὁ Ἰησοῦς. Nominative subject of ἐποίησεν.
ἐν Κανὰ. Locative.
τῆς Γαλιλαίας. Partitive genitive qualifying Κανὰ (see 2:1).
καὶ. Coordinating conjunction.
ἐφανέρωσεν. Aor act ind 3rd sg φανερόω.
τὴν δόξαν. Accusative direct object of ἐφανέρωσεν.
αὐτοῦ. Possessive genitive qualifying δόξαν.
καὶ. Coordinating conjunction.
ἐπίστευσαν. Aor act ind 3rd pl πιστεύω.
εἰς αὐτὸν. Goal of actions or feelings directed toward someone (BDAG, 290.4.c.β). For πιστεύειν εἰς + accusative ("trust or believe in someone"), see 1:12 on εἰς τὸ ὄνομα.
οἱ μαθηταὶ. Nominative subject of ἐπίστευσαν.
αὐτοῦ. Genitive of relationship qualifying μαθηταὶ.

John 2:12-17

¹²After this, he himself, his mother, his brothers, and his disciples went down to Capernaum; and they remained there for a few days. ¹³And the Passover of the Jews was near, and Jesus went up to Jerusalem. ¹⁴And he found in the temple those who were selling cattle, sheep, and pigeons, and the money-changers sitting. ¹⁵And after he made a whip of cords, he drove them all out of the temple, along with the sheep and the cattle; and he scattered the coins of the money changers and overturned their tables. ¹⁶And he said to those who were selling pigeons, "Take these things out of here! Stop making the house of my Father a house of merchandise!" ¹⁷His disciples remembered that it was written, "Zeal for your house will consume me."

2:12 Μετὰ τοῦτο κατέβη εἰς Καφαρναοὺμ αὐτὸς καὶ ἡ μήτηρ αὐτοῦ καὶ οἱ ἀδελφοὶ [αὐτοῦ] καὶ οἱ μαθηταὶ αὐτοῦ καὶ ἐκεῖ ἔμειναν οὐ πολλὰς ἡμέρας.

Μετὰ τοῦτο. Temporal. Fronted as a temporal frame. This verse is connected to the previous one by asyndeton.
κατέβη. Aor act ind 3rd sg καταβαίνω.
εἰς Καφαρναοὺμ. Locative.
αὐτὸς καὶ ἡ μήτηρ . . . καὶ οἱ ἀδελφοὶ . . . καὶ οἱ μαθηταὶ. Compound nominative subject of κατέβη. κατέβη is singular because it precedes four named subjects, agreeing with the first (BDF §135). αὐτὸς functions as

an intensive pronoun ("he himself") that differentiates Jesus from other three subjects (BDAG, 152.1.c).

αὐτοῦ ... [αὐτοῦ] ... αὐτοῦ. Genitives of relationship, the first qualifying μήτηρ, the second qualifying ἀδελφοί, and the third qualifying μαθηταί. The genitive pronoun after ἀδελφοί is absent in 𝔓⁶⁶*.⁷⁵ B Ψ 0162, but the external support for its presence is also strong (𝔓⁶⁶ᶜ A N Γ Δ Θ *f* ¹·¹³ 33 565 𝔐 lat sy et al.).

καί. Coordinating conjunction that links two clauses.

ἐκεῖ. Adverb of place. Fronted as a spatial frame.

ἔμειναν. Aor act ind 3rd pl μένω. The embedded subject of the verb ("they") refers to the compound nominative subject in the preceding clause.

οὐ πολλὰς ἡμέρας. This is an example of litotes, i.e., making a statement by negating the opposite idea: "not for many days" = "for a few days."

οὐ. Negative particle.

πολλὰς ἡμέρας. Accusative indicating extent of time.

2:13 Καὶ ἐγγὺς ἦν τὸ πάσχα τῶν Ἰουδαίων, καὶ ἀνέβη εἰς Ἱεροσόλυμα ὁ Ἰησοῦς.

Καί. Coordinating conjunction.

ἐγγύς. Predicate adverb indicating close temporal proximity (see 2:1 on ἐκεῖ). Fronted for emphasis.

ἦν. Impf act ind 3rd sg εἰμί.

τὸ πάσχα. Nominative subject of ἦν. This is the first Passover recorded in the FG (see 6:4 and 11:55).

τῶν Ἰουδαίων. Subjective genitive qualifying πάσχα ("the Passover that the Jews celebrate") or attributive genitive ("Jewish Passover"). On the meaning of this term, see 2:6.

καί. Coordinating conjunction.

ἀνέβη. Aor act ind 3rd sg ἀναβαίνω. In this context, ἀναβαίνω ("go up, ascend") indicates movement on "the road to Jerusalem, located on high ground" (BDAG, 58.1.a.α). Barrett notes that the verb functions almost like "a technical term for pilgrimage to the capital" (197).

εἰς Ἱεροσόλυμα. Locative.

ὁ Ἰησοῦς. Nominative subject of ἀνέβη.

2:14 Καὶ εὗρεν ἐν τῷ ἱερῷ τοὺς πωλοῦντας βόας καὶ πρόβατα καὶ περιστερὰς καὶ τοὺς κερματιστὰς καθημένους,

Καί. Coordinating conjunction.

εὗρεν. Aor act ind 3rd sg εὑρίσκω.

ἐν τῷ ἱερῷ. Locative. Elsewhere in the FG, this PP occurs in 5:14; 7:28; 8:20; 10:23; 11:56; 18:20.

τοὺς πωλοῦντας. Pres act ptc masc acc pl πωλέω (substantival). Accusative direct object of εὗρεν.

βόας καὶ πρόβατα καὶ περιστεράς. Accusative direct objects of πωλοῦντας.

καί. Coordinating conjunction.

τοὺς κερματιστάς. Accusative direct object of εὗρεν. κερματιστής ("money changer") is a NT *hapax legomenon*.

καθημένους. Pres mid ptc masc acc pl κάθημαι (predicative). The participle stands in the second predicate position (see 1:29 on ἐρχόμενον), functioning as the accusative complement to τοὺς κερματιστὰς in a double accusative object-complement construction.

2:15 καὶ ποιήσας φραγέλλιον ἐκ σχοινίων πάντας ἐξέβαλεν ἐκ τοῦ ἱεροῦ τά τε πρόβατα καὶ τοὺς βόας, καὶ τῶν κολλυβιστῶν ἐξέχεεν τὸ κέρμα καὶ τὰς τραπέζας ἀνέτρεψεν,

καί. Coordinating conjunction.

ποιήσας. Aor act ptc masc nom sg ποιέω (temporal or attendant circumstance). On participles that precede the main verb, see ἐμβλέψας in 1:36.

φραγέλλιον. Accusative direct object of ποιήσας. φραγέλλιον ("whip" or "lash") is a Latin loanword *flagellum* that occurs only here in the NT. The addition of ὡς before φραγέλλιον in 𝔓[66.75] L N W[s] 0162 *f*[1] 33 lat et al. probably serves to soften the image of Jesus (Metzger, 173).

ἐκ σχοινίων. Source, denoting "the material of which someth[ing] is made" (BDAG, 297.3.h). σχοινίον ("rope" or "cord") occurs only here and in Acts 27:32.

πάντας. Accusative direct object of ἐξέβαλεν. The masculine form indicates that the adjective refers to people. Fronted for emphasis.

ἐξέβαλεν. Aor act ind 3rd sg ἐκβάλλω.

ἐκ τοῦ ἱεροῦ. Separation.

τά ... πρόβατα. Accusative direct object of ἐξέβαλεν.

τε ... καί. A combination of the enclitic particle and a coordinating conjunction that is used to connect "concepts, usu[ally] of the same kind or corresponding as opposites" (BDAG, 993.2.c.α).

τοὺς βόας. Accusative direct object of ἐξέβαλεν.

καί. Coordinating conjunction.

τῶν κολλυβιστῶν. Possessive genitive qualifying κέρμα. Fronted as a topical frame. κολλυβιστής is the term for a "money changer" that also occurs in the synoptic accounts of the temple incident (Matt 21:12// Mark 11:15)

ἐξέχεεν. Aor act ind 3rd sg ἐκχέω. ἐκχέω ("pour out") here means "scatter" the coins on the ground (BDAG, 312.1.b).

τὸ κέρμα. Accusative direct object of ἐξέχεεν.

καί. Coordinating conjunction.

τὰς τραπέζας. Accusative direct object of ἀνέτρεψεν. The article may be possessive (Harris 2015, 63).

ἀνέτρεψεν. Aor act ind 3rd sg ἀνατρέπω.

2:16 καὶ τοῖς τὰς περιστερὰς πωλοῦσιν εἶπεν· ἄρατε ταῦτα ἐντεῦθεν, μὴ ποιεῖτε τὸν οἶκον τοῦ πατρός μου οἶκον ἐμπορίου.

καί. Coordinating conjunction.

τοῖς . . . πωλοῦσιν. Pres act ptc masc dat pl πωλέω (substantival). Dative indirect object of εἶπεν. Fronted as a topical frame.

τὰς περιστεράς. Accusative direct object of πωλοῦσιν.

εἶπεν. Aor act ind 3rd sg λέγω.

ἄρατε. Aor act impv 2nd pl αἴρω.

ταῦτα. Accusative direct object of ἄρατε. The demonstrative pronoun is anaphoric.

ἐντεῦθεν. Adverb of place.

μή. Negative particle introducing prohibition.

ποιεῖτε. Pres act impv 2nd pl ποιέω (prohibition). The imperfective aspect of the present tense indicates that the prohibited action is viewed as an ongoing process, but "[w]hether or not the action had already begun is not a part of the ontology of either tense of the imperative" (Wallace 1996, 716; cf. Porter 1989, 335–61). Such a conclusion can be made only based on the context. Since here Jesus regards the activity of selling sacrificial animals and currency exchange in the temple precincts to be analogous to the activity of merchants in a marketplace, his prohibition effectively means to stop an action that has already started (Wallace 1996, 724; Aubrey, 512, considers this to be an example of "the STOP DOING X usage with causative predicates").

τὸν οἶκον. Accusative direct object of ποιεῖτε in a double accusative object-complement construction.

τοῦ πατρός. Possessive genitive qualifying οἶκον.

μου. Genitive of relationship qualifying πατρός.

οἶκον. Accusative complement to τὸν οἶκον in a double accusative object-complement construction.

ἐμπορίου. Descriptive genitive qualifying οἶκον ("a house in which merchandise is sold" [Wallace 1996, 80]) or epexegetical genitive ("a house which is a place for business"). ἐμπόριον ("place where business is carried on, *market*" [BDAG, 325]) is a NT *hapax legomenon*.

2:17 ἐμνήσθησαν οἱ μαθηταὶ αὐτοῦ ὅτι γεγραμμένον ἐστίν· ὁ ζῆλος τοῦ οἴκου σου καταφάγεταί με.

ἐμνήσθησαν. Aor mid ind 3rd pl μιμνῄσκομαι. On the voice, see "Deponency" in the Series Introduction. In this context, μιμνῄσκομαι means "to recall information from memory, remember, recollect, remind oneself" (BDAG, 652.1). This verse is connected to the previous one by asyndeton.

οἱ μαθηταὶ. Nominative subject of ἐμνήσθησαν.

αὐτοῦ. Genitive of relationship qualifying μαθηταὶ.

ὅτι. Introduces the clausal complement (indirect discourse) of ἐμνήσθησαν.

γεγραμμένον ἐστίν. In the FG, γεγραμμένον, preceded or followed by ἐστίν, is a standard introductory formula for scriptural quotations (2:17; 6:31, 45; 10:34; 12:14). McKay thinks that "John's preference for ἐστὶν γεγραμμένον as against the synoptists' γέγραπται is only a feature of style affecting rhythm and word order, and therefore possibly emphasis and emotional effect, but not the aspectual (or even tense) value of the verb form" (1981, 292). Runge, however, argues that the copular (periphrastic) perfect ἐστὶν γεγραμμένον is less dynamic than the simple perfect γέγραπται because it portrays the written form "as an ongoing state (which results from a completed event)" (2016, 317).

γεγραμμένον. Prf pass ptc neut nom sg γράφω (perfect periphrastic). This is the only instance in the FG of a fronted γεγραμμένον. According to Runge, "[w]hen part or all of a participial clause is placed before the copula, the effect is to give it focal prominence, provided its default position is after the copula" (2016, 321). It is, however, difficult to demonstrate that the introductory formula in which γεγραμμένον is preposed (this verse) gives more prominence to what is written in Scripture than the formulas in which γεγραμμένον follows ἐστίν (6:31, 45; 10:34; 12:14).

ἐστίν. Pres act ind 3rd sg εἰμί. The present tense from the direct discourse is retained (see 1:39 on μένει).

ὁ ζῆλος τοῦ οἴκου σου καταφάγεταί με. A quotation of LXX Ps 68:10a [69:10a MT] (ὁ ζῆλος τοῦ οἴκου σου κατέφαγέν με). The quotation agrees with the LXX except for the change of the verb from the aorist active κατέφαγεν to the future middle καταφάγεται. The reason for this change, as Frey aptly explains, lies "in the notion—which belongs to the quotation in the narrated situation of the temple cleansing—that

Jesus will actually suffer death because of his zeal for God's 'house'" (2018, 80).

ὁ ζῆλος. Nominative subject of καταφάγεται. Fronted as a topical frame. This is the only occurrence of this noun in the FG. In this context, ζῆλος ("zeal, ardor" [BDAG, 427.1]) refers to Jesus' actions in vv. 15-16, but the term may also be viewed as a double entendre that refers not only to the zeal of Jesus but also to the zeal of the Jews, which ultimately leads them to seek Jesus' death (Lappenga, 141–59).

τοῦ οἴκου. Objective genitive qualifying ζῆλος ("the zeal for your house").

σου. Possessive genitive qualifying οἴκου.

καταφάγεται. Fut mid ind 3rd sg κατεσθίω. καταφάγεταί, which has an acute accent on the antepenult, acquired an additional accent, the acute, on the ultima from the enclitic με (Smyth §183; Carson 1985, 48). The future tense, which the evangelist uses instead of the aorist tense (see above), turns the verb κατεσθίω into a proleptic reference to Jesus' death (Frey 2018, 80).

με. Accusative direct object of καταφάγεταί.

John 2:18-22

[18]Then the Jews answered and said to him, "What sign do you show to us that you have the right to do these things?" [19]Jesus answered and said to them, "Destroy this temple, and in three days I will raise it up." [20]The Jews then said, "For forty-six years this temple has been under construction, and you will raise it up in three days?" [21]But he was speaking about the temple of his body. [22]So when he was raised from the dead, his disciples remembered that he had said this, and they believed the Scripture and the words that Jesus had spoken.

2:18 Ἀπεκρίθησαν οὖν οἱ Ἰουδαῖοι καὶ εἶπαν αὐτῷ· τί σημεῖον δεικνύεις ἡμῖν ὅτι ταῦτα ποιεῖς;

Ἀπεκρίθησαν. Aor mid ind 3rd pl ἀποκρίνομαι. On the voice, see "Deponency" in the Series Introduction.

οὖν. Postpositive inferential conjunction and/or transitional particle (see 1:22 and 11:6).

οἱ Ἰουδαῖοι. Nominative subject of Ἀπεκρίθησαν. Like in other polemical accounts in the FG, the term οἱ Ἰουδαῖοι here refers to Jewish religious authorities hostile to Jesus. Since, however, in the FG this group of characters is not primarily determined through their ethnic and religious identity but through their antagonistic attitude toward

Jesus, they represent a literary construct that functions as a stereotype of rejection (von Wahlde, 33–60; Kysar, 83; Johnson, 1619–20; on the understanding of the Ἰουδαῖοι as an ἔθνος in the Greco-Roman world, see Mason, 457–512).

καὶ εἶπαν αὐτῷ. Pleonastic clause under Semitic influence, which functions as a redundant quotative frame (see 1:25 on καὶ εἶπαν αὐτῷ).

καί. Coordinating conjunction.

εἶπαν. Aor act ind 3rd pl λέγω.

αὐτῷ. Dative indirect object of εἶπαν.

τί σημεῖον. Accusative direct object of δεικνύεις. Fronted for emphasis. In this construction, the interrogative pronoun is used adjectivally ("What sign . . ."; cf. Wallace 1996, 346).

δεικνύεις. Pres act ind 2nd sg δείκνυμι.

ἡμῖν. Dative indirect object of δεικνύεις.

ὅτι. Introduces a clause that is epexegetical to τί σημεῖον δεικνύεις ἡμῖν: "What sign do you show to us that you have the authority to do these things?" (cf. NIV; NASB; CJB; GNT; see Wallace 1996, 459–60). Alternatively, if ὅτι in this verse corresponds to Hebrew כִּי (BDF §456.2), it introduces a causal clause that provides justification for the request for a sign: "What sign do you show to us, because you are doing these [things]?" (LEB).

ταῦτα. Accusative direct object of ποιεῖς. Fronted for emphasis.

ποιεῖς. Pres act ind 2nd sg ποιέω.

2:19 ἀπεκρίθη Ἰησοῦς καὶ εἶπεν αὐτοῖς· λύσατε τὸν ναὸν τοῦτον καὶ ἐν τρισὶν ἡμέραις ἐγερῶ αὐτόν.

ἀπεκρίθη. Aor mid ind 3rd sg ἀποκρίνομαι. On the voice, see "Deponency" in the Series Introduction. This verse is connected to the previous one by asyndeton.

Ἰησοῦς. Nominative subject of ἀπεκρίθη.

καὶ εἶπεν αὐτοῖς. Pleonastic clause under Semitic influence, which functions as a redundant quotative frame (see 1:25 on καὶ εἶπαν αὐτῷ).

καί. Coordinating conjunction.

εἶπεν. Aor act ind 3rd sg λέγω.

αὐτοῖς. Dative indirect object of εἶπεν.

λύσατε. Aor act impv 2nd pl λύω. According to BDF (§387.2), this imperative is the equivalent of a concessive clause: λύσατε τὸν ναὸν τοῦτον = ἐὰν καὶ λύσητε τὸν ναὸν τοῦτον (see also Robertson, 948). Wallace (1996, 489–91) calls it a "conditional imperative" because it is followed by καί and the future indicative. He, however, adds that such an imperative has not lost its injunctive force. It does not merely express a condition which, if met, will have a described consequence; it also conveys a desire of the speaker that this condition should be fulfilled. Wallace therefore proposes the following translation for λύσατε τὸν ναὸν τοῦτον καὶ ἐν τρισὶν ἡμέραις ἐγερῶ αὐτόν: "If you destroy this temple—and I *command* you to—in three days I will raise it up" (490). Rhetorically, the imperative is used here to express irony: by "inviting" his opponents to kill him, Jesus uses an ironic imperative that is common in the prophetic tradition (cf. 1 Kgs 18:27; Isa 6:9; 8:10; 29:9; Jer 23:28; 44:25; Amos 4:4-5). It can therefore rightly be called a "prophetic imperative" (Kerr, 87–88).

τὸν ναὸν τοῦτον. Accusative direct object of λύσατε. Unlike ἱερόν, which in the FG occurs in 2:14, 15; 5:14; 7:14, 28; 8:20, 59; 10:23; 11:56; 18:20, ναός is used only here and in the next two verses. Harris (2015, 66) argues that the demonstrative pronoun τοῦτον "is intentionally ambiguous, referring either to the actual temple or to Jesus' physical body (regarded as God's living temple)."

καί. Coordinating conjunction.

ἐν τρισὶν ἡμέραις. Temporal. Fronted for emphasis.

ἐγερῶ. Fut act ind 1st sg ἐγείρω.

αὐτόν. Accusative direct object of ἐγερῶ. The personal pronoun refers to τὸν ναὸν τοῦτον.

2:20 εἶπαν οὖν οἱ Ἰουδαῖοι· τεσσεράκοντα καὶ ἓξ ἔτεσιν οἰκοδομήθη ὁ ναὸς οὗτος, καὶ σὺ ἐν τρισὶν ἡμέραις ἐγερεῖς αὐτόν;

εἶπαν. Aor act ind 3rd pl λέγω.

οὖν. Postpositive inferential conjunction and/or transitional particle (see 1:22 and 11:6).

οἱ Ἰουδαῖοι. Nominative subject of εἶπαν. On the meaning of this term, see 2:19.

τεσσεράκοντα καὶ ἕξ. Indeclinable cardinal numbers ("forty and six").

ἔτεσιν. Dative of time. Fronted for emphasis. If this dative indicates the point in time when the action of the main verb is accomplished, as is typical in classical Greek (BDF §200), the sense of the clause would be "this temple was built forty-six years ago" (Köstenberger, 109–10; Wallace 1996, 560–61). This interpretation presumes that ναός does not refer to the entire temple structure but only to the sanctuary proper, which was completed in c. 18–17 BCE. If, however, the dative stands for the accusative indicating extent of time, as is common in Hellenistic Greek (Zerwick, §54), the sense of the clause would be "this temple has been built for forty-six years."

οἰκοδομήθη. Aor pass ind 3rd sg οἰκοδομέω. The primary agent of the action is not expressed.

ὁ ναὸς οὗτος. Nominative subject of οἰκοδομήθη. In this formulation, the demonstrative pronoun unambiguously refers to the physical structure of the Jerusalem temple.

καὶ. Coordinating conjunction.

σὺ. Nominative subject of ἐγερεῖς. Fronted as a topical frame.

ἐν τρισὶν ἡμέραις. Temporal (see 2:19). Fronted for emphasis.

ἐγερεῖς. Fut act ind 2nd sg ἐγείρω.

αὐτόν. Accusative direct object of ἐγερεῖς.

2:21 ἐκεῖνος δὲ ἔλεγεν περὶ τοῦ ναοῦ τοῦ σώματος αὐτοῦ.

ἐκεῖνος. Nominative subject of ἔλεγεν. The demonstrative pronoun refers to Ἰησοῦς from v. 19, acting as a third-person personal pronoun with a simple anaphoric force (Wallace 1996, 328–29).

δὲ. Marker of narrative development.

ἔλεγεν. Impf act ind 3rd sg λέγω. Du Toit argues that this imperfect is used in an explanation of the content of Jesus' words because "it is inherently linked to another verb—in this case, εἶπεν in v. 19" (226). On the function of the imperfect in the FG, see 1:39 on ἦν.

περὶ τοῦ ναοῦ. Reference.

τοῦ σώματος. Epexegetical genitive explaining ναοῦ ("concerning the temple, which is his body"; cf. BDF §167). The head noun states a larger category ("the temple"), which is in this context ambiguous because it could be both literal and figurative, while the genitive noun names a specific subcategory ("his body") that clarifies the ambiguity of the head noun by explaining its metaphorical character (Wallace 1996, 95–98). Since τοῦ ναοῦ is also in the genitive because it serves as the object of the preposition περί, there is a structural possibility that τοῦ σώματος may function as a genitive in apposition to τοῦ ναοῦ (Robertson, 399). But if that were the case, the appositional genitive, being completely equivalent to the first genitive, could be removed from the formulation without any loss of meaning, which would result in a sentence that does not explain anything.

αὐτοῦ. Possessive genitive qualifying σώματος.

2:22 ὅτε οὖν ἠγέρθη ἐκ νεκρῶν, ἐμνήσθησαν οἱ μαθηταὶ αὐτοῦ ὅτι τοῦτο ἔλεγεν, καὶ ἐπίστευσαν τῇ γραφῇ καὶ τῷ λόγῳ ὃν εἶπεν ὁ Ἰησοῦς.

ὅτε. Introduces a temporal clause, which is fronted as a temporal frame.

οὖν. Postpositive inferential conjunction and/or transitional particle (see 1:22 and 11:6).

ἠγέρθη. Aor pass ind 3rd sg ἐγείρω. Although Jesus' pronouncement in v. 19 (ἐγερῶ) and the repetition of his prediction in v. 20 (ἐγερεῖς) use the active voice of ἐγείρω, the evangelist's explanation employs the passive voice, suggesting that Jesus did not raise himself from the dead but was raised by God. The passive voice is also used in 21:14 (ἐγερθεὶς ἐκ νεκρῶν). These are the only instances in the FG in which ἐγείρω is applied to Jesus' resurrection. Elsewhere in the FG, the active forms of this verb are used to describe God's raising of the dead (5:21) or Jesus' raising of Lazarus (12:1, 9, 17).

ἐκ νεκρῶν. Separation.

ἐμνήσθησαν. Aor mid ind 3rd pl μιμνῄσκομαι. On the voice, see "Deponency" in the Series Introduction; on the meaning, see 2:17. A similar comment, which places the disciples' recollection and understanding of the past events in the time after Easter, occurs in 12:16.

οἱ μαθηταί. Nominative subject of ἐμνήσθησαν.

αὐτοῦ. Genitive of relationship qualifying μαθηταί.

ὅτι. Introduces the clausal complement (indirect discourse) of ἐμνήσθησαν.

τοῦτο. Accusative direct object of ἔλεγεν. The anaphoric near-demonstrative refers to Jesus' declaration in 2:19.

ἔλεγεν. Impf act ind 3rd sg λέγω (see 2:21).

καί. Coordinating conjunction.

ἐπίστευσαν. Aor act ind 3rd pl πιστεύω.

τῇ γραφῇ. Dative direct object of ἐπίστευσαν. The dative conveys the thing to which someone gives credence (BDAG, 816.1.a.δ). The article is anaphoric, but it is not clear whether it refers to the specific scriptural passage such as the quotation of LXX Ps 68:10 in v. 17 or to the whole of Scripture that could be properly understood only from a post-resurrection perspective (Novakovic, 192–93; Brown, 1:116). The noun γραφή (sg.) occurs more often in the FG (eleven times: 2:22; 7:38, 42; 10:35; 13:18; 17:12; 19:24, 28, 36, 37; 20:9) than in all the Synoptics together (only twice: Mark 12:10 and Luke 4:21).

καί. Coordinating conjunction.

τῷ λόγῳ. Dative direct object of ἐπίστευσαν (see τῇ γραφῇ above).

ὄν. Accusative direct object of εἶπεν. The antecedent of the relative pronoun is τῷ λόγῳ. This is an example of a non-attraction of the relative to the case of its antecedent, which usually happens "if the relative clause is more clearly separated from its antecedent by . . . the importance of its own content" (BDF §294.1), as here. The variant reading ᾧ (A K N P Wˢ Γ Δ Θ Ψ $f^{1.13}$ 𝔐 et al.) most likely arose out of the need to adjust the case of the relative to its antecedent, which was "a construction at least as popular in late as in classical Greek" (Robertson, 715).

εἶπεν. Aor act ind 3rd sg λέγω.

ὁ Ἰησοῦς. Nominative subject of εἶπεν.

John 2:23-25

²³Now while he was in Jerusalem at the Passover, during the festival, many believed in his name because they saw his signs that he was doing. ²⁴But Jesus himself was not entrusting himself to them because he knew them all ²⁵and because he did not need that anyone should testify about a person; for he himself knew what was in a person.

2:23 Ὡς δὲ ἦν ἐν τοῖς Ἱεροσολύμοις ἐν τῷ πάσχα ἐν τῇ ἑορτῇ, πολλοὶ ἐπίστευσαν εἰς τὸ ὄνομα αὐτοῦ θεωροῦντες αὐτοῦ τὰ σημεῖα ἃ ἐποίει·

Ὡς. Temporal conjunction (BDAG, 1105.8.b; BDF §455.2), introducing a clause that is fronted as a temporal frame.

δὲ. Marker of narrative development.

ἦν. Impf act ind 3rd sg εἰμί.

ἐν τοῖς Ἱεροσολύμοις. Locative. The article is anaphoric, referring to Jerusalem mentioned in 2:13.

ἐν τῷ πάσχα. Temporal (see 2:13).

ἐν τῇ ἑορτῇ. Temporal ("during the festival") or locative ("among the assembled multitude at the festival" [cf. LSJ, 601; Harris 2015, 69]).

πολλοί. Nominative subject of ἐπίστευσαν. Fronted as a topical frame.

ἐπίστευσαν. Aor act ind 3rd pl πιστεύω.

εἰς τὸ ὄνομα. Goal of actions or feelings directed toward someone (BDAG, 290.4.c.β). For πιστεύειν εἰς + accusative ("trust or believe in someone"), see 1:12 on εἰς τὸ ὄνομα. ὄνομα is synecdoche for the whole person. Elsewhere in the FG, the expression πιστεύειν εἰς τὸ ὄνομα occurs in 1:12 and 3:18.

αὐτοῦ. Possessive genitive qualifying ὄνομα.

θεωροῦντες. Pres act ptc masc nom pl θεωρέω (causal or temporal). On participles that follow the main verb, see βαπτίζων in 1:31.

αὐτοῦ. Subjective genitive qualifying σημεῖα. Zerwick calls this usage "pronominal prolepsis" because "the subject of a relative clause is anticipated by a pronoun in the main clause" (§206); cf. Luke 2:30; John 7:3.

τὰ σημεῖα. Accusative direct object of θεωροῦντες. The use of the term σημεῖα for Jesus' miracles is one of the distinctive features of the FG (see 2:11; 3:2; 4:48, 54; 6:2, 14, 26; 7:31; 9:16; 11:47; 12:18, 37; 20:30; cf. Barrett, 75–78; Keener, 1:272–79; Thompson, 65–68).

ἅ. Accusative direct object of ἐποίει.

ἐποίει. Impf act ind 3rd sg ποιέω. The imperfective aspect portrays Jesus' performance of his signs as an ongoing process. On the function of the imperfect in the FG, see 1:39 on ἦν.

2:24 αὐτὸς δὲ Ἰησοῦς οὐκ ἐπίστευεν αὐτὸν αὐτοῖς διὰ τὸ αὐτὸν γινώσκειν πάντας

αὐτὸς . . . Ἰησοῦς. Nominative subject of ἐπίστευεν. Fronted as a topical frame. αὐτὸς, standing in the predicate position to Ἰησοῦς, functions as an intensive pronoun ("Jesus himself"), "setting an item off fr[om] everything else through emphasis and contrast" (BDAG, 152.1).

δὲ. Marker of narrative development.

οὐκ. Negative particle normally used with indicative verbs.

ἐπίστευεν. Impf act ind 3rd sg πιστεύω. The verb here means "entrust" something (acc) to someone (dat) (BDAG, 818.3). The imperfective aspect of the verb form indicates that the situation is viewed from within, i.e., as unfolding. On the function of the imperfect in the FG, see 1:39 on ἦν.

αὐτὸν. Accusative direct object of ἐπίστευεν. αὐτὸν stands for ἑαυτὸν, as many witnesses try to clarify ($\mathfrak{P}^{66}$ ℵ² Aᶜ K N P Wˢ Γ Δ Θ Ψ $f^{1.13}$ 𝔐 et al.), while a few others omit it ($\mathfrak{P}^{75}$ 579). However, not only is the manuscript support for αὐτὸν quite strong (ℵ* A* B L 700) but this is also the most difficult reading.

αὐτοῖς. Dative indirect object of ἐπίστευεν.

διὰ τὸ. Used with the infinitive to denote cause (see γινώσκειν below).

αὐτὸν. Accusative subject of the infinitive γινώσκειν.

γινώσκειν. Pres act inf γινώσκω. Used with διὰ τὸ to indicate cause.

πάντας. Accusative direct object of γινώσκειν.

2:25 καὶ ὅτι οὐ χρείαν εἶχεν ἵνα τις μαρτυρήσῃ περὶ τοῦ ἀνθρώπου· αὐτὸς γὰρ ἐγίνωσκεν τί ἦν ἐν τῷ ἀνθρώπῳ.

καὶ. Coordinating conjunction.

ὅτι. Introduces a causal clause that offers another explanation for the assertion in v. 24 that Jesus would not entrust himself to those who believed in him because of the signs that he performed.

οὐ. Negative particle normally used with indicative verbs.

χρείαν. Accusative direct object of εἶχεν.

εἶχεν. Impf act ind 3rd sg ἔχω. χρείαν ἔχω (lit. "to have need of") is an idiom for "to need." On the function of the imperfect in the FG, see 1:39 on ἦν.

ἵνα. Introduces an epexegetical clause that clarifies the noun χρείαν (Wallace 1996, 476).

τις. Nominative subject of μαρτυρήσῃ.

μαρτυρήσῃ. Aor act subj 3rd sg μαρτυρέω. Subjunctive with ἵνα.

περὶ τοῦ ἀνθρώπου. Reference. The article is generic, referring to human beings as a class (Wallace 1996, 227–28).

αὐτὸς. Intensive pronoun that reinforces the implied subject of ἐγίνωσκεν ("he himself").

γὰρ. Postpositive conjunction that introduces an explanation for the previous assertion that Jesus needed no one to testify about anyone. Runge emphasizes that "the information introduced [by γάρ] does not advance the discourse but adds background information that strengthens or supports what precedes" (2010, 52).

ἐγίνωσκεν. Impf act ind 3rd sg γινώσκω. On the function of the imperfect in the FG, see 1:39 on ἦν.

τί. Nominative subject of ἦν. The interrogative pronoun introduces indirect discourse.

ἦν. Impf act ind 3rd sg εἰμί. The use of the imperfect after the verb of perception in the past tense (ἐγίνωσκεν) can be explained in two ways: (1) it could have been used, through a tense assimilation, instead of the present-tense ἐστιν, which in indirect discourse expresses the relative (i.e., contemporaneous) time from the point of view of the original speaker (BDF §324); (2) it could have been used to refer to that particular time, i.e., the time described by the plot of the narrative (§330).

ἐν τῷ ἀνθρώπῳ. Locative. The article is again generic (see περὶ τοῦ ἀνθρώπου above).

John 3:1-12

¹Now there was a man among the Pharisees, (his name was Nicodemus), a leader of the Jews. ²He came to him by night and said to him, "Rabbi, we know that you have come from God as a teacher, for no one can do these signs that you do unless God is with him." ³Jesus answered and said to him, "Truly, truly I say to you, unless someone is born from above,

he cannot see the kingdom of God." ⁴Nicodemus said to him, "How can a man be born when he is an old man? He can't enter into his mother's womb for the second time and be born, can he?" ⁵Jesus answered, "Truly, truly I say to you, unless someone is born from water and spirit, he cannot enter into the kingdom of God. ⁶What is born of the flesh is flesh, and what is born of the spirit is spirit. ⁷Do not be amazed that I said to you, 'It is necessary for all of you to be born from above.' ⁸The wind blows where it wishes, and you hear the sound of it, but you do not know where it comes from and where it goes. So is everyone who is born of the Spirit." ⁹Nicodemus answered and said to him, "How can these things happen?" ¹⁰Jesus answered and said to him, "You are the teacher of Israel, and you do not understand these things? ¹¹Truly, truly I say to you, we speak what we know, and we testify what we have seen, but you all do not accept our testimony. ¹²If I have told you earthly things and you do not believe, how will you believe if I tell you heavenly things?"

3:1 Ἦν δὲ ἄνθρωπος ἐκ τῶν Φαρισαίων, Νικόδημος ὄνομα αὐτῷ, ἄρχων τῶν Ἰουδαίων·

Ἦν. Impf act ind 3rd sg εἰμί. The use of ἦν is a common way in the FG to introduce a new character in the main narrative (see 4:46; 5:5; 11:1; cf. LXX Exod 2:1; 1 Sam 1:1; Job 1:1; Luke 14:2; Acts 9:10, 36; 16:1). On the function of the imperfect in the FG, see 1:39 on ἦν.

δὲ. Marker of narrative development.

ἄνθρωπος. Nominative subject of Ἦν.

ἐκ τῶν Φαρισαίων. Replaces the partitive genitive.

Νικόδημος. Predicate nominative in a verbless clause. Lit. "the name [belonging] to him [was] Nicodemus" = "his name was Nicodemus."

ὄνομα. Parenthetic nominative, which functions as the subject of a verbless explanatory clause embedded in another clause.

αὐτῷ. Dative of possession ("the name [belonging] to him").

ἄρχων. Nominative in apposition to ἄνθρωπος. The appositional information receives emphasis through right-dislocation (Runge 2010, 317–36). In this context, ἄρχων ("ruler, leader") denotes a member of the Sanhedrin who has administrative authority (BDAG, 140.2.a).

τῶν Ἰουδαίων. Genitive of subordination qualifying ἄρχων. The phrase ἄρχων τῶν Ἰουδαίων "seems to focus primarily upon the authority and status which such a person has, rather than merely upon his being a member of a deliberative body" (LN, 483 n. 13).

3:2 οὗτος ἦλθεν πρὸς αὐτὸν νυκτὸς καὶ εἶπεν αὐτῷ· ῥαββί, οἴδαμεν ὅτι ἀπὸ θεοῦ ἐλήλυθας διδάσκαλος· οὐδεὶς γὰρ δύναται ταῦτα τὰ σημεῖα ποιεῖν ἃ σὺ ποιεῖς, ἐὰν μὴ ᾖ ὁ θεὸς μετ' αὐτοῦ.

οὗτος. Nominative subject of ἦλθεν. Fronted as a topical frame. The demonstrative pronoun refers to Νικόδημος from the previous verse, acting as a third-person personal pronoun with a simple anaphoric force (Wallace 1996, 328–29). This verse is connected to the previous one by asyndeton.

ἦλθεν. Aor act ind 3rd sg ἔρχομαι.

πρὸς αὐτὸν. Locative (motion toward).

νυκτὸς. Genitive of time. The genitive indicates the kind of time ("by night") rather than a particular point in the night in which Nicodemus came to Jesus (Wallace 1996, 123–24).

καὶ. Coordinating conjunction.

εἶπεν. Aor act ind 3rd sg λέγω.

αὐτῷ. Dative indirect object of εἶπεν.

ῥαββί. Vocative of direct address.

οἴδαμεν. Prf act ind 1st pl οἶδα (see 1:26 on οἴδατε).

ὅτι. Introduces the clausal complement (indirect discourse) of οἴδαμεν.

ἀπὸ θεοῦ. Source.

ἐλήλυθας. Prf act ind 2nd sg ἔρχομαι.

διδάσκαλος. Nominative complement to the implied subject of ἐλήλυθας ("you have come as a teacher"). It receives emphasis through right-dislocation (Runge 2010, 317–36).

οὐδεὶς. Nominative subject of δύναται. The substantival pronoun marks the beginning of the apodosis of a third-class condition, which precedes the protasis.

γὰρ. Postpositive conjunction that introduces the explanation for the assertion that Jesus is a teacher who came from God. This explanation consists of a third-class conditional clause, which seeks to establish Jesus' divine origin on the basis of his miraculous signs.

δύναται. Pres mid ind 3rd sg δύναμαι.

ταῦτα τὰ σημεῖα. Accusative direct object of ποιεῖν. The use of the term σημεῖα for Jesus' miracles is one of the distinctive features of the FG (see 2:11, 23; 4:48, 54; 6:2, 14, 26; 7:31; 9:16; 11:47; 12:18, 37; 20:30; cf. Barrett, 75–78; Keener, 1:272–79; Thompson, 65–68).

ποιεῖν. Pres act inf ποιέω (complementary).

ἃ. Accusative direct object of ποιεῖς.

σὺ. Nominative subject of ποιεῖς.

ποιεῖς. Pres act ind 2nd sg ποιέω.

ἐάν. Introduces the protasis of a third-class condition.

μή. Negative particle normally used with non-indicative verbs. ἐὰν μή can be translated "unless."

ᾖ. Pres act subj 3rd sg εἰμί. Subjunctive with ἐάν.

ὁ θεός. Nominative subject of ᾖ.

μετ' αὐτοῦ. Association/accompaniment.

3:3 ἀπεκρίθη Ἰησοῦς καὶ εἶπεν αὐτῷ· ἀμὴν ἀμὴν λέγω σοι, ἐὰν μή τις γεννηθῇ ἄνωθεν, οὐ δύναται ἰδεῖν τὴν βασιλείαν τοῦ θεοῦ.

ἀπεκρίθη. Aor mid ind 3rd sg ἀποκρίνομαι. On the voice, see "Deponency" in the Series Introduction. This verse is connected to the previous one by asyndeton.

Ἰησοῦς. Nominative subject of ἀπεκρίθη.

καὶ εἶπεν αὐτῷ. Pleonastic clause under Semitic influence, which functions as a redundant quotative frame (see 1:25 on καὶ εἶπαν αὐτῷ).

καί. Coordinating conjunction.

εἶπεν. Aor act ind 3rd sg λέγω.

αὐτῷ. Dative indirect object of εἶπεν.

ἀμὴν ἀμὴν λέγω σοι. Metacomment (see 1:51).

ἀμὴν ἀμήν. Asseverative particles that mark the beginning of Jesus' solemn declaration (see 1:51).

λέγω. Pres act ind 1st sg λέγω.

σοι. Dative indirect object of λέγω.

ἐάν. Introduces the protasis of a third-class condition.

μή. Negative particle normally used with non-indicative verbs. ἐὰν μή can be translated "unless."

τις. Nominative subject of γεννηθῇ. The indefinite pronoun is here used substantivally, i.e., as a true pronoun (Wallace 1996, 347).

γεννηθῇ. Aor pass subj 3rd sg γεννάω. Subjunctive with ἐάν.

ἄνωθεν. Adverb of place that can indicate "a source that is above, *from above*" (BDAG, 92.1) and/or "a subsequent point of time involving repetition, *again, anew*" (92.4). If the term is deliberately ambiguous (Barrett, 205–6; Thompson, 81; Hagner, 283), this works only in Greek because there is no Aramaic equivalent that has two meanings. While Jesus' explanation (3:5-8) indicates that the intended meaning of ἄνωθεν is "from above," as elsewhere in the FG (3:31; 19:11, 23), Nicodemus' misunderstanding (3:4) shows that he takes it to mean "again." The adverb therefore functions as a double entendre, which, by causing misunderstanding, provides occasion for further explanation and moves the conversation forward. For other examples of words with multiple meanings which are typically misunderstood by Jesus' audience, see 4:14-15; 6:33-34; 8:21-22; 11:11-13, 23-24; 14:7-8.

οὐ. Negative particle normally used with indicative verbs. It marks the beginning of the apodosis of a third-class condition.

δύναται. Pres mid ind 3rd sg δύναμαι.

ἰδεῖν. Aor act inf ὁράω (complementary).

τὴν βασιλείαν. Accusative direct object of ἰδεῖν. The expression ἡ βασιλεία τοῦ θεοῦ, the central theme of Jesus' proclamation in the Synoptic Gospels, occurs in the FG only here and in 3:5.

τοῦ θεοῦ. Subjective genitive qualifying βασιλείαν.

3:4 Λέγει πρὸς αὐτὸν [ὁ] Νικόδημος· πῶς δύναται ἄνθρωπος γεννηθῆναι γέρων ὤν; μὴ δύναται εἰς τὴν κοιλίαν τῆς μητρὸς αὐτοῦ δεύτερον εἰσελθεῖν καὶ γεννηθῆναι;

Λέγει. Pres act ind 3rd sg λέγω. The historical present calls attention to the absurdity of Nicodemus' reply, which shows that he misunderstood Jesus' statement about being born from above (see 1:15 on μαρτυρεῖ). This verse is connected to the previous one by asyndeton.

πρὸς αὐτόν. Locative (motion toward). The PP functions like an indirect object of Λέγει.

[ὁ] Νικόδημος. Nominative subject of Λέγει. The article is printed within square brackets because the external evidence for (א A K Γ Δ $f^{1.13}$ 565 700 et al.) and against ($\mathfrak{P}^{66.75}$ B L N W^s Θ Ψ 050 579 et al.) its presence in the text is evenly balanced.

πῶς. Interrogative particle.

δύναται. Pres mid 3rd sg δύναμαι.

ἄνθρωπος. Nominative subject of δύναται.

γεννηθῆναι. Aor pass inf γεννάω (complementary).

γέρων. Predicative nominative. γέρων denotes "an adult male, with emphasis upon advanced age" (LN 9.30).

ὤν. Pres act ptc masc nom sg εἰμί (temporal). On participles that follow the main verb, see βαπτίζων in 1:31.

μὴ. Negative particle that introduces a question that expects a negative answer.

δύναται. Pres mid ind 3rd sg δύναμαι.

εἰς τὴν κοιλίαν. Locative. κοιλία means "the uterus—'womb'" (LN 8.69).

τῆς μητρός. Possessive genitive qualifying κοιλίαν.

αὐτοῦ. Genitive of relationship qualifying μητρός.

δεύτερον. Adverbial accusative ("for the second time" [BDAG, 221.2]).

εἰσελθεῖν. Aor act inf εἰσέρχομαι (complementary).
καί. Coordinating conjunction.
γεννηθῆναι. Aor pass inf γεννάω (complementary).

3:5 ἀπεκρίθη Ἰησοῦς· ἀμὴν ἀμὴν λέγω σοι, ἐὰν μή τις γεννηθῇ ἐξ ὕδατος καὶ πνεύματος, οὐ δύναται εἰσελθεῖν εἰς τὴν βασιλείαν τοῦ θεοῦ.

ἀπεκρίθη. Aor mid ind 3rd sg ἀποκρίνομαι. On the voice, see "Deponency" in the Series Introduction. This verse is connected to the previous one by asyndeton.
Ἰησοῦς. Nominative subject of ἀπεκρίθη.
ἀμὴν ἀμὴν λέγω σοι. Metacomment (see 1:51).
ἀμὴν ἀμήν. Asseverative particles that mark the beginning of Jesus' solemn declaration (see 1:51).
λέγω. Pres act ind 1st sg λέγω.
σοι. Dative indirect object of σοι.
ἐάν. Introduces the protasis of a third-class condition. ἐὰν μή can be translated "unless."
μή. Negative particle normally used with non-indicative verbs. ἐὰν μή can be translated "unless."
τις. Nominative subject of γεννηθῇ. The indefinite pronoun is here used substantivally, i.e., as a true pronoun (Wallace 1996, 347).
γεννηθῇ. Aor pass subj 3rd sg γεννάω. Subjunctive with ἐάν.
ἐξ ὕδατος καὶ πνεύματος. Source/origin. The single preposition ἐκ that governs both nouns indicates that they are regarded as a conceptual unit (Harris 2015, 73).
οὐ. Negative particle normally used with indicative verbs. It marks the beginning of the apodosis of a third-class condition.
δύναται. Pres mid ind 3rd sg δύναμαι.
εἰσελθεῖν. Aor act inf εἰσέρχομαι (complementary).
εἰς τὴν βασιλείαν. Locative.
τοῦ θεοῦ. Subjective genitive qualifying βασιλείαν.

3:6 τὸ γεγεννημένον ἐκ τῆς σαρκὸς σάρξ ἐστιν, καὶ τὸ γεγεννημένον ἐκ τοῦ πνεύματος πνεῦμά ἐστιν.

τὸ γεγεννημένον. Prf pass ptc neut nom sg γεννάω (substantival). Nominative subject of ἐστιν. "The neuter is sometimes used with reference to persons if it is not the individuals but a general quality that is to be emphasized" (BDF §138.1). Zerwick (§141) adds that "the use of the neuter lays down an absolute and universal principle based on the distinction and separateness, each in its own sphere, of the natural and supernatural orders." The perfect tense of the participle, along with the PP that follows, conveys the idea that the past event (the birth) is determinative for the current state (the nature) of a person, but the stative aspect of the verb form, along with the predicative nominative, shifts the emphasis toward the latter: "what has been born and now presents itself that way" (Harris 2015, 73). This verse is connected to the previous one by asyndeton.

ἐκ τῆς σαρκὸς. Source/origin.

σάρξ. Predicate nominative. Fronted for emphasis. σάρξ is a qualitative predicate nominative because the emphasis is on human nature of those who are born of the flesh (see 1:14).

ἐστιν. Pres act ind 3rd sg εἰμί.

καὶ. Coordinating conjunction.

τὸ γεγεννημένον. Prf pass ptc neut nom sg γεννάω (substantival). Nominative subject of ἐστιν (see above).

ἐκ τοῦ πνεύματος. Source/origin.

πνεῦμά. Predicate nominative. Fronted for emphasis. πνεῦμά is a qualitative predicate nominative because the emphasis is on spiritual nature of those who are born of the Spirit. πνεῦμά, which has a circumflex accent on the penult, acquired an additional accent, the acute, on the ultima from the enclitic ἐστιν (Smyth §183; Carson 1985, 48).

ἐστιν. Pres act ind 3rd sg εἰμί.

3:7 μὴ θαυμάσῃς ὅτι εἶπόν σοι· δεῖ ὑμᾶς γεννηθῆναι ἄνωθεν.

μὴ. Negative particle introducing prohibition. This verse is connected to the previous one by asyndeton.

θαυμάσῃς. Aor act subj 2nd sg θαυμάζω (prohibitive subjunctive). The perfective aspect of the aorist tense indicates that marveling is seen as a complete action, not an action that has not yet started as it is assumed in the traditional view of the aorist in prohibitions. Wallace (1996, 717 n. 15) illustrates the inadequacy of such a view by offering a translation that follows the traditional canon: "Do not start to marvel," remarking that "Nicodemus already was marveling." The persistence of the traditional understanding can be seen in Harris' recent exegetical guide to John, in which he argues that Jesus' command represents a "'categorical prohibition' to prevent an action from beginning, with the aorist perhaps being ingressive, 'Do not begin to marvel'" (2015, 73).

ὅτι. Introduces the clausal complement of θαυμάσῃς.

εἶπόν. Aor act ind 1st sg λέγω. εἶπόν, which has a circumflex accent on the penult, acquired an additional accent, the acute, on the ultima from the enclitic σοι (Smyth §183; Carson 1985, 48).

σοι. Dative indirect object of εἶπόν.

δεῖ. Pres act ind 3rd sg δεῖ (impersonal).

ὑμᾶς. Accusative subject of the infnitive γεννηθῆναι. Note the shift from the second-person singular personal pronoun σοι to the second-person plural personal pronoun ὑμᾶς.

γεννηθῆναι. Aor pass inf γεννάω. If δεῖ is regarded as an impersonal verb, the function of the infinitive is complementary (Culy, Parsons, and Stigall, 98). Porter calls the combinations of δεῖ, μέλλω, θέλω, and δύναμαι with infinitives "catenative constructions" and emphasizes that in them "the verbal aspects of the main verb and the infinitive are to be included in the semantics of the syntactical unit" (197). Alternatively, the infinitival clause, ὑμᾶς γεννηθῆναι ἄνωθεν, could be viewed as the subject of δεῖ ("for you to be born from above is necessary"), but in such a case it is misleading to call δεῖ an impersonal verb (*pace* Wallace 1996, 600–601).

ἄνωθεν. Adverb of place that can indicate "a source that is above, *from above*" (BDAG, 92.1) and/or "a subsequent point of time involving repetition, *again, anew*" (92.4); see 3:3.

3:8 τὸ πνεῦμα ὅπου θέλει πνεῖ καὶ τὴν φωνὴν αὐτοῦ ἀκούεις, ἀλλ' οὐκ οἶδας πόθεν ἔρχεται καὶ ποῦ ὑπάγει· οὕτως ἐστὶν πᾶς ὁ γεγεννημένος ἐκ τοῦ πνεύματος.

τὸ πνεῦμα. Nominative subject of πνεῖ. Here πνεῦμα denotes "air in movement," i.e., "wind" (BDAG, 832.1.a). This verse is connected to the previous one by asyndeton.

ὅπου. Particle denoting place.

θέλει. Pres act ind 3rd sg θέλω.

πνεῖ. Pres act ind 3rd sg πνέω. Here the present tense describes "action occurring at any time" (Porter 1994, 32–33).

καὶ. Coordinating conjunction.

τὴν φωνὴν. Accusative direct object of ἀκούεις.

αὐτοῦ. Possessive genitive qualifying φωνήν. The anaphoric pronoun refers to τὸ πνεῦμα.

ἀκούεις. Pres act ind 2nd sg ἀκούω.

ἀλλ'. Marker of contrast.

οὐκ. Negative particle normally used with indicative verbs.

οἶδας. Prf act ind 2nd sg οἶδα (see 1:26 on οἴδατε).

πόθεν. Interrogative adverb of place ("from where").

ἔρχεται. Pres mid ind 3rd sg ἔρχομαι.
καί. Coordinating conjunction.
ποῦ. Interrogative adverb of place ("where").
ὑπάγει. Pres act ind 3rd sg ὑπάγω.
οὕτως. Predicate adverb of manner (see 2:1 on ἐκεῖ).
ἐστὶν. Pres act ind 3rd sg εἰμί.
πᾶς ὁ γεγεννημένος. Nominative subject of ἐστὶν. "In constructions where πᾶς is followed by an articular participle one could take either πᾶς or the participle as substantival. If πᾶς is viewed as substantival, the participle will be attributive. Since the nominative singular πᾶς does not require the article to make it substantival, and indeed is never articular, either analysis is acceptable" (Culy 2004, 56; cf. BDF §413.2; Robertson, 772–73). In this and other similar constructions in the FG, I will regard πᾶς as attributive and the articular participle as a noun.

ὁ γεγεννημένος. Prf pass ptc masc nom sg γεννάω (substantival). On the function of this participle, see πᾶς ὁ γεγεννημένος above.

ἐκ τοῦ πνεύματος. Source/origin. Here πνεῦμα denotes "God's being as controlling influence, with focus on association with humans" (BDAG, 834.5).

3:9 Ἀπεκρίθη Νικόδημος καὶ εἶπεν αὐτῷ· πῶς δύναται ταῦτα γενέσθαι;

Ἀπεκρίθη. Aor mid ind 3rd sg ἀποκρίνομαι. On the voice, see "Deponency" in the Series Introduction. This verse is connected to the previous one by asyndeton.

Νικόδημος. Nominative subject of Ἀπεκρίθη.

καὶ εἶπεν αὐτῷ. Pleonastic clause under Semitic influence, which functions as a redundant quotative frame (see 1:25 on καὶ εἶπαν αὐτῷ).

καί. Coordinating conjunction.
εἶπεν. Aor act ind 3rd sg λέγω.
αὐτῷ. Dative indirect object of εἶπεν.
πῶς. Interrogative particle.
δύναται. Pres mid ind 3rd sg δύναμαι. Neuter plural subjects typically take singular verbs (see 1:28 on ἐγένετο).
ταῦτα. Nominative subject of δύναται.
γενέσθαι. Aor mid inf γίνομαι (complementary).

3:10 ἀπεκρίθη Ἰησοῦς καὶ εἶπεν αὐτῷ· σὺ εἶ ὁ διδάσκαλος τοῦ Ἰσραὴλ καὶ ταῦτα οὐ γινώσκεις;

ἀπεκρίθη. Aor mid ind 3rd sg ἀποκρίνομαι. On the voice, see "Deponency" in the Series Introduction. This verse is connected to the previous one by asyndeton.

Ἰησοῦς. Nominative subject of ἀπεκρίθη.

καί. Coordinating conjunction.

καὶ εἶπεν αὐτῷ. Pleonastic clause under Semitic influence, which functions as a redundant quotative frame (see 1:25 on καὶ εἶπαν αὐτῷ).

καί. Coordinating conjunction.

εἶπεν. Aor act ind 3rd sg λέγω.

αὐτῷ. Dative indirect object of εἶπεν.

σύ. Nominative subject of εἶ. The personal pronoun is emphatic, perhaps suggesting an implicit "not I" vis-à-vis the designation that Nicodemus gave to Jesus in 3:2 (Zerwick and Grosvenor, 292). Alternatively, the emphasis may not be on a contrast between Nicodemus and Jesus but between Nicodemus' lack of basic comprehension of the activity of the Spirit and his status as the universally recognized teacher of Israel.

εἶ. Pres act ind 2nd sg εἰμί.

ὁ διδάσκαλος. Predicate nominative. The article is either anaphoric, identifying Nicodemus as the well-known teacher of Israel (Harris 2015, 74) or, par excellence, identifying him as "the number one professor on the Gallup poll" (Wallace 1996, 223).

τοῦ Ἰσραήλ. Objective genitive qualifying διδάσκαλος ("the one who teaches Israel") or possessive genitive ("the teacher who belongs to Israel").

καί. Coordinating conjunction.

ταῦτα. Accusative direct object of γινώσκεις.

οὐ. Negative particle normally used with indicative verbs.

γινώσκεις. Pres act ind 2nd sg γινώσκω. The verb stands in final, emphatic position.

3:11 ἀμὴν ἀμὴν λέγω σοι ὅτι ὃ οἴδαμεν λαλοῦμεν καὶ ὃ ἑωράκαμεν μαρτυροῦμεν, καὶ τὴν μαρτυρίαν ἡμῶν οὐ λαμβάνετε.

ἀμὴν ἀμὴν λέγω σοι. Metacomment (see 1:51).

ἀμὴν ἀμήν. Asseverative particles that mark the beginning of Jesus' solemn declaration (see 1:51). This verse is connected to the previous one by asyndeton.

λέγω. Pres act ind 1st sg λέγω.

σοι. Dative indirect object of λέγω.

ὅτι. ὅτι-*recitativum* that introduces the clausal complement (direct discourse) of λέγω.

ὅ. The relative pronoun introduces a headless relative clause that, in its entirety (ὅ οἴδαμεν), serves as the direct object of λαλοῦμεν. Within its clause, ὅ is the accusative direct object of οἴδαμεν.

οἴδαμεν. Prf act ind 1st pl οἶδα. Although the verb (λέγω) and its indirect object (σοι) at the beginning of this verse are in the singular, all verbs that follow are in the plural; on the meaning, see 1:26 on οἴδατε.

λαλοῦμεν. Pres act ind 1st pl λαλέω.

καὶ. Coordinating conjunction.

ὅ. The relative pronoun introduces a headless relative clause that, in its entirety (ὅ ἑωράκαμεν), serves as the direct object of μαρτυροῦμεν. Within its clause, ὅ is the accusative direct object of ἑωράκαμεν.

ἑωράκαμεν. Perf act ind 1st pl ὁράω.

μαρτυροῦμεν. Pres act ind 1st pl μαρτυρέω.

καὶ. Coordinating conjunction that links two clauses that stand in adversative relationship (see 1:5).

τὴν μαρτυρίαν. Accusative direct object of λαμβάνετε.

ἡμῶν. Subjective genitive qualifying μαρτυρίαν.

οὐ. Negative particle normally used with indicative verbs.

λαμβάνετε. Pres act ind 2nd pl λαμβάνω. The second-person plural verb form indicates that Jesus no longer addresses Nicodemus alone but speaks to a wider audience.

3:12 εἰ τὰ ἐπίγεια εἶπον ὑμῖν καὶ οὐ πιστεύετε, πῶς ἐὰν εἴπω ὑμῖν τὰ ἐπουράνια πιστεύσετε;

This verse consists of two parallel conditional clauses that function as the premises of the *a minore ad maius* rhetorical argument, known as *qal wahomer* (קל וחומר) in the rabbinic literature.

First-class condition	Third-class condition
Protasis: εἰ τὰ ἐπίγεια εἶπον ὑμῖν	Protasis: ἐὰν εἴπω ὑμῖν τὰ ἐπουράνια
Apodosis: καὶ οὐ πιστεύετε (assertion)	Apodosis: πῶς . . . πιστεύσετε (question)

The first-class condition establishes that the audience does not believe when Jesus tells them earthly things. This negative outcome functions as the "lighter" (less significant) step in the argument, from which Jesus draws the inference about the "weightier" (more significant) issue—the question regarding the audience's reaction to his message about heavenly things. The question-form of the apodosis of the third-class condition is rhetorically effective: if the listeners refuse to believe his talk about earthly things, how much more will they refuse to believe his talk about heavenly things! Thus, the apodosis of the third-class condition conveys an anticipation that the rejection of Jesus' preaching about heavenly things will be even greater than the rejection of his preaching about earthly things.

εἰ. Introduces the protasis of a first-class condition. This verse is connected to the previous one by asyndeton.

τὰ ἐπίγεια. Accusative direct object of εἶπον. The nominalized adjective refers to "what is characteristic of the earth as opposed to heavenly" (BDAG, 368.1).

εἶπον. Aor act ind 1st sg λέγω.

ὑμῖν. Dative indirect object of εἶπον.

καί. Coordinating conjunction.

οὐ. Negative particle normally used with indicative verbs.

πιστεύετε. Pres act ind 2nd pl πιστεύω.

πῶς. Interrogative particle.

ἐάν. Introduces the protasis of a third-class condition.

εἴπω. Aor act subj 1st sg λέγω. Subjunctive with ἐάν.

ὑμῖν. Dative indirect object of εἴπω.

τὰ ἐπουράνια. Accusative direct object of εἴπω. The nominalized adjective refers to "things in heaven" (BDAG, 388.2.b.α).

πιστεύσετε. Fut act ind 2nd pl πιστεύω.

John 3:13-21

[13]"And no one has ascended into heaven except the one who came down from heaven, the Son of Man. [14]And just as Moses lifted up the serpent in the wilderness, in this manner must the Son of Man be lifted up, [15]in order that everyone who believes might have in him eternal life." [16]For in this way God loved the world, so that he gave his only Son, in order that everyone who believes in him should not perish but should have eternal life, [17]for God did not send the Son into the world in order that he might condemn the world but in order that the world might be saved through him. [18]The one who believes in him is not condemned; but the one who does not believe has already been condemned, because he has not believed in the name of the only Son of God. [19]And the judgment is this: that the light has come into the world, and people loved darkness rather than the light because their deeds were evil. [20]For everyone who does wicked things hates the light and does not come to the light, so

that his deeds may not be exposed. ²¹But the one who practices the truth comes to the light, so that his deeds may be clearly seen, namely, that they are performed in God.

Some English translations regard this section as the continuation of Jesus' monologue (NRSV; REB; CEB; HCSB; ESV), while others treat vv. 13-15 as the conclusion of Jesus' speech and vv. 16-21 as the narrator's commentary (RSV; NIV; NET; LEB). After v. 12, however, there are no textual indications, such as the use of the first/second-person pronouns and verbs, that Jesus continues to address Nicodemus or a larger audience. It is therefore better to regard these verses as a theological reflection of the Fourth Evangelist (Talbert, 104). A similar phenomenon occurs in 3:31-36, where the evangelist offers another commentary on the one who comes from heaven.

3:13 καὶ οὐδεὶς ἀναβέβηκεν εἰς τὸν οὐρανὸν εἰ μὴ ὁ ἐκ τοῦ οὐρανοῦ καταβάς, ὁ υἱὸς τοῦ ἀνθρώπου.

καὶ. Coordinating conjunction.

οὐδεὶς . . . εἰ μὴ. A point/counterpoint set that corrects the negated clause ("nobody has ascended into heaven") by introducing an exception ("except the one who came down from heaven"). "The negated statement is not entirely true without the inclusion of the excepted element" (Runge 2010, 83). The combination of the negative + exception has significant rhetorical impact because Jesus does not merely assert that the Son of Man ascended into heaven. By making a generalizing claim that is not entirely true, he also highlights the reason why the Son of Man is an exception: he is the only one who descended from heaven. In this way, the excepted element is effectively emphasized. Runge argues that this rhetorical effect is achieved by placing the exceptive clause after the negated clause (85).

οὐδεὶς. Nominative subject of ἀναβέβηκεν.

ἀναβέβηκεν. Prf act ind 3rd sg ἀναβαίνω. Since the excepted clause in the point/counterpoint set presumes that the negated statement is applicable to only one person, i.e., the Son of Man, the traditional interpretation of the perfect tense, which holds that the verb describes a past action with present result, seems to imply that Jesus had already ascended into heaven at the time of his conversation with Nicodemus (Burkett, 82; Michaels, 195). To avoid this straightforward conclusion, some scholars have suggested that ἀναβέβηκεν is a timeless or gnomic perfect (Brown, 1:132; Ridderbos, 136) or that it refers to Jesus' ascension as a past event from the post-Easter perspective (Frey 1997–2000,

2:133, 254; Barrett, 213; Schnackenburg, 1:393). The verbal aspect theory, which holds that Greek verb tenses do not grammaticalize temporal information, offers another alternative. Pierce and Reynolds argue that, because the primary meaning of the perfect is not past action with present results, "all possible time values must be assessed in light of the immediate and broader contexts. In the case of John 3.13, present is the most plausible time value to associate with ἀναβέβηκεν" (154). This proposal, however, is quite similar to what traditional grammarians call a timeless/gnomic perfect, as Pierce and Reynolds (154) recognize. The only difference is that it uses the verbal aspect theory to support it.

εἰς τὸν οὐρανόν. Locative.

ὁ ... καταβάς. Aor act ptc masc nom sg καταβαίνω (substantival). The substantival participle functions as the second, excepted, nominative subject of ἀναβέβηκεν. Since the time of a participle is relative to the time of the main verb, the aorist participle "usually denotes *antecedent* time to that of the controlling verb" (Wallace 1996, 614; cf. Robertson, 1111). In addition, Porter argues that "[i]f a participle occurs before the finite verb on which it depends (or another verb which forms the governing or head term of the construction), the participle tends to refer to antecedent (preceding) action" (1994, 188). Both principles are applicable to ὁ ... καταβάς because this aorist participle precedes the main verb in a reconstructed elliptical structure of the excepted clause (εἰ μὴ ὁ ἐκ τοῦ οὐρανοῦ καταβάς [ἀναβέβηκεν εἰς τὸν οὐρανόν]), suggesting that the descent of the Son of Man precedes his ascent to heaven (Pierce and Reynolds, 154–55).

ἐκ τοῦ οὐρανοῦ. Source/origin. The PP modifies καταβάς.

ὁ υἱὸς. Nominative in apposition to ὁ ... καταβάς. The appositional information receives emphasis through right-dislocation.

τοῦ ἀνθρώπου. Genitive of relationship qualifying υἱός. This genitive is followed by the participial clause ὁ ὢν ἐν τῷ οὐρανῷ in a number of manuscripts (K N Γ Δ Θ Ψ 050 $f^{1.13}$ 565 579 700 892 𝔐 latt sy$^{c.p.h}$ et al.). Although this expansion represents the more difficult reading (because it stands in tension with the narrative plot of the FG) that could have been omitted by the later copyists, it is probably better to regard it "as an interpretative gloss, reflecting later Christological development" (Metzger, 175). The shorter reading also has strong external support by the Alexandrian textual family and other early witnesses ($\mathfrak{P}^{66.75}$ ℵ B L T W^s 083 086 33 1241 et al.).

3:14 Καὶ καθὼς Μωϋσῆς ὕψωσεν τὸν ὄφιν ἐν τῇ ἐρήμῳ, οὕτως ὑψωθῆναι δεῖ τὸν υἱὸν τοῦ ἀνθρώπου,

Καί. Coordinating conjunction.

καθώς. Introduces a comparative clause in a left-dislocation, which provides the frame of reference for the clause that follows (Runge 2010, 301). The comparative clause, καθὼς Μωϋσῆς ὕψωσεν τὸν ὄφιν ἐν τῇ ἐρήμῳ, refers to Num 21:4-9, which describes how Israelites bitten by venomous serpents were cured by looking at "a serpent of bronze" (נְחַשׁ נְחֹשֶׁת; ὄφιν χαλκοῦν) that Moses made and "put upon a standard" (וַיְשִׂמֵהוּ עַל־הַנֵּס; ἔστησεν αὐτὸν ἐπὶ σημείου).

Μωϋσῆς. Nominative subject of ὕψωσεν. Fronted as a topical frame.

ὕψωσεν. Aor act ind 3rd sg ὑψόω. The verb means "to cause something to become high—'to raise up, to lift up'" (LN 81.5).

τὸν ὄφιν. Accusative direct object of ὕψωσεν.

ἐν τῇ ἐρήμῳ. Locative.

οὕτως. Adverb of manner ("in this manner, thus, so") that functions as a correlative to καθώς (BDAG, 741.1.a).

ὑψωθῆναι. Aor pass inf ὑψόω (complementary). The primary agent of the action is not expressed. On the function of the infinitive with δεῖ, see 3:7 on γεννηθῆναι. ὑψωθῆναι is placed in a marked position, which, as Runge explains, "ensures that it receives extra attention" (2010, 279). The placement of ὑψωθῆναι in a position of prominence provides support for the idea that, in this sentence, "the point of comparison is not the serpent but the lifting up" (Brown, 1:214). The verb ὑψόω is used here and elsewhere in the FG (8:28; 12:32) in reference to Jesus' crucifixion. The idea of elevation inherent in the meaning of the verb allows the evangelist to associate the lifting up of the victim on the cross with the idea of exaltation and glorification.

δεῖ. Pres act ind 3rd sg δεῖ (impersonal).

τὸν υἱόν. Accusative subject of the infinitive ὑψωθῆναι.

τοῦ ἀνθρώπου. Genitive of relationship qualifying υἱόν.

3:15 ἵνα πᾶς ὁ πιστεύων ἐν αὐτῷ ἔχῃ ζωὴν αἰώνιον.

ἵνα. Introduces a purpose clause.

πᾶς ὁ πιστεύων. Nominative subject of ἔχῃ. Fronted as a topical frame. On πᾶς + articular participle, see 3:8 on πᾶς ὁ γεγεννημένος.

ὁ πιστεύων. Pres act ptc masc nom sg πιστεύω (substantival). On the function of this participle, see πᾶς ὁ πιστεύων above.

ἐν αὐτῷ. If this PP modifies πιστεύων, ἐν stands for εἰς to convey goal of actions or feelings directed toward someone (BDAG, 327.3). In that case, πιστεύω + ἐν is equivalent to πιστεύω + εἰς (Wallace 1996, 359; BDAG, 816.1.a.ε). Since, however, nowhere else in the FG is πιστεύω followed by ἐν, it is probably better to take ἐν αὐτῷ with ἔχῃ (BDAG, 817.2.a.ε; Harris 2015, 75; Barrett, 214; Moule, 80–81). In that case, the function of the PP is causal ("that every one who believes shall in him [i.e. resting upon him as the cause] have eternal life" [Metzger, 175]). The variant reading εἰς αὐτόν ($\mathfrak{P}^{63\text{vid}}$ ℵ A K N Γ Δ Θ Ψ 086 $f^{1.13}$ 33 565 700 𝔐) was most likely adopted by some scribes to solve the interpretive difficulties caused by πιστεύων + ἐν.

ἔχῃ. Pres act subj 3rd sg ἔχω. Subjunctive with ἵνα.

ζωὴν αἰώνιον. Accusative direct object of ἔχῃ. This is the first occurrence of the phrase ζωὴν αἰώνιον in the FG (see 3:16, 36; 4:14, 36; 5:24, 39; 6:27, 40, 47, 54, 68; 10:28; 12:25, 50; 17:2, 3). With only one exception (ἡ αἰώνιος ζωὴ in 17:3), this formulation is always anarthrous, with the adjective αἰώνιος in the fourth attributive position (noun-adjective) (Wallace 1996, 310–11).

3:16 οὕτως γὰρ ἠγάπησεν ὁ θεὸς τὸν κόσμον, ὥστε τὸν υἱὸν τὸν μονογενῆ ἔδωκεν, ἵνα πᾶς ὁ πιστεύων εἰς αὐτὸν μὴ ἀπόληται ἀλλ' ἔχῃ ζωὴν αἰώνιον.

οὕτως. Adverb of manner, which could (1) refer to what precedes ("in this manner, thus, so" [BDAG, 741.1]); (2) pertain to what follows ("in this way, as follows" [742.2]); or (3) mark a relatively high degree when it is placed before a verb ("so intensely" [742.3]). Many English translations and commentaries understand οὕτως in the third sense, i.e., as an adverb conveying the intensity of God's love: "For God so loved the world that he gave his only Son" (NRSV; ESV; cf. NIV; ASV; CEB; KJV; NASB); "For God loved the world so much that he gave his only Son" (GNT; cf. NCV; Schnackenburg, 1:398; Brown, 1:129). This interpretation has been challenged by Gundry and Howell, who argue that οὕτως does not have an intensifying function when it is followed by a finite verb and combined with ὥστε followed by another finite verb, as here. Rather, "in such circumstances οὕτως means 'in this way' as a matter of manner other than high degree" (25), and "it is used retrospectively" (26). If, then, the force of οὕτως is anaphoric, the clause οὕτως γὰρ ἠγάπησεν ὁ θεὸς τὸν κόσμον could be understood as a summation of v. 14: "God loved the world by way of determining . . . that the Son of Man be lifted up just as Moses lifted up the serpent in the wilderness" (35).

γὰρ. Postpositive conjunction that introduces the explanation of the previous assertions in vv. 14-15. This means that John 3:16, regarded by many as the most important verse in the FG that sums up its entire message, is "not the primary proposition in Jesus' argument. Instead, 3:16 provides the rationale for why the Son of Man was lifted up" (Runge 2010, 278).

ἠγάπησεν. Aor act ind 3rd sg ἀγαπάω. The verb ἀγαπάω and its cognate noun ἀγάπη occur more often in the FG (forty-four times) than in all the Synoptics together (twenty-eight times).

ὁ θεὸς. Nominative subject of ἠγάπησεν.

τὸν κόσμον. Accusative direct object of ἠγάπησεν. On the portrayal of the world in the FG, see 1:10 on ἐν τῷ κόσμῳ. This is the only reference to God's love for the world in the FG.

ὥστε. If the clause introduced with ὥστε is dependent, it probably expresses result. The uncertainty about its function is caused by the unusual combination of ὥστε and the indicative verb form, which occurs only here and in Gal 2:13 (BDAG, 1107.2.a.α). A result clause is usually conveyed with ὥστε + infinitive. If the clause introduced with ὥστε is independent, it expresses a conclusion drawn from the preceding assertion (BDAG, 1107.1.a). This usage is much more common in the NT (cf. Matt 12:12; 19:6; 23:31; Mark 2:28; 10:8; Rom 7:4, 12; 13:2; 1 Cor 3:7; 7:38; 11:27; 14:22; Gal 3:9, 24; 4:7, 16). My translation above presumes that ὥστε introduces a result clause.

τὸν υἱὸν τὸν μονογενῆ. Accusative direct object of ἔδωκεν. The adjective μονογενῆ ("pert[aining] to being the only one of its kind or class, *unique* (*in kind*)" [BDAG, 658.2]) stands in the second attributive position (see 1:9 on τὸ φῶς τὸ ἀληθινόν). The head noun τὸν υἱὸν restricts this meaning to familial relationships, referring "to the only child of one's parents" (TDNT 4:738; see also 1:14 on μονογενοῦς).

ἔδωκεν. Aor act ind 3rd sg δίδωμι.

ἵνα. Introduces a purpose-result clause. This type of clause "indicates both the intention and its sure accomplishment" (Wallace 1996, 473; cf. Porter 1994, 235). The reason for this classification is not a different syntax of the ἵνα clause but its theological message: it does not merely convey the divine purpose, but it also expresses the author's certainty about the intended outcome.

πᾶς ὁ πιστεύων. Nominative subject of ἀπόληται. Fronted as a topical frame. On πᾶς + articular participle, see 3:8 on πᾶς ὁ γεγεννημένος.

ὁ πιστεύων. Pres act ptc masc nom sg πιστεύω (substantival). On the function of this participle, see πᾶς ὁ πιστεύων above.

εἰς αὐτόν. Goal of actions or feelings directed toward someone (BDAG, 290.4.c.β). For πιστεύειν εἰς + accusative ("trust or believe in someone"), see 1:12 on εἰς τὸ ὄνομα.

μὴ . . . ἀλλ'. A point/counterpoint set ("not this . . . but that") that negates the incorrect assertion ("everyone who believes in the Son of God may perish") and replaces it with the correct one ("everyone who believes in the Son of God may have eternal life"). On the function of ἀλλά in a point/counterpoint set, see 1:8.

    ἀπόληται. Aor mid subj 3rd sg ἀπόλλυμι. Subjunctive with ἵνα.

    ἔχῃ. Pres act subj 3rd sg ἔχω. Subjunctive with ἵνα.

    ζωὴν αἰώνιον. Accusative direct object of ἔχῃ. On the use of this phrase in the FG, see 3:15 on ζωὴν αἰώνιον.

3:17 οὐ γὰρ ἀπέστειλεν ὁ θεὸς τὸν υἱὸν εἰς τὸν κόσμον ἵνα κρίνῃ τὸν κόσμον, ἀλλ' ἵνα σωθῇ ὁ κόσμος δι' αὐτοῦ.

    οὐ . . . ἀλλ'. A point/counterpoint set ("not this . . . but that") that negates the incorrect claim (God sent the Son into the world to condemn the world) and replaces it with the correct one (God sent the Son into the world that the world might be saved through him). On the function of ἀλλά in a point/counterpoint set, see 1:8.

    γὰρ. Postpositive conjunction that introduces an explanation of the preceding verse.

    ἀπέστειλεν. Aor act ind 3rd sg ἀποστέλλω.

    ὁ θεὸς. Nominative subject of ἀπέστειλεν.

    τὸν υἱὸν. Accusative direct object of ἀπέστειλεν.

    εἰς τὸν κόσμον. Locative. See 10:36 and 17:18 for other examples of the combination ἀποστέλλω + εἰς τὸν κόσμον in the FG. On the portrayal of the world in the FG, see 1:10 on ἐν τῷ κόσμῳ.

    ἵνα. Introduces a purpose clause.

    κρίνῃ. Aor act subj 3rd sg κρίνω. Subjunctive with ἵνα. The implied subject of the verb is the Son. The emphasis of κρίνω ("judge, decide, condemn") in this context falls on condemnation and punishment (BDAG, 568.5.b.α).

    τὸν κόσμον. Accusative direct object of κρίνῃ.

    ἵνα. Introduces a purpose clause.

    σωθῇ. Aor pass subj 3rd sg σῴζω. Subjunctive with ἵνα.

    ὁ κόσμος. Nominative subject of σωθῇ.

    δι' αὐτοῦ. Secondary (intermediate) agency. This formulation suggests that the primary (ultimate) agent of salvation is God.

3:18 ὁ πιστεύων εἰς αὐτὸν οὐ κρίνεται· ὁ δὲ μὴ πιστεύων ἤδη κέκριται, ὅτι μὴ πεπίστευκεν εἰς τὸ ὄνομα τοῦ μονογενοῦς υἱοῦ τοῦ θεοῦ.

ὁ πιστεύων. Pres act ptc masc nom sg πιστεύω (substantival). Nominative subject of κρίνεται. Fronted as a topical frame. This verse is connected to the previous one by asyndeton.

εἰς αὐτὸν. Goal of actions or feelings directed toward someone (BDAG, 290.4.c.β). For πιστεύειν εἰς + accusative ("trust or believe in someone"), see 1:12 on εἰς τὸ ὄνομα.

οὐ. Negative particle normally used with indicative verbs.

κρίνεται. Pres pass ind 3rd sg κρίνω. The imperfective aspect of the present tense indicates that not experiencing condemnation is viewed as an unfolding process in the life of a believer.

ὁ ... πιστεύων. Pres act ptc masc nom sg πιστεύω (substantival). Fronted as a topical frame. Nominative subject of κέκριται.

δὲ. Marker of narrative development with a contrastive nuance.

μὴ. Negative particle normally used with non-indicative verbs.

ἤδη. Temporal adverb ("already").

κέκριται. Prf pass ind 3rd sg κρίνω. The stative aspect of the perfect tense marks this verb for prominence and indicates, along with ἤδη, that κέκριται describes the current state of an unbeliever who "(already) stands condemned" (Harris 2015, 79).

ὅτι. Introduces a causal clause.

μὴ. This negative particle is irregular because μή is normally used with non-indicative verbs. Several explanations have been offered of this phenomenon. BDF (428.5) asserts that the use of μή in declarative clauses with ὅτι is quite common in Koine Greek. Moulton suggests that μή is used here because ὅτι μὴ πεπίστευκεν functions as a charge, in contrast to ὅτι οὐ πεπίστευκεν in 1 John 5:10, which states a simple fact (MHT 1:171). In Moule's (155) view, μὴ πεπίστευκεν has been influenced by the participial phrase ὁ μὴ πιστεύων that occurs just before it.

πεπίστευκεν. Prf act ind 3rd sg πιστεύω. The use of the perfect tense functions again as a thematic marker, alerting the audience to the significance of faith. While the contextual indicators show that the verb describes the refusal to believe as a past event, the emphasis falls on the state of disbelief that characterizes such a person's way of life.

εἰς τὸ ὄνομα. Goal of actions or feelings directed toward someone (BDAG, 290.4.c.β). For πιστεύειν εἰς + accusative ("trust or believe in someone"), see 1:12 on εἰς τὸ ὄνομα. ὄνομα is synecdoche for the whole person. Elsewhere in the FG, the expression πιστεύειν εἰς τὸ ὄνομα occurs in 1:12 and 2:23.

τοῦ μονογενοῦς υἱοῦ. Possessive genitive qualifying ὄνομα. For the meaning of this designation, see 3:16 on τὸν υἱὸν τὸν μονογενῆ.

τοῦ θεοῦ. Genitive of relationship qualifying υἱοῦ.

3:19 αὕτη δέ ἐστιν ἡ κρίσις ὅτι τὸ φῶς ἐλήλυθεν εἰς τὸν κόσμον καὶ ἠγάπησαν οἱ ἄνθρωποι μᾶλλον τὸ σκότος ἢ τὸ φῶς· ἦν γὰρ αὐτῶν πονηρὰ τὰ ἔργα.

αὕτη. Predicate nominative. The demonstrative pronoun agrees with the nominative subject ἡ κρίσις. Its force is cataphoric, i.e., it points to the judgment that will be introduced in this verse. In equative clauses, cataphoric demonstratives typically function as predicates (Culy 2004, 11). Runge emphasizes that "it is not the part of speech used that achieves added prominence, but rather the non-default use of the expression to point forward" (2010, 68). The rhetorical effect would have been significantly weakened had the evangelist simply said, "The judgment is that the light has come." By using the forward-pointing demonstrative αὕτη, the author sent a structural signal to the reader to pay attention to the explanation of the judgment that follows.

δέ. Marker of narrative development.

ἐστιν. Pres act ind 3rd sg εἰμί.

ἡ κρίσις. Nominative subject of ἐστίν. In this context, κρίσις denotes "the basis for rendering a judgment," although it can also be rendered as "how judgment works" or "the reason for God judging" (LN 30.111). Elsewhere in the FG, κρίσις is mentioned in 5:22, 24, 27, 29, 30; 7:24; 8:16; 12:31; 16:8, 11.

ὅτι. Introduces an epexegetical clause that explains αὕτη ("The judgment is this: that the light has come . . .") or, alternatively, a clause that is appositional to αὕτη because it could substitute for it ("The judgment is *that* the light has come . . ."; Wallace 1996, 459).

τὸ φῶς. Nominative subject of τὸ φῶς.

ἐλήλυθεν. Prf act ind 3rd sg ἔρχομαι.

εἰς τὸν κόσμον. Locative.

καί. Coordinating conjunction.

ἠγάπησαν. Aor act ind 3rd pl ἀγαπάω.

οἱ ἄνθρωποι. Nominative subject of ἠγάπησαν.

μᾶλλον. Comparative of the adverb μάλα ("more, rather").

τὸ σκότος. Accusative direct object of ἠγάπησαν.

ἤ. Particle denoting comparison (BDAG, 432.2).

τὸ φῶς. Accusative direct object of an implied ἠγάπησαν: "People loved darkness more than [they loved] the light."

ἦν. Impf act ind 3rd sg εἰμί. Neuter plural subjects typically take singular verbs (see 1:28 on ἐγένετο). On the function of the imperfect in the FG, see 1:39 on ἦν.

γὰρ. Postpositive conjunction that introduces the explanation why people loved darkness more than light.

αὐτῶν. Subjective genitive qualifying ἔργα. The preposed pronoun is thematically salient (Levinsohn 2000, 64).

πονηρά. Predicate adjective.

τὰ ἔργα. Nominative subject of ἦν.

3:20 πᾶς γὰρ ὁ φαῦλα πράσσων μισεῖ τὸ φῶς καὶ οὐκ ἔρχεται πρὸς τὸ φῶς, ἵνα μὴ ἐλεγχθῇ τὰ ἔργα αὐτοῦ·

πᾶς ... ὁ ... πράσσων. Nominative subject of μισεῖ. Fronted as a topical frame. On πᾶς + articular participle, see 3:8 on πᾶς ὁ γεγεννημένος.

ὁ ... πράσσων. Pres act ptc masc nom sg πράσσω (substantival). On the function of this participle, see πᾶς ... ὁ ... πράσσων above.

γὰρ. Postpositive conjunction that introduces additional explanation why those whose deeds are evil loved darkness more than light.

φαῦλα. Accusative direct object of πράσσων.

μισεῖ. Pres act ind 3rd sg μισέω. Contextual factors indicate that the present-tense verbs in this and the next verse describe "regularly recurring actions" (Porter 1994, 32), i.e., the typical attitude of those who commit worthless or truthful deeds.

τὸ φῶς. Accusative direct object of μισεῖ.

καὶ. Coordinating conjunction.

οὐκ. Negative particle normally used with indicative verbs.

ἔρχεται. Pres mid ind 3rd sg ἔρχομαι.

πρὸς τὸ φῶς. Locative (motion toward).

ἵνα. Introduces a purpose clause.

μὴ. Negative particle normally used with non-indicative verbs.

ἐλεγχθῇ. Aor pass subj 3rd sg ἐλέγχω. Subjunctive with ἵνα. Neuter plural subjects typically take singular verbs (see 1:28 on ἐγένετο).

τὰ ἔργα. Nominative subject of ἐλεγχθῇ.

αὐτοῦ. Subjective genitive qualifying ἔργα.

3:21 ὁ δὲ ποιῶν τὴν ἀλήθειαν ἔρχεται πρὸς τὸ φῶς, ἵνα φανερωθῇ αὐτοῦ τὰ ἔργα ὅτι ἐν θεῷ ἐστιν εἰργασμένα.

ὁ ... ποιῶν. Pres act ptc masc nom sg ποιέω (substantival). Nominative subject of ἔρχεται. Fronted as a topical frame.

δὲ. Marker of narrative development.

τὴν ἀλήθειαν. Accusative direct object of ποιῶν.
ἔρχεται. Pres mid ind 3rd sg ἔρχομαι.
πρὸς τὸ φῶς. Locative (motion toward).
ἵνα. Introduces a purpose clause.
φανερωθῇ. Aor pass subj 3rd sg φανερόω. Subjunctive with ἵνα. Neuter plural subjects typically take singular verbs (see 1:28 on ἐγένετο). In this context, φανερόω means "to make appear, to make visible, to cause to be seen" (LN 24.19).
αὐτοῦ. Subjective genitive qualifying ἔργα. The preposed pronoun is thematically salient (Levinsohn 2000, 64).
τὰ ἔργα. Nominative subject of φανερωθῇ.
ὅτι. Introduces a nominal clause that stands in apposition to ἔργα.
ἐν θεῷ. Locative ("before God," "in the presence of God"; cf. BDAG, 327.1.e), close personal relationship ("in communion with God"; cf. 327.4.c), or agency ("with the help of God"; cf. 329.6). Fronted for emphasis.
ἐστιν. Pres act ind 3rd sg εἰμί.
εἰργασμένα. Prf pass ptc neut nom pl ἐργάζομαι (perfect periphrastic).

John 3:22-30

²²After these things, Jesus and his disciples came into the Judean countryside, and he remained there with them and was baptizing. ²³John too was baptizing at Aenon, near Salim, because water was plentiful there, and they were coming and being baptized. ²⁴(For John had not yet been thrown into prison.) ²⁵Then a dispute arose on the part of John's disciples with a Jew concerning purification. ²⁶And they came to John and said to him, "Rabbi, the one who was with you across the Jordan, about whom you have testified—look, he is baptizing, and all are coming to him." ²⁷John answered and said, "A person cannot receive even one thing unless it is given to him from heaven. ²⁸You yourselves testify about me, that I said, 'I am not the Messiah,' but, 'I am sent ahead of him.' ²⁹The one who has the bride is the bridegroom. The friend of the bridegroom, who stands and listens to him, rejoices greatly because of the bridegroom's voice. So this joy of mine has been fulfilled. ³⁰It is necessary for him to increase, but for me to decrease."

3:22 Μετὰ ταῦτα ἦλθεν ὁ Ἰησοῦς καὶ οἱ μαθηταὶ αὐτοῦ εἰς τὴν Ἰουδαίαν γῆν καὶ ἐκεῖ διέτριβεν μετ' αὐτῶν καὶ ἐβάπτιζεν.

Μετὰ ταῦτα. Temporal. This PP is routinely used in the FG to refer to the previous events (cf. 5:1, 14; 6:1; 7:1; 13:7; 21:1). Fronted as a temporal frame. This verse is connected to the previous one by asyndeton.

ἦλθεν. Aor act ind 3rd sg ἔρχομαι.

ὁ Ἰησοῦς καὶ οἱ μαθηταὶ. Compound nominative subject of ἦλθεν. When the verb precedes its two (or more) subjects, as here, it is in the singular, agreeing with the first (BDF §135). The verb in the singular could also indicate that the author regarded the first-named subject as being the more important of the two (Wallace 1996, 401).

αὐτοῦ. Genitive of relationship qualifying μαθηταί.

εἰς τὴν Ἰουδαίαν γῆν. Locative. The adjective Ἰουδαίαν ("Jewish" or "Judean") stands in the first attributive position (see 2:10 on τὸν καλὸν οἶνον). γῆν probably refers here to a region or countryside (BDAG, 196.3).

καὶ. Coordinating conjunction.

ἐκεῖ. Adverb of place. Fronted as a spatial frame.

διέτριβεν. Impf act ind 3rd sg διατρίβω. The verb means "to remain or stay in a place, with the implication of some type of activity" (LN 85.61). This is the first in a series of several imperfects that create the setting for the main event, which is introduced by the aorist Ἐγένετο in 3:25 (du Toit, 220–21). According to du Toit, providing "background information by setting the scene (milieu, context) for events and other features that follow in the main storyline" is one of the major functions of the imperfect in the narrative portions of the FG (219).

μετ' αὐτῶν. Association/accompaniment.

καὶ. Coordinating conjunction.

ἐβάπτιζεν. Impf act ind 3rd sg βαπτίζω. In light of the disclaimer in 4:2, ἐβάπτιζεν probably means that Jesus was engaged in baptismal activity through his disciples. On the function of this imperfect, see διέτριβεν above.

3:23 Ἦν δὲ καὶ ὁ Ἰωάννης βαπτίζων ἐν Αἰνὼν ἐγγὺς τοῦ Σαλείμ, ὅτι ὕδατα πολλὰ ἦν ἐκεῖ, καὶ παρεγίνοντο καὶ ἐβαπτίζοντο·

Ἦν. Impf act ind 3rd sg εἰμί. On the function of this imperfect, see διέτριβεν in 3:22.

δὲ. Marker of narrative development.

καὶ. Adverbial use (adjunctive).

ὁ Ἰωάννης. Nominative subject of Ἦν.

βαπτίζων. Pres act ptc masc nom sg βαπτίζω (imperfect periphrastic).
ἐν Αἰνών. Locative.
ἐγγὺς τοῦ Σαλείμ. Locative. ἐγγὺς is an improper preposition (see 1:3 on χωρὶς αὐτοῦ) that indicates geographic proximity.
ὅτι. Introduces a causal clause.
ὕδατα πολλά. Nominative subject of ἦν. Fronted for emphasis. The adjective πολλά stands in the fourth attributive position (see 3:15 on ζωὴν αἰώνιον).
ἦν. Impf act ind 3rd sg εἰμί. Neuter plural subjects typically take singular verbs (see 1:28 on ἐγένετο). On the function of this imperfect, see διέτριβεν in 3:22.
ἐκεῖ. Predicate adverb of place (see 2:1 on ἐκεῖ).
καὶ. Coordinating conjunction.
παρεγίνοντο. Impf mid ind 3rd pl παραγίνομαι. The subject of the verb is not expressed, but the context indicates that it is people. The imperfective aspect of the verb portrays their coming to be baptized as an ongoing process. On the function of this imperfect, see διέτριβεν in 3:22.
καὶ. Coordinating conjunction.
ἐβαπτίζοντο. Impf pass ind 3rd pl βαπτίζω (see παρεγίνοντο above).

3:24 οὔπω γὰρ ἦν βεβλημένος εἰς τὴν φυλακὴν ὁ Ἰωάννης.

οὔπω γὰρ ἦν βεβλημένος εἰς τὴν φυλακὴν ὁ Ἰωάννης. Parenthetical editorial comment that interrupts the plot of the narrative to explain to the audience that knows about John's imprisonment that the events that are being narrated happened before that incident.
οὔπω. Adverb of time ("not yet"). Fronted for emphasis.
γὰρ. Postpositive conjunction that introduces a clarification about the timing of John's baptismal activity.
ἦν. Impf act ind 3rd sg εἰμί. On the function of the imperfect in the FG, see 1:39 on ἦν.
βεβλημένος. Prf pass ptc masc nom sg βάλλω (pluperfect periphrastic).
εἰς τὴν φυλακὴν. Locative.
ὁ Ἰωάννης. Nominative subject of ἦν.

3:25 Ἐγένετο οὖν ζήτησις ἐκ τῶν μαθητῶν Ἰωάννου μετὰ Ἰουδαίου περὶ καθαρισμοῦ.

Ἐγένετο. Aor mid ind 3rd sg γίνομαι.
οὖν. Postpositive inferential conjunction and/or transitional particle (see 1:22 and 11:6).

ζήτησις. Nominative subject of Ἐγένετο. ζήτησις denotes an "express[ion of] forceful differences of opinion without necessarily having a presumed goal of seeking a solution" (LN 44.440).

ἐκ τῶν μαθητῶν. Source, indicating that the controversy originated with John's disciples (Zerwick and Grosvenor, 293; Barrett, 221) or, less likely, the partitive use standing for τισὶν ἐκ τῶν μαθητῶν, indicating that the controversy began between some of John's disciples (Zerwick and Grosvenor, 293; cf. BDF §164.2).

Ἰωάννου. Genitive of relationship qualifying μαθητῶν.

μετὰ Ἰουδαίου. Association/accompaniment. The plural Ἰουδαίων has strong support in some early witnesses ($\mathfrak{P}^{66}$ ℵ* Θ $f^{1.13}$ 565 latt sy^c sa^{mss} bo Or), but, as Metzger (185) remarks, "it is more likely that the singular (which is unique in John) would have been changed to the more customary plural than vice versa" (Barrett, 221).

περὶ καθαρισμοῦ. Reference. καθαρισμός denotes "cleans[ing] from ritual contamination or impurity" (LN 53.28). In the following verses, however, the dispute is not about purification but about the relative significance of Jesus and John.

3:26 καὶ ἦλθον πρὸς τὸν Ἰωάννην καὶ εἶπαν αὐτῷ· ῥαββί, ὃς ἦν μετὰ σοῦ πέραν τοῦ Ἰορδάνου, ᾧ σὺ μεμαρτύρηκας, ἴδε οὗτος βαπτίζει καὶ πάντες ἔρχονται πρὸς αὐτόν.

καὶ. Coordinating conjunction.

ἦλθον. Aor act ind 3rd pl ἔρχομαι. The implied subject is John's disciples mentioned in the previous verse.

πρὸς τὸν Ἰωάννην. Locative (motion toward).

καὶ. Coordinating conjunction.

εἶπαν. Aor act ind 3rd pl λέγω.

αὐτῷ. Dative indirect object of εἶπαν.

ῥαββί. Vocative of direct address.

ὅς. The relative pronoun introduces the first headless relative clause that, in its entirety (ὃς ἦν μετὰ σοῦ πέραν τοῦ Ἰορδάνου), serves as the subject of βαπτίζει in a left-dislocation (see Runge 2010, 287–313). The left-dislocation of the relative clause shifts focus to the identity of Jesus as the one who was with John across the Jordan. Within its clause, ὅς is the nominative subject of ἦν.

ἦν. Impf act ind 3rd sg εἰμί.

μετὰ σοῦ. Association/accompaniment.

πέραν τοῦ Ἰορδάνου. Locative (see 1:28). πέραν is an improper preposition (see 1:3 on χωρὶς αὐτοῦ) that specifies the location where John was with Jesus (BDAG, 796.b.β).

ᾧ. The relative pronoun introduces the second headless relative clause that, in its entirety (ᾧ σὺ μεμαρτύρηκας), serves as the apposition to the first headless relative clause in a left-dislocation. The left-dislocation of the relative clause shifts focus on the identity of Jesus as the one who to whom John testified. Within its clause, ᾧ is the dative complement of μεμαρτύρηκας, denoting the person about whom someone speaks favorably (BDAG, 618.2.a).

σὺ. Nominative subject of μεμαρτύρηκας. Fronted as a topical frame.

μεμαρτύρηκας. Prf act ind 2nd sg μαρτυρέω. Like in 1:34, to which this verse refers, the stative aspect of the perfect tense of μαρτυρέω highlights John's role of witness bearing and draws attention to his confession of Jesus' divine identity.

ἴδε. An interjection (originally aor act impv 2nd sg ὁράω) that is "used when more than one pers[on] is addressed, and when that which is to be observed is in the nom[inative]" (BDAG, 466).

οὗτος. Nominative subject of βαπτίζει, resuming two headless relative clauses (see above). The anaphoric demonstrative reinforces what is already made prominent through the left-dislocation of the relative clauses. Fronted as a topical frame.

βαπτίζει. Pres act ind 3rd sg βαπτίζω. The imperfective aspect of the verb form portrays baptizing as an unfolding activity that is marked for prominence; see 3:22 on ἐβάπτιζεν.

καὶ. Coordinating conjunction.

πάντες. Nominative subject of ἔρχονται.

ἔρχονται. Pres mid 3rd pl ἔρχομαι.

πρὸς αὐτόν. Locative (motion toward).

3:27 Ἀπεκρίθη Ἰωάννης καὶ εἶπεν· οὐ δύναται ἄνθρωπος λαμβάνειν οὐδὲ ἓν ἐὰν μὴ ᾖ δεδομένον αὐτῷ ἐκ τοῦ οὐρανοῦ.

Ἀπεκρίθη. Aor mid ind 3rd sg ἀποκρίνομαι. On the voice, see "Deponency" in the Series Introduction. This verse is connected to the previous one by asyndeton.

Ἰωάννης. Nominative subject of Ἀπεκρίθη.

καὶ εἶπεν. Pleonastic clause under Semitic influence, which functions as a redundant quotative frame (see 1:25 on καὶ εἶπαν αὐτῷ).

καὶ. Coordinating conjunction.

εἶπεν. Aor act ind 3rd sg λέγω.

οὐ. Negative particle normally used with indicative verbs.

δύναται. Pres mid ind 3rd sg δύναμαι.

ἄνθρωπος. Nominative subject of δύναται.

λαμβάνειν. Pres act inf λαμβάνω (complementary).

οὐδὲ. A combination of the negative particle οὐ and the postpositive conjunction δέ (LN 69.7). It negates ἕν. οὐδὲ ἕν ("not even one thing") is equivalent to οὐδέν, but it is more emphatic (Robertson, 750–51). "If in the same clause one or more *compound* negatives follow a negative with the same verb, the compound negative simply confirms the firsts negative" (Smyth §2761).

ἕν. Accusative direct object of λαμβάνειν.

ἐὰν. Introduces the protasis of a third-class condition.

μὴ. Negative particle normally used with non-indicative verbs. ἐὰν μή can be translated "unless."

ᾖ. Pres act subj 3rd sg εἰμί. Subjunctive with ἐάν.

δεδομένον. Prf pass ptc neut nom sg δίδωμι (perfect periphrastic). Fanning notes that this participle "emphasizes the *resulting state* and only implies the anterior occurrence" (396).

αὐτῷ. Dative indirect object of δεδομένον.

ἐκ τοῦ οὐρανοῦ. Source.

3:28 αὐτοὶ ὑμεῖς μοι μαρτυρεῖτε ὅτι εἶπον [ὅτι] οὐκ εἰμὶ ἐγὼ ὁ χριστός, ἀλλ' ὅτι ἀπεσταλμένος εἰμὶ ἔμπροσθεν ἐκείνου.

αὐτοὶ ὑμεῖς. Nominative subject of μαρτυρεῖτε. Fronted for emphasis. αὐτοί functions as an intensive pronoun, emphasizing the identity of the subject—the addressees of John's words ("you yourselves"). This verse is connected to the previous one by asyndeton.

μοι. Dative complement of μαρτυρεῖτε, identifying the person about whom someone speaks favorably (BDAG, 618.2.a); see 3:26 on ᾧ.

μαρτυρεῖτε. Pres act ind 2nd pl μαρτυρέω.

ὅτι. Introduces the clausal complement (indirect discourse) of μαρτυρεῖτε.

εἶπον. Aor act ind 1st sg λέγω.

[ὅτι]. If ὅτι is original (it is absent in ℵ A D K L N Wˢ ΓΔ Θ Ψ 086 f^1 𝔐 et al.), it serves as ὅτι-*recitativum* that introduces the first clausal complement (direct discourse) of εἶπον.

οὐκ ... ἀλλ'. A point/counterpoint set ("not this ... but that") that negates the incorrect assertion ("I am the Messiah") and replaces it with the correct one ("I am sent ahead of him"). On the function of ἀλλά in a point/counterpoint set, see 1:8.

εἰμὶ. Pres act ind 1st sg εἰμί.

ἐγώ. Nominative subject of εἰμί. The personal pronoun has the identifying function.

ὁ χριστός. Predicate nominative.

ὅτι. ὅτι-*recitativum* that introduces the second clausal complement (direct discourse) of εἶπον.

ἀπεσταλμένος. Prf pass ptc masc nom sg ἀποστέλλω (perfect periphrastic).

εἰμί. Pres act ind 1st sg εἰμί.

ἔμπροσθεν ἐκείνου. Locative. ἔμπροσθεν is an adverb of place ("in front, ahead" [BDAG, 325.1.a]) that here functions as an improper preposition (see 1:3 on χωρὶς αὐτοῦ; cf. 325.1.b.ε).

3:29 ὁ ἔχων τὴν νύμφην νυμφίος ἐστίν· ὁ δὲ φίλος τοῦ νυμφίου ὁ ἑστηκὼς καὶ ἀκούων αὐτοῦ χαρᾷ χαίρει διὰ τὴν φωνὴν τοῦ νυμφίου. αὕτη οὖν ἡ χαρὰ ἡ ἐμὴ πεπλήρωται.

ὁ ἔχων. Pres act ptc masc nom sg ἔχω (substantival). Nominative subject of ἐστίν. This verse is connected to the previous one by asyndeton.

τὴν νύμφην. Accusative direct object of ἔχων.

νυμφίος. Predicative nominative. Fronted for emphasis.

ἐστίν. Pres act ind 3rd sg εἰμί.

ὁ . . . φίλος. Nominative subject of χαίρει.

δὲ. Marker of narrative development.

τοῦ νυμφίου. Genitive of relationship qualifying φίλος.

ὁ ἑστηκὼς καὶ ἀκούων. Both attributive participles modify ὁ . . . φίλος, standing in the second attributive position (see 1:29 on ὁ αἴρων).

ἑστηκώς. Prf act ptc masc nom sg ἵστημι (attributive).

ἀκούων. Pres act ptc masc nom sg ἀκούω (attributive).

αὐτοῦ. Genitive direct object of ἀκούων.

χαρᾷ. Cognate dative with χαίρει. Fronted for emphasis. This "emphatic reinforcement of the verbal notion" is a subcategory of the dative of manner, which is used in the LXX and the NT to render the Hebrew absolute infinitive (Zerwick §60).

χαίρει. Pres act ind 3rd sg χαίρω.

διὰ τὴν φωνὴν. Causal.

τοῦ νυμφίου. Possessive genitive qualifying φωνὴν.

αὕτη . . . ἡ χαρὰ ἡ ἐμὴ. Nominative subject of πεπλήρωται. The demonstrative αὕτη refers to the nearest contextual antecedent—the joy of the bridegroom's friend. It stands in its usual predicate position, separated from the noun it qualifies only by a postpositive οὖν. The possessive adjective ἐμὴ stands in the second attributive position (see 1:9 on τὸ φῶς τὸ ἀληθινόν).

οὖν. Postpositive inferential conjunction and/or transitional particle (see 1:22 and 11:6).

πεπλήρωται. Prf pass ind 3rd sg πληρόω. The verb stands in final, emphatic position.

3:30 ἐκεῖνον δεῖ αὐξάνειν, ἐμὲ δὲ ἐλαττοῦσθαι.

ἐκεῖνον. Accusative subject of the infinitive αὐξάνειν. Fronted as a topical frame. The demonstrative pronoun refers to Jesus, acting as a third-person personal pronoun with a simple anaphoric force (Wallace 1996, 328–29). This verse is connected to the previous one by asyndeton.

δεῖ. Pres act ind 3rd sg δεῖ (impersonal).

αὐξάνειν. Pres act inf αὐξάνω (complementary). On the function of the infinitive with δεῖ, see 3:7 on γεννηθῆναι. αὐξάνω is here used in the intransitive sense and means "to become more important, to enjoy greater respect or honor" (LN 87.37).

ἐμὲ. Accusative subject of the infinitive ἐλαττοῦσθαι. Fronted as a topical frame.

δὲ. Marker of narrative development.

ἐλαττοῦσθαι. Pres mid inf ἐλαττόω (complementary). On the function of the infinitive with δεῖ, see 3:7 on γεννηθῆναι. ἐλαττόω means "to become less important" with regard to status or rank (LN 87.69). According to BDAG (314.3), ἐλαττοῦσθαι occurs here in the passive voice that has intransitive sense: "diminish, become less." However, considering the recent discussion about deponent verbs (see "Deponency" in the Series Introduction), it seems more appropriate to classify this verb as middle rather than passive without a distinctive passive idea.

John 3:31-36

³¹The one who comes from above is above all; the one who is from the earth belongs to the earth and speaks in earthly terms. The one who comes from heaven is above all. ³²What he has seen and heard, this he testifies, yet no one accepts his testimony. ³³The one who received his testimony certified that God is true. ³⁴For the one whom God sent speaks the words of God, for he gives the Spirit without measure. ³⁵The Father loves the Son and has given all things into his hand. ³⁶One who believes in the Son has eternal life; one who disobeys the Son will not experience life, but God's wrath remains on him.

Because there is no explicit indication at which point John's speech ends, some English translations (CEB; CJB; NKJV; NCV), as well as some scholars (e.g., Barrett, 224), regard these verses as a continuation of John's homily. Since, however, this section does not contain any first/

second-person pronouns and verbs and, in addition, mentions various themes that appear in the first half of the chapter, it is more plausible to treat it as the evangelist's reflection on and the summary of the topics addressed in the entirety of chapter 3 (Brown, 1:159–60).

3:31 Ὁ ἄνωθεν ἐρχόμενος ἐπάνω πάντων ἐστίν· ὁ ὢν ἐκ τῆς γῆς ἐκ τῆς γῆς ἐστιν καὶ ἐκ τῆς γῆς λαλεῖ. ὁ ἐκ τοῦ οὐρανοῦ ἐρχόμενος [ἐπάνω πάντων ἐστίν]·

Ὁ . . . ἐρχόμενος. Pres mid ptc masc nom sg ἔρχομαι (substantival). Nominative subject of ἐστίν. Fronted as a topical frame. This verse is connected to the previous one by asyndeton.

ἄνωθεν. Adverb of place that here designates "a source that is above, *from above*" (BDAG, 92.1); cf. 3:3, 7 where it functions as a double entendre. The placement of the adverb between the article and the participle shows that it serves as an attributive modifier of ἐρχόμενος (see 1:15 on ὀπίσω μου).

ἐπάνω πάντων. Advantage. ἐπάνω is an improper preposition (see 1:3 on χωρὶς αὐτοῦ) denoting superiority in status (BDAG, 359.3).

ἐστίν. Pres act ind 3rd sg εἰμί.

ὁ ὤν. Pres act ptc masc nom sg εἰμί (substantival). Nominative subject of ἐστιν. Fronted as a topical frame.

ἐκ τῆς γῆς. Source/origin. The PP modifies ὁ ὤν ("the one who is from the earth").

ἐκ τῆς γῆς. Replaces the partitive genitive. This PP modifies ἐστιν ("is of the earth" = "belongs to the earth").

ἐστιν. Pres act ind 3rd sg εἰμί.

καὶ. Coordinating conjunction.

ἐκ τῆς γῆς. Source of insight (BDAG, 297.3.g.β). The PP modifies λαλεῖ ("speaks in earthly terms").

λαλεῖ. Pres act ind 3rd sg λαλέω.

ὁ . . . ἐρχόμενος. Pres mid ptc masc nom sg ἔρχομαι (substantival). Nominative subject of ἐστίν. Fronted as a topical frame.

ἐκ τοῦ οὐρανοῦ. Source. The PP, placed between the article and the participle, functions as an attributive modifier of ἐρχόμενος (see 1:15 on ὀπίσω μου).

[ἐπάνω πάντων ἐστίν]. These words are attested by $\mathfrak{P}^{36\text{vid}.66}$ $\aleph^2$ A B K L W^s Γ Δ Θ Ψ 083 086 f^{13} 33 $\mathfrak{M}$ et al., but it is omitted in $\mathfrak{P}^{75}$ $\aleph^*$ D f^1 565 it sy^c sa Hipp Or^{pt} Eus. Without this phrase, ὁ ἐκ τοῦ οὐρανοῦ ἐρχόμενος functions as the subject of μαρτυρεῖ in the next verse. A scribe could have added these words because they occur after the first Ὁ . . . ἐρχόμενος or deleted the phrase from the base text because of perceived redundancy.

Because the external evidence and transcriptional probabilities for both readings are quite balanced (Metzger, 175–76), the words are placed within square brackets in NA[28]/UBS[5] but not in SBLGNT.

ἐπάνω πάντων. Advantage (see above).

ἐστίν. Pres act ind 3rd sg εἰμί.

3:32 ὃ ἑώρακεν καὶ ἤκουσεν τοῦτο μαρτυρεῖ, καὶ τὴν μαρτυρίαν αὐτοῦ οὐδεὶς λαμβάνει.

ὅ. The relative pronoun introduces the headless relative clause that, in its entirety (ὃ ἑώρακεν καὶ ἤκουσεν), serves as the direct object of μαρτυρεῖ in a left-dislocation (see Runge 2010, 287–313). The left-dislocation of the relative clause highlights the content of the testimony of the one who comes from heaven. Within its clause, ὅ is the direct object of ἑώρακεν and ἤκουσεν. This verse is connected to the previous one by asyndeton.

ἑώρακεν. Prf act ind 3rd sg ὁράω. The stative aspect of the perfect tense gives more prominence to what the one coming from heaven has seen than to what he has heard (McKay 1981, 319; 1994, 50; Porter 1989, 250; BDF §342.2). It also "expresses that what the Son 'has seen'... stays enduringly before his eyes" (Frey 2018, 81).

καὶ. Coordinating conjunction.

ἤκουσεν. Aor act ind 3rd sg ἀκούω.

τοῦτο. Accusative direct object of μαρτυρεῖ, resuming ὃ ἑώρακεν καὶ ἤκουσεν. The anaphoric demonstrative reinforces what is already made prominent through the left-dislocation of the relative clause.

μαρτυρεῖ. Pres act ind 3rd sg μαρτυρέω. The verb stands in final, emphatic position.

καὶ. Coordinating conjunction. The clauses joined by this conjunction are antithetical to each other, but this is not a special case of the so-called adversative καί (*pace* Harris 2015, 83; see 1:5).

τὴν μαρτυρίαν. Accusative direct object of λαμβάνει.

αὐτοῦ. Subjective genitive qualifying μαρτυρίαν.

οὐδεὶς. Nominative subject of λαμβάνει. The next verse shows that this οὐδεὶς is not absolute.

λαμβάνει. Pres act ind 3rd sg λαμβάνω.

3:33 ὁ λαβὼν αὐτοῦ τὴν μαρτυρίαν ἐσφράγισεν ὅτι ὁ θεὸς ἀληθής ἐστιν.

ὁ λαβών. Aor act ptc masc nom sg λαμβάνω (substantival). Nominative subject of ἐσφράγισεν. Fronted as a topical frame. This verse is connected to the previous one by asyndeton.

αὐτοῦ. Subjective genitive qualifying μαρτυρίαν. The preposed pronoun is thematically salient (Levinsohn 2000, 64).

τὴν μαρτυρίαν. Accusative direct object of λαβών.

ἐσφράγισεν. Aor act ind 3rd sg σφραγίζω. The primary sense of the verb is "to provide with a seal as a security measure" (BDAG, 980.1) or "to mark with a seal as a means of identification" (980.3), but in this context it means "to certify that someth[ing] is so, *attest, certify, acknowledge*" (980.4).

ὅτι. Introduces the clausal complement (direct object clause) of ἐσφράγισεν (Wallace 1996, 454).

ὁ θεός. Nominative subject of ἐστιν.

ἀληθής. Predicate adjective. Fronted for emphasis.

ἐστιν. Pres act ind 3rd sg εἰμί.

3:34 ὃν γὰρ ἀπέστειλεν ὁ θεὸς τὰ ῥήματα τοῦ θεοῦ λαλεῖ, οὐ γὰρ ἐκ μέτρου δίδωσιν τὸ πνεῦμα.

ὅν. The relative pronoun introduces the headless relative clause that, in its entirety (ὃν γὰρ ἀπέστειλεν ὁ θεός), serves as the subject of λαλεῖ. Within its clause, ὅν is the direct object of ἀπέστειλεν.

γάρ. Postpositive conjunction that introduces an explanation of the preceding acknowledgment that God is true.

ἀπέστειλεν. Aor act ind 3rd sg ἀποστέλλω.

ὁ θεός. Nominative subject of ἀπέστειλεν.

τὰ ῥήματα. Accusative direct object of λαλεῖ.

τοῦ θεοῦ. Subjective genitive qualifying ῥήματα.

λαλεῖ. Pres act ind 3rd sg λαλέω.

οὐ. Negative particle that negates the PP ἐκ μέτρου.

γάρ. Postpositive conjunction that introduces a clause that offers the justification for the assertion that the one sent by God speaks God's words.

ἐκ μέτρου. Means (lit. "by measure" = "sparingly" [BDAG, 298.6.c]). The negated prepositional phrase is an example of litotes: "not by measure" = "bountifully."

δίδωσιν. Pres act ind 3rd sg δίδωμι. The next verse indicates that the implied subject of δίδωσιν is God (Harris 2015, 85; *pace* Brown, 1:158, who thinks that the Son is the giver because "gifts from the Father to the Son are normally expressed in John by the perfect ... or the aorist"). Some scribes, who wanted to clarify that God was the subject of δίδωσιν, added ὁ θεὸς between δίδωσιν and τὸ πνεῦμα (A C² D K Γ Δ Θ Ψ 086 f^{13} 700 892 𝔐 et al.), but the shorter reading has much stronger textual support (Metzger, 176).

τὸ πνεῦμα. Accusative direct object of δίδωσιν.

3:35 ὁ πατὴρ ἀγαπᾷ τὸν υἱὸν καὶ πάντα δέδωκεν ἐν τῇ χειρὶ αὐτοῦ.

ὁ πατήρ. Nominative subject of ἀγαπᾷ. Fronted as a topical frame. This verse is connected to the previous one by asyndeton.

ἀγαπᾷ. Pres act ind 3rd sg ἀγαπάω. Elsewhere in the FG, the Father's love for the Son is expressed in 5:20; 10:17; 15:9, 17:23-24, 26.

τὸν υἱόν. Accusative direct object of ἀγαπᾷ.

καί. Coordinating conjunction.

πάντα. Accusative direct object of δέδωκεν.

δέδωκεν. Prf act ind 3rd sg δίδωμι. Porter calls attention to the dynamic created through the use of the present tense of δίδωμι in v. 34 (δίδωσιν) and the perfect tense (δέδωκεν) in this verse and adds that "[a]s a result of God's loving he has created the state of having given all things" (1989, 277). Frey underscores that the resultative aspect of the perfect tense "expresses that what the Father 'has given' to the Son ... is definitely in his hand" (2018, 81).

ἐν τῇ χειρί. Locative.

αὐτοῦ. Possessive genitive qualifying χειρί. The antecedent is τὸν υἱόν. The sense of the statement that God "has given all things into his hand" is that God "has placed all things under his authority" (NET; cf. REB).

3:36 ὁ πιστεύων εἰς τὸν υἱὸν ἔχει ζωὴν αἰώνιον· ὁ δὲ ἀπειθῶν τῷ υἱῷ οὐκ ὄψεται ζωήν, ἀλλ' ἡ ὀργὴ τοῦ θεοῦ μένει ἐπ' αὐτόν.

ὁ πιστεύων. Pres act ptc masc nom sg πιστεύω (substantival). Nominative subject of ἔχει. Fronted as a topical frame. The imperfective aspect of the present-tense participle depicts believing as a process without regard for its beginning. This verse is connected to the previous one by asyndeton.

εἰς τὸν υἱόν. Goal of actions or feelings directed toward someone (BDAG, 290.4.c.β). For πιστεύειν εἰς + accusative ("trust or believe in someone"), see 1:12 on εἰς τὸ ὄνομα.

ἔχει. Pres act ind 3rd sg ἔχω. The combination ἔχω + ζωὴν αἰώνιον is frequently used in the FG to assert that for a believer the future hope is also a present reality (3:15, 16, 36; 5:24, 39; 6:40, 47, 54).

ζωὴν αἰώνιον. Accusative direct object of ἔχει. On the use of this phrase in the FG, see 3:15 on ζωὴν αἰώνιον.

ὁ . . . ἀπειθῶν. Pres act ptc masc nom sg ἀπειθέω (substantival). Nominative subject of ὄψεται. Fronted as a topical frame. ἀπειθέω denotes "unwillingness or refusal to comply with the demands of some authority" (LN 36.23). The imperfective aspect of the present-tense participle depicts disobeying as a process without regard for its beginning.

δέ. Marker of narrative development.

τῷ υἱῷ. Dative complement of ἀπειθῶν. The dative specifies the person to whom someone is disobedient (BDAG, 99).

οὐκ . . . ἀλλ'. A point/counterpoint set ("not this . . . but that") that negates the incorrect assertion (the one who disobeys the Son will see life) and replaces it with the correct one (the one who disobeys the Son must endure God's wrath). On the function of ἀλλά in a point/counterpoint set, see 1:8.

ὄψεται. Fut mid ind 3rd sg ὁράω. The meaning of ὁράω in this context is a figurative extension of its literal sense ("to see"): "to experience an event or state, normally in negative expressions indicating what one will not experience" (LN 90.79).

ζωήν. Accusative direct object of ὄψεται.

ἡ ὀργὴ. Nominative subject of μένει.

τοῦ θεοῦ. Subjective genitive qualifying ὀργὴ.

μένει. Pres act ind 3rd sg μένω.

ἐπ' αὐτόν. Locative.

John 4:1-3

¹Now when Jesus learned that the Pharisees had heard that Jesus was making and baptizing more disciples than John, ²(although Jesus himself was not baptizing, but his disciples), ³he left Judea and departed again to Galilee.

4:1 Ὡς οὖν ἔγνω ὁ Ἰησοῦς ὅτι ἤκουσαν οἱ Φαρισαῖοι ὅτι Ἰησοῦς πλείονας μαθητὰς ποιεῖ καὶ βαπτίζει ἢ Ἰωάννης

Ὡς. Temporal conjunction (BDAG, 1105.8.a; BDF §455.2), introducing a clause that is fronted as a temporal frame.

οὖν. Postpositive inferential conjunction and/or transitional particle (see 1:22 and 11:6).

ἔγνω. Aor act ind 3rd sg γινώσκω.

ὁ Ἰησοῦς. Nominative subject of ἔγνω.

ὅτι. Introduces the clausal complement (indirect discourse) of ἔγνω.

ἤκουσαν. Aor act ind 3rd pl ἀκούω.

οἱ Φαρισαῖοι. Nominative subject of ἤκουσαν.

ὅτι. Introduces the clausal complement (indirect discourse) of ἤκουσαν. This indirect discourse is embedded within the previous indirect discourse.

Ἰησοῦς. Nominative subject of ποιεῖ.

πλείονας μαθητὰς. Accusative direct object of ποιεῖ and βαπτίζει. Fronted for emphasis. πλείονας is masc acc pl of πλείων, a comparative of πολύς.

ποιεῖ. Pres act ind 3rd sg ποιέω. The present tense is retained from the direct discourse (see 1:39 on μένει). Wallace (1996, 458, 539) calls attention to the difference between the historical present, which is aspectually flat, and the present tense retained in indirect discourse, which maintains its aspectual force. The imperfective aspect of ποιεῖ depicts making disciples as an unfolding activity.

καὶ. Coordinating conjunction.

βαπτίζει. Pres act ind 3rd sg βαπτίζω. The present tense is retained from the direct discourse (see 1:39 on μένει). The imperfective aspect depicts baptizing as an unfolding activity.

ἤ. Particle denoting comparison (BDAG, 432.2).

Ἰωάννης. Nominative subject of an elliptical clause that presumes the repetition of the main verbs: "Jesus was making and baptizing more disciples than John [was making and baptizing]."

4:2 —καίτοιγε Ἰησοῦς αὐτὸς οὐκ ἐβάπτιζεν ἀλλ' οἱ μαθηταὶ αὐτοῦ—

καίτοιγε Ἰησοῦς αὐτὸς οὐκ ἐβάπτιζεν ἀλλ' οἱ μαθηταὶ αὐτοῦ. Parenthetical editorial gloss that provides a correction to the account about Jesus' baptismal activity that the Pharisees received.

καίτοιγε. Adversative conjunction ("although") that is created from the classical conjunction καίτοι and the emphatic particle γε (BDAG, 496.2.i.δ; BDF §450.3).

Ἰησοῦς αὐτὸς. Nominative subject of ἐβάπτιζεν. αὐτὸς functions as an intensive pronoun ("Jesus himself"), pointing out a contrast between Jesus and his disciples and anticipating the incorrect inference that Jesus personally baptized (BDAG, 152.1.c).

οὐκ . . . ἀλλ'. A point/counterpoint set ("not this . . . but that") that negates the incorrect supposition (Jesus himself was baptizing) and replaces it with the correct one (Jesus' disciples were baptizing). On the function of ἀλλά in a point/counterpoint set, see 1:8.

ἐβάπτιζεν. Impf act ind 3rd sg βαπτίζω. On the function of the imperfect in the FG, see 1:39 on ἦν.

οἱ μαθηταί. Nominative subject of an implied ἐβάπτιζον.

αὐτοῦ. Genitive of relationship qualifying μαθηταί.

4:3 ἀφῆκεν τὴν Ἰουδαίαν καὶ ἀπῆλθεν πάλιν εἰς τὴν Γαλιλαίαν.

ἀφῆκεν. Aor act ind 3rd sg ἀφίημι. The implied subject is ὁ Ἰησοῦς from 4:1.

τὴν Ἰουδαίαν. Accusative direct object of ἀφῆκεν.

καὶ. Coordinating conjunction.

ἀπῆλθεν. Aor act ind 3rd sg ἀπέρχομαι.

πάλιν. Adverb "pert[aining] to return to a position or state" (BDAG, 752.1).

εἰς τὴν Γαλιλαίαν. Locative.

John 4:4-26

[4]Now it was necessary for him to pass through Samaria. [5]So he came to a town in Samaria called Sychar, near the piece of land that Jacob gave to Joseph, his son. [6]Jacob's well was there. Then Jesus, because he had become tired from the journey, simply sat down at the well. It was about the sixth hour. [7]A woman from Samaria came to draw water. Jesus said to her, "Give me a drink." [8]For his disciples had gone away into the town so that they could buy food. [9]Then the Samaritan woman said to him, "How is it that you, although you are a Jew, ask a drink from me, although I am a Samaritan woman?" (For Jews do not associate with Samaritans.) [10]Jesus answered and said to her, "If you knew the gift of God and who it is that is saying to you, 'Give me a drink,' you would have asked him, and he would have given you living water." [11]The woman said to him, "Sir, you have no bucket, and the well is deep. From where, then, do you get this living water? [12]Surely you are not greater than our father Jacob, are you, who gave us the well and drank from it himself, and his sons and his livestock?" [13]Jesus answered and said to her, "Everyone who drinks of this water will be thirsty again. [14]But whoever drinks of the water that I will give to him will never be thirsty for eternity, but the water that I will give to him will become in him a well of water springing up to eternal life." [15]The woman said to him, "Sir, give me this water, so that I may not be thirsty nor come here to draw water." [16]He said to her, "Go, call your husband, and come here." [17]The woman answered and said to him, "I don't have a husband." Jesus said to her, "You have said rightly, 'I don't have a husband.' [18]For you had five husbands, and the one whom you now have is not your husband. What you have said is true." [19]The woman said to him, "I perceive that you are a prophet. [20]Our

fathers worshipped on this mountain, but you say that in Jerusalem is the place where it is necessary to worship." ²¹Jesus said to her, "Believe me, woman, that the hour is coming when you will worship the Father neither on this mountain nor in Jerusalem. ²²You worship what you do not know. We worship what we know, because salvation is from the Jews. ²³But the hour is coming and now is [here], when the true worshippers will worship the Father in spirit and truth, for indeed the Father seeks such people as his worshippers. ²⁴God is spirit, and those who worship him must worship in spirit and in truth." ²⁵The woman said to him, "I know that the Messiah (who is called Christ) is coming. Whenever he comes, he will proclaim all things to us." ²⁶Jesus said to her, "I, the one talking to you, am he."

4:4 Ἔδει δὲ αὐτὸν διέρχεσθαι διὰ τῆς Σαμαρείας.

Ἔδει. Impf act ind 3rd sg δεῖ (impersonal). On the function of the imperfect in the FG, see 1:39 on ἦν.

δὲ. Marker of narrative development.

αὐτὸν. Accusative subject of the infinitive διέρχεσθαι.

διέρχεσθαι. Pres mid inf διέρχομαι (complementary). On the function of the infinitive with δεῖ, see 3:7 on γεννηθῆναι.

διὰ τῆς Σαμαρείας. Spatial.

4:5 Ἔρχεται οὖν εἰς πόλιν τῆς Σαμαρείας λεγομένην Συχὰρ πλησίον τοῦ χωρίου ὃ ἔδωκεν Ἰακὼβ [τῷ] Ἰωσὴφ τῷ υἱῷ αὐτοῦ·

Ἔρχεται. Pres mid ind 3rd sg ἔρχομαι. The historical present marks a transition to a new geographical setting (see 1:15 on μαρτυρεῖ).

οὖν. Postpositive inferential conjunction and/or transitional particle (see 1:22 and 11:6).

εἰς πόλιν. Locative. Since the larger context indicates that Jesus did not actually enter the town (see 4:16, 28-30), εἰς stands for πρός, indicating a motion toward Sychar (Harris 2015, 89; Zerwick §97).

τῆς Σαμαρείας. Partitive genitive qualifying πόλιν. Samaria denotes the territory within which Sychar lies (MHT 3:210).

λεγομένην. Pres pass ptc fem acc sg λέγω (attributive). The participle modifies πόλιν, standing in the fourth attributive position (see 1:6 on ἀπεσταλμένος).

Συχὰρ. Accusative complement to πόλιν in a double accusative subject-complement construction. Such constructions are common in passive clauses that are derived from the (real or hypothetical) active clauses that employ double accusative object-complement constructions.

For example, when the active sentence τις λέγει τὴν πόλιν Συχὰρ is transformed into a passive formulation ἡ πόλις λέγεται Συχὰρ, the direct object becomes the nominative subject, and the accusative complement becomes the nominative complement (Culy 2009). Since in this PP (εἰς πόλιν . . . λεγομένην Συχὰρ) πόλιν is accusative as the object of the preposition εἰς but serves as the conceptual subject of the passive participle λεγομένην, it requires a complement in the same case.

πλησίον τοῦ χωρίου. Locative. πλησίον ("near, close to") is an improper preposition (see 1:3 on χωρὶς αὐτοῦ).

ὅ. Accusative direct object of ἔδωκεν. The relative pronoun is not attracted to its antecedent τοῦ χωρίου.

ἔδωκεν. Aor act ind 3rd sg δίδωμι.

Ἰακώβ. Nominative subject of ἔδωκεν.

[τῷ] Ἰωσὴφ. Dative indirect object of ἔδωκεν. The article, which is attested in some manuscripts ($\mathfrak{P}^{66.75}$ ℵ B), is probably a scribal addition to clarify that the indeclinable noun Ἰωσὴφ is in the dative.

τῷ υἱῷ. Dative in apposition to τῷ Ἰωσὴφ.

αὐτοῦ. Genitive of relationship qualifying υἱῷ.

4:6 ἦν δὲ ἐκεῖ πηγὴ τοῦ Ἰακώβ. ὁ οὖν Ἰησοῦς κεκοπιακὼς ἐκ τῆς ὁδοιπορίας ἐκαθέζετο οὕτως ἐπὶ τῇ πηγῇ· ὥρα ἦν ὡς ἕκτη.

ἦν. Impf act ind 3rd sg εἰμί. On the function of the imperfect in the FG, see 1:39 on ἦν.

δὲ. Marker of narrative development.

ἐκεῖ. Predicate adverb of place (see 2:1 on ἐκεῖ).

πηγὴ. Nominative subject of ἦν. πηγή denotes "a source of someth[ing] that gushes out or flows, *spring, fountain, flow*" (BDAG, 810.1.a).

τοῦ Ἰακώβ. Possessive genitive.

ὁ . . . Ἰησοῦς. Nominative subject of ἐκαθέζετο.

οὖν. Postpositive inferential conjunction and/or transitional particle (see 1:22 and 11:6).

κεκοπιακὼς. Prf act ptc masc nom sg κοπιάω (causal). Wallace (1996, 631) notes that adverbial perfect participles almost always indicate the cause of the action of the main verb. κοπιάω means "to be tired or weary, as the result of hard or difficult endeavor" (LN 23.78). The stative aspect of the perfect participle draws attention to Jesus' state of weariness. On participles that precede the main verb, see ἐμβλέψας in 1:36.

ἐκ τῆς ὁδοιπορίας. Causal. ὁδοιπορία means "journey, trip" (LN 15.20).

ἐκαθέζετο. Impf mid ind 3rd sg καθέζομαι. The verb could mean "to be in a seated position or to take such a position" (LN 17.12). According to BDAG (490, 2), καθέζομαι here means "to take a seated position, *sit down*," so that the imperfect has an aorist nuance: "I sat down" (BDF §101).

οὕτως. Adverb of manner, which here means "without further ado, just, simply" (BDAG, 742.4).

ἐπὶ τῇ πηγῇ. Locative.

ὥρα. Nominative subject of ἦν.

ἦν. Impf act ind 3rd sg εἰμί. On the function of the imperfect in the FG, see 1:39 on ἦν.

ὡς. Particle used with numerals to denote an estimate ("about, approximately").

ἕκτη. Predicate adjective. ἕκτη (from ἕκτος) is an ordinal number meaning "sixth"; "the sixth hour of a day" = 12 p.m. based on a customary reckoning of the twelve-hour day from sunrise (6 a.m.) to sunset (6 p.m.).

4:7 Ἔρχεται γυνὴ ἐκ τῆς Σαμαρείας ἀντλῆσαι ὕδωρ. λέγει αὐτῇ ὁ Ἰησοῦς· δός μοι πεῖν·

Ἔρχεται. Pres mid ind 3rd sg ἔρχομαι. The historical present signals a change of scene, accentuating the appearance of a new character—a Samaritan woman (Battle, 128); on this function of the nonspeech historical presents in the FG, see 6:19 on θεωροῦσιν. This verse is connected to the previous one by asyndeton.

γυνή. Nominative subject of Ἔρχεται. The anarthrous γυνή is indefinite because the approaching woman is portrayed only as a member of her class—the people of Samaria (Wallace 1996, 244).

ἐκ τῆς Σαμαρείας. Source/origin. The PP has attributive function qualifying γυνή ("a woman from Samaria" = "a Samaritan woman").

ἀντλῆσαι. Aor act inf ἀντλέω (purpose).

ὕδωρ. Accusative direct object of ἀντλῆσαι.

λέγει. Pres act ind 3rd sg λέγω. This and most of the verb forms of λέγω in this chapter are in the historical present. They call attention to the dialogue between Jesus and the Samaritan woman and other characters that converse with Jesus (see 1:15 on μαρτυρεῖ).

αὐτῇ. Dative indirect object of λέγει.

ὁ Ἰησοῦς. Nominative subject of λέγει.

δός. Aor act impv 2nd sg δίδωμι.

μοι. Dative indirect object of δός.

πεῖν. Aor act inf πίνω (purpose). πεῖν is a postclassical contracted form of πιεῖν (BDF §31.2). Moule (127) says that this infinitive is used as a noun but without an article ("a drink"), although it is easier to understand it as a verb with the implied τι ("to give something to drink").

4:8 οἱ γὰρ μαθηταὶ αὐτοῦ ἀπεληλύθεισαν εἰς τὴν πόλιν ἵνα τροφὰς ἀγοράσωσιν.

οἱ . . . μαθηταί. Nominative subject of ἀπεληλύθεισαν. Fronted as a topical frame.

γάρ. Postpositive conjunction that introduces the explanation why Jesus was alone at the well asking the woman for a drink of water.

αὐτοῦ. Genitive of relationship qualifying μαθηταί.

ἀπεληλύθεισαν. Plprf act ind 3rd pl ἀπέρχομαι. The pluperfect describes a state of affairs that was the result of an action that occurred before the narrated events (Harris 2015, 90).

εἰς τὴν πόλιν. Locative.

ἵνα. Introduces a purpose clause.

τροφάς. Accusative direct object of ἀγοράσωσιν.

ἀγοράσωσιν. Aor act subj 3rd pl ἀγοράζω. Subjunctive with ἵνα.

4:9 λέγει οὖν αὐτῷ ἡ γυνὴ ἡ Σαμαρῖτις· πῶς σὺ Ἰουδαῖος ὢν παρ' ἐμοῦ πεῖν αἰτεῖς γυναικὸς Σαμαρίτιδος οὔσης; οὐ γὰρ συγχρῶνται Ἰουδαῖοι Σαμαρίταις.

λέγει. Pres act ind 3rd sg λέγω. The historical present (see 4:7).

οὖν. Postpositive inferential conjunction and/or transitional particle (see 1:22 and 11:6).

αὐτῷ. Dative indirect object of λέγει.

ἡ γυνὴ ἡ Σαμαρῖτις. The article is anaphoric, referring back to the anarthrous γυνή in v. 7 (Wallace 1996, 218). Σαμαρῖτις, which can also be a noun, functions here as an adjective ("the Samaritan woman"), standing in the second attributive position (see 1:9 on τὸ φῶς τὸ ἀληθινόν).

πῶς. Interrogative particle.

σύ. Nominative subject of αἰτεῖς.

Ἰουδαῖος. Predicate nominative.

ὤν. Pres act ptc masc nom sg εἰμί. The participle is either concessive ("although you are a Jew") or attributive modifying σύ ("you, who are a Jew").

παρ' ἐμοῦ. Agency. Combined with αἰτέω, παρά + genitive here serves as "a marker of the agentive source of an activity, though often remote and indirect 'from, by, of'" (LN 90.14).

πεῖν. Aor act inf πίνω (purpose).

αἰτεῖς. Pres act ind 2nd sg αἰτέω.

γυναικὸς Σαμαρίτιδος. Predicate genitive. Like above, Σαμαρίτιδος functions as an adjective ("a Samaritan woman"), standing in the fourth attributive position (see 3:15 on ζωὴν αἰώνιον).

οὔσης. Pres act ptc fem gen sg εἰμί (attributive). The participle is either concessive ("although I am a Samaritan woman") or attributive modifying ἐμοῦ in the previous PP ("from me, who am a Samaritan woman").

οὐ γὰρ συγχρῶνται Ἰουδαῖοι Σαμαρίταις. Parenthetical editorial comment that interrupts the plot of the narrative to explain to the audience the antagonistic relationship between Jews and Samaritans. This explanatory clause is omitted in ℵ* D a b e j, but most manuscripts include it. Metzger notes that "[t]he omission, if not accidental, may reflect scribal opinion that the statement is not literally exact and therefore should be deleted" (177).

οὐ. Negative particle normally used with indicative verbs.

γὰρ. Postpositive conjunction that introduces an explanation why the Samaritan woman was so surprised by Jesus' request.

συγχρῶνται. Pres mid ind 3rd pl συγχράομαι. The verb means "to associate with one another, normally involving spatial proximity and/or joint activity, and usually implying some kind of reciprocal relation or involvement" (LN 34.1; cf. BDAG, 953.2). An alternative meaning is proposed by Daube, who contends that συγχράομαι refers to a common use of vessels for food and drink, which was avoided by Jews because they considered Samaritans ritually impure (Brown, 1:166, 170; REB: "Jews do not share drinking vessels with Samaritans;" NET: "Jews use nothing in common with Samaritans"). This understanding is criticized by Louw and Nida, who argue that "[s]uch an interpretation . . . is based upon etymological arguments for which there seems to be no certain justification in general Greek usage" (LN 34.1).

Ἰουδαῖοι. Nominative subject of συγχρῶνται.

Σαμαρίταις. Dative of association.

4:10 ἀπεκρίθη Ἰησοῦς καὶ εἶπεν αὐτῇ· εἰ ᾔδεις τὴν δωρεὰν τοῦ θεοῦ καὶ τίς ἐστιν ὁ λέγων σοι· δός μοι πεῖν, σὺ ἂν ᾔτησας αὐτὸν καὶ ἔδωκεν ἄν σοι ὕδωρ ζῶν.

ἀπεκρίθη. Aor mid ind 3rd sg ἀποκρίνομαι. On the voice, see "Deponency" in the Series Introduction. This verse is connected to the previous one by asyndeton.

Ἰησοῦς. Nominative subject of ἀπεκρίθη.

καὶ εἶπεν αὐτῇ. Pleonastic clause under Semitic influence, which functions as a redundant quotative frame (see 1:25 on καὶ εἶπαν αὐτῷ).
καὶ. Coordinating conjunction.
εἶπεν. Aor act ind 3rd sg λέγω.
αὐτῇ. Dative indirect object of εἶπεν.
εἰ. Introduces the protasis of a second-class (contrary-to-fact) condition. Typically, the present contrary-to-fact conditions have the imperfect in both the protasis and the apodosis, while the past contrary-to-fact conditions have the aorist in both the protasis and the apodosis. Wallace (1996, 695 n. 25) notes that, of the five occurrences in the NT when pluperfect is used in the protasis (Matt 24:43; Luke 12:39; John 4:10; 8:19; Acts 26:32), four involve the pluperfect of οἶδα, as here. Since this pluperfect has the imperfect meaning (see below), and since the second verb in the protasis is in the present tense, while both verbs in the apodosis are in the aorist, the whole construction represents a mixed form. The protasis states something that is not true in the present time, i.e., at the time when Jesus was speaking (the woman does not know the gift of God, and she does not know Jesus' identity), but the apodosis refers to something that was not true in the past, i.e., at the time before Jesus spoke (the woman did not ask for living water).

ᾔδεις. Plprf act ind 2nd sg οἶδα. In the FG, every occurrence of the pluperfect within direct discourse is a pluperfect of οἶδα (1:31, 33; 4:10; 8:19 [2x]; 11:42). The pluperfect tense has the imperfect meaning (see 1:26 on οἴδατε).

τὴν δωρεὰν. Accusative direct object of ᾔδεις.
τοῦ θεοῦ. Subjective genitive qualifying δωρεὰν.
καὶ. Coordinating conjunction.
τίς. Predicate nominative. The interrogative pronoun has an identifying function in an indirect question. "Interrogatives, by their nature, indicate the unknown component and hence cannot be the subject" (Wallace 1996, 40 n. 12).
ἐστιν. Pres act ind 3rd sg εἰμί.
ὁ λέγων. Pres act ptc masc nom sg λέγω (substantival). Nominative subject of ἐστιν.
σοι. Dative indirect object of λέγων.
δός μοι πεῖν. Direct discourse embedded within another direct discourse (see 4:7).
δός. Aor act impv 2nd sg δίδωμι.
μοι. Dative indirect object of δός.
πεῖν. Aor act inf πίνω (purpose).

σύ. Nominative subject of ᾔτησας. The emphatic personal pronoun (BDF §277.1) marks the beginning of the apodosis of a second-class (contrary-to-fact) condition.

ἄν. Marker of contingency in the apodosis of the second-class condition.

ᾔτησας. Aor act ind 2nd sg αἰτέω.

αὐτόν. Accusative direct object of ᾔτησας.

καί. Coordinating conjunction.

ἔδωκεν. Aor act ind 3rd sg δίδωμι.

ἄν. Marker of contingency in the apodosis of the second-class condition.

σοι. Dative indirect object of ἔδωκεν.

ὕδωρ. Accusative direct object of ἔδωκεν. The noun is anarthrous because the concept of living water is introduced here for the first time (Wallace 1996, 218).

ζῶν. Pres act ptc neut acc sg ζάω (attributive). The participle modifies ὕδωρ, standing in the fourth attributive position (see 1:6 on ἀπεσταλμένος). The expression ὕδωρ ζῶν functions as a double entendre (it could mean "living water" in spiritual sense and/or "flowing water" in literal sense as opposed to stagnant water found in a well), which, by causing misunderstanding, provides occasion for further explanation and moves the conversation forward. On the OT background of this expression, see McHugh (273–79). For other examples of words with multiple meanings that are typically misunderstood by Jesus' audience, see 3:3-4; 6:33-34; 8:21-22; 11:11-13, 23-24; 14:7-8.

4:11 Λέγει αὐτῷ [ἡ γυνή]· κύριε, οὔτε ἄντλημα ἔχεις καὶ τὸ φρέαρ ἐστὶν βαθύ· πόθεν οὖν ἔχεις τὸ ὕδωρ τὸ ζῶν;

Λέγει. Pres act ind 3rd sg λέγω. The historical present (see 4:7). This verse is connected to the previous one by asyndeton.

αὐτῷ. Dative indirect object of Λέγει.

[ἡ γυνή]. Nominative subject of Λέγει. ἡ γυνή is missing in 𝔓⁷⁵ B sy^s, while ℵ* has ἐκείνη. Intrinsic probabilities cannot resolve the matter because a scribe could have added ἡ γυνή to clarify the subject of the verb or delete the noun to prune the text of superfluous words (Metzger, 177).

κύριε. Vocative of direct address.

οὔτε . . . καί. A correlative set consisting of a negative (οὔτε ἄντλημα ἔχεις) and a positive element (τὸ φρέαρ ἐστὶν βαθύ). BDF (§445.3) notes that "[t]he correlation of negative and positive members is . . . admissible, though it is not common in the NT."

ἄντλημα. Accusative direct object of ἔχεις. ἄντλημα denotes "a container or vessel for drawing water" (LN 6.123).

ἔχεις. Pres act ind 2nd sg ἔχω.

τὸ φρέαρ. Nominative subject of ἐστίν. In this account, φρέαρ ("a construction consisting of a vertical shaft, covered with a stone, for water supply, *a well*" [BDAG, 1065.1]) and πηγή (see 4:6) are used interchangeably (LN §7.57), but the term φρέαρ is rhetorically more effective at this point of the conversation because it allows the woman to focus on the depth of the shaft and point out that Jesus needs a bucket, which he does not have.

ἐστίν. Pres act ind 3rd sg εἰμί.

βαθύ. Predicate adjective.

πόθεν. Interrogative adverb of place.

οὖν. Postpositive inferential conjunction.

ἔχεις. Pres act ind 2nd sg ἔχω.

τὸ ὕδωρ. Accusative direct object of ἔχεις. The article is anaphoric, referring back to ὕδωρ ζῶν from the previous verse (Wallace 1996, 218).

τὸ ζῶν. Pres act ptc neut acc sg ζάω (attributive). The participle modifies τὸ ὕδωρ, standing in the second attributive position (see 1:29 on ὁ αἴρων).

4:12 μὴ σὺ μείζων εἶ τοῦ πατρὸς ἡμῶν Ἰακώβ, ὃς ἔδωκεν ἡμῖν τὸ φρέαρ καὶ αὐτὸς ἐξ αὐτοῦ ἔπιεν καὶ οἱ υἱοὶ αὐτοῦ καὶ τὰ θρέμματα αὐτοῦ;

μὴ. Negative particle that introduces a question that expects a negative answer. This verse is connected to the previous one by asyndeton.

σὺ. Nominative subject of εἶ. Fronted as a topical frame.

μείζων. Predicate adjective. μείζων is a comparative from μέγας.

εἶ. Pres act ind 2nd sg εἰμί.

τοῦ πατρὸς. Genitive of comparison.

ἡμῶν. Genitive of relationship qualifying πατρὸς. The first-person plural personal pronoun is exclusive because the woman does not include her conversation partner—Jesus—in it (Wallace 1996, 398).

Ἰακώβ. Genitive in apposition to τοῦ πατρὸς.

ὅς. Nominative subject of ἔδωκεν. The antecedent of the relative is Ἰακώβ.

ἔδωκεν. Aor act ind 3rd sg δίδωμι.

ἡμῖν. Dative indirect object of ἔδωκεν. The first-person plural personal pronoun is exclusive (see ἡμῶν above).

τὸ φρέαρ. Accusative direct object of ἔδωκεν. On the meaning of this term, see 4:11.

καί. Coordinating conjunction.

αὐτὸς ... καὶ οἱ υἱοὶ ... καὶ τὰ θρέμματα. Compound nominative subject of ἔπιεν. αὐτὸς functions as an intensive pronoun ("he himself"). When the verb stands between the first subject, which is in the singular, and the second subject, which is in the plural, as here, it is in the singular, agreeing with the first (BDF §135).

ἐξ αὐτοῦ. Source.

ἔπιεν. Aor act ind 3rd sg πίνω.

αὐτοῦ. Genitive of relationship qualifying υἱοί.

αὐτοῦ. Possessive genitive qualifying θρέμματα.

4:13 ἀπεκρίθη Ἰησοῦς καὶ εἶπεν αὐτῇ· πᾶς ὁ πίνων ἐκ τοῦ ὕδατος τούτου διψήσει πάλιν·

ἀπεκρίθη. Aor mid ind 3rd sg ἀποκρίνομαι. On the voice, see "Deponency" in the Series Introduction. This verse is connected to the previous one by asyndeton.

Ἰησοῦς. Nominative subject of ἀπεκρίθη.

καὶ εἶπεν αὐτῇ. Pleonastic clause under Semitic influence, which functions as a redundant quotative frame (see 1:25 on καὶ εἶπαν αὐτῷ).

καί. Coordinating conjunction.

εἶπεν. Aor act ind 3rd sg λέγω.

αὐτῇ. Dative indirect object of εἶπεν.

πᾶς ὁ πίνων. Nominative subject of διψήσει. Fronted as a topical frame. On πᾶς + articular participle, see 3:8 on πᾶς ὁ γεγεννημένος.

ὁ πίνων. Pres act ptc masc nom sg πίνω (substantival). On the function of this participle, see πᾶς ὁ πίνων above.

ἐκ τοῦ ὕδατος τούτου. Source.

διψήσει. Fut act ind 3rd sg διψάω. This future tense has gnomic force because it presents the recurrence of thirst as a natural process (Porter 1994, 44).

πάλιν. Adverb denoting "a falling back into a previous state or a return to a previous activity" (BDAG, 752.1.b).

4:14 ὃς δ' ἂν πίῃ ἐκ τοῦ ὕδατος οὗ ἐγὼ δώσω αὐτῷ, οὐ μὴ διψήσει εἰς τὸν αἰῶνα, ἀλλὰ τὸ ὕδωρ ὃ δώσω αὐτῷ γενήσεται ἐν αὐτῷ πηγὴ ὕδατος ἁλλομένου εἰς ζωὴν αἰώνιον.

ὅς ... ἄν. Nominative subject of πίῃ. The particle ἄν marks the relative pronoun ὅς, indicating that "the element of contingency is not that of time but of person" (Wallace 1996, 478). This construction is used to designate a generic subject ("whoever").

John 4:12-14

δ'. Marker of narrative development with a contrastive nuance.

πίῃ. Aor act subj 3rd sg πίνω. Subjunctive with ἄν.

ἐκ τοῦ ὕδατος. Source.

οὗ. Direct object of δώσω, which is in the genitive rather than the accusative because the case of the relative pronoun has been attracted to the case of its antecedent, ὕδατος.

ἐγὼ. Nominative subject of δώσω.

δώσω. Fut act ind 1st sg δίδωμι.

αὐτῷ. Dative indirect object of δώσω.

οὐ μὴ . . . ἀλλὰ. A point/counterpoint set that emphatically negates the assumption that a person who drinks of the water that Jesus will give to him will be thirsty and replaces it with the claim that the water that Jesus will give to that person will become in him a well of water springing up to eternal life. οὐ μή "is the most definite form of negation regarding the future" (BDF §365; cf. Zerwick §444). It is usually followed by the aorist subjunctive, but it could sometimes be followed by the future indicative, as here (Wallace 1996, 468). On the function of ἀλλά in a point/counterpoint set, see 1:8.

διψήσει. Fut act ind 3rd sg διψάω.

εἰς τὸν αἰῶνα. Temporal.

τὸ ὕδωρ. Nominative subject of γενήσεται.

ὅ. Accusative direct object of δώσω. The antecedent of the relative pronoun is τὸ ὕδωρ.

δώσω. Fut act ind 1st sg δίδωμι.

αὐτῷ. Dative indirect object of δώσω.

γενήσεται. Fut mid ind 3rd sg γίνομαι.

ἐν αὐτῷ. Locative.

πηγὴ. Predicate nominative. Jesus has substituted the term τὸ φρέαρ, which the woman used in vv. 11-12, with the term πηγὴ, which shifts the focus from the depth of the cistern to its source—a spring of fresh, flowing water (McHugh, 274; Brown, 1:170).

ὕδατος. Genitive of content qualifying πηγὴ ("spring full of water") or genitive of product ("spring that produces water").

ἁλλομένου. Pres mid ptc neut gen sg ἅλλομαι (attributive). The participle modifies ὕδατος, standing in the fourth attributive position (see 1:6 on ἀπεσταλμένος). ἅλλομαι denotes "the action of water forming bubbles and welling up from underneath the ground—'to bubble up, to well up'" (LN §14.30).

εἰς ζωὴν αἰώνιον. Goal or result. On the use of this phrase in the FG, see 3:15 on ζωὴν αἰώνιον.

4:15 Λέγει πρὸς αὐτὸν ἡ γυνή· κύριε, δός μοι τοῦτο τὸ ὕδωρ, ἵνα μὴ διψῶ μηδὲ διέρχωμαι ἐνθάδε ἀντλεῖν.

Λέγει. Pres act ind 3rd sg λέγω. The historical present (see 4:7). This verse is connected to the previous one by asyndeton.

πρὸς αὐτὸν. Locative (motion toward). The PP functions like an indirect object of Λέγει.

ἡ γυνή. Nominative subject of Λέγει.

κύριε. Vocative of direct address.

δός. Aor act impv 2nd sg δίδωμι.

μοι. Dative indirect object of δός.

τοῦτο τὸ ὕδωρ. Accusative direct object of δός. The demonstrative refers to the water that Jesus gives, described in the previous verse.

ἵνα. Introduces a purpose clause.

μὴ . . . μηδὲ. Negative particles that are used with non-indicative verbs; μηδὲ also indicates development ("neither . . . nor").

διψῶ. Pres act subj 1st sg διψάω. Subjunctive with ἵνα.

διέρχωμαι. Pres mid subj 1st sg διέρχομαι. Subjunctive with ἵνα.

ἐνθάδε. Adverb of place.

ἀντλεῖν. Pres act inf ἀντλέω (purpose).

4:16 λέγει αὐτῇ· ὕπαγε φώνησον τὸν ἄνδρα σου καὶ ἐλθὲ ἐνθάδε.

λέγει. Pres act ind 3rd sg λέγω. The historical present (see 4:7). This verse is connected to the previous one by asyndeton.

αὐτῇ. Dative indirect object of λέγει.

ὕπαγε. Pres act impv 2nd sg ὑπάγω.

φώνησον. Aor act impv 2nd sg φωνέω. This imperative is connected to the previous one by asyndeton (BDF §461.1).

τὸν ἄνδρα. Accusative direct object of φώνησον. Louw and Nida note that "ἀνήρ in the meaning of 'husband' is normally clearly marked by context, usually involving a so-called 'possessive marker'" (LN 10.53), as here.

σου. Genitive of relationship qualifying ἄνδρα.

καὶ. Coordinating conjunction.

ἐλθὲ. Aor act impv 2nd sg ἔρχομαι.

ἐνθάδε. Adverb of place.

4:17 ἀπεκρίθη ἡ γυνὴ καὶ εἶπεν αὐτῷ· οὐκ ἔχω ἄνδρα. λέγει αὐτῇ ὁ Ἰησοῦς· καλῶς εἶπας ὅτι ἄνδρα οὐκ ἔχω·

ἀπεκρίθη. Aor mid ind 3rd sg ἀποκρίνομαι. On the voice, see "Deponency" in the Series Introduction. This verse is connected to the previous one by asyndeton.

ἡ γυνὴ. Nominative subject of ἀπεκρίθη.

καὶ εἶπεν αὐτῷ. Pleonastic clause under Semitic influence, which functions as a redundant quotative frame (see 1:25 on καὶ εἶπαν αὐτῷ).

καὶ. Coordinating conjunction.

εἶπεν. Aor act ind 3rd sg λέγω.

αὐτῷ. Dative indirect object of εἶπεν.

οὐκ. Negative particle normally used with indicative verbs.

ἔχω. Pres act ind 1st sg ἔχω.

ἄνδρα. Accusative direct object of ἔχω. Like in the previous verse, ἄνδρα means "husband."

λέγει. Pres act ind 3rd sg λέγω. The historical present (see 4:7).

αὐτῇ. Dative indirect object of λέγει.

ὁ Ἰησοῦς. Nominative subject of λέγει.

καλῶς. Adverb of manner.

εἶπας. Aor act ind 2nd sg λέγω.

ὅτι. ὅτι-*recitativum* that introduces the clausal complement (direct discourse) of εἶπας.

ἄνδρα. Accusative direct object of ἔχω. The word order in Jesus' quotation of the woman's words is altered so that the direct object is now placed before the verb. By restructuring the clause, the speaker (Jesus) places the focal information from the previous clause—the noun ἄνδρα—in a marked position. Runge explains that in discourse analysis emphasis means "[a]ttracting extra attention to what was already most important. . . . The primary way that emphasis is communicated in Koiné Greek is through restructuring the information of the clause to place the focal information in a specially marked position. The emphasized information stands out more because the expected ordering of the clause has been violated" (2010, 272).

οὐκ. Negative particle normally used with indicative verbs.

ἔχω. Pres act ind 1st sg ἔχω. The verb stands in final, emphatic position.

4:18 πέντε γὰρ ἄνδρας ἔσχες καὶ νῦν ὃν ἔχεις οὐκ ἔστιν σου ἀνήρ· τοῦτο ἀληθὲς εἴρηκας.

πέντε . . . ἄνδρας. Accusative direct object of ἔσχες. Fronted for emphasis. ἀνήρ continues to denote "husband" because the text indicates when this is not the case, as the next clause shows (*pace* Harris 2015, 92, who claims that here ἄνδρας means "men as partners").

γὰρ. Postpositive conjunction that introduces a clause that explains why Jesus concurred with the woman's assertion that she did not have a husband.

ἔσχες. Aor act ind 2nd sg ἔχω.

καὶ. Coordinating conjunction.

νῦν. Adverb of time. νῦν is placed before ὃν for emphasis (hyperbaton), because the elements that belong to a dependent clause normally come after the subordinating conjunction (BDF §475.2).

ὅν. The relative pronoun introduces the headless relative clause that, in its entirety (νῦν ὃν ἔχεις), serves as the subject of ἔστιν. Fronted as a topical frame. In this conversation, Jesus does not use the term ἀνήρ for a man who is not married to the woman; rather, he refers to him descriptively, with the help of the relative clause ("the one whom you now have"). Within its clause, ὅν is the direct object of ἔχεις.

ἔχεις. Pres act ind 2nd sg ἔχω.

οὐκ. Negative particle normally used with indicative verbs.

ἔστιν. Pres act ind 3rd sg εἰμί. The enclitic ἐστιν is accented ἔστιν when it comes at the beginning of a sentence, when it expresses existence, or when it follows ἀλλ', εἰ, καί, οὐκ, ὅτι, or τοῦτ'. The third condition is fulfilled here.

σου. Genitive of relationship qualifying ἀνήρ. The preposed pronoun is thematically salient (Levinsohn 2000, 64).

ἀνήρ. Predicate nominative.

τοῦτο. Accusative direct object of εἴρηκας.

ἀληθὲς. Accusative complement to τοῦτο in a double accusative object-complement construction (lit. "you have said this as something true" = "what you have said is true"; cf. BDF §292). Alternatively, ἀληθὲς could be regarded as adverbial accusative ("this you have spoken truly"; cf. Wallace 1996, 293).

εἴρηκας. Prf act ind 2nd sg λέγω.

4:19 Λέγει αὐτῷ ἡ γυνή· κύριε, θεωρῶ ὅτι προφήτης εἶ σύ.

Λέγει. Pres act ind 3rd sg λέγω. The historical present (see 4:7). This verse is connected to the previous one by asyndeton.

αὐτῷ. Dative indirect object of λέγει.
ἡ γυνή. Nominative subject of λέγει.
κύριε. Vocative of direct address.
θεωρῶ. Pres act ind 1st sg θεωρέω. The verb means "to come to the understanding of someth[ing], *notice, perceive, observe, find*" (BDAG, 454.2).
ὅτι. Introduces the clausal complement (indirect discourse) of θεωρῶ.
προφήτης. Predicate nominative. Fronted for emphasis. According to Wallace, προφήτης "is the most likely candidate of an indefinite preverbal PN in the NT" because the woman comes to this conclusion based on Jesus' supernatural knowledge of her past, but he also suggests that "the sense may be better characterized as indefinite-qualitative" (1996, 265–66; cf. Harris 2015, 92).
εἶ. Pres act ind 2nd sg εἰμί.
σύ. Nominative subject of εἶ.

4:20 οἱ πατέρες ἡμῶν ἐν τῷ ὄρει τούτῳ προσεκύνησαν· καὶ ὑμεῖς λέγετε ὅτι ἐν Ἱεροσολύμοις ἐστὶν ὁ τόπος ὅπου προσκυνεῖν δεῖ.

οἱ πατέρες. Nominative subject of προσεκύνησαν. Fronted as a topical frame. This verse is connected to the previous one by asyndeton.
ἡμῶν. Genitive of relationship qualifying πατέρες. The first-person plural personal pronoun is exclusive and contrastive, distinguishing the Samaritans ("our fathers") from the Jews.
ἐν τῷ ὄρει τούτῳ. Locative. Fronted for emphasis.
προσεκύνησαν. Aor act ind 3rd pl προσκυνέω.
καί. Coordinating conjunction. This is not a special case of the so-called adversative καί (Harris 2015, 92) but an observation about the semantic relationship of the clauses joined by καί (see 1:5).
ὑμεῖς. Nominative subject of λέγετε. The second-person plural personal pronoun is exclusive and contrastive, distinguishing the Jews ("you") from the Samaritans.
λέγετε. Pres act ind 2nd pl λέγω.
ὅτι. Introduces the clausal complement (indirect discourse) of λέγετε.
ἐν Ἱεροσολύμοις. Locative. Fronted for emphasis.
ἐστὶν. Pres act ind 3rd sg εἰμί.
ὁ τόπος. Nominative subject of ἐστὶν.
ὅπου. Particle denoting place.
προσκυνεῖν. Pres act inf προσκυνέω (complementary). On the function of the infinitive with δεῖ, see 3:7 on γεννηθῆναι.

δεῖ. Pres act ind 3rd sg δεῖ (impersonal). The verb stands in final, emphatic position.

4:21 λέγει αὐτῇ ὁ Ἰησοῦς· πίστευέ μοι, γύναι, ὅτι ἔρχεται ὥρα ὅτε οὔτε ἐν τῷ ὄρει τούτῳ οὔτε ἐν Ἱεροσολύμοις προσκυνήσετε τῷ πατρί.

λέγει. Pres act ind 3rd sg λέγω. The historical present (see 4:7). This verse is connected to the previous one by asyndeton.

αὐτῇ. Dative indirect object of λέγει.

ὁ Ἰησοῦς. Nominative subject of λέγει.

πίστευέ. Pres act impv 2nd sg πιστεύω. πίστευέ, which has an acute accent on the antepenult, acquired an additional accent, the acute, on the ultima from the enclitic μοι (Smyth §183; Carson 1985, 48).

μοι. Dative complement of πίστευέ. The dative indicates the person "to whom one gives credence or whom one believes" (BDAG, 816.1.b).

γύναι. Vocative of direct address.

ὅτι. Introduces the clausal complement (indirect discourse) of πίστευέ.

ἔρχεται. Pres mid ind 3rd sg ἔρχομαι. The present tense is here used for an action that is extended into the future.

ὥρα. Nominative subject of ἔρχεται.

ὅτε. Introduces a temporal clause.

οὔτε . . . οὔτε. "Neither . . . nor" (BDAG, 740).

ἐν τῷ ὄρει τούτῳ. Locative.

ἐν Ἱεροσολύμοις. Locative.

προσκυνήσετε. Fut act ind 2nd pl προσκυνέω. προσκυνέω ("[fall down and] worship, do obeisance to, prostrate oneself before, do reverence to, welcome respectfully" [BDAG, 882]) can be used with both the dative (4:21, 23a; 9:38) and the accusative (4:22, 23b, 24). The alteration of the datives and the accusatives in vv. 21–23 speaks against the idea that "the dative direct object is used with προσκυνέω when true Deity is the object of worship . . . and when false deity is worshipped, the accusative direct object is used" (Wallace 1996, 172). It is more likely that this is stylistic variation that has no theological implications (Barrett 236–37).

τῷ πατρί. Dative direct object of προσκυνήσετε.

4:22 ὑμεῖς προσκυνεῖτε ὃ οὐκ οἴδατε· ἡμεῖς προσκυνοῦμεν ὃ οἴδαμεν, ὅτι ἡ σωτηρία ἐκ τῶν Ἰουδαίων ἐστίν.

ὑμεῖς προσκυνεῖτε ὃ οὐκ οἴδατε· ἡμεῖς προσκυνοῦμεν ὃ οἴδαμεν. These two clauses are connected by asyndeton.

ὑμεῖς. Nominative subject of προσκυνεῖτε. The second-person plural personal pronoun is exclusive and contrastive, distinguishing the Samaritans ("you") from the Jews ("we"). ὑμεῖς and ἡμεῖς are also emphatic, although in cases when pronouns are contrasted, as here, "[t]he amount of emphasis will vary very greatly according to circumstances and may sometimes vanish entirely so far as we can determine" (Robertson, 677). This verse is connected to the previous one by asyndeton.

προσκυνεῖτε. Pres act ind 2nd pl προσκυνέω.

ὅ. The relative pronoun introduces a headless relative clause that, in its entirety (ὃ οὐκ οἴδατε), serves as the direct object of προσκυνεῖτε. Within its clause, ὅ is the accusative direct object of οἴδατε. Although the relative clause ὃ οὐκ οἴδατε refers to God, ὅ is neuter rather than masculine. This is a case of the use of abstract for concrete (Robertson, 713). See Acts 17:23 (Ἀγνώστῳ θεῷ. ὃ οὖν ἀγνοοῦντες εὐσεβεῖτε, τοῦτο ἐγὼ καταγγέλλω ὑμῖν), which also uses the neuter relative pronoun for God as the object of worship.

οὐκ. Negative particle normally used with indicative verbs.

οἴδατε. Prf act ind 2nd pl οἶδα (see 1:26 on οἴδατε).

ἡμεῖς. Nominative subject of προσκυνοῦμεν. The first-person plural personal pronoun is exclusive and contrastive, distinguishing the Jews ("we") from the Samaritans ("you").

προσκυνοῦμεν. Pres act ind 1st pl προσκυνέω.

ὅ. The relative pronoun introduces a headless relative clause that, in its entirety (ὃ οἴδαμεν), serves as the direct object of προσκυνοῦμεν. Within its clause, ὅ is the accusative direct object of οἴδαμεν. On the neuter gender of the relative pronoun, see ὅ above.

οἴδαμεν. Prf act ind 1st pl οἶδα (see 1:26 on οἴδατε).

ὅτι. Introduces a causal clause.

ἡ σωτηρία. Nominative subject of ἐστίν. Wallace notes that the article with the abstract noun σωτηρία highlights its quality as "the only salvation worth considering and the one that needs no clarification because it is well known" (1996, 226).

ἐκ τῶν Ἰουδαίων. Source. Fronted for emphasis. In this context, the term "the Jews" is "no more than a religious, nationalistic designation" that distinguishes them from the Samaritans (Brown, 1:lxxi).

ἐστίν. Pres act ind 3rd sg εἰμί.

4:23 ἀλλ' ἔρχεται ὥρα καὶ νῦν ἐστιν, ὅτε οἱ ἀληθινοὶ προσκυνηταὶ προσκυνήσουσιν τῷ πατρὶ ἐν πνεύματι καὶ ἀληθείᾳ· καὶ γὰρ ὁ πατὴρ τοιούτους ζητεῖ τοὺς προσκυνοῦντας αὐτόν.

ἀλλ'. Marker of contrast.

ἔρχεται ὥρα καὶ νῦν ἐστιν. This clause, which also occurs in 5:25, expresses the tension between the expectation of an hour that is still in the future (see ἔρχεται below and the references to "the last day" in 6:39, 40, 44, 54; 11:24; 12:48) and the experience of salvation in the present (see νῦν below; cf. Frey 1997–2000, 2:2–5).

ἔρχεται. Pres mid ind 3rd sg ἔρχομαι. The present tense is here used for an action that is extended into the future.

ὥρα. Nominative subject of ἔρχεται.

καί. Coordinating conjunction.

νῦν. Adverb of time that functions as a temporal marker, focusing on "time coextensive with the event of the narrative" (BDAG, 681.1.a).

ἐστιν. Pres act ind 3rd sg εἰμί.

ὅτε. Introduces a temporal clause.

οἱ ἀληθινοὶ προσκυνηταί. Nominative subject of προσκυνήσουσιν. Fronted as a topical frame. The adjective ἀληθινοί ("genuine, authentic, real" [BDAG, 43.3]) stands in the first attributive position (see 2:10 on τὸν καλὸν οἶνον).

προσκυνήσουσιν. Fut act ind 3rd pl προσκυνέω.

τῷ πατρί. Dative direct object of προσκυνήσουσιν.

ἐν πνεύματι καὶ ἀληθείᾳ. State or condition (BDAG, 327.2.b). Since ἐν is not repeated before ἀληθείᾳ, the two nouns form a conceptual unit, but they do not represent a hendiadys (e.g., "in the Spirit of Truth" or "in the true Spirit"; cf. Harris 2015, 93; Barrett, 239).

καὶ γάρ. A combination of conjunctions for *etenim* ("for indeed," "actually"), "in which καί has completely lost its force" (BDF §452.3).

ὁ πατήρ. Nominative subject of ζητεῖ.

τοιούτους. Accusative direct object of ζητεῖ in a double accusative object-complement construction. The adjective τοιοῦτος ("of such kind, such as these") is used as a substantive ("people of this kind"; cf. Zerwick and Grosvenor, 296).

ζητεῖ. Pres act ind 3rd sg ζητέω.

τοὺς προσκυνοῦντας. Pres act ptc masc acc pl προσκυνέω (substantival). Accusative complement to τοιούτους in a double accusative object-complement construction.

αὐτόν. Accusative direct object of προσκυνοῦντας.

4:24 πνεῦμα ὁ θεός, καὶ τοὺς προσκυνοῦντας αὐτὸν ἐν πνεύματι καὶ ἀληθείᾳ δεῖ προσκυνεῖν.

πνεῦμα. Predicate nominative. Fronted for emphasis. The anarthrous πνεῦμα is qualitative, describing God's essence (Wallace 1996, 270). πνεῦμα ὁ θεός is not a convertible proposition that presumes complete interchangeability between the subject and the predicate nominative (Harris 2015, 93). This verse is connected to the previous one by asyndeton.

ὁ θεός. Nominative subject of an implied ἐστίν in a verbless clause.

καὶ. Coordinating conjunction.

τοὺς προσκυνοῦντας. Pres act ptc masc acc pl προσκυνέω (substantival). Accusative subject of the infinitive προσκυνεῖν.

αὐτὸν. Accusative direct object of προσκυνοῦντας.

ἐν πνεύματι καὶ ἀληθείᾳ. State or condition (see 4:23). Fronted for emphasis.

δεῖ. Pres act ind 3rd sg δεῖ (impersonal).

προσκυνεῖν. Pres act inf προσκυνέω (complementary). On the function of the infinitive with δεῖ, see 3:7 on γεννηθῆναι.

4:25 Λέγει αὐτῷ ἡ γυνή· οἶδα ὅτι Μεσσίας ἔρχεται ὁ λεγόμενος χριστός· ὅταν ἔλθῃ ἐκεῖνος, ἀναγγελεῖ ἡμῖν ἅπαντα.

Λέγει. Pres act ind 3rd sg λέγω. The historical present (see 4:7). This verse is connected to the previous one by asyndeton.

αὐτῷ. Dative indirect object of Λέγει.

ἡ γυνή. Nominative subject of Λέγει.

οἶδα. Prf act ind 1st sg οἶδα (see 1:26 on οἴδατε).

ὅτι. Introduces the clausal complement (indirect discourse) of οἶδα.

Μεσσίας. Nominative subject of ἔρχεται; on the meaning of the term, see 1:41 on τὸν Μεσσίαν. Fronted for emphasis.

ἔρχεται. Pres mid ind 3rd sg ἔρχομαι. The present tense describes an event that, from the woman's perspective, still lies in the future.

ὁ λεγόμενος. Pres pass ptc masc nom sg λέγω (attributive). The participle modifies Μεσσίας, standing in the third attributive position (see 1:18 on ὁ ὤν).

χριστός. Nominative complement to Μεσσίας in a double nominative subject-complement construction. Such constructions are common in passive clauses that are derived from the (real or hypothetical) active clauses that employ double accusative object-complement constructions. For example, when the active sentence τις λέγει Μεσσίαν χριστόν is transformed into a passive sentence Μεσσίας λέγεται χριστός, the direct object (Μεσσίαν) becomes the nominative subject (Μεσσίας), and the accusative complement (χριστόν) becomes the nominative complement (χριστός) (Culy 2009).

ὅταν. Introduces an indefinite temporal clause.

ἔλθῃ. Aor act subj 3rd sg ἔρχομαι. Subjunctive with ὅταν.

ἐκεῖνος. Nominative subject of ἔλθῃ. The demonstrative pronoun refers to Μεσσίας, acting as a third-person personal pronoun with a simple anaphoric force (Wallace 1996, 328–29).

ἀναγγελεῖ. Fut act ind 3rd sg ἀναγγέλλω. The verb means to "disclose, announce, proclaim, teach" (BDAG, 59.2).

ἡμῖν. Dative indirect object of ἀναγγελεῖ.

ἅπαντα. Accusative direct object of ἀναγγελεῖ.

4:26 λέγει αὐτῇ ὁ Ἰησοῦς· ἐγώ εἰμι, ὁ λαλῶν σοι.

λέγει. Pres act ind 3rd sg λέγω. The historical present (see 4:7). This verse is connected to the previous one by asyndeton.

αὐτῇ. Dative indirect object of λέγει.

ὁ Ἰησοῦς. Nominative subject of λέγει.

ἐγώ. Nominative subject of εἰμι. Fronted for emphasis. The personal pronoun has the identifying function.

εἰμι. Pres act ind 1st sg εἰμί.

ὁ λαλῶν. Pres act ptc masc nom sg λαλέω (substantival). Nominative in apposition to ἐγώ, which receives additional emphasis through right-dislocation.

σοι. Dative indirect object of λαλῶν.

John 4:27-30

[27]And at that moment his disciples came and were astonished because he was speaking with a woman, though no one said, "What do you want?" or "Why are you speaking with her?" [28]Then the woman left her water jar and went away into the town and said to the people, [29]"Come, see a man who told me everything that I ever did. Could this perhaps be the Messiah?" [30]They went out of the town and were coming to him.

4:27 Καὶ ἐπὶ τούτῳ ἦλθαν οἱ μαθηταὶ αὐτοῦ καὶ ἐθαύμαζον ὅτι μετὰ γυναικὸς ἐλάλει· οὐδεὶς μέντοι εἶπεν· τί ζητεῖς ἢ τί λαλεῖς μετ' αὐτῆς;

Καὶ. Coordinating conjunction.

ἐπὶ τούτῳ. Temporal.

ἦλθαν. Aor act ind 3rd pl ἔρχομαι.

οἱ μαθηταὶ. Nominative subject of ἦλθαν.

αὐτοῦ. Genitive of relationship qualifying μαθηταί.

καὶ. Coordinating conjunction.

ἐθαύμαζον. Impf act ind 3rd pl θαυμάζω. The imperfect tense portrays the astonishment of the disciples as an unfolding action. On the function of the imperfect in the FG, see 1:39 on ἦν.

ὅτι. Introduces a causal clause. Many English translations (NRSV; ASV; CEB; HCSB; ESV; KJV; LEB) presume that ὅτι introduces the clausal complement (indirect discourse) of ἐθαύμαζον. This reading, however, requires regarding ἐλάλει as the retained past tense from the direct discourse that should be translated with the pluperfect in English ("that he had been speaking with a woman"), which is not appropriate to the situation since at the moment of the disciples' arrival (see ἐπὶ τούτῳ) Jesus was still engaged in the conversation with the Samaritan woman (Wallace 1996, 461, 553 n. 31). If this were an indirect discourse, we would expect the present-tense λαλεῖ and not the imperfect ἐλάλει (Harris 2015, 96).

μετὰ γυναικὸς. Association/accompaniment. Wallace notes that "[t]here is no need for the article to be used to make the object of a proposition definite," but he adds that "this is not to say that all prepositional objects are definite" (1996, 247). In this case, the anarthrous noun is indefinite, indicating that the disciples were not surprised that Jesus spoke with this particular woman but with any woman (Wallace 1996, 208, 247).

ἐλάλει. Impf act ind 3rd sg λαλέω. On the function of the imperfect in the FG, see 1:39 on ἦν.

οὐδεὶς. Nominative subject of εἶπεν. Fronted for emphasis.

μέντοι. Adverbial particle with adversative sense ("though, to be sure, indeed" [BDAG, 630.2]).

εἶπεν. Aor act ind 3rd sg λέγω.

τί. Accusative direct object of ζητεῖς.

ζητεῖς. Pres act ind 2nd sg ζητέω.

ἤ. Marker of an alternative/disjunctive particle (BDAG, 432.1).

τί. Adverbial accusative ("why") or accusative direct object of λαλεῖς ("what").

λαλεῖς. Pres act ind 2nd sg λαλέω.

μετ' αὐτῆς. Association/accompaniment.

4:28 ἀφῆκεν οὖν τὴν ὑδρίαν αὐτῆς ἡ γυνὴ καὶ ἀπῆλθεν εἰς τὴν πόλιν καὶ λέγει τοῖς ἀνθρώποις·

ἀφῆκεν. Aor act ind 3rd sg ἀφίημι.

οὖν. Postpositive inferential conjunction and/or transitional particle (see 1:22 and 11:6).

τὴν ὑδρίαν. Accusative direct object of ἀφῆκεν.

αὐτῆς. Possessive genitive qualifying ὑδρίαν.
ἡ γυνὴ. Nominative subject of ἀφῆκεν.
καὶ. Coordinating conjunction.
ἀπῆλθεν. Aor act ind 3rd sg ἀπέρχομαι.
εἰς τὴν πόλιν. Locative.
καὶ. Coordinating conjunction.
λέγει. Pres act ind 3rd sg λέγω. The historical present (see 4:7).
τοῖς ἀνθρώποις. Dative indirect object of λέγει.

4:29 δεῦτε ἴδετε ἄνθρωπον ὃς εἶπέν μοι πάντα ὅσα ἐποίησα, μήτι οὗτός ἐστιν ὁ χριστός;

δεῦτε. An adverb ("come here! come on!"), used as hortatory particle followed by the plural (imperative or aorist subjunctive) (BDAG, 220).
ἴδετε. Aor act impv 2nd pl ὁράω.
ἄνθρωπον. Accusative direct object of ἴδετε.
ὅς. Nominative subject of εἶπέν.
εἶπέν. Aor act ind 3rd sg λέγω. εἶπέν, which has a circumflex accent on the penult, acquired an additional accent, the acute, on the ultima from the enclitic μοι (Smyth §183; Carson 1985, 48).
μοι. Dative indirect object of εἶπέν.
πάντα. Accusative direct object of εἶπέν.
ὅσα. Accusative direct object of ἐποίησα. The antecedent of the correlative pronoun ("as many as") is πάντα. πάντα ὅσα = "all things that" (BDAG, 729.2).
ἐποίησα. Aor act ind 1st sg ποιέω.
μήτι. Negative particle that introduces a question that expects a negative answer. μήτι is "somewhat more emphatic than the simple μή," but it is also used in "questions in which the questioner is in doubt concerning the answer," as here (BDAG, 649). Robertson remarks that "[t]he woman does not mean to imply flatly that Jesus is not the Messiah by using μή τι, but she raises the question and throws a cloud of uncertainty and curiosity over it with a woman's keen instinct. In a word, μή is just the negative to use when one does not wish to be too positive" (1167).
οὗτός. Nominative subject of ἐστιν. Fronted for emphasis. The anaphoric demonstrative refers to the nearest contextual antecedent, i.e., ὃς εἶπέν μοι πάντα ὅσα ἐποίησα. οὗτός, which has a circumflex accent on the penult, acquired an additional accent, the acute, on the ultima from the enclitic ἐστιν (Smyth §183; Carson 1985, 48).
ἐστιν. Pres act ind 3rd sg εἰμί.
ὁ χριστός. Predicate nominative.

4:30 ἐξῆλθον ἐκ τῆς πόλεως καὶ ἤρχοντο πρὸς αὐτόν.

ἐξῆλθον. Aor act ind 3rd pl ἐξέρχομαι. This verse is connected to the previous one by asyndeton.

ἐκ τῆς πόλεως. Separation.

καί. Coordinating conjunction.

ἤρχοντο. Impf mid ind 3rd pl ἔρχομαι. The imperfective aspect portrays Samaritans' coming toward Jesus as an action in progress (cf. NRSV: "they . . . were on their way to him"). Du Toit argues that "[t]his imperfect creates the expectation that an event will follow. But this only happens in vv. 39-40, after the intervening discussion between Jesus and his disciples (vv. 31-38). . . . The imperfect ἤρχοντο keeps the two parts of the narrative together, and thus establishes cohesion in the text" (222).

πρὸς αὐτόν. Locative (motion toward).

John 4:31-38

³¹In the meantime, the disciples were asking him, saying, "Rabbi, eat something." ³²But he said to them, "I have food to eat which you do not know." ³³So the disciples began to say to one another, "No one brought him anything to eat, did they?" ³⁴Jesus said to them, "My food is that I should do the will of the one who sent me and complete his work. ³⁵Do you not say, 'There are yet four months, and the harvest is coming?' Look, I say to you, lift up your eyes and look at the fields, that they are white for harvesting. ³⁶The reaper is already receiving wages and is gathering fruit for eternal life, so that the sower and the reaper may rejoice together. ³⁷For in this matter the saying is true, 'It is one who sows and another who reaps.' ³⁸I sent you to reap what you have not labored for. Others have labored, and you have entered their labor."

4:31 Ἐν τῷ μεταξὺ ἠρώτων αὐτὸν οἱ μαθηταὶ λέγοντες· ῥαββί, φάγε.

Ἐν τῷ μεταξύ. Temporal. Fronted as a temporal frame. The article τῷ functions as a nominalizer, changing the adverb μεταξὺ ("between") into the object of the preposition Ἐν (lit. "in the between" = "in the meantime"). This verse is connected to the previous one by asyndeton.

ἠρώτων. Impf act ind 3rd pl ἐρωτάω. ἐρωτάω ("to ask, request") is usually followed by a participle of λέγω, which introduces a request in the form of direct discourse, as here (BDAG, 395.2). On the function of the imperfect in the FG, see 1:39 on ἦν.

αὐτόν. Accusative direct object of ἠρώτων.
οἱ μαθηταί. Nominative subject of ἠρώτων.
λέγοντες. Pres act ptc masc nom pl λέγω (pleonastic).
ῥαββί. Vocative of direct address.
φάγε. Aor act impv 2nd sg ἐσθίω.

4:32 ὁ δὲ εἶπεν αὐτοῖς· ἐγὼ βρῶσιν ἔχω φαγεῖν ἣν ὑμεῖς οὐκ οἴδατε.

ὁ δὲ. A construction that is frequently used in narrative literature to indicate the change of the speaker in a dialogue. The nominative article stands in place of a third-person singular personal pronoun and functions as the subject of εἶπεν. Its force is anaphoric, referring to Jesus who has just been asked to eat.
εἶπεν. Aor act ind 3rd sg λέγω.
αὐτοῖς. Dative indirect object of εἶπεν.
ἐγώ. Nominative subject of ἔχω. The first-person singular personal pronoun is emphatic and contrastive, differentiating Jesus from his disciples. Fronted as a topical frame.
βρῶσιν. Accusative direct object of ἔχω. Fronted for emphasis.
ἔχω. Pres act ind 1st sg ἔχω.
φαγεῖν. Aor act inf ἐσθίω (epexegetical to βρῶσιν).
ἥν. Accusative direct object of οἴδατε. The antecedent of the relative pronoun is βρῶσιν.
ὑμεῖς. Nominative subject of οἴδατε. The second-person plural personal pronoun is contrastive, differentiating the disciples from Jesus.
οὐκ. Negative particle normally used with indicative verbs.
οἴδατε. Prf act ind 2nd pl οἶδα (see 1:26 on οἴδατε).

4:33 ἔλεγον οὖν οἱ μαθηταὶ πρὸς ἀλλήλους· μή τις ἤνεγκεν αὐτῷ φαγεῖν;

ἔλεγον. Impf act ind 3rd pl λέγω. On the function of the imperfect in the FG, see 1:39 on ἦν.
οὖν. Postpositive inferential conjunction and/or transitional particle (see 1:22 and 11:6).
οἱ μαθηταί. Nominative subject of ἔλεγον.
πρὸς ἀλλήλους. Locative (motion toward). The PP functions like an indirect object of ἔλεγον.
μή. Negative particle that introduces a question that expects a negative answer.
τις. Nominative subject of ἤνεγκεν.
ἤνεγκεν. Aor act ind 3rd sg φέρω.

αὐτῷ. Dative indirect object of ἤνεγκεν.
φαγεῖν. Aor act inf ἐσθίω (complementary).

4:34 λέγει αὐτοῖς ὁ Ἰησοῦς· ἐμὸν βρῶμά ἐστιν ἵνα ποιήσω τὸ θέλημα τοῦ πέμψαντός με καὶ τελειώσω αὐτοῦ τὸ ἔργον.

λέγει. Pres act ind 3rd sg λέγω. The historical present (see 4:7). This verse is connected to the previous one by asyndeton.
αὐτοῖς. Dative indirect object of λέγει.
ὁ Ἰησοῦς. Nominative subject of λέγει.
ἐμὸν βρῶμά. Nominative subject of ἐστιν. βρῶμά, which has a circumflex accent on the penult, acquired an additional accent, the acute, on the ultima from the enclitic ἐστιν (Smyth §183; Carson 1985, 48).
ἐστιν. Pres act ind 3rd sg εἰμί.
ἵνα. Introduces a substantival clause that functions as the predicate nominative clause: "My food is [*that* I should do the will of the one who sent me and complete his work]" (Wallace 1996, 475).
ποιήσω. Aor act subj 1st sg ποιέω. Subjunctive with ἵνα.
τὸ θέλημα. Accusative direct object of ποιήσω. The nominal phrase τὸ θέλημα τοῦ πέμψαντός με also occurs in 5:30; 6:38, 39.
τοῦ πέμψαντός. Aor act ptc masc gen sg πέμπω (substantival). Subjective genitive qualifying θέλημα. πέμψαντός, which has an acute accent on the antepenult, acquired an additional accent, the acute, on the ultima from the enclitic με (Smyth §183; Carson 1985, 48). The use of the participial forms of πέμπω to either identify or describe God as the one who sent Jesus is a unique feature of the FG (4:34; 5:23, 24, 30, 37; 6:38, 39, 44; 7:16, 18, 28, 33; 8:16, 18, 26, 29; 9:4; 12:44, 45, 49; 13:20; 14:24; 15:21; 16:5).
με. Accusative direct object of πέμψαντός.
καὶ. Coordinating conjunction.
τελειώσω. Aor act subj 1st sg τελειόω. Subjunctive with ἵνα.
αὐτοῦ. Possessive ("his work") or subjective genitive ("the work that he is doing") qualifying ἔργον. The preposed pronoun is thematically salient (Levinsohn 2000, 64).
τὸ ἔργον. Accusative direct object of τελειώσω.

4:35 οὐχ ὑμεῖς λέγετε ὅτι ἔτι τετράμηνός ἐστιν καὶ ὁ θερισμὸς ἔρχεται; ἰδοὺ λέγω ὑμῖν, ἐπάρατε τοὺς ὀφθαλμοὺς ὑμῶν καὶ θεάσασθε τὰς χώρας ὅτι λευκαί εἰσιν πρὸς θερισμόν. ἤδη

οὐχ. Negative particle that introduces a question that expects an affirmative answer. This verse is connected to the previous one by asyndeton.

ὑμεῖς. Nominative subject of λέγετε. Fronted for emphasis.

λέγετε. Pres act ind 2nd pl λέγω.

ὅτι. Introduces the clausal complement (direct [NRSV; REB; NET; ESV] or indirect [DBY; WYC] discourse) of λέγετε.

ἔτι. Adverb ("yet, still").

τετράμηνός. Nominative subject of ἐστιν. τετράμηνός ("lasting four months") is here used as a substantive for a period of four months (BDAG, 1001; BDF §241.3; LN 67.176). τετράμηνός, which has an acute accent on the antepenult, acquired an additional accent, the acute, on the ultima from the enclitic ἐστιν (Smyth §183; Carson 1985, 48).

ἐστιν. Pres act ind 3rd sg εἰμί.

καὶ. Coordinating conjunction.

ὁ θερισμὸς. Nominative subject of ἔρχεται.

ἔρχεται. Pres mid ind 3rd sg ἔρχομαι. The verb stands in final, emphatic position. The present tense is here used to express the future expectation.

ἰδοὺ. An interjection (originally ἰδοῦ [aor mid impv 2nd sg ὁράω] but accented with the acute rather than the circumflex) that "draws attention to what follows" (BDAG, 468).

λέγω ὑμῖν. Metacomment (see Runge 2010, 101–24).

λέγω. Pres act ind 1st sg λέγω.

ὑμῖν. Dative indirect object of λέγω.

ἐπάρατε. Aor act impv 2nd pl ἐπαίρω.

τοὺς ὀφθαλμοὺς. Accusative direct object of ἐπάρατε.

ὑμῶν. Possessive genitive qualifying ὀφθαλμοὺς.

καὶ. Coordinating conjunction.

θεάσασθε. Aor mid impv 2nd pl θεάομαι.

τὰς χώρας. Accusative direct object of θεάσασθε, which functions as an anticipation of the conceptional subject of the ὅτι clause that follows (Zerwick §207). χώρα denotes "land under cultivation or used for pasture" (LN 1.95).

ὅτι. Introduces the clausal complement of θεάσασθε.

λευκαί. Predicate adjective. Fronted for emphasis. Louw and Nida note that the Greek text speaks "of fields being 'white for the harvest,' but in a number of languages it would be quite impossible to use the same term for the ripe condition of a harvest as in the case of the color of wool or snow" (LN 79.27).

εἰσιν. Pres act ind 3rd pl εἰμί.

πρὸς θερισμόν. Purpose.

ἤδη. Temporal adverb ("already, now"). The punctuation in NA[28]/UBS[5] and SBLGNT suggests that the adverb belongs to v. 36, although it can also make good sense with what precedes. It seems that the latter view was held by some scribes (A C³ K N Γ Δ Θ f¹·¹³ 565 579 700 892 𝔐 lat et al.), who tried to prevent taking ἤδη with what follows by inserting καί at the beginning of v. 36. The version without καί not only has better textual support (𝔓⁶⁶·⁷⁵ ℵ B C* D L Wˢ Ψ 083 33 it) but also reflects the evangelist's habit of starting a sentence with ἤδη (4:51; 7:14; 9:22; 15:3; cf. Metzger, 177–78).

4:36 ὁ θερίζων μισθὸν λαμβάνει καὶ συνάγει καρπὸν εἰς ζωὴν αἰώνιον, ἵνα ὁ σπείρων ὁμοῦ χαίρῃ καὶ ὁ θερίζων.

ὁ θερίζων. Pres act ptc masc nom sg θερίζω (substantival). Nominative subject of λαμβάνει. This verse is connected to the previous one by asyndeton.

μισθὸν. Accusative direct object of λαμβάνει. Fronted for emphasis.

λαμβάνει. Pres act ind 3rd sg λαμβάνω.

καὶ. Coordinating conjunction.

συνάγει. Pres act ind 3rd sg συνάγω.

καρπὸν. Accusative direct object of συνάγει. καρπός denotes "harvest, crop, fruit, grain" (LN 43.15).

εἰς ζωὴν αἰώνιον. Goal or result. On the use of this phrase in the FG, see 3:15 on ζωὴν αἰώνιον.

ἵνα. Introduces a result clause (Porter, 235 n. 2; Wallace 1996, 473–74, regards it as a purpose-result clause).

ὁ σπείρων . . . καὶ ὁ θερίζων. Compound nominative subject of χαίρῃ. When the verb stands between the first subject and the second subject, as here, it agrees with the first (BDF §135). Wallace (1996, 402) argues that this word order and verbal agreement give prominence to the first-named subject, i.e., the sower.

ὁ σπείρων. Pres act ptc masc nom sg σπείρω (substantival).

ὁ θερίζων. Pres act ptc masc nom sg θερίζω (substantival).

ὁμοῦ. Adverb that pertains to being simultaneous ("together at the same time [as], in company [with]" [BDAG, 709.2]).

χαίρῃ. Pres act subj 3rd sg χαίρω. Subjunctive with ἵνα.

4:37 ἐν γὰρ τούτῳ ὁ λόγος ἐστὶν ἀληθινὸς ὅτι ἄλλος ἐστὶν ὁ σπείρων καὶ ἄλλος ὁ θερίζων.

ἐν . . . τούτῳ. Reference. The demonstrative pronoun is cataphoric, referring to the explanation that follows.

γὰρ. Postpositive conjunction introducing a clause that provides support for the previous verse.

ὁ λόγος. Nominative subject of ἐστίν.
ἐστίν. Pres act ind 3rd sg εἰμί.
ἀληθινὸς. Predicate adjective.
ὅτι. ὅτι-*recitativum* that introduces the content of λόγος.
ἄλλος. Predicate adjective. Fronted for emphasis.
ἐστίν. Pres act ind 3rd sg εἰμί.
ὁ σπείρων. Pres act ptc masc nom sg σπείρω (substantival). Nominative subject of ἐστίν.
καὶ. Coordinating conjunction.
ἄλλος. Predicate adjective. Fronted for emphasis.
ὁ θερίζων. Pres act ptc masc nom sg θερίζω (substantival). Nominative subject of an implied ἐστίν.

4:38 ἐγὼ ἀπέστειλα ὑμᾶς θερίζειν ὃ οὐχ ὑμεῖς κεκοπιάκατε· ἄλλοι κεκοπιάκασιν καὶ ὑμεῖς εἰς τὸν κόπον αὐτῶν εἰσεληλύθατε.

ἐγὼ. Nominative subject of ἀπέστειλα. Fronted as a topical frame. This verse is connected to the previous one by asyndeton.
ἀπέστειλα. Aor act ind 1st sg ἀποστέλλω.
ὑμᾶς. Accusative direct object of ἀπέστειλα.
θερίζειν. Pres act inf θερίζω (purpose).
ὅ. The relative pronoun introduces a headless relative clause that, in its entirety (ὃ οὐχ ὑμεῖς κεκοπιάκατε), serves as the direct object of θερίζειν. Within its clause, ὅ is the accusative of respect (lit. "with respect to which").
οὐχ. Negative particle normally used with indicative verbs.
ὑμεῖς. Nominative subject of κεκοπιάκατε. Fronted for emphasis.
κεκοπιάκατε. Prf act ind 2nd pl κοπιάω. Both occurrences of κοπιάω in this verse are in the perfect tense, highlighting their prominence. Fanning describes the past action presumed by this perfect as "unbounded" because it "has no natural end-point" (119). Yet, although the end result is less obvious than with other verbs, it "may lie in the realm of *responsibility* on the part of the subject for having done the action" (148).
ἄλλοι. Nominative subject of κεκοπιάκασιν. Fronted for emphasis.
κεκοπιάκασιν. Prf act ind 3rd pl κοπιάω.
καὶ. Coordinating conjunction.
ὑμεῖς. Nominative subject of εἰσεληλύθατε. The second-person plural personal pronoun is contrastive, distinguishing Jesus' disciples ("you") from "others who have labored."
εἰς τὸν κόπον. Locative.
αὐτῶν. Subjective genitive qualifying κόπον.

εἰσεληλύθατε. Prf act ind 2nd pl εἰσέρχομαι. The stative aspect of the perfect tense marks this verb for prominence.

John 4:39-42

³⁹Many of the Samaritans from that town believed in him because of the word of the woman when she testified, "He told me all things that I did." ⁴⁰So when the Samaritans came to him, they began asking him to stay with them. And he stayed there two days. ⁴¹And many more believed because of his word. ⁴²They said to the woman, "No longer do we believe because of your talk, for we ourselves have heard [him], and we know that this one is truly the Savior of the world."

4:39 Ἐκ δὲ τῆς πόλεως ἐκείνης πολλοὶ ἐπίστευσαν εἰς αὐτὸν τῶν Σαμαριτῶν διὰ τὸν λόγον τῆς γυναικὸς μαρτυρούσης ὅτι εἶπέν μοι πάντα ἃ ἐποίησα.

Ἐκ ... τῆς πόλεως ἐκείνης. Source. Fronted as a spatial frame.

δὲ. Marker of narrative development.

πολλοὶ. Nominative subject of ἐπίστευσαν. Fronted for emphasis.

ἐπίστευσαν. Aor act ind 3rd pl πιστεύω.

εἰς αὐτὸν. Goal of actions or feelings directed toward someone (BDAG, 290.4.c.β). For πιστεύειν εἰς + accusative ("trust or believe in someone"), see 1:12 on εἰς τὸ ὄνομα.

τῶν Σαμαριτῶν. Partitive genitive qualifying πολλοί.

διὰ τὸν λόγον. Causal.

τῆς γυναικὸς. Subjective genitive qualifying λόγον.

μαρτυρούσης. Pres act ptc fem gen sg μαρτυρέω (temporal). The participle is not attributive, as some translations presume (ASV; KJV; NET; LEB), because in such a case it should have been articular like τῆς γυναικὸς (Wallace 1996, 241 n. 64; *pace* Harris 2015, 98, who suggests that the participle may be substantival "with τῆς understood").

ὅτι. ὅτι-*recitativum* that introduces the clausal complement (direct discourse) of μαρτυρούσης.

εἶπέν. Aor act ind 3rd sg λέγω. εἶπέν, which has a circumflex accent on the penult, acquired an additional accent, the acute, on the ultima from the enclitic μοι (Smyth §183; Carson 1985, 48).

μοι. Dative indirect discourse of εἶπέν.

πάντα. Accusative direct object of εἶπέν.

ἃ. Accusative direct object of ἐποίησα. The antecedent of the relative pronoun is πάντα.

ἐποίησα. Aor act ind 1st sg ποιέω.

4:40 ὡς οὖν ἦλθον πρὸς αὐτὸν οἱ Σαμαρῖται, ἠρώτων αὐτὸν μεῖναι παρ' αὐτοῖς· καὶ ἔμεινεν ἐκεῖ δύο ἡμέρας.

ὡς. Temporal conjunction (BDAG, 1105.8.a; BDF §455.2), introducing a clause that is fronted as a temporal frame.

οὖν. Postpositive inferential conjunction and/or transitional particle (see 1:22 and 11:6). Poythress argues that οὖν is "the unmarked way of continuing the narrative whenever there is a shift to a new agent" (328), but since οὖν can be used in contexts in which there is no change of agent, as here, it is probably more accurate to say with Buth that "a very high frequency of sentences with οὖν have a different subject from the previous sentence" (1992, 150).

ἦλθον. Aor act ind 3rd pl ἔρχομαι.

πρὸς αὐτόν. Locative (motion toward).

οἱ Σαμαρῖται. Nominative subject of ἦλθον.

ἠρώτων. Impf act ind 3rd pl ἐρωτάω. On the function of the imperfect in the FG, see 1:39 on ἦν.

αὐτόν. Accusative direct object of ἠρώτων.

μεῖναι. Aor act inf μένω (indirect discourse).

παρ' αὐτοῖς. Association.

καί. Coordinating conjunction.

ἔμεινεν. Aor act ind 3rd sg μένω.

ἐκεῖ. Adverb of place.

δύο ἡμέρας. Accusative indicating extent of time.

4:41 καὶ πολλῷ πλείους ἐπίστευσαν διὰ τὸν λόγον αὐτοῦ,

καί. Coordinating conjunction.

πολλῷ. Dative of measure. It precedes the comparative adjective πλείους and indicates "the extent to which the comparison is true" (Wallace 1996, 166–67): lit. "more by much" = "many more."

πλείους. Nominative subject of ἐπίστευσαν. πλείους is a contracted form of πλείονες, a nom pl comparative of πολύς.

ἐπίστευσαν. Aor act ind 3rd pl πιστεύω.

διὰ τὸν λόγον. Causal (see 4:39)

αὐτοῦ. Subjective genitive qualifying λόγον.

4:42 τῇ τε γυναικὶ ἔλεγον ὅτι οὐκέτι διὰ τὴν σὴν λαλιὰν πιστεύομεν, αὐτοὶ γὰρ ἀκηκόαμεν καὶ οἴδαμεν ὅτι οὗτός ἐστιν ἀληθῶς ὁ σωτὴρ τοῦ κόσμου.

τῇ ... γυναικὶ. Dative indirect object of ἔλεγον. Fronted as a topical frame.

τε. Enclitic coordinating particle.

ἔλεγον. Impf act ind 3rd pl λέγω. The imperfective aspect of the verb form calls attention "not on the fact that this was or was not said (aorist) but on the exposition on *what* was said" (Zerwick §272). On the function of the imperfect in the FG, see 1:39 on ἦν.

ὅτι. ὅτι-*recitativum* that introduces the clausal complement (direct discourse) of ἔλεγον.

οὐκέτι. Negative adverb of time ("no longer, no further").

διὰ τὴν σὴν λαλιὰν. Causal. The possessive adjective σὴν stands in the first attributive position (see 2:10 on τὸν καλὸν οἶνον).

πιστεύομεν. Pres act ind 1st pl πιστεύω.

αὐτοὶ. Intensive pronoun that reinforces the implied subject of ἀκηκόαμεν ("we ourselves"). Fronted for emphasis.

γὰρ. Postpositive conjunction that introduces and explanation for the previous clause.

ἀκηκόαμεν. Prf act ind 1st pl ἀκούω. The stative aspect of the perfect tense gives prominence to the state of the Samaritans, highlighting the contrast between firsthand knowledge and someone else's testimony.

καὶ. Coordinating conjunction.

οἴδαμεν. Prf act ind 1st pl οἶδα (see 1:26 on οἴδατε).

ὅτι. Introduces the clausal complement (indirect discourse) of οἴδαμεν.

οὗτός. Nominative subject of ἐστιν. Fronted as a topical frame. The anaphoric demonstrative refers to Jesus. οὗτός, which has a circumflex accent on the penult, acquired an additional accent, the acute, on the ultima from the enclitic ἐστιν (Smyth §183; Carson 1985, 48).

ἐστιν. Pres act ind 3rd sg εἰμί.

ἀληθῶς. Adverb ("truly, really").

ὁ σωτὴρ. Nominative subject of ἐστιν.

τοῦ κόσμου. Objective genitive qualifying σωτὴρ. On the portrayal of the world in the FG, see 1:10 on ἐν τῷ κόσμῳ.

John 4:43-45

[43]After the two days, he departed from there to Galilee. [44]For Jesus himself testified that a prophet has no honor in his own country. [45]So when

he came to Galilee, the Galileans welcomed him, because they had seen all the things that he did in Jerusalem at the festival, for they themselves had also gone to the festival.

4:43 Μετὰ δὲ τὰς δύο ἡμέρας ἐξῆλθεν ἐκεῖθεν εἰς τὴν Γαλιλαίαν·

Μετὰ . . . τὰς δύο ἡμέρας. Temporal. Fronted as a temporal frame. The article is anaphoric, referring to δύο ἡμέρας in 4:40.
δὲ. Marker of narrative development.
ἐξῆλθεν. Aor act ind 3rd sg ἐξέρχομαι.
ἐκεῖθεν. Adverb of place ("from there").
εἰς τὴν Γαλιλαίαν. Locative.

4:44 αὐτὸς γὰρ Ἰησοῦς ἐμαρτύρησεν ὅτι προφήτης ἐν τῇ ἰδίᾳ πατρίδι τιμὴν οὐκ ἔχει.

αὐτὸς . . . Ἰησοῦς. Nominative subject of ἐμαρτύρησεν. αὐτὸς, standing in the predicate position to Ἰησοῦς, functions as an intensive pronoun ("Jesus himself"), "setting an item off fr[om] everything else through emphasis and contrast" (BDAG, 152.1). Fronted as a topical frame.
γὰρ. Postpositive conjunction that introduces an explanation of the previous verse.
ἐμαρτύρησεν. Aor act ind 3rd sg μαρτυρέω.
ὅτι. Introduces the clausal complement (indirect discourse) of ἐμαρτύρησεν.
προφήτης. Nominative subject of ἔχει. Fronted as a topical frame.
ἐν τῇ ἰδίᾳ πατρίδι. Locative. The adjective ἰδίᾳ ("one's own") stands in the first attributive position (see 2:10 on τὸν καλὸν οἶνον).
τιμὴν. Accusative direct object of ἔχει.
οὐκ. Negative particle normally used with indicative verbs.
ἔχει. Pres act ind 3rd sg ἔχω.

4:45 ὅτε οὖν ἦλθεν εἰς τὴν Γαλιλαίαν, ἐδέξαντο αὐτὸν οἱ Γαλιλαῖοι πάντα ἑωρακότες ὅσα ἐποίησεν ἐν Ἱεροσολύμοις ἐν τῇ ἑορτῇ, καὶ αὐτοὶ γὰρ ἦλθον εἰς τὴν ἑορτήν.

ὅτε. Introduces a temporal clause, which is fronted as a temporal frame.
οὖν. Postpositive inferential conjunction and/or transitional particle (see 1:22 and 11:6).
ἦλθεν. Aor act ind 3rd sg ἔρχομαι.
εἰς τὴν Γαλιλαίαν. Locative.

ἐδέξαντο. Aor mid ind 3rd pl δέχομαι.
αὐτόν. Accusative direct object of ἐδέξαντο.
οἱ Γαλιλαῖοι. Nominative subject of ἐδέξαντο.
πάντα. Accusative direct object of ἑωρακότες. Fronted for emphasis.
ἑωρακότες. Prf act ptc masc nom pl ὁράω (causal). On participles that follow the main verb, see βαπτίζων in 1:31.
ὅσα. Accusative direct object of ἐποίησεν. The antecedent of the correlative pronoun ("as many as") is πάντα. πάντα ὅσα = "all things that" (BDAG, 729.2).
ἐποίησεν. Aor act ind 3rd sg ποιέω.
ἐν Ἱεροσολύμοις. Locative.
ἐν τῇ ἑορτῇ. Temporal ("during the festival") or locative ("among the assembled multitude at the festival" [cf. LSJ, 601]); see 2:23.
καί. Adverbial use (adjunctive).
αὐτοί. Intensive pronoun that reinforces the implied subject of ἦλθον ("they themselves"). Fronted for emphasis.
γάρ. Postpositive conjunction that introduces a clause that explains how the Galileans knew about the mighty deeds that Jesus performed in Jerusalem.
ἦλθον. Aor act ind 3rd pl ἔρχομαι.
εἰς τὴν ἑορτήν. Locative.

John 4:46-54

⁴⁶Then he came again to Cana in Galilee, where he had made the water wine. And there was a certain royal official, whose son was sick in Capernaum. ⁴⁷When he heard that Jesus had come from Judea to Galilee, he went to him and asked that he come down and heal his son, for he was about to die. ⁴⁸Then Jesus said to him, "Unless you [people] see signs and wonders, you will never believe." ⁴⁹The royal official said to him, "Sir, come down before my child dies." ⁵⁰Jesus said to him, "Go, your son is going to live." The man believed the word that Jesus said to him and started on his way. ⁵¹Now while he was going down, his slaves met him, saying that his child was alive. ⁵²So he inquired from them the hour at which he began to get better. Then they said to him, "Yesterday at the seventh hour the fever left him." ⁵³Then the father knew that it was that hour at which Jesus said to him, "Your son is going to live," and he himself believed along with his whole household. ⁵⁴Jesus again did this as the second sign when he came from Judea to Galilee.

4:46 Ἦλθεν οὖν πάλιν εἰς τὴν Κανὰ τῆς Γαλιλαίας, ὅπου ἐποίησεν τὸ ὕδωρ οἶνον. καὶ ἦν τις βασιλικὸς οὗ ὁ υἱὸς ἠσθένει ἐν Καφαρναούμ.

Ἦλθεν. Aor act ind 3rd sg ἔρχομαι.

οὖν. Postpositive inferential conjunction and/or transitional particle (see 1:22 and 11:6).

πάλιν. Adverb "pert[aining] to return to a position or state" (BDAG, 752.1).

εἰς τὴν Κανὰ. Locative.

τῆς Γαλιλαίας. Partitive genitive qualifying Κανὰ (see 2:1).

ὅπου. Particle denoting place.

ἐποίησεν. Aor act ind 3rd sg ποιέω.

τὸ ὕδωρ. Accusative direct object of ἐποίησεν in a double accusative object-complement construction.

οἶνον. Accusative complement to τὸ ὕδωρ in a double accusative object-complement construction.

καὶ. Coordinating conjunction.

ἦν. Impf act ind 3rd sg εἰμί. The use of ἦν is a common way in the FG to introduce a new character in the main narrative (see 3:1; 5:5; 11:1; cf. LXX Exod 2:1; 1 Sam 1:1; Job 1:1; Luke 14:2; Acts 9:10, 36; 16:1). On the function of the imperfect in the FG, see 1:39 on ἦν.

τις βασιλικὸς. Nominative subject of ἦν. The adjective βασιλικός ("royal") functions as a noun denoting a "royal official, official of a king" (LN 37.84). The indefinite pronoun τις is used adjectivally.

οὗ. Genitive of relationship qualifying υἱὸς.

ὁ υἱὸς. Nominative subject of ἠσθένει. Fronted as a topical frame.

ἠσθένει. Impf act ind 3rd sg ἀσθενέω. On the function of the imperfect in the FG, see 1:39 on ἦν.

ἐν Καφαρναούμ. Locative.

4:47 οὗτος ἀκούσας ὅτι Ἰησοῦς ἥκει ἐκ τῆς Ἰουδαίας εἰς τὴν Γαλιλαίαν ἀπῆλθεν πρὸς αὐτὸν καὶ ἠρώτα ἵνα καταβῇ καὶ ἰάσηται αὐτοῦ τὸν υἱόν, ἤμελλεν γὰρ ἀποθνῄσκειν.

οὗτος. Nominative subject of ἀπῆλθεν. The demonstrative pronoun refers to τις βασιλικὸς from the previous verse, acting as a third-person personal pronoun with a simple anaphoric force (Wallace 1996, 328–29). This verse is connected to the previous one by asyndeton.

ἀκούσας. Aor act ptc masc nom sg ἀκούω (temporal or causal). On participles that precede the main verb, see ἐμβλέψας in 1:36.

ὅτι. Introduces the clausal complement (indirect discourse) of ἀκούσας.

Ἰησοῦς. Nominative subject of ἥκει.

ἥκει. Pres act ind 3rd sg ἥκω. The present tense is retained from the direct discourse (see 1:39 on μένει).

ἐκ τῆς Ἰουδαίας. Separation.

εἰς τὴν Γαλιλαίαν. Locative.

ἀπῆλθεν. Aor act ind 3rd sg ἀπέρχομαι.

πρὸς αὐτόν. Locative (motion toward).

καί. Coordinating conjunction.

ἠρώτα. Impf act ind 3rd sg ἐρωτάω. The use of the imperfect tense stands out in the context dominated by the aorist verb forms. Its imperfective aspect conveys an action in progress, without any indication when it started (e.g., "started begging him") or whether it was repeated (e.g., "kept urging him") as is usually assumed in traditional commentaries (Harris 2015, 101). On the function of the imperfect in the FG, see 1:39 on ἦν.

ἵνα. Introduces a direct object clause of ἠρώτα. This use is also known as a "content ἵνα clause" because it gives the content to ἠρώτα (Wallace 1996, 475).

καταβῇ. Aor act subj 3rd sg καταβαίνω. Subjunctive with ἵνα. In this context, καταβαίνω refers to going down from Cana to Capernaum.

καί. Coordinating conjunction.

ἰάσηται. Aor mid subj 3rd sg ἰάομαι. Subjunctive with ἵνα.

αὐτοῦ. Genitive of relationship qualifying υἱόν. The preposed pronoun is thematically salient (Levinsohn 2000, 64).

τὸν υἱόν. Accusative direct object of ἰάσηται.

ἤμελλεν. Impf act ind 3rd sg μέλλω. The augment in the imperfect verb forms of μέλλω vacillates between ἠ- and ἐ- (BDF §66.3).

γάρ. Postpositive conjunction that introduces an explanation of the official's request.

ἀποθνῄσκειν. Pres act inf ἀποθνῄσκω (complementary).

4:48 εἶπεν οὖν ὁ Ἰησοῦς πρὸς αὐτόν· ἐὰν μὴ σημεῖα καὶ τέρατα ἴδητε, οὐ μὴ πιστεύσητε.

εἶπεν. Aor act ind 3rd sg λέγω.

οὖν. Postpositive inferential conjunction and/or transitional particle (see 1:22 and 11:6).

ὁ Ἰησοῦς. Nominative subject of εἶπεν.

πρὸς αὐτόν. Locative (motion toward). The PP functions like an indirect object of εἶπεν.

ἐάν. Introduces the protasis of a third-class condition. The punctuation in NA[28]/UBS[5] and SBLGNT, followed by most English translations, understands this conditional clause as a statement, but it could also be regarded as a question (cf. REB; NLT).

μὴ. Negative particle normally used with non-indicative verbs. ἐὰν μή can be translated "unless."

σημεῖα καὶ τέρατα. Accusative direct object of ἴδητε. Fronted for emphasis. The use of the term σημεῖα for Jesus' miracles is one of the distinctive features of the FG (see 2:11, 23; 3:2; 4:54; 6:2, 14, 26; 7:31; 9:16; 11:47; 12:18, 37; 20:30; cf. Barrett, 75–78; Keener, 1:272–79; Thompson, 65–68).

ἴδητε. Aor act subj 2nd pl ὁράω. Subjunctive with ἐάν. The second plural form of this and the next verb indicates that the Johannine Jesus is no longer addressing the royal official but a wider audience.

οὐ μὴ. Emphatic negation, which is usually followed by the aorist subjunctive. It marks the beginning of the apodosis of a third-class condition.

πιστεύσητε. Aor act subj 2nd pl πιστεύω. Used with οὐ μὴ to express emphatic negation. The verb stands in final, emphatic position. For the use of the second plural verb form, see ἴδητε above.

4:49 λέγει πρὸς αὐτὸν ὁ βασιλικός· κύριε, κατάβηθι πρὶν ἀποθανεῖν τὸ παιδίον μου.

λέγει. Pres act ind 3rd sg λέγω. The historical present (see 4:7). This verse is connected to the previous one by asyndeton.

πρὸς αὐτὸν. Locative (motion toward). The PP functions like an indirect object of λέγει.

ὁ βασιλικός. Nominative subject of λέγει. The article is anaphoric, referring to τις βασιλικὸς introduced in 4:46.

κύριε. Vocative of direct address.

κατάβηθι. Aor act impv 2nd sg καταβαίνω.

πρὶν. Subordinating conjunction ("before").

ἀποθανεῖν. Aor act inf ἀποθνῄσκω. Used with πρὶν to denote subsequent time.

τὸ παιδίον. Accusative subject of the infinitive ἀποθανεῖν. The diminutive παιδίον denotes a very young child, "normally below the age of puberty" (BDAG, 749.1).

μου. Genitive of relationship qualifying παιδίον.

4:50 λέγει αὐτῷ ὁ Ἰησοῦς· πορεύου, ὁ υἱός σου ζῇ. Ἐπίστευσεν ὁ ἄνθρωπος τῷ λόγῳ ὃν εἶπεν αὐτῷ ὁ Ἰησοῦς καὶ ἐπορεύετο.

λέγει. Pres act ind 3rd sg λέγω. The historical present (see 4:7). This verse is connected to the previous one by asyndeton.

αὐτῷ. Dative indirect object of λέγει.

ὁ Ἰησοῦς. Nominative subject of λέγει.

πορεύου. Pres mid impv 2nd sg πορεύομαι. The imperfective aspect of the present imperative functions as a semantic marker, but its significance should not be pressed too much because in the NT the imperatives of πορεύομαι regularly occur in the present tense (twenty-three times).

ὁ υἱός. Nominative subject of ζῇ.

σου. Genitive of relationship qualifying υἱός.

ζῇ. Pres act ind 3rd sg ζάω. The present tense is used here for the action that is carrying over into the future.

Ἐπίστευσεν. Aor act ind 3rd sg πιστεύω.

ὁ ἄνθρωπος. Nominative subject of Ἐπίστευσεν. The article is anaphoric, referring to ὁ βασιλικός in the previous verse.

τῷ λόγῳ. Dative direct object of Ἐπίστευσεν. The dative conveys the thing to which someone gives credence (BDAG, 816.1.a.δ).

ὅν. Accusative direct object of εἶπεν.

εἶπεν. Aor act ind 3rd sg λέγω.

αὐτῷ. Dative indirect object of εἶπεν.

ὁ Ἰησοῦς. Nominative subject of εἶπεν.

καὶ. Coordinating conjunction.

ἐπορεύετο. Impf mid ind 3rd sg πορεύομαι. The imperfective aspect, which depicts the official's return home as a process, is well suited here because, as the next verse indicates, his journey back was interrupted by the news of his son's recovery.

4:51 ἤδη δὲ αὐτοῦ καταβαίνοντος οἱ δοῦλοι αὐτοῦ ὑπήντησαν αὐτῷ λέγοντες ὅτι ὁ παῖς αὐτοῦ ζῇ.

ἤδη. Temporal adverb ("already, now").

δὲ. Marker of narrative development.

αὐτοῦ. Genitive subject of καταβαίνοντος.

καταβαίνοντος. Pres act ptc masc gen sg καταβαίνω (genitive absolute, temporal). As is fairly common in Hellenistic Greek, this genitive absolute is not truly absolute by the standards of classical usage (which is "limited to the sentences where the noun or pronoun to which the participle refers does not appear either as subject or in any other capacity" [BDF §423]), because the genitive subject of the participle reappears first as the possessive genitive that modifies the nominative subject of the main clause and then as the dative complement of the main verb (MHT, 3:322). As Harris (2015, 102) shows, the genitive absolute clause could have been easily incorporated into the main sentence: οἱ δοῦλοι αὐτοῦ ὑπήντησαν αὐτῷ ἤδη καταβαινόντῳ ("his slaves met him while he was still going down").

οἱ δοῦλοι. Nominative subject of ὑπήντησαν.

αὐτοῦ. Possessive genitive qualifying δοῦλοι.

ὑπήντησαν. Aor act ind 3rd pl ὑπαντάω. ὑπαντάω ("to go to meet someone") takes its object in dative.

αὐτῷ. Dative complement of ὑπήντησαν.

λέγοντες. Pres act ptc masc nom pl λέγω (manner). On participles that follow the main verb, see βαπτίζων in 1:31.

ὅτι. Introduces the clausal complement (indirect discourse) of λέγοντες.

ὁ παῖς. Nominative subject of ζῇ. The variant υἱός ($\mathfrak{P}^{66c}$ D K L N 33 579 et al.) is probably the result of scribal assimilation of παῖς, which in the FG does not appear anywhere else, to the term υἱός, which has been used throughout this account (vv. 46, 47, 50, 53; cf. Metzger, 178).

αὐτοῦ. Genitive of relationship qualifying παῖς. Many manuscripts have σου instead of αὐτοῦ, either in the combination παῖς σου (Γ Δ Θ Ψ f^1 565 700 1424 𝔐 et al.) or υἱός σου ($\mathfrak{P}^{66c}$ D K L N 33 579 et al.), because the copyists interpreted the ὅτι clause as the actual report of the servants (Metzger, 178).

ζῇ. Pres act ind 3rd sg ζάω. The verb stands in final, emphatic position. The present tense is retained from the direct discourse (see 1:39 on μένει).

4:52 ἐπύθετο οὖν τὴν ὥραν παρ' αὐτῶν ἐν ᾗ κομψότερον ἔσχεν· εἶπαν οὖν αὐτῷ ὅτι ἐχθὲς ὥραν ἑβδόμην ἀφῆκεν αὐτὸν ὁ πυρετός.

ἐπύθετο. Aor mid ind 3rd sg πυνθάνομαι. The verb means to "inquire, ask" τὶ παρά τινος.

οὖν. Postpositive inferential conjunction and/or transitional particle (see 1:22 and 11:6).

τὴν ὥραν. Accusative direct object of ἐπύθετο.

παρ' αὐτῶν. Source of information (BDAG, 756.A.3.a.γ).

ἐν ᾗ. Temporal.

κομψότερον. Adverb of the comparative of κομψός ("fine"), meaning "better." κομψότερον ἔχειν (lit. "to have better") means to "feel better" (BDAG, 422.10.b) or to "begin to improve" (BDAG, 558). Fronted for emphasis.

ἔσχεν. Aor act ind 3rd sg ἔχω.

εἶπαν. Aor act ind 3rd pl λέγω.

οὖν. Postpositive inferential conjunction and/or transitional particle (see 1:22 and 11:6).

αὐτῷ. Dative indirect object of εἶπαν.

ὅτι. ὅτι-*recitativum* that introduces the clausal complement (direct discourse) of εἶπαν.

ἐχθὲς. Adverb of time ("yesterday").

ὥραν ἑβδόμην. Accusative indicating the point in time ("the seventh hour" = 1 p.m. based on a customary reckoning of the twelve-hour day from sunrise [6 a.m.] to sunset [6 p.m.]). This is an atypical use of the accusative, which usually indicates the extent of time. Fronted for emphasis.

ἀφῆκεν. Aor act ind 3rd sg ἀφίημι.

αὐτὸν. Accusative direct object of ἀφῆκεν.

ὁ πυρετός. Nominative subject of ἀφῆκεν.

4:53 ἔγνω οὖν ὁ πατὴρ ὅτι [ἐν] ἐκείνῃ τῇ ὥρᾳ ἐν ᾗ εἶπεν αὐτῷ ὁ Ἰησοῦς· ὁ υἱός σου ζῇ, καὶ ἐπίστευσεν αὐτὸς καὶ ἡ οἰκία αὐτοῦ ὅλη.

ἔγνω. Aor act ind 3rd sg γινώσκω.

οὖν. Postpositive inferential conjunction and/or transitional particle (see 1:22 and 11:6).

ὁ πατὴρ. Nominative subject of ἔγνω.

ὅτι. Introduces the clausal complement (indirect discourse) of ἔγνω. The ὅτι clause is elliptical, with the verb ἦν implied ("that [it was] in that hour . . ."; cf. MHT, 3:304).

[ἐν] ἐκείνῃ τῇ ὥρᾳ. Temporal. Square brackets indicate that the evidence for ($\mathfrak{P}^{66\ 2}$ ℵ A D K L N W^s Γ Δ Θ Ψ 078 f^{13} 33 565 1241 1424 𝔐 et al.) and against ($\mathfrak{P}^{75}$ ℵ* B C T 892 et al.) the inclusion of the preposition ἐν is evenly balanced.

ἐν ᾗ. Temporal. The antecedent of the relative pronoun is τῇ ὥρᾳ.

εἶπεν. Aor act ind 3rd sg λέγω.

αὐτῷ. Dative indirect object of εἶπεν.

ὁ Ἰησοῦς. Nominative subject of εἶπεν.

ὁ υἱός. Nominative subject of ζῇ.

σου. Genitive of relationship qualifying υἱός.

ζῇ. Pres act ind 3rd sg ζάω.

καὶ. Coordinating conjunction.

ἐπίστευσεν. Aor act ind 3rd sg πιστεύω.

αὐτὸς καὶ ἡ οἰκία . . . ὅλη. Compound nominative subject of ἐπίστευσεν. αὐτὸς functions as an intensive pronoun ("he himself"). When the verb precedes the compound subject, it is in the singular, agreeing with the first (BDF §135). The verb in the singular could also indicate that the author regarded the first-named subject as being more important of the two (Wallace 1996, 401).

αὐτοῦ. Possessive genitive qualifying οἰκία.

4:54 Τοῦτο [δὲ] πάλιν δεύτερον σημεῖον ἐποίησεν ὁ Ἰησοῦς ἐλθὼν ἐκ τῆς Ἰουδαίας εἰς τὴν Γαλιλαίαν.

Τοῦτο. Accusative direct object of ἐποίησεν (see 2:11 on Ταύτην). Wallace (1996, 187, 242 n. 66) rightly criticizes English versions, such as NRSV, ASV, NASB, and NIV, which translate Τοῦτο as if it were the subject of the sentence ("This was the second sign that Jesus did").

[δὲ]. Marker of narrative development. Square brackets indicate that the evidence for ($\mathfrak{P}^{66.75}$ B C* T W^s 078^c f^{13} 1241 pbo bo^{pt} Or) and against (ℵ A C² D K L N Γ Δ Θ Ψ 078*^{vid} f^1 33 565 700 892 1424 𝔐 latt sys a bo^{pt}) the inclusion of this conjunction is evenly balanced.

πάλιν. Adverb "pert[aining] to repetition in the same (or similar) manner" (BDAG, 752.2). This adverb relates Jesus' healing of the royal official's son to the changing of the water to wine that was mentioned at the outset of this pericope: Ἦλθεν οὖν πάλιν εἰς τὴν Κανὰ τῆς Γαλιλαίας, ὅπου ἐποίησεν τὸ ὕδωρ οἶνον (4:46).

δεύτερον σημεῖον. Accusative complement to Τοῦτο in a double accusative object-complement construction. The use of the term σημεῖα for Jesus' miracles is one of the distinctive features of the FG (see 2:11, 23; 3:2; 4:48; 6:2, 14, 26; 7:31; 9:16; 11:47; 12:18, 37; 20:30; cf. Barrett, 75–78; Keener, 1:272–79; Thompson, 65–68).

ἐποίησεν. Aor act ind 3rd sg ποιέω.

ὁ Ἰησοῦς. Nominative subject of ἐποίησεν.

ἐλθών. Aor act ptc masc nom sg ἔρχομαι (temporal). On participles that follow the main verb, see βαπτίζων in 1:31.

ἐκ τῆς Ἰουδαίας. Separation.

εἰς τὴν Γαλιλαίαν. Locative.

John 5:1-18

[1]After these things, there was a festival of the Jews, and Jesus went up to Jerusalem. [2]Now there is in Jerusalem, near the Sheep Gate, a pool called in Aramaic Bethzatha, which has five colonnades. [3]In these were lying a large number of those who were sick—blind, lame, paralyzed. [5]Now a certain man was there who had been thirty-eight years in his sickness. [6]When Jesus saw him lying there and knew that he had already

been in that condition for a long time, he said to him, "Do you want to become well?" ⁷The sick man answered him, "Sir, I have nobody that, when the water is stirred up, could put me into the pool. While I am going [there], another goes down before me." ⁸Jesus said to him, "Get up, take up your mat, and walk!" ⁹And at once the man became well, and he took up his mat and began walking. Now it was a Sabbath on that day. ¹⁰Therefore the Jews were saying to the man who had been cured, "It is the Sabbath, and it is not permitted for you to carry your mat." ¹¹But he answered them, "The one who made me well—that one said to me, 'Take up your mat and walk!'" ¹²They asked him, "Who is the man who said to you, 'Take it up and walk'?" ¹³But the one who was healed did not know who it was, for Jesus had withdrawn quietly while a crowd was in the place. ¹⁴After these things, Jesus found him in the temple and said to him, "Look, you have become well! Sin no more, lest something worse happen to you." ¹⁵The man went away and announced to the Jews that it was Jesus who had made him well. ¹⁶And on account of this the Jews began to persecute Jesus, because he was doing these things on the Sabbath. ¹⁷But Jesus answered them, "My Father is working until now, and I too am working." ¹⁸So on account of this the Jews were seeking even more to kill him, because he not only was breaking the Sabbath but also was calling God his own Father, thus making himself equal to God.

5:1 Μετὰ ταῦτα ἦν ἑορτὴ τῶν Ἰουδαίων καὶ ἀνέβη Ἰησοῦς εἰς Ἱεροσόλυμα.

Μετὰ ταῦτα. Temporal (see 3:22). Fronted as a temporal frame. This verse is connected to the previous one by asyndeton.

ἦν. Impf act ind 3rd sg εἰμί. On the function of the imperfect in the FG, see 1:39 on ἦν.

ἑορτὴ. Nominative subject of ἦν. The anarthrous noun has the strongest external support, but some scribes (ℵ C L Δ Ψ f^1 33 892 1424 *pm*) tried to identify the festival, perhaps with the Passover, by adding the article ἡ (Metzger, 178).

τῶν Ἰουδαίων. Subjective genitive qualifying ἑορτὴ ("a festival that the Jews celebrate") or attributive genitive ("Jewish festival").

καὶ. Coordinating conjunction.

ἀνέβη. Aor act ind 3rd sg ἀναβαίνω. On the meaning of the verb, see 2:13.

Ἰησοῦς. Nominative subject of ἀνέβη.

εἰς Ἱεροσόλυμα. Locative.

5:2 Ἔστιν δὲ ἐν τοῖς Ἱεροσολύμοις ἐπὶ τῇ προβατικῇ κολυμβήθρα ἡ ἐπιλεγομένη Ἑβραϊστὶ Βηθζαθὰ πέντε στοὰς ἔχουσα.

Ἔστιν. Pres act ind 3rd sg εἰμί. Schnackenburg aptly remarks that "[i]t is hardly possible to conclude from the use of the present-tense ἔστιν that the structure was still in existence at the time that the story was written since it may be a present historic" (2:460 n. 9; *pace* Wallace 1990).

δὲ. Marker of narrative development.

ἐν τοῖς Ἱεροσολύμοις. Locative.

ἐπὶ τῇ προβατικῇ. Locative. The adjective προβατικός ("pertaining to sheep") is here used in an elliptical expression for ἡ προβατικὴ πύλη (BDAG, 865; BDF §241.6; LN 4.23).

κολυμβήθρα. Nominative subject of Ἔστιν. κολυμβήθρα is "a relatively large construction for impounding water—'pool' (primarily used for bathing)" (LN 7.58).

ἡ ἐπιλεγομένη. Pres pass ptc fem nom sg ἐπιλέγω (attributive). The participle modifies κολυμβήθρα, standing in the third attributive position (see 1:18 on ὁ ὤν). Robertson notes that in such constructions "the substantive is indefinite and general, while the attribute makes a particular application" (777).

Ἑβραϊστὶ. Adverb ("in Hebrew/Aramaic" [BDAG, 270]).

Βηθζαθὰ. Nominative complement to κολυμβήθρα in a double nominative subject-complement construction (see 1:41 on χριστός). The name of the pool is transmitted in three variants: (1) Βηθεσδά (A C K N Γ Δ Θ $f^{1.13}$ 565 700 𝔐 et al.), (2) Βηθσαϊδά ($\mathfrak{P}^{75}$ B T W^s et al.), and (3) Βηθζαθά (א [L] 33 it). Βηθσαϊδά is probably a scribal assimilation to the Galilean town mention in 1:44. UBS[5] and NT[28] adopted Βηθζαθά as "the least unsatisfactory reading" (Metzger, 178), while SBLGNT preferred Βηθεσδά because of its wide textual support.

πέντε στοὰς. Accusative direct object of ἔχουσα. στοά denotes "a covered colonnade, open normally on one side, where people could stand, sit, or walk, protected from the weather and the heat of the sun" (LN 7.40).

ἔχουσα. Pres act ptc fem nom sg ἔχω (attributive). The participle modifies κολυμβήθρα, standing in the fourth attributive position (see 1:6 on ἀπεσταλμένος).

5:3 ἐν ταύταις κατέκειτο πλῆθος τῶν ἀσθενούντων, τυφλῶν, χωλῶν, ξηρῶν.

ἐν ταύταις. Locative. Fronted as a spatial frame. This verse is connected to the previous one by asyndeton.
κατέκειτο. Impf mid ind 3rd sg κατάκειμαι.
πλῆθος. Nominative subject of κατέκειτο.
τῶν ἀσθενούντων. Pres act ptc masc gen pl ἀσθενέω (substantival). Partitive genitive.
τυφλῶν, χωλῶν, ξηρῶν. Genitives in apposition to ἀσθενούντων. After ξηρῶν, many witnesses have ἐκδεχομένων τὴν τοῦ ὕδατος κίνησιν (A^c C^3 D K W^s Γ Δ Θ Ψ 078 $f^{1.13}$ 33 565 579 700 𝔐 lat sy^{p.h} et al.). Since, however, this reading does not occur in the oldest and most reliable manuscripts, it is most likely a scribal emendation seeking to clarify v. 7 (Metzger, 179).

5:4 [ἄγγελος γὰρ κατὰ καιρὸν κατέβαινεν ἐν τῇ κολυμβήθρᾳ, καὶ ἐτάρασσεν τὸ ὕδωρ· ὁ οὖν πρῶτος ἐμβὰς μετὰ τὴν ταραχὴν τοῦ ὕδατος, ὑγιὴς ἐγίνετο, ᾧ δήποτε κατείχετο νοσήματι.]

This verse is not printed in NA²⁸/UBS⁵ and SBLGNT because it is generally regarded as an early scribal gloss that became part of the textual tradition under the influence of v. 7. There are four main reasons for this verdict: (1) the verse is absent from the earliest and most reliable textual witnesses, such as 𝔓⁶⁶ and 𝔓⁷⁵, (2) many scribes have marked it with asterisks or obeli to indicate that it is spurious, (3) it contains many non-Johannine words, and (4) it is transmitted in a wide range of divergent variants (Metzger, 179).

5:5 ἦν δέ τις ἄνθρωπος ἐκεῖ τριάκοντα [καὶ] ὀκτὼ ἔτη ἔχων ἐν τῇ ἀσθενείᾳ αὐτοῦ·

ἦν. Impf act ind 3rd sg εἰμί. The use of ἦν is a common way in the FG to introduce a new character in the main narrative (see 3:1; 4:46; 11:1; cf. LXX Exod 2:1; 1 Sam 1:1; Job 1:1; Luke 14:2; Acts 9:10, 36; 16:1). On the function of the imperfect in the FG, see 1:39 on ἦν.
δέ. Marker of narrative development.
τις ἄνθρωπος. Nominative subject of ἦν.
ἐκεῖ. Predicate adverb of place (see 2:1 on ἐκεῖ).
τριάκοντα [καὶ] ὀκτὼ ἔτη. Accusative indicating extent of time. Fronted for emphasis. Square brackets indicate that the evidence for

(א A C D L T Δ Ψ 078 $f^{1.13}$ 33 565 et al.) and against (B K Γ Θ 892 1424 et al.) the inclusion of καί is evenly balanced.

ἔχων. Pres act ptc masc nom sg ἔχω (attributive). The participle modifies ἄνθρωπος, standing in the fourth attributive position (see 1:6 on ἀπεσταλμένος). When ἔχω is combined with temporal indications of time, as here, it refers to a certain state or condition (BDAG, 422.7.b). Lit. "who had had thirty-eight years in his sickness" = "who had been thirty-eight years in his sickness."

ἐν τῇ ἀσθενείᾳ. State or condition (BDAG, 327.2.b).

αὐτοῦ. Possessive genitive broadly defined qualifying ἀσθενείᾳ ("his illnesses" = "the illnesses from which he suffered").

5:6 τοῦτον ἰδὼν ὁ Ἰησοῦς κατακείμενον καὶ γνοὺς ὅτι πολὺν ἤδη χρόνον ἔχει, λέγει αὐτῷ· θέλεις ὑγιὴς γενέσθαι;

τοῦτον. Accusative direct object of ἰδών. The demonstrative pronoun refers to τις ἄνθρωπος from the previous verse, acting as a third-person personal pronoun with a simple anaphoric force (Wallace 1996, 328–29). This verse is connected to the previous one by asyndeton.

ἰδών. Aor act ptc masc nom sg ὁράω (temporal). On participles that precede the main verb, see ἐμβλέψας in 1:36.

ὁ Ἰησοῦς. Nominative subject of λέγει.

κατακείμενον. Pres mid/pass ptc masc acc sg κατάκειμαι (predicative). The participle functions as the accusative complement to τοῦτον in a double accusative object-complement construction.

καί. Coordinating conjunction.

γνούς. Aor act ptc masc nom sg γινώσκω (temporal or causal). On participles that precede the main verb, see ἐμβλέψας in 1:36.

ὅτι. Introduces the clausal complement (indirect discourse) of γνούς.

πολὺν ... χρόνον. Accusative indicating extent of time. Lit. "that he already had a long time (behind him)" = "that he had already been in that condition for a long time." Fronted for emphasis.

ἤδη. Temporal adverb ("already, now").

ἔχει. Pres act ind 3rd sg ἔχω. The present tense is retained from the direct discourse (see 1:39 on μένει). The imperfective aspect of the verb form portrays the situation of the sick man as still in progress (Fanning, 217).

λέγει. Pres act ind 3rd sg λέγω. The historical present calls attention to Jesus' question that follows (see 1:15 on μαρτυρεῖ).

αὐτῷ. Dative indirect object of λέγει.

θέλεις. Pres act ind 2nd sg θέλω.

ὑγιής. Predicate adjective. Fronted for emphasis.
γενέσθαι. Aor mid inf γίνομαι (complementary).

5:7 ἀπεκρίθη αὐτῷ ὁ ἀσθενῶν· κύριε, ἄνθρωπον οὐκ ἔχω ἵνα ὅταν ταραχθῇ τὸ ὕδωρ βάλῃ με εἰς τὴν κολυμβήθραν· ἐν ᾧ δὲ ἔρχομαι ἐγώ, ἄλλος πρὸ ἐμοῦ καταβαίνει.

ἀπεκρίθη. Aor mid ind 3rd sg ἀποκρίνομαι. On the voice, see "Deponency" in the Series Introduction. This verse is connected to the previous one by asyndeton.
αὐτῷ. Dative indirect object of ἀπεκρίθη.
ὁ ἀσθενῶν. Pres act ptc masc nom sg ἀσθενέω (substantival). Nominative subject of ἀπεκρίθη. The imperfective aspect of the present participle depicts the illness of the man as an ongoing condition.
κύριε. Vocative of direct address.
ἄνθρωπον. Accusative direct object of ἔχω. ἄνθρωπον οὐκ ἔχω stands for οὐδένα ἔχω.
οὐκ. Negative particle normally used with indicative verbs.
ἔχω. Pres act ind 1st sg ἔχω. The verb stands in final, emphatic position.
ἵνα. Introduces an epexegetical clause that explains the clause ἄνθρωπον οὐκ ἔχω. In classical Greek, an epexegetical ἵνα clause is equivalent to an epexegetical infinitive (Wallace 1996, 476; BDF §379).
ὅταν. Introduces an indefinite temporal clause, which is fronted as a temporal frame.
ταραχθῇ. Aor pass subj 3rd sg ταράσσω. Subjunctive with ὅταν. The primary agent of the verb is not expressed.
τὸ ὕδωρ. Nominative subject of ταραχθῇ.
βάλῃ. Aor act subj 3rd sg βάλλω. Subjunctive with ἵνα.
με. Accusative direct object of βάλῃ.
εἰς τὴν κολυμβήθραν. Locative.
ἐν ᾧ. Temporal. ἐν ᾧ is an ellipsis for ἐν ᾧ χρόνῳ (lit. "during which time" = "while").
δέ. Marker of narrative development.
ἔρχομαι. Pres mid ind 1st sg ἔρχομαι.
ἐγώ. Nominative subject of ἔρχομαι. The personal pronoun is emphatic.
ἄλλος. Nominative subject of καταβαίνει.
πρὸ ἐμοῦ. Temporal.
καταβαίνει. Pres act ind 3rd sg καταβαίνω.

5:8 λέγει αὐτῷ ὁ Ἰησοῦς· ἔγειρε ἆρον τὸν κράβαττόν σου καὶ περιπάτει.

λέγει. Pres act ind 3rd sg λέγω. This verse is connected to the previous one by asyndeton.

αὐτῷ. Dative indirect object of λέγει.

ὁ Ἰησοῦς. Nominative subject of λέγει.

ἔγειρε. Pres act impv 2nd sg ἐγείρω. The imperfective aspect of the present imperative functions as a semantic marker, but its significance should not be overstated because in the NT the imperatives of ἐγείρω are regularly in the present tense (eighteen out of twenty).

ἆρον. Aor act impv 2nd sg αἴρω. This imperative is connected to the previous one by asyndeton. See 4:16 for a similar succession of two imperatives. The combination ἔγειρε ἆρον also occurs in Mark 2:11.

τὸν κράβαττόν. Accusative direct object of ἆρον. κράβαττόν, which has an acute accent on the antepenult, acquired an additional accent, the acute, on the ultima from the enclitic σου (Smyth §183; Carson 1985, 48).

σου. Possessive genitive qualifying κράβαττόν.

καὶ. Coordinating conjunction.

περιπάτει. Pres act impv 2nd sg περιπατέω. The present tense of the imperative is marked for prominence. Wallace (1996, 717) uses this imperative as an illustration of the inadequacy of the traditional view, which presumes that the present imperative commands to continue an action that has already begun: "'Take up [aorist ἆρον] your mattress and *continue walking* [present: περιπάτει].' But how could the lame man *continue* walking if he had not done so for thirty-eight years?"

5:9 καὶ εὐθέως ἐγένετο ὑγιὴς ὁ ἄνθρωπος καὶ ἦρεν τὸν κράβαττον αὐτοῦ καὶ περιεπάτει. Ἦν δὲ σάββατον ἐν ἐκείνῃ τῇ ἡμέρᾳ.

καὶ. Coordinating conjunction.

εὐθέως. Temporal adverb ("immediately, at once"). Fronted for emphasis.

ἐγένετο. Aor mid ind 3rd sg γίνομαι.

ὑγιὴς. Predicate adjective.

ὁ ἄνθρωπος. Nominative subject of ἐγένετο.

καὶ. Coordinating conjunction.

ἦρεν. Aor act ind 3rd sg αἴρω.

τὸν κράβαττον. Accusative direct object of ἦρεν.

αὐτοῦ. Possessive genitive qualifying κράβαττον.

καὶ. Coordinating conjunction.

περιεπάτει. Impf act ind 3rd sg περιπατέω. The context indicates that the imperfect marks the beginning of the cured man's walking, which is portrayed as an action in progress.

Ἦν. Impf act ind 3rd sg εἰμί. On the function of the imperfect in the FG, see 1:39 on ἦν.

δὲ. Marker of narrative development.

σάββατον. Nominative subject of Ἦν.

ἐν ἐκείνῃ τῇ ἡμέρᾳ. Temporal.

5:10 ἔλεγον οὖν οἱ Ἰουδαῖοι τῷ τεθεραπευμένῳ· σάββατόν ἐστιν, καὶ οὐκ ἔξεστίν σοι ἆραι τὸν κράβαττόν σου.

ἔλεγον. Impf act ind 3rd pl λέγω. On the function of the imperfect in the FG, see 1:39 on ἦν.

οὖν. While in most instances in the FG it is not easy to distinguish between the inferential and transitional functions of οὖν, the inferential role is more pronounced here because the complaint of the Jewish leaders is presented as the consequence of the previous remark that the healing of the man occurred on the Sabbath.

οἱ Ἰουδαῖοι. Nominative subject of ἔλεγον.

τῷ τεθεραπευμένῳ. Prf pass ptc masc dat sg θεραπεύω (substantival). Dative indirect object of ἔλεγον. The stative aspect of the perfect participle highlights the restoration to health of the man who was cured by Jesus. This descriptive substantive functions as a changed reference to the participant who was in the preceding narrative portrayed as a sick man (see ὁ ἀσθενῶν in v. 7), which has the rhetorical effect of recharacterizing him and highlighting his new condition (Runge 2010, 349–63).

σάββατόν. Nominative subject of ἐστιν. Fronted for emphasis. σάββατόν, which has an acute accent on the antepenult, acquired an additional accent, the acute, on the ultima from the enclitic ἐστιν (Smyth §183; Carson 1985, 48).

ἐστιν. Pres act ind 3rd sg εἰμί.

καὶ. Coordinating conjunction.

οὐκ. Negative particle normally used with indicative verbs.

ἔξεστίν. Pres act ind 3rd sg ἔξεστιν (impersonal). ἔξεστιν means "it is right, is authorized, is permitted, is proper" and can be followed by a dative of person and an infinitive, as here (BDAG, 348.1.b). ἔξεστίν, which has an acute accent on the antepenult, acquired an additional accent, the acute, on the ultima from the enclitic σοι (Smyth §183; Carson 1985, 48).

σοι. Dative complement of ἔξεστίν.

ἆραι. Aor act inf αἴρω (complementary). Alternatively, ἆραι could be understood as the subject of ἔξεστιν, but since ἔξεστιν is an impersonal verb, it is better to regard it as complementary (see 3:7 on γεννηθῆναι).

τὸν κράβαττόν. Accusative direct object of ἆραι. κράβαττόν, which has an acute accent on the antepenult, acquired an additional accent, the acute, on the ultima from the enclitic σου (Smyth §183; Carson 1985, 48).

σου. Possessive genitive qualifying κράβαττόν.

5:11 ὁ δὲ ἀπεκρίθη αὐτοῖς· ὁ ποιήσας με ὑγιῆ ἐκεῖνός μοι εἶπεν· ἆρον τὸν κράβαττόν σου καὶ περιπάτει.

ὁ δὲ. A construction used in narrative literature to indicate the change of the speaker in a dialogue. The nominative article stands in place of a third-person singular personal pronoun and functions as the subject of ἀπεκρίθη.

ἀπεκρίθη. Aor mid ind 3rd sg ἀποκρίνομαι. On the voice, see "Deponency" in the Series Introduction.

αὐτοῖς. Dative indirect object of ἀπεκρίθη.

ὁ ποιήσας. Aor act ptc masc nom sg ποιέω (substantival). Nominative subject of εἶπεν in a left-dislocation, resumed by ἐκεῖνός. On the function of left-dislocations, see 1:33 on ὁ πέμψας.

με. Accusative direct object of ποιήσας in a double accusative object-complement construction.

ὑγιῆ. Accusative complement to με in a double accusative object-complement construction.

ἐκεῖνός. Nominative subject of εἶπεν, resuming ὁ ποιήσας. Fronted for emphasis. The anaphoric demonstrative reinforces what is already made prominent through the left-dislocation of ὁ ποιήσας. ἐκεῖνός, which has a circumflex accent on the penult, acquired an additional accent, the acute, on the ultima from the enclitic μοι (Smyth §183; Carson 1985, 48).

μοι. Dative indirect object of εἶπεν.

εἶπεν. Aor act ind 3rd sg λέγω.

ἆρον. Aor act impv 2nd sg αἴρω.

τὸν κράβαττόν. Accusative direct object of ἆρον. κράβαττόν, which has an acute accent on the antepenult, acquired an additional accent, the acute, on the ultima from the enclitic σου (Smyth §183; Carson 1985, 48).

σου. Possessive genitive qualifying κράβαττόν.

καὶ. Coordinating conjunction.

περιπάτει. Pres act impv 2nd sg περιπατέω.

5:12 ἠρώτησαν αὐτόν· τίς ἐστιν ὁ ἄνθρωπος ὁ εἰπών σοι· ἆρον καὶ περιπάτει;

ἠρώτησαν. Aor act ind 3rd pl ἐρωτάω. This verse is connected to the previous one by asyndeton.

αὐτόν. Accusative direct object of ἠρώτησαν.

τίς. Predicate nominative. Fronted for emphasis. "Interrogatives, by their nature, indicate the unknown component and hence cannot be the subject" (Wallace, 40 n. 12).

ἐστιν. Pres act ind 3rd sg εἰμί.

ὁ ἄνθρωπος. Nominative subject of ἐστιν.

ὁ εἰπών. Aor act ptc masc nom sg λέγω (attributive). The participle modifies ὁ ἄνθρωπος, standing in the second attributive position (see 1:29 on ὁ αἴρων).

σοι. Dative indirect object of εἰπών.

ἆρον. Aor act impv 2nd sg αἴρω. Many witnesses add τὸν κρά(β)ατ(τ)όν σου after ἆρον (A^c C^3 D K N Δ Θ Ψ $f^{1.13}$ 33 565 579 𝔐 latt sy et al.), but this is most likely a later addition to conform the text to the previous verse.

καὶ. Coordinating conjunction.

περιπάτει. Pres act impv 2nd sg περιπατέω.

5:13 ὁ δὲ ἰαθεὶς οὐκ ᾔδει τίς ἐστιν, ὁ γὰρ Ἰησοῦς ἐξένευσεν ὄχλου ὄντος ἐν τῷ τόπῳ.

ὁ ... ἰαθεὶς. Aor pass ptc masc nom sg ἰάομαι (substantival). Nominative subject of ᾔδει. This descriptive substantive functions as another changed reference to the previously sick man (see τῷ τεθεραπευμένῳ in v. 10), which highlights his restoration to health (Runge 2010, 349–63).

δὲ. Marker of narrative development.

οὐκ. Negative particle normally used with indicative verbs.

ᾔδει. Plprf act ind 3rd sg οἶδα. The pluperfect of οἶδα is rendered by the imperfect.

τίς. Predicate nominative. The interrogative pronoun has an identifying function in an indirect question.

ἐστιν. Pres act ind 3rd sg εἰμί. The present tense is retained from the direct question (see 1:39 on μένει).

ὁ ... Ἰησοῦς. Nominative subject of ἐξένευσεν.

γὰρ. Postpositive conjunction that introduces the explanation of the previous clause.

ἐξένευσεν. Aor act ind 3rd sg ἐκνεύω. The verb means "to withdraw quietly, to slip out" (LN 15.60).

ὄχλου. Genitive subject of ὄντος. Alternatively, this could be a genitive of separation ("he withdrew quietly away from a crowd").

ὄντος. Pres act ptc masc gen sg εἰμί (genitive absolute, temporal or causal). If ὄχλου is understood as a genitive of separation, ὄντος is attributive ("away from the crowd which was in that place").

ἐν τῷ τόπῳ. Locative.

5:14 μετὰ ταῦτα εὑρίσκει αὐτὸν ὁ Ἰησοῦς ἐν τῷ ἱερῷ καὶ εἶπεν αὐτῷ· ἴδε ὑγιὴς γέγονας, μηκέτι ἁμάρτανε, ἵνα μὴ χεῖρόν σοί τι γένηται.

μετὰ ταῦτα. Temporal (see 3:22). Fronted as a temporal frame. The demonstrative pronoun is anaphoric, referring to the healing, described in vv. 1-9, and the cured man's conversation with the Jews, described in vv. 10-13. This verse is connected to the previous one by asyndeton.

εὑρίσκει. Pres act ind 3rd sg εὑρίσκω. The historical present gives prominence to the encounter between Jesus and the healed man.

αὐτὸν. Accusative direct object of εὑρίσκει.

ὁ Ἰησοῦς. Nominative subject of εὑρίσκει.

ἐν τῷ ἱερῷ. Locative. Elsewhere in the FG, this PP occurs in 2:14; 7:28; 8:20; 10:23; 11:56; 18:20.

καὶ. Coordinating conjunction.

εἶπεν. Aor act ind 3rd sg λέγω.

αὐτῷ. Dative indirect object of εἶπεν.

ἴδε. An interjection (originally aor act impv 2nd sg ὁράω) that is "used when more than one pers[on] is addressed, and when that which is to be observed is in the nom[inative]" (BDAG, 466).

ὑγιὴς. Predicate adjective. Fronted for emphasis.

γέγονας. Prf act ind 2nd sg γίνομαι. The stative aspect of the perfect tense gives prominence to the new situation—a state of health—of the man.

μηκέτι. Negative adverb that includes temporal component ("no longer, not from now on"). When it is used with the present imperative, as here, it indicates the prohibition of the continuation of an action that is already in progress.

ἁμάρτανε. Pres act impv 2nd sg ἁμαρτάνω.

ἵνα. Introduces a purpose clause.

μὴ. Negative particle normally used with non-indicative verbs. ἵνα μὴ can be translated "lest."

χεῖρόν. Predicate adjective. Fronted for emphasis. χεῖρόν is the comparative from κακός. χεῖρόν, which has a circumflex accent on the penult, acquired an additional accent, the acute, on the ultima from the enclitic σοί (Smyth §183; Carson 1985, 48).

σοί. Dative of disadvantage. Lit. "lest something become worse to your detriment" = "lest something worse happen to you." The enclitic σοί is accented because it is followed by the enclitic τι. "When several enclitics occur in succession, each receives an accent from the following, only the last having no accent" (Smyth §185).

τι. Nominative subject of γένηται. τι functions here as a true indefinite pronoun.

γένηται. Aor mid subj 3rd sg γίνομαι. Subjunctive with ἵνα.

5:15 ἀπῆλθεν ὁ ἄνθρωπος καὶ ἀνήγγειλεν τοῖς Ἰουδαίοις ὅτι Ἰησοῦς ἐστιν ὁ ποιήσας αὐτὸν ὑγιῆ.

ἀπῆλθεν. Aor act ind 3rd sg ἀπέρχομαι. This verse is connected to the previous one by asyndeton.

ὁ ἄνθρωπος. Nominative subject of ἀπῆλθεν.

καὶ. Coordinating conjunction.

ἀνήγγειλεν. Aor act ind 3rd sg ἀναγγέλλω.

τοῖς Ἰουδαίοις. Dative indirect object of ἀνήγγειλεν.

ὅτι. Introduces the clausal complement (indirect discourse) of ἀνήγγειλεν.

Ἰησοῦς. Predicate nominative (Fee 1970, 176). Fronted for emphasis.

ἐστιν. Pres act ind 3rd sg εἰμί. The present tense is retained from the direct discourse (see 1:39 on μένει).

ὁ ποιήσας. Aor act ptc masc nom sg ποιέω (substantival). Nominative subject of ἐστιν.

αὐτὸν. Accusative direct object of ποιήσας in a double accusative object-complement construction.

ὑγιῆ. Accusative complement to αὐτὸν in a double accusative object-complement construction.

5:16 καὶ διὰ τοῦτο ἐδίωκον οἱ Ἰουδαῖοι τὸν Ἰησοῦν, ὅτι ταῦτα ἐποίει ἐν σαββάτῳ.

καὶ. Coordinating conjunction.

διὰ τοῦτο. Causal. The near-demonstrative pronoun is cataphoric, pointing to the explanation that follows.

ἐδίωκον. Impf act ind 3rd pl διώκω. The verb marks the beginning of the open hostility of the Jewish authorities toward Jesus. Campbell claims that the imperfects ἐδίωκον and ἐποίει in this verse provide supplemental or background material for the narrative proper, which is related from an external point of view through the aorist verb forms (2007, 91–95). Yet this offline information that interrupts the plot of the narrative is essential for the proper understanding of the events recounted in the mainline of the narrative proper. This background information may be remote, as Campbell argues, but, as he acknowledges, it "has the effect of drawing the reader into the narrative as an internal view is presented" (2007, 93).

οἱ Ἰουδαῖοι. Nominative subject of ἐδίωκον.

τὸν Ἰησοῦν. Accusative direct object of ἐδίωκον.

ὅτι. Introduces a causal clause.

ταῦτα. Accusative direct object of ἐποίει. The demonstrative pronoun is anaphoric, referring to the healing described in vv. 1-9.

ἐποίει. Impf act ind 3rd sg ποιέω.

ἐν σαββάτῳ. Temporal.

5:17 Ὁ δὲ [Ἰησοῦς] ἀπεκρίνατο αὐτοῖς· ὁ πατήρ μου ἕως ἄρτι ἐργάζεται κἀγὼ ἐργάζομαι·

Ὁ ... [Ἰησοῦς]. Nominative subject of ἀπεκρίνατο. Square brackets indicate some doubts about the authenticity of Ἰησοῦς because it is missing in some witnesses ($\mathfrak{P}^{75}$ ℵ B W 892 1241 pbo) and attested by others ($\mathfrak{P}^{66}$ A D K L N Γ Δ Θ Ψ $f^{1.13}$ 33 𝔐 latt et al.).

δὲ. Marker of narrative development.

ἀπεκρίνατο. Aor mid ind 3rd sg ἀποκρίνομαι.

αὐτοῖς. Dative indirect object of ἀπεκρίνατο.

ὁ πατήρ. Nominative subject of ἐργάζεται.

μου. Genitive of relationship qualifying πατήρ.

ἕως ἄρτι. Temporal. Fronted for emphasis. ἕως serves as an improper preposition (see 1:3 on χωρὶς αὐτοῦ) and the adverb ἄρτι as a substantive. ἕως ἄρτι = "until now" (BDAG, 423.1.b.γ).

ἐργάζεται. Pres mid ind 3rd sg ἐργάζομαι. The imperfective aspect of the present tense gives prominence to God's working, which is presented as an action in progress extending from the past into the present (Harris 2015, 109–10).

κἀγώ. Formed by crasis from καὶ ἐγώ. καί has both coordinating and adjunctive function ("and I also"). ἐγώ is the nominative subject of ἐργάζομαι.

ἐργάζομαι. Pres mid ind 1st sg ἐργάζομαι. This verb is also marked for prominence, portraying Jesus' working as an unfolding activity.

5:18 διὰ τοῦτο οὖν μᾶλλον ἐζήτουν αὐτὸν οἱ Ἰουδαῖοι ἀποκτεῖναι, ὅτι οὐ μόνον ἔλυεν τὸ σάββατον, ἀλλὰ καὶ πατέρα ἴδιον ἔλεγεν τὸν θεὸν ἴσον ἑαυτὸν ποιῶν τῷ θεῷ.

διὰ τοῦτο. Causal. The demonstrative pronoun is cataphoric, pointing to the ὅτι clause that follows (see 5:16).

οὖν. Postpositive inferential conjunction and/or transitional particle (see 1:22 and 11:6).

μᾶλλον. Comparative of the adverb μάλα ("to a greater or higher degree, more" [BDAG, 613.1]). Fronted for emphasis.

ἐζήτουν. Impf act ind 3rd pl ζητέω. The imperfective aspect marks the verb for prominence and presents the action as unfolding. On the function of the imperfect in the FG, see 1:39 on ἦν. In the FG, ζητέω is used six times with the complimentary infinitive ἀποκτεῖναι (5:18; 7:1, 19, 20, 25; 8:37).

αὐτόν. Accusative direct object of ἀποκτεῖναι.

οἱ Ἰουδαῖοι. Nominative subject of ἐζήτουν.

ἀποκτεῖναι. Aor act inf ἀποκτείνω (complementary).

ὅτι. Introduces a causal clause.

οὐ μόνον . . . ἀλλὰ καί. A point/counterpoint set ("not only . . . but also") that corrects the first assertion (Jesus was breaking the Sabbath) by supplementing it by another assertion (Jesus was calling God his own Father). On the function of ἀλλά in a point/counterpoint set, see 1:8.

ἔλυεν. Impf act ind 3rd sg λύω. The verb form depicts the action as unfolding. In this context, λύω denotes "the failure to conform to a law or regulation, with a possible implication of regarding it as invalid" (LN 36.30). BDAG's suggestion that λύω means "abolish" because "Jesus is accused not of breaking the Sabbath, but of doing away w[ith] it as an ordinance" (607.4) is probably too strong given the parallel expression in 5:16, which merely claims that Jesus "was doing these things on the Sabbath." See also the Sabbath controversy described in ch. 9, in which Jesus is accused not of abolishing the Sabbath but of not observing it: τὸ σάββατον οὐ τηρεῖ (9:16).

τὸ σάββατον. Accusative direct object of ἔλυεν.

πατέρα ἴδιον. Accusative complement to τὸν θεόν in a double accusative object-complement construction. Fronted for emphasis.

ἔλεγεν. Impf act ind 3rd sg λέγω. On the function of the imperfect in the FG, see 1:39 on ἦν.

τὸν θεόν. Accusative direct object of ἔλεγεν in a double accusative object-complement construction.

ἴσον. Accusative complement to ἑαυτόν in a double accusative object-complement construction. Fronted for emphasis.

ἑαυτόν. Accusative direct object of ποιῶν in a double accusative object-complement construction.

ποιῶν. Pres act ptc masc nom sg ποιέω (result). On participles that follow the main verb, see βαπτίζων in 1:31.

τῷ θεῷ. Dative complement of ἴσον.

John 5:19-29

[19]Then Jesus answered and said to them, "Truly, truly I say to you, the Son can do nothing on his own unless it is something he sees the Father doing. For whatever he does—these things also the Son does in like manner. [20]For the Father loves the Son and shows him all that he himself does. And greater works than these he will show him, so that you will be amazed. [21]For just as the Father raises the dead and makes them alive, so also the Son makes alive whomever he wants. [22]Furthermore, the Father judges no one but has given all judgment to the Son, [23]so that all may honor the Son just as they honor the Father. The one who does not honor the Son does not honor the Father who sent him. [24]Truly, truly I say to you, the one who hears my word and believes the one who sent me has eternal life and does not come into judgment but has passed from death to life. [25]Truly, truly I say to you, the hour is coming and is now here, when the dead will hear the voice of the Son of God, and those who hear will live. [26]For just as the Father has life in himself, so also he has granted to the Son to have life in himself. [27]And he gave authority to him to render judgment, because he is the Son of Man. [28]Do not be amazed at this, because an hour is coming when all who are in the tombs will hear his voice [29]and will come out—those who have done good to the resurrection of life, and those who have done evil to the resurrection of judgment."

5:19 Ἀπεκρίνατο οὖν ὁ Ἰησοῦς καὶ ἔλεγεν αὐτοῖς· ἀμὴν ἀμὴν λέγω ὑμῖν, οὐ δύναται ὁ υἱὸς ποιεῖν ἀφ' ἑαυτοῦ οὐδὲν ἐὰν μή τι βλέπῃ τὸν πατέρα ποιοῦντα· ἃ γὰρ ἂν ἐκεῖνος ποιῇ, ταῦτα καὶ ὁ υἱὸς ὁμοίως ποιεῖ.

Ἀπεκρίνατο. Aor mid ind 3rd sg ἀποκρίνομαι.

οὖν. Postpositive inferential conjunction and/or transitional particle (see 1:22 and 11:6).

ὁ Ἰησοῦς. Nominative subject of Ἀπεκρίνατο.

καὶ ἔλεγεν αὐτοῖς. Pleonastic clause under Semitic influence, which functions as a redundant quotative frame (see 1:25 on καὶ εἶπαν αὐτῷ).

καὶ. Coordinating conjunction.

ἔλεγεν. Impf act ind 3rd sg λέγω. On the function of the imperfect in the FG, see 1:39 on ἦν.

αὐτοῖς. Dative indirect object of ἔλεγεν.

ἀμὴν ἀμὴν λέγω ὑμῖν. Metacomment (see 1:51).

ἀμὴν ἀμὴν. Asseverative particles that mark the beginning of Jesus' solemn declaration (see 1:51).

λέγω. Pres act ind 1st sg λέγω.

ὑμῖν. Dative indirect object of λέγω.

οὐ. Negative particle normally used with indicative verbs. It marks the beginning of the apodosis of a third-class condition, which precedes the protasis.

δύναται. Pres mid ind 3rd sg δύναμαι.

ὁ υἱὸς. Nominative subject of δύναται.

ποιεῖν. Pres act inf ποιέω (complementary).

ἀφ' ἑαυτοῦ. Agency. The preposition ἀπό indicates an agent responsible for something (BDAG, 107.5.e.α). The prepositional phrases ἀφ' ἑαυτοῦ and ἀπ' ἐμαυτοῦ occur only in the FG (5:19, 30; 7:17, 18, 28; 8:28; 10:18; 11:51; 14:10; 15:4; 16:13).

οὐδὲν. Accusative direct object of ποιεῖν. The two negatives οὐ . . . οὐδὲν do not cancel but reinforce each other: lit. "the Son cannot do nothing on his own" = "the Son can do nothing on his own" (see 3:27 on οὐδὲ).

ἐάν. Introduces the protasis of a third-class condition.

μή. Negative particle normally used with non-indicative verbs. ἐὰν μή can be translated "unless."

τι. Accusative direct object of ποιοῦντα.

βλέπῃ. Pres act subj 3rd sg βλέπω. Subjunctive with ἐάν.

τὸν πατέρα. Accusative direct object of βλέπῃ.

ποιοῦντα. Pres act ptc masc acc sg ποιέω (predicative). The participle stands in the second predicate position (see 1:29 on ἐρχόμενον), functioning as the accusative complement to τὸν πατέρα in a double accusative object-complement construction.

ἃ . . . ἄν. The relative pronoun followed by the particle of contingency introduces a headless indefinite relative clause in a left-dislocation, resumed by ἐκεῖνός. On the function of left-dislocations, see 1:33 on ὁ πέμψας. The relative clause in its entirety (ἃ γὰρ ἂν ἐκεῖνος ποιῇ) serves as the direct object of ποιεῖ. Within its clause, ἃ is the accusative direct object of ποιῇ.

γὰρ. Postpositive conjunction that indicates that the headless indefinite relative clause functions as an explanation for Jesus' previous assertion that the Son can do only what he sees the Father doing.

ἐκεῖνος. Nominative subject of ποιῇ. The demonstrative pronoun refers to τὸν πατέρα, acting as a third-person personal pronoun with a simple anaphoric force (Wallace 1996, 328–29).

ποιῇ. Pres act subj 3rd sg ποιέω. Subjunctive with ἄν.

ταῦτα. Accusative direct object of ποιεῖ, resuming the indefinite relative clause ἃ γὰρ ἂν ἐκεῖνος ποιῇ. The anaphoric demonstrative reinforces what is already made prominent through the left-dislocation of the relative clause.

καὶ. Adverbial use (adjunctive).

ὁ υἱὸς. Nominative subject of ποιεῖ.

ὁμοίως. Adverb of manner ("likewise, in the same way").

ποιεῖ. Pres act ind 3rd sg ποιέω.

5:20 ὁ γὰρ πατὴρ φιλεῖ τὸν υἱὸν καὶ πάντα δείκνυσιν αὐτῷ ἃ αὐτὸς ποιεῖ, καὶ μείζονα τούτων δείξει αὐτῷ ἔργα, ἵνα ὑμεῖς θαυμάζητε.

ὁ... πατὴρ. Nominative subject of φιλεῖ. Fronted as a topical frame.

γὰρ. Postpositive conjunction that introduces the explanation of the previous assertion.

φιλεῖ. Pres act ind 3rd sg φιλέω. In the FG, φιλέω and ἀγαπάω are interchangeable (Barrett, 259; Frey 2009, 176; Harris 2015, 112); see, e.g., 3:35, which has ὁ πατὴρ ἀγαπᾷ τὸν υἱόν.

τὸν υἱὸν. Accusative direct object of φιλεῖ.

καὶ. Coordinating conjunction.

πάντα. Accusative direct object of δείκνυσιν. Fronted for emphasis.

δείκνυσιν. Pres act ind 3rd sg δείκνυμι.

αὐτῷ. Dative indirect object of δείκνυσιν.

ἃ. Accusative direct object of ποιεῖ. The antecedent of the relative pronoun is πάντα.

αὐτὸς. Intensive pronoun that reinforces the implied subject of ποιεῖ ("he himself").

ποιεῖ. Pres act ind 3rd sg ποιέω.

καὶ. Coordinating conjunction.

μείζονα ... ἔργα. Accusative direct object of δείξει. μείζονα is the comparative adjective from μέγας.

τούτων. Genitive of comparison.

δείξει. Fut act ind 3rd sg δείκνυμι.

αὐτῷ. Dative indirect object of δείξει.

ἵνα. Introduces a result clause (Harris 2015, 113).

ὑμεῖς. Nominative subject of θαυμάζητε. The personal pronoun is emphatic.

θαυμάζητε. Pres act subj 2nd pl θαυμάζω. Subjunctive with ἵνα.

5:21 ὥσπερ γὰρ ὁ πατὴρ ἐγείρει τοὺς νεκροὺς καὶ ζῳοποιεῖ, οὕτως καὶ ὁ υἱὸς οὓς θέλει ζῳοποιεῖ.

ὥσπερ. Introduces the protasis of a comparison, the apodosis of which is introduced by οὕτως καὶ (BDAG, 1106.a). The comparative clause is placed in a left-dislocation, which provides the frame of reference for the clause that follows (Runge 2010, 301).

γὰρ. Postpositive conjunction that indicates that the ὥσπερ . . . οὕτως καὶ comparison offers the corroboration for the previous assertion.

ὁ πατὴρ. Nominative subject of ἐγείρει.

ἐγείρει. Pres act ind 3rd sg ἐγείρω.

τοὺς νεκροὺς. Accusative direct object of ἐγείρει.

καὶ. Coordinating conjunction.

ζῳοποιεῖ. Pres act ind 3rd sg ζῳοποιέω.

οὕτως καὶ. Introduces the apodosis of a comparison (see ὥσπερ above). καὶ is adverbial (adjunctive).

ὁ υἱὸς. Nominative subject of ζῳοποιεῖ.

οὓς. The relative pronoun introduces a headless relative clause that, in its entirety (οὓς θέλει), serves as the direct object of ζῳοποιεῖ. Within its clause, οὓς is the accusative direct object of θέλει.

θέλει. Pres act ind 3rd sg θέλω.

ζῳοποιεῖ. Pres act ind 3rd sg ζῳοποιέω.

5:22 οὐδὲ γὰρ ὁ πατὴρ κρίνει οὐδένα, ἀλλὰ τὴν κρίσιν πᾶσαν δέδωκεν τῷ υἱῷ,

οὐδὲ . . . ἀλλὰ. A point/counterpoint set ("not this . . . but that") that negates the incorrect assertion ("the Father judges people") and replaces it with the correct one ("he has given all judgment to the Son"). οὐδὲ is a combination of the negative particle "οὐ . . . and the postpositive conjunction δέ" (LN 69.7). On the function of ἀλλά in a point/counterpoint set, see 1:8.

γὰρ. Postpositive conjunction that introduces further support for the previous assertion.

ὁ πατὴρ. Nominative subject of κρίνει.

κρίνει. Pres act ind 3rd sg κρίνω.

οὐδένα. Accusative direct object of κρίνει. The two negatives οὐδὲ . . . οὐδένα reinforce each other (see 3:27 on οὐδὲ).

τὴν κρίσιν πᾶσαν. Accusative direct object of δέδωκεν. The pronominal adjective πᾶσαν has attributive function although it stands in the second predicate position (article-noun-adjective), because the pronominal adjectives such as πᾶς are exceptions to the rules about the relation of the adjective to the noun when the article is present (Wallace 1996, 308). Elsewhere in the FG, κρίσις is mentioned in 3:19; 5:24, 27, 29, 30; 7:24; 8:16; 12:31; 16:8, 11.

δέδωκεν. Prf act ind 3rd sg δίδωμι. In a discourse dominated by the present-tense verbs, the perfect tense calls attention to the new situation created by the Father's turning over of the function of judging to the Son.

τῷ υἱῷ. Dative indirect object of δέδωκεν.

5:23 ἵνα πάντες τιμῶσιν τὸν υἱὸν καθὼς τιμῶσιν τὸν πατέρα. ὁ μὴ τιμῶν τὸν υἱὸν οὐ τιμᾷ τὸν πατέρα τὸν πέμψαντα αὐτόν.

ἵνα. Introduces a purpose clause.
πάντες. Nominative subject of τιμῶσιν.
τιμῶσιν. Pres act subj 3rd pl τιμάω. Subjunctive with ἵνα.
τὸν υἱόν. Accusative direct object of τιμῶσιν.
καθώς. Introduces a comparative clause.
τιμῶσιν. Pres act ind 3rd pl τιμάω.
τὸν πατέρα. Accusative direct object of τιμῶσιν.
ὁ . . . τιμῶν. Pres act ptc masc nom sg τιμάω (substantival). Nominative subject of τιμᾷ. This clause is connected to the preceding one by asyndeton.

μή. Negative particle normally used with non-indicative verbs. It modifies the substantival participle τιμῶν ("the one who does not honor").

τὸν υἱόν. Accusative direct object of τιμῶν.
οὐ. Negative particle normally used with indicative verbs.
τιμᾷ. Pres act ind 3rd sg τιμάω.
τὸν πατέρα. Accusative direct object of τιμᾷ.

τὸν πέμψαντα. Aor act ptc masc acc sg πέμπω (attributive). The participle modifies τὸν πατέρα, standing in the second attributive position (see 1:29 on ὁ αἴρων). On the use of the participial forms of πέμπω to either identify or describe God in the FG, see τοῦ πέμψαντός in 4:34.

αὐτόν. Accusative direct object of πέμψαντα.

5:24 Ἀμὴν ἀμὴν λέγω ὑμῖν ὅτι ὁ τὸν λόγον μου ἀκούων καὶ πιστεύων τῷ πέμψαντί με ἔχει ζωὴν αἰώνιον καὶ εἰς κρίσιν οὐκ ἔρχεται, ἀλλὰ μεταβέβηκεν ἐκ τοῦ θανάτου εἰς τὴν ζωήν.

Ἀμὴν ἀμὴν λέγω ὑμῖν. Metacomment (see 1:51).
Ἀμὴν ἀμήν. Asseverative particles that mark the beginning of Jesus' solemn declaration (see 1:51). This verse is connected to the previous one by asyndeton.

λέγω. Pres act ind 1st sg λέγω.

ὑμῖν. Dative indirect object of λέγω.

ὅτι. Introduces the clausal complement (direct [NRSV; REB; NET; ASV; ESV; NASB; NIV] or indirect [CEB; LEB] discourse) of λέγω.

ὁ ... ἀκούων καὶ πιστεύων. Nominative subject of ἔχει. According to the Granville Sharp rule, the article that governs two substantival participles joined by καί indicates that both participles have the same referent. In the article-substantive-καί-substantive combination, which Wallace (1996, 270–72) calls the "TSKS construction," both substantives (which can be substantival adjectives, substantival participles, or nouns) refer to the same person only if neither is impersonal, neither is plural, and neither is a proper name.

ἀκούων. Pres act ptc masc nom sg ἀκούω (substantival). On the function of this participle, see ὁ ... ἀκούων καὶ πιστεύων above.

τὸν λόγον. Accusative direct object of ἀκούων.

μου. Subjective genitive qualifying λόγον.

πιστεύων. Pres act ptc masc nom sg πιστεύω (substantival). On the syntactical function of this participle, see ὁ ... ἀκούων καὶ πιστεύων above.

τῷ πέμψαντι. Aor act ptc masc dat sg πέμπω (substantival). Dative complement of πιστεύων. The dative indicates the person "to whom one gives credence or whom one believes" (BDAG, 816.1.b). πέμψαντί, which has an acute accent on the antepenult, acquired an additional accent, the acute, on the ultima from the enclitic με (Smyth §183; Carson 1985, 48). On the use of the participial forms of πέμπω to either identify or describe God in the FG, see τοῦ πέμψαντός in 4:34.

με. Accusative direct object of πέμψαντί.

ἔχει. Pres act ind 3rd sg ἔχω.

ζωὴν αἰώνιον. Accusative direct object of ἔχει. On the use of this phrase in the FG, see 3:15 on ζωὴν αἰώνιον.

καί. Coordinating conjunction.

εἰς κρίσιν. Locative. Fronted for emphasis.

οὐκ ... ἀλλά. A point/counterpoint set ("not this ... but that") that negates the incorrect assertion (the one who hears and believes comes under judgment) and replaces it with the correct one (the one who hears and believes has passed from death to life). On the function of ἀλλά in a point/counterpoint set, see 1:8.

ἔρχεται. Pres mid ind 3rd sg ἔρχομαι.

μεταβέβηκεν. Perf act ind 3rd sg μεταβαίνω. The perfect tense is marked for prominence in the context dominated by the present-tense verb forms. Its stative aspect accentuates the transition from one state or condition (death) to another (life).

ἐκ τοῦ θανάτου. Separation.
εἰς τὴν ζωήν. Locative.

5:25 ἀμὴν ἀμὴν λέγω ὑμῖν ὅτι ἔρχεται ὥρα καὶ νῦν ἐστιν ὅτε οἱ νεκροὶ ἀκούσουσιν τῆς φωνῆς τοῦ υἱοῦ τοῦ θεοῦ καὶ οἱ ἀκούσαντες ζήσουσιν.

ἀμὴν ἀμὴν λέγω ὑμῖν. Metacomment (see 1:51).

ἀμὴν ἀμὴν. Asseverative particles that mark the beginning of Jesus' solemn declaration (see 1:51). This verse is connected to the previous one by asyndeton.

λέγω. Pres act ind 1st sg λέγω.

ὑμῖν. Dative indirect object of λέγω.

ὅτι. Introduces the clausal complement (direct [NRSV; REB; NET; ASV; ESV; NASB; NIV] or indirect [CEB; LEB] discourse) of λέγω.

ἔρχεται ὥρα καὶ νῦν ἐστιν. This clause, which also occurs in 4:23, expresses the tension between the expectation of an hour that is still in the future (see ἔρχεται below and the references to "the last day" in 6:39, 40, 44, 54; 11:24; 12:48) and the experience of salvation in the present (see νῦν below; cf. Frey 1997–2000, 2:2–5).

ἔρχεται. Pres mid ind 3rd sg ἔρχομαι. The present tense is here used for an action that is extended into the future (Caragounis 2004, 276).

ὥρα. Nominative subject of ἔρχεται.

καὶ. Coordinating conjunction.

νῦν. Adverb of time that functions as a temporal marker, focusing on "time coextensive with the event of the narrative" (BDAG, 681.1.a).

ἐστιν. Pres act ind 3rd sg εἰμί.

ὅτε. Introduces a temporal clause.

οἱ νεκροί. Nominative subject of ἀκούσουσιν.

ἀκούσουσιν. Fut act ind 3rd pl ἀκούω.

τῆς φωνῆς. Genitive direct object of ἀκούσουσιν.

τοῦ υἱοῦ. Possessive genitive or genitive of source qualifying τῆς φωνῆς.

τοῦ θεοῦ. Genitive of relationship qualifying τοῦ υἱοῦ.

καὶ. Coordinating conjunction.

οἱ ἀκούσαντες. Aor act ptc masc nom pl ἀκούω (substantival). Nominative subject of ζήσουσιν.

ζήσουσιν. Fut act ind 3rd pl ζάω.

5:26 ὥσπερ γὰρ ὁ πατὴρ ἔχει ζωὴν ἐν ἑαυτῷ, οὕτως καὶ τῷ υἱῷ ἔδωκεν ζωὴν ἔχειν ἐν ἑαυτῷ.

ὥσπερ. Introduces the protasis of a comparison, the apodosis of which is introduced by οὕτως καὶ (BDAG, 1106.a). The comparative clause is placed in a left-dislocation, which provides the frame of reference for the clause that follows (Runge 2010, 301).

γάρ. Postpositive conjunction that introduces an explanation of the previous assertion.

ὁ πατήρ. Nominative subject of ἔχει.

ἔχει. Pres act ind 3rd sg ἔχω.

ζωήν. Accusative direct object of ἔχει.

ἐν ἑαυτῷ. Locative.

οὕτως καὶ. Introduces the apodosis of a comparison (see ὥσπερ above). καὶ is adverbial (adjunctive).

τῷ υἱῷ. Dative indirect object of ἔδωκεν.

ἔδωκεν. Aor act ind 3rd sg δίδωμι.

ζωήν. Accusative direct object of ἔχειν.

ἔχειν. Pres act inf ἔχω. The infinitival clause ζωὴν ἔχειν ἐν ἑαυτῷ functions as the direct object of ἔδωκεν: "He has granted to the Son (the privilege) of having life in himself" (BDAG, 243.13; cf. Wallace 1996, 602).

ἐν ἑαυτῷ. Locative.

5:27 καὶ ἐξουσίαν ἔδωκεν αὐτῷ κρίσιν ποιεῖν, ὅτι υἱὸς ἀνθρώπου ἐστίν.

καὶ. Coordinating conjunction.

ἐξουσίαν. Accusative direct object of ἔδωκεν. Fronted for emphasis.

ἔδωκεν. Aor act ind 3rd sg δίδωμι.

αὐτῷ. Dative indirect object of ἔδωκεν.

κρίσιν. Accusative direct object of ποιεῖν.

ποιεῖν. Pres act inf ποιέω. The infinitival clause, κρίσιν ποιεῖν, is epexegetical to ἐξουσίαν.

ὅτι. Introduces a causal clause.

υἱός. Predicate nominative. Fronted for emphasis. One reason why υἱός is anarthrous could be Colwell's rule, which states that "[d]efinite predicate nouns which precede the verb usually lack the article" (20; for the implications of Colwell's rule, see 1:1 on θεός). Another reason could be that this may be an allusion to LXX Dan 7:13, in which the designation υἱὸς ἀνθρώπου is also anarthrous (Harris 2015, 114).

ἀνθρώπου. Genitive of relationship qualifying υἱός.

ἐστίν. Pres act ind 3rd sg εἰμί.

5:28 μὴ θαυμάζετε τοῦτο, ὅτι ἔρχεται ὥρα ἐν ᾗ πάντες οἱ ἐν τοῖς μνημείοις ἀκούσουσιν τῆς φωνῆς αὐτοῦ

μὴ. Negative particle normally used with non-indicative verbs. This verse is connected to the previous one by asyndeton.

θαυμάζετε. Pres act impv 2nd pl θαυμάζω. Aubrey notes that "it is not clear that the state being prohibited is one that the audience was already in. The imperfective prohibition in John 5:38 comes at a point mid-monologue for Jesus, and we have no access to the experience or feelings of his disciples. One possibility for why the author chose the imperfective here rather than the normal perfective used for specific commands/prohibitions would be to imply to the reader that the disciples in listening to Jesus expressed surprise at his words" (503–4).

τοῦτο. Accusative direct object of θαυμάζετε. The transitive use of θαυμάζω takes the accusative of the thing wondered at (BDAG, 444.1.b). τοῦτο could be anaphoric, referring to vv. 25–27 (Barrett, 263; Frey 1997–2000, 3:330–31), or cataphoric, referring to the ὅτι clause that follows.

ὅτι. If τοῦτο is anaphoric, ὅτι introduces a causal clause. If τοῦτο is cataphoric, ὅτι introduces a nominal clause that stands in apposition to this demonstrative (Wallace 1996, 458–59).

ἔρχεται. Pres mid ind 3rd sg ἔρχομαι. The present tense is used here to describe an event that is expected to occur in the future.

ὥρα. Nominative subject of ἔρχεται.

ἐν ᾗ. Temporal.

πάντες οἱ ἐν τοῖς μνημείοις. The article functions as a nominalizer, changing the prepositional phrase ἐν τοῖς μνημείοις into the nominative subject of ἀκούσουσιν (v. 29). The pronominal adjective πάντες has attributive function although it stands in the first predicate position (adjective-article-noun) (Wallace 1996, 307–8).

ἐν τοῖς μνημείοις. Locative.

ἀκούσουσιν. Fut act ind 3rd pl ἀκούω.

τῆς φωνῆς. Genitive direct object of ἀκούσουσιν.

αὐτοῦ. Possessive genitive or genitive of source qualifying φωνῆς.

5:29 καὶ ἐκπορεύσονται οἱ τὰ ἀγαθὰ ποιήσαντες εἰς ἀνάστασιν ζωῆς, οἱ δὲ τὰ φαῦλα πράξαντες εἰς ἀνάστασιν κρίσεως.

καὶ. Coordinating conjunction.

ἐκπορεύσονται. Fut mid ind 3rd pl ἐκπορεύομαι.

οἱ . . . ποιήσαντες. Aor act ptc masc nom pl ποιέω (substantival). Nominative in apposition to πάντες οἱ ἐν τοῖς μνημείοις (v. 28).

τὰ ἀγαθά. Accusative direct object of ποιήσαντες.
εἰς ἀνάστασιν. Goal (BDAG, 290.4.a).
ζωῆς. Genitive of purpose or result qualifying ἀνάστασιν (BDF §166).
οἱ . . . πράξαντες. Aor act ptc masc nom pl πράσσω (substantival). Nominative in apposition to πάντες οἱ ἐν τοῖς μνημείοις (v. 28).
δέ. Marker of narrative development.
τὰ φαῦλα. Accusative direct object of πράξαντες.
εἰς ἀνάστασιν. Goal (BDAG, 290.4.a).
κρίσεως. Genitive of purpose or result qualifying ἀνάστασιν (BDF §166).

John 5:30-47

³⁰"I can do nothing on my own. As I hear, I judge, and my judgment is just, because I do not seek my own will but the will of the one who sent me. ³¹If I testify about myself, my testimony is not true. ³²There is another who testifies about me, and I know that the testimony which he testifies about me is true. ³³You have sent messengers to John, and he has testified to the truth. ³⁴I do not accept human testimony, but I say these things in order that you may be saved. ³⁵He was the burning and shining lamp, and you wanted to rejoice for a while in his light. ³⁶But I have a testimony greater than that of John. For the works that the Father has given to me that I should complete them—the very works that I am doing—testify about me that the Father has sent me. ³⁷And the Father who sent me—that one has testified about me. You have never heard his voice or seen his form, ³⁸and you do not have his word abiding in you, because whom he has sent—this one you do not believe. ³⁹You search the Scriptures because you think that in them you have eternal life; they too are the ones that testify about me. ⁴⁰Yet you do not want to come to me so that you may have life. ⁴¹I do not accept glory from human beings. ⁴²But I know you, that you do not have the love of God in you. ⁴³I have come in my Father's name, and you do not accept me. If another comes in his own name, you will accept him. ⁴⁴How can you believe when you accept honor from one another and do not seek the honor that comes from the only God? ⁴⁵Do not think that I will accuse you to the Father. The one who accuses you is Moses, on whom you have set your hope. ⁴⁶For if you believed Moses, you would believe me, because he wrote about me. ⁴⁷But if you do not believe his writings, how will you believe my words?"

5:30 Οὐ δύναμαι ἐγὼ ποιεῖν ἀπ' ἐμαυτοῦ οὐδέν· καθὼς ἀκούω κρίνω, καὶ ἡ κρίσις ἡ ἐμὴ δικαία ἐστίν, ὅτι οὐ ζητῶ τὸ θέλημα τὸ ἐμὸν ἀλλὰ τὸ θέλημα τοῦ πέμψαντός με.

Οὐ. Negative particle normally used with indicative verbs. This verse is connected to the previous one by asyndeton.

δύναμαι. Pres mid ind 1st sg δύναμαι.

ἐγώ. Nominative subject of δύναμαι. The personal pronoun is emphatic.

ποιεῖν. Pres act inf ποιέω (complementary).

ἀπ' ἐμαυτοῦ. Agency (see 5:19 on ἀφ' ἑαυτοῦ).

οὐδέν. Accusative direct object of ποιεῖν. The two negatives Οὐ ... οὐδέν reinforce each other: lit. "I cannot do nothing on my own" = "I can do nothing on my own" (see 3:27 on οὐδὲ).

καθώς. Introduces a comparative clause.

ἀκούω. Pres act ind 1st sg ἀκούω.

κρίνω. Pres act ind 1st sg κρίνω.

καί. Coordinating conjunction.

ἡ κρίσις ἡ ἐμή. Nominative subject of ἐστίν. The possessive adjective stands in the second attributive position (see 1:9 on τὸ φῶς τὸ ἀληθινόν).

δικαία. Predicate adjective. Fronted for emphasis.

ἐστίν. Pres act ind 3rd sg εἰμί.

ὅτι. Introduces a causal clause.

οὐ ... ἀλλά. A point/counterpoint set ("not this ... but that") that negates the incorrect assertion (Jesus seeks to do his own will) and replaces it with the correct one (Jesus seeks to do the will of him who sent him). On the function of ἀλλά in a point/counterpoint set, see 1:8.

ζητῶ. Pres act ind 1st sg ζητέω.

τὸ θέλημα τὸ ἐμόν. Accusative direct object of ζητῶ. The possessive adjective stands in the second attributive position (see 1:9 on τὸ φῶς τὸ ἀληθινόν).

τὸ θέλημα. Accusative direct object of an implied ζητῶ. The nominal phrase τὸ θέλημα τοῦ πέμψαντός με also occurs in 4:34; 6:38, 39.

τοῦ πέμψαντός. Aor act ptc masc gen sg πέμπω (substantival). Subjective genitive qualifying θέλημα. πέμψαντός, which has an acute accent on the antepenult, acquired an additional accent, the acute, on the ultima from the enclitic με (Smyth §183; Carson 1985, 48). On the use of the participial forms of πέμπω to either identify or describe God in the FG, see τοῦ πέμψαντός in 4:34.

με. Accusative direct object of πέμψαντός.

John 5:30-32

5:31 Ἐὰν ἐγὼ μαρτυρῶ περὶ ἐμαυτοῦ, ἡ μαρτυρία μου οὐκ ἔστιν ἀληθής·

Ἐάν. Introduces the protasis of a third-class condition. Wallace suggests that "the present tense in the apodosis (ἔστιν) permits this to be taken as a fifth class condition" (1996, 471), also known as the present general condition, in which "the speaker gives no indication about the likelihood of its fulfillment" (470). This classification seems appropriate to this context because Jesus is not talking about a situation that could happen but makes a simple conditional statement: "If A, then B." This verse is connected to the previous one by asyndeton.

ἐγώ. Nominative subject of μαρτυρῶ. Fronted for emphasis.

μαρτυρῶ. Pres act subj 1st sg μαρτυρέω. Subjunctive with ἐάν.

περὶ ἐμαυτοῦ. Reference.

ἡ μαρτυρία. Nominative subject of ἔστιν. It marks the beginning of the apodosis of a third-class condition.

μου. Subjective genitive qualifying μαρτυρία.

οὐκ. Negative particle normally used with indicative verbs.

ἔστιν. Pres act ind 3rd sg εἰμί. The enclitic ἐστιν is accented ἔστιν when it comes at the beginning of a sentence, when it expresses existence, or when it follows ἀλλ᾽, εἰ, καί, οὐκ, ὅτι, or τοῦτ᾽. The third condition is fulfilled here.

ἀληθής. Predicate adjective.

5:32 ἄλλος ἐστὶν ὁ μαρτυρῶν περὶ ἐμοῦ, καὶ οἶδα ὅτι ἀληθής ἐστιν ἡ μαρτυρία ἣν μαρτυρεῖ περὶ ἐμοῦ.

ἄλλος. Predicate adjective. Fronted for emphasis. This verse is connected to the previous one by asyndeton.

ἐστίν. Pres act ind 3rd sg εἰμί.

ὁ μαρτυρῶν. Pres act ptc masc nom sg μαρτυρέω (substantival). Nominative subject of ἐστίν.

περὶ ἐμοῦ. Reference.

καί. Coordinating conjunction.

οἶδα. Prf act ind 1st sg οἶδα (see 1:26 on οἴδατε). Two variants, the plurals οἴδατε (ℵ* D a aur e q sy^c) and οἴδαμεν (1424), are scribal corrections seeking to strengthen Jesus' argument by showing that his hearers also know that the testimony about him is true (Metzger, 180).

ὅτι. Introduces the clausal complement (indirect discourse) of οἶδα.

ἀληθής. Predicate adjective. Fronted for emphasis.

ἐστίν. Pres act ind 3rd sg εἰμί.

ἡ μαρτυρία. Nominative subject of ἐστίν.

ἦν. Accusative direct object of μαρτυρεῖ.
μαρτυρεῖ. Pres act ind 3rd sg μαρτυρέω.
περὶ ἐμοῦ. Reference.

5:33 ὑμεῖς ἀπεστάλκατε πρὸς Ἰωάννην, καὶ μεμαρτύρηκεν τῇ ἀληθείᾳ·

ὑμεῖς. Nominative subject of ἀπεστάλκατε. Fronted as a topical frame, which sharpens the contrast between the addressees and the speaker. This verse is connected to the previous one by asyndeton.
ἀπεστάλκατε. Perf act ind 2nd pl ἀποστέλλω. The stative aspect of this and the next verb form gives prominence to John's testimony about Jesus.
πρὸς Ἰωάννην. Locative (motion toward).
καί. Coordinating conjunction.
μεμαρτύρηκεν. Perf act ind 3rd sg μαρτυρέω.
τῇ ἀληθείᾳ. Dative complement of μεμαρτύρηκεν (BDAG, 618.1.a.α) or dative of interest (Haubeck and von Siebenthal, 541).

5:34 ἐγὼ δὲ οὐ παρὰ ἀνθρώπου τὴν μαρτυρίαν λαμβάνω, ἀλλὰ ταῦτα λέγω ἵνα ὑμεῖς σωθῆτε.

ἐγώ. Nominative subject of λαμβάνω. Fronted as a topical frame, which draws attention to the contrast between Jesus (ἐγώ) and the Jews (ὑμεῖς).
δέ. Marker of narrative development.
οὐ . . . ἀλλά. A point/counterpoint set ("not this . . . but that") that negates the incorrect assertion (Jesus needs human testimony) and replaces it with the correct one (Jesus accepts John's testimony in order that his hearers might be saved). On the function of ἀλλά in a point/counterpoint set, see 1:8.
παρὰ ἀνθρώπου. Source. Fronted for emphasis.
τὴν μαρτυρίαν. Accusative direct object of λαμβάνω.
λαμβάνω. Pres act ind 1st sg λαμβάνω.
ταῦτα. Accusative direct object of λέγω.
λέγω. Pres act ind 1st sg λέγω.
ἵνα. Introduces a purpose clause.
ὑμεῖς. Nominative subject of σωθῆτε.
σωθῆτε. Aor pass subj 2nd pl σῴζω. Subjunctive with ἵνα.

5:35 ἐκεῖνος ἦν ὁ λύχνος ὁ καιόμενος καὶ φαίνων, ὑμεῖς δὲ ἠθελήσατε ἀγαλλιαθῆναι πρὸς ὥραν ἐν τῷ φωτὶ αὐτοῦ.

ἐκεῖνος. Nominative subject of ἦν. The demonstrative pronoun refers to John. This verse is connected to the previous one by asyndeton.

ἦν. Impf act ind 3rd sg εἰμί. On the function of the imperfect in the FG, see 1:39 on ἦν.

ὁ λύχνος ὁ καιόμενος καὶ φαίνων. Predicate nominative. The articular predicate nominative underscores the uniqueness of John (BDF §273.1). Two attributive participles joined by καί modify ὁ λύχνος, standing in the second attributive position (see 1:29 on ὁ αἴρων).

καιόμενος. Pres mid ptc masc nom sg καίω (attributive).

φαίνων. Pres act ptc masc nom sg φαίνω (attributive).

ὑμεῖς. Nominative subject of ἠθελήσατε. Fronted for emphasis.

δὲ. Marker of narrative development.

ἠθελήσατε. Aor act ind 2nd pl θέλω. On the augment, see 1:43 on ἠθέλησεν.

ἀγαλλιαθῆναι. Aor pass inf ἀγαλλιάω (complementary). ἀγαλλιάω means to "exult, be glad, overjoyed" (BDAG, 4).

πρὸς ὥραν. Temporal ("for a short time"). In this context, ὥρα denotes "an indefinite unit of time which is relatively short—'a while'" (LN 67.148).

ἐν τῷ φωτὶ. Causal, expressing the object of the joy (BDAG, 4).

αὐτοῦ. Subjective genitive qualifying φωτὶ ("the light that he shed").

5:36 Ἐγὼ δὲ ἔχω τὴν μαρτυρίαν μείζω τοῦ Ἰωάννου· τὰ γὰρ ἔργα ἃ δέδωκέν μοι ὁ πατὴρ ἵνα τελειώσω αὐτά, αὐτὰ τὰ ἔργα ἃ ποιῶ μαρτυρεῖ περὶ ἐμοῦ ὅτι ὁ πατήρ με ἀπέσταλκεν.

Ἐγὼ. Nominative subject of ἔχω. Fronted as a topical frame.

δὲ. Marker of narrative development.

ἔχω. Pres act ind 1st sg ἔχω.

τὴν μαρτυρίαν. Accusative direct object of ἔχω.

μείζω. μείζω (an alternative form of μείζονα) is acc fem sg comparative adjective from μέγας. It modifies μαρτυρίαν, standing in the second predicate position (article-noun-adjective) (Wallace 1996, 308). ἔχω τὴν μαρτυρίαν μείζω is equivalent to ἡ μαρτυρία, ἣν ἔχω, μείζων ἐστίν ("the testimony, which I have, is greater") or ἔχω μαρτυρίαν, ἣ μείζων ἐστίν ("I have a testimony, which is greater") (Zerwick §186; Haubeck and von Siebenthal, 541). It seems that some scribes considered the syntax of the sentence a bit convoluted (see τοῦ Ἰωάννου below) and tried to clarify it by changing the accusative μείζω to the nominative μείζων ($\mathfrak{P}^{66}$ A B N W Ψ f^{13} 33 579 1241), but the resulting clause ("I, who am greater than John, have the testimony") does not fit the context (Metzger, 180).

τοῦ Ἰωάννου. This genitive is part of an abbreviated comparison: "a testimony greater than that given by John," which could be expressed in Greek as μείζω τῆς τοῦ Ἰωάννου (BDF §185.1). Consequently, τοῦ Ἰωάννου is not a genitive of comparison (because Jesus does not compare God's testimony with John's persona) but a subjective genitive that modifies the elided genitive of comparison (because Jesus compares God's testimony with John's testimony).

τὰ ... ἔργα. Nominative subject of μαρτυρεῖ.

γὰρ. Postpositive conjunction that introduces the explanation of Jesus' statement that he has a testimony greater than John's.

ἅ. Accusative direct object of δέδωκέν. The antecedent of the relative pronoun is τὰ ... ἔργα.

δέδωκέν. Prf act ind 3rd sg δίδωμι. δέδωκέν, which has an acute accent on the antepenult, acquired an additional accent, the acute, on the ultima from the enclitic μοι (Smyth §183; Carson 1985, 48).

μοι. Dative indirect object of δέδωκέν.

ὁ πατήρ. Nominative subject of δέδωκέν.

ἵνα. Introduces a purpose clause.

τελειώσω. Aor act subj 1st sg τελειόω. Subjunctive with ἵνα.

αὐτά. Accusative direct object of τελειώσω. The antecedent of the personal pronoun is τὰ ... ἔργα.

αὐτὰ τὰ ἔργα. Nominative in apposition to τὰ ... ἔργα. αὐτὰ functions as an intensive pronoun ("the works themselves, the very deeds").

ἅ. Accusative direct object of ποιῶ. The antecedent of the relative pronoun is αὐτὰ τὰ ἔργα.

ποιῶ. Pres act ind 1st sg ποιέω.

μαρτυρεῖ. Pres act ind 3rd sg μαρτυρέω. Neuter plural subjects typically take singular verbs (see 1:28 on ἐγένετο).

περὶ ἐμοῦ. Reference.

ὅτι. Introduces the clausal complement (indirect discourse) of μαρτυρεῖ.

ὁ πατήρ. Nominative subject of ἀπέσταλκεν.

με. Accusative direct object of ἀπέσταλκεν.

ἀπέσταλκεν. Perf act ind 3rd sg ἀποστέλλω.

5:37 καὶ ὁ πέμψας με πατὴρ ἐκεῖνος μεμαρτύρηκεν περὶ ἐμοῦ. οὔτε φωνὴν αὐτοῦ πώποτε ἀκηκόατε οὔτε εἶδος αὐτοῦ ἑωράκατε,

καί. Coordinating conjunction, but it could also be adverbial (adjunctive) (Harris 2015, 118).

ὁ ... πατήρ. Nominative subject of μεμαρτύρηκεν in a left-dislocation, resumed by ἐκεῖνός (see Runge 2010, 287–313). The left-dislocation shifts focus on the Father who sent Jesus.

πέμψας. Aor act ptc masc nom sg πέμπω (attributive). The participle modifies πατήρ, standing in the first attributive position (article-attributive participle-noun) (Wallace 1996, 306, 618). On the use of the participial forms of πέμπω to either identify or describe God in the FG, see τοῦ πέμψαντός in 4:34. ὁ πέμψας με πατὴρ is a common Johannine expression (5:37; 8:16, 18; 12:49; 14:24).

με. Accusative direct object of πέμψας.

ἐκεῖνος. Nominative subject of μεμαρτύρηκεν, resuming ὁ ... πατήρ. The anaphoric demonstrative reinforces what is already made prominent through the left-dislocation of ὁ πέμψας με πατὴρ.

μεμαρτύρηκεν. Perf act ind 3rd sg μαρτυρέω.

περὶ ἐμοῦ. Reference.

οὔτε ... οὔτε. "Neither ... nor" (BDAG, 740).

φωνὴν. Accusative direct object of ἀκηκόατε. Fronted for emphasis.

αὐτοῦ. Possessive genitive qualifying φωνήν.

πώποτε. Indefinite adverb of time.

ἀκηκόατε. Perf act ind 2nd pl ἀκούω.

εἶδος. Accusative direct object of ἑωράκατε. Fronted for emphasis.

αὐτοῦ. Possessive genitive qualifying εἶδος.

ἑωράκατε. Perf act ind 2nd pl ὁράω.

5:38 καὶ τὸν λόγον αὐτοῦ οὐκ ἔχετε ἐν ὑμῖν μένοντα, ὅτι ὃν ἀπέστειλεν ἐκεῖνος, τούτῳ ὑμεῖς οὐ πιστεύετε.

καὶ. Coordinating conjunction.

τὸν λόγον. Accusative direct object of ἔχετε. Fronted for emphasis.

αὐτοῦ. Subjective genitive qualifying λόγον.

οὐκ. Negative particle normally used with indicative verbs.

ἔχετε. Pres act ind 2nd pl ἔχω.

ἐν ὑμῖν. Locative.

μένοντα. Pres act ptc masc acc sg μένω (predicative). The participle stands in the second predicate position (see 1:29 on ἐρχόμενον), functioning as the accusative complement to τὸν λόγον in a double accusative object-complement construction.

ὅτι. Introduces a causal clause.

ὃν. The relative pronoun introduces a headless relative clause that, in its entirety (ὃν ἀπέστειλεν ἐκεῖνος), serves as the complement of πιστεύετε in a left-dislocation (see Runge 2010, 287–313), resumed by τούτῳ. The left-dislocation of the relative clause shifts focus on Jesus' identity as the one who has been sent by the Father. Within its clause, ὅν is the accusative direct object of ἀπέστειλεν.

ἀπέστειλεν. Aor act ind 3rd sg ἀποστέλλω.

ἐκεῖνος. Nominative subject of ἀπέστειλεν. The demonstrative pronoun refers to ὁ ... πατήρ from the previous verse, acting as a third-person personal pronoun with a simple anaphoric force (Wallace 1996, 328–29).

τούτῳ. Dative complement of πιστεύετε, resuming the relative clause ὅν ἀπέστειλεν ἐκεῖνος. The dative indicates the person "to whom one gives credence or whom one believes" (BDAG, 816.1.b).

ὑμεῖς. Nominative subject of πιστεύετε. The personal pronoun is emphatic.

οὐ. Negative particle normally used with indicative verbs.

πιστεύετε. Pres act ind 2nd pl πιστεύω. The verb stands in final, emphatic position.

5:39 ἐραυνᾶτε τὰς γραφάς, ὅτι ὑμεῖς δοκεῖτε ἐν αὐταῖς ζωὴν αἰώνιον ἔχειν· καὶ ἐκεῖναί εἰσιν αἱ μαρτυροῦσαι περὶ ἐμοῦ·

ἐραυνᾶτε. Pres act ind 2nd pl (or pres act impv 2nd pl) ἐραυνάω. The verb means "to make a careful or thorough effort to learn someth[ing]," "search, examine, investigate" (BDAG, 389). Most English translations understand it as indicative, but some take it as imperative (CEB; KJV; RHE; WBT). This verse is connected to the previous one by asyndeton.

τὰς γραφάς. Accusative direct object of ἐραυνᾶτε.

ὅτι. Introduces a causal clause.

ὑμεῖς. Nominative subject of δοκεῖτε. Fronted as a topical frame.

δοκεῖτε. Pres act ind 2nd pl δοκέω.

ἐν αὐταῖς. Locative.

ζωὴν αἰώνιον. Accusative direct object of ἔχειν. Fronted for emphasis. On the use of this phrase in the FG, see 3:15 on ζωὴν αἰώνιον.

ἔχειν. Pres act inf ἔχω (complementary). The implied accusative subject of the infinitive is ὑμᾶς.

καί. Adverbial (adjunctive) or simply connective.

ἐκεῖναί. Nominative subject of εἰσιν. Fronted for emphasis. The demonstrative pronoun refers to τὰς γραφάς, acting as a third-person personal pronoun with a simple anaphoric force (Wallace 1996, 328–29). ἐκεῖναί, which has a circumflex accent on the penult, acquired an additional accent, the acute, on the ultima from the enclitic εἰσιν (Smyth §183; Carson 1985, 48).

εἰσιν. Pres act ind 3rd pl εἰμί.

αἱ μαρτυροῦσαι. Pres act ptc fem nom pl μαρτυρέω (substantival). The article indicates that the participle functions as the predicate nominative. Without the article, it would be a present periphrasis with εἰσιν (BDF §273.3).

περὶ ἐμοῦ. Reference.

5:40 καὶ οὐ θέλετε ἐλθεῖν πρός με ἵνα ζωὴν ἔχητε.

καὶ. Coordinating conjunction. This is not a special case of the so-called adversative καί (*pace* Haubeck and von Siebenthal, 542) but the standard use of καί joining two clauses that stand in tension with each other (see 1:5).

οὐ. Negative particle normally used with indicative verbs.

θέλετε. Pres act ind 2nd pl θέλω.

ἐλθεῖν. Aor act inf ἔρχομαι (complementary).

πρός με. Locative (motion toward).

ἵνα. Introduces a purpose clause.

ζωήν. Accusative direct object of ἔχητε. Fronted for emphasis.

ἔχητε. Pres act subj 2nd pl ἔχω. Subjunctive with ἵνα.

5:41 Δόξαν παρὰ ἀνθρώπων οὐ λαμβάνω,

Δόξαν. Accusative direct object of λαμβάνω. This verse is connected to the previous one by asyndeton.

παρὰ ἀνθρώπων. Source.

οὐ. Negative particle normally used with indicative verbs.

λαμβάνω. Pres act ind 1st sg λαμβάνω. The verb stands in final, emphatic position.

5:42 ἀλλ᾽ ἔγνωκα ὑμᾶς ὅτι τὴν ἀγάπην τοῦ θεοῦ οὐκ ἔχετε ἐν ἑαυτοῖς.

ἀλλ᾽. Marker of contrast.

ἔγνωκα. Prf act ind 1st sg γινώσκω.

ὑμᾶς. Accusative direct object of ἔγνωκα, which functions as an anticipation of the conceptual subject of the ὅτι clause that follows: ἔγνωκα ὑμᾶς ὅτι . . . οὐκ ἔχετε = ἔγνωκα ὅτι ὑμεῖς . . . οὐκ ἔχετε (Zerwick §207; see also 4:35 on τὰς χώρας).

ὅτι. Introduces the clausal complement (indirect discourse) of ἔγνωκα.

τὴν ἀγάπην. Accusative direct object of ἔχετε.

τοῦ θεοῦ. Objective ("love for God") or subjective genitive ("God's love") qualifying ἀγάπην.

οὐκ. Negative particle normally used with indicative verbs.

ἔχετε. Pres act ind 2nd pl ἔχω.
ἐν ἑαυτοῖς. Locative.

5:43 ἐγὼ ἐλήλυθα ἐν τῷ ὀνόματι τοῦ πατρός μου, καὶ οὐ λαμβάνετέ με· ἐὰν ἄλλος ἔλθῃ ἐν τῷ ὀνόματι τῷ ἰδίῳ, ἐκεῖνον λήμψεσθε.

ἐγώ. Nominative subject of ἐλήλυθα. Fronted as a topical frame. This verse is connected to the previous one by asyndeton.
ἐλήλυθα. Prf act ind 1st sg ἔρχομαι.
ἐν τῷ ὀνόματι. Instrumental.
τοῦ πατρός. Possessive genitive qualifying ὀνόματι.
μου. Genitive of relationship qualifying πατρός.
καί. Coordinating conjunction.
οὐ. Negative particle normally used with indicative verbs.
λαμβάνετε. Pres act ind 2nd pl λαμβάνω. λαμβάνετέ, which has an acute accent on the antepenult, acquired an additional accent, the acute, on the ultima from the enclitic με (Smyth §183; Carson 1985, 48).
με. Accusative direct object of λαμβάνετέ.
ἐάν. Introduces the protasis of a third-class condition.
ἄλλος. Nominative subject of ἔλθῃ. Fronted for emphasis.
ἔλθῃ. Aor act subj 3rd sg ἔρχομαι. Subjunctive with ἐάν.
ἐν τῷ ὀνόματι τῷ ἰδίῳ. Instrumental. The adjective ἰδίῳ stands in the second attributive position (see 1:9 on τὸ φῶς τὸ ἀληθινόν).
ἐκεῖνον. Accusative direct object of λήμψεσθε. Fronted for emphasis. The demonstrative pronoun refers to ἄλλος. It marks the beginning of the apodosis of a third-class condition.
λήμψεσθε. Fut mid ind 2nd pl λαμβάνω.

5:44 πῶς δύνασθε ὑμεῖς πιστεῦσαι δόξαν παρὰ ἀλλήλων λαμβάνοντες, καὶ τὴν δόξαν τὴν παρὰ τοῦ μόνου θεοῦ οὐ ζητεῖτε;

πῶς. Interrogative particle. This verse is connected to the previous one by asyndeton.
δύνασθε. Pres mid ind 2nd pl δύναμαι.
ὑμεῖς. Nominative subject of δύνασθε.
πιστεῦσαι. Aor act inf πιστεύω (complementary).
δόξαν. Accusative direct object of λαμβάνοντες.
παρὰ ἀλλήλων. Source. Fronted for emphasis.
λαμβάνοντες. Pres act ptc masc nom pl λαμβάνω (temporal, causal, or conditional). On participles that follow the main verb, see βαπτίζων in 1:31.
καί. Coordinating conjunction.

τὴν δόξαν. Accusative direct object of ζητεῖτε. In this context, δόξα means "honor as enhancement or recognition of status or performance, *fame, recognition, renown, honor, prestige*" (BDAG, 257.3).

τὴν παρὰ τοῦ μόνου θεοῦ. The article functions as an adjectivizer, changing the prepositional phrase παρὰ τοῦ μόνου θεοῦ into an attributive modifier of δόξαν.

παρὰ τοῦ μόνου θεοῦ. Source. The adjective μόνου stands in the first attributive position (see 2:10 on τὸν καλὸν οἶνον).

οὐ. Negative particle normally used with indicative verbs.

ζητεῖτε. Pres act ind 2nd pl ζητέω. The verb stands in final, emphatic position.

5:45 Μὴ δοκεῖτε ὅτι ἐγὼ κατηγορήσω ὑμῶν πρὸς τὸν πατέρα· ἔστιν ὁ κατηγορῶν ὑμῶν Μωϋσῆς, εἰς ὃν ὑμεῖς ἠλπίκατε.

Μὴ. Negative particle used with non-indicative verbs. This verse is connected to the previous one by asyndeton.

δοκεῖτε. Pres act impv 2nd pl δοκέω.

ὅτι. Introduces the clausal complement (indirect discourse) of δοκεῖτε.

ἐγώ. Nominative subject of κατηγορήσω. Fronted as a topical frame.

κατηγορήσω. Fut act ind 1st sg κατηγορέω. κατηγορήσω τί τινος means to "accuse someone of a thing" (BDAG, 533.1.a).

ὑμῶν. Genitive complement of κατηγορήσω, indicating the person accused of something (see above).

πρὸς τὸν πατέρα. Locative (motion toward): "Do not think that I will bring charges against you to the Father."

ἔστιν. Pres act ind 3rd sg εἰμί. The enclitic ἐστιν is accented ἔστιν when it comes at the beginning of a sentence, when it expresses existence, or when it follows ἀλλ', εἰ, καί, οὐκ, ὅτι, or τοῦτ'. The first condition is fulfilled here.

ὁ κατηγορῶν. Pres act ptc masc nom sg κατηγορέω (substantival). Nominative subject of ἔστιν.

ὑμῶν. Objective genitive qualifying ὁ κατηγορῶν.

Μωϋσῆς. Predicative nominative.

εἰς ὅν. Goal of actions or feelings directed toward someone (BDAG, 290.4.c.β).

ὑμεῖς. Nominative subject of ἠλπίκατε. Fronted as a topical frame.

ἠλπίκατε. Prf act ind 2nd pl ἐλπίζω. The verb stands in final, emphatic position. The perfective aspect of the verb form gives prominence to the state characterized by hope that is "concurrent with the reference time of the clause with no reference to any prior event" (Crellin, 432).

5:46 εἰ γὰρ ἐπιστεύετε Μωϋσεῖ, ἐπιστεύετε ἄν ἐμοί· περὶ γὰρ ἐμοῦ ἐκεῖνος ἔγραψεν.

εἰ. Introduces the protasis of a second-class (contrary-to-fact) condition. This is the present contrary-to-fact condition, which typically has the imperfect in both the protasis and the apodosis, as here. It assumes something that is not true in the present, i.e., at the time when Jesus was speaking: if the Jews believed Moses (but they do not), they would believe Jesus (but they do not).

γὰρ. The postpositive conjunction indicates that the second-class condition functions as the explanation for Jesus' assertion that the one who accuses the Jews is Moses.

ἐπιστεύετε. Impf act ind 2nd pl πιστεύω. The verb marks the beginning of the apodosis of a second-class (contrary-to-fact) condition.

Μωϋσεῖ. Dative complement of ἐπιστεύετε. The dative indicates the person "to whom one gives credence or whom one believes" (BDAG, 816.1.b).

ἐπιστεύετε. Impf act ind 2nd pl πιστεύω.

ἄν. Marker of contingency in the apodosis of the second-class condition.

ἐμοί. Dative complement of ἐπιστεύετε (see Μωϋσεῖ above).

περὶ ... ἐμοῦ. Reference.

γὰρ. Postpositive conjunction that introduces the justification for the previous conditional clause.

ἐκεῖνος. Nominative subject of ἔγραψεν. Fronted for emphasis. The demonstrative pronoun refers to Moses, acting as a third-person personal pronoun with a simple anaphoric force (Wallace 1996, 328–29).

ἔγραψεν. Aor act ind 3rd sg γράφω.

5:47 εἰ δὲ τοῖς ἐκείνου γράμμασιν οὐ πιστεύετε, πῶς τοῖς ἐμοῖς ῥήμασιν πιστεύσετε;

εἰ. Introduces the protasis of the first-class condition. This class of conditions assumes that the protasis is true for the sake of the argument and draws the conclusion from that supposition. In this verse, though, the apodosis is not a statement about what will happened if the condition in the protasis is fulfilled but a question that, on the semantic level, seems to be open ended. On the pragmatic level, however, the entire conditional clause serves as a rabbinic *qal wahomer* argument (see 3:12). The protasis, which presumes that the Jews do not believe what Moses wrote, functions as the "lighter" (less significant) step in the argument, from which Jesus draws the inference about the "weightier" (more significant) issue—believing what Jesus says—which is phrased as a rhetorical question that anticipates that the answer will be negative.

δὲ. Marker of narrative development.

τοῖς ... γράμμασιν. Dative direct object of πιστεύετε. The dative conveys the thing to which someone gives credence (BDAG, 816.1.a.δ). Fronted for emphasis.

ἐκείνου. Subjective genitive qualifying γράμμασιν ("the writings which he wrote"). The demonstrative pronoun refers to Moses, acting as a third-person personal pronoun with a simple anaphoric force (Wallace 1996, 328–29).

οὐ. Negative particle normally used with indicative verbs.

πιστεύετε. Pres act ind 2nd pl πιστεύω.

πῶς. Interrogative particle. It marks the beginning of the apodosis of the first-class condition.

τοῖς ἐμοῖς ῥήμασιν. Dative direct object of πιστεύσετε (see τοῖς ... γράμμασιν above). Fronted for emphasis. The possessive adjective ἐμοῖς stands in the first attributive position (see 2:10 on τὸν καλὸν οἶνον).

πιστεύσετε. Fut act ind 2nd pl πιστεύω.

John 6:1-15

¹After these things, Jesus went away to the other side of the Sea of Galilee, that is, [the Sea] of Tiberias. ²A large crowd was following him, because they were observing the signs that he was doing on the sick. ³Jesus went up to the mountain and sat down there with his disciples. ⁴Now the Passover, the festival of the Jews, was near. ⁵When Jesus lifted up his eyes and saw that a large crowd was coming to him, he said to Philip, "Where are we to buy bread so that these people may eat?" ⁶He said this to test him, for he himself knew what he was about to do. ⁷Philip answered him, "Two hundred denarii worth of bread is not sufficient for them, so that each one could get a little." ⁸One of his disciples, Andrew, the brother of Simon Peter, said to him, ⁹"A youth is here who has five barley loaves and two fish, but what are these for so many?" ¹⁰Jesus said, "Have the people sit down." Now there was plenty of grass in the place. So the men sat down—with reference to number about five thousand. ¹¹Then Jesus took the loaves and, after he gave thanks, he distributed them to those who were seated; in the same way also of the fish, as much as they wanted. ¹²When they were fully satisfied, he said to his disciples, "Gather up the pieces that are left over so that nothing is wasted." ¹³Then they gathered them up and filled twelve baskets with pieces from the five barley loaves which were left by those who had eaten. ¹⁴So when the people saw the sign that he had done, they said, "This one is truly the prophet who is

coming into the world." ¹⁵Then Jesus, because he knew that they were about to come and seize him in order to make him king, withdrew again to the mountain by himself.

6:1 Μετὰ ταῦτα ἀπῆλθεν ὁ Ἰησοῦς πέραν τῆς θαλάσσης τῆς Γαλιλαίας τῆς Τιβεριάδος.

Μετὰ ταῦτα. Temporal (see 3:22). Fronted as a temporal frame. This verse is connected to the previous one by asyndeton.

ἀπῆλθεν. Aor act ind 3rd sg ἀπέρχομαι.

ὁ Ἰησοῦς. Nominative subject of ἀπῆλθεν.

πέραν τῆς θαλάσσης. Locative. πέραν is an improper preposition (see 1:3 on χωρὶς αὐτοῦ).

τῆς Γαλιλαίας. Partitive genitive qualifying θαλάσσης. This genitive is missing in some witnesses (ℵ 0210 bo^ms), but the omission is most likely an attempt to remove the ambiguity created by two successive genitives.

τῆς Τιβεριάδος. Epexegetical genitive, identifying the city in Galilee—Tiberias—after which the Sea of Galilee is sometimes named. 𝔓⁶⁶* omits this genitive, while some copyists add εἰς τὰ μέρη before τῆς Τιβεριάδος (D Θ 892 b e j r¹). Both corrections seek to give some clarity to the text that has two identifications of the same sea.

6:2 ἠκολούθει δὲ αὐτῷ ὄχλος πολύς, ὅτι ἐθεώρουν τὰ σημεῖα ἃ ἐποίει ἐπὶ τῶν ἀσθενούντων.

ἠκολούθει. Impf act ind 3rd sg ἀκολουθέω. All three verbs in this verse are imperfects, which are semantically marked for prominence compared to the aorist verb forms (ἀπῆλθεν and ἀνῆλθεν) that are used in the framing narrative (vv. 1 and 3).

δὲ. Marker of narrative development.

αὐτῷ. Dative direct object of ἠκολούθει.

ὄχλος πολύς. Nominative subject of ἠκολούθει.

ὅτι. Introduces a causal clause.

ἐθεώρουν. Impf act ind 3rd pl θεωρέω. The plural verb form is a *constructio ad sensum* because the implied subject, ὄχλος πολύς, is a collective noun (BDF §134.1).

τὰ σημεῖα. Accusative direct object of ἐθεώρουν. The use of the term σημεῖα for Jesus' miracles is one of the distinctive features of the FG (see 2:11, 23; 3:2; 4:48, 54; 6:14, 26; 7:31; 9:16; 11:47; 12:18, 37; 20:30; cf. Barrett, 75–78; Keener, 1:272–79; Thompson, 65–68).

ἅ. Accusative direct object of ἐποίει.

ἐποίει. Impf act ind 3rd sg ποιέω.
ἐπὶ τῶν ἀσθενούντων. Locative.
τῶν ἀσθενούντων. Pres act ptc masc gen pl ἀσθενέω (substantival).

6:3 ἀνῆλθεν δὲ εἰς τὸ ὄρος Ἰησοῦς καὶ ἐκεῖ ἐκάθητο μετὰ τῶν μαθητῶν αὐτοῦ.

ἀνῆλθεν. Aor act ind 3rd sg ἀνέρχομαι.
δὲ. Marker of narrative development.
εἰς τὸ ὄρος. Locative.
Ἰησοῦς. Nominative subject of ἀνῆλθεν.
καὶ. Coordinating conjunction.
ἐκεῖ. Adverb of place.
ἐκάθητο. Impf mid ind 3rd sg κάθημαι.
μετὰ τῶν μαθητῶν. Association/accompaniment.
αὐτοῦ. Genitive of relationship qualifying μαθητῶν.

6:4 ἦν δὲ ἐγγὺς τὸ πάσχα, ἡ ἑορτὴ τῶν Ἰουδαίων.

ἦν. Impf act ind 3rd sg εἰμί. On the function of the imperfect in the FG, see 1:39 on ἦν.
δὲ. Marker of narrative development.
ἐγγὺς. Predicate adverb indicating close temporal proximity (see 2:1 on ἐκεῖ).
τὸ πάσχα. Nominative subject of ἦν. This is the second Passover recorded in the FG (see 2:13 and 11:55).
ἡ ἑορτὴ. Nominative in apposition to τὸ πάσχα.
τῶν Ἰουδαίων. Subjective genitive ("the festival that the Jews celebrate") or attributive genitive ("the Jewish festival") qualifying ἑορτὴ.

6:5 Ἐπάρας οὖν τοὺς ὀφθαλμοὺς ὁ Ἰησοῦς καὶ θεασάμενος ὅτι πολὺς ὄχλος ἔρχεται πρὸς αὐτὸν λέγει πρὸς Φίλιππον· πόθεν ἀγοράσωμεν ἄρτους ἵνα φάγωσιν οὗτοι;

Ἐπάρας. Aor act ptc masc nom sg ἐπαίρω (temporal). On participles that precede the main verb, see ἐμβλέψας in 1:36.
οὖν. Postpositive inferential conjunction and/or transitional particle (see 1:22 and 11:6).
τοὺς ὀφθαλμοὺς. Accusative direct object of Ἐπάρας.
ὁ Ἰησοῦς. Nominative subject of λέγει.
καὶ. Coordinating conjunction.
θεασάμενος. Aor mid ptc masc nom sg θεάομαι (temporal). On participles that precede the main verb, see ἐμβλέψας in 1:36.

ὅτι. Introduces that clausal complement (indirect discourse) of θεασάμενος.

πολὺς ὄχλος. Nominative subject of ἔρχεται.

ἔρχεται. Pres mid ind 3rd sg ἔρχομαι. The present tense is retained from direct discourse (see 1:39 on μένει).

πρὸς αὐτὸν. Locative (motion toward).

λέγει. Pres act ind 3rd sg λέγω. The historical present calls attention to Jesus' words to Philip (see 1:15 on μαρτυρεῖ).

πρὸς Φίλιππον. Locative (motion toward). The PP functions like an indirect object of λέγει.

πόθεν. Interrogative adverb of place. Fronted for emphasis.

ἀγοράσωμεν. Aor act subj 1st pl ἀγοράζω (deliberative subjunctive).

ἄρτους. Accusative direct object of ἀγοράσωμεν.

ἵνα. Introduces a purpose clause.

φάγωσιν. Aor act subj 3rd pl ἐσθίω. Subjunctive with ἵνα.

οὗτοι. Nominative subject of φάγωσιν.

6:6 τοῦτο δὲ ἔλεγεν πειράζων αὐτόν· αὐτὸς γὰρ ᾔδει τί ἔμελλεν ποιεῖν.

τοῦτο. Accusative direct object of ἔλεγεν. The near-demonstrative pronoun is anaphoric, referring to Jesus' question in v. 5. Fronted as a topical frame.

δὲ. Marker of narrative development.

ἔλεγεν. Impf act ind 3rd sg λέγω. On the function of the imperfect in the FG, see 1:39 on ἦν.

πειράζων. Pres act ptc masc nom sg πειράζω (purpose). On participles that follow the main verb, see βαπτίζων in 1:31.

αὐτόν. Accusative direct object of πειράζων.

αὐτὸς. Intensive pronoun that reinforces the implied subject of ᾔδει ("he himself").

γὰρ. Postpositive conjunction that introduces the explanation of the preceding assertion.

ᾔδει. Plprf act ind 3rd sg οἶδα. The pluperfect of οἶδα is rendered by the imperfect.

τί. Accusative direct object of ποιεῖν.

ἔμελλεν. Impf act ind 3rd sg μέλλω.

ποιεῖν. Pres act inf ποιέω (complementary).

6:7 ἀπεκρίθη αὐτῷ [ὁ] Φίλιππος· διακοσίων δηναρίων ἄρτοι οὐκ ἀρκοῦσιν αὐτοῖς ἵνα ἕκαστος βραχύ [τι] λάβῃ.

ἀπεκρίθη. Aor mid ind 3rd sg ἀποκρίνομαι. On the voice, see "Deponency" in the Series Introduction. This verse is connected to the previous one by asyndeton.

αὐτῷ. Dative indirect object of ἀπεκρίθη.

[ὁ] Φίλιππος. Nominative subject of ἀπεκρίθη. Scribal evidence for ($\mathfrak{P}^{66}$ ℵ L N W 892) and against ὁ ($\mathfrak{P}^{75}$ A B D K Γ Δ Θ Ψ $f^{1.13}$ 33 565 579 700 1241 1424 $\mathfrak{M}$) was probably caused by the presence of the article with this proper noun in 1:44 and its absence in 1:43, 45, 48; 6:5.

διακοσίων δηναρίων. Genitive of price qualifying ἄρτοι (lit. "bread worth two hundred denarii"). Two hundred denarii is the amount that a laborer could earn in approximately eight months.

ἄρτοι. Nominative subject of ἀρκοῦσιν.

οὐκ. Negative particle normally used with indicative verbs.

ἀρκοῦσιν. Pres act ind 3rd pl ἀρκέω.

αὐτοῖς. Dative of interest.

ἵνα. Introduces a result clause (BDF §393.2).

ἕκαστος. Nominative subject of λάβῃ.

βραχύ [τι]. Accusative direct object of λάβῃ. The adjective βραχύ, which here pertains "to being low in quantity" (BDAG, 183, 3), qualifies the indefinitive pronoun τι ("a little, a bite, a mouthful"). τι is attested in a number of manuscripts ($\mathfrak{P}^{66}$ ℵ A K L N W Γ Δ Θ Ψ $f^{1.13}$ 33 565 $\mathfrak{M}$ et al.), but it is absent in some important witnesses ($\mathfrak{P}^{75}$ B D it).

λάβῃ. Aor act subj 3rd sg λαμβάνω. Subjunctive with ἵνα.

6:8 λέγει αὐτῷ εἷς ἐκ τῶν μαθητῶν αὐτοῦ, Ἀνδρέας ὁ ἀδελφὸς Σίμωνος Πέτρου·

λέγει. Pres act ind 3rd sg λέγω. The historical present draws attention to Andrew's words (see 1:15 on μαρτυρεῖ). This verse is connected to the previous one by asyndeton.

αὐτῷ. Dative indirect object of λέγει.

εἷς. Nominative subject of λέγει. εἷς stands for τις.

ἐκ τῶν μαθητῶν. Replaces the partitive genitive.

αὐτοῦ. Genitive of relationship qualifying μαθητῶν.

Ἀνδρέας. Nominative in apposition to εἷς. Placed in a right-dislocation.

ὁ ἀδελφὸς. Nominative in apposition to Ἀνδρέας. It receives additional emphasis through right-dislocation.

Σίμωνος Πέτρου. Genitive of relationship qualifying ἀδελφός.

6:9 ἔστιν παιδάριον ὧδε ὃς ἔχει πέντε ἄρτους κριθίνους καὶ δύο ὀψάρια· ἀλλὰ ταῦτα τί ἐστιν εἰς τοσούτους;

ἔστιν. Pres act ind 3rd sg εἰμί. The enclitic ἐστιν is accented ἔστιν when it comes at the beginning of a sentence, when it expresses existence, or when it follows ἀλλ', εἰ, καί, οὐκ, ὅτι, or τοῦτ'. The first two conditions are fulfilled here. This verse is connected to the previous one by asyndeton.

παιδάριον. Nominative subject of ἔστιν. παιδάριον could denote "a youth, who is no longer a child" (BDAG, 748.1.b) or a "young slave" (BDAG, 748.2).

ὧδε. Predicate adverb of place (see 2:1 on ἐκεῖ).

ὅς. Nominative subject of ἔχει. The antecedent is παιδάριον. The masculine gender of the relative is a *constructio ad sensum* (BDF §296).

ἔχει. Pres act ind 3rd sg ἔχω.

πέντε ἄρτους κριθίνους. Accusative direct object of ἔχει. The adjective κριθίνους ("made of barley flour") stands in the fourth attributive position (see 3:15 on ζωὴν αἰώνιον).

καὶ. Coordinating conjunction.

δύο ὀψάρια. Accusative direct object of ἔχει. ὀψάριον is a diminutive of ὄψον ("cooked food"), which in this context probably refers to preserved fish (BDAG, 746).

ἀλλὰ. Marker of contrast.

ταῦτα. Nominative subject of ἐστιν. The demonstrative is anaphoric, referring to πέντε ἄρτους κριθίνους καὶ δύο ὀψάρια.

τί. Predicate nominative (BDF §299.1). Fronted for emphasis.

ἐστιν. Pres act ind 3rd sg εἰμί.

εἰς τοσούτους. Reference.

6:10 εἶπεν ὁ Ἰησοῦς· ποιήσατε τοὺς ἀνθρώπους ἀναπεσεῖν. ἦν δὲ χόρτος πολὺς ἐν τῷ τόπῳ. ἀνέπεσαν οὖν οἱ ἄνδρες τὸν ἀριθμὸν ὡς πεντακισχίλιοι.

εἶπεν. Aor act ind 3rd sg λέγω. This verse is connected to the previous one by asyndeton.

ὁ Ἰησοῦς. Nominative subject of εἶπεν.

ποιήσατε. Aor act impv 2nd pl ποιέω. The use of ποιέω here is focused on causality. "The result of the action is indicated by the acc[usative] and inf[initive]; *make (to), cause (someone) to, bring it about that*" (BDAG, 840.2.h.α).

τοὺς ἀνθρώπους. Accusative direct object of ποιήσατε or accusative subject of the infinitive ἀναπεσεῖν.

ἀναπεσεῖν. Aor act inf ἀναπίπτω (complementary to ποιήσατε).
ἦν. Impf act ind 3rd sg εἰμί. On the function of the imperfect in the FG, see 1:39 on ἦν.
δὲ. Marker of narrative development.
χόρτος πολὺς. Nominative subject of ἦν.
ἐν τῷ τόπῳ. Locative.
ἀνέπεσαν. Aor act ind 3rd pl ἀναπίπτω.
οὖν. Postpositive inferential conjunction and/or transitional particle (see 1:22 and 11:6).
οἱ ἄνδρες. Nominative subject of ἀνέπεσαν.
τὸν ἀριθμὸν. Accusative of respect.
ὡς. Particle used with numerals to denote an estimate ("about, approximately").
πεντακισχίλιοι. The cardinal adjective ("five thousand") modifies οἱ ἄνδρες, standing in the second predicate position (see 5:36 on μείζω).

6:11 ἔλαβεν οὖν τοὺς ἄρτους ὁ Ἰησοῦς καὶ εὐχαριστήσας διέδωκεν τοῖς ἀνακειμένοις ὁμοίως καὶ ἐκ τῶν ὀψαρίων ὅσον ἤθελον.

ἔλαβεν. Aor act ind 3rd sg λαμβάνω.
οὖν. Postpositive inferential conjunction and/or transitional particle (see 1:22 and 11:6).
τοὺς ἄρτους. Accusative direct object of ἔλαβεν.
ὁ Ἰησοῦς. Nominative subject of ἔλαβεν.
καὶ. Coordinating conjunction.
εὐχαριστήσας. Aor act ptc masc nom sg εὐχαριστέω (temporal). On participles that precede the main verb, see ἐμβλέψας in 1:36.
διέδωκεν. Aor act ind 3rd sg διαδίδωμι.
τοῖς ἀνακειμένοις. Pres mid ptc masc dat pl ἀνάκειμαι (substantival). Dative indirect object of διέδωκεν.
ὁμοίως. Adverb of manner ("likewise, in the same way").
καὶ. Adverbial use (adjunctive).
ἐκ τῶν ὀψαρίων. Replaces the partitive genitive.
ὅσον. Adverbial accusative ("as much as"; BDAG, 729.2).
ἤθελον. Impf act ind 3rd pl θέλω. On the augment, see 1:43 on ἠθέλησεν.

6:12 ὡς δὲ ἐνεπλήσθησαν, λέγει τοῖς μαθηταῖς αὐτοῦ· συναγάγετε τὰ περισσεύσαντα κλάσματα, ἵνα μή τι ἀπόληται.

ὡς. Temporal conjunction (BDAG, 1105.8.a; BDF §455.2), introducing a clause that is fronted as a temporal frame.

δέ. Marker of narrative development.
ἐνεπλήσθησαν. Aor pass ind 3rd pl ἐμπί(μ)πλημι.
λέγει. Pres act ind 3rd sg λέγω. The historical present draws attention to Jesus' words to his disciples (see 1:15 on μαρτυρεῖ).
τοῖς μαθηταῖς. Dative indirect object of λέγει.
αὐτοῦ. Genitive of relationship qualifying μαθηταῖς.
συναγάγετε. Aor act impv 2nd pl συνάγω.
τὰ ... κλάσματα. Accusative direct object of συναγάγετε.
περισσεύσαντα. Aor act ptc neut acc pl περισσεύω (attributive). The participle modifies κλάσματα ("fragments, pieces"), standing in the first attributive position (see 5:37 on πέμψας).
ἵνα. Introduces a purpose clause.
μή. Negative particle normally used with non-indicative verbs.
τι. Nominative subject of ἀπόληται.
ἀπόληται. Aor mid subj 3rd sg ἀπόλλυμι. Subjunctive with ἵνα.

6:13 συνήγαγον οὖν καὶ ἐγέμισαν δώδεκα κοφίνους κλασμάτων ἐκ τῶν πέντε ἄρτων τῶν κριθίνων ἃ ἐπερίσσευσαν τοῖς βεβρωκόσιν.

συνήγαγον. Aor act ind 3rd pl συνάγω.
οὖν. Postpositive inferential conjunction.
καί. Coordinating conjunction.
ἐγέμισαν. Aor act ind 3rd pl γεμίζω.
δώδεκα κοφίνους. Accusative direct object of ἐγέμισαν.
κλασμάτων. Genitive of content qualifying κοφίνους.
ἐκ τῶν πέντε ἄρτων τῶν κριθίνων. Replaces the partitive genitive. The article is anaphoric, referring to πέντε ἄρτους κριθίνους in v. 9. The adjective κριθίνων now stands in the second attributive position (see 1:9 on τὸ φῶς τὸ ἀληθινόν).
ἅ. Nominative subject of ἐπερίσσευσαν. The antecedent is κλασμάτων.
ἐπερίσσευσαν. Aor act ind 3rd pl περισσεύω.
τοῖς βεβρωκόσιν. Prf act ptc masc dat pl βιβρώσκω (substantival). Dative of agency ("which were left by those who have eaten") or, perhaps, dative of respect ("which were left in the case of those who have eaten" [Harris 2015, 124–25]). βιβρώσκω ("to consume solid food" [LN 23.3]) is a NT *hapax legomenon*.

6:14 Οἱ οὖν ἄνθρωποι ἰδόντες ὃ ἐποίησεν σημεῖον ἔλεγον ὅτι οὗτός ἐστιν ἀληθῶς ὁ προφήτης ὁ ἐρχόμενος εἰς τὸν κόσμον.

Οἱ ... ἄνθρωποι. Nominative subject of ἔλεγον. Fronted as a topical frame.

οὖν. Postpositive inferential conjunction and/or transitional particle (see 1:22 and 11:6).

ἰδόντες. Aor act ptc masc nom pl ὁράω (temporal or causal). On participles that precede the main verb, see ἐμβλέψας in 1:36.

ὃ. Accusative direct object of ἐποίησεν. The relative pronoun introduces an internally headed relative clause because its antecedent (σημεῖον) is incorporated into the relative clause (Culy, Parsons, and Stigall, 115). When this happens, "the article going with the noun must be omitted and the noun itself then attracted to the case of the relative" (BDF §294.5). In this instance, however, the attraction did not occur because both the relative pronoun and its antecedent function as the accusative direct objects of their respective verbs: ἰδόντες ὃ ἐποίησεν σημεῖον = ἰδόντες τὸ σημεῖον ὃ ἐποίησεν ("when the people saw the sign that he had done"). Alternatively, ὃ ἐποίησεν σημεῖον could be regarded as a headless relative clause that, in its entirety, serves as the direct object of ἰδόντες ("when the people saw what he had done as a sign").

ἐποίησεν. Aor act ind 3rd sg ποιέω.

σημεῖον. If σημεῖον is understood as the antecedent of ὃ that is incorporated into the relative clause, it functions as the accusative direct object of ἰδόντες. If ὃ ἐποίησεν σημεῖον is viewed as a headless relative clause, σημεῖον functions as the accusative complement to ὃ in a double accusative object-complement construction. The use of the term σημεῖα for Jesus' miracles is one of the distinctive features of the FG (see 2:11, 23; 3:2; 4:48, 54; 6:2, 26; 7:31; 9:16; 11:47; 12:18, 37; 20:30; cf. Barrett, 75–78; Keener, 1:272–79; Thompson, 65–68).

ἔλεγον. Impf act ind 3rd pl λέγω. On the function of the imperfect in the FG, see 1:39 on ἦν.

ὅτι. ὅτι-*recitativum* that introduces the clausal complement (direct discourse) of ἔλεγον.

οὗτός. Nominative subject of ἐστιν. Fronted as a topical frame. The demonstrative pronoun refers to Jesus. οὗτός, which has a circumflex accent on the penult, acquired an additional accent, the acute, on the ultima from the enclitic ἐστιν (Smyth §183; Carson 1985, 48).

ἐστιν. Pres act ind 3rd sg εἰμί.

ἀληθῶς. Adverb ("truly, really").

ὁ προφήτης. Predicate nominative. The article is anaphoric in a broad sense, referring to the prophetic figure known to the audience (see 1:21; 7:40).

ὁ ἐρχόμενος. Pres mid ptc masc nom sg ἔρχομαι (attributive). The participle modifies ὁ προφήτης, standing in the second attributive position (see 1:29 on ὁ αἴρων).

εἰς τὸν κόσμον. Locative.

6:15 Ἰησοῦς οὖν γνοὺς ὅτι μέλλουσιν ἔρχεσθαι καὶ ἁρπάζειν αὐτὸν ἵνα ποιήσωσιν βασιλέα, ἀνεχώρησεν πάλιν εἰς τὸ ὄρος αὐτὸς μόνος.

Ἰησοῦς. Nominative subject of ἀνεχώρησεν.

οὖν. Postpositive inferential conjunction and/or transitional particle (see 1:22 and 11:6).

γνοὺς. Aor act ptc masc nom sg γινώσκω (causal or temporal). On participles that precede the main verb, see ἐμβλέψας in 1:36.

ὅτι. Introduces the clausal complement (indirect discourse) of γνοὺς.

μέλλουσιν. Pres act ind 3rd pl μέλλω. The present tense is retained from the direct discourse (see 1:39 on μένει).

ἔρχεσθαι. Pres mid inf ἔρχομαι (complementary).

καὶ. Coordinating conjunction.

ἁρπάζειν. Pres act inf ἁρπάζω (complementary). ἁρπάζω means "to grab or seize suddenly so as to remove or gain control, snatch / take away" (BDAG, 134.2).

αὐτὸν. Accusative direct object of ἁρπάζειν.

ἵνα. Introduces a purpose clause.

ποιήσωσιν. Aor act subj 3rd pl ποιέω. Subjunctive with ἵνα.

βασιλέα. Accusative complement to an implied αὐτόν in a double accusative object-complement construction.

ἀνεχώρησεν. Aor act ind 3rd sg ἀναχωρέω.

πάλιν. Adverb "pert[aining] to return to a position or state" (BDAG, 752.1).

εἰς τὸ ὄρος. Locative.

αὐτὸς μόνος. Nominative in apposition to Ἰησοῦς. αὐτὸς functions as an intensive pronoun, which is modified by the adjective μόνος, portraying Jesus as a solitary figure ("he alone" = "by himself"; cf. BDAG, 152.1.e).

John 6:16-21

[16]When evening came, his disciples went down to the sea, [17]and, after they got into a boat, they were on their way across the sea to Capernaum. And it had already become dark, and Jesus had not yet come to them. [18]The sea was becoming rough because a strong wind was blowing. [19]Then, when they had rowed about twenty-five or thirty stadia, they saw Jesus walking on the sea and coming near the boat, and they were afraid. [20]But he said to them, "It is I. Do not be afraid!" [21]Then they wanted to take him into the boat, and immediately the boat came to the land to which they were going.

6:16 Ὡς δὲ ὀψία ἐγένετο κατέβησαν οἱ μαθηταὶ αὐτοῦ ἐπὶ τὴν θάλασσαν

Ὡς. Temporal conjunction (BDAG, 1105.8.a; BDF §455.2).
δὲ. Marker of narrative development.
ὀψία. Nominative subject of ἐγένετο.
ἐγένετο. Aor mid ind 3rd sg γίνομαι.
κατέβησαν. Aor act ind 3rd pl καταβαίνω.
οἱ μαθηταὶ. Nominative subject of κατέβησαν.
αὐτοῦ. Genitive of relationship qualifying μαθηταὶ.
ἐπὶ τὴν θάλασσαν. Locative.

6:17 καὶ ἐμβάντες εἰς πλοῖον ἤρχοντο πέραν τῆς θαλάσσης εἰς Καφαρναούμ. καὶ σκοτία ἤδη ἐγεγόνει καὶ οὔπω ἐληλύθει πρὸς αὐτοὺς ὁ Ἰησοῦς,

καὶ. Coordinating conjunction.
ἐμβάντες. Aor act ptc masc nom pl ἐμβαίνω (temporal). On participles that precede the main verb, see ἐμβλέψας in 1:36.
εἰς πλοῖον. Locative.
ἤρχοντο. Impf mid ind 3rd pl ἔρχομαι. The imperfective aspect of the verb form portrays the crossing of the sea as an unfolding action.
πέραν τῆς θαλάσσης. Locative (see 6:1). πέραν is an improper preposition (see 1:3 on χωρὶς αὐτοῦ).
εἰς Καφαρναούμ. Locative.
καὶ. Coordinating conjunction.
σκοτία. Nominative subject of ἐγεγόνει.
ἤδη. Temporal adverb ("already, now").
ἐγεγόνει. Plprf act ind 3rd sg γίνομαι. The pluperfect verb form focuses on a "state which existed in the past, with implication of a prior occurrence which produced it" (Fanning, 306).
καὶ. Coordinating conjunction.
οὔπω. Adverb of time ("not yet").
ἐληλύθει. Plprf act ind 3rd sg ἔρχομαι. In this context, the combination of the pluperfect of ἔρχομαι and οὔπω highlights the nonoccurrence of Jesus' arrival in the antecedent past (Fanning, 307).
πρὸς αὐτοὺς. Locative (motion toward).
ὁ Ἰησοῦς. Nominative subject of ἐληλύθει.

John 6:16-21

6:18 ἥ τε θάλασσα ἀνέμου μεγάλου πνέοντος διεγείρετο.

ἥ . . . θάλασσα. Nominative subject of διεγείρετο. Fronted as a topical frame. The definite article, a proclitic that normally has no accent, here has an acute accent because it precedes the enclitic τε (Smyth §180; Harris 1985, 49).

τε. Enclitic coordinating particle.

ἀνέμου μεγάλου. Genitive subject of πνέοντος. Fronted for emphasis.

πνέοντος. Pres act ptc masc gen sg πνέω (genitive absolute, causal).

διεγείρετο. Impf pass ind 3rd sg διεγείρω. The passive voice of διεγείρω (lit. "was awakened") is here metaphorically applied to the arousal of the sea. Mark 4:39 uses the passive participle of the same verb to describe Jesus' awakening from sleep when a sea storm threatened the boat in which he was with his disciples. The imperfective aspect of διεγείρω calls attention to sea turbulence as a situation in progress.

6:19 ἐληλακότες οὖν ὡς σταδίους εἴκοσι πέντε ἢ τριάκοντα θεωροῦσιν τὸν Ἰησοῦν περιπατοῦντα ἐπὶ τῆς θαλάσσης καὶ ἐγγὺς τοῦ πλοίου γινόμενον, καὶ ἐφοβήθησαν.

ἐληλακότες. Prf act ptc masc nom pl ἐλαύνω (temporal). On participles that precede the main verb, see ἐμβλέψας in 1:36.

οὖν. Postpositive inferential conjunction and/or transitional particle (see 1:22 and 11:6).

ὡς. Particle used with numerals to denote an estimate ("about, approximately").

σταδίους. Accusative indicating extent of space. στάδιον is "a measure of distance of about 192 meters" (BDAG, 940.1).

εἴκοσι πέντε. Cardinal number ("twenty-five").

ἤ. Marker of an alternative/disjunctive particle (BDAG, 432.1).

τριάκοντα. Cardinal number ("thirty").

θεωροῦσιν. Pres act ind 3rd pl θεωρέω. The historical present marks Jesus' appearance in a scene in which the disciples are struggling against a rough sea and the strong wind. According to Levinsohn, one of the most common functions of the nonspeech historical present in the FG is to "*activate* a participant by introducing him or her to the scene of a previous interaction between participants" (2000, 208).

τὸν Ἰησοῦν. Accusative direct object of θεωροῦσιν.

περιπατοῦντα. Pres act ptc masc acc sg περιπατέω (predicative). The participle stands in the second predicate position (see 1:29 on ἐρχόμενον), functioning as the first accusative complement to τὸν Ἰησοῦν in a double accusative object-complement construction.

ἐπὶ τῆς θαλάσσης. Locative.

καὶ. Coordinating conjunction.

ἐγγὺς τοῦ πλοίου. Locative. Fronted for emphasis. ἐγγὺς is an improper preposition (see 1:3 on χωρὶς αὐτοῦ) that indicates spatial proximity.

γινόμενον. Pres mid ptc masc acc sg γίγνομαι (predicative). The participle stands in the second predicate position (see 1:29 on ἐρχόμενον), functioning as the second accusative complement to τὸν Ἰησοῦν in a double accusative object-complement construction.

καὶ. Coordinating conjunction.

ἐφοβήθησαν. Aor mid ind 3rd pl φοβέομαι. On the voice, see "Deponency" in the Series Introduction.

6:20 ὁ δὲ λέγει αὐτοῖς· ἐγώ εἰμι· μὴ φοβεῖσθε.

ὁ δὲ. A construction used in narrative literature to indicate the change of speaker in a dialogue. The nominative article stands in place of a third-person singular personal pronoun and functions as the subject of λέγει.

λέγει. Pres act ind 3rd sg λέγω. The historical present grants prominence to Jesus' declaration that follows (see 1:15 on μαρτυρεῖ).

αὐτοῖς. Dative indirect object of λέγει.

ἐγώ. Nominative subject of εἰμι. The personal pronoun has the identifying function. Fronted for emphasis.

εἰμι. Pres act ind 1st sg εἰμί.

μὴ. Negative particle introducing prohibition.

φοβεῖσθε. Pres mid impv 2nd pl φοβέομαι (prohibition). On the voice, see "Deponency" in the Series Introduction. Since the narrator has already informed the audience that the disciples were afraid (v. 19), this imperative is a command to stop an action that is already in progress (Porter 1989, 335–61). The imperatives of φοβέομαι are commonly used for this purpose (BDF §336.3).

6:21 ἤθελον οὖν λαβεῖν αὐτὸν εἰς τὸ πλοῖον, καὶ εὐθέως ἐγένετο τὸ πλοῖον ἐπὶ τῆς γῆς εἰς ἣν ὑπῆγον.

ἤθελον. Impf act ind 3rd pl θέλω. On the augment, see 1:43 on ἠθέλησεν.

οὖν. Postpositive inferential conjunction and/or transitional particle (see 1:22 and 11:6).

λαβεῖν. Aor act inf λαμβάνω (complementary).

αὐτὸν. Accusative direct object of λαβεῖν.

εἰς τὸ πλοῖον. Locative.

καί. Coordinating conjunction.

εὐθέως. Temporal adverb ("immediately, at once"). Fronted for emphasis.

ἐγένετο. Aor mid ind 3rd sg γίνομαι.

τὸ πλοῖον. Nominative subject of ἐγένετο.

ἐπὶ τῆς γῆς. Locative.

εἰς ἥν. Locative. The antecedent of the relative pronoun is τῆς γῆς.

ὑπῆγον. Impf act ind 3rd pl ὑπάγω. On the function of the imperfect in the FG, see 1:39 on ἦν.

John 6:22-24

²²On the next day, the crowd that remained on the other side of the sea saw that no other boat had been there except one, and that Jesus had not entered the boat with his disciples, but his disciples had gone away alone. ²³Other boats from Tiberias came near the place where they had eaten the bread after the Lord had given thanks. ²⁴So when the crowd saw that neither Jesus nor his disciples were there, they got into the boats and came to Capernaum to look for Jesus.

6:22 Τῇ ἐπαύριον ὁ ὄχλος ὁ ἑστηκὼς πέραν τῆς θαλάσσης εἶδον ὅτι πλοιάριον ἄλλο οὐκ ἦν ἐκεῖ εἰ μὴ ἕν καὶ ὅτι οὐ συνεισῆλθεν τοῖς μαθηταῖς αὐτοῦ ὁ Ἰησοῦς εἰς τὸ πλοῖον ἀλλὰ μόνοι οἱ μαθηταὶ αὐτοῦ ἀπῆλθον·

Τῇ ἐπαύριον. The article functions as a nominalizer, changing the adverb ἐπαύριον ("tomorrow") into the dative of time (see 1:29). Fronted as a temporal frame. This verse is connected to the previous one by asyndeton.

ὁ ὄχλος. Nominative subject of εἶδον.

ὁ ἑστηκώς. Prf act ptc masc nom sg ἵστημι (attributive). The participle modifies ὁ ὄχλος, standing in the second attributive position (see 1:29 on ὁ αἴρων).

πέραν τῆς θαλάσσης. Locative (see 6:1). πέραν is an improper preposition (see 1:3 on χωρὶς αὐτοῦ).

εἶδον. Aor act ind 3rd pl ὁράω. The plural verb form is a *constructio ad sensum* because the subject (ὁ ὄχλος) is a collective noun (BDF §134.1).

ὅτι. Introduces the first clausal complement (indirect discourse) of εἶδον.

πλοιάριον ἄλλο. Nominative subject of ἦν. πλοιάριον is a diminutive of πλοῖον ("small ship, boat, skiff").

οὐκ ... εἰ μή. A point/counterpoint set that corrects the negated clause ("no other boat had been there") by introducing an exception ("except one"); on the function of the excepted element, see 3:13 on οὐδεὶς ... εἰ μή.

ἦν. Impf act ind 3rd sg εἰμί. The imperfect verb form is retained from the (reconstructed) direct discourse (see 1:39 on μένει). In English, the imperfect is pushed "one slot" back and translated with the pluperfect.

ἐκεῖ. Predicate adverb of place (see 2:1 on ἐκεῖ).

ἕν. The second, excepted, nominative subject of ἦν. ἕν is an ellipsis for ἓν πλοιάριον ("one boat").

καί. Coordinating conjunction.

ὅτι. Introduces the second clausal complement (indirect discourse) of εἶδον.

οὐ ... ἀλλά. A point/counterpoint set ("not this ... but that") that negates the incorrect assertion (Jesus entered the boat with his disciples) and replaces it with the correct one (Jesus' disciples departed alone). On the function of ἀλλά in a point/counterpoint set, see 1:8.

συνεισῆλθεν. Aor act ind 3rd sg συνεισέρχομαι. The aorist verb form is retained from the (reconstructed) direct discourse (see 1:39 on μένει). In English, the aorist is pushed "one slot" back and translated with the pluperfect.

τοῖς μαθηταῖς. Dative of association.

αὐτοῦ. Genitive of relationship qualifying μαθηταῖς.

ὁ Ἰησοῦς. Nominative subject of συνεισῆλθεν.

εἰς τὸ πλοῖον. Locative.

μόνοι. Predicate nominative.

οἱ μαθηταί. Nominative subject of ἀπῆλθον.

αὐτοῦ. Genitive of relationship qualifying μαθηταί.

ἀπῆλθον. Aor act ind 3rd pl ἀπέρχομαι. The aorist verb form is retained from the (reconstructed) direct discourse (see 1:39 on μένει). In English, the aorist is pushed "one slot" back and translated with the pluperfect.

6:23 ἄλλα ἦλθεν πλοιά[ρια] ἐκ Τιβεριάδος ἐγγὺς τοῦ τόπου ὅπου ἔφαγον τὸν ἄρτον εὐχαριστήσαντος τοῦ κυρίου.

ἄλλα ... πλοιά[ρια]. Nominative subject of ἦλθεν. The manuscript evidence for πλοῖα ($\mathfrak{P}^{75}$ ℵ B W Ψ lat) and πλοιάρια (A D K L N Γ Δ Θ $f^{1.13}$ 33 565 1241 1424 𝔐 et al.) is evenly balanced, which is reflected in the presence of square brackets in NA^{28}/UBS^5 (but not in SBLGNT).

ἦλθεν. Aor act ind 3rd sg ἔρχομαι. Neuter plural subjects typically take singular verbs (see 1:28 on ἐγένετο).

ἐκ Τιβεριάδος. Separation.
ἐγγὺς τοῦ τόπου. Locative. ἐγγὺς is an improper preposition (see 1:3 on χωρὶς αὐτοῦ) that indicates spatial proximity.
ὅπου. Particle denoting place.
ἔφαγον. Aor act ind 3rd pl ἐσθίω.
τὸν ἄρτον. Accusative direct object of ἔφαγον.
εὐχαριστήσαντος. Aor act ptc masc gen sg εὐχαριστέω (genitive absolute, temporal).
τοῦ κυρίου. Genitive subject of εὐχαριστήσαντος.

6:24 ὅτε οὖν εἶδεν ὁ ὄχλος ὅτι Ἰησοῦς οὐκ ἔστιν ἐκεῖ οὐδὲ οἱ μαθηταὶ αὐτοῦ, ἐνέβησαν αὐτοὶ εἰς τὰ πλοιάρια καὶ ἦλθον εἰς Καφαρναοὺμ ζητοῦντες τὸν Ἰησοῦν.

ὅτε. Introduces a temporal clause that resumes Τῇ ἐπαύριον ὁ ὄχλος in v. 22. This is an example of anacoluthon after an intervening sentence in v. 23 "where there is no question of a lapse of memory" (BDF §467).

οὖν. Postpositive inferential conjunction and/or transitional particle (see 1:22 and 11:6).

εἶδεν. Aor act ind 3rd sg ὁράω.

ὁ ὄχλος. Nominative subject of εἶδεν.

ὅτι. Introduces the clausal complement (indirect discourse) of εἶδεν.

Ἰησοῦς . . . οἱ μαθηταὶ. Compound nominative subject of ἔστιν. When the verb stands between the first subject and the second subject, as here, it agrees with the first (BDF §135). Wallace (1996, 402) argues that this word order and verbal agreement give prominence to the first-named subject, Jesus.

οὐκ . . . οὐδὲ. "Neither . . . nor." οὐδὲ is a combination of the negative particle οὐ and the marker of narrative development δέ.

ἔστιν. Pres act ind 3rd sg εἰμί. The present tense is retained from the (reconstructed) direct discourse (see 1:39 on μένει). The enclitic ἐστιν is accented ἔστιν when it comes at the beginning of a sentence, when it expresses existence, or when it follows ἀλλ', εἰ, καί, οὐκ, ὅτι, or τοῦτ'. The third condition is fulfilled here.

ἐκεῖ. Predicate adverb of place (see 2:1 on ἐκεῖ).

αὐτοῦ. Genitive of relationship qualifying μαθηταί.

ἐνέβησαν. Aor act ind 3rd pl ἐμβαίνω.

αὐτοί. This third-person personal pronoun is not emphatic but redundant with the pronominal notion embedded in ἐνέβησαν (Wallace 1996, 323).

εἰς τὰ πλοιάρια. Locative.

καὶ. Coordinating conjunction.
ἦλθον. Aor act ind 3rd pl ἔρχομαι.
εἰς Καφαρναοὺμ. Locative.
ζητοῦντες. Pres act ptc masc nom pl ζητέω (purpose). On participles that follow the main verb, see βαπτίζων in 1:31.
τὸν Ἰησοῦν. Accusative direct object of ζητοῦντες.

John 6:25-29

25And when they found him on the other side of the sea, they said to him, "Rabbi, when did you get here?" 26Jesus answered them and said, "Truly, truly I say to you, you are looking for me, not because you saw signs, but because you ate of the loaves and were satisfied. 27Work not for the food that perishes but for the food that endures for eternal life, which the Son of Man will give to you. For on this one the Father, God, has set his seal of approval." 28Then they said to him, "What shall we do that we might perform the works that God requires?" 29Jesus answered and said to them, "This is the work that God requires—that you believe in the one whom he has sent."

6:25 καὶ εὑρόντες αὐτὸν πέραν τῆς θαλάσσης εἶπον αὐτῷ· ῥαββί, πότε ὧδε γέγονας;

καὶ. Coordinating conjunction.
εὑρόντες. Aor act ptc masc nom pl εὑρίσκω (temporal). On participles that precede the main verb, see ἐμβλέψας in 1:36.
αὐτὸν. Accusative direct object of εὑρόντες.
πέραν τῆς θαλάσσης. Locative (see 6:1). πέραν is an improper preposition (see 1:3 on χωρὶς αὐτοῦ).
εἶπον. Aor act ind 3rd pl λέγω.
αὐτῷ. Dative indirect object of εἶπον.
ῥαββί. Vocative of direct address.
πότε. Interrogative adverb of time.
ὧδε. Predicate adverb of place (see 2:1 on ἐκεῖ).
γέγονας. Prf act ind 2nd sg γίνομαι.

6:26 Ἀπεκρίθη αὐτοῖς ὁ Ἰησοῦς καὶ εἶπεν· ἀμὴν ἀμὴν λέγω ὑμῖν, ζητεῖτέ με οὐχ ὅτι εἴδετε σημεῖα, ἀλλ' ὅτι ἐφάγετε ἐκ τῶν ἄρτων καὶ ἐχορτάσθητε.

Ἀπεκρίθη. Aor mid ind 3rd sg ἀποκρίνομαι. On the voice, see "Deponency" in the Series Introduction. This verse is connected to the previous one by asyndeton.

αὐτοῖς. Dative indirect object of Ἀπεκρίθη.

ὁ Ἰησοῦς. Nominative subject of Ἀπεκρίθη and εἶπεν.

καὶ εἶπεν. Pleonastic clause under Semitic influence, which functions as a redundant quotative frame (see 1:25 on καὶ εἶπαν αὐτῷ).

καὶ. Coordinating conjunction.

εἶπεν. Aor act ind 3rd sg λέγω.

ἀμὴν ἀμὴν λέγω ὑμῖν. Metacomment (see 1:51).

ἀμὴν ἀμὴν. Asseverative particles that mark the beginning of Jesus' solemn declaration (see 1:51).

λέγω. Pres act ind 1st sg λέγω.

ὑμῖν. Dative indirect object of λέγω.

ζητεῖτέ. Pres act ind 2nd pl ζητέω. ζητεῖτέ, which has a circumflex accent on the penult, acquired an additional accent, the acute, on the ultima from the enclitic με (Smyth §183; Carson 1985, 48).

με. Accusative direct object of ζητεῖτέ.

οὐχ . . . ἀλλ᾽. A point/counterpoint set ("not this . . . but that") that negates the incorrect causal clause ("because you saw signs") and replaces it with the correct one ("because you ate your fill of bread"). On the function of ἀλλά in a point/counterpoint set, see 1:8.

ὅτι. Introduces a causal clause.

εἴδετε. Aor act ind 2nd pl ὁράω.

σημεῖα. Accusative direct object of εἴδετε. The use of the term σημεῖα for Jesus' miracles is one of the distinctive features of the FG (see 2:11, 23; 3:2; 4:48, 54; 6:2, 14, 26; 7:31; 9:16; 11:47; 12:18, 37; 20:30; cf. Barrett, 75–78; Keener, 1:272–79; Thompson, 65–68).

ὅτι. Introduces a causal clause.

ἐφάγετε. Aor act ind 2nd pl ἐσθίω.

ἐκ τῶν ἄρτων. Replaces the partitive genitive.

καὶ. Coordinating conjunction.

ἐχορτάσθητε. Aor pass ind 2nd pl χορτάζω. The verb means "to eat, resulting in a state of being satisfied—'to eat one's fill'" (LN 23.15).

6:27 ἐργάζεσθε μὴ τὴν βρῶσιν τὴν ἀπολλυμένην ἀλλὰ τὴν βρῶσιν τὴν μένουσαν εἰς ζωὴν αἰώνιον, ἣν ὁ υἱὸς τοῦ ἀνθρώπου ὑμῖν δώσει· τοῦτον γὰρ ὁ πατὴρ ἐσφράγισεν ὁ θεός.

ἐργάζεσθε. Pres mid impv 2nd pl ἐργάζομαι. This verse is connected to the previous one by asyndeton.

μὴ . . . ἀλλὰ. A point/counterpoint set ("not this . . . but that") that negates the wrong kind of food that one should work for (the food that perishes) and replaces it with the right kind of food (the food that endures for eternal life). On the function of ἀλλά in a point/counterpoint set, see 1:8.

τὴν βρῶσιν. Accusative direct object of ἐργάζεσθε.

τὴν ἀπολλυμένην. Pres mid ptc fem acc sg ἀπόλλυμι (attributive). The participle modifies τὴν βρῶσιν, standing in the second attributive position (see 1:29 on ὁ αἴρων).

τὴν βρῶσιν. Accusative direct object of ἐργάζεσθε.

τὴν μένουσαν. Pres act ptc fem acc sg μένω (attributive). The participle modifies τὴν βρῶσιν, standing in the second attributive position (see 1:29 on ὁ αἴρων).

εἰς ζωὴν αἰώνιον. Goal or result. On the use of this phrase in the FG, see 3:15 on ζωὴν αἰώνιον.

ἥν. Accusative direct object of δώσει. The antecedent of the relative pronoun is ζωὴν αἰώνιον.

ὁ υἱός. Nominative subject of δώσει.

τοῦ ἀνθρώπου. Genitive of relationship qualifying υἱός.

ὑμῖν. Dative indirect object of δώσει.

δώσει. Fut act ind 3rd sg δίδωμι. The variant with the present-tense δίδωσιν, attested by some witnesses (א D e ff² j), is most likely the result of an assimilation to 6:32 (Metzger, 182).

τοῦτον. Accusative direct object of ἐσφράγισεν.

γάρ. Postpositive conjunction that introduces an explanation of the claim that the Son of Man, i.e., Jesus, will give the food that endures for eternal life.

ὁ πατήρ. Nominative subject of ἐσφράγισεν.

ἐσφράγισεν. Aor act ind 3rd sg σφραγίζω.

ὁ θεός. Nominative in apposition to ὁ πατήρ, which receives emphasis through right-dislocation.

6:28 εἶπον οὖν πρὸς αὐτόν· τί ποιῶμεν ἵνα ἐργαζώμεθα τὰ ἔργα τοῦ θεοῦ;

εἶπον. Aor act ind 3rd pl λέγω.

οὖν. Postpositive inferential conjunction and/or transitional particle (see 1:22 and 11:6).

πρὸς αὐτόν. Locative (motion toward). The PP functions like an indirect object of εἶπον.

τί. Interrogative pronoun functioning as the accusative direct object of ποιῶμεν.

ποιῶμεν. Pres act subj 1st pl ποιέω (deliberative subjunctive).

ἵνα. Introduces a purpose clause.

ἐργαζώμεθα. Pres mid subj 1st pl ἐργάζομαι. Subjunctive with ἵνα.

τὰ ἔργα. Accusative direct object of ἐργαζώμεθα.

τοῦ θεοῦ. Subjective genitive qualifying ἔργα ("the works that God demands").

6:29 ἀπεκρίθη [ὁ] Ἰησοῦς καὶ εἶπεν αὐτοῖς· τοῦτό ἐστιν τὸ ἔργον τοῦ θεοῦ, ἵνα πιστεύητε εἰς ὃν ἀπέστειλεν ἐκεῖνος.

ἀπεκρίθη. Aor mid ind 3rd sg ἀποκρίνομαι. On the voice, see "Deponency" in the Series Introduction. This verse is connected to the previous one by asyndeton.

[ὁ] Ἰησοῦς. Nominative subject of ἀπεκρίθη. The article is printed within square brackets because the external evidence for (A B D K L N T Θ $f^{1.13}$ et al.) and against ($\mathfrak{P}^{75}$ ℵ W Γ Δ Ψ 565 700 𝔐 et al.) its presence in the text is evenly balanced.

καὶ εἶπεν αὐτοῖς. Pleonastic clause under Semitic influence, which functions as a redundant quotative frame (see 1:25 on καὶ εἶπαν αὐτῷ).

καὶ. Coordinating conjunction.

εἶπεν. Aor act ind 3rd sg λέγω.

αὐτοῖς. Dative indirect object of εἶπεν.

τοῦτό. Nominative subject of ἐστιν. Fronted for emphasis. The demonstrative pronoun is cataphoric, pointing toward the explanation of the work of God that follows. τοῦτό, which has a circumflex accent on the penult, acquired an additional accent, the acute, on the ultima from the enclitic ἐστιν (Smyth §183; Carson 1985, 48).

ἐστιν. Pres act ind 3rd sg εἰμί.

τὸ ἔργον. Predicate nominative.

τοῦ θεοῦ. Subjective genitive qualifying ἔργον ("the works that God demands").

ἵνα. Introduces an epexegetical clause that explains τὸ ἔργον τοῦ θεοῦ.

πιστεύητε. Pres act subj 2nd pl πιστεύω. Subjunctive with ἵνα.

εἰς ὃν. Goal of actions or feelings directed toward someone (BDAG, 290.4.c.β). For πιστεύειν εἰς + accusative ("trust or believe in someone"), see 1:12 on εἰς τὸ ὄνομα. εἰς ὃν is an ellipsis for εἰς τοῦτον ὃν (Haubeck and von Siebenthal, 546; Harris 2015, 131); thus, ὃν has a double function, serving as both the object of the preposition εἰς and the accusative direct object of ἀπέστειλεν.

ἀπέστειλεν. Aor act ind 3rd sg ἀποστέλλω.

ἐκεῖνος. Nominative subject of ἀπέστειλεν. As is usual in the FG, the demonstrative pronoun acts as a third-person personal pronoun with a simple anaphoric force (Wallace 1996, 328–29), but in this context the far-demonstrative also serves to distinguish its referent (God) from the referent of the relative pronoun ὅν (Jesus) that stands closer to the verb.

John 6:30-35

³⁰So they said to him, "What, then, are you going to do for a sign, so that we may see and believe you? What work are you performing? ³¹Our fathers ate the manna in the wilderness, as it is written, 'He gave them bread from heaven to eat.'" ³²Then Jesus said to them, "Truly, truly I say to you, it was not Moses who gave you the bread from heaven, but my Father gives you the true bread that is from heaven. ³³For the bread of God is the one who comes down from heaven and gives life to the world." ³⁴So they said to him, "Sir, always give us this bread!" ³⁵Jesus said to them, "I am the bread of life. The one who comes to me will never be hungry, and the one who believes in me will never be thirsty."

6:30 Εἶπον οὖν αὐτῷ· τί οὖν ποιεῖς σὺ σημεῖον, ἵνα ἴδωμεν καὶ πιστεύσωμέν σοι; τί ἐργάζῃ;

Εἶπον. Aor act ind 3rd pl λέγω.

οὖν. Postpositive inferential conjunction and/or transitional particle (see 1:22 and 11:6).

αὐτῷ. Dative indirect object of Εἶπον.

τί. Interrogative pronoun functioning as the accusative direct object of ποιεῖς in a double-accusative object-complement construction.

οὖν. Postpositive inferential conjunction.

ποιεῖς. Pres act ind 2nd sg ποιέω. The present tense has a futuristic meaning because Jesus' interlocutors apparently do not regard the miracles that he performed so far as legitimizing signs.

σὺ. Nominative subject of ποιεῖς. The personal pronoun is emphatic and contrastive, juxtaposing Jesus to οἱ πατέρες ἡμῶν in v. 31.

σημεῖον. Accusative complement to τί in a double-accusative object-complement construction.

ἵνα. Introduces a purpose clause.

ἴδωμεν. Aor act subj 1st pl ὁράω. Subjunctive with ἵνα.

καὶ. Coordinating conjunction.

πιστεύσωμέν. Aor act subj 1st pl πιστεύω. Subjunctive with ἵνα. πιστεύσωμέν, which has an acute accent on the antepenult, acquired an additional accent, the acute, on the ultima from the enclitic σοι (Smyth §183; Carson 1985, 48).

σοι. Dative complement of πιστεύσωμεν. The dative indicates the person "to whom one gives credence or whom one believes" (BDAG, 816.1.b).

τί. Accusative direct object of ἐργάζῃ.

ἐργάζῃ. Pres mid ind 2nd sg ἐργάζομαι. The present tense has the futuristic meaning (see ποιεῖς above).

6:31 οἱ πατέρες ἡμῶν τὸ μάννα ἔφαγον ἐν τῇ ἐρήμῳ, καθώς ἐστιν γεγραμμένον· ἄρτον ἐκ τοῦ οὐρανοῦ ἔδωκεν αὐτοῖς φαγεῖν.

οἱ πατέρες. Nominative subject of ἔφαγον. The noun refers to the Exodus generation. This verse is connected to the previous one by asyndeton.

ἡμῶν. Genitive of relationship qualifying πατέρες.

τὸ μάννα. Accusative direct object of ἔφαγον. Fronted for emphasis.

ἔφαγον. Aor act ind 3rd pl ἐσθίω.

ἐν τῇ ἐρήμῳ. Locative.

καθώς ἐστιν γεγραμμένον. The OT introductory formula (cf. 2:17; 6:45; 10:34; 12:14).

καθώς. Introduces a comparative clause.

ἐστιν. Pres act ind 3rd sg εἰμί.

γεγραμμένον. Prf pass ptc neut nom sg γράφω (perfect periphrastic).

ἄρτον ἐκ τοῦ οὐρανοῦ ἔδωκεν αὐτοῖς φαγεῖν. A combination of the elements of the quotations of LXX Exod 16:4a (ἐγὼ ὕω ὑμῖν ἄρτους ἐκ τοῦ οὐρανοῦ), LXX Ps 77:24 [78:24 MT] (καὶ ἔβρεξεν αὐτοῖς μαννα φαγεῖν καὶ ἄρτον οὐρανοῦ ἔδωκεν αὐτοῖς), and LXX Neh 9:15a (ἄρτον ἐξ οὐρανοῦ ἔδωκας αὐτοῖς).

ἄρτον. Accusative direct object of ἔδωκεν. Fronted for emphasis.

ἐκ τοῦ οὐρανοῦ. Source.

ἔδωκεν. Aor act ind 3rd sg δίδωμι.

αὐτοῖς. Dative indirect object of ἔδωκεν.

φαγεῖν. Aor act inf ἐσθίω (purpose).

6:32 εἶπεν οὖν αὐτοῖς ὁ Ἰησοῦς· ἀμὴν ἀμὴν λέγω ὑμῖν, οὐ Μωϋσῆς δέδωκεν ὑμῖν τὸν ἄρτον ἐκ τοῦ οὐρανοῦ, ἀλλ' ὁ πατήρ μου δίδωσιν ὑμῖν τὸν ἄρτον ἐκ τοῦ οὐρανοῦ τὸν ἀληθινόν·

εἶπεν. Aor act ind 3rd sg λέγω.

οὖν. Postpositive inferential conjunction and/or transitional particle (see 1:22 and 11:6).

αὐτοῖς. Dative indirect object of εἶπεν.

ὁ Ἰησοῦς. Nominative subject of εἶπεν.

ἀμὴν ἀμὴν λέγω ὑμῖν. Metacomment (see 1:51).

ἀμὴν ἀμὴν. Asseverative particles that mark the beginning of Jesus' solemn declaration (see 1:51).

λέγω. Pres act ind 1st sg λέγω.

ὑμῖν. Dative indirect object of λέγω.

οὐ . . . ἀλλ'. A point/counterpoint set ("not this . . . but that") that negates the first, incorrect, assertion ("Moses gave you the bread from heaven") and replaces it with the second, correct, assertion ("my Father gives you the true bread from heaven"). On the function of ἀλλά in a point/counterpoint set, see 1:8.

Μωϋσῆς. Nominative subject of δέδωκεν. Fronted for emphasis.

δέδωκεν. Prf act ind 3rd sg δίδωμι. Although in this context the perfect tense primarily describes the past event (Porter 1989, 261), its present relevance is subtly insinuated by the second plural pronoun ὑμῖν, which draws Jesus' audience into the foundational narrative (cf. οἱ πατέρες ἡμῶν and αὐτοῖς in v. 31). The verb form is semantically marked, calling attention to the agent—Moses—who did not perform the action of giving the bread from heaven.

ὑμῖν. Dative indirect object of δέδωκεν.

τὸν ἄρτον. Accusative direct object of δέδωκεν.

ἐκ τοῦ οὐρανοῦ. Source.

ὁ πατήρ. Nominative subject of δίδωσιν. Fronted for emphasis.

μου. Genitive of relationship qualifying πατήρ.

δίδωσιν. Pres act ind 3rd sg δίδωμι. The present tense describes an event that is contemporaneous with the plot of the narrative. The imperfective aspect functions as a semantic marker, creating a contrasting parallel between the past event (see δέδωκεν above) and the present experience.

ὑμῖν. Dative indirect object of δίδωσιν.

τὸν ἄρτον . . . τὸν ἀληθινόν. Accusative direct object of δίδωσιν. The adjective stands in the second attributive position (see 1:9 on τὸ φῶς τὸ ἀληθινόν).

ἐκ τοῦ οὐρανοῦ. Source. The PP, embedded in the nominal phrase τὸν ἄρτον . . . τὸν ἀληθινόν, functions as the attributive modifier of τὸν ἄρτον. While in the preceding clause the PP functions adverbially, clarifying the origin of the act of giving, here it functions attributively, explaining the origin of the true bread.

6:33 ὁ γὰρ ἄρτος τοῦ θεοῦ ἐστιν ὁ καταβαίνων ἐκ τοῦ οὐρανοῦ καὶ ζωὴν διδοὺς τῷ κόσμῳ.

ὁ . . . ἄρτος. Nominative subject of ἐστιν. Fronted as a topical frame.

γάρ. Postpositive conjunction that introduces the explanation of the previous assertion that the Father gives the true bread that is from heaven.

τοῦ θεοῦ. Possessive genitive ("God's bread") or genitive of producer ("bread supplied by God") qualifying ἄρτος.

ἐστιν. Pres act ind 3rd sg εἰμί.

ὁ καταβαίνων ... καὶ ... διδούς. Predicate nominative. Two substantival participles governed by one article and joined by καί form a TSKS (article-substantive-καί-substantive) construction. In such formulations, according to the Granville Sharp rule, the single article indicates that both participles have the same referent; see 5:24 on ὁ ... ἀκούων καὶ πιστεύων. The masculine gender of the substantival participles is not required by the masculine gender of ὁ ... ἄρτος (*pace* Michaels, 372), because ὁ καταβαίνων ... καὶ ... διδούς functions as the predicate nominative and is therefore not dependent on the gender of the subject of ἐστιν (see, e.g., ἡ ζωὴ ἦν τὸ φῶς τῶν ἀνθρώπων [1:4]; πνεῦμα ὁ θεός [6:33]). Even so, the masculine gender of the participial phrase creates a double entendre that causes misunderstanding, because ὁ καταβαίνων ... καὶ ... διδούς could refer to the physical bread supplied by God from heaven (i.e., the manna mentioned in v. 31) and/or to a personalized bread from heaven, anticipating Jesus' explicit claims in v. 35 (ἐγώ εἰμι ὁ ἄρτος τῆς ζωῆς) and v. 51 (ἐγώ εἰμι ὁ ἄρτος ὁ ζῶν ὁ ἐκ τοῦ οὐρανοῦ καταβάς). For other examples of words with multiple meanings that are typically misunderstood by Jesus' audience, see 3:3-4; 4:14-15; 8:21-22; 11:11-13, 23-24; 14:7-8.

καταβαίνων. Pres act ptc masc nom sg καταβαίνω (substantival).

διδούς. Pres act ptc masc nom sg δίδωμι (substantival).

ἐκ τοῦ οὐρανοῦ. Source/origin.

ζωὴν. Accusative direct object of διδούς. Fronted for emphasis.

τῷ κόσμῳ. Dative indirect object of διδούς. On the portrayal of the world in the FG, see 1:10 on ἐν τῷ κόσμῳ.

6:34 εἶπον οὖν πρὸς αὐτόν· κύριε, πάντοτε δὸς ἡμῖν τὸν ἄρτον τοῦτον.

εἶπον. Aor act ind 3rd pl λέγω.

οὖν. Postpositive inferential conjunction and/or transitional particle (see 1:22 and 11:6).

πρὸς αὐτόν. Locative (motion toward). The PP functions like an indirect object of εἶπον.

κύριε. Vocative of direct address.

πάντοτε. Adverb of time ("always, at all times").

δός. Aor act impv 2nd sg δίδωμι.

ἡμῖν. Dative indirect object of δός.

τὸν ἄρτον τοῦτον. Accusative direct object of δός.

6:35 εἶπεν αὐτοῖς ὁ Ἰησοῦς· ἐγώ εἰμι ὁ ἄρτος τῆς ζωῆς· ὁ ἐρχόμενος πρὸς ἐμὲ οὐ μὴ πεινάσῃ, καὶ ὁ πιστεύων εἰς ἐμὲ οὐ μὴ διψήσει πώποτε.

εἶπεν. Aor act ind 3rd sg λέγω. This verse is connected to the previous one by asyndeton.

αὐτοῖς. Dative indirect object of εἶπεν.

ὁ Ἰησοῦς. Nominative subject of εἶπεν.

ἐγώ εἰμι ὁ ἄρτος τῆς ζωῆς. This is the first of Jesus' "I am" pronouncements in the FG with an explicit predicate; for other statements of this type, see 6:48, 51; 8:12; 10:7, 9, 11, 14; 11:25; 14:6; 15:1, 5. In this group of sayings, Jesus identifies himself with the help of various metaphors that express human quest for salvation.

ἐγώ. Nominative subject of εἰμι. Fronted for emphasis. Boring (689) argues that ἐγώ is the predicate and translates ἐγώ εἰμι ὁ ἄρτος τῆς ζωῆς as "the bread of life, it is I" (689). However, in an equative clause that has a pronoun and an articular noun, as here, "the pronoun has greatest priority: It will be the S[ubject] regardless of what grammatical tag the other substantive has" (Wallace 1996, 44).

εἰμι. Pres act ind 1st sg εἰμί.

ὁ ἄρτος. Predicate nominative.

τῆς ζωῆς. Genitive of product ("bread that generates life") or descriptive genitive ("bread characterized by life") qualifying ἄρτος.

ὁ ἐρχόμενος. Pres mid ptc masc nom sg ἔρχομαι (substantival). Nominative subject of πεινάσῃ. Fronted as a topical frame. This clause is connected to the preceding one by asyndeton.

πρὸς ἐμὲ. Locative (motion toward).

οὐ μὴ. Emphatic negation, which is usually followed by the aorist subjunctive.

πεινάσῃ. Aor act subj 3rd sg πεινάω. Used with οὐ μὴ to express emphatic negation.

καί. Coordinating conjunction.

ὁ πιστεύων. Pres act ptc masc nom sg πιστεύω (substantival). Nominative subject of διψήσει. Fronted as a topical frame.

εἰς ἐμὲ. Goal of actions or feelings directed toward someone (BDAG, 290.4.c.β). For πιστεύειν εἰς + accusative ("trust or believe in someone"), see 1:12 on εἰς τὸ ὄνομα.

οὐ μὴ. Emphatic negation, which is usually followed by the aorist subjunctive, but it could sometimes be followed by the future indicative, as here (Wallace 1996, 468; BDF §365).

διψήσει. Fut act ind 3rd sg διψάω.

πώποτε. Indefinite adverb of time.

John 6:36-40

³⁶"But I said to you that though you have seen me, yet you do not believe. ³⁷Everyone whom the Father gives to me will come to me, and the one who comes to me I will never throw out, ³⁸because I have come down from heaven not that I should do my own will, but the will of the one who sent me. ³⁹This is the will of the one who sent me—that everyone whom he has given me, I should not lose any of them, but raise them up on the last day. ⁴⁰For this is the will of my Father—that everyone who sees the Son and believes in him should have eternal life, and I will raise him up on the last day."

6:36 Ἀλλ' εἶπον ὑμῖν ὅτι καὶ ἑωράκατέ [με] καὶ οὐ πιστεύετε.

Ἀλλ'. Marker of contrast.

εἶπον. Aor act ind 1st sg λέγω.

ὑμῖν. Dative indirect object of εἶπον.

ὅτι. Introduces the clausal complement (indirect discourse) of εἶπον.

καὶ . . . καὶ. "Both . . . and," which can be translated here "though . . . yet" (Zerwick and Grosvenor, 305).

ἑωράκατέ. Prf act ind 2nd pl ὁράω.

[με]. Accusative direct object of ἑωράκατέ. The variant without με, attested by some manuscripts (ℵ A a b e q sy^{s.c}), better fits the tenor of the FG because it presumes that Jesus speaks about the signs that people have seen (cf. 6:26). The variant with με, however, has stronger textual support and represents the *lectio difficilior*. Square brackets in NA²⁸/UBS⁵ indicate that a decision between these two readings is difficult (Metzger, 182), while their absence in SBLGNT show the editors' preference for the variant with με.

οὐ. Negative particle normally used with indicative verbs.

πιστεύετε. Pres act ind 2nd pl πιστεύω.

6:37 πᾶν ὃ δίδωσίν μοι ὁ πατὴρ πρὸς ἐμὲ ἥξει, καὶ τὸν ἐρχόμενον πρὸς ἐμὲ οὐ μὴ ἐκβάλω ἔξω,

πᾶν. Nominative subject of ἥξει. The neuter singular is sometimes used with reference to persons, as here, "if it is not the individuals but a general quality that is to be emphasized" (BDF §138.1). For other examples of this usage in the FG, see 3:6; 6:39; 17:2, 24. This verse is connected to the previous one by asyndeton.

ὅ. Accusative direct object of δίδωσίν. The neuter agrees with its antecedent πᾶν, although it refers to a person (see above).

δίδωσίν. Pres act ind 3rd sg δίδωμι. δίδωσίν, which has an acute accent on the antepenult, acquired an additional accent, the acute, on the ultima from the enclitic μοι (Smyth §183; Carson 1985, 48).

μοι. Dative indirect object of δίδωσίν.
ὁ πατὴρ. Nominative subject of δίδωσίν.
πρὸς ἐμὲ. Locative (motion toward).
ἥξει. Fut act ind 3rd sg ἥκω.
καὶ. Coordinating conjunction.
τὸν ἐρχόμενον. Pres mid ptc masc acc sg ἔρχομαι (substantival). Accusative direct object of ἐκβάλω.
πρὸς ἐμὲ. Locative (motion toward).
οὐ μὴ ἐκβάλω ἔξω. Litotes for προσλήμψομαι (Harris 2015, 135).
οὐ μὴ. Emphatic negation, which is usually followed by the aorist subjunctive.
ἐκβάλω. Aor act subj 1st sg ἐκβάλλω. Used with οὐ μὴ to express emphatic negation.
ἔξω. Adverb of place ("out, outside").

6:38 ὅτι καταβέβηκα ἀπὸ τοῦ οὐρανοῦ οὐχ ἵνα ποιῶ τὸ θέλημα τὸ ἐμὸν ἀλλὰ τὸ θέλημα τοῦ πέμψαντός με.

ὅτι. Introduces a causal clause.
καταβέβηκα. Prf act ind 1st sg καταβαίνω.
ἀπὸ τοῦ οὐρανοῦ. Source/origin.
οὐχ . . . ἀλλὰ. A point/counterpoint set ("not this . . . but that") that negates the incorrect explanation of the purpose of Jesus' descent from heaven ("to do my own will") and replaces it with the correct explanation of his purpose ("to do the will of the one who sent him"). On the function of ἀλλὰ in a point/counterpoint set, see 1:8.
ἵνα. Introduces a purpose clause.
ποιῶ. Pres act subj 1st sg ποιέω. Subjunctive with ἵνα.
τὸ θέλημα τὸ ἐμὸν. Accusative direct object of ποιῶ. The possessive adjective stands in the second attributive position (see 1:9 on τὸ φῶς τὸ ἀληθινόν).
τὸ θέλημα. Accusative direct object of an implied ποιῶ. The nominal phrase τὸ θέλημα τοῦ πέμψαντός με also occurs in 4:34; 5:30; 6:39.
τοῦ πέμψαντός. Aor act ptc masc gen sg πέμπω (substantival). Subjective genitive qualifying θέλημα. πέμψαντός, which has an acute accent on the antepenult, acquired an additional accent, the acute, on the ultima from the enclitic με (Smyth §183; Carson 1985, 48). On the use of the participial forms of πέμπω to either identify or describe God in the FG, see τοῦ πέμψαντός in 4:34.
με. Accusative direct object of πέμψαντός.

6:39 τοῦτο δέ ἐστιν τὸ θέλημα τοῦ πέμψαντός με, ἵνα πᾶν ὃ δέδωκέν μοι μὴ ἀπολέσω ἐξ αὐτοῦ, ἀλλ' ἀναστήσω αὐτὸ [ἐν] τῇ ἐσχάτῃ ἡμέρᾳ.

τοῦτο. Nominative subject of ἐστιν. Fronted for emphasis. The near-demonstrative pronoun is cataphoric, pointing to the explanation of God's will that follows.

δέ. Marker of narrative development.

ἐστιν. Pres act ind 3rd sg εἰμί.

τὸ θέλημα. Predicate nominative. The nominal phrase τὸ θέλημα τοῦ πέμψαντός με also occurs in 4:34; 5:30; 6:38.

τοῦ πέμψαντός. Aor act ptc masc gen sg πέμπω (substantival). Subjective genitive qualifying θέλημα. πέμψαντός, which has an acute accent on the antepenult, acquired an additional accent, the acute, on the ultima from the enclitic με (Smyth §183; Carson 1985, 48). On the use of the participial forms of πέμπω to either identify or describe God in the FG, see τοῦ πέμψαντός in 4:34.

με. Accusative direct object of πέμψαντός.

ἵνα. Introduces an epexegetical clause that explains τὸ θέλημα τοῦ πέμψαντός με.

πᾶν. Pendent nominative in a left-dislocation (Runge 2010, 287–313). On the neuter gender, see 6:37.

ὅ. Accusative direct object of δέδωκεν. The neuter agrees with its antecedent πᾶν, although it refers to a person (see above). The entire relative clause ὃ δέδωκέν μοι is, like πᾶν to which it refers, in a left-dislocation.

δέδωκεν. Prf act ind 3rd sg δίδωμι. δέδωκέν, which has an acute accent on the antepenult, acquired an additional accent, the acute, on the ultima from the enclitic μοι (Smyth §183; Carson 1985, 48). The perfect tense, which is semantically marked, "expresses that what the Father 'has given' to the Son ... is definitely in his hand" (Frey 2018, 81).

μοι. Dative indirect object of δέδωκεν.

μὴ ... ἀλλ'. A point/counterpoint set ("not this ... but that") that negates the incorrect explanation of the divine will regarding those who have been given to Jesus (he should lose some of them) and replaces it with the correct explanation of the divine will (he should raise them up on the last day). On the function of ἀλλά in a point/counterpoint set, see 1:8.

ἀπολέσω. Aor act subj 1st sg ἀπόλλυμι. Subjunctive with ἵνα.

ἐξ αὐτοῦ. Replaces the partitive genitive. αὐτοῦ is resumptive, referring to πᾶν. The anaphoric personal pronoun reinforces what is already made prominent through the left-dislocation of πᾶν ὃ δέδωκέν μοι.

ἀναστήσω. Aor act subj 1st sg ἀνίστημι. Subjunctive with ἵνα.

αὐτό. Accusative direct object of ἀναστήσω. Like αὐτοῦ above, αὐτὸ is resumptive, referring to πᾶν.

[ἐν] τῇ ἐσχάτῃ ἡμέρᾳ. Temporal. Square brackets indicate that the evidence for (א A D K N f^{13} 33 1241 et al.) and against ($\mathfrak{P}^{66.75}$ B C L T W Γ Δ Θ Ψ f^1 565 579 700 892 et al.) the inclusion of the preposition ἐν is evenly balanced. The PP "on the last day" occurs only in the FG (6:39, 40, 44; 11:24; 12:48; cf. τῇ ἐσχάτῃ ἡμέρᾳ in 6:54). Other NT expressions use the plural "the last days" (ἐν ταῖς ἐσχάταις ἡμέραις [Acts 2:17]; ἐν ἐσχάταις ἡμέραις [2 Tim 3:1; Jas 5:3]; ἐπ' ἐσχάτου τῶν ἡμερῶν [Heb 1:2]; ἐπ' ἐσχάτων τῶν ἡμερῶν [2 Pet 3:3]).

6:40 τοῦτο γάρ ἐστιν τὸ θέλημα τοῦ πατρός μου, ἵνα πᾶς ὁ θεωρῶν τὸν υἱὸν καὶ πιστεύων εἰς αὐτὸν ἔχῃ ζωὴν αἰώνιον, καὶ ἀναστήσω αὐτὸν ἐγὼ [ἐν] τῇ ἐσχάτῃ ἡμέρᾳ.

τοῦτο. Nominative subject of ἐστιν. Fronted for emphasis. The near-demonstrative pronoun is cataphoric, pointing to the explanation of God's will that follows.

γάρ. Postpositive conjunction that introduces the support for the previous statement. For the most part, however, this verse repeats the assertions of v. 39.

ἐστιν. Pres act ind 3rd sg εἰμί.

τὸ θέλημα. Predicate nominative.

τοῦ πατρός. Subjective genitive qualifying θέλημα.

μου. Genitive of relationship qualifying πατρός.

ἵνα. Introduces an epexegetical clause that explains τὸ θέλημα τοῦ πατρός μου.

πᾶς ὁ θεωρῶν . . . καὶ πιστεύων. Nominative subject of ἔχῃ. Two substantival participles governed by one article and joined by καί form a TSKS (article-substantive-καί-substantive) construction. In such formulations, according to the Granville Sharp rule, the single article indicates that both participles have the same referent; see 5:24 on ὁ . . . ἀκούων καὶ πιστεύων. On πᾶς + articular participle, see 3:8 on πᾶς ὁ γεγεννημένος.

θεωρῶν. Pres act ptc masc nom sg θεωρέω (substantival). On the function of this participle, see πᾶς ὁ θεωρῶν . . . καὶ πιστεύων above.

τὸν υἱὸν. Accusative direct object of θεωρῶν.

πιστεύων. Pres act ptc masc nom sg πιστεύω (substantival). On the function of this participle, see πᾶς ὁ θεωρῶν . . . καὶ πιστεύων above.

εἰς αὐτὸν. Goal of actions or feelings directed toward someone (BDAG, 290.4.c.β). For πιστεύειν εἰς + accusative ("trust or believe in someone"), see 1:12 on εἰς τὸ ὄνομα.

ἔχῃ. Pres act subj 3rd sg ἔχω. Subjunctive with ἵνα.

ζωὴν αἰώνιον. Accusative direct object of ἔχῃ. On the use of this phrase in the FG, see 3:15 on ζωὴν αἰώνιον.

καί. Coordinating conjunction.

ἀναστήσω. Aor act subj 1st sg ἀνίστημι with an implied ἵνα, continuing to explain the will of God by restating the counterpoint from 6:39, or fut act ind 1st sg ἀνίστημι in an independent clause. The abrupt switch from the third-person to the first-person subject supports taking ἀναστήσω αὐτὸν ἐγὼ [ἐν] τῇ ἐσχάτῃ ἡμέρᾳ as a separate clause that expresses promise like in 6:44, 54.

αὐτόν. Accusative direct object of ἀναστήσω.

ἐγώ. Nominative subject of ἀναστήσω. The personal pronoun is emphatic.

[ἐν] τῇ ἐσχάτῃ ἡμέρᾳ. Temporal. Like in the previous verse, the evidence for ($\mathfrak{P}^{66}$ ℵ A D K L N Ψ f^{13} 33 1241 et al.) and against ($\mathfrak{P}^{75}$ B C T W Γ Δ Θ 1 565 579 700 892 1424 𝔐 et al.) the inclusion of the preposition ἐν is evenly balanced. On the use of this PP in the FG, see 6:39 on [ἐν] τῇ ἐσχάτῃ ἡμέρᾳ.

John 6:41-51

[41]Then the Jews began to grumble about him because he said, "I am the bread that came down from heaven." [42]And they were saying, "Is not this one Jesus, the son of Joseph, whose father and mother we know? How can he now say, 'I have come down from heaven'?" [43]Jesus answered and said to them, "Do not grumble among yourselves. [44]No one can come to me unless the Father who sent me draws him, and I will raise him up on the last day. [45]It is written in the prophets, 'And they will all be taught by God.' Everyone who hears from the Father and learns comes to me. [46]Not that anyone has seen the Father except the one who is from God—this one has seen the Father. [47]Truly, truly I say to you, the one who believes has eternal life. [48]I am the bread of life. [49]Our fathers ate the manna in the wilderness and they died. [50]This is the bread that comes down from heaven, so that someone may eat of it and not die. [51]I am the living bread that came down from heaven. If anyone eats of this bread, he will live forever. And the bread that I will give is my flesh for the life of the world."

6:41 Ἐγόγγυζον οὖν οἱ Ἰουδαῖοι περὶ αὐτοῦ ὅτι εἶπεν· ἐγώ εἰμι ὁ ἄρτος ὁ καταβὰς ἐκ τοῦ οὐρανοῦ,

Ἐγόγγυζον. Impf act ind 3rd pl γογγύζω. The verb means "to express one's discontent—'to complain, to grumble, complaint'" (LN 33.382). On the function of the imperfect in the FG, see 1:39 on ἦν.

οὖν. Postpositive inferential conjunction and/or transitional particle (see 1:22 and 11:6).

οἱ Ἰουδαῖοι. Nominative subject of Ἐγόγγυζον.

περὶ αὐτοῦ. Reference.

ὅτι. Introduces a causal clause.

εἶπεν. Aor act ind 3rd sg λέγω.

ἐγώ. Nominative subject of εἰμί. Fronted for emphasis.

εἰμι. Pres act ind 1st sg εἰμί.

ὁ ἄρτος. Predicate nominative.

ὁ καταβὰς. Aor act ptc masc nom sg καταβαίνω (attributive). The participle modifies ὁ ἄρτος, standing in the second attributive position (see 1:29 on ὁ αἴρων). Since "the temporal reference of a participle is established relative to its use in context" (Porter 1994, 187), the aorist participle, because it refers to Jesus, describes an action that is antecedent to Jesus' declarative statement ἐγώ εἰμι ὁ ἄρτος.

ἐκ τοῦ οὐρανοῦ. Source/origin.

6:42 καὶ ἔλεγον· οὐχ οὗτός ἐστιν Ἰησοῦς ὁ υἱὸς Ἰωσήφ, οὗ ἡμεῖς οἴδαμεν τὸν πατέρα καὶ τὴν μητέρα; πῶς νῦν λέγει ὅτι ἐκ τοῦ οὐρανοῦ καταβέβηκα;

καὶ. Coordinating conjunction.

ἔλεγον. Impf act ind 3rd pl λέγω. On the function of the imperfect in the FG, see 1:39 on ἦν.

οὐχ. Negative particle that introduces a question that expects an affirmative answer.

οὗτός. Nominative subject of ἐστιν. οὗτός, which has a circumflex accent on the penult, acquired an additional accent, the acute, on the ultima from the enclitic ἐστιν (Smyth §183; Carson 1985, 48). Robertson (697) thinks that this οὗτος is contemptuous. Runge, conversely, argues that this usage is "better explained as marking the participant as being thematically salient, as being in the spotlight" (2010, 373 n. 22).

ἐστιν. Pres act ind 3rd sg εἰμί.

Ἰησοῦς. Predicate nominative.

ὁ υἱὸς. Nominative in apposition to Ἰησοῦς.

Ἰωσήφ. Genitive of relationship qualifying υἱὸς.

οὗ. Genitive of relationship qualifying πατέρα and μητέρα. The antecedent of the relative is Ἰησοῦς.

ἡμεῖς. Nominative subject of οἴδαμεν. Fronted for emphasis.

οἴδαμεν. Prf act ind 1st pl οἶδα (see 1:26 on οἴδατε).

τὸν πατέρα. Accusative direct object of οἴδαμεν.

καί. Coordinating conjunction.

τὴν μητέρα. Accusative direct object of οἴδαμεν.

πῶς. Interrogative particle.

νῦν. Adverb of time.

λέγει. Pres act ind 3rd sg λέγω.

ὅτι. ὅτι-*recitativum* that introduces the clausal complement (direct discourse) of λέγει.

ἐκ τοῦ οὐρανοῦ. Source/origin. Fronted for emphasis.

καταβέβηκα. Prf act ind 1st sg καταβαίνω.

6:43 ἀπεκρίθη Ἰησοῦς καὶ εἶπεν αὐτοῖς· μὴ γογγύζετε μετ' ἀλλήλων.

ἀπεκρίθη. Aor mid ind 3rd sg ἀποκρίνομαι. On the voice, see "Deponency" in the Series Introduction. This verse is connected to the previous one by asyndeton.

Ἰησοῦς. Nominative subject of ἀπεκρίθη.

καὶ εἶπεν αὐτοῖς. Pleonastic clause under Semitic influence, which functions as a redundant quotative frame (see 1:25 on καὶ εἶπαν αὐτῷ).

καί. Coordinating conjunction.

εἶπεν. Aor act ind 3rd sg λέγω.

αὐτοῖς. Dative indirect object of εἶπεν.

μή. Negative particle normally used with non-indicative verbs.

γογγύζετε. Pres act impv 2nd pl γογγύζω. Since v. 41 indicates that the Jews began to complain, the present imperative undoubtedly means that they should stop grumbling.

μετ' ἀλλήλων. Association/accompaniment.

6:44 οὐδεὶς δύναται ἐλθεῖν πρός με ἐὰν μὴ ὁ πατὴρ ὁ πέμψας με ἑλκύσῃ αὐτόν, κἀγὼ ἀναστήσω αὐτὸν ἐν τῇ ἐσχάτῃ ἡμέρᾳ.

οὐδείς. Nominative subject of δύναται. Fronted for emphasis. It marks the beginning of the apodosis of a third-class condition, which precedes the protasis. This verse is connected to the previous one by asyndeton.

δύναται. Pres mid ind 3rd sg δύναμαι.

ἐλθεῖν. Aor act inf ἔρχομαι (complementary).

πρός με. Locative (motion toward).

ἐάν. Introduces the protasis of a third-class condition.

μή. Negative particle normally used with non-indicative verbs. ἐὰν μή can be translated "unless."

ὁ πατήρ. Nominative subject of ἑλκύσῃ.

ὁ πέμψας. Aor act ptc masc nom sg πέμπω (attributive). The participle modifies ὁ πατήρ, standing in the second attributive position (see 1:29 on ὁ αἴρων). On the use of the participial forms of πέμπω to either identify or describe God in the FG, see τοῦ πέμψαντός in 4:34.

με. Accusative direct object of πέμψας.

ἑλκύσῃ. Aor act subj 3rd sg ἕλκω. Subjunctive with ἐάν. The literal meaning of ἕλκω ("to move an object from one area to another in a pulling motion" [BDAG, 318.1]) is extended figuratively to denote "to draw a pers[on] in the direction of values for inner life" (BDAG, 318.2).

αὐτόν. Accusative direct object of ἑλκύσῃ.

κἀγώ. Formed by crasis from καὶ ἐγώ. καί is a coordinating conjunction; ἐγώ is the nominative subject of ἀναστήσω. The personal pronoun is emphatic.

ἀναστήσω. Fut act ind 1st sg ἀνίστημι (see 6:40).

αὐτόν. Accusative direct object of ἀναστήσω.

ἐν τῇ ἐσχάτῃ ἡμέρᾳ. Temporal. On the use of this PP in the FG, see 6:39 on [ἐν] τῇ ἐσχάτῃ ἡμέρᾳ.

6:45 ἔστιν γεγραμμένον ἐν τοῖς προφήταις· καὶ ἔσονται πάντες διδακτοὶ θεοῦ· πᾶς ὁ ἀκούσας παρὰ τοῦ πατρὸς καὶ μαθὼν ἔρχεται πρὸς ἐμέ.

ἔστιν γεγραμμένον. The standard OT introductory formula (cf. 2:17; 6:31; 10:34; 12:14).

ἔστιν. Pres act ind 3rd sg εἰμί. The enclitic ἐστιν is accented ἔστιν when it comes at the beginning of a sentence, when it expresses existence, or when it follows ἀλλ', εἰ, καί, οὐκ, ὅτι, or τοῦτ'. The first condition is fulfilled here. This verse is connected to the previous one by asyndeton.

γεγραμμένον. Prf pass ptc neut nom sg γράφω (perfect periphrastic).

ἐν τοῖς προφήταις. Locative.

καὶ ἔσονται πάντες διδακτοὶ θεοῦ. A paraphrastic quotation of LXX Isa 54:13 (καὶ πάντας τοὺς υἱούς σου διδακτοὺς θεοῦ).

καί. Coordinating conjunction.

ἔσονται. Fut mid ind 3rd pl εἰμί.

πάντες. Nominative subject of ἔσονται.

διδακτοί. Predicate adjective.

θεοῦ. Genitive of agency ("taught by God"), which is typically used with verbal adjectives that have the characteristically passive ending -τος (BDF §183); cf. 1 Thess 4:9 (θεοδίδακτοί); 1 Cor 2:13 (διδακτοῖς πνεύματος).

πᾶς ὁ ἀκούσας . . . καὶ μαθών. Nominative subject of ἔρχεται. Two substantival participles governed by one article and joined by καί form a TSKS (article-substantive-καί-substantive) construction. In such formulations, according to the Granville Sharp rule, the single article indicates that both participles have the same referent; see 5:24 on ὁ . . . ἀκούων καὶ πιστεύων. Although both participles are in the aorist tense, the indefinite adjective πᾶς ("every") shows that they have a generalizing function, like other articular participles in FG that are preceded by πᾶς. "A general rule of thumb [with substantival participles] is that the more particular (as opposed to generic) the referent, the more of the verbal aspect is still seen" (Wallace 1996, 620). Since the function of these two participles is more generic, they do not refer to some antecedent actions relative to the context (e.g., "Everyone who has heard and learned from the Father comes to me" [NRSV; ESV]) but describe activities whose temporal references are irrelevant. On πᾶς + articular participle, see 3:8 on πᾶς ὁ γεγεννημένος.

ἀκούσας. Aor act ptc masc nom sg ἀκούω (substantival). On the function of this participle, see πᾶς ὁ ἀκούσας . . . καὶ μαθών above.

παρὰ τοῦ πατρός. Source.

μαθών. Aor act ptc masc nom sg μανθάνω (substantival). On the function of this participle, see πᾶς ὁ ἀκούσας . . . καὶ μαθών above.

ἔρχεται. Pres mid ind 3rd sg ἔρχομαι.

πρὸς ἐμέ. Locative (motion toward).

6:46 οὐχ ὅτι τὸν πατέρα ἑώρακέν τις εἰ μὴ ὁ ὢν παρὰ τοῦ θεοῦ, οὗτος ἑώρακεν τὸν πατέρα.

οὐχ ὅτι. An ellipsis for οὐ λέγω ὅτι (BDF §480.5).

οὐχ . . . εἰ μή. A point/counterpoint set that corrects the negated clause ("not that anyone has seen the Father") by introducing an exception ("except the one who is from God"); on the function of the excepted element, see 3:13 on οὐδεὶς . . . εἰ μή.

ὅτι. Introduces the clausal complement (indirect discourse) of an implied λέγω (see οὐχ ὅτι above).

τὸν πατέρα. Accusative direct object of first ἑώρακέν.

ἑώρακέν. Prf act ind 3rd sg ὁράω. ἑώρακέν, which has an acute accent on the antepenult, acquired an additional accent, the acute, on the ultima from the enclitic τις (Smyth §183; Carson 1985, 48).

τις. Nominative subject of the first ἑώρακεν.

ὁ ὤν. Pres act ptc masc nom sg εἰμί (substantival). The participle functions as the second, excepted, nominative subject of the first ἑώρακεν.

παρὰ τοῦ θεοῦ. Source/origin (BDAG, 756.A.1).

οὗτος. Nominative subject of the second ἑώρακεν. Fronted for emphasis. The demonstrative refers to ὁ ὤν παρὰ τοῦ θεοῦ.

ἑώρακεν. Prf act ind 3rd sg ὁράω.

τὸν πατέρα. Accusative direct object of the second ἑώρακεν.

6:47 Ἀμὴν ἀμὴν λέγω ὑμῖν, ὁ πιστεύων ἔχει ζωὴν αἰώνιον.

Ἀμὴν ἀμὴν λέγω ὑμῖν. Metacomment (see 1:51).

Ἀμὴν ἀμὴν. Asseverative particles that mark the beginning of Jesus' solemn declaration (see 1:51). This verse is connected to the previous one by asyndeton.

λέγω. Pres act ind 1st sg λέγω.

ὑμῖν. Dative indirect object of λέγω.

ὁ πιστεύων. Pres act ptc masc nom sg πιστεύω (substantival). After this participle, many witnesses add εἰς ἐμέ (A C² D K N Γ Δ Ψ $f^{1.13}$ 33 565 𝔐 et al.), but the shorter text has stronger textual support ($\mathfrak{P}^{66.75\text{vid}}$ ℵ B C* L T W Θ 892 et al.). Moreover, "[i]f the words had been present in the original text, no good reason can be suggested to account for their omission" (Metzger, 183).

ἔχει. Pres act ind 3rd sg ἔχω.

ζωὴν αἰώνιον. Accusative direct object of ἔχει. On the use of this phrase in the FG, see 3:15 on ζωὴν αἰώνιον.

6:48 Ἐγώ εἰμι ὁ ἄρτος τῆς ζωῆς.

Ἐγώ εἰμι ὁ ἄρτος τῆς ζωῆς. This is a verbatim repetition of Jesus' "I am" pronouncement in 6:35; for other statements of this type, see 6:51; 8:12; 10:7, 9, 11, 14; 11:25; 14:6; 15:1, 5.

Ἐγώ. Nominative subject of εἰμί. Fronted for emphasis. This verse is connected to the previous one by asyndeton.

εἰμί. Pres act ind 1st sg εἰμί.

ὁ ἄρτος. Predicate nominative.

τῆς ζωῆς. Genitive of product or descriptive genitive qualifying ἄρτος (see 6:35).

6:49 οἱ πατέρες ὑμῶν ἔφαγον ἐν τῇ ἐρήμῳ τὸ μάννα καὶ ἀπέθανον·

οἱ πατέρες. Nominative subject of ἔφαγον. οἱ πατέρες refers to the Exodus generation. Jesus modifies the assertion of the Jews in v. 31 (οἱ πατέρες ἡμῶν τὸ μάννα ἔφαγον ἐν τῇ ἐρήμῳ) by adding the second verb, ἀπέθανον ("they died"), which becomes the focus of the argument that follows. This verse is connected to the previous one by asyndeton.

ὑμῶν. Genitive of relationship qualifying πατέρες.
ἔφαγον. Aor act ind 3rd pl ἐσθίω.
ἐν τῇ ἐρήμῳ. Locative.
τὸ μάννα. Accusative direct object of ἔφαγον.
καί. Coordinating conjunction.
ἀπέθανον. Aor act ind 3rd pl ἀποθνήσκω.

6:50 οὗτός ἐστιν ὁ ἄρτος ὁ ἐκ τοῦ οὐρανοῦ καταβαίνων, ἵνα τις ἐξ αὐτοῦ φάγῃ καὶ μὴ ἀποθάνῃ.

οὗτός. Nominative subject of ἐστιν. Fronted for emphasis. οὗτός, which has a circumflex accent on the penult, acquired an additional accent, the acute, on the ultima from the enclitic ἐστιν (Smyth §183; Carson 1985, 48). This verse is connected to the previous one by asyndeton.
ἐστιν. Pres act ind 3rd sg εἰμί.
ὁ ἄρτος. Predicate nominative.
ὁ ... καταβαίνων. Pres act ptc masc nom sg καταβαίνω (attributive). The participle modifies ὁ ἄρτος, standing in the second attributive position (see 1:29 on ὁ αἴρων).
ἐκ τοῦ οὐρανοῦ. Source. The PP modifies καταβαίνων.
ἵνα. Introduces either a result or purpose clause.
τις. Nominative subject of φάγῃ.
ἐξ αὐτοῦ. Replaces the partitive genitive qualifying τις ("some of it").
φάγῃ. Aor act subj 3rd sg ἐσθίω. Subjunctive with ἵνα.
καί. Coordinating conjunction.
μή. Negative particle normally used with non-indicative verbs.
ἀποθάνῃ. Aor act subj 3rd sg ἀποθνήσκω. Subjunctive with ἵνα. The verb stands in final, emphatic position.

6:51 ἐγώ εἰμι ὁ ἄρτος ὁ ζῶν ὁ ἐκ τοῦ οὐρανοῦ καταβάς· ἐάν τις φάγῃ ἐκ τούτου τοῦ ἄρτου ζήσει εἰς τὸν αἰῶνα, καὶ ὁ ἄρτος δὲ ὃν ἐγὼ δώσω ἡ σάρξ μού ἐστιν ὑπὲρ τῆς τοῦ κόσμου ζωῆς.

ἐγώ εἰμι ὁ ἄρτος ὁ ζῶν ὁ ἐκ τοῦ οὐρανοῦ καταβάς. This is one of Jesus' "I am" pronouncements in the FG with an explicit predicate; for other statements of this type, see 6:35, 48; 8:12; 10:7, 9, 11, 14; 11:25; 14:6; 15:1, 5.
ἐγώ. Nominative subject of εἰμι. Fronted for emphasis. This verse is connected to the previous one by asyndeton.

εἰμι. Pres act ind 1st sg εἰμί.

ὁ ἄρτος. Predicate nominative.

ὁ ζῶν. Pres act ptc masc nom sg ζάω (attributive). The participle modifies ὁ ἄρτος, standing in the second attributive position (see 1:29 on ὁ αἴρων).

ὁ . . . καταβάς. Aor act ptc masc nom sg καταβαίνω (attributive). The participle also modifies ἄρτος, standing in the second attributive position (see above); on the temporal reference of the participle, see 6:41 on ὁ καταβάς.

ἐκ τοῦ οὐρανοῦ. Source/origin. The PP modifies καταβάς.

ἐάν. Introduces the protasis of a third-class condition. This clause is connected to the preceding one by asyndeton.

τις. Nominative subject of φάγῃ.

φάγῃ. Aor act subj 3rd sg ἐσθίω. Subjunctive with ἐάν.

ἐκ τούτου τοῦ ἄρτου. Replaces the partitive genitive ("some of this bread").

ζήσει. Fut act ind 3rd sg ζάω. The verb marks the beginning of the apodosis of a third-class condition.

εἰς τὸν αἰῶνα. Temporal.

καί. Coordinating conjunction.

ὁ ἄρτος. Nominative subject of ἐστιν.

δέ. Marker of narrative development.

ὄν. Accusative direct object of δώσω. The antecedent of the relative pronoun is ὁ ἄρτος.

ἐγώ. Nominative subject of δώσω. Emphatic use.

δώσω. Fut act ind 1st sg δίδωμι.

ἡ σάρξ. Predicate nominative. Fronted for emphasis.

μού. Possessive genitive qualifying σάρξ. The enclitic μού is accented because it is followed by the enclitic ἐστιν. "When several enclitics occur in succession, each receives an accent from the following, only the last having no accent" (Smyth §185).

ἐστιν. Pres act ind 3rd sg εἰμί.

ὑπὲρ τῆς . . . ζωῆς. Representation ("on behalf of the life of the world"). For the prepositional phrases with ὑπέρ in the FG, see 10:11, 15; 11:50, 51, 52; 13:37, 38; 15:13; 17:19; 18:15.

τοῦ κόσμου. Subjective genitive qualifying ζωῆς. Barrett (298) suggests that "ὑπὲρ τῆς τοῦ κόσμου ζωῆς is equivalent to ἵνα ὁ κόσμος ζῇ."

John 6:52-58

⁵²Then the Jews began to clash severely among themselves, saying, "How can this man give us his flesh to eat?" ⁵³So Jesus said to them, "Truly,

truly I say to you, unless you eat the flesh of the Son of Man and drink his blood, you do not have life in you. ⁵⁴The one who eats my flesh and drinks my blood has eternal life, and I will raise him up on the last day. ⁵⁵For my flesh is true food, and my blood is true drink. ⁵⁶The one who eats my flesh and drinks my blood resides in me and I in him. ⁵⁷Just as the living Father sent me, and I live because of the Father, so also the one who eats me—that one also will live because of me. ⁵⁸This is the bread that came down from heaven, not like the bread that the fathers ate and died. The one who eats this bread will live forever."

6:52 Ἐμάχοντο οὖν πρὸς ἀλλήλους οἱ Ἰουδαῖοι λέγοντες· πῶς δύναται οὗτος ἡμῖν δοῦναι τὴν σάρκα [αὐτοῦ] φαγεῖν;

Ἐμάχοντο. Impf mid ind 3rd pl μάχομαι. The verb means "to clash severely, struggle, fight" (LN 39.23).

οὖν. Postpositive inferential conjunction and/or transitional particle (see 1:22 and 11:6).

πρὸς ἀλλήλους. Locative (motion toward).

οἱ Ἰουδαῖοι. Nominative subject of Ἐμάχοντο.

λέγοντες. Pres act ptc masc nom pl λέγω (pleonastic).

πῶς. Interrogative particle.

δύναται. Pres mid ind 3rd sg δύναμαι.

οὗτος. Nominative subject of δύναται.

ἡμῖν. Indirect object of δύναται.

δοῦναι. Aor act inf δίδωμι (complementary).

τὴν σάρκα. Accusative direct object of δοῦναι.

[αὐτοῦ]. Possessive genitive qualifying σάρκα. Metzger explains that the word is printed within square brackets because the external evidence for and against its presence "is so evenly balanced, and . . . considerations of internal probabilities are not decisive" (183).

φαγεῖν. Aor act inf ἐσθίω (purpose).

6:53 εἶπεν οὖν αὐτοῖς ὁ Ἰησοῦς· ἀμὴν ἀμὴν λέγω ὑμῖν, ἐὰν μὴ φάγητε τὴν σάρκα τοῦ υἱοῦ τοῦ ἀνθρώπου καὶ πίητε αὐτοῦ τὸ αἷμα, οὐκ ἔχετε ζωὴν ἐν ἑαυτοῖς.

εἶπεν. Aor act ind 3rd sg λέγω.

οὖν. Postpositive inferential conjunction and/or transitional particle (see 1:22 and 11:6).

αὐτοῖς. Dative indirect object of εἶπεν.

ὁ Ἰησοῦς. Nominative subject of εἶπεν.

ἀμὴν ἀμὴν λέγω ὑμῖν. Metacomment (see 1:51).

ἀμὴν ἀμήν. Asseverative particles that mark the beginning of Jesus' solemn declaration (see 1:51).
λέγω. Pres act ind 1st sg λέγω.
ὑμῖν. Dative indirect object of λέγω.
ἐάν. Introduces the protasis of a third-class condition.
μή. Negative particle normally used with non-indicative verbs. ἐὰν μή can be translated "unless."
φάγητε. Aor act subj 2nd pl ἐσθίω. Subjunctive with ἐάν.
τὴν σάρκα. Accusative direct object of φάγητε.
τοῦ υἱοῦ. Possessive genitive qualifying σάρκα.
τοῦ ἀνθρώπου. Genitive of relationship qualifying υἱοῦ.
καί. Coordinating conjunction.
πίητε. Aor act subj 2nd pl πίνω. Subjunctive with ἐάν.
αὐτοῦ. Possessive genitive qualifying αἷμα. The preposed pronoun is thematically salient (Levinsohn 2000, 64).
τὸ αἷμα. Accusative direct object of πίητε.
οὐκ. Negative particle normally used with indicative verbs. It marks the beginning of the apodosis of a third-class condition.
ἔχετε. Pres act ind 2nd pl ἔχω.
ζωήν. Accusative direct object of ἔχετε.
ἐν ἑαυτοῖς. Locative. The reflexive pronoun ἑαυτοῖς stands for ὑμῖν αὐτοῖς (MHT 3:42; Zerwick §209; Haubeck and von Siebenthal, 547).

6:54 ὁ τρώγων μου τὴν σάρκα καὶ πίνων μου τὸ αἷμα ἔχει ζωὴν αἰώνιον, κἀγὼ ἀναστήσω αὐτὸν τῇ ἐσχάτῃ ἡμέρᾳ.

ὁ τρώγων . . . καὶ πίνων. Nominative subject of ἔχει. Two substantival participles governed by one article and joined by καί form a TSKS (article-substantive-καί-substantive) construction. In such formulations, according to the Granville Sharp rule, the single article indicates that both participles have the same referent; see 5:24 on ὁ . . . ἀκούων καὶ πιστεύων. This verse is connected to the previous one by asyndeton.
τρώγων. Pres act ptc masc nom sg τρώγω (substantival). τρώγω ("to bite or chew food, eat" [BDAG, 1019]) is more graphic than ἐσθίω, but there is no significant difference in meaning between these two verbs.
μου. Possessive genitive qualifying σάρκα. The preposed pronoun is thematically salient (Levinsohn 2000, 64).
τὴν σάρκα. Accusative direct object of τρώγων.
καί. Coordinating conjunction.
πίνων. Pres act ptc masc nom sg πίνω (substantival).
μου. Possessive genitive qualifying αἷμα. The preposed pronoun is thematically salient (Levinsohn 2000, 64).

τὸ αἷμα. Accusative direct object of πίνων.

ἔχει. Pres act ind 3rd sg ἔχω.

ζωὴν αἰώνιον. Accusative direct object of ἔχει. On the use of this phrase in the FG, see 3:15 on ζωὴν αἰώνιον.

κἀγώ. Formed by crasis from καὶ ἐγώ. καί is a coordinating conjunction; ἐγώ is the nominative subject of ἀναστήσω. The personal pronoun is emphatic.

ἀναστήσω. Fut act ind 1st sg ἀνίστημι (see 6:40).

αὐτόν. Accusative direct object of ἀναστήσω.

τῇ ἐσχάτῃ ἡμέρᾳ. Dative of time. On the use of this expression in the FG, see 6:39 on [ἐν] τῇ ἐσχάτῃ ἡμέρᾳ.

6:55 ἡ γὰρ σάρξ μου ἀληθής ἐστιν βρῶσις, καὶ τὸ αἷμά μου ἀληθής ἐστιν πόσις.

ἡ ... σάρξ. Nominative subject of ἐστιν.

γάρ. Postpositive conjunction that introduces an explanation of the preceding assertion.

μου. Possessive genitive qualifying σάρξ.

ἀληθής ... βρῶσις. Predicate nominative. The adjective ἀληθής stands in the first (anarthrous) attributive position (see 2:6 on λίθιναι ὑδρίαι). By metonymy, βρῶσις ("eating") here denotes "food" (Harris 2015, 142).

ἐστιν. Pres act ind 3rd sg εἰμί.

καί. Coordinating conjunction.

τὸ αἷμά. Nominative subject of ἐστιν. αἷμά, which has a circumflex accent on the penult, acquired an additional accent, the acute, on the ultima from the enclitic μου (Smyth §183; Carson 1985, 48).

μου. Possessive genitive qualifying αἷμά.

ἀληθής ... πόσις. Predicate nominative. The adjective ἀληθής stands in the first (anarthrous) attributive position (see ἀληθής ... βρῶσις above). By metonymy, πόσις ("drinking") here denotes "drink" (Harris 2015, 142).

ἐστιν. Pres act ind 3rd sg εἰμί.

6:56 ὁ τρώγων μου τὴν σάρκα καὶ πίνων μου τὸ αἷμα ἐν ἐμοὶ μένει κἀγὼ ἐν αὐτῷ.

ὁ τρώγων ... καὶ πίνων. Nominative subject of μένει (see 6:54). This verse is connected to the previous one by asyndeton.

ὁ τρώγων. Pres act ptc masc nom sg τρώγω (substantival).

μου. Possessive genitive qualifying σάρκα. The preposed pronoun is thematically salient (Levinsohn 2000, 64).

τὴν σάρκα. Accusative direct object of τρώγων.

καί. Coordinating conjunction.

πίνων. Pres act ptc masc nom sg πίνω (substantival).

μου. Possessive genitive qualifying αἷμα. The preposed pronoun is thematically salient (Levinsohn 2000, 64).

τὸ αἷμα. Accusative direct object of πίνων.

ἐν ἐμοί. State of being characterized by close association with Jesus (BDAG, 327.4.a).

μένει. Pres act ind 3rd sg μένω.

κἀγώ. Formed by crasis from καὶ ἐγώ. καί is a coordinating conjunction; ἐγώ is the nominative subject of an implied μένω.

ἐν αὐτῷ. State of being gripped by Jesus' spiritual presence (BDAG, 327.4.a).

6:57 καθὼς ἀπέστειλέν με ὁ ζῶν πατὴρ κἀγὼ ζῶ διὰ τὸν πατέρα, καὶ ὁ τρώγων με κἀκεῖνος ζήσει δι' ἐμέ.

καθώς. Introduces a comparative clause. This verse is connected to the previous one by asyndeton.

ἀπέστειλέν. Aor act ind 3rd sg ἀποστέλλω. ἀπέστειλέν, which has an acute accent on the antepenult, acquired an additional accent, the acute, on the ultima from the enclitic με (Smyth §183; Carson 1985, 48).

με. Accusative direct object of ἀπέστειλέν.

ὁ ... πατήρ. Nominative subject of ἀπέστειλέν.

ζῶν. Pres act ptc masc nom sg ζάω (attributive). The participle modifies πατήρ, standing in the first attributive position (see 5:37 on πέμψας).

κἀγώ. Formed by crasis from καὶ ἐγώ. καί is a coordinating conjunction; ἐγώ is the nominative subject of ζῶ.

ζῶ. Pres act ind 1st sg ζάω.

διὰ τὸν πατέρα. Causal or intermediate agency instead of διά + genitive (BDAG, 226, 2.d.β).

καί. Adverbial use (adjunctive).

ὁ τρώγων. Pres act ptc masc nom sg τρώγω (substantival). Nominative subject of ζήσει in a left-dislocation, resumed by κἀκεῖνος (see Runge 2010, 287–313). The left-dislocation shifts focus on the act of "eating" Jesus.

με. Accusative direct object of τρώγων.

κἀκεῖνος. Formed by crasis from καὶ ἐκεῖνος. καί is adverbial (adjunctive); ἐκεῖνος is the nominative subject of ζήσει, resuming ὁ τρώγων. The anaphoric demonstrative reinforces what is already made prominent through the left-dislocation of ὁ τρώγων.

ζήσει. Fut act ind 3rd sg ζάω.

δι' ἐμέ. Causal or intermediate agency (see διὰ τὸν πατέρα above).

6:58 οὗτός ἐστιν ὁ ἄρτος ὁ ἐξ οὐρανοῦ καταβάς, οὐ καθὼς ἔφαγον οἱ πατέρες καὶ ἀπέθανον· ὁ τρώγων τοῦτον τὸν ἄρτον ζήσει εἰς τὸν αἰῶνα.

οὗτός. Nominative subject of ἐστιν. Fronted for emphasis. The near-demonstrative pronoun refers to Jesus, who spoke of himself in vv. 53-57. οὗτός, which has a circumflex accent on the penult, acquired an additional accent, the acute, on the ultima from the enclitic ἐστιν (Smyth §183; Carson 1985, 48). This verse is connected to the previous one by asyndeton.

ἐστιν. Pres act ind 3rd sg εἰμί.

ὁ ἄρτος. Predicate nominative.

ὁ . . . καταβάς. Aor act ptc masc nom sg καταβαίνω (attributive). The participle modifies ἄρτος, standing in the second attributive position (see 1:29 on ὁ αἴρων); on the temporal reference of the participle, see 6:41 on ὁ καταβάς.

ἐξ οὐρανοῦ. Source/origin. The PP modifies καταβάς.

οὐ. The negative particle modifies the elliptical construction after καθώς, which requires the repetition of ὁ ἄρτος and the addition of the relative pronoun ὅν serving as the accusative direct object of ἔφαγον: οὐ καθὼς [ὁ ἄρτος ὅν] ἔφαγον οἱ πατέρες καὶ ἀπέθανον ("not like [the bread which] the fathers ate and died").

καθώς. Introduces a comparative clause.

ἔφαγον. Aor act ind 3rd pl ἐσθίω.

οἱ πατέρες. Nominative subject of ἔφαγον. As in the previous references to οἱ πατέρες in this chapter (vv. 31, 49), the noun refers to the Exodus generation. Unlike the previous references, however, here is οἱ πατέρες not followed by the genitive of a personal pronoun (ἡμῶν or ὑμῶν) indicating relationship. A number of scribes sought to correct this anomaly by adding ὑμῶν (D 33 e sy[s.c] sa[mss] ly pbo bo[mss]) or ὑμῶν (ἡμῶν Γ 579 1424) τὸ μάννα (K N Γ Δ Θ Ψ $f^{1.13}$ 565 579 1241 1424 𝔐 lat sy[p.h] et al.) after οἱ πατέρες under the influence of 6:49 (οἱ πατέρες ὑμῶν ἔφαγον ἐν τῇ ἐρήμῳ τὸ μάννα καὶ ἀπέθανον) (Metzger, 183).

καί. Coordinating conjunction.

ἀπέθανον. Aor act ind 3rd pl ἀποθνήσκω.

ὁ τρώγων. Pres act ptc masc nom sg τρώγω (substantival). Nominative subject of ζήσει.

τοῦτον τὸν ἄρτον. Accusative direct object of τρώγων.

ζήσει. Fut act ind 3rd sg ζάω.

εἰς τὸν αἰῶνα. Temporal.

John 6:59-71

⁵⁹He said these things in the synagogue while he was teaching in Capernaum. ⁶⁰Then many of his disciples, when they heard it, said, "This saying is hard. Who can listen to it?" ⁶¹But Jesus, because he knew in himself that his disciples were grumbling about this, said to them, "Does this offend you? ⁶²Then what if you see the Son of Man ascending where he was before? ⁶³The spirit is the one that gives life; the flesh profits nothing. The words that I have spoken to you are spirit, and they are life. ⁶⁴But there are some of you who do not believe." For Jesus knew from the beginning who were the ones who did not believe, and who was the one who would betray him. ⁶⁵And he said, "Because of this I have told you that no one can come to me unless it has been granted to him by the Father." ⁶⁶As a result of this, many of his disciples turned back and were no longer walking about with him. ⁶⁷So Jesus said to the Twelve, "You do not want to go away too, do you?" ⁶⁸Simon Peter answered him, "Lord, to whom shall we go? You have the words of eternal life, ⁶⁹and we believe and know that you are the Holy One of God." ⁷⁰Jesus answered them, "Did I not choose you, the Twelve? Yet one of you is a devil." ⁷¹Now he was speaking about Judas son of Simon Iscariot, for this one, one of the Twelve, was going to betray him.

6:59 Ταῦτα εἶπεν ἐν συναγωγῇ διδάσκων ἐν Καφαρναούμ.

Ταῦτα. Accusative direct object of εἶπεν. This verse is connected to the previous one by asyndeton.

εἶπεν. Aor act ind 3rd sg λέγω.

ἐν συναγωγῇ. Locative. Since "[t]here is no need for the article to be used to make the object of a preposition definite" (Wallace 1996, 247), the anarthrous συναγωγῇ does not mean that the noun is indefinite.

διδάσκων. Pres act ptc masc nom sg διδάσκω (temporal). On participles that follow the main verb, see βαπτίζων in 1:31.

ἐν Καφαρναούμ. Locative.

6:60 Πολλοὶ οὖν ἀκούσαντες ἐκ τῶν μαθητῶν αὐτοῦ εἶπαν· σκληρός ἐστιν ὁ λόγος οὗτος· τίς δύναται αὐτοῦ ἀκούειν;

Πολλοὶ. Nominative subject of εἶπαν.

οὖν. Postpositive inferential conjunction and/or transitional particle (see 1:22 and 11:6).

ἀκούσαντες. Aor act ptc masc nom pl ἀκούω (temporal or substantival). The direct object of ἀκούσαντες must be supplied from the context: "these things" (referring to Ταῦτα in the previous verse) or "it" (referring to ὁ λόγος οὗτος that follows).

ἐκ τῶν μαθητῶν. Replaces the partitive genitive.

αὐτοῦ. Genitive of relationship qualifying μαθητῶν.

εἶπαν. Aor act ind 3rd pl λέγω.

σκληρός. Predicate adjective. Fronted for emphasis.

ἐστιν. Pres act ind 3rd sg εἰμί.

ὁ λόγος οὗτος. Nominative subject of ἐστιν.

τίς. Nominative subject of δύναται.

δύναται. Pres mid ind 3rd sg δύναμαι.

αὐτοῦ. Genitive direct object of ἀκούειν. The personal pronoun refers to ὁ λόγος οὗτος.

ἀκούειν. Pres act inf ἀκούω (complementary).

6:61 εἰδὼς δὲ ὁ Ἰησοῦς ἐν ἑαυτῷ ὅτι γογγύζουσιν περὶ τούτου οἱ μαθηταὶ αὐτοῦ εἶπεν αὐτοῖς· τοῦτο ὑμᾶς σκανδαλίζει;

εἰδώς. Prf act ptc masc nom sg οἶδα (causal or perhaps temporal [cf. NET; KJV]). As usual, the perfect tense of οἶδα has the present meaning (see 1:26 on οἴδατε). On participles that precede the main verb, see ἐμβλέψας in 1:36.

δέ. Marker of narrative development.

ὁ Ἰησοῦς. Nominative subject of εἶπεν.

ἐν ἑαυτῷ. Locative (lit. "within himself"; cf. BDAG, 327.1.f).

ὅτι. Introduces the clausal complement (indirect discourse) of εἰδώς.

γογγύζουσιν. Pres act ind 3rd pl γογγύζω. The present tense is retained from the direct discourse (see 1:39 on μένει). On the meaning, see 6:41 on Ἐγόγγυζον.

περὶ τούτου. Reference.

οἱ μαθηταί. Nominative subject of γογγύζουσιν.

αὐτοῦ. Genitive of relationship qualifying μαθηταί.

εἶπεν. Aor act ind 3rd sg λέγω.

αὐτοῖς. Dative indirect object of εἶπεν.

τοῦτο. Nominative subject of σκανδαλίζει. Fronted for emphasis.

ὑμᾶς. Accusative direct object of σκανδαλίζει.

σκανδαλίζει. Pres act ind 3rd sg σκανδαλίζω. In this context, σκανδαλίζω probably means "to cause someone to no longer believe," but it could also mean "to cause offense" (LN 31.78). The only other occurrence of σκανδαλίζω in the FG is in 16:1.

6:62 ἐὰν οὖν θεωρῆτε τὸν υἱὸν τοῦ ἀνθρώπου ἀναβαίνοντα ὅπου ἦν τὸ πρότερον;

ἐάν. Introduces the protasis of a third-class condition, which is formulated as an elliptical question that does not have the apodosis. This omission is a form of aposiopesis, "a breaking-off of speech due to strong emotion or to modesty" (BDF §482). The audience is supposed to supply the missing part, such as, "would you then still take offense?" (BDF §482), or simply τί in front of the protasis ("What then [will you think/do/say] if you see . . . ?") (Harris 2015, 145).

οὖν. Postpositive inferential conjunction and/or transitional particle (see 1:22 and 11:6).

θεωρῆτε. Pres act subj 2nd pl θεωρέω. Subjunctive with ἐάν.

τὸν υἱὸν. Accusative direct object of θεωρῆτε.

τοῦ ἀνθρώπου. Genitive of relationship qualifying υἱόν.

ἀναβαίνοντα. Pres act ptc masc acc sg ἀναβαίνω (predicative). The participle stands in the second predicate position (see 1:29 on ἐρχόμενον), functioning as the accusative complement to τὸν υἱὸν in a double accusative object-complement construction.

ὅπου. Particle denoting place.

ἦν. Impf act ind 3rd sg εἰμί.

τὸ πρότερον. The article functions as a nominalizer, changing the adverb πρότερον into the accusative indicating extent of time ("during former time, before").

6:63 τὸ πνεῦμά ἐστιν τὸ ζῳοποιοῦν, ἡ σὰρξ οὐκ ὠφελεῖ οὐδέν· τὰ ῥήματα ἃ ἐγὼ λελάληκα ὑμῖν πνεῦμά ἐστιν καὶ ζωή ἐστιν.

τὸ πνεῦμά. Nominative subject of ἐστιν. Fronted for emphasis. πνεῦμά, which has a circumflex accent on the penult, acquired an additional accent, the acute, on the ultima from the enclitic ἐστιν (Smyth §183; Carson 1985, 48). This verse is connected to the previous one by asyndeton.

ἐστιν. Pres act ind 3rd sg εἰμί.

τὸ ζῳοποιοῦν. Pres act ptc neut nom sg ζῳοποιέω (substantival). Predicate nominative.

ἡ σὰρξ. Nominative subject of ὠφελεῖ. ἡ σὰρξ does not refer to Jesus' flesh but to human nature in general.

οὐκ. Negative particle normally used with indicative verbs.

ὠφελεῖ. Pres act ind 3rd sg ὠφελέω. The verb means "to provide assistance, with emphasis upon the resulting benefit—'to help'" (LN 35.2).

οὐδέν. Accusative direct object of ὠφελεῖ. Two negatives (οὐκ . . . οὐδέν) do not cancel but reinforce each other (see 3:27 on οὐδὲ).

τὰ ῥήματα. Nominative subject of ἐστιν.

ἃ. Accusative direct object of λελάληκα.

ἐγὼ. Nominative subject of λελάληκα. The personal pronoun is emphatic.

λελάληκα. Prf act ind 1st sg λαλέω. Frey argues that the resultative aspect of the perfect tense conveys that what Jesus "'has spoken' (λελάληκα: 6.63; 8.40; 14.25; 15.3, 11; 16.1, 4, 6, 25, 33; 18.20) is enduringly valid revelation. The use of the perfect here results from an authorial choice of the linguistic expression. It characterizes the Johannine style and expresses, beyond this, the constitutive relatedness of the post-Easter community to the enduringly valid word and work of Christ and his connection back to the initiative of the Father, who sent and authorized him" (2018, 81).

ὑμῖν. Dative indirect object of λελάληκα.

πνεῦμά. Predicate nominative. Fronted for emphasis. πνεῦμά is a qualitative preverbal predicate nominative because the emphasis is on the spirit-giving character of Jesus' words. πνεῦμά, which has a circumflex accent on the penult, acquired an additional accent, the acute, on the ultima from the enclitic ἐστιν (Smyth §183; Carson 1985, 48).

ἐστιν. Pres act ind 3rd sg εἰμί. Neuter plural subjects typically take singular verbs (see 1:28 on ἐγένετο).

καὶ. Coordinating conjunction.

ζωή. Predicate nominative. Fronted for emphasis. This preverbal predicate nominative is most likely qualitative because the emphasis is on the life-giving character of Jesus' words.

ἐστιν. Pres act ind 3rd sg εἰμί. The copula is repeated to indicate that in this context πνεῦμα and ζωή are regarded as distinct, though complementary, concepts (Harris 2015, 146).

6:64 ἀλλ' εἰσὶν ἐξ ὑμῶν τινες οἳ οὐ πιστεύουσιν. ᾔδει γὰρ ἐξ ἀρχῆς ὁ Ἰησοῦς τίνες εἰσὶν οἱ μὴ πιστεύοντες καὶ τίς ἐστιν ὁ παραδώσων αὐτόν.

ἀλλ'. Marker of contrast.

εἰσὶν. Pres act ind 3rd pl εἰμί.

ἐξ ὑμῶν. Replaces the partitive genitive.

τινες. Nominative subject of εἰσὶν.

οἵ. The relative pronoun introduces a headless relative clause that, in its entirety (οἳ οὐ πιστεύουσιν), serves as the predicate nominative. Within its clause, οἵ is the nominative subject of πιστεύουσιν.

οὐ. Negative particle normally used with indicative verbs.

πιστεύουσιν. Pres act ind 3rd pl πιστεύω. Both uses of πιστεύω in this verse are absolute, i.e., they are not accompanied by a PP or a noun/pronoun indicating the object of belief.

ᾔδει. Plprf act ind 3rd sg οἶδα. The pluperfect of οἶδα is rendered by the imperfect.

γάρ. Postpositive conjunction that introduces an explanation of Jesus' assertion that there are some who do not believe.

ἐξ ἀρχῆς. Temporal.

ὁ Ἰησοῦς. Nominative subject of ᾔδει.

τίνες. Nominative subject of εἰσὶν.

εἰσὶν. Pres act ind 3rd pl εἰμί.

οἱ ... πιστεύοντες. Pres act ptc masc nom pl πιστεύω (substantival). Predicate nominative.

μὴ. Negative particle normally used with non-indicative verbs.

καὶ. Coordinating conjunction.

τίς. Predicate nominative. "Interrogatives, by their nature, indicate the unknown component and hence cannot be the subject" (Wallace 1996, 40 n. 12).

ἐστιν. Pres act ind 3rd sg εἰμί.

ὁ παραδώσων. Fut act ptc masc nom sg παραδίδωμι (substantival). Nominative subject of ἐστιν. There are only six more occurrences of the future substantival participles in the NT (Luke 22:49; Acts 20:22; 1 Cor 15:37; Heb 3:5; 13:17; 1 Pet 3:13).

αὐτόν. Accusative direct object of παραδώσων.

6:65 καὶ ἔλεγεν· διὰ τοῦτο εἴρηκα ὑμῖν ὅτι οὐδεὶς δύναται ἐλθεῖν πρός με ἐὰν μὴ ᾖ δεδομένον αὐτῷ ἐκ τοῦ πατρός.

καὶ. Coordinating conjunction.

ἔλεγεν. Impf act ind 3rd sg λέγω. On the function of the imperfect in the FG, see 1:39 on ἦν.

διὰ τοῦτο. Causal. The demonstrative pronoun is anaphoric, referring to Jesus' assertions in vv. 63-64a. In this context, the PP διὰ τοῦτο functions as a connective; on this function of διὰ τοῦτο, see 1:31.

εἴρηκα. Prf act ind 1st sg λέγω. εἴρηκα refers back to v. 44.

ὑμῖν. Dative indirect object of εἴρηκα.

ὅτι. Introduces the clausal complement (indirect discourse) of εἴρηκα.

οὐδεὶς. Nominative subject of δύναται. Fronted for emphasis.

δύναται. Pres mid ind 3rd sg δύναμαι.
ἐλθεῖν. Aor act inf ἔρχομαι (complementary).
πρός με. Locative (motion toward).
ἐάν. Introduces the protasis of a third-class condition.
μή. Negative particle normally used with non-indicative verbs.
ᾖ. Pres act subj 3rd sg εἰμί. Subjunctive with ἐάν.
δεδομένον. Prf pass ptc neut nom sg δίδωμι (perfect periphrastic).
αὐτῷ. Dative indirect object of δεδομένον.
ἐκ τοῦ πατρός. Personal agency. ἐκ stands for παρά (Zerwick and Grosvenor, 306).

6:66 Ἐκ τούτου πολλοὶ [ἐκ] τῶν μαθητῶν αὐτοῦ ἀπῆλθον εἰς τὰ ὀπίσω καὶ οὐκέτι μετ' αὐτοῦ περιεπάτουν.

Ἐκ τούτου. Causal ("because of this") or temporal ("from this time on"). This verse is connected to the previous one by asyndeton.
πολλοί. Nominative subject of ἀπῆλθον.
[ἐκ] τῶν μαθητῶν. Replaces the partitive genitive. The preposition ἐκ is printed within square brackets because the external evidence for ($\mathfrak{P}^{66}$ B T f^1 33 565) and against (ℵ C D K L N W Γ Δ Θ Ψ f^{13} 𝔐 et al.) its presence in the text is evenly balanced.
αὐτοῦ. Genitive of relationship qualifying μαθητῶν.
ἀπῆλθον. Aor act ind 3rd pl ἀπέρχομαι.
εἰς τὰ ὀπίσω. Locative (lit. "to the things behind"). The article functions as a nominalizer, changing the adverb ὀπίσω ("behind") into the object of the preposition εἰς.
καί. Coordinating conjunction.
οὐκέτι. Negative adverb of time ("no longer, no further").
μετ' αὐτοῦ. Association/accompaniment.
περιεπάτουν. Impf act ind 3rd pl περιπατέω. The imperfective aspect of the verb portrays going about with Jesus as an ongoing process.

6:67 εἶπεν οὖν ὁ Ἰησοῦς τοῖς δώδεκα· μὴ καὶ ὑμεῖς θέλετε ὑπάγειν;

εἶπεν. Aor act ind 3rd sg λέγω.
οὖν. Postpositive inferential conjunction and/or transitional particle (see 1:22 and 11:6).
ὁ Ἰησοῦς. Nominative subject of εἶπεν.
τοῖς δώδεκα. Dative indirect object of εἶπεν. This is the first appearance of the Twelve in the FG. After this verse, they are mentioned only three more times (6:70, 71; 20:24).

μή. Negative particle that introduces a question that expects a negative answer.

καί. Adverbial use (adjunctive).

ὑμεῖς. Nominative subject of θέλετε. The second-person plural personal pronoun is emphatic and contrastive, differentiating the Twelve from other disciples of Jesus.

θέλετε. Pres act ind 2nd pl θέλω.

ὑπάγειν. Pres act inf ὑπάγω (complementary).

6:68 ἀπεκρίθη αὐτῷ Σίμων Πέτρος· κύριε, πρὸς τίνα ἀπελευσόμεθα; ῥήματα ζωῆς αἰωνίου ἔχεις,

ἀπεκρίθη. Aor mid ind 3rd sg ἀποκρίνομαι. On the voice, see "Deponency" in the Series Introduction. This verse is connected to the previous one by asyndeton.

αὐτῷ. Dative indirect object of ἀπεκρίθη.

Σίμων Πέτρος. Nominative subject of ἀπεκρίθη.

κύριε. Vocative of direct address.

πρὸς τίνα. Locative (motion toward).

ἀπελευσόμεθα. Fut mid ind 1st pl ἀπέρχομαι. This is a deliberative (modal) use of the future tense for rhetorical purposes. Although the future is a non-aspectual tense form that conveys the expectation of the occurrence of an event subsequent to a certain reference point, it can sometimes have a secondary function, as here, which stems "from the natural connection between future time and ... contingency, possibility, intention, and other non-assertive modal forces" (Fanning, 123).

ῥήματα. Accusative direct object of ἔχεις. Fronted for emphasis.

ζωῆς αἰωνίου. Genitive of purpose ("words that lead to eternal life") or descriptive genitive ("words characterized by eternal life") qualifying ῥήματα. On the use of this phrase in the FG, see 3:15 on ζωὴν αἰώνιον.

ἔχεις. Pres act ind 2nd sg ἔχω.

6:69 καὶ ἡμεῖς πεπιστεύκαμεν καὶ ἐγνώκαμεν ὅτι σὺ εἶ ὁ ἅγιος τοῦ θεοῦ.

καί. Coordinating conjunction.

ἡμεῖς. Nominative subject of πεπιστεύκαμεν. The first-person personal pronoun is emphatic and contrastive, differentiating the speaker's group [= the Twelve] from other disciples of Jesus who left him.

πεπιστεύκαμεν. Prf act ind 1st pl πιστεύω. Campbell, who holds that the distinguishing semantic quality of the perfect tense is heightened proximity with intensive implicature (2007, 195–201), proposes the following rendering of this verse: "[W]e *truly* believe and know that you are the Holy One of God" (202). Barrett suggests that the sense of πεπιστεύκαμεν is "[w]e are in state of faith and knowledge; we have recognized the truth and hold it" (306), but Porter may be right when he objects that "[t]he second half is unnecessary" (1989, 255; cf. Thomson, 68, who argues that πεπιστεύκαμεν "has a stative sense close to that of the present πιστεύομεν"). Indeed, the emphasis falls on the present state of belief of the Twelve rather than on their entrance into this state.

καί. Coordinating conjunction.

ἐγνώκαμεν. Prf act ind 1st pl γινώσκω. The perfect tense is again semantically marked, conveying the state of comprehension of Jesus' identity.

ὅτι. Introduces the clausal complement (indirect discourse) of ἐγνώκαμεν.

σύ. Nominative subject of εἶ. The second-person singular pronoun emphasizes Jesus' distinctiveness.

εἶ. Pres act ind 2nd sg εἰμί.

ὁ ἅγιος. Predicate nominative.

τοῦ θεοῦ. Genitive of relationship qualifying ἅγιος. In the synoptic tradition, only the demons confess that Jesus is ὁ ἅγιος τοῦ θεοῦ (Mark 1:24//Luke 4:34). In some manuscripts, this declaration is expanded by ὁ χριστός in front of it ($\mathfrak{P}^{66}$ sa^{mss} ly bo) or replaced with ὁ χριστός ὁ υἱὸς τοῦ θεοῦ τοῦ ζῶντος (Κ Ν Γ Δ Θ^c Ψ f^{13} 579 700 892 1241 1424 $\mathfrak{M}$ sy$^{p.h}$ bo^{mss}). Nonetheless, the reading ὁ ἅγιος τοῦ θεοῦ has the best textual support ($\mathfrak{P}^{75}$ ℵ B C* D L W sa^{ms} pbo), while other variants reflect the influence of John 1:49; 11:27; and Matt 16:26 (Metzger, 184).

6:70 ἀπεκρίθη αὐτοῖς ὁ Ἰησοῦς· οὐκ ἐγὼ ὑμᾶς τοὺς δώδεκα ἐξελεξάμην; καὶ ἐξ ὑμῶν εἷς διάβολός ἐστιν.

ἀπεκρίθη. Aor mid ind 3rd sg ἀποκρίνομαι. On the voice, see "Deponency" in the Series Introduction. This verse is connected to the previous one by asyndeton.

αὐτοῖς. Dative indirect object of ἀπεκρίθη.

ὁ Ἰησοῦς. Nominative subject of ἀπεκρίθη.

οὐκ. Negative particle that introduces a question that expects an affirmative answer.

ἐγώ. Nominative subject of ἐξελεξάμην. Fronted for emphasis.

ὑμᾶς. Accusative direct object of ἐξελεξάμην.

τοὺς δώδεκα. Accusative in apposition to ὑμᾶς. This is the second of the four references to the Twelve in the FG (6:67, 70, 71; 20:24).

ἐξελεξάμην. Aor mid ind 1st sg ἐκλέγω.

καί. Coordinating conjunction.
ἐξ ὑμῶν. Replaces the partitive genitive.
εἷς. Nominative subject of ἐστιν.
διάβολός. Predicate nominative. Fronted for emphasis. The anarthrous form of the noun does not preclude the possibility that διάβολός is definite because, according to Colwell's rule, "[d]efinite predicate nouns which precede the verb usually lack the article" (20). However, Wallace's (1996, 249, 265) argument for the definiteness of διάβολός based on its monadic character is not persuasive because Jesus does not identify one of his disciples with the devil himself but portrays him as "a wicked person who has a number of characteristics typical of the Devil—'a devil'" (LN 88.124). The evangelist characterizes Judas as a person who has fallen under the devil's influence and became the devil's tool when he decided to betray Jesus (13:2, 27). διάβολός, which has an acute accent on the antepenult, acquired an additional accent, the acute, on the ultima from the enclitic ἐστιν (Smyth §183; Carson 1985, 48).
ἐστιν. Pres act ind 3rd sg εἰμί.

6:71 ἔλεγεν δὲ τὸν Ἰούδαν Σίμωνος Ἰσκαριώτου· οὗτος γὰρ ἔμελλεν παραδιδόναι αὐτόν, εἷς ἐκ τῶν δώδεκα.

ἔλεγεν. Impf act ind 3rd sg λέγω. On the function of the imperfect in the FG, see 1:39 on ἦν.
δὲ. Marker of narrative development.
τὸν Ἰούδαν. Accusative of respect.
Σίμωνος Ἰσκαριώτου. Genitive of relationship in an elliptical construction ("[son of] Simon Iscariot"). In the FG, Judas is identified as the son of Simon Iscariot twice more (13:2, 26). In the Gospels, Ἰσκαριώτης is also Judas' surname (Matt 10:4; 26:14; Luke 22:3; John 12:4; 14:22), which is "usu[ally] taken to refer to the place of his origin, *from Kerioth* (in southern Judea)" (BDAG, 480). Some scribes (ℵ* Θ *f*¹³ sy^hmg) certainly understood it that way because they replaced Ἰσκαριώτου with ἀπὸ Καρυώτου (אִישׁ קְרִיּוֹת).
οὗτος. Nominative subject of ἔμελλεν.
γὰρ. Postpositive conjunction that introduces an explanation for the assertion that Jesus spoke about Judas.
ἔμελλεν. Impf act ind 3rd sg μέλλω.
παραδιδόναι. Pres act inf παραδίδωμι (complementary).
αὐτόν. Accusative direct object of παραδιδόναι.
εἷς. Nominative in apposition to οὗτος.
ἐκ τῶν δώδεκα. Replaces the partitive genitive. In the FG, only two disciples are identified as "one of the Twelve": Judas (here) and Thomas

(20:24). This is the third of the four references to the Twelve in the FG (6:67, 70, 71; 20:24).

John 7:1-9

¹And after these things Jesus was going about in Galilee. For he did not want to go about in Judea, because the Jews were seeking to kill him. ²Now the festival of the Jews, the Feast of Tabernacles, was near. ³So his brothers said to him, "Depart from here and go to Judea, so that your disciples also may see your works that you are doing. ⁴For no one does anything secretly when he seeks to be known publicly. If you are doing these things, show yourself to the world!" ⁵For not even his brothers believed in him. ⁶Then Jesus said to them, "My time has not yet come, but your time is always ready. ⁷The world cannot hate you, but it hates me, because I testify about it that its works are evil. ⁸You go up to the festival! I am not going up to this festival, because my time is not yet completed." ⁹After he said these things, he himself remained in Galilee.

7:1 Καὶ μετὰ ταῦτα περιεπάτει ὁ Ἰησοῦς ἐν τῇ Γαλιλαίᾳ· οὐ γὰρ ἤθελεν ἐν τῇ Ἰουδαίᾳ περιπατεῖν, ὅτι ἐζήτουν αὐτὸν οἱ Ἰουδαῖοι ἀποκτεῖναι.

Καὶ. Coordinating conjunction.

μετὰ ταῦτα. Temporal (see 3:22). Fronted as a temporal frame.

περιεπάτει. Impf act ind 3rd sg περιπατέω. On the function of the imperfect in the FG, see 1:39 on ἦν.

ὁ Ἰησοῦς. Nominative subject of περιεπάτει.

ἐν τῇ Γαλιλαίᾳ. Locative.

οὐ. Negative particle normally used with indicative verbs.

γὰρ. Postpositive conjunction that introduces a clause that explains why Jesus went about in Galilee.

ἤθελεν. Impf act ind 3rd sg θέλω. On the augment, see 1:43 on ἠθέλησεν. Instead of ἤθελεν, some manuscripts (W it sy^c Chr^com) have εἶχεν ἐξουσίαν. Although internal probabilities favor εἶχεν ἐξουσίαν because ἐξουσίαν ἔχειν occurs elsewhere in the FG (10:18 [2x]; 19:10 [2x], 11) and because this is the more difficult reading, the external evidence overwhelmingly supports ἤθελεν (Metzger, 184–85).

ἐν τῇ Ἰουδαίᾳ. Locative.

περιπατεῖν. Pres act inf περιπατέω (complementary).

ὅτι. Introduces a causal clause.

ἐζήτουν. Impf act ind 3rd pl ζητέω. The imperfective aspect marks the verb for prominence and presents the action as unfolding. On the function of the imperfect in the FG, see 1:39 on ἦν. In the FG, ζητέω is used six times with the complimentary infinitive ἀποκτεῖναι (5:18; 7:1, 19, 20, 25; 8:37).

αὐτὸν. Accusative direct object of ἀποκτεῖναι.
οἱ Ἰουδαῖοι. Nominative subject of ἐζήτουν. The noun refers to the Jewish leaders in Judea.
ἀποκτεῖναι. Aor act inf ἀποκτείνω (complementary).

7:2 Ἦν δὲ ἐγγὺς ἡ ἑορτὴ τῶν Ἰουδαίων ἡ σκηνοπηγία.

Ἦν. Impf act ind 3rd sg εἰμί. On the function of the imperfect in the FG, see 1:39 on ἦν.
δὲ. Marker of narrative development.
ἐγγὺς. Predicate adverb indicating close temporal proximity (see 2:1 on ἐκεῖ).
ἡ ἑορτὴ. Nominative subject of Ἦν.
τῶν Ἰουδαίων. Subjective genitive ("the festival that the Jews celebrate") or attributive genitive ("the Jewish festival") qualifying ἑορτὴ.
ἡ σκηνοπηγία. Nominative in apposition to ἡ ἑορτὴ.

7:3 εἶπον οὖν πρὸς αὐτὸν οἱ ἀδελφοὶ αὐτοῦ· μετάβηθι ἐντεῦθεν καὶ ὕπαγε εἰς τὴν Ἰουδαίαν, ἵνα καὶ οἱ μαθηταί σου θεωρήσουσιν σοῦ τὰ ἔργα ἃ ποιεῖς·

εἶπον. Aor act ind 3rd pl λέγω.
οὖν. Postpositive inferential conjunction and/or transitional particle (see 1:22 and 11:6).
πρὸς αὐτὸν. Locative (motion toward). The PP functions like an indirect object of εἶπον.
οἱ ἀδελφοὶ. Nominative subject of εἶπον.
αὐτοῦ. Genitive of relationship qualifying ἀδελφοὶ.
μετάβηθι. Aor act impv 2nd sg μεταβαίνω. The verb means "to transfer from one place to another" (BDAG, 638.1).
ἐντεῦθεν. Adverb of place.
καὶ. Coordinating conjunction.
ὕπαγε. Pres act impv 2nd sg ὑπάγω.
εἰς τὴν Ἰουδαίαν. Locative.
ἵνα. Introduces a purpose clause.
καὶ. Adverbial use (adjunctive).
οἱ μαθηταί. Nominative subject of θεωρήσουσιν.
σου. Genitive of relationship qualifying μαθηταί.

θεωρήσουσιν. Fut act ind 3rd pl θεωρέω. In Hellenistic Greek, the future tense is sometimes used instead of the subjunctive with ἵνα (BDF §369.2; Zerwick §340). The aorist subjunctive variant θεωρήσωσιν ($\mathfrak{P}^{66}$ B² K Γ Θ Ψ 070 $f^{1.13}$ 565 579 700 892 1241 𝔐) is most likely a scribal correction in agreement with the rules for the ἵνα clauses in classical Greek.

σοῦ. Subjective genitive qualifying ἔργα. The pronoun is accented and fronted for emphasis. It functions as a pronominal prolepsis because "the subject of a relative clause is anticipated by a pronoun in the main clause" (Zerwick §206); see 2:23 on αὐτοῦ.

τὰ ἔργα. Accusative direct object of θεωρήσουσιν.

ἅ. Accusative direct object of ποιεῖς. The antecedent of the relative pronoun is τὰ ἔργα.

ποιεῖς. Pres act ind 2nd sg ποιέω.

7:4 οὐδεὶς γάρ τι ἐν κρυπτῷ ποιεῖ καὶ ζητεῖ αὐτὸς ἐν παρρησίᾳ εἶναι. εἰ ταῦτα ποιεῖς, φανέρωσον σεαυτὸν τῷ κόσμῳ.

οὐδεὶς. Nominative subject of ποιεῖ.

γάρ. Postpositive conjunction that introduces an explanation of the previous request.

τι. Accusative direct object of ποιεῖ.

ἐν κρυπτῷ. Manner (lit. "in the hidden" = "secretly"). The adjective κρυπτός is here used as a substantive.

ποιεῖ. Pres act ind 3rd sg ποιέω.

καὶ. Coordinating conjunction. Since καὶ connects two clauses that stand in tension with each other, it could be translated with an adversative "and yet" or with a subordinate conjunction "when" (Zerwick and Grosvenor, 307).

ζητεῖ. Pres act ind 3rd sg ζητέω.

αὐτὸς. Nominative subject of ζητεῖ.

ἐν παρρησίᾳ. Manner ("in public" = "publicly").

εἶναι. Pres act inf εἰμί (complementary).

εἰ. Introduces the protasis of a first-class condition. This class of conditions assumes that the protasis is true for the sake of the argument and draws the conclusion from that supposition.

ταῦτα. Accusative direct object of ποιεῖς. Fronted for emphasis.

ποιεῖς. Pres act ind 2nd sg ποιέω.

φανέρωσον. Aor act impv 2nd sg φανερόω. The imperative marks the beginning of the apodosis of a first-class condition.

σεαυτὸν. Accusative direct object of φανέρωσον.

τῷ κόσμῳ. Dative indirect object of φανέρωσον.

7:5 οὐδὲ γὰρ οἱ ἀδελφοὶ αὐτοῦ ἐπίστευον εἰς αὐτόν.

οὐδὲ. A combination of the negative particle οὐ and the marker of narrative development δέ.

γάρ. Postpositive conjunction that introduces a parenthetical clause that explains why Jesus' brothers urged him to demonstrate publicly his miraculous power.

οἱ ἀδελφοί. Nominative subject of ἐπίστευον. Fronted for emphasis.

αὐτοῦ. Genitive of relationship qualifying ἀδελφοί.

ἐπίστευον. Impf act ind 3rd pl πιστεύω. On the function of the imperfect in the FG, see 1:39 on ἦν.

εἰς αὐτόν. Goal of actions or feelings directed toward someone (BDAG, 290.4.c.β). For πιστεύειν εἰς + accusative ("trust or believe in someone"), see 1:12 on εἰς τὸ ὄνομα.

7:6 λέγει οὖν αὐτοῖς ὁ Ἰησοῦς· ὁ καιρὸς ὁ ἐμὸς οὔπω πάρεστιν, ὁ δὲ καιρὸς ὁ ὑμέτερος πάντοτέ ἐστιν ἕτοιμος.

λέγει. Pres act ind 3rd sg λέγω. The historical present gives prominence to Jesus' words that follow (see 1:15 on μαρτυρεῖ).

οὖν. Postpositive inferential conjunction and/or transitional particle (see 1:22 and 11:6).

αὐτοῖς. Dative indirect object of λέγει.

ὁ Ἰησοῦς. Nominative subject of λέγει.

ὁ καιρὸς ὁ ἐμός. Nominative subject of πάρεστιν. Fronted as a topical frame. καιρός denotes "a moment or period as especially appropriate," i.e., "the right, proper, favorable time" (BDAG, 497.1.b). The possessive adjective ἐμός stands in the second attributive position (see 1:9 on τὸ φῶς τὸ ἀληθινόν).

οὔπω. Adverb of time ("not yet").

πάρεστιν. Pres act ind 3rd sg πάρειμι. The verb means to "be present" (BDAG, 773.1).

ὁ . . . καιρὸς ὁ ὑμέτερος. Nominative subject of ἐστιν. Fronted as a topical frame. The possessive adjective ὑμέτερος stands in the second attributive position (see 1:9 on τὸ φῶς τὸ ἀληθινόν).

δέ. Marker of narrative development.

πάντοτέ. Adverb of time ("always"). πάντοτε, which has an acute accent on the antepenult, acquired an additional accent, the acute, on the ultima from the enclitic ἐστιν (Smyth §183; Carson 1985, 48).

ἐστιν. Pres act ind 3rd sg εἰμί.

ἕτοιμος. Predicate adjective.

7:7 οὐ δύναται ὁ κόσμος μισεῖν ὑμᾶς, ἐμὲ δὲ μισεῖ, ὅτι ἐγὼ μαρτυρῶ περὶ αὐτοῦ ὅτι τὰ ἔργα αὐτοῦ πονηρά ἐστιν.

οὐ. Negative particle normally used with indicative verbs. This verse is connected to the previous one by asyndeton.
δύναται. Pres mid ind 3rd sg δύναμαι.
ὁ κόσμος. Nominative subject of δύναται. On the portrayal of the world in the FG, see 1:10 on ἐν τῷ κόσμῳ.
μισεῖν. Pres act inf μισέω (complementary).
ὑμᾶς. Accusative direct object of μισεῖν.
ἐμὲ. Accusative direct object of μισεῖ.
δὲ. Marker of narrative development.
μισεῖ. Pres act ind 3rd sg μισέω.
ὅτι. Introduces a causal clause.
ἐγώ. Nominative subject of μαρτυρῶ. Fronted for emphasis.
μαρτυρῶ. Pres act ind 1st sg μαρτυρέω.
περὶ αὐτοῦ. Reference. αὐτοῦ refers to ὁ κόσμος.
ὅτι. Introduces the clausal complement (indirect discourse) of μαρτυρῶ.
τὰ ἔργα. Nominative subject of ἐστιν.
αὐτοῦ. Subjective genitive qualifying ἔργα. αὐτοῦ refers to ὁ κόσμος.
πονηρά. Predicate adjective. Fronted for emphasis.
ἐστιν. Pres act ind 3rd sg εἰμί. Neuter plural subjects typically take singular verbs (see 1:28 on ἐγένετο).

7:8 ὑμεῖς ἀνάβητε εἰς τὴν ἑορτήν· ἐγὼ οὐκ ἀναβαίνω εἰς τὴν ἑορτὴν ταύτην, ὅτι ὁ ἐμὸς καιρὸς οὔπω πεπλήρωται.

ὑμεῖς. Nominative subject of ἀνάβητε. The personal pronoun is emphatic and contrastive, differentiating the addressees of Jesus' words (his brothers) from him. This verse is connected to the previous one by asyndeton.
ἀνάβητε. Aor act impv 2nd pl ἀναβαίνω. On the meaning of the verb, see 2:13 on ἀνέβη.
εἰς τὴν ἑορτήν. Locative.
ἐγώ. Nominative subject of ἀναβαίνω. This personal pronoun is emphatic and contrastive, differentiating the speaker (Jesus) from his brothers.
οὐκ. Negative particle normally used with indicative verbs.
ἀναβαίνω. Pres act ind 1st sg ἀναβαίνω. This is traditionally seen as a futuristic present (BDF §323.3), but it is perhaps more accurate to say that the action "is regarded as already under way, even if only in intention" (Fanning, 223).

εἰς τὴν ἑορτὴν ταύτην. Locative.

ὅτι. Introduces a causal clause.

ὁ ἐμὸς καιρός. Nominative subject of πεπλήρωται. The possessive adjective ἐμὸς stands in the first attributive position (see 2:10 on τὸν καλὸν οἶνον).

οὔπω. Adverb of time ("not yet").

πεπλήρωται. Prf pass ind 3rd sg πληρόω. The passive meaning of this verb is such that "no agency is to be implied" (Wallace 1996, 436).

7:9 ταῦτα δὲ εἰπὼν αὐτὸς ἔμεινεν ἐν τῇ Γαλιλαίᾳ.

ταῦτα. Accusative direct object of εἰπών.

δὲ. Marker of narrative development.

εἰπών. Aor act ptc masc nom sg λέγω (temporal). On participles that precede the main verb, see ἐμβλέψας in 1:36.

αὐτός. Intensive pronoun that reinforces the implied subject of ἔμεινεν ("he himself"), differentiating Jesus from his brothers (BDAG, 152.1.c).

ἔμεινεν. Aor act ind 3rd sg μένω.

ἐν τῇ Γαλιλαίᾳ. Locative.

John 7:10-13

[10]But after his brothers had gone up to the festival, then he also went up, not publicly but (as it were) secretly. [11]So the Jews were looking for him at the festival and were saying, "Where is he?" [12]And a subdued debate about him was considerable among the crowds. Some were saying, "He is a good man," others were saying, "No, but he is deceiving the crowd." [13]Yet no one was speaking openly about him for fear of the Jews.

7:10 Ὡς δὲ ἀνέβησαν οἱ ἀδελφοὶ αὐτοῦ εἰς τὴν ἑορτήν, τότε καὶ αὐτὸς ἀνέβη οὐ φανερῶς ἀλλ' [ὡς] ἐν κρυπτῷ.

Ὡς. Temporal conjunction (BDAG, 1105.8.a; BDF §455.2), which introduces a temporal clause in a left-dislocation, resumed by τότε.

δὲ. Marker of contrast (LN 89.124).

ἀνέβησαν. Aor act ind 3rd pl ἀναβαίνω. On the meaning of the verb, see 2:13 on ἀνέβη.

οἱ ἀδελφοί. Nominative subject of ἀνέβησαν.

αὐτοῦ. Genitive of relationship qualifying ἀδελφοί.

εἰς τὴν ἑορτήν. Locative.

τότε. Adverb of time, which resumes the temporal clause Ὡς δὲ ἀνέβησαν οἱ ἀδελφοὶ αὐτοῦ εἰς τὴν ἑορτήν. Fronted for emphasis. Runge explains that "[t]he entity introduced in the dislocation is complex enough that there might be confusion over where the dislocation ends and the main clause begins. Placing the pronominal element in a frame of reference marks the transition, making it easier for the reader to recognize the process by making the discontinuity stand out" (2010, 297).

καί. Adverbial use (adjunctive).

αὐτός. Nominative subject of ἀνέβη. The third-person personal pronoun is redundant with the pronominal notion embedded in ἀνέβη (see 6:24). It is used here as a "switch-reference device, signifying a change in subject to someone or something that had been mentioned previously" (Young, 75).

ἀνέβη. Aor act ind 3rd sg ἀναβαίνω.

οὐ . . . ἀλλ'. A point/counterpoint set ("not this . . . but that") that that negates the incorrect description of the manner of Jesus' arrival to the festival ("publicly") and replaces it with the correct description of his arrival ("secretly"). On the function of ἀλλά in a point/counterpoint set, see 1:8.

φανερῶς. Adverb of manner ("pertaining to the manner by which something can easily be known by the public, with the implication that the related events take place in the open—'publicly, openly'" [LN 28.63])

[ὡς]. Comparative particle. Square brackets indicate that the evidence for and against the inclusion of this particle is balanced. While the external support for its presence ($\mathfrak{P}^{66.75\text{vid}}$ B K L N T W Γ Δ Θ Ψ 070 0105 $f^{1.13}$ 𝔐 lat sy$^{p.h}$ et al.) is more compelling than for its omission (ℵ D 1424 it sy$^{s.c}$ sa ly cw pbo), intrinsic probability favors the text without ὡς "since a copyist may have inserted the word in order to soften the force of the expression ἐν κρυπτῷ" (Metzger, 185).

ἐν κρυπτῷ. Manner ("pertaining to not being able to be known by the public but known by some in-group or by those immediately involved—'in secret, in private, secretly, privately'" [LN 28.71]).

7:11 οἱ οὖν Ἰουδαῖοι ἐζήτουν αὐτὸν ἐν τῇ ἑορτῇ καὶ ἔλεγον· ποῦ ἐστιν ἐκεῖνος;

οἱ . . . Ἰουδαῖοι. Nominative subject of ἐζήτουν.

οὖν. Postpositive inferential conjunction and/or transitional particle (see 1:22 and 11:6).

ἐζήτουν. Impf act ind 3rd pl ζητέω. On the function of the imperfect in the FG, see 1:39 on ἦν. Although in this context the verb ζητέω simply means "to look / search for," Dennis (164) argues that it carries malicious intent. He derives this conclusion from other uses of ζητέω in the FG, which typically describe the pursuit of Jesus for violent purposes, such as to kill him (5:18; 7:1, 19, 20, 25; 8:37), to arrest him (7:30), or to stone him (11:8).

αὐτόν. Accusative direct object of ἐζήτουν.

ἐν τῇ ἑορτῇ. Locative ("at the festival") or temporal ("during the festival").

καί. Coordinating conjunction.

ἔλεγον. Impf act ind 3rd pl λέγω. On the function of the imperfect in the FG, see 1:39 on ἦν.

ποῦ. Interrogative adverb of place.

ἐστιν. Pres act ind 3rd sg εἰμί.

ἐκεῖνος. Nominative subject of ἐστιν. The demonstrative pronoun refers to Jesus, acting as a third-person personal pronoun with a simple anaphoric force (Wallace 1996, 328–29).

7:12 καὶ γογγυσμὸς περὶ αὐτοῦ ἦν πολὺς ἐν τοῖς ὄχλοις· οἱ μὲν ἔλεγον ὅτι ἀγαθός ἐστιν, ἄλλοι [δὲ] ἔλεγον· οὔ, ἀλλὰ πλανᾷ τὸν ὄχλον.

καί. Coordinating conjunction.

γογγυσμός. Nominative subject of ἦν. γογγυσμός denotes "utterance made in a low tone of voice" that could refer to both satisfaction and discontent, as here (BDAG, 204).

περὶ αὐτοῦ. Reference.

ἦν. Impf act ind 3rd sg εἰμί. On the function of the imperfect in the FG, see 1:39 on ἦν.

πολύς. Predicate adjective.

ἐν τοῖς ὄχλοις. Locative.

οἱ μέν. Nominative subject of the first ἔλεγον. The article stands in place of a third-person personal pronoun. The particle μέν has an identifying and mildly contrastive function, distinguishing one group of speakers from another (see ἄλλοι [δέ] below). Levinsohn claims that "[t]he presence of μέν not only anticipates a corresponding sentence containing δέ but frequently, in narrative, it also downgrades the importance of the sentence containing μέν" (2000, 170). Runge, however, contends that "[t]he downgrading effect that Levinsohn asserts is better explained by the nature of the offline information that it often introduces than by the particle itself" (2010, 76 n. 7). In this verse, both clauses containing the μέν and δέ particles are characterized by a parallel structure, including the imperfect ἔλεγον, which suggests that their rhetorical functions are similar.

ἔλεγον. Impf act ind 3rd pl λέγω. On the function of the imperfect in the FG, see 1:39 on ἦν.

ὅτι. ὅτι-*recitativum* that introduces the clausal complement (direct discourse) of ἔλεγον.

ἀγαθός. Predicate adjective. Fronted for emphasis.

ἐστιν. Pres act ind 3rd sg εἰμί.

ἄλλοι [δὲ]. Nominative subject of the second ἔλεγον (see οἱ μὲν above). The external evidence for ($\mathfrak{P}^{75vid}$ B N T W Θ $f^{1.13}$ et al.) and against ($\mathfrak{P}^{66}$ ℵ D K L Γ Δ Ψ 𝔐 et al.) the presence of the particle δὲ in the text is evenly balanced.

ἔλεγον. Impf act ind 3rd pl λέγω. On the function of the imperfect in the FG, see 1:39 on ἦν.

οὔ. Negative particle with an accent, as here, means "no."

ἀλλὰ. Marker of contrast.

πλανᾷ. Pres act ind 3rd sg πλανάω.

τὸν ὄχλον. Accusative direct object of πλανᾷ.

7:13 οὐδεὶς μέντοι παρρησίᾳ ἐλάλει περὶ αὐτοῦ διὰ τὸν φόβον τῶν Ἰουδαίων.

οὐδεὶς. Nominative subject of ἐλάλει. This verse is connected to the previous one by asyndeton.

μέντοι. Adverbial particle that is mostly adversative ("though, to be sure, yet").

παρρησίᾳ. Dative of manner ("openly, publicly").

ἐλάλει. Impf act ind 3rd sg λαλέω. On the function of the imperfect in the FG, see 1:39 on ἦν.

περὶ αὐτοῦ. Reference.

διὰ τὸν φόβον. Causal.

τῶν Ἰουδαίων. Objective genitive qualifying φόβον (BDF §163).

John 7:14-24

[14]When the festival was already at the midpoint, Jesus went up to the temple and began to teach. [15]Then the Jews were amazed, saying, "How does this man have such learning although he has never studied?" [16]So Jesus answered and said, "My teaching is not mine but from the one who sent me. [17]If anyone wants to do the will of God, he will know about this teaching, whether it is from God or I am speaking on my own. [18]The one who speaks on his own seeks his own glory. But the one who seeks the glory of the one who sent him—this one is sincere, and falsehood is not in him. [19]Has not Moses given you the law? Yet none of you practices the law. Why do you seek to kill me?" [20]The crowd answered, "You have a demon! Who is seeking to kill you?" [21]Jesus answered and said to

them, "I performed one work, and all of you are astonished. ²²For this reason Moses has given you circumcision—not that it is from Moses, but from the fathers—and you circumcise a man on the Sabbath. ²³If a man receives circumcision on the Sabbath so that the law of Moses may not be broken, are you angry with me because I made a whole man well on the Sabbath? ²⁴Do not judge according to the appearance, but judge with right judgment."

7:14 Ἤδη δὲ τῆς ἑορτῆς μεσούσης ἀνέβη Ἰησοῦς εἰς τὸ ἱερὸν καὶ ἐδίδασκεν.

Ἤδη. Adverb of time ("already").

δὲ. Marker of narrative development.

τῆς ἑορτῆς. Genitive subject of μεσούσης.

μεσούσης. Pres act ptc fem gen sg μεσόω (genitive absolute, temporal). μεσόω is a NT *hapax legomenon* that means to "be in/at the middle" (BDAG, 635).

ἀνέβη. Aor act ind 3rd sg ἀναβαίνω.

Ἰησοῦς. Nominative subject of ἀνέβη.

εἰς τὸ ἱερὸν. Locative.

καὶ. Coordinating conjunction.

ἐδίδασκεν. Impf act ind 3rd sg διδάσκω. The context indicates that the imperfect marks the beginning of Jesus' teaching in the temple, which is portrayed as an action in progress.

7:15 ἐθαύμαζον οὖν οἱ Ἰουδαῖοι λέγοντες· πῶς οὗτος γράμματα οἶδεν μὴ μεμαθηκώς;

ἐθαύμαζον. Impf act ind 3rd pl θαυμάζω. On the function of the imperfect in the FG, see 1:39 on ἦν.

οὖν. Postpositive inferential conjunction and/or transitional particle (see 1:22 and 11:6).

οἱ Ἰουδαῖοι. Nominative subject of ἐθαύμαζον.

λέγοντες. Pres act ptc masc nom pl λέγω (manner). On participles that follow the main verb, see βαπτίζων in 1:31.

πῶς. Interrogative particle.

οὗτος. Nominative subject of οἶδεν.

γράμματα. Accusative direct object of οἶδεν. Fronted for emphasis. γράμματα ("letters of the alphabet") refers here to "the body of information acquired in school or from the study of writings" (LN 27.21). The Jews were not surprised that Jesus could read but that he had advanced scriptural knowledge that could be mastered only through a training with a rabbinic scholar.

οἶδεν. Prf act ind 3rd sg οἶδα (see 1:26 on οἴδατε).

μὴ. Negative particle normally used with non-indicative verbs.

μεμαθηκώς. Prf act ptc masc nom sg μανθάνω (concessive). μανθάνω means "to acquire information as the result of instruction, whether in an informal or formal context" (LN 27.12). In this verse, the verb most likely refers to a formal training in rabbinic techniques of scriptural interpretation (Harris 2015, 153–54). On participles that follow the main verb, see βαπτίζων in 1:31.

7:16 ἀπεκρίθη οὖν αὐτοῖς [ὁ] Ἰησοῦς καὶ εἶπεν· ἡ ἐμὴ διδαχὴ οὐκ ἔστιν ἐμὴ ἀλλὰ τοῦ πέμψαντός με·

ἀπεκρίθη. Aor mid ind 3rd sg ἀποκρίνομαι. On the voice, see "Deponency" in the Series Introduction.

οὖν. Postpositive inferential conjunction and/or transitional particle (see 1:22 and 11:6).

αὐτοῖς. Dative indirect object of ἀπεκρίθη.

[ὁ] Ἰησοῦς. Nominative subject of ἀπεκρίθη. Although the article is attested in a number of witnesses ($\mathfrak{P}^{66}$ D K L N T W Γ Δ Θ Ψ $f^{1.13}$ 𝔐 et al.), it is absent in Sinaiticus and Vaticanus.

καὶ εἶπεν. Pleonastic clause under Semitic influence, which functions as a redundant quotative frame (see 1:25 on καὶ εἶπαν αὐτῷ).

καὶ. Coordinating conjunction.

εἶπεν. Aor act ind 3rd sg λέγω.

ἡ ἐμὴ διδαχὴ. Nominative subject of ἔστιν. The possessive adjective ἐμὴ stands in the first attributive position (see 2:10 on τὸν καλὸν οἶνον).

οὐκ ... ἀλλὰ. A point/counterpoint set ("not this ... but that") that that negates the incorrect description of the source of Jesus' teaching ("it is mine") and replaces it with the correct one ("it is of the one who sent me"). On the function of ἀλλά in a point/counterpoint set, see 1:8.

ἔστιν. Pres act ind 3rd sg εἰμί. The enclitic ἐστιν is accented ἔστιν when it comes at the beginning of a sentence, when it expresses existence, or when it follows ἀλλ', εἰ, καί, οὐκ, ὅτι, or τοῦτ'. The third condition is fulfilled here.

ἐμὴ. Predicate adjective.

τοῦ πέμψαντός. Aor act ptc masc gen sg πέμπω (substantival). Genitive of source qualifying διδαχὴ. πέμψαντός, which has an acute accent on the antepenult, acquired an additional accent, the acute, on the ultima from the enclitic με (Smyth §183; Carson 1985, 48). On the use of the participial forms of πέμπω to either identify or describe God in the FG, see τοῦ πέμψαντός in 4:34.

με. Accusative direct object of πέμψαντός.

7:17 ἐάν τις θέλῃ τὸ θέλημα αὐτοῦ ποιεῖν, γνώσεται περὶ τῆς διδαχῆς πότερον ἐκ τοῦ θεοῦ ἐστιν ἢ ἐγὼ ἀπ' ἐμαυτοῦ λαλῶ.

ἐάν. Introduces the protasis of a third-class condition. This verse is connected to the previous one by asyndeton.

τις. Nominative subject of θέλῃ.

θέλῃ. Pres act subj 3rd sg θέλω. Subjunctive with ἐάν.

τὸ θέλημα. Accusative direct object of ποιεῖν.

αὐτοῦ. Subjective genitive qualifying θέλημα.

ποιεῖν. Pres act inf ποιέω (complementary).

γνώσεται. Fut mid ind 3rd sg γινώσκω. It marks the beginning of the apodosis of a third-class condition.

περὶ τῆς διδαχῆς. Reference. The article is anaphoric, referring to ἡ ἐμὴ διδαχὴ in 7:16.

πότερον. Interrogative adverb. It is used in a disjunctive question πότερον ... ἤ ("whether ... or") (BDAG, 856). A NT *hapax legomenon*.

ἐκ τοῦ θεοῦ. Source/origin.

ἐστιν. Pres act ind 3rd sg εἰμί.

ἤ. Marker of an alternative/disjunctive particle (BDAG, 432.1).

ἐγώ. Nominative subject of λαλῶ.

ἀπ' ἐμαυτοῦ. Agency (see 5:19 on ἀφ' ἑαυτοῦ).

λαλῶ. Pres act ind 1st sg λαλέω.

7:18 ὁ ἀφ' ἑαυτοῦ λαλῶν τὴν δόξαν τὴν ἰδίαν ζητεῖ· ὁ δὲ ζητῶν τὴν δόξαν τοῦ πέμψαντος αὐτὸν οὗτος ἀληθής ἐστιν καὶ ἀδικία ἐν αὐτῷ οὐκ ἔστιν.

ὁ ... λαλῶν. Pres act ptc masc nom sg λαλέω (substantival). Nominative subject of ζητεῖ. Fronted as a topical frame. This verse is connected to the previous one by asyndeton.

ἀφ' ἑαυτοῦ. Agency (see 5:19 on ἀφ' ἑαυτοῦ).

τὴν δόξαν τὴν ἰδίαν. Accusative direct object of ζητεῖ. Fronted for emphasis. The adjective ἰδίαν stands in the second attributive position (see 1:9 on τὸ φῶς τὸ ἀληθινόν).

ζητεῖ. Pres act ind 3rd sg ζητέω.

ὁ ... ζητῶν. Pres act ptc masc nom sg ζητέω (substantival). Nominative subject of ἐστιν in a left-dislocation, resumed by οὗτος (see Runge 2010, 287–313). The left-dislocation shifts focus on the characterization of a genuine emissary. On the function of left-dislocations, see 1:33 on ὁ πέμψας.

δὲ. Marker of narrative development.

τὴν δόξαν. Accusative direct object of ζητῶν.

τοῦ πέμψαντος. Aor act ptc masc gen sg πέμπω (substantival). Possessive genitive qualifying δόξαν. On the use of the participial forms of πέμπω to either identify or describe God in the FG, see τοῦ πέμψαντός in 4:34.

αὐτὸν. Accusative direct object of πέμψαντος. The personal pronoun refers to ὁ . . . ζητῶν.

οὗτος. Nominative subject of ἐστιν, resuming ὁ . . . ζητῶν. The anaphoric demonstrative reinforces what is already made prominent through the left-dislocation of ὁ . . . ζητῶν.

ἀληθής. Predicate nominative. Fronted for emphasis.

ἐστιν. Pres act ind 3rd sg εἰμί.

καὶ. Coordinating conjunction.

ἀδικία. Nominative subject of ἔστιν.

ἐν αὐτῷ. Locative. The personal pronoun refers to ὁ . . . ζητῶν.

οὐκ. Negative particle normally used with indicative verbs.

ἔστιν. Pres act ind 3rd sg εἰμί. The enclitic ἐστιν is accented ἔστιν when it comes at the beginning of a sentence, when it expresses existence, or when it follows ἀλλ', εἰ, καί, οὐκ, ὅτι, or τοῦτ'. The last two conditions are fulfilled here.

7:19 Οὐ Μωϋσῆς δέδωκεν ὑμῖν τὸν νόμον; καὶ οὐδεὶς ἐξ ὑμῶν ποιεῖ τὸν νόμον. τί με ζητεῖτε ἀποκτεῖναι;

Οὐ. Negative particle that introduces a question that expects an affirmative answer. This verse is connected to the previous one by asyndeton.

Μωϋσῆς. Nominative subject of δέδωκεν. Fronted for emphasis.

δέδωκεν. Prf act ind 3rd sg δίδωμι. By crediting the subject of the verb—Moses—for giving the law, the perfect tense, which is semantically marked, refers to a past event, but the emphasis falls on the condition of the recipients, i.e., on their state of possessing the law that they are supposed to obey (Fanning, 295–96).

ὑμῖν. Dative indirect object of δέδωκεν.

τὸν νόμον. Accusative direct object of δέδωκεν.

καὶ. Coordinating conjunction joining two clauses that stand in tension with each other (see 1:5).

οὐδεὶς. Nominative subject of ποιεῖ. Fronted for emphasis.

ἐξ ὑμῶν. Replaces the partitive genitive.

ποιεῖ. Pres act ind 3rd sg ποιέω.

τὸν νόμον. Accusative direct object of ποιεῖ.
τί. Adverbial use of the interrogative pronoun ("why?").
με. Accusative direct object of ἀποκτεῖναι.
ζητεῖτε. Pres act ind 2nd pl ζητέω. In the FG, ζητέω is used six times with the complimentary infinitive ἀποκτεῖναι (5:18; 7:1, 19, 20, 25; 8:37).
ἀποκτεῖναι. Aor act inf ἀποκτείνω (complementary).

7:20 ἀπεκρίθη ὁ ὄχλος· δαιμόνιον ἔχεις· τίς σε ζητεῖ ἀποκτεῖναι;

ἀπεκρίθη. Aor mid ind 3rd sg ἀποκρίνομαι. On the voice, see "Deponency" in the Series Introduction. This verse is connected to the previous one by asyndeton.
ὁ ὄχλος. Nominative subject of ἀπεκρίθη.
δαιμόνιον. Accusative direct object of ἔχεις. Fronted for emphasis.
ἔχεις. Pres act ind 2nd sg ἔχω.
τίς. Nominative subject of ζητεῖ.
σε. Accusative direct object of ζητεῖ.
ζητεῖ. Pres act ind 3rd sg ζητέω (see 7:19).
ἀποκτεῖναι. Aor act inf ἀποκτείνω (complementary).

7:21 ἀπεκρίθη Ἰησοῦς καὶ εἶπεν αὐτοῖς· ἓν ἔργον ἐποίησα καὶ πάντες θαυμάζετε.

ἀπεκρίθη. Aor mid ind 3rd sg ἀποκρίνομαι. On the voice, see "Deponency" in the Series Introduction. This verse is connected to the previous one by asyndeton.
Ἰησοῦς. Nominative subject of ἀπεκρίθη.
καὶ εἶπεν αὐτοῖς. Pleonastic clause under Semitic influence, which functions as a redundant quotative frame (see 1:25 on καὶ εἶπαν αὐτῷ).
καί. Coordinating conjunction.
εἶπεν. Aor act ind 3rd sg λέγω.
αὐτοῖς. Dative indirect object of εἶπεν.
ἓν ἔργον. Accusative direct object of ἐποίησα. This is probably a reference to Jesus' healing of the sick man on the Sabbath in 5:5-9. Fronted for emphasis.
ἐποίησα. Aor act ind 1st sg ποιέω.
καί. Coordinating conjunction.
πάντες. Adjective that modifies the implied subject ("you") of θαυμάζετε.
θαυμάζετε. Pres act ind 2nd pl θαυμάζω.

7:22 διὰ τοῦτο Μωϋσῆς δέδωκεν ὑμῖν τὴν περιτομήν– οὐχ ὅτι ἐκ τοῦ Μωϋσέως ἐστὶν ἀλλ' ἐκ τῶν πατέρων– καὶ ἐν σαββάτῳ περιτέμνετε ἄνθρωπον.

διὰ τοῦτο. Causal. If the PP belongs with the previous verse, the demonstrative pronoun is anaphoric, referring to Jesus' healing on the Sabbath: καὶ πάντες θαυμάζετε διὰ τοῦτο ("and all of you are shocked on that account" [Brown, 1:310]). If the PP belongs with v. 22, as suggested by the punctuation adopted in NA[28]/UBS[5] and SBLGNT, τοῦτο is cataphoric, referring to the explanation that follows. Since, however, the reason for the commandment of circumcision is not clearly stated, the connection between Jesus' healing and circumcision could be either negative (i.e., circumcision as a precedent for breaking the Sabbath law) or positive (i.e., circumcision as "a type of the complete renewal of human nature" [Barrett, 319]).

Μωϋσῆς. Nominative subject of δέδωκεν.
δέδωκεν. Prf act ind 3rd sg δίδωμι; see 7:19.
ὑμῖν. Dative indirect object of δέδωκεν.
τὴν περιτομήν. Accusative direct object of δέδωκεν.
οὐχ ὅτι ἐκ τοῦ Μωϋσέως ἐστὶν ἀλλ' ἐκ τῶν πατέρων. Parenthetical clause that interrupts the plot of the narrative. The purpose of this editorial gloss is to clarify to the audience that although circumcision is a commandment in the Mosaic law (Lev 12:3), the rite itself was practiced since the patriarchs (Gen 17:12).

οὐχ ὅτι. An ellipsis for οὐ λέγω ὅτι (BDF §480.5); see 6:46.
οὐχ . . . ἀλλ'. A point/counterpoint set ("not this . . . but that") that negates the inaccurate explanation of the origin of circumcision (it is from Moses) and replaces it with the accurate explanation (it is from the patriarchs). On the function of ἀλλά in a point/counterpoint set, see 1:8.
ὅτι. Introduces the clausal complement (indirect discourse) of an implied λέγω (see οὐχ ὅτι above).
ἐκ τοῦ Μωϋσέως. Source/origin.
ἐστίν. Pres act ind 3rd sg εἰμί.
ἐκ τῶν πατέρων. Source/origin.
καί. Coordinating conjunction.
ἐν σαββάτῳ. Temporal.
περιτέμνετε. Pres act in 2nd pl περιτέμνω.
ἄνθρωπον. Accusative direct object of περιτέμνετε. Here ἄνθρωπος refers to a male infant, who had to be circumcised on the eighth day after birth.

7:23 εἰ περιτομὴν λαμβάνει ἄνθρωπος ἐν σαββάτῳ ἵνα μὴ λυθῇ ὁ νόμος Μωϋσέως, ἐμοὶ χολᾶτε ὅτι ὅλον ἄνθρωπον ὑγιῆ ἐποίησα ἐν σαββάτῳ;

εἰ. Introduces the protasis of a first-class condition. This verse is connected to the previous one by asyndeton.
περιτομὴν. Accusative direct object of λαμβάνει.
λαμβάνει. Pres act ind 3rd sg λαμβάνω.
ἄνθρωπος. Nominative subject of λαμβάνει.
ἐν σαββάτῳ. Temporal.
ἵνα. Introduces a purpose clause.
μὴ. Negative particle normally used with non-indicative verbs.
λυθῇ. Aor pass subj 3rd sg λύω. Subjunctive with ἵνα. In this context, λύω refers to "the failure to conform to a law or regulation, with a possible implication of regarding it as invalid—'to break (a law), to transgress'" (LN 36.30).
ὁ νόμος. Nominative subject of λυθῇ.
Μωϋσέως. Attributive genitive ("the Mosaic Law") or a genitive of origin ("the law that Moses wrote") qualifying νόμος.
ἐμοὶ. Dative complement of χολᾶτε.
χολᾶτε. Pres act ind 2nd pl χολάω. χολάω is a NT *hapax legomenon* that means to "be angry with" + dat (BDAG, 1086).
ὅτι. Introduces a causal clause.
ὅλον ἄνθρωπον. Accusative direct object of ἐποίησα.
ὑγιῆ. Accusative complement to ὅλον ἄνθρωπον in a double accusative object-complement construction.
ἐποίησα. Aor act ind 1st sg ποιέω.
ἐν σαββάτῳ. Temporal.

7:24 μὴ κρίνετε κατ' ὄψιν, ἀλλὰ τὴν δικαίαν κρίσιν κρίνετε.

μὴ ... ἀλλὰ. A point/counterpoint set ("not this ... but that") that prohibits judging according to the appearance and commands judging with right judgment. On the function of ἀλλά in a point/counterpoint set, see 1:8. This verse is connected to the previous one by asyndeton.
κρίνετε. Pres act impv 2nd pl κρίνω.
κατ' ὄψιν. Standard.
τὴν δικαίαν κρίσιν. Cognate accusative (accusative of the inner object). Fronted for emphasis.
κρίνετε. Pres act impv 2nd pl κρίνω.

John 7:25-31

[25]Then some of the inhabitants of Jerusalem began to say, "Is this not the one whom they are seeking to kill? [26]And look, he is speaking openly, and they say nothing to him! Can it be that the authorities really know that this is the Messiah? [27]Yet we know this one, where he is from. But the Messiah, whenever he comes, no one knows where he is from." [28]Then Jesus cried out while he was teaching in the temple and speaking, "You both know me and know where I am from. Yet I have not come on my own, but the one who sent me is trustworthy, whom you do not know. [29]I know him, because I am from him, and he sent me." [30]So they were seeking to seize him, but no one laid a hand on him, because his hour had not yet come. [31]Yet many of the crowd believed in him and were saying, "The Messiah, whenever he comes, will not do more signs than those which this man has done, will he?"

7:25 Ἔλεγον οὖν τινες ἐκ τῶν Ἱεροσολυμιτῶν· οὐχ οὗτός ἐστιν ὃν ζητοῦσιν ἀποκτεῖναι;

Ἔλεγον. Impf act ind 3rd pl λέγω. On the function of the imperfect in the FG, see 1:39 on ἦν.

οὖν. Postpositive inferential conjunction and/or transitional particle (see 1:22 and 11:6).

τινες. Nominative subject of Ἔλεγον.

ἐκ τῶν Ἱεροσολυμιτῶν. Replaces the partitive genitive.

οὐχ. Negative particle that introduces a question that expects an affirmative answer.

οὗτός. Nominative subject of ἐστιν. Fronted for emphasis. οὗτός, which has a circumflex accent on the penult, acquired an additional accent, the acute, on the ultima from the enclitic ἐστιν (Smyth §183; Carson 1985, 48).

ἐστιν. Pres act ind 3rd sg εἰμί.

ὃν. The relative pronoun introduces a headless relative clause that, in its entirety (ὃν ζητοῦσιν ἀποκτεῖναι), serves as the predicate nominative. Within its clause, ὃν is the accusative direct object of ἀποκτεῖναι.

ζητοῦσιν. Pres act ind 3rd pl ζητέω. In the FG, ζητέω is used six times with the complimentary infinitive ἀποκτεῖναι (5:18; 7:1, 19, 20, 25; 8:37).

ἀποκτεῖναι. Aor act inf ἀποκτείνω (complementary).

7:26 καὶ ἴδε παρρησίᾳ λαλεῖ καὶ οὐδὲν αὐτῷ λέγουσιν. μήποτε ἀληθῶς ἔγνωσαν οἱ ἄρχοντες ὅτι οὗτός ἐστιν ὁ χριστός;

καὶ. Coordinating conjunction.

ἴδε. An interjection (originally aor act impv 2nd sg ὁράω) that is "used when more than one pers[on] is addressed, and when that which is to be observed is in the nom[inative]" (BDAG, 466).

παρρησίᾳ. Dative of manner ("openly, publicly").

λαλεῖ. Pres act ind 3rd sg λαλέω.

καὶ. Coordinating conjunction.

οὐδὲν. Accusative direct object of λέγουσιν.

αὐτῷ. Dative indirect object of λέγουσιν.

λέγουσιν. Pres act ind 3rd pl λέγω.

μήποτε. Marker of inquiry that signals that a negative answer is expected but also conveys some uncertainty: "Can it be?" (BDF §427.2; BDAG, 648.3.a).

ἀληθῶς. Adverb ("truly, really").

ἔγνωσαν. Aor act ind 3rd pl γινώσκω. In this context, the aorist ἔγνωσαν does not refer to the past but describes the current knowledge of the Jewish leaders (Campbell 2007, 120).

οἱ ἄρχοντες. Nominative subject of ἔγνωσαν.

ὅτι. Introduces the clausal complement (indirect discourse) of ἔγνωσαν.

οὗτός. Nominative subject of ἐστιν. Fronted for emphasis. οὗτός, which has a circumflex accent on the penult, acquired an additional accent, the acute, on the ultima from the enclitic ἐστιν (Smyth §183; Carson 1985, 48).

ἐστιν. Pres act ind 3rd sg εἰμί.

ὁ χριστός. Predicate nominative.

7:27 ἀλλὰ τοῦτον οἴδαμεν πόθεν ἐστίν· ὁ δὲ χριστὸς ὅταν ἔρχηται οὐδεὶς γινώσκει πόθεν ἐστίν.

ἀλλὰ. Marker of contrast.

τοῦτον. Accusative direct object of οἴδαμεν. τοῦτον functions as a pronominal prolepsis because "the subject of a relative clause is anticipated by a pronoun in the main clause" (Zerwick §206). τοῦτον οἴδαμεν πόθεν ἐστίν ("we know this one, where he is from") = οἴδαμεν πόθεν οὗτός ἐστιν ("we know where this one is from").

οἴδαμεν. Prf act ind 1st pl οἶδα (see 1:26 on οἴδατε).

πόθεν. Interrogative adverb of place.

ἐστίν. Pres act ind 3rd sg εἰμί.

ὁ ... χριστὸς. Nominative subject of ἔρχηται in a left-dislocation (see Runge 2010, 287–313). Runge argues that two basic uses of left-dislocations in the NT are (1) "streamlining the introduction of a complex entity into one clause instead of two," and (2) "thematically highlighting the introduction of an entity because of its significance for the discourse" (2010, 291). Both functions can be discerned here. On the one hand, ὁ ... χριστὸς merges the indefinite temporal clause, ὅταν ἔρχηται, and the declarative clause, οὐδεὶς γινώσκει πόθεν ἐστίν, into one clause. On the other hand, it grants prominence to the main subject matter of both clauses—the identity of the Messiah.

δὲ. Marker of narrative development.
ὅταν. Introduces an indefinite temporal clause.
ἔρχηται. Pres mid subj 3rd sg ἔρχομαι. Subjunctive with ὅταν.
οὐδεὶς. Nominative subject of γινώσκει.
γινώσκει. Pres act ind 3rd sg γινώσκω.
πόθεν. Interrogative adverb of place.
ἐστίν. Pres act ind 3rd sg εἰμί.

7:28 ἔκραξεν οὖν ἐν τῷ ἱερῷ διδάσκων ὁ Ἰησοῦς καὶ λέγων· κἀμὲ οἴδατε καὶ οἴδατε πόθεν εἰμί· καὶ ἀπ' ἐμαυτοῦ οὐκ ἐλήλυθα, ἀλλ' ἔστιν ἀληθινὸς ὁ πέμψας με, ὃν ὑμεῖς οὐκ οἴδατε·

ἔκραξεν. Aor act ind 3rd sg κράζω.
οὖν. Postpositive inferential conjunction and/or transitional particle (see 1:22 and 11:6).
ἐν τῷ ἱερῷ. Locative. Elsewhere in the FG, this PP occurs in 2:14; 5:14; 8:20; 10:23; 11:56; 18:20.
διδάσκων. Pres act ptc masc nom sg διδάσκω (temporal or manner). On participles that follow the main verb, see βαπτίζων in 1:31.
ὁ Ἰησοῦς. Nominative subject of ἔκραξεν.
καὶ. Coordinating conjunction.
λέγων. Pres act ptc masc nom sg λέγω. If καὶ links λέγων and διδάσκων, their functions are probably the same (temporal or manner). If, despite the καὶ, λέγων is connected to ἔκραξεν (so Haubeck and von Siebenthal, 551), it is probably pleonastic, like in 7:37 (ἔκραξεν λέγων); see also 1:15 (κέκραγεν λέγων). My translation reflects the first alternative and presumes that both participles are temporal.
κἀμὲ. Formed by crasis from καὶ ἐμέ. καὶ and the next καὶ form the καὶ ... καὶ construction ("both ... and"; cf. BDF §444.3). ἐμέ is the accusative direct object of the first οἴδατε.
οἴδατε. Prf act ind 2nd pl οἶδα (see 1:26 on οἴδατε).
οἴδατε. Prf act ind 2nd pl οἶδα (see 1:26 on οἴδατε).
πόθεν. Interrogative adverb of place.
εἰμί. Pres act ind 1st sg εἰμί.
καὶ. Coordinating conjunction linking two clauses that stand in adversative relationship (see 1:5).
ἀπ' ἐμαυτοῦ. Agency (see 5:19 on ἀφ' ἑαυτοῦ).

οὐκ . . . ἀλλ'. A point/counterpoint set ("not this . . . but that") that negates the assertion that Jesus came on his own and replaces it with the assertion that the one who sent him is trustworthy. On the function of ἀλλά in a point/counterpoint set, see 1:8.

ἐλήλυθα. Prf act ind 1st sg ἔρχομαι. The verb stands in final, emphatic position.

ἔστιν. Pres act ind 3rd sg εἰμί. The enclitic ἐστιν is accented ἔστιν when it comes at the beginning of a sentence, when it expresses existence, or when it follows ἀλλ', εἰ, καί, οὐκ, ὅτι, or τοῦτ'. The first two conditions are fulfilled here.

ἀληθινὸς. Predicate adjective.

ὁ πέμψας. Aor act ptc masc nom sg πέμπω (substantival). Nominative subject of ἔστιν. On the use of the participial forms of πέμπω to either identify or describe God in the FG, see τοῦ πέμψαντός in 4:34.

με. Accusative direct object of πέμψας.

ὃν. Accusative direct object of οἴδατε.

ὑμεῖς. Nominative subject of οἴδατε. The personal pronoun is emphatic and contrastive, highlighting the difference between Jesus and his interlocutors.

οὐκ. Negative particle normally used with indicative verbs.

οἴδατε. Prf act ind 2nd pl οἶδα (see 1:26 on οἴδατε). The verb stands in final, emphatic position.

7:29 ἐγὼ οἶδα αὐτόν, ὅτι παρ' αὐτοῦ εἰμι κἀκεῖνός με ἀπέστειλεν.

ἐγώ. Nominative subject of οἶδα. The personal pronoun is emphatic and contrastive, distinguishing Jesus, who knows God, from his interlocutors, who do not (see 7:28). This verse is connected to the previous one by asyndeton.

οἶδα. Prf act ind 1st sg οἶδα (see 1:26 on οἴδατε).

αὐτόν. Nominative subject of οἶδα.

ὅτι. Introduces a causal clause.

παρ' αὐτοῦ. Source/origin (BDAG, 756.A.1).

εἰμι. Pres act ind 1st sg εἰμί.

κἀκεῖνός. Formed by crasis from καὶ ἐκεῖνος. καὶ is connective. ἐκεῖνος is the nominative subject of ἀπέστειλεν, functioning as a third-person personal pronoun with a simple anaphoric force (Wallace 1996, 328–29). κἀκεῖνός, which has a circumflex accent on the penult, acquired an additional accent, the acute, on the ultima from the enclitic με (Smyth §183; Carson 1985, 48).

με. Accusative direct object of ἀπέστειλεν.

ἀπέστειλεν. Aor act ind 3rd sg ἀποστέλλω. The verb stands in final, emphatic position.

7:30 Ἐζήτουν οὖν αὐτὸν πιάσαι, καὶ οὐδεὶς ἐπέβαλεν ἐπ' αὐτὸν τὴν χεῖρα, ὅτι οὔπω ἐληλύθει ἡ ὥρα αὐτοῦ.

Ἐζήτουν. Impf act ind 3rd pl ζητέω. On the function of the imperfect in the FG, see 1:39 on ἦν.

οὖν. Postpositive inferential conjunction and/or transitional particle (see 1:22 and 11:6).

αὐτὸν. Accusative direct object of πιάσαι.

πιάσαι. Aor act inf πιάζω (complementary). The verb πιάζω ("seize, arrest, take into custody" [BDAG, 812.2]) is not found in the Synoptics. In the FG, it is used either as a complementary infinitive (7:30, 44; 10:39) or by itself (7:32; 8:20; 11:57).

καὶ. Coordinating conjunction linking two clauses that stand in adversative relationship (see 1:5).

οὐδεὶς. Nominative subject of ἐπέβαλεν. Fronted for emphasis.

ἐπέβαλεν. Aor act ind 3rd sg ἐπιβάλλω.

ἐπ' αὐτὸν. Locative.

τὴν χεῖρα. Accusative direct object of ἐπέβαλεν.

ὅτι. Introduces a causal clause.

οὔπω. Adverb of time ("not yet").

ἐληλύθει. Plprf act ind 3rd sg ἔρχομαι. In this context, the combination of the pluperfect of ἔρχομαι and οὔπω highlights the nonoccurrence of the coming of Jesus' hour in the antecedent past (Fanning, 307).

ἡ ὥρα. Nominative subject of ἐληλύθει. On the arrival of Jesus' hour, see ἡ ὥρα in 12:23.

αὐτοῦ. Genitive of purpose qualifying ὥρα ("the hour destined for him").

7:31 Ἐκ τοῦ ὄχλου δὲ πολλοὶ ἐπίστευσαν εἰς αὐτὸν καὶ ἔλεγον· ὁ χριστὸς ὅταν ἔλθῃ μὴ πλείονα σημεῖα ποιήσει ὧν οὗτος ἐποίησεν;

Ἐκ τοῦ ὄχλου. Replaces the partitive genitive.

δὲ. Marker of narrative development with a contrastive nuance.

πολλοὶ. Nominative subject of ἐπίστευσαν. Fronted for emphasis.

ἐπίστευσαν. Aor act ind 3rd pl πιστεύω.

εἰς αὐτὸν. Goal of actions or feelings directed toward someone (BDAG, 290.4.c.β). For πιστεύειν εἰς + accusative ("trust or believe in someone"), see 1:12 on εἰς τὸ ὄνομα.

καὶ. Coordinating conjunction.

ἔλεγον. Impf act ind 3rd pl λέγω. On the function of the imperfect in the FG, see 1:39 on ἦν.

ὁ χριστὸς. Nominative subject of ἔλθῃ and ποιήσει in a left-dislocation (see Runge 2010, 287–313). ὁ χριστὸς joins the indefinite temporal clause ὅταν ἔλθῃ and the question μὴ πλείονα σημεῖα ποιήσει ὧν οὗτος ἐποίησεν into one clause. It also grants prominence to the Messiah, which functions as the subject of both clauses (291).

ὅταν. Introduces an indefinite temporal clause.

ἔλθῃ. Aor act subj 3rd sg ἔρχομαι. Subjunctive with ὅταν.

μὴ. Negative particle that introduces a question that expects a negative answer.

πλείονα σημεῖα. Accusative direct object of ποιήσει. πλείονα is neut acc pl of πλείων, a comparative of πολύς. The use of the term σημεῖα for Jesus' miracles is one of the distinctive features of the FG (see 2:11, 23; 3:2; 4:48, 54; 6:2, 14, 26; 9:16; 11:47; 12:18, 37; 20:30; cf. Barrett, 75–78; Keener, 1:272–79; Thompson, 65–68).

ποιήσει. Fut act ind 3rd sg ποιέω. Since this future tense is used within a question, it expresses uncertainty (Campbell 2007, 156; see also 6:68 on ἀπελευσόμεθα).

ὧν. Genitive of comparison. The relative pronoun is attracted to the case of its omitted antecedent demonstrative: ὧν = τούτων/ἐκείνων ἅ (BDF §294.4). The comparative construction πλείονα σημεῖα . . . ὧν corresponds to πλείονα σημεῖα . . . ἢ ἅ (Ramelli, 339).

οὗτος. Nominative subject of ἐποίησεν. Fronted for emphasis.

ἐποίησεν. Aor act ind 3rd sg ποιέω.

John 7:32-36

[32] The Pharisees heard the crowd murmuring these things about him, and the chief priests and the Pharisees sent officers to take him into custody. [33] Then Jesus said, "I am still with you for a short time, and then I am going to the one who sent me. [34] You will seek me, and you will not find me, and where I am, you cannot come." [35] Then the Jews said to one another, "Where does this man intend to go that we will not find him? He is not intending to go to the dispersed among the Greeks and teach the Greeks, is he? [36] What is this saying that he said, 'You will seek me, and you will not find me, and where I am, you cannot come'?"

7:32 ἤκουσαν οἱ Φαρισαῖοι τοῦ ὄχλου γογγύζοντος περὶ αὐτοῦ ταῦτα, καὶ ἀπέστειλαν οἱ ἀρχιερεῖς καὶ οἱ Φαρισαῖοι ὑπηρέτας ἵνα πιάσωσιν αὐτόν.

ἤκουσαν. Aor act ind 3rd pl ἀκούω. This verse is connected to the previous one by asyndeton.

οἱ Φαρισαῖοι. Nominative subject of ἤκουσαν.

τοῦ ὄχλου. Genitive direct object of ἤκουσαν.

γογγύζοντος. Pres act ptc masc gen sg γογγύζω (predicative). The participle modifies τοῦ ὄχλου, standing in the second predicate position (see 1:29 on ἐρχόμενον). The combination τοῦ ὄχλου γογγύζοντος is equivalent to a double accusative object-complement construction; the direct object (τοῦ ὄχλου) and its complement (γογγύζοντος) are genitives because this case is required by the governing verb ἤκουσαν.

περὶ αὐτοῦ. Reference.

ταῦτα. Accusative direct object of γογγύζοντος.

καὶ. Coordinating conjunction.

ἀπέστειλαν. Aor act ind 3rd pl ἀποστέλλω.

οἱ ἀρχιερεῖς καὶ οἱ Φαρισαῖοι. Compound nominative subject of ἀπέστειλαν.

ὑπηρέτας. Accusative direct object of ἀπέστειλαν. Since the chief priests and the Pharisees were two major groups represented in the Sanhedrin, ὑπηρέτας ("servants, assistants") most likely refers to their representatives rather than to the temple police consisting of the Levites, as presumed in many English translations (TDNT 8:540).

ἵνα. Introduces a purpose clause.

πιάσωσιν. Aor act subj 3rd pl πιάζω. Subjunctive with ἵνα. On the meaning and the use of this verb in the FG, see 7:30 on πιάσαι.

αὐτόν. Accusative direct object of πιάσωσιν.

7:33 Εἶπεν οὖν ὁ Ἰησοῦς· ἔτι χρόνον μικρὸν μεθ' ὑμῶν εἰμι καὶ ὑπάγω πρὸς τὸν πέμψαντά με.

Εἶπεν. Aor act ind 3rd sg λέγω.

οὖν. Postpositive inferential conjunction and/or transitional particle (see 1:22 and 11:6).

ὁ Ἰησοῦς. Nominative subject of Εἶπεν.

ἔτι. Adverb ("yet, still").

χρόνον μικρὸν. Accusative indicating extent of time.

μεθ' ὑμῶν. Association/accompaniment.

εἰμι. Pres act ind 1st sg εἰμί.

καί. Coordinating conjunction. Since it links two clauses that stand in chronological sequence, it is sometimes regarded as an example of "the temporal use of καί in parataxis" (MHT 2:421–22).

ὑπάγω. Pres act ind 1st sg ὑπάγω. Since in this verse ὑπάγω ("go away") refers to Jesus' going to the Father, i.e., to his death, the present tense describes an action that is expected to occur in the future.

πρὸς τὸν πέμψαντά. Locative (motion toward).

τὸν πέμψαντά. Aor act ptc masc acc sg πέμπω (substantival). πέμψαντά, which has an acute accent on the antepenult, acquired an additional accent, the acute, on the ultima from the enclitic με (Smyth §183; Carson 1985, 48). On the use of the participial forms of πέμπω to either identify or describe God in the FG, see τοῦ πέμψαντός in 4:34.

με. Accusative direct object of πέμψαντά.

7:34 ζητήσετέ με καὶ οὐχ εὑρήσετέ [με], καὶ ὅπου εἰμὶ ἐγὼ ὑμεῖς οὐ δύνασθε ἐλθεῖν.

ζητήσετέ. Fut act ind 2nd pl ζητέω. ζητήσετέ, which has an acute accent on the antepenult, acquired an additional accent, the acute, on the ultima from the enclitic με (Smyth §183; Carson 1985, 48). This verse is connected to the previous one by asyndeton.

με. Accusative direct object of ζητήσετέ.

καί. Coordinating conjunction.

οὐχ. Negative particle normally used with indicative verbs.

εὑρήσετέ. Fut act ind 2nd pl εὑρίσκω. εὑρήσετέ, which has an acute accent on the antepenult, acquired an additional accent, the acute, on the ultima from the enclitic με (Smyth §183; Carson 1985, 48).

[με]. Accusative direct object of εὑρήσετέ. The personal pronoun is printed within square brackets because the evidence for (𝔓⁷⁵ B N T 0105 565 sy) and against (𝔓⁶⁶ ℵ D K L W Γ Δ Θ Ψ f¹·¹³ 𝔐) its presence in the text is evenly balanced.

καί. Coordinating conjunction.

ὅπου. Particle denoting place.

εἰμί. Pres act ind 1st sg εἰμί.

ἐγώ. Nominative subject of εἰμί. The personal pronoun is contrastive, distinguishing Jesus from his audience.

ὑμεῖς. Nominative subject of δύνασθε. The personal pronoun is contrastive, distinguishing Jesus' audience from him.

οὐ. Negative particle normally used with indicative verbs.

δύνασθε. Pres mid ind 2nd pl δύναμαι.

ἐλθεῖν. Aor act inf ἔρχομαι (complementary).

7:35 εἶπον οὖν οἱ Ἰουδαῖοι πρὸς ἑαυτούς· ποῦ οὗτος μέλλει πορεύεσθαι ὅτι ἡμεῖς οὐχ εὑρήσομεν αὐτόν; μὴ εἰς τὴν διασπορὰν τῶν Ἑλλήνων μέλλει πορεύεσθαι καὶ διδάσκειν τοὺς Ἕλληνας;

εἶπον. Aor act ind 3rd pl λέγω.

οὖν. Postpositive inferential conjunction and/or transitional particle (see 1:22 and 11:6).

οἱ Ἰουδαῖοι. Nominative subject of εἶπον.

πρὸς ἑαυτούς. Locative (motion toward). The PP functions like an indirect object of εἶπον.

ποῦ. Interrogative adverb of place.

οὗτος. Nominative subject of μέλλει.

μέλλει. Pres act ind 3rd sg μέλλω.

πορεύεσθαι. Pres mid inf πορεύομαι (complementary).

ὅτι. Introduces the causal clause that gives "the reason why a question is asked" (Zerwick §420).

ἡμεῖς. Nominative subject of εὑρήσομεν. The personal pronoun is contrastive, differentiating between the Jewish leaders (ἡμεῖς) and Jesus (οὗτος).

οὐχ. Negative particle normally used with indicative verbs.

εὑρήσομεν. Fut act ind 1st pl εὑρίσκω.

αὐτόν. Accusative direct object of εὑρήσομεν.

μὴ. Negative particle that introduces a question that expects a negative answer.

εἰς τὴν διασπορὰν. Locative. διασπορά denotes either the "state or condition of being scattered" (BDAG, 236.1) or "the place in which the dispersed are found" (236.2).

τῶν Ἑλλήνων. Genitive of direction ("the dispersion among the Greeks") or genitive of reference ("the dispersion with regard to the Greeks") qualifying διασπορὰν.

μέλλει. Pres act ind 3rd sg μέλλω.

πορεύεσθαι. Pres mid inf πορεύομαι (complementary).

καὶ. Coordinating conjunction.

διδάσκειν. Pres act inf διδάσκω (complementary).

τοὺς Ἕλληνας. Accusative direct object of διδάσκειν.

7:36 τίς ἐστιν ὁ λόγος οὗτος ὃν εἶπεν· ζητήσετέ με καὶ οὐχ εὑρήσετέ [με], καὶ ὅπου εἰμὶ ἐγὼ ὑμεῖς οὐ δύνασθε ἐλθεῖν;

τίς. Predicate nominative. "Interrogatives, by their nature, indicate the unknown component and hence cannot be the subject" (Wallace 1996, 40 n. 12). This verse is connected to the previous one by asyndeton.

ἐστιν. Pres act ind 3rd sg εἰμί.

ὁ λόγος οὗτος. Nominative subject of ἐστιν. ὁ λόγος οὗτος refers to Jesus' assertions in 7:34, which are here repeated verbatim.

ὅν. Accusative direct object of εἶπεν. The antecedent of the relative pronoun is ὁ λόγος οὗτος.

εἶπεν. Aor act ind 3rd sg λέγω.

ζητήσετέ. Fut act ind 2nd pl ζητέω. ζητήσετέ, which has an acute accent on the antepenult, acquired an additional accent, the acute, on the ultima from the enclitic με (Smyth §183; Carson 1985, 48).

με. Accusative direct object of ζητήσετέ.

καὶ. Coordinating conjunction.

οὐχ. Negative particle normally used with indicative verbs.

εὑρήσετέ. Fut act ind 2nd pl εὑρίσκω. εὑρήσετέ, which has an acute accent on the antepenult, acquired an additional accent, the acute, on the ultima from the enclitic με (Smyth §183; Carson 1985, 48).

[με]. Accusative direct object of εὑρήσετέ. Like in 7:34, the external evidence for ($\mathfrak{P}^{75}$ B T f^1 565 892 et al.) and against ($\mathfrak{P}^{66}$ ℵ D K L W Γ Δ Θ Ψ $f^{1.13}$ 𝔐 et al.) the presence of με after εὑρήσετέ is evenly balanced.

καὶ. Coordinating conjunction.

ὅπου. Particle denoting place.

εἰμὶ. Pres act ind 1st sg εἰμί.

ἐγώ. Nominative subject of εἰμί.

ὑμεῖς. Nominative subject of δύνασθε.

οὐ. Negative particle normally used with indicative verbs.

δύνασθε. Pres mid ind 2nd pl δύναμαι.

ἐλθεῖν. Aor act inf ἔρχομαι (complementary).

John 7:37-39

³⁷On the last day of the festival, the great day, Jesus was standing and cried out, saying, "If anyone is thirsty, let him come to me and drink. ³⁸The one who believes in me, just as the Scripture said, 'Rivers of living water will flow out of his heart.'" ³⁹He said this about the Spirit, whom those who believed in him were about to receive; for the Spirit was not yet there, because Jesus was not yet glorified.

7:37 Ἐν δὲ τῇ ἐσχάτῃ ἡμέρᾳ τῇ μεγάλῃ τῆς ἑορτῆς εἱστήκει ὁ Ἰησοῦς καὶ ἔκραξεν λέγων· ἐάν τις διψᾷ ἐρχέσθω πρός με καὶ πινέτω.

Ἐν . . . τῇ ἐσχάτῃ ἡμέρᾳ. Temporal. Fronted as a temporal frame. The adjective ἐσχάτῃ stands in the first attributive position (see 2:10 on τὸν καλὸν οἶνον).

John 7:37-39

δέ. Marker of narrative development.

τῇ μεγάλῃ. Dative in apposition to τῇ ἐσχάτῃ ἡμέρᾳ. The repetition of ἡμέρα is implied: τῇ μεγάλῃ [ἡμέρᾳ]. In this formulation, the adjective μεγάλη also stands in the first attributive position (see Ἐν . . . τῇ ἐσχάτῃ ἡμέρᾳ above).

τῆς ἑορτῆς. Partitive genitive qualifying ἡμέρᾳ.

εἱστήκει. Plprf act ind 3rd sg ἵστημι. The pluperfect has the imperfect meaning.

ὁ Ἰησοῦς. Nominative subject of εἱστήκει.

καί. Coordinating conjunction.

ἔκραξεν. Aor act ind 3rd sg κράζω.

λέγων. Pres act ptc masc nom sg λέγω (pleonastic).

ἐάν. Introduces the protasis of a third-class condition.

τις. Nominative subject of διψᾷ.

διψᾷ. Pres act subj 3rd sg διψάω. Subjunctive with ἐάν.

ἐρχέσθω. Pres mid impv 3rd sg ἔρχομαι. The verb marks the beginning of the apodosis of a third-class condition.

πρός με. Locative (motion toward).

καί. Coordinating conjunction.

πινέτω. Pres act impv 3rd sg πίνω.

7:38 ὁ πιστεύων εἰς ἐμέ, καθὼς εἶπεν ἡ γραφή, ποταμοὶ ἐκ τῆς κοιλίας αὐτοῦ ῥεύσουσιν ὕδατος ζῶντος.

ὁ πιστεύων. Pres act ptc masc nom sg πιστεύω (substantival). Verses 37-38 can be punctuated in two ways: (1) the full stop could be placed at the end of v. 37 (supported by Origen, Athanasius, and most of the Eastern fathers and adopted by NA[28]/UBS[5] and SBLGNT); (2) the full stop could be placed after ὁ πιστεύων εἰς ἐμέ (supported by Justin, Hippolytus, Tertullian, Irenaeus, and other Western fathers). If ὁ πιστεύων belongs with v. 38 (the first option), it begins a new sentence and functions as the pendent nominative in a left-dislocation, which is resumed by αὐτοῦ (ASV; KJV; RSV; NASB; ESV). If ὁ πιστεύων belongs with v. 37 (the second option), it serves as the nominative subject of πινέτω (cf. NRSV; NEB; NET; LEB; Brown, 1:320-23). For theological implications of these alternatives, see αὐτοῦ below. My translation follows the punctuation in NA[28]/UBS[5]. This verse is connected to the previous one by asyndeton.

εἰς ἐμέ. Goal of actions or feelings directed toward someone (BDAG, 290.4.c.β). For πιστεύειν εἰς + accusative ("trust or believe in someone"), see 1:12 on εἰς τὸ ὄνομα.

John 7:37-39

καθὼς εἶπεν ἡ γραφή. The OT introductory formula that occurs only here (cf. 7:42).

καθώς. Introduces a comparative clause.

εἶπεν. Aor act ind 3rd sg λέγω.

ἡ γραφή. Nominative subject of εἶπεν.

ποταμοὶ ἐκ τῆς κοιλίας αὐτοῦ ῥεύσουσιν ὕδατος ζῶντος. Although the introductory formula indicates that this is a scriptural quotation, it is impossible to tell which OT text is quoted. Similar ideas can be found in Ps 78:15-16 (77:15-16 [LXX]); Prov 18:4; Isa 12:3; 43:19-20; 44:3; 55:1; 58:11; Jer 2:13; 17:13; Ezek 47:1-2; Zech 14:8.

ποταμοί. Nominative subject of ῥεύσουσιν.

ἐκ τῆς κοιλίας. Source. κοιλία (lit. "belly, stomach") here denotes "seat of inward life, of feelings and desire," whose functional equivalent in English is "heart" (BDAG, 550–51.3).

αὐτοῦ. Possessive genitive qualifying κοιλίας. If ὁ πιστεύων belongs with v. 38 (the first option above), αὐτοῦ is resumptive, referring to "the one who believes." On this reading, the believer becomes the source of the living water. The resumptive pronoun αὐτοῦ is placed in an unmarked position (following the verb), which occurs relatively infrequently in the FG (here and in 15:2; 17:2). Much more common are left-dislocations that have the resumptive pronoun in a marked position (at the beginning of the clause). If ὁ πιστεύων belongs with v. 37 (the second option above), αὐτοῦ refers to Jesus. On this reading, Jesus himself is the source of the living water (christological interpretation).

ῥεύσουσιν. Fut act ind 3rd pl ῥέω.

ὕδατος. Genitive of content qualifying ποταμοί ("rivers full of living water").

ζῶντος. Pres act ptc neut gen sg ζάω (attributive). The participle modifies ὕδατος, standing in the fourth attributive position (see 1:6 on ἀπεσταλμένος).

7:39 τοῦτο δὲ εἶπεν περὶ τοῦ πνεύματος ὃ ἔμελλον λαμβάνειν οἱ πιστεύσαντες εἰς αὐτόν· οὔπω γὰρ ἦν πνεῦμα, ὅτι Ἰησοῦς οὐδέπω ἐδοξάσθη.

τοῦτο. Accusative direct object of εἶπεν. The near-demonstrative pronoun refers to Jesus' declarations in vv. 37-38.

δέ. Marker of narrative development.

εἶπεν. Aor act ind 3rd sg λέγω.

περὶ τοῦ πνεύματος. Reference.

ὅ. Accusative direct object of λαμβάνειν. The antecedent of the relative pronoun is τοῦ πνεύματος.

ἔμελλον. Impf act ind 3rd pl μέλλω.

λαμβάνειν. Pres act inf λαμβάνω (complementary).

οἱ πιστεύσαντες. Aor act ptc masc nom pl πιστεύω (substantival). Nominative subject of ἔμελλον. Although many witnesses have πιστεύοντες (ℵ D K N Γ Δ Θ Ψ 0105 ƒ¹·¹³ 33 565 579 1241 1424 𝔐 et al.), intrinsic probability favors πιστεύσαντες (attested by 𝔓⁶⁶ B L T W sa^mss pbo) because it is more likely that a scribe would change the aorist participle into the present participle than vice versa.

εἰς αὐτόν. Goal of actions or feelings directed toward someone (BDAG, 290.4.c.β). For πιστεύειν εἰς + accusative ("trust or believe in someone"), see 1:12 on εἰς τὸ ὄνομα.

οὔπω. Adverb of time ("not yet").

γάρ. Postpositive conjunction that introduces the explanation for the previous assertion.

ἦν. Impf act ind 3rd sg εἰμί. On the function of the imperfect in the FG, see 1:39 on ἦν.

πνεῦμα. Nominative subject of ἦν. The most common variant is the addition of ἅγιον after πνεῦμα (𝔓⁶⁶* L Nᶜ W Γ Δ 0105 ƒ¹·¹³ 33 565 1241 1424 𝔐 et al.). Other modifications, such as the addition of the participle δεδομένον (B e q sy^h** et al.) or the PP ἐπ᾽ αὐτούς (D*·¹ f), seek to clarify that the evangelist does not deny the existence of the Spirit before Jesus' glorification (Metzger, 186).

ὅτι. Introduces a causal clause.

Ἰησοῦς. Nominative subject of ἐδοξάσθη.

οὐδέπω. Adverb of time (οὐδέπω = οὔπω).

ἐδοξάσθη. Aor pass ind 3rd sg δοξάζω. The unexpressed primary agent of the action is most likely God (see 11:4 on δοξασθῇ). In this context, glorification refers to Jesus' death and resurrection. A similar usage of this verb can be found in 12:16, 23; 13:31, 32; 17:1. Van der Watt argues that in all these instances δοξάζω functions as a double entendre that "eliminates the shame of the cross, emphasizes the necessary link between the cross and resurrection, and defines the whole process in terms of the (pre-existent) glory of Christ" (2005, 480–81).

John 7:40-44

⁴⁰Then some of the crowd, when they heard these words, began to say, "This is really the prophet." ⁴¹Others were saying, "This is the Messiah." But still others said, "Surely not, for the Messiah does not come from Galilee, does he? ⁴²Has not the Scripture said that the Messiah comes from the offspring of David and from Bethlehem, the village where David was?" ⁴³So there was a division in the crowd because of him.

⁴⁴Some of them wanted to take him into custody, but no one laid hands on him.

7:40 Ἐκ τοῦ ὄχλου οὖν ἀκούσαντες τῶν λόγων τούτων ἔλεγον· οὗτός ἐστιν ἀληθῶς ὁ προφήτης·

Ἐκ τοῦ ὄχλου. Replaces the partitive genitive (ἐκ τοῦ ὄχλου = τινὲς ἐκ τοῦ ὄχλου).

οὖν. Postpositive inferential conjunction and/or transitional particle (see 1:22 and 11:6).

ἀκούσαντες. Aor act ptc masc nom pl ἀκούω (temporal). On participles that precede the main verb, see ἐμβλέψας in 1:36.

τῶν λόγων τούτων. Genitive direct object of ἀκούσαντες.

ἔλεγον. Impf act ind 3rd pl λέγω. On the function of the imperfect in the FG, see 1:39 on ἦν.

οὗτός. Nominative subject of ἐστιν. Fronted as a topical frame. οὗτός, which has a circumflex accent on the penult, acquired an additional accent, the acute, on the ultima from the enclitic ἐστιν (Smyth §183; Carson 1985, 48).

ἐστιν. Pres act ind 3rd sg εἰμί.

ἀληθῶς. Adverb ("truly, really").

ὁ προφήτης. Predicate nominative. The article is anaphoric in a broad sense, referring to the prophetic figure known to the audience (see 1:21; 6:14).

7:41 ἄλλοι ἔλεγον· οὗτός ἐστιν ὁ χριστός, οἱ δὲ ἔλεγον· μὴ γὰρ ἐκ τῆς Γαλιλαίας ὁ χριστὸς ἔρχεται;

ἄλλοι. Nominative subject of ἔλεγον. This verse is connected to the previous one by asyndeton.

ἔλεγον. Impf act ind 3rd pl λέγω. On the function of the imperfect in the FG, see 1:39 on ἦν.

οὗτός. Nominative subject of ἐστιν. Fronted as a topical frame. οὗτός, which has a circumflex accent on the penult, acquired an additional accent, the acute, on the ultima from the enclitic ἐστιν (Smyth §183; Carson 1985, 48).

ἐστιν. Pres act ind 3rd sg εἰμί.

ὁ χριστός. Predicate nominative.

οἱ δὲ. A construction that is frequently used in narrative literature to indicate the change of the speaker in a dialogue. The nominative article stands in place of a third-person personal pronoun and functions as the subject of ἔλεγον.

ἔλεγον. Impf act ind 3rd pl λέγω. On the function of the imperfect in the FG, see 1:39 on ἦν.

μὴ. Negative particle that introduces a question that expects a negative answer.

γὰρ. Postpositive conjunction that indicates that the question raised by this group explains why they doubted that Jesus could be the Messiah. The combination μὴ γάρ occurs only four times in the NT (here; 1 Cor 11:22; Jas 1:7; 1 Pet 4:15).

ἐκ τῆς Γαλιλαίας. Source/origin. Fronted for emphasis.

ὁ χριστὸς. Nominative subject of ἔρχεται.

ἔρχεται. Pres mid ind 3rd sg ἔρχομαι.

7:42 οὐχ ἡ γραφὴ εἶπεν ὅτι ἐκ τοῦ σπέρματος Δαυὶδ καὶ ἀπὸ Βηθλέεμ τῆς κώμης ὅπου ἦν Δαυὶδ ἔρχεται ὁ χριστός;

οὐχ. Negative particle that introduces a question that expects an affirmative answer. This verse is connected to the previous one by asyndeton.

ἡ γραφὴ. Nominative subject of εἶπεν.

εἶπεν. Aor act ind 3rd sg λέγω.

ὅτι. Introduces the clausal complement (indirect discourse) of εἶπεν.

ἐκ τοῦ σπέρματος. Source/origin.

Δαυὶδ. Genitive of relationship or genitive of source qualifying σπέρματος. Δαυίδ is an indeclinable proper noun.

καὶ. Coordinating conjunction.

ἀπὸ Βηθλέεμ. Locative. Βηθλέεμ is an indeclinable proper noun.

τῆς κώμης. Genitive in apposition to Βηθλέεμ.

ὅπου. Particle denoting place.

ἦν. Impf act ind 3rd sg εἰμί.

Δαυὶδ. Nominative subject of ἦν.

ἔρχεται. Pres mid ind 3rd sg ἔρχομαι.

ὁ χριστός. Nominative subject of ἔρχεται.

7:43 σχίσμα οὖν ἐγένετο ἐν τῷ ὄχλῳ δι' αὐτόν·

σχίσμα. Nominative subject of ἐγένετο. Fronted for emphasis.

οὖν. Postpositive inferential conjunction and/or transitional particle (see 1:22 and 11:6).

ἐγένετο. Aor mid ind 3rd sg γίνομαι.

ἐν τῷ ὄχλῳ. Locative.

δι' αὐτόν. Causal.

7:44 τινὲς δὲ ἤθελον ἐξ αὐτῶν πιάσαι αὐτόν, ἀλλ' οὐδεὶς ἐπέβαλεν ἐπ' αὐτὸν τὰς χεῖρας.

τινὲς. Nominative subject of ἤθελον.

δὲ. Marker of narrative development.

ἤθελον. Impf act ind 3rd pl θέλω. On the augment, see 1:43 on ἠθέλησεν.

ἐξ αὐτῶν. Replaces the partitive genitive.

πιάσαι. Aor act inf πιάζω (complementary). On the meaning and the use of this verb in the FG, see 7:30 on πιάσαι.

αὐτόν. Accusative direct object of πιάσαι.

ἀλλ'. Marker of contrast.

οὐδεὶς. Nominative subject of ἐπέβαλεν.

ἐπέβαλεν. Aor act ind 3rd sg ἐπιβάλλω.

ἐπ' αὐτὸν. Locative.

τὰς χεῖρας. Accusative direct object of ἐπέβαλεν.

John 7:45-52

⁴⁵Then the officers went back to the chief priests and Pharisees, and they said to them, "Why did you not bring him?" ⁴⁶The officers answered, "Never has a man spoken like this." ⁴⁷Then the Pharisees answered them, "You have not also been deceived, have you? ⁴⁸None of the leaders or of the Pharisees have believed in him, have they? ⁴⁹But this crowd that does not know the law is accursed." ⁵⁰Nicodemus, who had gone to him before, said to them because he was one of them, ⁵¹"Our law does not condemn a man unless it first hears from him and finds out what he has been doing, does it?" ⁵²They answered and said to him, "You are not also from Galilee, are you? Search and see that a prophet does not arise from Galilee."

7:45 Ἦλθον οὖν οἱ ὑπηρέται πρὸς τοὺς ἀρχιερεῖς καὶ Φαρισαίους, καὶ εἶπον αὐτοῖς ἐκεῖνοι· διὰ τί οὐκ ἠγάγετε αὐτόν;

Ἦλθον. Aor act ind 3rd pl ἔρχομαι.

οὖν. Postpositive inferential conjunction and/or transitional particle (see 1:22 and 11:6).

οἱ ὑπηρέται. Nominative subject of Ἦλθον. The article is anaphoric, referring to ὑπηρέτας mentioned in 7:32.

πρὸς τοὺς ἀρχιερεῖς καὶ Φαρισαίους. Locative (motion toward). The single article that governs both nouns indicates that the chief priests and Pharisees are here regarded as two distinct, though conceptually united, groups (Wallace 1996, 278–79).

καί. Coordinating conjunction.

εἶπον. Aor act ind 3rd pl λέγω.

αὐτοῖς. Dative indirect object of εἶπον. The personal pronoun refers to οἱ ὑπηρέται.

ἐκεῖνοι. Nominative subject of εἶπον. The antecedent of the demonstrative is τοὺς ἀρχιερεῖς καὶ Φαρισαίους, although this is the nearest group of characters in the context. Wallace suggests that "ἐκεῖνος is used, most likely, because the officers had been dispatched to find Jesus in v 32 and were nearer in the writer's mind than was the Sanhedrin" that remains, as it were, "behind the scene" in the plot of the narrative (1996, 327).

διὰ τί. Causal.

οὐκ. Negative particle normally used with indicative verbs.

ἠγάγετε. Aor act ind 2nd pl ἄγω.

αὐτόν. Accusative direct object of ἠγάγετε.

7:46 ἀπεκρίθησαν οἱ ὑπηρέται· οὐδέποτε ἐλάλησεν οὕτως ἄνθρωπος.

ἀπεκρίθησαν. Aor mid ind 3rd pl ἀποκρίνομαι. On the voice, see "Deponency" in the Series Introduction. This verse is connected to the previous one by asyndeton.

οἱ ὑπηρέται. Nominative subject of ἀπεκρίθησαν.

οὐδέποτε. Temporal adverb ("never").

ἐλάλησεν. Prf act ind 3rd sg λαλέω.

οὕτως. Adverb of manner ("in this manner, thus, so").

ἄνθρωπος. Nominative subject of ἐλάλησεν.

7:47 ἀπεκρίθησαν οὖν αὐτοῖς οἱ Φαρισαῖοι· μὴ καὶ ὑμεῖς πεπλάνησθε;

ἀπεκρίθησαν. Aor mid ind 3rd pl ἀποκρίνομαι. On the voice, see "Deponency" in the Series Introduction.

οὖν. Postpositive inferential conjunction and/or transitional particle (see 1:22 and 11:6).

αὐτοῖς. Dative indirect object of ἀπεκρίθησαν.

οἱ Φαρισαῖοι. Nominative subject of ἀπεκρίθησαν.

μή. Negative particle that introduces a question that expects a negative answer.

καί. Adverbial use (adjunctive).

ὑμεῖς. Nominative subject of πεπλάνησθε. The personal pronoun is emphatic.

πεπλάνησθε. Prf pass ind 2nd pl πλανάω. The unexpressed primary (ultimate) agent is Jesus.

7:48 μή τις ἐκ τῶν ἀρχόντων ἐπίστευσεν εἰς αὐτὸν ἢ ἐκ τῶν Φαρισαίων;

μή. Negative particle that introduces a question that expects a negative answer. This verse is connected to the previous one by asyndeton.

τις. Nominative subject of ἐπίστευσεν.

ἐκ τῶν ἀρχόντων. Replaces the partitive genitive.

ἐπίστευσεν. Aor act ind 3rd sg πιστεύω.

εἰς αὐτόν. Goal of actions or feelings directed toward someone (BDAG, 290.4.c.β). For πιστεύειν εἰς + accusative ("trust or believe in someone"), see 1:12 on εἰς τὸ ὄνομα.

ἤ. Marker of an alternative/disjunctive particle (BDAG, 432.1).

ἐκ τῶν Φαρισαίων. Replaces the partitive genitive.

7:49 ἀλλ' ὁ ὄχλος οὗτος ὁ μὴ γινώσκων τὸν νόμον ἐπάρατοί εἰσιν.

ἀλλ'. Marker of contrast.

ὁ ὄχλος οὗτος. Nominative subject of εἰσιν.

ὁ... γινώσκων. Pres act ptc masc nom sg γινώσκω (attributive). The participle modifies ὁ ὄχλος, standing in the second attributive position (see 1:29 on ὁ αἴρων).

μή. Negative particle normally used with non-indicative verbs.

τὸν νόμον. Accusative direct object of γινώσκων.

ἐπάρατοί. Predicate nominative. Fronted for emphasis. ἐπάρατοί, which has an acute accent on the antepenult, acquired an additional accent, the acute, on the ultima from the enclitic εἰσιν (Smyth §183; Carson 1985, 48).

εἰσιν. Pres act ind 3rd pl εἰμί. The plural verb form is a *constructio ad sensum* because the subject (ὁ ὄχλος οὗτος) is a collective noun (BDF §134.1).

7:50 λέγει Νικόδημος πρὸς αὐτούς, ὁ ἐλθὼν πρὸς αὐτὸν [τὸ] πρότερον, εἷς ὢν ἐξ αὐτῶν·

λέγει. Pres act ind 3rd sg λέγω. The historical present gives prominence to Nicodemus' words that follow (see 1:15 on μαρτυρεῖ). This verse is connected to the previous one by asyndeton.

Νικόδημος. Nominative subject of λέγει.

πρὸς αὐτούς. Locative (motion toward). The PP functions like an indirect object of λέγει.

ὁ ἐλθών. Aor act ptc masc nom sg ἔρχομαι (attributive). The participle modifies Νικόδημος, standing in the third attributive position (see 1:18 on ὁ ὤν).

πρὸς αὐτόν. Locative (motion toward).

[τὸ] πρότερον. The article functions as a nominalizer, changing the adverb πρότερον into the accusative indicating extent of time ("during former time, before"). Its external attestation, however, is evenly balanced between the copies that have it ($\mathfrak{P}^{66}$ L W Θ $f^{1.13}$ 565 892) and those that do not ($\mathfrak{P}^{75}$ ℵ² B T).

εἷς. Predicate nominative.

ὤν. Pres act ptc masc nom sg εἰμί. The participle is not attributive, as many English translations presume (e.g., NRSV: "and who was one of them"), because it is not preceded by an article (see ὁ ἐλθών above). If ὤν modifies the previous participial phrase (ὁ ἐλθὼν πρὸς αὐτὸν [τὸ] πρότερον), it is probably concessive ("although he was one of them"), indicating that Nicodemus came to Jesus despite being one of the leaders who have just declared that none of them believed in Jesus. If ὤν modifies the main clause (λέγει Νικόδημος πρὸς αὐτούς), it is probably causal ("because he was one of them"), indicating that Nicodemus could speak with authority to other Jewish leaders because he was one of them. The second option is preferable because the participial clause seems to be "an instance of the common Johannine practice of identifying characters already encountered" in the narrative (Brown, 1:325), rather than an insinuation of Nicodemus' status as a secret believer.

ἐξ αὐτῶν. Replaces the partitive genitive. When the PP with ἐκ is combined with εἶναι, it means to "belong to someone or someth[ing]" (BDAG, 297.4.a.δ).

7:51 μὴ ὁ νόμος ἡμῶν κρίνει τὸν ἄνθρωπον ἐὰν μὴ ἀκούσῃ πρῶτον παρ' αὐτοῦ καὶ γνῷ τί ποιεῖ;

μή. Negative particle that introduces a question that expects a negative answer. It marks the beginning of the apodosis of a third-class condition, which here precedes the protasis. This verse is connected to the previous one by asyndeton.

ὁ νόμος. Nominative subject of κρίνει.

ἡμῶν. Possessive genitive qualifying νόμος.

κρίνει. Pres act ind 3rd sg κρίνω. In this context, κρίνω means "to judge a person to be guilty and liable to punishment—'to judge as guilty, to condemn'" (LN 56.30).

τὸν ἄνθρωπον. Accusative direct object of κρίνει. The article could be generic ("any person") or anaphoric ("the accused person").

ἐάν. Introduces the protasis of a third-class condition.

μή. Negative particle normally used with non-indicative verbs. ἐὰν μή can be translated "unless."

ἀκούσῃ. Aor act subj 3rd sg ἀκούω. Subjunctive with ἐάν. ἀκούω is used here as a legal term, "to give a judicial hearing in a legal matter—'to hear a case, to provide a legal hearing, to hear a case in court'" (LN 56.13). The implied subject of the verb is ὁ νόμος.

πρῶτον. Adverbial accusative.

παρ' αὐτοῦ. Source.

καί. Coordinating conjunction.

γνῷ. Aor act subj 3rd sg γινώσκω. Subjunctive with ἐάν. The implied subject of the verb is ὁ νόμος.

τί. Accusative direct object of ποιεῖ.

ποιεῖ. Pres act ind 3rd sg ποιέω. The present tense is retained from the direct discourse (see 1:39 on μένει).

7:52 ἀπεκρίθησαν καὶ εἶπαν αὐτῷ· μὴ καὶ σὺ ἐκ τῆς Γαλιλαίας εἶ; ἐραύνησον καὶ ἴδε ὅτι ἐκ τῆς Γαλιλαίας προφήτης οὐκ ἐγείρεται.

ἀπεκρίθησαν. Aor mid ind 3rd pl ἀποκρίνομαι. On the voice, see "Deponency" in the Series Introduction. This verse is connected to the previous one by asyndeton.

καὶ εἶπαν αὐτῷ. Pleonastic clause under Semitic influence, which functions as a redundant quotative frame (see 1:25 on καὶ εἶπαν αὐτῷ).

καί. Coordinating conjunction.

εἶπαν. Aor act ind 3rd pl λέγω.

αὐτῷ. Dative indirect object of εἶπαν.

μή. Negative particle that introduces a question that expects a negative answer.

καί. Adverbial use (adjunctive).

σύ. Nominative subject of εἶ. The personal pronoun is emphatic and contrastive, distinguishing Nicodemus from other members of the Sanhedrin.

ἐκ τῆς Γαλιλαίας. Source/origin.

εἶ. Pres act ind 2nd sg εἰμί.

ἐραύνησον. Aor act impv 2nd sg ἐραυνάω. Wallace (1996, 489, 491) regards ἐραύνησον as a type of conditional imperative ("if X, then Y will happen") even though it is not followed by καί and the future indicative but by καί and another imperative. A similar explanation is offered by Zerwick and Grosvenor, who suggest that "under Sem. influence the second of two impvs often contains the result of the former, 'inquire and you will see'" (310).

καί. Coordinating conjunction.

ἴδε. Aor act impv 2nd sg ὁράω.

ὅτι. Introduces the clausal complement (indirect discourse) of ἴδε.

ἐκ τῆς Γαλιλαίας. Source/origin.

προφήτης. Nominative subject of ἐγείρεται. The anarthrous προφήτης, which is attested by most manuscripts, refers to an unspecified prophet from Galilee. Although the variant ὁ προφήτης has weak external support ($\mathfrak{P}^{66^*}$), some scholars (Brown, 1:325; Schnackenburg, 2:161) prefer it because it refers to the prophet like Moses (cf. Deut 18:15), which is a prominent concept in the FG. Moreover, the assertion that no prophet would ever come from Galilee is problematic in light of 2 Kgs 14:25, which says that Jonah was from the Galilean town Gath-hepher (cf. Josh 19:13).

οὐκ. Negative particle normally used with indicative verbs.

ἐγείρεται. Pres mid ind 3rd sg ἐγείρω. On the voice, see "Deponency" in the Series Introduction. The intransitive sense of ἐγείρω is often used to describe the appearance of a prophet (cf. Matt 11:11; 24:24; Luke 7:16). The verb stands in final, emphatic position.

John 7:53–8:11

7:53 And they went each to his own house, 8:1 while Jesus went to the Mount of Olives. ²Early in the morning he came back to the temple, and all the people were coming to him. And he sat down and began to teach them. ³Now the scribes and the Pharisees brought a woman who had been caught while committing adultery and, after they made her stand in the middle, ⁴they said to him, "Teacher, this woman was caught in the very act, committing adultery. ⁵In the law, Moses commanded us to stone such women. What then do you say?" ⁶Now they were saying this to test him, so that they could have some charge to bring against him. Jesus bent down and began to write on the ground with his finger. ⁷When they continued questioning him, he straightened up and said to them, "Let the one who is without sin among you be the first to throw a stone at her." ⁸And again he bent down and continued writing on the ground. ⁹When they heard this, they began to go away, one by one, beginning with the older ones; and he was left alone, and the woman standing in the middle. ¹¹Jesus straightened up and said to her, "Woman, where are they? Did no one condemn you?" ¹²She said, "No one, sir." Jesus said, "Neither do I condemn you. Go, and from now on sin no more."

This account, known as the *Pericope adulterae* (Pericope of the adulteress), is almost certainly a non-Johannine composition that was added to the FG at some later point in the transmission process. It is absent from the earliest, and quite diversified, manuscripts ($\mathfrak{P}^{66.75}$ ℵ A^vid B C^vid L^c N T W Δ^c Θ Ψ 0141 0211 33 131 565 1241 1333 1424^txt sy sa ly pbo^pt Or Hier^mss et al.). In the copies that include this account, it is usually inserted after John 7:52 (D K L*^vid Γ Δ*^vid 118 174 209 579 700 892 𝔐 lat bo^pt et al.), but occasionally it is placed after John 7:36 (225), 21:25 (1 1582), or Luke 21:38 (f^{13}). In most copies that have it, it is marked with asterisks or obeli, betraying the copyists' awareness that the account was not original. The non-Johannine vocabulary and style of the narrative support the conclusion that it is not composed by the Fourth Evangelist. Since, however, most scholars regard it as a piece of a very old dominical tradition that circulated orally, it is printed within double square brackets in NA^28/UBS^5 Greek NT to indicate that this is not an original part of the FG (Metzger, 187–89; von Soden, 486–524).

7:53 Καὶ ἐπορεύθησαν ἕκαστος εἰς τὸν οἶκον αὐτοῦ,

Καὶ. Coordinating conjunction.
ἐπορεύθησαν. Aor mid ind 3rd pl πορεύομαι. On the voice, see "Deponency" in the Series Introduction. The plural verb form is a *constructio ad sensum* because the subject consists of multiple individuals ("each of them").
ἕκαστος. Nominative subject of ἐπορεύθησαν.
εἰς τὸν οἶκον. Locative.
αὐτοῦ. Possessive genitive qualifying οἶκον.

8:1 Ἰησοῦς δὲ ἐπορεύθη εἰς τὸ ὄρος τῶν ἐλαιῶν.

Ἰησοῦς. Nominative subject of ἐπορεύθη.
δὲ. Marker of narrative development.
ἐπορεύθη. Aor mid ind 3rd sg πορεύομαι. On the voice, see "Deponency" in the Series Introduction.
εἰς τὸ ὄρος. Locative.
τῶν ἐλαιῶν. Epexegetical genitive qualifying ὄρος ("the mountain which is called Olives / Olive Trees"). τὸ ὄρος τῶν ἐλαιῶν is the most common reference to the Mount of Olives in the NT (Matt 21:1; 24:3; 26:30; Mark 11:1; 13:3; 14:26; Luke 19:37; 22:39; John 8:1). The second designation is τὸ ὄρος τὸ καλούμενον Ἐλαιῶν, which occurs only in Luke (19:29; 21:37).

8:2 Ὄρθρου δὲ πάλιν παρεγένετο εἰς τὸ ἱερὸν καὶ πᾶς ὁ λαὸς ἤρχετο πρὸς αὐτόν, καὶ καθίσας ἐδίδασκεν αὐτούς.

Ὄρθρου. Genitive of time. ὄρθρος means "dawn, early morning."
δὲ. Marker of narrative development.
πάλιν. Adverb "pert[aining] to return to a position or state" (BDAG, 752.1).
παρεγένετο. Aor mid ind 3rd sg παραγίνομαι.
εἰς τὸ ἱερὸν. Locative.
καὶ. Coordinating conjunction.
πᾶς ὁ λαὸς. Nominative subject of ἤρχετο.
ἤρχετο. Impf mid ind 3rd sg ἔρχομαι.
πρὸς αὐτόν. Locative (motion toward).
καὶ. Coordinating conjunction.
καθίσας. Aor act ptc masc nom sg καθίζω (attendant circumstance or temporal). On participles that precede the main verb, see ἐμβλέψας in 1:36.
ἐδίδασκεν. Impf act ind 3rd sg διδάσκω.
αὐτούς. Accusative direct object of ἐδίδασκεν.

8:3 Ἄγουσιν δὲ οἱ γραμματεῖς καὶ οἱ Φαρισαῖοι γυναῖκα ἐπὶ μοιχείᾳ κατειλημμένην καὶ στήσαντες αὐτὴν ἐν μέσῳ

Ἄγουσιν. Pres act ind 3rd pl ἄγω. The historical present marks the narrative transition to a new scene and calls attention to the appearance of the scribes and Pharisees who brought a woman caught in adultery.
δὲ. Marker of narrative development.
οἱ γραμματεῖς καὶ οἱ Φαρισαῖοι. Compound nominative subject of Ἄγουσιν.
γυναῖκα. Accusative direct object of Ἄγουσιν.
ἐπὶ μοιχείᾳ. Temporal ("at the time of adultery").
κατειλημμένην. Prf pass ptc fem acc sg καταλαμβάνω (attributive). The participle modifies γυναῖκα, standing in the fourth attributive position (see 1:6 on ἀπεσταλμένος). καταλαμβάνω means "to seize and take control of—'to catch, to seize, to arrest'" (LN 37.108).
καὶ. Coordinating conjunction.
στήσαντες. Aor act ptc masc nom pl ἵστημι (temporal). On participles that precede the main verb, see ἐμβλέψας in 1:36.
αὐτὴν. Accusative direct object of στήσαντες.
ἐν μέσῳ. Locative.

8:4 λέγουσιν αὐτῷ· διδάσκαλε, αὕτη ἡ γυνὴ κατείληπται ἐπ' αὐτοφώρῳ μοιχευομένη·

λέγουσιν. Pres act ind 3rd pl λέγω. The historical present gives prominence to the accusation of the scribes and the Pharisees. This verse is connected to the previous one by asyndeton.
αὐτῷ. Dative indirect object of λέγουσιν.
διδάσκαλε. Vocative of direct address.
αὕτη ἡ γυνὴ. Nominative subject of κατείληπται.
κατείληπται. Prf pass ind 3rd sg καταλαμβάνω.
ἐπ' αὐτοφώρῳ. Temporal ("[caught] in the act" [BDAG, 154]). A NT *hapax legomenon*.
μοιχευομένη. Pres mid ptc fem nom sg μοιχεύω (predicative). The participle stands in the second predicate position (see 1:29 on ἐρχόμενον), functioning as the nominative complement to ἡ γυνὴ in a double nominative subject-complement construction (see 1:41 on χριστός).

8:5 ἐν δὲ τῷ νόμῳ ἡμῖν Μωϋσῆς ἐνετείλατο τὰς τοιαύτας λιθάζειν. σὺ οὖν τί λέγεις;

ἐν ... τῷ νόμῳ. Locative. Fronted as a spatial frame.
δὲ. Marker of narrative development.
ἡμῖν. Dative indirect object of ἐνετείλατο.
Μωϋσῆς. Nominative subject of ἐνετείλατο.
ἐνετείλατο. Aor mid ind 3rd sg ἐντέλλομαι.
τὰς τοιαύτας. Accusative direct object of λιθάζειν.
λιθάζειν. Pres act inf λιθάζω (complementary).
σὺ. Nominative subject of λέγεις. The personal pronoun is emphatic.
οὖν. Postpositive inferential conjunction.
τί. Accusative direct object of λέγεις.
λέγεις. Pres act ind 2nd sing λέγω.

8:6 τοῦτο δὲ ἔλεγον πειράζοντες αὐτόν, ἵνα ἔχωσιν κατηγορεῖν αὐτοῦ. ὁ δὲ Ἰησοῦς κάτω κύψας τῷ δακτύλῳ κατέγραφεν εἰς τὴν γῆν.

τοῦτο. Accusative direct object of ἔλεγον.
δὲ. Marker of narrative development.
ἔλεγον. Impf act ind 3rd pl λέγω.
πειράζοντες. Pres act ptc masc nom pl πειράζω (purpose). On participles that follow the main verb, see βαπτίζων in 1:31.
αὐτόν. Accusative direct object of πειράζοντες.
ἵνα. Introduces a purpose clause.

ἔχωσιν. Pres act subj 3rd pl ἔχω. Subjunctive with ἵνα. ἔχω with the infinitive means "to be in a position to do someth[ing], *can, be able*" (BDAG, 421.5).

κατηγορεῖν. Pres act inf κατηγορέω. The infinitival clause, κατηγορεῖν αὐτοῦ, functions as the direct object of ἔχωσιν. In this context, κατηγορέω means to "bring charges in court" against someone (in genitive) (BDAG, 533.1.a).

αὐτοῦ. Genitive complement of κατηγορεῖν.

ὁ ... Ἰησοῦς. Nominative subject of κατέγραφεν.

δέ. Marker of narrative development.

κάτω. Adverb ("downward, down").

κύψας. Aor act ptc masc nom sg κύπτω (attendant circumstance). On participles that precede the main verb, see ἐμβλέψας in 1:36.

τῷ δακτύλῳ. Dative of means/instrument.

κατέγραφεν. Impf act ind 3rd sg καταγράφω.

εἰς τὴν γῆν. Locative.

8:7 ὡς δὲ ἐπέμενον ἐρωτῶντες αὐτόν, ἀνέκυψεν καὶ εἶπεν αὐτοῖς· ὁ ἀναμάρτητος ὑμῶν πρῶτος ἐπ' αὐτὴν βαλέτω λίθον.

ὡς. Temporal conjunction (BDAG, 1105.8.b; BDF §455.2), introducing a clause that is fronted as a temporal frame.

δέ. Marker of narrative development.

ἐπέμενον. Impf act ind 3rd pl ἐπιμένω.

ἐρωτῶντες. Pres act ptc masc nom pl ἐρωτάω (complementary). This use of the participle is relatively rare in the NT and typically occurs with verbs expressing a consummative or progressive idea, as here (Wallace 1996, 646).

αὐτόν. Accusative direct object of ἐρωτῶντες.

ἀνέκυψεν. Aor act ind 3rd sg ἀνακύπτω.

καί. Coordinating conjunction.

εἶπεν. Aor act ind 3rd sg λέγω.

αὐτοῖς. Dative indirect object of εἶπεν.

ὁ ἀναμάρτητος. Nominative subject of βαλέτω. Fronted as a topical frame. The adjective ἀναμάρτητος ("without sin") is here used as a substantive. A NT *hapax legomenon*.

ὑμῶν. Partitive genitive qualifying ὁ ἀναμάρτητος.

πρῶτος. Predicate adjective in relation to ὁ ἀναμάρτητος, indicating sequence (BDF §243).

ἐπ' αὐτήν. Locative.

βαλέτω. Aor act impv 3rd sg βάλλω.

λίθον. Accusative direct object of βαλέτω.

8:8 καὶ πάλιν κατακύψας ἔγραφεν εἰς τὴν γῆν.

καὶ. Coordinating conjunction.

πάλιν. Adverb "pert[aining] to repetition in the same (or similar) manner" (BDAG, 752.2).

κατακύψας. Aor act ptc masc nom sg κατακύπτω (attendant circumstance). On participles that precede the main verb, see ἐμβλέψας in 1:36.

ἔγραφεν. Impf act ind 3rd sg γράφω. The imperfective aspect of the verb portrays Jesus' writing on the ground as an action in progress. Runge argues that "if a language has a three-way contrast between imperfective (present and imperfect) forms, simple perfect (present perfect and pluperfect) forms and copular perfect (copula plus perfect participle) constructions, then I would expect them to differ in dynamicity" (2016, 316–17). In his view, the imperfective aspect, which portrays an ongoing event, is the most dynamic of the three.

εἰς τὴν γῆν. Locative. Some manuscripts (U Π 73 331 363 700 782 1592 et al.), trying to satisfy the natural curiosity about the content of Jesus' writing on the ground, add ἑνὸς ἑκάστου αὐτῶν τὰς ἁμαρτίας ("the sins of each of them") after γῆν (Metzger, 190).

8:9 οἱ δὲ ἀκούσαντες ἐξήρχοντο εἷς καθ' εἷς ἀρξάμενοι ἀπὸ τῶν πρεσβυτέρων καὶ κατελείφθη μόνος καὶ ἡ γυνὴ ἐν μέσῳ οὖσα.

οἱ δὲ. A construction that marks the continuation of the narrative (BDF §251). The nominative article stands in place of a third-person personal pronoun and functions as the subject of ἐξήρχοντο. Its force is anaphoric, referring to the scribes and the Pharisees.

ἀκούσαντες. Aor act ptc masc nom pl ἀκούω (temporal). On participles that precede the main verb, see ἐμβλέψας in 1:36.

ἐξήρχοντο. Impf mid ind 3rd pl ἐξέρχομαι.

εἷς καθ' εἷς. A colloquial distributive expression: "one by one," "one after another" (BDAG, 293.5.e). The second εἷς is an undeclined nominative that stands for the accusative (ἕνα) that would be expected after the preposition κατά, which was a common practice in Koine Greek (Robertson, 282).

ἀρξάμενοι. Aor mid ptc masc nom pl ἄρχω (manner). On participles that follow the main verb, see βαπτίζων in 1:31.

ἀπὸ τῶν πρεσβυτέρων. Used with ἄρχομαι, ἀπό indicates a starting point (BDAG, 105.2.c). The adjective πρεσβύτερος (comparative of πρέσβυς), which is here used as a substantive, refers to persons who are "relatively advanced in age," i.e., "the older ones" (BDAG, 862.1.a).

καὶ. Coordinating conjunction.

κατελείφθη. Aor pass ind 3rd sg καταλείπω.

μόνος. Nominative complement to the implied subject of κατελείφθη (see 1:41 on χριστός).

καί. Coordinating conjunction.

ἡ γυνή. Nominative subject of an implied κατελείφθη.

ἐν μέσῳ. Locative. Since the woman's accusers have left, the PP no longer means "in the midst" of them, as in v. 3, "but she remains standing, as it were, in the centre of the stage" (Barrett, 592).

οὖσα. Pres act ptc fem nom sg εἰμί (manner). On participles that follow the main verb, see βαπτίζων in 1:31.

8:10 ἀνακύψας δὲ ὁ Ἰησοῦς εἶπεν αὐτῇ· γύναι, ποῦ εἰσιν; οὐδείς σε κατέκρινεν;

ἀνακύψας. Aor act ptc masc nom sg ἀνακύπτω (attendant circumstance or temporal). On participles that precede the main verb, see ἐμβλέψας in 1:36.

δέ. Marker of narrative development.

ὁ Ἰησοῦς. Nominative subject of εἶπεν.

εἶπεν. Aor act ind 3rd sg λέγω.

αὐτῇ. Dative indirect object of εἶπεν.

γύναι. Vocative of direct address.

ποῦ. Interrogative adverb of place.

εἰσιν. Pres act ind 3rd pl εἰμί.

οὐδείς. Nominative subject of κατέκρινεν. Fronted for emphasis.

σε. Accusative direct object of κατέκρινεν.

κατέκρινεν. Aor act ind 3rd sg κατακρίνω.

8:11 ἡ δὲ εἶπεν· οὐδείς, κύριε. εἶπεν δὲ ὁ Ἰησοῦς· οὐδὲ ἐγώ σε κατακρίνω· πορεύου, [καὶ] ἀπὸ τοῦ νῦν μηκέτι ἁμάρτανε.

ἡ δέ. A construction used in narrative literature to indicate the change of the speaker in a dialogue.

εἶπεν. Aor act ind 3rd sg λέγω.

οὐδείς. Nominative subject in a verbless clause.

κύριε. Vocative of direct address.

εἶπεν. Aor act ind 3rd sg λέγω.

δέ. Marker of narrative development.

ὁ Ἰησοῦς. Nominative subject of εἶπεν.

οὐδέ. A combination of the negative particle οὐ and the marker of narrative development δέ.

ἐγώ. Nominative subject of κατακρίνω. Fronted for emphasis.

σε. Accusative direct object of κατακρίνω.
κατακρίνω. Pres act ind 1st sg κατακρίνω.
πορεύου. Pres mid impv 2nd sg πορεύομαι.
[καὶ]. Coordinating conjunction. It is printed within square brackets because it is absent in some manuscripts (D ff² bo^pt) while attested in others (Γ 1 700 892 *pm* c d r¹ bo^ms).
ἀπὸ τοῦ νῦν. Temporal. The article functions as a nominalizer, changing the adverb νῦν into the object of the preposition ἀπὸ.
μηκέτι. Temporal adverb ("no longer").
ἁμάρτανε. Pres act impv 2nd sg ἁμαρτάνω.

John 8:12-20

¹²Then Jesus spoke to them again, saying, "I am the light of the world. The one who follows me will never walk in darkness but will have the light of life." ¹³Then the Pharisees said to him, "You are testifying about yourself. Your testimony is not true." ¹⁴Jesus answered and said to them, "Even if I testify about myself, my testimony is true, because I know where I came from and where I am going. But you do not know where I come from or where I am going. ¹⁵You judge according to human standards; I do not judge anyone. ¹⁶Yet even if I judge, my judgment is true, because I am not alone, but I and the Father who sent me. ¹⁷And in your law it is written that the testimony of two people is true. ¹⁸I am the one who testifies about myself, and the Father who sent me testifies about me." ¹⁹They continued to say, "Where is your father?" Jesus answered, "You know neither me nor my Father. If you knew me, you would know my Father also." ²⁰He spoke these words in the treasury while he was teaching in the temple, and no one took him into custody, because his hour had not yet come.

8:12 Πάλιν οὖν αὐτοῖς ἐλάλησεν ὁ Ἰησοῦς λέγων· ἐγώ εἰμι τὸ φῶς τοῦ κόσμου· ὁ ἀκολουθῶν ἐμοὶ οὐ μὴ περιπατήσῃ ἐν τῇ σκοτίᾳ, ἀλλ᾽ ἕξει τὸ φῶς τῆς ζωῆς.

Πάλιν. Adverb "pert[aining] to repetition in the same (or similar) manner" (BDAG, 752.2). Fronted for emphasis.
οὖν. Postpositive inferential conjunction and/or transitional particle (see 1:22 and 11:6).
αὐτοῖς. Dative indirect object of ἐλάλησεν.
ἐλάλησεν. Aor act ind 3rd sg λαλέω.
ὁ Ἰησοῦς. Nominative subject of ἐλάλησεν.
λέγων. Pres act ptc masc nom sg λέγω (pleonastic).

ἐγώ εἰμι τὸ φῶς τοῦ κόσμου. This is one of Jesus' "I am" pronouncements in the FG with an explicit predicate; for other statements of this type, see 6:35, 48, 51; 10:7, 9, 11, 14; 11:25; 14:6; 15:1, 5.

ἐγώ. Nominative subject of εἰμι. Fronted for emphasis.

εἰμι. Pres act ind 1st sg εἰμί.

τὸ φῶς. Predicate nominative.

τοῦ κόσμου. Objective genitive qualifying φῶς ("the light that illuminates the world"). On the portrayal of the world in the FG, see 1:10 on ἐν τῷ κόσμῳ.

ὁ ἀκολουθῶν. Pres act ptc masc nom sg ἀκολουθέω (substantival). Nominative subject of περιπατήσῃ. Fronted as a topical frame. This clause is connected to the preceding one by asyndeton.

ἐμοί. Dative direct object of ἀκολουθῶν.

οὐ μὴ. Emphatic negation, which is usually followed by the aorist subjunctive.

περιπατήσῃ. Aor act subj 3rd sg περιπατέω. Used with οὐ μὴ to express emphatic negation.

ἐν τῇ σκοτίᾳ. Locative.

ἀλλ'. Marker of contrast.

ἕξει. Fut act ind 3rd sg ἔχω.

τὸ φῶς. Accusative direct object of ἕξει.

τῆς ζωῆς. Genitive of purpose qualifying φῶς ("the light that leads to life") or epexegetical genitive explaining φῶς ("the light which is the life"; cf. Zerwick and Grosvenor, 311).

8:13 Εἶπον οὖν αὐτῷ οἱ Φαρισαῖοι· σὺ περὶ σεαυτοῦ μαρτυρεῖς· ἡ μαρτυρία σου οὐκ ἔστιν ἀληθής.

Εἶπον. Aor act ind 3rd pl λέγω.

οὖν. Postpositive inferential conjunction and/or transitional particle (see 1:22 and 11:6).

αὐτῷ. Dative indirect object of Εἶπον.

οἱ Φαρισαῖοι. Nominative subject of Εἶπον.

σὺ. Nominative subject of μαρτυρεῖς. The personal pronoun is emphatic.

περὶ σεαυτοῦ. Reference.

μαρτυρεῖς. Pres act ind 2nd sg μαρτυρέω.

ἡ μαρτυρία. Nominative subject of ἔστιν.

σου. Subjective genitive qualifying μαρτυρία.

οὐκ. Negative particle normally used with indicative verbs.

ἔστιν. Pres act ind 3rd sg εἰμί. The enclitic ἐστιν is accented ἔστιν when it comes at the beginning of a sentence, when it expresses existence, or when it follows ἀλλ', εἰ, καί, οὐκ, ὅτι, or τοῦτ'. The third condition is fulfilled here.

ἀληθής. Predicate adjective.

8:14 ἀπεκρίθη Ἰησοῦς καὶ εἶπεν αὐτοῖς· κἂν ἐγὼ μαρτυρῶ περὶ ἐμαυτοῦ, ἀληθής ἐστιν ἡ μαρτυρία μου, ὅτι οἶδα πόθεν ἦλθον καὶ ποῦ ὑπάγω· ὑμεῖς δὲ οὐκ οἴδατε πόθεν ἔρχομαι ἢ ποῦ ὑπάγω.

ἀπεκρίθη. Aor mid ind 3rd sg ἀποκρίνομαι. On the voice, see "Deponency" in the Series Introduction. This verse is connected to the previous one by asyndeton.

Ἰησοῦς. Nominative subject of ἀπεκρίθη.

καὶ εἶπεν αὐτοῖς. Pleonastic clause under Semitic influence, which functions as a redundant quotative frame (see 1:25 on καὶ εἶπαν αὐτῷ).

καί. Coordinating conjunction.

εἶπεν. Aor act ind 3rd sg λέγω.

αὐτοῖς. Dative indirect object of εἶπεν.

κἄν. Formed by crasis from καὶ ἐάν. καί is ascensive ("even"). Louw and Nida call κἄν "an emphatic marker of concession—'even if, even though'" (LN 89.73). ἐάν introduces the protasis of a third-class condition.

ἐγώ. Nominative subject of μαρτυρῶ. Fronted for emphasis.

μαρτυρῶ. Pres act subj 1st sg μαρτυρέω. Subjunctive with ἐάν.

περὶ ἐμαυτοῦ. Reference.

ἀληθής. Predicate adjective, which marks the beginning of the apodosis of a third-class condition. Fronted for emphasis.

ἐστιν. Pres act ind 3rd sg εἰμί.

ἡ μαρτυρία. Nominative subject of ἐστιν.

μου. Subjective genitive qualifying μαρτυρία.

ὅτι. Introduces a causal clause.

οἶδα. Prf act ind 1st sg οἶδα (see 1:26 on οἴδατε).

πόθεν. Interrogative adverb of place.

ἦλθον. Aor act ind 1st sg ἔρχομαι.

καί. Coordinating conjunction.

ποῦ. Interrogative adverb of place.

ὑπάγω. Pres act ind 1st sg ὑπάγω. Fanning notes that this present tense describes "a process going on in the present with its (stated or implied) termination to be reached only in the future" and adds that "this type of futuristic present is not due to a rhetorical transfer of time-reference... but to the aspect-value of the present" (222). On the meaning of ὑπάγω, see 7:33.

ὑμεῖς. Nominative subject of οἴδατε. The personal pronoun is emphatic and contrastive, distinguishing Jesus' interlocutors from him.
δέ. Marker of narrative development.
οὐκ. Negative particle normally used with indicative verbs.
οἴδατε. Prf act ind 2nd pl οἶδα (see 1:26 on οἴδατε).
πόθεν. Interrogative adverb of place.
ἔρχομαι. Pres mid ind 1st sg ἔρχομαι.
ἤ. Disjunctive particle. ἤ "comes close to the force of a copulative conjunction, especially in negative clauses" (BDF §446).
ποῦ. Interrogative adverb of place.
ὑπάγω. Pres act ind 1st sg ὑπάγω.

8:15 ὑμεῖς κατὰ τὴν σάρκα κρίνετε, ἐγὼ οὐ κρίνω οὐδένα.

ὑμεῖς. Nominative subject of κρίνετε. The personal pronoun is emphatic and contrastive (see 8:14). This verse is connected to the previous one by asyndeton.
κατὰ τὴν σάρκα. Standard. Lit. "according to the flesh" = "according to human standards." Apart from this occurrence, κατὰ σάρκα (without the article) appears only in the Pauline corpus (Rom 1:3; 4:1; 8:4, 5, 12, 13; 9:3, 5; 1 Cor 1:26; 10:18; 2 Cor 1:17; 5:16; 10:2, 3; 11:18; Gal 4:23, 29; Eph 6:5; Col 3:22).
κρίνετε. Pres act ind 2nd pl κρίνω.
ἐγώ. Nominative subject of κρίνω. The personal pronoun is emphatic and contrastive.
οὐ. Negative particle normally used with indicative verbs.
κρίνω. Pres act ind 1st sg κρίνω.
οὐδένα. Accusative direct object of κρίνω. The two negatives οὐ ... οὐδένα do not cancel but reinforce each other (see 3:27 on οὐδέ).

8:16 καὶ ἐὰν κρίνω δὲ ἐγώ, ἡ κρίσις ἡ ἐμὴ ἀληθινή ἐστιν, ὅτι μόνος οὐκ εἰμί, ἀλλ' ἐγὼ καὶ ὁ πέμψας με πατήρ.

καί. Adverbial use (ascensive).
ἐάν. Introduces the protasis of a third-class condition.
κρίνω. Aor/pres act subj 1st sg κρίνω. Subjunctive with ἐάν.
δέ. Marker of narrative development with a contrastive nuance. It comes fourth in the sentence in order not to disrupt the flow of the protasis (BDF §475.2).
ἐγώ. Nominative subject of κρίνω. The personal pronoun is emphatic and contrastive.

ἡ κρίσις ἡ ἐμή. Nominative subject of ἐστιν. It marks the beginning of the apodosis of a third-class condition. The possessive adjective ἐμή stands in the second attributive position (see 1:9 on τὸ φῶς τὸ ἀληθινόν). Elsewhere in the FG, κρίσις is mentioned in 3:19; 5:22, 24, 27, 29, 30; 7:24; 12:31; 16:8, 11.

ἀληθινή. Predicate adjective. Fronted for emphasis.

ἐστιν. Pres act ind 3rd sg εἰμί.

ὅτι. Introduces a causal clause.

μόνος. Predicate adjective.

οὐκ ... ἀλλ'. A point/counterpoint set ("not this ... but that") that negates the incorrect perception of the nature of Jesus' judgment ("I alone judge") and replaces it with the correct one ("I and the Father who sent me judge"). On the function of ἀλλά in a point/counterpoint set, see 1:8.

εἰμί. Pres act ind 1st sg εἰμί.

ἐγὼ καὶ ὁ ... πατήρ. Compound nominative subject of an implied copulative. πατήρ is absent from ℵ* D sy[s.c], but since all other manuscripts have it, its omission is probably the result of scribal oversight (Metzger, 191).

πέμψας. Aor act ptc masc nom sg πέμπω (attributive). The participle modifies πατήρ, standing in the first attributive position (see 5:37 on πέμψας). The alternative, which views ὁ πέμψας as a substantival participle and πατήρ as its apposition ("ὁ πέμψας ... me, the Father" [Harris 2015, 169]; "the One who sent me, the Father" [MSG]) is doubtful because in the FG πατήρ is always articular (e.g., 3:35; 4:23, 53; 5:17, 20, 21, 22, 26, 36; 6:27, 32, 37). The only exception is the vocative πάτερ (11:41; 12:27, 28; 17:1, 5, 11, 21, 24, 25). Elsewhere in the FG, ὁ πέμψας με πατὴρ occurs in 5:37; 8:18; 12:49; 14:24.

με. Accusative direct object of πέμψας.

8:17 καὶ ἐν τῷ νόμῳ δὲ τῷ ὑμετέρῳ γέγραπται ὅτι δύο ἀνθρώπων ἡ μαρτυρία ἀληθής ἐστιν.

καὶ. Coordinating conjunction.

ἐν τῷ νόμῳ ... τῷ ὑμετέρῳ. Locative. The possessive adjective ὑμετέρῳ stands in the second attributive position (see 1:9 on τὸ φῶς τὸ ἀληθινόν).

δὲ. Marker of narrative development. It stands fifth in the sentence, highlighting ἐν τῷ νόμῳ (Barrett, 339).

γέγραπται. Prf pass ind 3rd sg γράφω. γέγραπται is a standard introductory formula for scriptural quotations in the Synoptic Gospels, but in the FG it is used only here (with regard to the law) and in 20:31 (with regard to the Johannine narrative). The stative aspect of the perfect tense is semantically marked and highlights the authoritative status of the law ("it stands written") rather than the past action of writing it (see 7:19 on δέδωκεν). At the same time, however, the evangelist's choice of the simple perfect rather than the periphrastic perfect indicates that "it is not the stative existence of the written form that is to the fore, but the fact that the testimony of two people is validated in 'your own law'" (Runge 2016, 318–19). What follows is not an actual quotation but a legal principle that informs the regulations in Deut 17:6; 19:15.

ὅτι. Introduces a nominal clause that functions as the subject of γέγραπται: "[*That* the testimony of two people is true] is written in your law" (Wallace 1996, 453–54).

δύο ἀνθρώπων. Subjective genitive qualifying μαρτυρία. Fronted for emphasis.

ἡ μαρτυρία. Nominative subject of ἐστιν.

ἀληθής. Predicate adjective. Fronted for emphasis.

ἐστιν. Pres act ind 3rd sg εἰμί.

8:18 ἐγώ εἰμι ὁ μαρτυρῶν περὶ ἐμαυτοῦ καὶ μαρτυρεῖ περὶ ἐμοῦ ὁ πέμψας με πατήρ.

ἐγώ. Nominative subject of εἰμι. The personal pronoun is emphatic because it identifies the first witness that validates Jesus' testimony. This verse is connected to the previous one by asyndeton.

εἰμι. Pres act ind 1st sg εἰμί.

ὁ μαρτυρῶν. Pres act ptc masc nom sg μαρτυρέω (substantival). Predicate nominative.

περὶ ἐμαυτοῦ. Reference.

καί. Coordinating conjunction.

μαρτυρεῖ. Pres act ind 3rd sg μαρτυρέω.

περὶ ἐμοῦ. Reference.

ὁ . . . πατήρ. Nominative subject of μαρτυρεῖ. The placement of the noun at the end of the clause is emphatic because it identifies the second witness that validates Jesus' testimony.

πέμψας. Aor act ptc masc nom sg πέμπω (attributive). The participle modifies πατήρ, standing in the first attributive position (see 5:37 on πέμψας). On the use of the participial forms of πέμπω to either identify or describe God in the FG, see τοῦ πέμψαντός in 4:34. ὁ πέμψας με πατήρ is a common Johannine expression (5:37; 8:16, 18; 12:49; 14:24).

με. Accusative direct object of πέμψας.

8:19 ἔλεγον οὖν αὐτῷ· ποῦ ἐστιν ὁ πατήρ σου; ἀπεκρίθη Ἰησοῦς· οὔτε ἐμὲ οἴδατε οὔτε τὸν πατέρα μου· εἰ ἐμὲ ᾔδειτε, καὶ τὸν πατέρα μου ἂν ᾔδειτε.

ἔλεγον. Impf act ind 3rd pl λέγω. Fanning (289–90) suggests that the sequence of the aorist and perfect tenses of λέγω in 8:13 (Εἶπον) and here (ἔλεγον) follows the pattern "they said . . . they continued to say." On the function of the imperfect in the FG, see 1:39 on ἦν.

οὖν. Postpositive inferential conjunction and/or transitional particle (see 1:22 and 11:6).

αὐτῷ. Dative indirect object of ἔλεγον.

ποῦ. Interrogative adverb of place.

ἐστιν. Pres act ind 3rd sg εἰμί.

ὁ πατήρ. Nominative subject of ἐστιν.

σου. Genitive of relationship qualifying πατήρ.

ἀπεκρίθη. Aor mid ind 3rd sg ἀποκρίνομαι. On the voice, see "Deponency" in the Series Introduction.

Ἰησοῦς. Nominative subject of ἀπεκρίθη.

οὔτε . . . οὔτε. "Neither . . . nor" (BDAG, 740).

ἐμὲ. Accusative direct object of οἴδατε.

οἴδατε. Prf act ind 2nd pl οἶδα (see 1:26 on οἴδατε).

τὸν πατέρα. Accusative direct object of οἴδατε.

μου. Genitive of relationship qualifying πατέρα.

εἰ. Introduces the protasis of a second-class (contrary-to-fact) condition. Typically, the present contrary-to-fact conditions have the imperfect in both the protasis and the apodosis, while the past contrary-to-fact conditions have the aorist in both the protasis and the apodosis. Wallace (1996, 695 n. 25) notes that of the five occurrences in the NT when pluperfect is used in the protasis (Matt 24:43; Luke 12:39; John 4:10; 8:19; Acts 26:32), four involve the pluperfect of οἶδα, as here. Since this pluperfect has the imperfect meaning (see below), this should be regarded as the present contrary-to-fact condition. It assumes that neither the protasis nor the apodosis is true in the present, i.e., at the time when Jesus was speaking: if the Pharisees knew Jesus (but they do not), they would know his Father too (but they do not).

ἐμὲ. Accusative direct object of ᾔδειτε.

ᾔδειτε. Plprf act ind 2nd pl οἶδα. The pluperfect has the imperfect meaning.

καὶ. Adverbial use (adjunctive).

τὸν πατέρα. Accusative direct object of ᾔδειτε.

μου. Genitive of relationship qualifying πατέρα.

ἄν. Marker of contingency in the apodosis of the second-class condition.

ᾔδειτε. Plprf act ind 2nd pl οἶδα. The pluperfect has the imperfect meaning.

8:20 Ταῦτα τὰ ῥήματα ἐλάλησεν ἐν τῷ γαζοφυλακίῳ διδάσκων ἐν τῷ ἱερῷ· καὶ οὐδεὶς ἐπίασεν αὐτόν, ὅτι οὔπω ἐληλύθει ἡ ὥρα αὐτοῦ.

Ταῦτα τὰ ῥήματα. Accusative direct object of ἐλάλησεν. This verse is connected to the previous one by asyndeton.

ἐλάλησεν. Aor act ind 3rd sg λαλέω.

ἐν τῷ γαζοφυλακίῳ. Locative. If γαζοφυλάκιον denotes "a room in the Temple used as a treasury," the PP means "in the treasury"; if it designates "the offering boxes rather than the treasure itself," the PP means "near where the offering boxes were" (LN 7.33).

διδάσκων. Pres act ptc masc nom sg διδάσκω (temporal). On participles that follow the main verb, see βαπτίζων in 1:31.

ἐν τῷ ἱερῷ. Locative. Elsewhere in the FG, this PP occurs in 2:14; 5:14; 7:28; 10:23; 11:56; 18:20.

καὶ. Coordinating conjunction.

οὐδεὶς. Nominative subject of ἐπίασεν. Fronted for emphasis.

ἐπίασεν. Aor act ind 3rd sg πιάζω. On the meaning and the use of this verb in the FG, see 7:30 on πιάσαι.

αὐτόν. Accusative direct object of ἐπίασεν.

ὅτι. Introduces a causal clause.

οὔπω. Adverb of time ("not yet").

ἐληλύθει. Plprf act ind 3rd sg ἔρχομαι. In this context, the combination of the pluperfect of ἔρχομαι and οὔπω highlights the nonoccurrence of the coming of Jesus' hour in the antecedent past (Fanning, 307).

ἡ ὥρα. Nominative subject of ἐληλύθει. On the arrival of Jesus' hour, see ἡ ὥρα in 12:23.

αὐτοῦ. Genitive of purpose qualifying ὥρα ("the hour destined for him").

John 8:21-30

[21]So he said to them again, "I am going away, and you will seek me, and you will die in your sin. Where I am going, you cannot come." [22]Then the Jews said, "Will he kill himself, since he says, 'Where I am going, you cannot come'?" [23]And he said to them, "You are from below; I am from above. You are from this world; I am not from this world. [24]Therefore I told you that you would die in your sins. For unless you believe that I

am [he], you will die in your sins." ²⁵So they said to him, "Who are you?" Jesus said to them, "Just what I have been saying to you from the beginning. ²⁶I have many things to say and to judge concerning you. But the one who sent me is true, and what I heard from him—these things I speak to the world." ²⁷They did not understand that he had been speaking to them about the Father. ²⁸So Jesus said to them, "When you have lifted up the Son of Man, then you will know that I am [he], and that I do nothing on my own. But just as the Father taught me, I speak these things. ²⁹And the one who sent me is with me. He has not left me alone, because I always do the things that are pleasing to him." ³⁰While he was saying these things, many believed in him.

8:21 Εἶπεν οὖν πάλιν αὐτοῖς· ἐγὼ ὑπάγω καὶ ζητήσετέ με, καὶ ἐν τῇ ἁμαρτίᾳ ὑμῶν ἀποθανεῖσθε· ὅπου ἐγὼ ὑπάγω ὑμεῖς οὐ δύνασθε ἐλθεῖν.

Εἶπεν. Aor act ind 3rd sg λέγω.

οὖν. Postpositive inferential conjunction and/or transitional particle (see 1:22 and 11:6).

πάλιν. Adverb "pert[aining] to repetition in the same (or similar) manner" (BDAG, 752.2).

αὐτοῖς. Dative indirect object of Εἶπεν.

ἐγώ. Nominative subject of ὑπάγω. Fronted as a topical frame.

ὑπάγω. Pres act ind 1st sg ὑπάγω (see 8:14). Like in 7:33 and 8:14, ὑπάγω ("go away") refers to Jesus' going to the Father, i.e., to his death. In this context, the verb functions as a double entendre because it causes misunderstanding by Jesus' audience, giving occasion for further explanation. For other examples of words with multiple meanings that are typically misunderstood by Jesus' audience, see 3:3-4; 4:14-15; 6:33-34; 11:11-13, 23-24; 14:7-8.

καί. Coordinating conjunction.

ζητήσετέ. Fut act ind 2nd pl ζητέω. ζητήσετέ, which has an acute accent on the antepenult, acquired an additional accent, the acute, on the ultima from the enclitic με (Smyth §183; Carson 1985, 48).

με. Accusative direct object of ζητήσετέ.

καί. Coordinating conjunction.

ἐν τῇ ἁμαρτίᾳ. State/condition ("in your state of sin") or causal ("because of your sin").

ὑμῶν. Subjective genitive qualifying ἁμαρτίᾳ.

ἀποθανεῖσθε. Fut mid ind 2nd pl ἀποθνῄσκω.

ὅπου. Particle denoting place.

ἐγώ. Nominative subject of ὑπάγω. The personal pronoun emphasizes the contrast between Jesus (ἐγώ) and his addressees (ὑμεῖς).

ὑπάγω. Pres act ind 1st sg ὑπάγω (see 8:14).

ὑμεῖς. Nominative subject of δύνασθε. ὑμεῖς is contrasted to ἐγώ (see above).

οὐ. Negative particle normally used with indicative verbs.

δύνασθε. Pres mid ind 2nd pl δύναμαι.

ἐλθεῖν. Aor act inf ἔρχομαι (complementary).

8:22 ἔλεγον οὖν οἱ Ἰουδαῖοι· μήτι ἀποκτενεῖ ἑαυτόν, ὅτι λέγει· ὅπου ἐγὼ ὑπάγω ὑμεῖς οὐ δύνασθε ἐλθεῖν;

ἔλεγον. Impf act ind 3rd pl λέγω. Fanning calls the alteration between the aorist and imperfect tenses of λέγω in 8:21-28 "the give-and-take of dialogue, in contrast to the simple narration provided by the aorist" (286).

οὖν. Postpositive inferential conjunction and/or transitional particle (see 1:22 and 11:6).

οἱ Ἰουδαῖοι. Nominative subject of ἔλεγον. In this context, οἱ Ἰουδαῖοι consists either entirely or partially of the Pharisees mentioned in 8:13.

μήτι. Negative particle that introduces a question that expects a negative answer. μήτι is "somewhat more emphatic than the simple μή," but it is also used in "questions in which the questioner is in doubt concerning the answer" (BDAG, 649).

ἀποκτενεῖ. Fut act ind 3rd sg ἀποκτείνω.

ἑαυτόν. Accusative direct object of ἀποκτενεῖ. The reflexive pronoun indicates that οἱ Ἰουδαῖοι misinterpret Jesus' statement about going away to mean the he will commit suicide.

ὅτι. Introduces a causal clause that gives "the reason why a question is asked" (Zerwick §420).

λέγει. Pres act ind 3rd sg λέγω.

ὅπου. Particle denoting place.

ἐγώ. Nominative subject of ὑπάγω. The personal pronoun is contrastive (see 8:21).

ὑπάγω. Pres act ind 1st sg ὑπάγω (see 8:14).

ὑμεῖς. Nominative subject of δύνασθε. The personal pronoun is contrastive (see 8:21).

οὐ. Negative particle normally used with indicative verbs.

δύνασθε. Pres mid ind 2nd pl δύναμαι.

ἐλθεῖν. Aor act inf ἔρχομαι (complementary).

8:23 καὶ ἔλεγεν αὐτοῖς· ὑμεῖς ἐκ τῶν κάτω ἐστέ, ἐγὼ ἐκ τῶν ἄνω εἰμί· ὑμεῖς ἐκ τούτου τοῦ κόσμου ἐστέ, ἐγὼ οὐκ εἰμὶ ἐκ τοῦ κόσμου τούτου.

καὶ. Coordinating conjunction.
ἔλεγεν. Impf act ind 3rd sg λέγω (see 8:22 on ἔλεγον).
αὐτοῖς. Dative indirect object of ἔλεγεν.
ὑμεῖς. Nominative subject of ἐστέ. The personal pronoun emphasizes the contrast between the addressees (ὑμεῖς) and Jesus (ἐγώ).
ἐκ τῶν κάτω. Source/origin that determines the character of a person (Zerwick §§134–35). The article functions as a nominalizer, changing the adverb κάτω ("below") into the object of the preposition ἐκ. Fronted for emphasis. This is the only occurrence of the expression τὰ κάτω in the NT. As Barrett explains, "τὰ κάτω means (as the second part of the verse shows) this world; not hell, but all that is not contained in the heavenly world" (341).
ἐστέ. Pres act ind 2nd pl εἰμί.
ἐγώ. Nominative subject of εἰμί. The personal pronoun is contrastive (see ὑμεῖς above).
ἐκ τῶν ἄνω. Source/origin that determines the character of a person (Zerwick §§134–35). The article functions as a nominalizer, changing the adverb ἄνω ("above") into the object of the preposition ἐκ. Fronted for emphasis. The expression τὰ ἄνω refers to the heavenly world (see Col 3:1-2; cf. Barrett, 341).
εἰμί. Pres act ind 1st sg εἰμί.
ὑμεῖς. Nominative subject of ἐστέ. The personal pronoun is contrastive (see ὑμεῖς above).
ἐκ τούτου τοῦ κόσμου. Source/origin that determines the character of a person (Zerwick §§134–35). Fronted for emphasis. On the portrayal of the world in the FG, see 1:10 on ἐν τῷ κόσμῳ.
ἐστέ. Pres act ind 2nd pl εἰμί.
ἐγώ. Nominative subject of εἰμί. The personal pronoun is contrastive (see ὑμεῖς above).
οὐκ. Negative particle normally used with indicative verbs.
εἰμὶ. Pres act ind 1st sg εἰμί.
ἐκ τοῦ κόσμου τούτου. Source/origin that determines the character of a person (Zerwick §§134–35).

8:24 εἶπον οὖν ὑμῖν ὅτι ἀποθανεῖσθε ἐν ταῖς ἁμαρτίαις ὑμῶν· ἐὰν γὰρ μὴ πιστεύσητε ὅτι ἐγώ εἰμι, ἀποθανεῖσθε ἐν ταῖς ἁμαρτίαις ὑμῶν.

εἶπον. Aor act ind 1st sg λέγω (see 8:22 on ἔλεγον).
οὖν. Postpositive inferential conjunction.

ὑμῖν. Dative indirect object of εἶπον.

ὅτι. Introduces the clausal complement (indirect discourse) of εἶπον.

ἀποθανεῖσθε. Fut mid ind 2nd pl ἀποθνήσκω.

ἐν ταῖς ἁμαρτίαις. State/condition ("in your state of sins") or causal ("because of your sins").

ὑμῶν. Subjective genitive qualifying ἁμαρτίαις.

ἐάν. Introduces the protasis of a third-class condition.

γάρ. Postpositive conjunction that indicates that the conditional clause provides an explanation for Jesus' claim that his interlocutors will die in their sins.

μή. Negative particle normally used with non-indicative verbs. ἐὰν μή can be translated "unless."

πιστεύσητε. Aor act subj 2nd pl πιστεύω. Subjunctive with ἐάν.

ὅτι. Introduces the clausal complement (indirect discourse) of πιστεύσητε.

ἐγώ. Nominative subject of εἰμι. Fronted for emphasis.

εἰμι. Pres act ind 1st sg εἰμί. In the OT, ἐγώ εἰμι functions as divine self-designation (cf. LXX Exod 3:14; Isa 41:4; 43:10; 46:4; 48:12).

ἀποθανεῖσθε. Fut mid ind 2nd pl ἀποθνήσκω.

ἐν ταῖς ἁμαρτίαις. State/condition ("in your state of sins") or causal ("because of your sins").

ὑμῶν. Subjective genitive qualifying ἁμαρτίαις.

8:25 Ἔλεγον οὖν αὐτῷ· σὺ τίς εἶ; εἶπεν αὐτοῖς ὁ Ἰησοῦς· τὴν ἀρχὴν ὅ τι καὶ λαλῶ ὑμῖν;

Ἔλεγον. Impf act ind 3rd pl λέγω (see 8:22 on ἔλεγον).

οὖν. Postpositive inferential conjunction and/or transitional particle (see 1:22 and 11:6).

αὐτῷ. Dative indirect object of Ἔλεγον.

σύ. Nominative subject of εἶ. The placement of the personal pronoun before τίς is emphatic (BDF §475.1).

τίς. Predicate nominative.

εἶ. Pres act ind 2nd sg εἰμί.

εἶπεν. Aor act ind 3rd sg λέγω (see 8:22 on ἔλεγον).

αὐτοῖς. Dative indirect object of εἶπεν.

ὁ Ἰησοῦς. Nominative subject of εἶπεν.

τὴν ἀρχήν. Accusative of respect ("with reference to the beginning") that is equivalent to ἀπ' ἀρχῆς ("from the beginning"; cf. Moule, 34), adverbial accusative that is equivalent to ὅλως ("to begin with, entirely, at all"; cf. BDAG, 138.1.a), or a temporal use of the idiomatic adverbial accusative that is equivalent to ἀπ' ἀρχῆς/ἐξ ἀρχῆς ("in/at the beginning, from the beginning"; cf. Caragounis 2007, 139, 142–47). τὴν ἀρχὴν is placed before the relative clause to which it belongs for emphasis. Caragounis' translation of the exchange between the Jews and Jesus nicely approximates the sense and the word order of the Greek text: "Who are you?" "[I am] From the beginning!—precisely what I have been saying (speaking) to you" (2007, 147).

ὅ τι. Since the oldest Greek copies do not have division between words, these three letters could be read either as two words or as one word. (1) If they are read as two words (ὅ τι), this is a combination of the relative pronoun and the indefinite pronoun introducing a headless relative clause. Within its clause, ὅ τι ("that which") functions as the accusative direct object of λαλῶ. Jesus' answer could be understood as a statement with an implied ἐγώ εἰμι, "[I am] what I have been saying to you from the beginning" (cf. LEB; NIV; RSV; GNT; NCV; REB; Brown, 346; BDAG, 138.1.a), or as a question, "What have I been saying to you from the beginning?" (NASB). (2) If these three letters are read as one word (ὅτι), ὅτι functions as an equivalent to τί ("Why?") introducing a counterquestion (BDF §300.2). This reading, favored by most Greek fathers, interprets τὴν ἀρχὴν adverbially: "Why do I speak to you at all?" (NRSV). While this translation makes good sense as Jesus' reply to the question of the Jews ("Who are you?"), it is undermined by the next sentence that he speaks in v. 27: "I have much to say about you" (Caragounis 2007, 141–42). Neither solution completely satisfies, but it seems that understanding the clause as a statement rather than as a question is the less problematic of the two.

καὶ. Adverbial use (ascensive).

λαλῶ. Pres act ind 1st sg λαλέω. The temporal marker τὴν ἀρχὴν indicates that λαλῶ refers to an action that began at some point in the past, while the imperfective aspect of the present tense suggests that this action, i.e., Jesus' bearing witness to himself, is still in progress. This usage is equivalent to the progressive perfect in English (Caragounis 2007, 145).

ὑμῖν. Dative indirect object of λαλῶ.

8:26 πολλὰ ἔχω περὶ ὑμῶν λαλεῖν καὶ κρίνειν, ἀλλ' ὁ πέμψας με ἀληθής ἐστιν, κἀγὼ ἃ ἤκουσα παρ' αὐτοῦ ταῦτα λαλῶ εἰς τὸν κόσμον.

πολλὰ. Accusative direct object of ἔχω. Fronted for emphasis. This verse is connected to the previous one by asyndeton.

ἔχω. Pres act ind 1st sg ἔχω.

περὶ ὑμῶν. Reference.

λαλεῖν. Pres act inf λαλέω (complementary).

καί. Coordinating conjunction.

κρίνειν. Pres act inf κρίνω (complementary).

ἀλλ'. Marker of contrast.

ὁ πέμψας. Aor act ptc masc nom sg πέμπω (substantival). Nominative subject of ἐστιν. On the use of the participial forms of πέμπω to either identify or describe God in the FG, see τοῦ πέμψαντός in 4:34.

με. Accusative direct object of πέμψας.

ἀληθής. Predicate adjective. Fronted for emphasis.

ἐστιν. Pres act ind 3rd sg εἰμί.

κἀγώ. Formed by crasis from καὶ ἐγώ. καί is a coordinating conjunction; ἐγώ is the nominative subject of λαλῶ.

ἅ. The relative pronoun introduces the headless relative clause that, in its entirety (ἃ ἤκουσα παρ' αὐτοῦ), serves as the direct object of λαλῶ in a left-dislocation (see Runge 2010, 287–313). The left-dislocation of the relative clause highlights the fact that Jesus declares only what he has heard from the one who sent him. Within its clause, ἅ is the accusative direct object of ἤκουσα.

ἤκουσα. Aor act ind 1st sg ἀκούω.

παρ' αὐτοῦ. Source.

ταῦτα. Accusative direct object of λαλῶ, resuming ἃ ἤκουσα παρ' αὐτοῦ. Fronted for emphasis.

λαλῶ. Pres act ind 1st sg λαλέω.

εἰς τὸν κόσμον. εἰς stands for πρός (Zerwick and Grosvenor, 312; Zerwick §97). The PP functions like an indirect object of λαλῶ. On the portrayal of the world in the FG, see 1:10 on ἐν τῷ κόσμῳ.

8:27 οὐκ ἔγνωσαν ὅτι τὸν πατέρα αὐτοῖς ἔλεγεν.

οὐκ. Negative particle normally used with indicative verbs. This verse is connected to the previous one by asyndeton.

ἔγνωσαν. Aor act ind 3rd pl γινώσκω.

ὅτι. Introduces the clausal complement (indirect discourse) of ἔγνωσαν.

τὸν πατέρα. Accusative of respect. λέγω + accusative is used to indicate the person about whom someone speaks (BDAG, 588.1.b.β). Fronted for emphasis.

αὐτοῖς. Dative indirect object of ἔλεγεν.

ἔλεγεν. Impf act ind 3rd sg λέγω. The imperfect is retained from the direct discourse (see 1:39 on μένει), which refers to Jesus' previous declaration (Wallace 1996, 552–53).

8:28 εἶπεν οὖν [αὐτοῖς] ὁ Ἰησοῦς· ὅταν ὑψώσητε τὸν υἱὸν τοῦ ἀνθρώπου, τότε γνώσεσθε ὅτι ἐγώ εἰμι, καὶ ἀπ' ἐμαυτοῦ ποιῶ οὐδέν, ἀλλὰ καθὼς ἐδίδαξέν με ὁ πατὴρ ταῦτα λαλῶ.

εἶπεν. Aor act ind 3rd sg λέγω (see 8:22 on ἔλεγον).

οὖν. Postpositive inferential conjunction and/or transitional particle (see 1:22 and 11:6).

[αὐτοῖς]. Dative indirect object of εἶπεν. The personal pronoun is printed within square brackets because the manuscript evidence for its presence ($\mathfrak{P}^{66c.75}$ ℵ D K N Γ Δ Θ Ψ f^{13} 33 579 700 1424 𝔐 lat sy co) and its absence ($\mathfrak{P}^{66*}$ B L T W f^1 565 892 1241 a) is evenly balanced.

ὁ Ἰησοῦς. Nominative subject of εἶπεν.

ὅταν. Introduces an indefinite temporal clause in a left-dislocation, which is resumed by the temporal adverb τότε. Runge explains that the temporal clause is dislocated because it is too complex to be placed in a marked position. "The left-dislocation allows the information to be introduced, and the pro-adverb is simple enough to be emphasized" (2010, 310).

ὑψώσητε. Aor act subj 2nd pl ὑψόω. Subjunctive with ὅταν. On the meaning of the verb ὑψόω in reference to Jesus' crucifixion, see ὑψωθῆναι in 3:14. Kysar nicely captures the irony and double meaning of ὑψώσητε in this verse: "When you execute me as a common criminal in the most demeaning way, you will bring about my exaltation, the revelation of my true identity" (52–53).

τὸν υἱὸν. Accusative direct object of ὑψώσητε.

τοῦ ἀνθρώπου. Genitive of relationship qualifying υἱόν.

τότε. Adverb of time, which resumes the temporal clause ὅταν ὑψώσητε τὸν υἱὸν τοῦ ἀνθρώπου. Fronted for emphasis. On the function of the resumptive element, see 7:10 on τότε.

γνώσεσθε. Fut mid ind 2nd pl γινώσκω.

ὅτι. Introduces the clausal complement (indirect discourse) of γνώσεσθε.

ἐγώ. Nominative subject of εἰμι. Fronted for emphasis.

εἰμι. Pres act ind 1st sg εἰμί.

καὶ. Coordinating conjunction.

ἀπ' ἐμαυτοῦ. Agency (see 5:19 on ἀφ' ἑαυτοῦ). Fronted for emphasis.

ποιῶ. Pres act ind 1st sg ποιέω.

οὐδέν. Accusative direct object of ποιῶ.

ἀλλὰ. Marker of contrast.

καθὼς. Introduces a comparative clause.

ἐδίδαξέν. Aor act ind 3rd sg διδάσκω. ἐδίδαξέν, which has an acute accent on the antepenult, acquired an additional accent, the acute, on the ultima from the enclitic με (Smyth §183; Carson 1985, 48).

με. Accusative direct object of ἐδίδαξέν.

ὁ πατὴρ. Nominative subject of ἐδίδαξέν.

ταῦτα. Accusative direct object of λαλῶ. The demonstrative pronoun refers to the comparative clause καθὼς ἐδίδαξέν με ὁ πατήρ. Fronted for emphasis.

λαλῶ. Pres act ind 1st sg λαλέω.

8:29 καὶ ὁ πέμψας με μετ' ἐμοῦ ἐστιν· οὐκ ἀφῆκέν με μόνον, ὅτι ἐγὼ τὰ ἀρεστὰ αὐτῷ ποιῶ πάντοτε.

καὶ. Coordinating conjunction.

ὁ πέμψας. Aor act ptc masc nom sg πέμπω (substantival). Nominative subject of ἐστιν. On the use of the participial forms of πέμπω to either identify or describe God in the FG, see τοῦ πέμψαντός in 4:34.

με. Accusative direct object of πέμψας.

μετ' ἐμοῦ. Association/accompaniment.

ἐστιν. Pres act ind 3rd sg εἰμί.

οὐκ. Negative particle normally used with indicative verbs.

ἀφῆκέν. Aor act ind 3rd sg ἀφίημι. ἀφῆκέν, which has a circumflex accent on the penult, acquired an additional accent, the acute, on the ultima from the enclitic με (Smyth §183; Carson 1985, 48).

με. Accusative direct object of ἀφῆκέν in a double accusative object-complement construction.

μόνον. Accusative complement to με in a double accusative object-complement construction.

ὅτι. Introduces a causal clause.

ἐγώ. Nominative subject of ποιῶ. Fronted for emphasis.

τὰ ἀρεστά. Accusative direct object of ποιῶ.

αὐτῷ. Dative complement to ἀρεστά.

ποιῶ. Pres act ind 1st sg ποιέω.

πάντοτε. Adverb of time ("always, at all times").

8:30 Ταῦτα αὐτοῦ λαλοῦντος πολλοὶ ἐπίστευσαν εἰς αὐτόν.

Ταῦτα. Accusative direct object of λαλοῦντος. This verse is connected to the previous one by asyndeton.

αὐτοῦ. Genitive subject of λαλοῦντος.

λαλοῦντος. Pres act ptc masc gen sg λαλέω (genitive absolute, temporal).

πολλοί. Nominative subject of ἐπίστευσαν. Fronted for emphasis.

ἐπίστευσαν. Aor act ind 3rd pl πιστεύω.

εἰς αὐτόν. Goal of actions or feelings directed toward someone (BDAG, 290.4.c.β). For πιστεύειν εἰς + accusative ("trust or believe in someone"), see 1:12 on εἰς τὸ ὄνομα.

John 8:31-36

³¹Then Jesus said to the Jews who had believed him, "If you continue in my word, you are truly my disciples, ³²and you will know the truth, and the truth will set you free." ³³They answered him, "We are the offspring of Abraham and have never been enslaved to anyone. How do you say, 'You will become free'?" ³⁴Jesus answered them, "Truly, truly I say to you, everyone who commits sin is a slave to sin. ³⁵The slave does not remain in the household forever; the son remains forever. ³⁶So if the Son sets you free, you will be really free."

8:31 Ἔλεγεν οὖν ὁ Ἰησοῦς πρὸς τοὺς πεπιστευκότας αὐτῷ Ἰουδαίους· ἐὰν ὑμεῖς μείνητε ἐν τῷ λόγῳ τῷ ἐμῷ, ἀληθῶς μαθηταί μού ἐστε

Ἔλεγεν. Impf act ind 3rd sg λέγω. Levinsohn regards this imperfect as a prime example of occasions "when it is not obvious that the event described can be viewed as being incomplete" (2000, 175). He suggests that the primary function of such imperfects is markedness: "The message to the reader in this case is that, because the writer did not select the *natural* way of portraying a completed event (with, say, an aorist), there must be 'added implicatures'" (175; cf. Levinsohn 2016, 169–70, where he says that the effect of using the imperfect at this point of the narrative is foregrounding).

οὖν. Postpositive inferential conjunction and/or transitional particle (see 1:22 and 11:6).

ὁ Ἰησοῦς. Nominative subject of Ἔλεγεν.

πρὸς τοὺς . . . Ἰουδαίους. Locative (motion toward). The PP functions like an indirect object of Ἔλεγεν.

πεπιστευκότας. Prf act ptc masc acc pl πιστεύω (attributive). The participle modifies Ἰουδαίους, standing in the first attributive position (see 5:37 on πέμψας). On the meaning of the perfect tense of πιστεύω, see 6:69 on πεπιστεύκαμεν. Regarding the perfect participle, Fanning notes that "it often emphasizes the *resulting state* and only implies the anterior occurrence" (416).

αὐτῷ. Dative complement of πεπιστευκότας. The dative indicates the person "to whom one gives credence or whom one believes" (BDAG,

816.1.b). There is no distinction between πιστεύω + dative and πιστεύω + εἰς with accusative (Harris 2012, 236).

ἐάν. Introduces the protasis of a third-class condition.

ὑμεῖς. Nominative subject of μείνητε. Fronted for emphasis.

μείνητε. Aor act subj 2nd pl μένω. Subjunctive with ἐάν.

ἐν τῷ λόγῳ τῷ ἐμῷ. State/condition. The possessive adjective ἐμῷ stands in the second attributive position (see 1:9 on τὸ φῶς τὸ ἀληθινόν).

ἀληθῶς. Adverb ("truly, really"). It marks the beginning of the apodosis of a third-class condition.

μαθηταί. Predicate nominative. Fronted for emphasis.

μού. Genitive of relationship qualifying μαθηταί. The enclitic μού is accented because it is followed by the enclitic ἐστε. "When several enclitics occur in succession, each receives an accent from the following, only the last having no accent" (Smyth §185).

ἐστε. Pres act ind 2nd pl εἰμί.

8:32 καὶ γνώσεσθε τὴν ἀλήθειαν, καὶ ἡ ἀλήθεια ἐλευθερώσει ὑμᾶς.

καί. Coordinating conjunction.

γνώσεσθε. Fut mid ind 2nd pl γινώσκω.

τὴν ἀλήθειαν. Accusative direct object of γνώσεσθε.

καί. Coordinating conjunction.

ἡ ἀλήθεια. Nominative subject of ἐλευθερώσει.

ἐλευθερώσει. Fut act ind 3rd sg ἐλευθερόω.

ὑμᾶς. Accusative direct object of ἐλευθερώσει.

8:33 ἀπεκρίθησαν πρὸς αὐτόν· σπέρμα Ἀβραάμ ἐσμεν καὶ οὐδενὶ δεδουλεύκαμεν πώποτε· πῶς σὺ λέγεις ὅτι ἐλεύθεροι γενήσεσθε;

ἀπεκρίθησαν. Aor mid ind 3rd pl ἀποκρίνομαι. On the voice, see "Deponency" in the Series Introduction. This verse is connected to the previous one by asyndeton.

πρὸς αὐτόν. Locative (motion toward). The PP functions like an indirect object of ἀπεκρίθησαν.

σπέρμα. Predicate nominative. Fronted for emphasis. σπέρμα . . . ἐσμεν is a *constructio ad sensum* because σπέρμα is a collective noun.

Ἀβραάμ. Genitive of relationship qualifying σπέρμα.

ἐσμεν. Pres act ind 1st pl εἰμί.

καί. Coordinating conjunction.

οὐδενί. Dative complement of δεδουλεύκαμεν. The dative denotes the person to whom someone is enslaved or subjected (BDAG, 259.1).

δεδουλεύκαμεν. Prf act ind 1st pl δουλεύω.

πώποτε. Indefinite adverb of time.
πῶς. Interrogative particle.
σὺ. Nominative subject of λέγεις. The personal pronoun is emphatic and contrastive, underscoring the difference of opinion between Jesus and his interlocutors.
λέγεις. Pres act ind 2nd sing λέγω.
ὅτι. ὅτι-*recitativum* that introduces the clausal complement (direct discourse) of λέγεις.
ἐλεύθεροι. Predicate adjective. Fronted for emphasis.
γενήσεσθε. Fut mid ind 2nd pl γίνομαι.

8:34 ἀπεκρίθη αὐτοῖς ὁ Ἰησοῦς· ἀμὴν ἀμὴν λέγω ὑμῖν ὅτι πᾶς ὁ ποιῶν τὴν ἁμαρτίαν δοῦλός ἐστιν τῆς ἁμαρτίας.

ἀπεκρίθη. Aor mid ind 3rd sg ἀποκρίνομαι. On the voice, see "Deponency" in the Series Introduction. This verse is connected to the previous one by asyndeton.
αὐτοῖς. Dative indirect object of ἀπεκρίθη.
ὁ Ἰησοῦς. Nominative subject of ἀπεκρίθη.
ἀμὴν ἀμὴν λέγω ὑμῖν. Metacomment (see 1:51).
ἀμὴν ἀμὴν. Asseverative particles that mark the beginning of Jesus' solemn declaration (see 1:51).
λέγω. Pres act ind 1st sg λέγω.
ὑμῖν. Dative indirect object of λέγω.
ὅτι. Introduces the clausal complement (direct [NRSV; NET; ASV; ESV; NASB; NIV] or indirect [REB; CEB; LEB] discourse) of λέγω.
πᾶς ὁ ποιῶν. Nominative subject of ἐστιν. On πᾶς + articular participle, see 3:8 on πᾶς ὁ γεγεννημένος.
ὁ ποιῶν. Pres act ptc masc nom sg ποιέω (substantival). On the function of this participle, see πᾶς ὁ ποιῶν above.
τὴν ἁμαρτίαν. Accusative direct object of ποιῶν.
δοῦλός. Predicate nominative. Fronted for emphasis. This anarthrous preverbal predicate nominative is most likely indefinite (Wallace 1996, 266). δοῦλός, which has a circumflex accent on the penult, acquired an additional accent, the acute, on the ultima from the enclitic ἐστιν (Smyth §183; Carson 1985, 48).
ἐστιν. Pres act ind 3rd sg εἰμί.
τῆς ἁμαρτίας. Objective genitive qualifying δοῦλός.

8:35 ὁ δὲ δοῦλος οὐ μένει ἐν τῇ οἰκίᾳ εἰς τὸν αἰῶνα, ὁ υἱὸς μένει εἰς τὸν αἰῶνα.

    ὁ . . . δοῦλος. Nominative subject of μένει. The article is generic. Fronted as a topical frame.
    δὲ. Marker of narrative development.
    οὐ. Negative particle normally used with indicative verbs.
    μένει. Pres act ind 3rd sg μένω.
    ἐν τῇ οἰκίᾳ. Locative.
    εἰς τὸν αἰῶνα. Temporal.
    ὁ υἱός. Nominative subject of μένει. The article is generic (see ὁ . . . δοῦλος above). Fronted as a topical frame.
    μένει. Pres act ind 3rd sg μένω.
    εἰς τὸν αἰῶνα. Temporal.

8:36 ἐὰν οὖν ὁ υἱὸς ὑμᾶς ἐλευθερώσῃ, ὄντως ἐλεύθεροι ἔσεσθε.

    ἐάν. Introduces the protasis of a third-class condition.
    οὖν. Postpositive inferential conjunction and/or transitional particle (see 1:22 and 11:6).
    ὁ υἱός. Nominative subject of ἐλευθερώσῃ. Since Jesus now addresses his audience (ὑμᾶς), ὁ υἱός most likely no longer refers to the generic son from the illustration in the previous verse but to Jesus himself.
    ὑμᾶς. Accusative direct object of ἐλευθερώσῃ.
    ἐλευθερώσῃ. Aor act subj 3rd sg ἐλευθερόω. Subjunctive with ἐάν.
    ὄντως. Adverb of the participle ὤν ("really, certainly, in truth"). It marks the beginning of the apodosis of a third-class condition.
    ἐλεύθεροι. Predicate adjective. Fronted for emphasis.
    ἔσεσθε. Fut mid ind 2nd pl εἰμί.

John 8:37-47

[37]"I know that you are the offspring of Abraham, but you seek to kill me, because my word makes no progress among you. [38]I speak the things that I have seen in the Father's presence; so also you, do the things that you have heard from the Father!" [39]They answered and said to him, "Our father is Abraham." Jesus said to them, "If you are the children of Abraham, you would be doing the deeds of Abraham. [40]Yet now you are seeking to kill me, a man who has told you the truth that I heard from God. Abraham did not do this! [41]You are doing the deeds of your father." Then they said to him, "We are not born from sexual immorality. We have one father—God." [42]Jesus said to them, "If God were your Father,

you would love me, for I came from God and I am here. For I did not come on my own, but he sent me. ⁴³Why do you not understand my way of speaking? It is because you cannot listen to my word. ⁴⁴You are from your father, the devil, and you want to do the desires of your father. He was a murderer from the beginning and did not stand in the truth, because truth is not in him. When he speaks the lie, he speaks from his own character, because he is a liar and the father of lies. ⁴⁵But because I tell the truth, you do not believe me. ⁴⁶Who among you convicts me concerning sin? If I tell the truth, why do you not believe me? ⁴⁷The one who is from God listens to the words of God. This is why you do not listen, because you are not from God."

8:37 Οἶδα ὅτι σπέρμα Ἀβραάμ ἐστε· ἀλλὰ ζητεῖτέ με ἀποκτεῖναι, ὅτι ὁ λόγος ὁ ἐμὸς οὐ χωρεῖ ἐν ὑμῖν.

Οἶδα. Prf act ind 1st sg οἶδα (see 1:26 on οἴδατε). This verse is connected to the previous one by asyndeton.

ὅτι. Introduces the clausal complement (indirect discourse) of Οἶδα.

σπέρμα. Predicate nominative. Fronted for emphasis. σπέρμα . . . ἐστε is a *constructio ad sensum* because σπέρμα is a collective noun (see 8:33).

Ἀβραάμ. Genitive of relationship qualifying σπέρμα.

ἐστε. Pres act ind 2nd pl εἰμί.

ἀλλὰ. Marker of contrast.

ζητεῖτέ. Pres act ind 2nd pl ζητέω. ζητεῖτέ, which has a circumflex accent on the penult, acquired an additional accent, the acute, on the ultima from the enclitic με (Smyth §183; Carson 1985, 48). In the FG, ζητέω is used six times with the complimentary infinitive ἀποκτεῖναι (5:18; 7:1, 19, 20, 25; 8:37).

με. Accusative direct object of ἀποκτεῖναι.

ἀποκτεῖναι. Aor act inf ἀποκτείνω (complementary).

ὅτι. Introduces a causal clause.

ὁ λόγος ὁ ἐμὸς. Nominative subject of χωρεῖ. The possessive adjective ἐμὸς stands in the second attributive position (see 1:9 on τὸ φῶς τὸ ἀληθινόν).

οὐ. Negative particle normally used with indicative verbs.

χωρεῖ. Pres act ind 3rd sg χωρέω. In this context, χωρέω ("to move on from one place to another—to move on, to advance") is used figuratively, referring to either making progress or finding an adequate place (LN 15.13).

ἐν ὑμῖν. Locative.

8:38 ἃ ἐγὼ ἑώρακα παρὰ τῷ πατρὶ λαλῶ· καὶ ὑμεῖς οὖν ἃ ἠκούσατε παρὰ τοῦ πατρὸς ποιεῖτε.

ἃ. The relative pronoun introduces the headless relative clause that, in its entirety (ἃ ἐγὼ ἑώρακα παρὰ τῷ πατρὶ), serves as the direct object of λαλῶ, which is fronted as a topical frame. Within its clause, ἃ is the accusative direct object of ἑώρακα. This verse is connected to the previous one by asyndeton.

ἐγώ. Nominative subject of ἑώρακα. The personal pronoun is emphatic and contrastive, highlighting the ἐγὼ ... ὑμεῖς antithesis.

ἑώρακα. Prf act ind 1st sg ὁράω.

παρὰ τῷ πατρί. Association (lit. "at the Father's side" = "in the Father's presence"; cf. Harris 2012, 173). Many English translations presume that the article is possessive or that the first-person singular personal pronoun μου is implied (RSV; REB; ASV; ESV; KJV; NASB; NCV; NLT). This was undoubtedly the understanding of various copyists who added μου after τῷ πατρὶ in the interest of clarity (ℵ K N Γ Δ Θ Ψ $f^{1.13}$ 565 700 1424 𝔐 it vg^d sy et al.). The reading without μου, however, is to be preferred on both external ($\mathfrak{P}^{66.75}$ B C L 070 vgst et al.) and internal grounds (Metzger, 192).

λαλῶ. Pres act ind 1st sg λαλέω. The verb stands in final, emphatic position.

καί. Coordinating conjunction or ascensive.

ὑμεῖς. Nominative subject of ποιεῖτε. The personal pronoun is emphatic and contrastive, highlighting the ἐγὼ ... ὑμεῖς antithesis.

οὖν. Postpositive inferential conjunction and/or transitional particle (see 1:22 and 11:6).

ἅ. The relative pronoun introduces the headless relative clause that, in its entirety (ἃ ἠκούσατε παρὰ τοῦ πατρὸς), serves as the direct object of ποιεῖτε, which is fronted as a topical frame. Within its clause, ἃ is the accusative direct object of ἠκούσατε.

ἠκούσατε. Aor act ind 2nd pl ἀκούω.

παρὰ τοῦ πατρός. Source. Many English translations again (see παρὰ τῷ πατρὶ above) postulate that the article is possessive or that the second-person plural personal pronoun ὑμῶν is implied (RSV; REB; ASV; ESV; KJV; NASB; NCV; NLT). The variants that include ὑμῶν make this assumption explicit, but the copyists disagreed on the exact wording of the PP: some wrote παρὰ τοῦ πατρὸς ὑμῶν (ℵ C K Θ $f^{1.13}$ 33 565 892 f), and others παρὰ τῷ πατρὶ ὑμῶν (D N Γ Δ Ψ 579 700 1424 𝔐 lat). The reading with ὑμῶν assumes that this verse anticipates v. 44, where Jesus declares that the father of these Jews is the devil. The reading without ὑμῶν, however, is not only well attested ($\mathfrak{P}^{66}$ B L W 070

Or) but also more difficult because it suggests that both prepositional phrases refer to the same Father.

ποιεῖτε. Pres act ind (or impv) 2nd pl ποιέω. The verb stands in final, emphatic position. The parallel structure of both clauses in this verse favors taking ποιεῖτε as an indicative. If so, Jesus' statement makes the best sense if we suppose that παρὰ τῷ πατρὶ and παρὰ τοῦ πατρὸς have different referents, i.e., that the articles are possessive—the former referring to the heavenly Father and the latter referring to another, still undisclosed, father. If both prepositional phrases have the same referent—the heavenly Father—Jesus' statement makes the best sense if we take ποιεῖτε as an imperative (NRSV: "as for you, you should do what you have heard from the Father"; NET: "as for you, practice the things you have heard from the Father!" cf. Brown, 1:356). My translation reflects the second view, because it preserves the rhetorical progression of Jesus' dialogue with the Jews.

8:39 Ἀπεκρίθησαν καὶ εἶπαν αὐτῷ· ὁ πατὴρ ἡμῶν Ἀβραάμ ἐστιν. λέγει αὐτοῖς ὁ Ἰησοῦς· εἰ τέκνα τοῦ Ἀβραάμ ἐστε, τὰ ἔργα τοῦ Ἀβραὰμ ἐποιεῖτε·

Ἀπεκρίθησαν. Aor mid ind 3rd pl ἀποκρίνομαι. On the voice, see "Deponency" in the Series Introduction. This verse is connected to the previous one by asyndeton.

καὶ εἶπαν αὐτῷ. Pleonastic clause under Semitic influence, which functions as a redundant quotative frame (see 1:25 on καὶ εἶπαν αὐτῷ).

καὶ. Coordinating conjunction.

εἶπαν. Aor act ind 3rd pl λέγω.

αὐτῷ. Dative indirect object of εἶπαν.

ὁ πατήρ. Nominative subject of ἐστιν. Wallace argues that "articular nouns and proper names seem to have equal priority. In instances where one substantive is articular and the other is a proper name . . . , word order may be the determining factor" (1996, 44), but he adds that "[i]t is possible that [ὁ πατὴρ ἡμῶν Ἀβραάμ ἐστιν] should be translated 'Abraham is our father'" (1996, 45 n. 26), as in some English translations (e.g., RSV, NRSV, REB, NET; ESV; KJV; LEB).

ἡμῶν. Genitive of relationship qualifying πατήρ.

Ἀβραάμ. Predicate nominative. Fronted for emphasis.

ἐστιν. Pres act ind 3rd sg εἰμί.

λέγει. Pres act ind 3rd sg λέγω. The historical present gives prominence to Jesus' reply to his interlocutors (see 1:15 on μαρτυρεῖ).

αὐτοῖς. Dative indirect object of λέγει.

ὁ Ἰησοῦς. Nominative subject of λέγει.

εἰ. Introduces the protasis of a first-class condition. This conditional sentence is of a mixed type: the protasis is a first-class (real) condition, which assumes the truthfulness of the claim of Jesus' interlocutors that they are Abraham's children, while the apodosis is a second-class (unreal, contrary-to-fact) condition without the customary ἄν (BDF §360.1), which assumes that the conduct that reflects Abrahamic paternity—i.e., doing "the deeds of Abraham"—is not true (Harris 2015, 177). This is one of several examples in the NT that demonstrate "the relative independence between protasis and apodosis" (Zerwick §329). The transmission history of the text, however, shows that some scribes tried to "correct" this mixture of different types of conditions by modifying either the protasis or the apodosis to comply with the grammatical rules governing the first-class or second-class conditions (see below).

τέκνα. Predicate nominative. Fronted for emphasis.

τοῦ Ἀβραάμ. Genitive of relationship qualifying τέκνα.

ἐστε. Pres act ind 2nd pl εἰμί. The variant ἦτε (C K N W Γ Δ Θ Ψ $f^{1.13}$ 33 565 579 700 892 1424 𝔐 it sy$^{p.h}$ et al.) is a scribal adjustment of the protasis to a second-class (contrary-to-fact) condition (Metzger, 192–93).

τὰ ἔργα. Accusative direct object of ἐποιεῖτε. It marks the beginning of the apodosis of a second-class condition.

τοῦ Ἀβραάμ. Subjective genitive qualifying ἔργα.

ἐποιεῖτε. Impf act ind 2nd pl ποιέω. The verb stands in final, emphatic position. Some copyists have added ἄν (ℵ^2 C K L N Δ Ψ $f^{1.13}$ 33 565 579 [700] 892 et al.) to comply with the Attic rules for second-class conditions, although this was no longer necessary (BDF §360.1). Others have deleted the augment ($\mathfrak{P}^{66}$ B* ff^2 vg Did^{pt}) because the imperative ποιεῖτε complies with the rules for first-class conditions and makes good sense of the sentence ("If you are Abraham's children, then do the deeds of Abraham!"). The imperfect ἐποιεῖτε without ἄν, however, has strong external support ($\mathfrak{P}^{75}$ ℵ* B^2 D W Γ Θ 070 1424 *pm* Epiph) and better explains the origin of other variants (Metzger, 192).

8:40 νῦν δὲ ζητεῖτέ με ἀποκτεῖναι ἄνθρωπον ὃς τὴν ἀλήθειαν ὑμῖν λελάληκα ἣν ἤκουσα παρὰ τοῦ θεοῦ· τοῦτο Ἀβραὰμ οὐκ ἐποίησεν.

νῦν. Adverb of time.

δὲ. Marker of narrative development.

ζητεῖτέ. Pres act ind 2nd pl ζητέω. ζητεῖτέ, which has a circumflex accent on the penult, acquired an additional accent, the acute, on the ultima from the enclitic με (Smyth §183; Carson 1985, 48).

με. Accusative direct object of ἀποκτεῖναι.

ἀποκτεῖναι. Aor act inf ἀποκτείνω (complementary).

ἄνθρωπον. Accusative in apposition to με, which receives emphasis through right-dislocation.

ὅς. Nominative subject of λελάληκα. The antecedent of the relative pronoun is με, which explains why the verb is first-person singular and not the expected third-person plural form (Harris 2015, 178).

τὴν ἀλήθειαν. Accusative direct object of λελάληκα. Fronted for emphasis.

ὑμῖν. Dative indirect object of λελάληκα.

λελάληκα. Prf act ind 1st sg λαλέω. On the significance of the verbal aspect of λελάληκα, see 6:63.

ἥν. Accusative direct object of ἤκουσα. The antecedent of the relative pronoun is τὴν ἀλήθειαν.

ἤκουσα. Aor act ind 1st sg ἀκούω.

παρὰ τοῦ θεοῦ. Source.

τοῦτο. Accusative direct object of ἐποίησεν.

Ἀβραάμ. Nominative subject of ἐποίησεν.

οὐκ. Negative particle normally used with indicative verbs.

ἐποίησεν. Aor act ind 3rd sg ποιέω. The verb stands in final, emphatic position.

8:41 ὑμεῖς ποιεῖτε τὰ ἔργα τοῦ πατρὸς ὑμῶν. Εἶπαν [οὖν] αὐτῷ· ἡμεῖς ἐκ πορνείας οὐ γεγεννήμεθα, ἕνα πατέρα ἔχομεν τὸν θεόν.

ὑμεῖς. Nominative subject of ποιεῖτε. Fronted for emphasis. This verse is connected to the previous one by asyndeton.

ποιεῖτε. Pres act ind 2nd pl ποιέω.

τὰ ἔργα. Accusative direct object of ποιεῖτε.

τοῦ πατρὸς. Subjective genitive qualifying ἔργα.

ὑμῶν. Genitive of relationship qualifying πατρός.

Εἶπαν. Aor act ind 3rd pl λέγω.

[οὖν]. Postpositive inferential conjunction and/or transitional particle (see 1:22 and 11:6). It is printed within square brackets because the external evidence for ($\mathfrak{P}^{66.75}$ C D K N Γ Δ Θ Ψ f^{13} 𝔐 et al.) and against (ℵ B L W 070 et al.) its inclusion is evenly balanced.

αὐτῷ. Dative indirect object of Εἶπαν.

ἡμεῖς. Nominative subject of γεγεννήμεθα. The personal pronoun is emphatic, contrastive, and exclusive, highlighting the difference between Jesus' opponents ("we") and Jesus (Wallace 1996, 398).

ἐκ πορνείας. Instrumental/impersonal agency ("born from fornication" = "conceived through unlawful sexual intercourse").

οὐ. Negative particle normally used with indicative verbs.

γεγεννήμεθα. Prf pass ind 1st pl γεννάω. The verb stands in final, emphatic position. The perfect tense is semantically marked, emphasizing the character of the past act (illegitimate conception) as a determining factor for the status of a person in the present (illegitimate children).

ἕνα πατέρα. Accusative direct object of ἔχομεν. ἕνα πατέρα is fronted for emphasis and functions as a forward-pointing reference to τὸν θεόν. Runge explains that the forward-pointing reference has "the pragmatic effect of attracting extra attention to the target" (2010, 62).

ἔχομεν. Pres act ind 1st pl ἔχω.

τὸν θεόν. Accusative in apposition to ἕνα πατέρα, which functions as a forward-pointing target (see ἕνα πατέρα above).

8:42 εἶπεν αὐτοῖς ὁ Ἰησοῦς· εἰ ὁ θεὸς πατὴρ ὑμῶν ἦν ἠγαπᾶτε ἂν ἐμέ, ἐγὼ γὰρ ἐκ τοῦ θεοῦ ἐξῆλθον καὶ ἥκω· οὐδὲ γὰρ ἀπ' ἐμαυτοῦ ἐλήλυθα, ἀλλ' ἐκεῖνός με ἀπέστειλεν.

εἶπεν. Aor act ind 3rd sg λέγω. This verse is connected to the previous one by asyndeton.

αὐτοῖς. Dative indirect object of εἶπεν.

ὁ Ἰησοῦς. Nominative subject of εἶπεν.

εἰ. Introduces the protasis of a second-class (contrary-to-fact) condition. Typically, the present contrary-to-fact conditions have the imperfect in both the protasis and the apodosis, while the past contrary-to-fact conditions have the aorist in both the protasis and the apodosis. Since both verbs here are the imperfects, this is a prime example of a present contrary-to-fact condition: if God were the Father of Jesus' opponents (but he is not), they would love Jesus (but they do not).

ὁ θεὸς. Nominative subject of ἦν.

πατὴρ. Predicate nominative. Fronted for emphasis.

ὑμῶν. Genitive of relationship qualifying πατὴρ.

ἦν. Impf act ind 3rd sg εἰμί.

ἠγαπᾶτε. Impf act ind 2nd pl ἀγαπάω. It marks the beginning of the apodosis of a second-class (contrary-to-fact) condition.

ἄν. Marker of contingency in the apodosis of the second-class condition.

ἐμέ. Accusative direct object of ἠγαπᾶτε.

ἐγώ. Nominative subject of ἐξῆλθον. Fronted for emphasis.

γάρ. Postpositive conjunction that introduces an explanation of the apodosis of the previous condition.

ἐκ τοῦ θεοῦ. Source/origin.

ἐξῆλθον. Aor act ind 1st sg ἐξέρχομαι.

καί. Coordinating conjunction.

ἥκω. Pres act ind 1st sg ἥκω. The verb stands in final, emphatic position. In this context, ἥκω ("to move toward and to arrive at a point" [LN 15.84]) probably means "to be in a place, as the result of having arrived" (85.10).

οὐδὲ . . . ἀλλ'. A point/counterpoint set ("not this . . . but that") that negates the incorrect conclusion that Jesus came on his own and replaces it with the correct conclusion that God sent him. οὐδὲ is a combination of the negative particle οὐ and the marker of narrative development δέ. On the function of ἀλλά in a point/counterpoint set, see 1:8.

γάρ. Postpositive conjunction that introduces supporting material for the previous explanatory clause.

ἀπ' ἐμαυτοῦ. Agency (see 5:19 on ἀφ' ἑαυτοῦ).

ἐλήλυθα. Prf act ind 1st sg ἔρχομαι.

ἐκεῖνός. Nominative subject of ἀπέστειλεν. The demonstrative pronoun, which is fronted for emphasis, refers to God. ἐκεῖνός, which has a circumflex accent on the penult, acquired an additional accent, the acute, on the ultima from the enclitic με (Smyth §183; Carson 1985, 48).

με. Accusative direct object of ἀπέστειλεν.

ἀπέστειλεν. Aor act ind 3rd sg ἀποστέλλω.

8:43 διὰ τί τὴν λαλιὰν τὴν ἐμὴν οὐ γινώσκετε; ὅτι οὐ δύνασθε ἀκούειν τὸν λόγον τὸν ἐμόν.

διὰ τί. Causal. This verse is connected to the previous one by asyndeton.

τὴν λαλιὰν τὴν ἐμήν. Accusative direct object of γινώσκετε. The possessive adjective ἐμήν stands in the second attributive position (see 1:9 on τὸ φῶς τὸ ἀληθινόν).

οὐ. Negative particle normally used with indicative verbs.

γινώσκετε. Pres act ind 2nd pl γινώσκω. The verb stands in final, emphatic position.

ὅτι. Introduces a causal clause.

οὐ. Negative particle normally used with indicative verbs.

δύνασθε. Pres mid ind 2nd pl δύναμαι.

ἀκούειν. Pres act inf ἀκούω (complementary).

τὸν λόγον τὸν ἐμόν. Accusative direct object of ἀκούειν. The possessive adjective ἐμόν stands in the second attributive position (see 1:9 on τὸ φῶς τὸ ἀληθινόν).

8:44 ὑμεῖς ἐκ τοῦ πατρὸς τοῦ διαβόλου ἐστὲ καὶ τὰς ἐπιθυμίας τοῦ πατρὸς ὑμῶν θέλετε ποιεῖν. ἐκεῖνος ἀνθρωποκτόνος ἦν ἀπ' ἀρχῆς καὶ ἐν τῇ ἀληθείᾳ οὐκ ἔστηκεν, ὅτι οὐκ ἔστιν ἀλήθεια ἐν αὐτῷ. ὅταν

λαλῇ τὸ ψεῦδος, ἐκ τῶν ἰδίων λαλεῖ, ὅτι ψεύστης ἐστὶν καὶ ὁ πατὴρ αὐτοῦ.

ὑμεῖς. Nominative subject of ἐστὲ. Fronted as a topical frame. This verse is connected to the previous one by asyndeton.

ἐκ τοῦ πατρὸς. Source/origin that determines the character of a person (Zerwick §§134–35). When the PP with ἐκ is combined with εἶναι, it means to "belong to someone or someth[ing]" (BDAG, 297.4.a.δ). In this context, the article is possessive ("from your father"). Fronted for emphasis.

τοῦ διαβόλου. Genitive in apposition to τοῦ πατρὸς ("from your father, the devil") or epexegetical genitive explaining τοῦ πατρὸς ("from your father, namely the devil").

ἐστὲ. Pres act ind 2nd pl εἰμί.

καὶ. Coordinating conjunction.

τὰς ἐπιθυμίας. Accusative direct object of ποιεῖν. Fronted for emphasis.

τοῦ πατρὸς. Subjective genitive qualifying ἐπιθυμίας.

ὑμῶν. Genitive of relationship qualifying πατρὸς.

θέλετε. Pres act ind 2nd pl θέλω.

ποιεῖν. Pres act inf ποιέω (complementary).

ἐκεῖνος. Nominative subject of ἦν. The demonstrative pronoun refers to the devil, acting as a third-person personal pronoun with a simple anaphoric force (Wallace 1996, 328–29).

ἀνθρωποκτόνος. Predicate nominative. Fronted for emphasis. ἀνθρωποκτόνος denotes "a person who murders another person—'murderer'" (LN 20.85).

ἦν. Impf act ind 3rd sg εἰμί.

ἀπ' ἀρχῆς. Temporal.

καὶ. Coordinating conjunction.

ἐν τῇ ἀληθείᾳ. State or condition (BDAG, 327.2.b).

οὐκ. Negative particle normally used with indicative verbs.

ἔστηκεν. Impf act ind 3rd sg στήκω ("stand, stand firm"), a late formation from ἔστηκα (the perfect of ἵστημι). Metzger (193) argues that the imperfect ἔστηκεν, attested by $\mathfrak{P}^{66}$ ℵ B* C D L N W Δ Θ Ψ 070 f^{13} 33 892 1241 1424 sy^h, "follows more naturally after ἦν than does the perfect-tense ἕστηκεν," attested by $\mathfrak{P}^{75}$ B^2 K Γ f^1 565 700 𝔐 sy^{hmg} Cl Or (BDF §14; Robertson, 224; Barrett, 349).

ὅτι. Introduces a causal clause.

οὐκ. Negative particle normally used with indicative verbs.

ἔστιν. Pres act ind 3rd sg εἰμί. The enclitic ἐστιν is accented ἔστιν when it comes at the beginning of a sentence, when it expresses existence, or when it follows ἀλλ᾽, εἰ, καί, οὐκ, ὅτι, or τοῦτ᾽. The last two conditions are fulfilled here.

ἀλήθεια. Nominative subject of ἔστιν.
ἐν αὐτῷ. Locative.
ὅταν. Introduces an indefinite temporal clause.
λαλῇ. Pres act subj 3rd sg λαλέω. Subjunctive with ὅταν.
τὸ ψεῦδος. Accusative direct object of λαλῇ.
ἐκ τῶν ἰδίων. Source/origin that determines the character of a person (Zerwick §§134–35). The article functions as a nominalizer, changing the adjective ἴδιος ("one's own") into the object of the preposition ἐκ ("from one's characteristic features" = "in keeping with his nature/character" [cf. Zerwick and Grosvenor, 313]).
λαλεῖ. Pres act ind 3rd sg λαλέω.
ὅτι. Introduces a causal clause.
ψεύστης. Predicate nominative. Fronted for emphasis.
ἐστὶν. Pres act ind 3rd sg εἰμί.
καὶ. Coordinating conjunction.
ὁ πατὴρ. Predicate nominative.
αὐτοῦ. Genitive of relationship qualifying πατήρ. Although αὐτοῦ could be masculine, referring to ψεύστης, it is probably neuter, referring to τὸ ψεῦδος, i.e., ὁ πατὴρ τοῦ ψεύδους ("the father of falsity/lies").

8:45 ἐγὼ δὲ ὅτι τὴν ἀλήθειαν λέγω, οὐ πιστεύετέ μοι.

ἐγώ. Pendent nominative or nominative subject of λέγω in a left-dislocation. The left-dislocation of the subject of the clause "attracts more attention to the topic than it would have otherwise received with one of the more conventional methods" (Runge 2010, 290).
δὲ. Marker of narrative development with a contrastive nuance.
ὅτι. Introduces a causal clause, which is positioned before the main clause. The fronting of the ὅτι clause places it in a position of prominence that creates a frame of reference for the clause that follows. The causal clause ὅτι τὴν ἀλήθειαν λέγω creates the expectation that Jesus will be believed, which is then reversed by Jesus' claim that the Pharisees do not believe him. In this way, the fronting of the ὅτι clause calls attention to Pharisaic unbelief, which, in turn, functions as a forward-pointing device to 8:47, where Jesus explains why refusing to believe the one who speaks the truth represents the natural response of those who are not from God (Runge 2010, 239–40).
τὴν ἀλήθειαν. Accusative direct object of λέγω. Fronted for emphasis.
λέγω. Pres act ind 1st sg λέγω.
οὐ. Negative particle normally used with indicative verbs.

πιστεύετέ. Pres act ind 2nd pl πιστεύω.

μοι. Dative complement of πιστεύετέ. The dative indicates the person "to whom one gives credence or whom one believes" (BDAG, 816.1.b).

8:46 τίς ἐξ ὑμῶν ἐλέγχει με περὶ ἁμαρτίας; εἰ ἀλήθειαν λέγω, διὰ τί ὑμεῖς οὐ πιστεύετέ μοι;

τίς. Nominative subject of ἐλέγχει. This verse is connected to the previous one by asyndeton.

ἐξ ὑμῶν. Replaces the partitive genitive.

ἐλέγχει. Pres act ind 3rd sg ἐλέγχω. In this context, ἐλέγχω means "to bring a pers[on] to the point of recognizing wrongdoing, *convict, convince* someone of someth[ing]" (BDAG, 315.2).

με. Accusative subject of ἐλέγχει.

περὶ ἁμαρτίας. Reference.

εἰ. Introduces the protasis of a first-class condition.

ἀλήθειαν. Accusative direct object of λέγω. Fronted for emphasis.

λέγω. Pres act ind 1st sg λέγω.

διὰ τί. Causal.

ὑμεῖς. Nominative subject of πιστεύετέ. The personal pronoun is emphatic and contrastive.

οὐ. Negative particle normally used with indicative verbs.

πιστεύετέ. Pres act ind 2nd pl πιστεύω. πιστεύετέ, which has an acute accent on the antepenult, acquired an additional accent, the acute, on the ultima from the enclitic μοι (Smyth §183; Carson 1985, 48).

μοι. Dative complement of πιστεύετέ. The dative indicates the person "to whom one gives credence or whom one believes" (BDAG, 816.1.b).

8:47 ὁ ὢν ἐκ τοῦ θεοῦ τὰ ῥήματα τοῦ θεοῦ ἀκούει· διὰ τοῦτο ὑμεῖς οὐκ ἀκούετε, ὅτι ἐκ τοῦ θεοῦ οὐκ ἐστέ.

ὁ ὤν. Pres act ptc masc nom sg εἰμί (substantival). Nominative subject of ἀκούει. This verse is connected to the previous one by asyndeton. Fronted as a topical frame.

ἐκ τοῦ θεοῦ. Source/origin (BDAG, 296.3.a). When the PP with ἐκ is combined with εἶναι, it means to "belong to someone or someth[ing]" (BDAG, 297.4.a.δ).

τὰ ῥήματα. Accusative direct object of ἀκούει.

τοῦ θεοῦ. Subjective genitive qualifying ῥήματα.

ἀκούει. Pres act ind 3rd sg ἀκούω. The verb stands in final, emphatic position.

διὰ τοῦτο. Causal. The demonstrative pronoun is cataphoric, referring to the ὅτι clause that follows.

ὑμεῖς. Nominative subject of ἀκούετε. The personal pronoun is emphatic and contrastive, underscoring a distinction between Jesus' interlocutors and a person who is from God.

οὐκ. Negative particle normally used with indicative verbs.

ἀκούετε. Pres act ind 2nd pl ἀκούω.

ὅτι. Introduces a causal clause.

ἐκ τοῦ θεοῦ. Source/origin (see above).

οὐκ. Negative particle normally used with indicative verbs.

ἐστέ. Pres act ind 2nd pl εἰμί.

John 8:48-59

⁴⁸The Jews answered and said to him, "Do we not say rightly that you are a Samaritan and have a demon?" ⁴⁹Jesus answered, "I do not have a demon, but I honor my Father, and you dishonor me. ⁵⁰I do not seek my own glory; there is one who seeks and judges. ⁵¹Truly, truly I say to you, if anyone keeps my word, he will never experience death." ⁵²Then the Jews said to him, "Now we know that you have a demon. Abraham and the prophets died, and you say, 'If anyone keeps my word, he will never experience death.' ⁵³You are not greater than our father Abraham who died, are you? And the prophets died. Whom do you make yourself out to be?" ⁵⁴Jesus answered, "If I glorify myself, my glory is nothing. My Father is the one who glorifies me, about whom you say, 'He is our God.' ⁵⁵Yet you do not know him, but I know him. And if I were to say that I do not know him, I would be a liar like you. But I know him, and I keep his word. ⁵⁶Abraham, our father, rejoiced at the prospect of seeing my day; and he saw it and was glad." ⁵⁷Then the Jews said to him, "You are not yet fifty years old, and you have seen Abraham?" ⁵⁸Jesus said to them, "Truly, truly I say to you, before Abraham came into existence, I am." ⁵⁹Then they took up stones to throw at him, but Jesus hid himself and went out of the temple.

8:48 Ἀπεκρίθησαν οἱ Ἰουδαῖοι καὶ εἶπαν αὐτῷ· οὐ καλῶς λέγομεν ἡμεῖς ὅτι Σαμαρίτης εἶ σὺ καὶ δαιμόνιον ἔχεις;

Ἀπεκρίθησαν. Aor mid ind 3rd pl ἀποκρίνομαι. On the voice, see "Deponency" in the Series Introduction. This verse is connected to the previous one by asyndeton.

οἱ Ἰουδαῖοι. Nominative subject of Ἀπεκρίθησαν.

καὶ εἶπαν αὐτῷ. Pleonastic clause under Semitic influence, which functions as a redundant quotative frame (see 1:25 on καὶ εἶπαν αὐτῷ).
καὶ. Coordinating conjunction.
εἶπαν. Aor act ind 3rd pl λέγω.
αὐτῷ. Dative indirect object of εἶπαν.
οὐ. Negative particle that introduces a question that expects an affirmative answer.
καλῶς. Adverb ("well, rightly").
λέγομεν. Pres act ind 1st pl λέγω.
ἡμεῖς. Nominative subject of λέγομεν. ἡμεῖς is contrasted to σὺ.
ὅτι. Introduces the clausal complement (indirect discourse) of λέγομεν.
Σαμαρίτης. Predicate nominative. Fronted for emphasis.
εἶ. Pres act ind 2nd sg εἰμί.
σὺ. Nominative subject of εἶ. The personal pronoun is contrastive (see ἡμεῖς above).
καὶ. Coordinating conjunction.
δαιμόνιον. Accusative direct object of ἔχεις. Fronted for emphasis.
ἔχεις. Pres act ind 2nd sg ἔχω.

8:49 ἀπεκρίθη Ἰησοῦς· ἐγὼ δαιμόνιον οὐκ ἔχω, ἀλλὰ τιμῶ τὸν πατέρα μου, καὶ ὑμεῖς ἀτιμάζετέ με.

ἀπεκρίθη. Aor mid ind 3rd sg ἀποκρίνομαι. On the voice, see "Deponency" in the Series Introduction. This verse is connected to the previous one by asyndeton.
Ἰησοῦς. Nominative subject of ἀπεκρίθη.
ἐγὼ. Nominative subject of ἔχω. Fronted as a topical frame.
δαιμόνιον. Accusative direct object of ἔχω.
οὐκ ... ἀλλὰ. A point/counterpoint set ("not this ... but that") that negates the incorrect assertion ("I have a demon") and replaces it with the correct one ("I honor my Father"). On the function of ἀλλά in a point/counterpoint set, see 1:8.
ἔχω. Pres act ind 1st sg ἔχω. The verb stands in final, emphatic position.
τιμῶ. Pres act ind 1st sg τιμάω.
τὸν πατέρα. Accusative direct object of τιμῶ.
μου. Genitive of relationship qualifying πατέρα.
καὶ. Coordinating conjunction.
ὑμεῖς. Nominative subject of ἀτιμάζετέ. Fronted as a topical frame.
ἀτιμάζετέ. Pres act ind 2nd pl ἀτιμάζω. ἀτιμάζετέ, which has an acute accent on the antepenult, acquired an additional accent, the acute, on the ultima from the enclitic με (Smyth §183; Carson 1985, 48).
με. Accusative direct object of ἀτιμάζετέ.

8:50 ἐγὼ δὲ οὐ ζητῶ τὴν δόξαν μου· ἔστιν ὁ ζητῶν καὶ κρίνων.

ἐγώ. Nominative subject of ζητῶ. Fronted as a topical frame.
δέ. Marker of narrative development.
οὐ. Negative particle normally used with indicative verbs.
ζητῶ. Pres act ind 1st sg ζητέω.
τὴν δόξαν. Accusative direct object of ζητῶ.
μου. Objective genitive qualifying δόξαν.
ἔστιν. Pres act ind 3rd sg εἰμί. The enclitic ἐστιν is accented ἔστιν when it comes at the beginning of a sentence, when it expresses existence, or when it follows ἀλλ', εἰ, καί, οὐκ, ὅτι, or τοῦτ'. The first two conditions are fulfilled here.
ὁ ζητῶν καὶ κρίνων. Nominative subject of ἔστιν. Two substantival participles governed by one article and joined by καί form a TSKS (article-substantive-καί-substantive) construction. In such formulations, according to the Granville Sharp rule, the single article indicates that both participles have the same referent; see 5:24 on ὁ . . . ἀκούων καὶ πιστεύων.
ζητῶν. Pres act ptc masc nom sg ζητέω (substantival).
κρίνων. Pres act ptc masc nom sg κρίνω (substantival).

8:51 ἀμὴν ἀμὴν λέγω ὑμῖν, ἐάν τις τὸν ἐμὸν λόγον τηρήσῃ, θάνατον οὐ μὴ θεωρήσῃ εἰς τὸν αἰῶνα.

ἀμὴν ἀμὴν λέγω ὑμῖν. Metacomment (see 1:51).
ἀμὴν ἀμήν. Asseverative particles that mark the beginning of Jesus' solemn declaration (see 1:51). This verse is connected to the previous one by asyndeton.
λέγω. Pres act ind 1st sg λέγω.
ὑμῖν. Dative indirect object of λέγω.
ἐάν. Introduces the protasis of a third-class condition.
τις. Nominative subject of τηρήσῃ.
τὸν ἐμὸν λόγον. Accusative direct object of τηρήσῃ. The possessive adjective ἐμόν stands in the first attributive position (see 2:10 on τὸν καλὸν οἶνον). Fronted for emphasis.
τηρήσῃ. Aor act subj 3rd sg τηρέω. Subjunctive with ἐάν.
θάνατον. Accusative direct object of θεωρήσῃ. It marks the beginning of the apodosis of a third-class condition.
οὐ μή. Emphatic negation, which is usually followed by the aorist subjunctive.
θεωρήσῃ. Aor act subj 3rd sg θεωρέω. Used with οὐ μή to express emphatic negation. The literal meaning of θεωρέω ("to observe") is here

extended figuratively: "to experience an event or state, normally in negative expressions indicating what one will not experience" (LN 90.79).

εἰς τὸν αἰῶνα. Temporal.

8:52 Εἶπον [οὖν] αὐτῷ οἱ Ἰουδαῖοι· νῦν ἐγνώκαμεν ὅτι δαιμόνιον ἔχεις. Ἀβραὰμ ἀπέθανεν καὶ οἱ προφῆται, καὶ σὺ λέγεις· ἐάν τις τὸν λόγον μου τηρήσῃ, οὐ μὴ γεύσηται θανάτου εἰς τὸν αἰῶνα.

Εἶπον. Aor act ind 3rd pl λέγω.

[οὖν]. Postpositive inferential conjunction and/or transitional particle (see 1:22 and 11:6). It is printed within square brackets because the external evidence for ($\mathfrak{P}^{75}$ D K L N Γ Δ Ψ 070 $f^{1.13}$ 𝔐 et al.) and against ($\mathfrak{P}^{66}$ ℵ B C W Θ 579 et al.) its inclusion is evenly balanced.

αὐτῷ. Dative indirect object of Εἶπον.

οἱ Ἰουδαῖοι. Nominative subject of Εἶπον.

νῦν. Adverb of time.

ἐγνώκαμεν. Prf act ind 1st pl γινώσκω. The perfect tense is semantically marked for prominence and emphasizes the present (νῦν) state of knowledge of the Jews. Yet, as McKay notes, unlike οἶδα, "ἔγνωκα, the perfect tense of γινώσκω, normally seems to differ in having an inbuilt reference to the event of acquisition of knowledge" (1981, 118). Fanning further clarifies that with stative verbs, such as γινώσκω, the perfect tense implies "the act of entrance which led into that state" (139). In this context, Jesus' declaration that a person who keeps his word will not experience death functions as a tipping point, i.e., an "entrance" into the state of "knowledge" of Jesus' interlocutors that he had a demon ("we have come to know and now know").

ὅτι. Introduces the clausal complement (indirect discourse) of ἐγνώκαμεν.

δαιμόνιον. Accusative direct object of ἔχεις. Fronted for emphasis.

ἔχεις. Pres act ind 2nd sg ἔχω.

Ἀβραάμ . . . καὶ οἱ προφῆται. Compound nominative subject of ἀπέθανεν. When the verb stands between the first subject, which is in the singular, and the second subject, which is in the plural, as here, it is in the singular, agreeing with the first (BDF §135).

ἀπέθανεν. Aor act ind 3rd sg ἀποθνήσκω.

καί. Coordinating conjunction linking two clauses that stand in adversative relationship (see 1:5).

σύ. Nominative subject of λέγεις. Fronted for emphasis.

λέγεις. Pres act ind 2nd sing λέγω.

ἐάν. Introduces the protasis of a third-class condition.

τις. Nominative subject of τηρήσῃ.

τὸν λόγον. Accusative direct object of τηρήσῃ. Fronted for emphasis.

μου. Subjective genitive qualifying λόγον ("words that I say") or possessive genitive ("my words").

τηρήσῃ. Aor act subj 3rd sg τηρέω.

οὐ μὴ. Emphatic negation, which is usually followed by the aorist subjunctive.

γεύσηται. Aor mid subj 3rd sg γεύομαι. Used with οὐ μὴ to express emphatic negation. The literal meaning of γεύομαι ("taste, partake of") is here extended figuratively: "to experience someth[ing] cognitively or emotionally" (BDAG, 195.2).

θανάτου. Genitive complement of γεύσηται.

εἰς τὸν αἰῶνα. Temporal.

8:53 μὴ σὺ μείζων εἶ τοῦ πατρὸς ἡμῶν Ἀβραάμ, ὅστις ἀπέθανεν; καὶ οἱ προφῆται ἀπέθανον. τίνα σεαυτὸν ποιεῖς;

μὴ. Negative particle that introduces a question that expects a negative answer. This verse is connected to the previous one by asyndeton.

σὺ. Nominative subject of εἶ. Fronted as a topical frame.

μείζων. Predicate adjective. μείζων is a comparative from μέγας.

εἶ. Pres act ind 2nd sg εἰμί.

τοῦ πατρὸς. Genitive of comparison.

ἡμῶν. Genitive of relationship qualifying πατρὸς.

Ἀβραάμ. Genitive in apposition to πατρὸς.

ὅστις. Nominative subject of ἀπέθανεν. The indefinite relative pronoun (ὅς + τις) is used here "with reference to a definite person where the relative clause expresses the general quality" (BDF §293.2).

ἀπέθανεν. Aor act ind 3rd sg ἀποθνῄσκω.

καὶ. Coordinating conjunction or adverbial (adjunctive; cf. NRSV; GW).

οἱ προφῆται. Nominative subject of ἀπέθανον.

ἀπέθανον. Aor act ind 3rd pl ἀποθνῄσκω.

τίνα. Accusative complement to σεαυτὸν in a double accusative object-complement construction.

σεαυτὸν. Accusative direct object of ποιεῖς in a double accusative object-complement construction.

ποιεῖς. Pres act ind 2nd sg ποιέω.

8:54 ἀπεκρίθη Ἰησοῦς· ἐὰν ἐγὼ δοξάσω ἐμαυτόν, ἡ δόξα μου οὐδέν ἐστιν· ἔστιν ὁ πατήρ μου ὁ δοξάζων με, ὃν ὑμεῖς λέγετε ὅτι θεὸς ἡμῶν ἐστιν,

ἀπεκρίθη. Aor mid ind 3rd sg ἀποκρίνομαι. On the voice, see "Deponency" in the Series Introduction. This verse is connected to the previous one by asyndeton.

Ἰησοῦς. Nominative subject of ἀπεκρίθη.

ἐάν. Introduces the protasis of a third-class condition.

ἐγώ. Nominative subject of δοξάσω. Fronted for emphasis.

δοξάσω. Aor act subj 1st sg δοξάζω. Subjunctive with ἐάν.

ἐμαυτόν. Accusative direct object of δοξάσω.

ἡ δόξα. Nominative subject of ἐστιν.

μου. Subjective and objective genitive qualifying δόξα because Jesus is both the glorifier and the glorified.

οὐδέν. Predicate nominative. Fronted for emphasis.

ἐστιν. Pres act ind 3rd sg εἰμί.

ἔστιν. Pres act ind 3rd sg εἰμί. The enclitic ἐστιν is accented ἔστιν when it comes at the beginning of a sentence, when it expresses existence, or when it follows ἀλλ', εἰ, καί, οὐκ, ὅτι, or τοῦτ'. The first condition is fulfilled here.

ὁ πατήρ. Nominative subject of ἔστιν.

μου. Genitive of relationship qualifying πατήρ.

ὁ δοξάζων. Pres act ptc masc nom sg δοξάζω (substantival). Predicate nominative.

με. Accusative direct object of δοξάζων.

ὅν. Accusative of respect. λέγω + accusative is used to indicate the person about whom someone speaks (BDAG, 588.1.b.β).

ὑμεῖς. Nominative subject of λέγετε. Fronted for emphasis.

λέγετε. Pres act ind 2nd pl λέγω.

ὅτι. ὅτι-*recitativum* that introduces the clausal complement (direct discourse) of λέγετε.

θεός. Predicate nominative.

ἡμῶν. Genitive of subordination qualifying θεός. The variant ὑμῶν (א B* D Ψ 700 1424 it vg^d bo^ms), which makes the clause after ὅτι an indirect discourse, is probably secondary because of the scribal tendency to change direct to indirect discourse rather than vice versa (Metzger, 193).

ἐστιν. Pres act ind 3rd sg εἰμί.

8:55 καὶ οὐκ ἐγνώκατε αὐτόν, ἐγὼ δὲ οἶδα αὐτόν. κἂν εἴπω ὅτι οὐκ οἶδα αὐτόν, ἔσομαι ὅμοιος ὑμῖν ψεύστης· ἀλλ' οἶδα αὐτὸν καὶ τὸν λόγον αὐτοῦ τηρῶ.

καὶ. Coordinating conjunction linking two clauses that stand in adversative relationship (see 1:5).
οὐκ. Negative particle normally used with indicative verbs.
ἐγνώκατε. Prf act ind 2nd pl γινώσκω. On the meaning of the perfect tense, see 8:52 on ἐγνώκαμεν.
αὐτόν. Accusative direct object of ἐγνώκατε.
ἐγὼ. Nominative subject of οἶδα. Fronted for emphasis.
δὲ. Marker of narrative development with a contrastive nuance.
οἶδα. Prf act ind 1st sg οἶδα (see 1:26 on οἴδατε).
αὐτόν. Accusative direct object of οἶδα.
κἂν. Formed by crasis from καὶ ἐάν. καὶ is a coordinating conjunction. ἐάν introduces the protasis of a third-class condition.
εἴπω. Aor act subj 1st sg λέγω. Subjunctive with ἐάν.
ὅτι. Introduces the clausal complement (indirect discourse) of εἴπω.
οὐκ. Negative particle normally used with indicative verbs.
οἶδα. Prf act ind 1st sg οἶδα (see 1:26 on οἴδατε).
αὐτόν. Accusative direct object of οἶδα.
ἔσομαι. Fut mid ind 1st sg εἰμί.
ὅμοιος . . . ψεύστης. Predicate nominative. The adjective ὅμοιος stands in the first (anarthrous) attributive position (see 2:6 on λίθιναι ὑδρίαι).
ὑμῖν. Dative complement of ὅμοιος.
ἀλλ'. Marker of contrast.
οἶδα. Prf act ind 1st sg οἶδα (see 1:26 on οἴδατε).
αὐτὸν. Accusative direct object of οἶδα.
καὶ. Coordinating conjunction.
τὸν λόγον. Accusative direct object of τηρῶ.
αὐτοῦ. Subjective genitive qualifying λόγον.
τηρῶ. Pres act ind 1st sg τηρέω. The verb stands in final, emphatic position.

8:56 Ἀβραὰμ ὁ πατὴρ ὑμῶν ἠγαλλιάσατο ἵνα ἴδῃ τὴν ἡμέραν τὴν ἐμήν, καὶ εἶδεν καὶ ἐχάρη.

Ἀβραὰμ. Nominative subject of ἠγαλλιάσατο. This verse is connected to the previous one by asyndeton.
ὁ πατὴρ. Nominative in apposition to Ἀβραάμ.
ὑμῶν. Genitive of relationship qualifying πατήρ.

ἠγαλλιάσατο. Aor mid ind 3rd sg ἀγαλλιάω.

ἵνα. Introduces a complementary clause that completes the meaning of ἠγαλλιάσατο. In classical Greek, a complementary ἵνα clause is equivalent to a complementary infinitive (Wallace 1996, 476, 664; BDF §392.1a). Zerwick (§410), however, regards this as an epexegetical ἵνα clause that explains the content of the verb ἠγαλλιάσατο, although he recognizes that such ἵνα clauses usually explain a noun or a pronoun. Another problem with Zerwick's classification is that the next clause (καὶ εἶδεν καὶ ἐχάρη) appears to be a mere repetition of the ἵνα clause (Harris 2015, 182). It seems therefore best to view the ἵνα clause as describing Abraham's longing, i.e., his anticipation of Jesus' day, and the next clause as describing the realization of this anticipation.

ἴδῃ. Aor act subj 3rd sg ὁράω. Subjunctive with ἵνα.

τὴν ἡμέραν τὴν ἐμήν. Accusative direct object of ἴδῃ. The possessive adjective ἐμήν stands in the second attributive position (see 1:9 on τὸ φῶς τὸ ἀληθινόν).

καί. Coordinating conjunction.

εἶδεν. Aor act ind 3rd sg ὁράω.

καί. Coordinating conjunction.

ἐχάρη. Aor mid ind 3rd sg χαίρω. "The verb χαίρω occurs in the active in the present tense, in the middle in the future tense, and in the 'passive' in the aorist tense. Historically, the variation may be accounted for by noting that the volitional nature of the future tense frequently led to the use of middle morphology (Cooper, 594; cited by Conrad, 8 n. 18), while -θη- forms (and the less common -η- forms) were originally aorist *intransitive* markers, which eventually came to be used to identify the aorist middle/passive" (Culy 2004, 143–44). On the voice, see also "Deponency" in the Series Introduction.

8:57 εἶπον οὖν οἱ Ἰουδαῖοι πρὸς αὐτόν· πεντήκοντα ἔτη οὔπω ἔχεις καὶ Ἀβραὰμ ἑώρακας;

εἶπον. Aor act ind 3rd pl λέγω.

οὖν. Postpositive inferential conjunction and/or transitional particle (see 1:22 and 11:6).

οἱ Ἰουδαῖοι. Nominative subject of εἶπον.

πρὸς αὐτόν. Locative (motion toward). The PP functions like an indirect object of εἶπον.

πεντήκοντα ἔτη. Accusative indicating extent of time. Lit. "you do not yet have fifty years" = "you are not yet fifty years old." Fronted for emphasis.

οὔπω. Adverb of time ("not yet").

ἔχεις. Pres act ind 2nd sg ἔχω.
καί. Coordinating conjunction.
Ἀβραάμ. Accusative direct object of ἑώρακας. Fronted for emphasis.
ἑώρακας. Prf act ind 2nd sg ὁράω. The variant ἑώρακέν σε ($\mathfrak{P}^{75}$ 070 *ℵ sy^s sa ly pbo) is probably a scribal assimilation to the previous verse, but the reading ἑώρακας not only has a stronger external support but also better conveys the perspective of the Jews because it affirms the superiority of Abraham (Metzger, 193). Porter argues that "[t]his text consciously exploits verbal aspect. The fact that the Jews question whether Jesus could see Abraham, using the Perfect, shows that they do not treat it as having continuing result. They are concerned with the apparent historical discrepancy between Jesus and Abraham in age" (1989, 261).

8:58 εἶπεν αὐτοῖς Ἰησοῦς· ἀμὴν ἀμὴν λέγω ὑμῖν, πρὶν Ἀβραὰμ γενέσθαι ἐγὼ εἰμί.

εἶπεν. Aor act ind 3rd sg λέγω. This verse is connected to the previous one by asyndeton.
αὐτοῖς. Dative indirect object of εἶπεν.
Ἰησοῦς. Nominative subject of εἶπεν.
ἀμὴν ἀμὴν λέγω ὑμῖν. Metacomment (see 1:51).
ἀμὴν ἀμὴν. Asseverative particles that mark the beginning of Jesus' solemn declaration (see 1:51).
λέγω. Pres act ind 1st sg λέγω.
ὑμῖν. Dative indirect object of λέγω.
πρὶν. Subordinating conjunction ("before").
Ἀβραάμ. Accusative subject of the infinitive γενέσθαι.
γενέσθαι. Aor mid inf γίνομαι. Used with πρὶν to denote subsequent time.
ἐγώ. Nominative subject of εἰμί. The personal pronoun is emphatic and contrastive, juxtaposing Jesus to Abraham.
εἰμί. Pres act ind 1st sg εἰμί. The verb stands in final, emphatic position. Although εἰμί refers to the time before Abraham's past, this is not a historical present because, as Wallace (1996, 530–31) explains, (1) there are no undisputed examples of the historical present of the equative verb εἰμί in the NT, and (2) all legitimate examples of the historical present in the NT are in the third person. In this context, ἐγὼ εἰμί functions as an explicit claim to preexistence and an equivalent to divine self-designation (LXX Deut 32:39; Isa 41:4; 43:10, 25; 46:4; 48:12; cf. Exod 3:14).

8:59 Ἦραν οὖν λίθους ἵνα βάλωσιν ἐπ' αὐτόν. Ἰησοῦς δὲ ἐκρύβη καὶ ἐξῆλθεν ἐκ τοῦ ἱεροῦ.

Ἦραν. Aor act ind 3rd pl αἴρω.
οὖν. Postpositive inferential conjunction and/or transitional particle (see 1:22 and 11:6). The inferential function of οὖν is more pronounced here because the attempt to stone Jesus is provoked by Jesus' claim to deity in the previous verse, which the Jews interpret as blasphemy.
λίθους. Accusative direct object of Ἦραν.
ἵνα. Introduces a purpose clause.
βάλωσιν. Aor act subj 3rd pl βάλλω. Subjunctive with ἵνα.
ἐπ' αὐτόν. Locative.
Ἰησοῦς. Nominative subject of ἐκρύβη.
δὲ. Marker of narrative development.
ἐκρύβη. Aor mid ind 3rd sg κρύπτω. On the voice, see "Deponency" in the Series Introduction. Although the verb could be passive, with God as the unexpressed primary agent ("he was hidden"; cf. HCSB; LEB; NLT), it is more likely that this is a θη-middle with a reflexive sense: "he hid himself" (BDF §471.4; NRSV; ASV; CEB; ESV; GNT; NCV; NIV; see 12:36).
καὶ. Coordinating conjunction.
ἐξῆλθεν. Aor act ind 3rd sg ἐξέρχομαι.
ἐκ τοῦ ἱεροῦ. Separation.

John 9:1-7

¹And as he was passing by, he saw a man blind from birth. ²And his disciples asked him, saying, "Rabbi, who sinned, this man or his parents, that he should be born blind?" ³Jesus answered and said, "Neither this man nor his parents sinned, but this happened so that God's works may be displayed in him. ⁴It is necessary for us to do the works of the one who sent me while it is day; night is coming when no one can work. ⁵As long as I am in the world, I am the light of the world." ⁶When he had said these things, he spat on the ground and made clay with the saliva and smeared the clay on his eyes ⁷and said to him, "Go, wash in the pool of Siloam" (which is translated "Sent"). So he went and washed and came back seeing.

9:1 Καὶ παράγων εἶδεν ἄνθρωπον τυφλὸν ἐκ γενετῆς.

Καὶ. Coordinating conjunction.
παράγων. Pres act ptc masc nom sg παράγω (temporal). The present participle describes an action (Jesus' passing by) that occurred concurrently with the action of the main verb.

εἶδεν. Aor act ind 3rd sg ὁράω.
ἄνθρωπον. Accusative direct object of εἶδεν.
τυφλὸν. The adjective stands in the second (anarthrous) predicate position to ἄνθρωπον (noun-adjective), which is common in equative clauses (i.e., "a man was blind"; cf. Wallace 1996, 311).
ἐκ γενετῆς. Temporal.

9:2 καὶ ἠρώτησαν αὐτὸν οἱ μαθηταὶ αὐτοῦ λέγοντες· ῥαββί, τίς ἥμαρτεν, οὗτος ἢ οἱ γονεῖς αὐτοῦ, ἵνα τυφλὸς γεννηθῇ;

καὶ. Coordinating conjunction.
ἠρώτησαν. Aor act ind 3rd pl ἐρωτάω.
αὐτὸν. Accusative direct object of ἠρώτησαν.
οἱ μαθηταὶ. Nominative subject of ἠρώτησαν.
αὐτοῦ. Genitive of relationship qualifying μαθηταὶ.
λέγοντες. Pres act ptc masc nom pl λέγω (pleonastic).
ῥαββί. Vocative of direct address.
τίς. Nominative subject of ἥμαρτεν.
ἥμαρτεν. Aor act ind 3rd sg ἁμαρτάνω.
οὗτος. Nominative subject of an implied ἥμαρτεν. The near-demonstrative οὗτος indicates spatial proximity.
ἢ. Marker of an alternative/disjunctive particle (BDAG, 432.1).
οἱ γονεῖς. Nominative subject of an implied ἥμαρτον.
αὐτοῦ. Genitive of relationship qualifying γονεῖς.
ἵνα. Introduces a result clause (Wallace 1996, 473; BDF §391.5; Caragounis 2004, 196).
τυφλὸς. Predicate adjective. Fronted for emphasis.
γεννηθῇ. Aor pass subj 3rd sg γεννάω. Subjunctive with ἵνα.

9:3 ἀπεκρίθη Ἰησοῦς· οὔτε οὗτος ἥμαρτεν οὔτε οἱ γονεῖς αὐτοῦ, ἀλλ' ἵνα φανερωθῇ τὰ ἔργα τοῦ θεοῦ ἐν αὐτῷ.

ἀπεκρίθη. Aor mid ind 3rd sg ἀποκρίνομαι. On the voice, see "Deponency" in the Series Introduction. This verse is connected to the previous one by asyndeton.
Ἰησοῦς. Nominative subject of ἀπεκρίθη.
οὔτε . . . οὔτε . . . ἀλλ'. A point/counterpoint set. The negative particles ("neither . . . nor") negate two incorrect conclusions ("this man sinned" and "his parents sinned"), while ἀλλ' introduces a corrective ("[this happened] so that God's works might be revealed in him"); see 1:8 on οὐκ . . . ἀλλ'.
οὗτος. Nominative subject of ἥμαρτεν.

ἥμαρτεν. Aor act ind 3rd sg ἁμαρτάνω.
οἱ γονεῖς. Nominative subject of an implied ἥμαρτον.
αὐτοῦ. Genitive of relationship qualifying γονεῖς.
ἵνα. Introduces a purpose clause. The ἵνα clause is elliptical, requiring an introduction, such as "[this happened] in order that . . ." or "[he was born blind] in order that . . ." (BDF §448.7).
φανερωθῇ. Aor pass subj 3rd sg φανερόω. Subjunctive with ἵνα. Neuter plural subjects typically take singular verbs (see 1:28 on ἐγένετο).
τὰ ἔργα. Nominative subject of φανερωθῇ.
τοῦ θεοῦ. Subjective genitive qualifying ἔργα.
ἐν αὐτῷ. Locative.

9:4 ἡμᾶς δεῖ ἐργάζεσθαι τὰ ἔργα τοῦ πέμψαντός με ἕως ἡμέρα ἐστίν· ἔρχεται νὺξ ὅτε οὐδεὶς δύναται ἐργάζεσθαι.

ἡμᾶς. Accusative subject of the infinitive ἐργάζεσθαι. The reading ἡμᾶς ($\mathfrak{P}^{66.75}$ ℵ* B [D] L W 070 sa pbo bo) is more difficult than the variant ἐμέ (¹ℵ A C K N Γ Δ Θ Ψ $f^{1.13}$ 33 565 579 𝔐 lat sy et al.), so that, as Metzger explains, "it is slightly more probable that copyists would have altered ἡμᾶς to ἐμέ than vice versa" (194). This verse is connected to the previous one by asyndeton.
δεῖ. Pres act ind 3rd sg δεῖ.
ἐργάζεσθαι. Pres mid inf ἐργάζομαι (complementary). On the function of the infinitive with δεῖ, see 3:7 on γεννηθῆναι.
τὰ ἔργα. Accusative direct object of ἐργάζεσθαι.
τοῦ πέμψαντός. Aor act ptc masc gen sg πέμπω (substantival). Subjective genitive qualifying ἔργα ("the works that the one who sent me demands"). πέμψαντός, which has an acute accent on the antepenult, acquired an additional accent, the acute, on the ultima from the enclitic με (Smyth §183; Carson 1985, 48). On the use of the participial forms of πέμπω to either identify or describe God in the FG, see τοῦ πέμψαντός in 4:34.
με. Accusative direct object of πέμψαντός.
ἕως. Temporal conjunction denoting contemporaneousness (BDAG, 423.2).
ἡμέρα. Nominative subject of ἐστίν.
ἐστίν. Pres act ind 3rd sg εἰμί.
ἔρχεται. Pres mid ind 3rd sg ἔρχομαι. This clause is connected to the preceding one by asyndeton.
νὺξ. Nominative subject of ἔρχεται.
ὅτε. Introduces a temporal clause.

οὐδεὶς. Nominative subject of δύναται.
δύναται. Pres mid ind 3rd sg δύναμαι.
ἐργάζεσθαι. Pres mid inf ἐργάζομαι (complementary).

9:5 ὅταν ἐν τῷ κόσμῳ ὦ, φῶς εἰμι τοῦ κόσμου.

ὅταν. Introduces an indefinite temporal clause that expresses duration ("as long as / while I am in the world"; cf. Robertson, 972), rather than specific circumstances, such as "as often as I am in the world" or "when I am in the world" (Barrett, 357). Fronted as a temporal frame. This verse is connected to the previous one by asyndeton.

ἐν τῷ κόσμῳ. Locative. On the portrayal of the world in the FG, see 1:10 on ἐν τῷ κόσμῳ.

ὦ. Pres act subj 1st sg εἰμί. Subjunctive with ὅταν.

φῶς. Predicate nominative. Fronted for emphasis. Although φῶς is anarthrous, it is probably definite because, according to Colwell's rule, the definiteness of a preverbal anarthrous predicate nominative cannot be excluded. In 8:12 (ἐγώ εἰμι τὸ φῶς τοῦ κόσμου) φῶς is articular because it follows the verb.

εἰμι. Pres act ind 1st sg εἰμί. The subject of the verb ("I") is grammaticalized in the verb form.

τοῦ κόσμου. Objective genitive qualifying φῶς ("the light that illuminates the world" = "I give light to the world"). The head noun and its modifier (φῶς . . . τοῦ κόσμου) are separated by the main verb.

9:6 Ταῦτα εἰπὼν ἔπτυσεν χαμαὶ καὶ ἐποίησεν πηλὸν ἐκ τοῦ πτύσματος καὶ ἐπέχρισεν αὐτοῦ τὸν πηλὸν ἐπὶ τοὺς ὀφθαλμοὺς

Ταῦτα. Accusative direct object of εἰπών. This verse is connected to the previous one by asyndeton.

εἰπών. Aor act ptc masc nom sg λέγω (temporal). On participles that precede the main verb, see ἐμβλέψας in 1:36.

ἔπτυσεν. Aor act ind 3rd sg πτύω.

χαμαὶ. Adverb ("to/on the ground" [BDAG, 1076.2]).

καὶ. Coordinating conjunction.

ἐποίησεν. Aor act ind 3rd sg ποιέω.

πηλὸν. Accusative direct object of ἐποίησεν.

ἐκ τοῦ πτύσματος. Means or source, denoting "the material of which someth[ing] is made" (BDAG, 297.3.h). πτύσμα ("saliva, spittle") is a NT *hapax legomenon*.

καὶ. Coordinating conjunction.

ἐπέχρισεν. Aor act ind 3rd sg ἐπιχρίω. The verb means "to smear or rub on substances such as salve or oil—'to put on, to smear on, to rub on, to anoint'" (LN 47.15).

αὐτοῦ. Possessive genitive that modifies ὀφθαλμοὺς ("his eyes"). αὐτοῦ refers to the man born blind introduced in 9:1 and discussed in 9:1-2, and not to Jesus (*pace* Harris 2015, 186, who suggests that αὐτοῦ may modify τὸν πηλὸν). In the formulation αὐτοῦ . . . τοὺς ὀφθαλμοὺς, the genitive is separated from its head noun by the direct object of the verb and the prepositional phrase. Such a separation of closely related elements gives greater emphasis to the word—here αὐτοῦ—that is "torn out of its natural context and made more independent" (BDF §473).

τὸν πηλὸν. Accusative direct object of ἐπέχρισεν. The article is anaphoric, referring to πηλὸν mentioned earlier.

ἐπὶ τοὺς ὀφθαλμοὺς. Locative.

9:7 καὶ εἶπεν αὐτῷ· ὕπαγε νίψαι εἰς τὴν κολυμβήθραν τοῦ Σιλωάμ (ὃ ἑρμηνεύεται ἀπεσταλμένος). ἀπῆλθεν οὖν καὶ ἐνίψατο καὶ ἦλθεν βλέπων.

καὶ. Coordinating conjunction.

εἶπεν. Aor act ind 3rd sg λέγω.

αὐτῷ. Dative indirect object of εἶπεν.

ὕπαγε. Pres act impv 2nd sg ὑπάγω.

νίψαι. Aor mid impv 2nd sg νίπτω. This imperative is connected to the previous one by asyndeton (BDF §461.1). See 4:16 for a similar succession of two imperatives.

εἰς τὴν κολυμβήθραν. Locative. If the PP goes with νίψαι, εἰς stands for ἐν (BDF §205). If the PP goes with ὕπαγε, εἰς has its usual sense ("go to the pool . . . and wash"; see 9:11).

τοῦ Σιλωάμ. Epexegetical genitive explaining κολυμβήθραν ("the pool which is called Siloam"). The indeclinable noun Σιλωάμ is a Greek transliteration of the Hebrew term שִׁלֹחַ.

ὃ ἑρμηνεύεται ἀπεσταλμένος. Parenthetical editorial comment that interrupts the plot of the narrative to explain the meaning of the name of the pool "Siloam." For similar parenthetical comments, see 1:38 and 1:41.

ὃ. Nominative subject of ἑρμηνεύεται. The relative pronoun refers to τοῦ Σιλωάμ.

ἑρμηνεύεται. Pres pass ind 3rd sg ἑρμηνεύω.

ἀπεσταλμένος. Prf pass ptc masc nom sg ἀποστέλλω (attributive). Nominative complement to ὃ in a double nominative subject-complement construction (see 1:41 on χριστός).

ἀπῆλθεν. Aor act ind 3rd sg ἀπέρχομαι.

οὖν. Postpositive inferential conjunction and/or transitional particle (see 1:22 and 11:6).

καί. Coordinating conjunction.

ἐνίψατο. Aor mid ind 3rd sg νίπτω.

καί. Coordinating conjunction.

ἦλθεν. Aor act ind 3rd sg ἔρχομαι.

βλέπων. Pres act ptc masc nom sg βλέπω (manner).

John 9:8-12

⁸Then the neighbors and those who had seen him before, that he was a beggar, were saying, "Is this not the one who used to sit and beg?" ⁹Some were saying, "This is he." Others were saying, "No, but he is like him." He kept saying, "I am he." ¹⁰So they were saying to him, "How then were your eyes opened?" ¹¹He answered, "The man called Jesus made clay and smeared my eyes and said to me, 'Go to Siloam and wash.' So I went and washed and gained my sight." ¹²And they said to him, "Where is he?" He said, "I do not know."

9:8 Οἱ οὖν γείτονες καὶ οἱ θεωροῦντες αὐτὸν τὸ πρότερον ὅτι προσαίτης ἦν ἔλεγον· οὐχ οὗτός ἐστιν ὁ καθήμενος καὶ προσαιτῶν;

Οἱ . . . γείτονες καὶ οἱ θεωροῦντες. Compound nominative subject of ἔλεγον.

οἱ θεωροῦντες. Pres act ptc masc nom pl θεωρέω (substantival). Since the ὅτι clause describes the situation that transpired before the action of the main clause (see ἦν below), the present participle "refers to the same prepast (pluperf[ect]) time that is expressed in the dependent clause by προσαίτης ἦν" (BDF §330).

οὖν. Postpositive inferential conjunction and/or transitional particle (see 1:22 and 11:6).

αὐτὸν. Accusative direct object of θεωροῦντες. αὐτὸν functions as a pronominal prolepsis because it anticipates the subject of the ὅτι clause that follows (Zerwick §206); see 2:23 on αὐτοῦ.

τὸ πρότερον. The article functions as a nominalizer, changing the adverb πρότερον into the accusative indicating extent of time ("during former time, before"); see 6:62.

ὅτι. Introduces the clausal complement (indirect discourse) of θεωροῦντες (most English translations). Two other possibilities are to regard ὅτι as standing for ὅτε ("those who had seen him before when he was a beggar"; cf. Zerwick §429) or introducing a causal clause (LEB: "those who saw him previously [because he was a beggar]").

προσαίτης. Predicate nominative. Fronted for emphasis. προσαίτης denotes "one who asks for charity—'beggar'" (LN 33.174).

ἦν. Impf act ind 3rd sg εἰμί. According to BDF (§330), "The imperfect after verbs of perception (and belief) is not in itself temporally relative. Since, however, the present expressed time contemporary with that of the verb of perception . . . , the imperfect was virtually limited to those cases where a time previous to the time of perception was to be indicated."

ἔλεγον. Impf act ind 3rd pl λέγω. All of the verb forms of λέγω in 9:8-10 are imperfects, calling attention to the ongoing character of the conversation among the neighbors, bystanders, and the man born blind.

οὐχ. Negative particle that introduces a question that expects an affirmative answer.

οὗτός. Nominative subject of ἐστιν. Fronted for emphasis. οὗτός, which has a circumflex accent on the penult, acquired an additional accent, the acute, on the ultima from the enclitic ἐστιν (Smyth §183; Carson 1985, 48).

ἐστιν. Pres act ind 3rd sg εἰμί.

ὁ καθήμενος καὶ προσαιτῶν. Predicate nominative. Two substantival participles governed by one article and joined by καί form a TSKS (article-substantive-καί-substantive) construction. In such formulations, according to the Granville Sharp rule, the single article indicates that both participles have the same referent; see 5:24 on ὁ . . . ἀκούων καὶ πιστεύων.

καθήμενος. Pres mid ptc masc nom sg κάθημαι (substantival).

προσαιτῶν. Pres act ptc masc nom sg προσαιτέω (substantival).

9:9 ἄλλοι ἔλεγον ὅτι οὗτός ἐστιν, ἄλλοι ἔλεγον· οὐχί, ἀλλ' ὅμοιος αὐτῷ ἐστιν. ἐκεῖνος ἔλεγεν ὅτι ἐγώ εἰμι.

ἄλλοι. Nominative subject of ἔλεγον. This verse is connected to the previous one by asyndeton.

ἔλεγον. Impf act ind 3rd pl λέγω (see 9:8).

ὅτι. ὅτι-*recitativum* that introduces the clausal complement (direct discourse) of ἔλεγον.

οὗτός. Nominative subject of ἐστιν. Fronted for emphasis. οὗτός, which has a circumflex accent on the penult, acquired an additional accent, the acute, on the ultima from the enclitic ἐστιν (Smyth §183; Carson 1985, 48).

ἐστιν. Pres act ind 3rd sg εἰμί. The implied predicate nominative is ὁ καθήμενος καὶ προσαιτῶν from the previous verse ("this is the one who used to sit and beg").

ἄλλοι. Nominative subject of ἔλεγον.

ἔλεγον. Impf act ind 3rd pl λέγω (see 9:8).

οὐχί. A negative reply ("no, by no means"), which is usually followed by ἀλλά (BDAG, 742.2); cf. Luke 1:60; 12:51; 13:3, 5; 16:30; Rom 3:27.

ἀλλ᾽. Marker of contrast.

ὅμοιος. Predicate adjective. Fronted for emphasis.

αὐτῷ. Dative complement of ὅμοιος.

ἐστιν. Pres act ind 3rd sg εἰμί.

ἐκεῖνος. Nominative subject of ἔλεγεν. The demonstrative pronoun refers to the man born blind, acting as a third-person personal pronoun with a simple anaphoric force (Wallace 1996, 328–29; BDF §291.6).

ἔλεγεν. Impf act ind 3rd sg λέγω (see 9:8).

ὅτι. ὅτι-*recitativum* that introduces the clausal complement (direct discourse) of ἔλεγεν.

ἐγώ. Nominative subject of εἰμι. The personal pronoun has an identifying function, confirming the correct and rejecting the incorrect identities proposed in the deliberations of his neighbors and acquaintances.

εἰμι. Pres act ind 1st sg εἰμί. The implied predicate nominative is ὁ καθήμενος καὶ προσαιτῶν from the previous verse ("I am the one who used to sit and beg").

9:10 ἔλεγον οὖν αὐτῷ· πῶς [οὖν] ἠνεῴχθησάν σου οἱ ὀφθαλμοί;

ἔλεγον. Impf act ind 3rd pl λέγω (see 9:8).

οὖν. Postpositive inferential conjunction and/or transitional particle (see 1:22 and 11:6).

αὐτῷ. Dative indirect object of ἔλεγον.

πῶς. Interrogative particle.

[οὖν]. Postpositive inferential conjunction and/or transitional particle (see 1:22 and 11:6). It is printed within square brackets because the external evidence for ($\mathfrak{P}^{66}$ ℵ C D L N Θ Ψ 070 et al.) and against ($\mathfrak{P}^{75}$ A B K W Γ Δ $f^{1.13}$ 33 565 𝔐 et al.) its inclusion is evenly balanced.

ἠνεῴχθησάν. Aor pass ind 3rd pl ἀνοίγω. Wallace suggests that the ultimate agent of the verb is suppressed for rhetorical effect—to draw the reader into the story (1996, 437 n. 96). ἠνεῴχθησάν, which has an acute accent on the antepenult, acquired an additional accent, the acute, on the ultima from the enclitic σου (Smyth §183; Carson 1985, 48).

σου. Possessive genitive qualifying ὀφθαλμοί. The preposed pronoun is thematically salient (Levinsohn 2000, 64).

οἱ ὀφθαλμοί. Nominative subject of ἠνεῴχθησάν.

9:11 ἀπεκρίθη ἐκεῖνος· ὁ ἄνθρωπος ὁ λεγόμενος Ἰησοῦς πηλὸν ἐποίησεν καὶ ἐπέχρισέν μου τοὺς ὀφθαλμοὺς καὶ εἶπέν μοι ὅτι ὕπαγε εἰς τὸν Σιλωὰμ καὶ νίψαι· ἀπελθὼν οὖν καὶ νιψάμενος ἀνέβλεψα.

ἀπεκρίθη. Aor mid ind 3rd sg ἀποκρίνομαι. On the voice, see "Deponency" in the Series Introduction. This verse is connected to the previous one by asyndeton.

ἐκεῖνος. Nominative subject of ἀπεκρίθη. The demonstrative pronoun refers to the man born blind, acting as a third-person personal pronoun with a simple anaphoric force (Wallace 1996, 328–29; BDF §291.6).

ὁ ἄνθρωπος. Nominative subject of ἐποίησεν.

ὁ λεγόμενος. Pres pass ptc masc nom sg λέγω (attributive). The participle modifies ὁ ἄνθρωπος, standing in the second attributive position (see 1:29 on ὁ αἴρων).

Ἰησοῦς. Nominative complement to ὁ ἄνθρωπος in a double nominative subject-complement construction (see 1:41 on χριστός).

πηλὸν. Accusative direct object of ἐποίησεν. Fronted for emphasis.

ἐποίησεν. Aor act ind 3rd sg ποιέω.

καὶ. Coordinating conjunction.

ἐπέχρισέν. Aor act ind 3rd sg ἐπιχρίω. ἐπέχρισέν, which has an acute accent on the antepenult, acquired an additional accent, the acute, on the ultima from the enclitic μου (Smyth §183; Carson 1985, 48).

μου. Possessive genitive qualifying ὀφθαλμούς. The preposed pronoun is thematically salient (Levinsohn 2000, 64).

τοὺς ὀφθαλμοὺς. Accusative direct object of ἐπέχρισέν.

καὶ. Coordinating conjunction.

εἶπέν. Aor act ind 3rd sg λέγω. εἶπέν, which has a circumflex accent on the penult, acquired an additional accent, the acute, on the ultima from the enclitic μοι (Smyth §183; Carson 1985, 48).

μοι. Dative indirect object of εἶπέν.

ὅτι. ὅτι-*recitativum* that introduces the clausal complement (direct discourse) of εἶπέν.

ὕπαγε. Pres act impv 2nd sg ὑπάγω.

εἰς τὸν Σιλωάμ. Locative.

καὶ. Coordinating conjunction.

νίψαι. Aor mid impv 2nd sg νίπτω. Like in 9:7, this imperative is connected to the previous one by asyndeton (BDF §461.1). See 4:16 for a similar succession of two imperatives.

ἀπελθών. Aor act ptc masc nom sg ἀπέρχομαι (attendant circumstance or temporal). On participles that precede the main verb, see ἐμβλέψας in 1:36.

οὖν. Postpositive inferential conjunction and/or transitional particle (see 1:22 and 11:6).

καί. Coordinating conjunction.

νιψάμενος. Aor mid ptc masc nom sg νίπτω (attendant circumstance or temporal). On participles that precede the main verb, see ἐμβλέψας in 1:36.

ἀνέβλεψα. Aor act ind 1st sg ἀναβλέπω. In this context, the prefix ἀνά in ἀναβλέπω ("regain sight, become able to see again") has completely lost its force (BDAG, 59.2.a.β).

9:12 καὶ εἶπαν αὐτῷ· ποῦ ἐστιν ἐκεῖνος; λέγει· οὐκ οἶδα.

καί. Coordinating conjunction.

εἶπαν. Aor act ind 3rd pl λέγω.

αὐτῷ. Dative indirect object of εἶπαν.

ποῦ. Interrogative adverb of place.

ἐστιν. Pres act ind 3rd sg εἰμί.

ἐκεῖνος. Nominative subject of ἐστιν. The demonstrative pronoun refers to Jesus, acting as a third-person personal pronoun with a simple anaphoric force (Wallace 1996, 328–29).

λέγει. Pres act ind 3rd sg λέγω. The historical present gives prominence to the man's response to his interlocutors (see 1:15 on μαρτυρεῖ).

οὐκ. Negative particle normally used with indicative verbs.

οἶδα. Prf act ind 1st sg οἶδα (see 1:26 on οἴδατε).

John 9:13-23

[13]They brought him—the man who had formerly been blind—to the Pharisees. [14]Now the day on which Jesus made the clay and opened his eyes was the Sabbath. [15]Then again the Pharisees too began to ask him how he gained his sight. He said to them, "He put clay on my eyes, and I washed, and I see." [16]So some of the Pharisees were saying, "This man is not from God because he does not keep the Sabbath." But others were saying, "How can a sinful man do such signs?" And there was a division among them. [17]So they said to the blind man again, "What do you say about him, since he opened your eyes?" He said, "He is a prophet." [18]So the Jews did not believe concerning him that he had been blind and had gained his sight until they called the parents of him—the man who had gained his sight. [19]And they asked them, saying, "Is this your son,

about whom you say that he was born blind? How then does he now see?" ²⁰So his parents answered and said, "We know that this is our son and that he was born blind. ²¹But how he now sees we do not know, or who opened his eyes we do not know. Ask him! He is of age; he will speak for himself." ²²His parents said these things because they feared the Jews; for the Jews had already agreed that if anyone should confess him as Messiah, he would be expelled from the synagogue. ²³This is why his parents said, "He is of age; ask him."

9:13 Ἄγουσιν αὐτὸν πρὸς τοὺς Φαρισαίους τόν ποτε τυφλόν.

Ἄγουσιν. Pres act ind 3rd pl ἄγω. The historical present marks the narrative transition to a new scene and calls attention to the appearance of the new group of characters—the Pharisees (Battle, 128). This verse is connected to the previous one by asyndeton.

αὐτὸν. Accusative direct object of Ἄγουσιν.

πρὸς τοὺς Φαρισαίους. Locative (motion toward).

τόν . . . τυφλόν. Accusative in apposition to αὐτὸν, which receives emphasis through right-dislocation.

ποτε. Enclitic particle involving generalization of time ("once, formerly"; BDAG, 856.1). Placed between the article and the noun, it has attributive function: lit. "the one formerly blind" = "the man who had formerly been blind."

9:14 ἦν δὲ σάββατον ἐν ᾗ ἡμέρᾳ τὸν πηλὸν ἐποίησεν ὁ Ἰησοῦς καὶ ἀνέῳξεν αὐτοῦ τοὺς ὀφθαλμούς.

ἦν. Impf act ind 3rd sg εἰμί. On the function of the imperfect in the FG, see 1:39 on ἦν.

δὲ. Marker of narrative development.

σάββατον. Predicate nominative. The implied subject of ἦν is ἡ ἡμέρα, but because it has been transferred to the relative clause, it is in the dative rather than in the nominative (see ἐν ᾗ ἡμέρᾳ below).

ἐν ᾗ ἡμέρᾳ. Temporal. The antecedent (ἡμέρα) of the relative pronoun (ᾗ) is transferred to the relative clause (Zerwick §18): ἐν ᾗ ἡμέρᾳ ("on which day") = ἡ ἡμέρα ἐν ᾗ ("the day, on which").

τὸν πηλὸν. Accusative direct object of ἐποίησεν. The article is anaphoric, referring to πηλὸν mentioned earlier in the narrative. Fronted for emphasis.

ἐποίησεν. Aor act ind 3rd sg ποιέω.

ὁ Ἰησοῦς. Nominative subject of ἐποίησεν.

καὶ. Coordinating conjunction.

ἀνέῳξεν. Aor act ind 3rd sg ἀνοίγω.
αὐτοῦ. Possessive genitive qualifying ὀφθαλμούς. The preposed pronoun is thematically salient (Levinsohn 2000, 64).
τοὺς ὀφθαλμούς. Accusative direct object of ἀνέῳξεν.

9:15 πάλιν οὖν ἠρώτων αὐτὸν καὶ οἱ Φαρισαῖοι πῶς ἀνέβλεψεν. ὁ δὲ εἶπεν αὐτοῖς· πηλὸν ἐπέθηκέν μου ἐπὶ τοὺς ὀφθαλμοὺς καὶ ἐνιψάμην καὶ βλέπω.

πάλιν. Adverb "pert[aining] to repetition in the same (or similar) manner" (BDAG, 752.2).
οὖν. Postpositive inferential conjunction and/or transitional particle (see 1:22 and 11:6).
ἠρώτων. Impf act ind 3rd pl ἐρωτάω. The imperfective aspect of the verb form portrays the interrogation of the formerly blind man as an ongoing process.
αὐτόν. Accusative direct object of ἠρώτων.
καί. Adverbial use (adjunctive).
οἱ Φαρισαῖοι. Nominative subject of ἠρώτων.
πῶς. Interrogative particle.
ἀνέβλεψεν. Aor act ind 3rd sg ἀναβλέπω. On the meaning of ἀναβλέπω in this context, see 9:11.
ὁ δέ. A construction used in narrative literature to indicate the change of the speaker in a dialogue. The nominative article stands in place of a third-person singular personal pronoun and functions as the subject of εἶπεν.
εἶπεν. Aor act ind 3rd sg λέγω.
αὐτοῖς. Dative indirect object of εἶπεν.
πηλόν. Accusative direct object of ἐπέθηκέν. Fronted for emphasis.
ἐπέθηκέν. Aor act ind 3rd sg ἐπιτίθημι. ἐπέθηκέν, which has an acute accent on the antepenult, acquired an additional accent, the acute, on the ultima from the enclitic μου (Smyth §183; Carson 1985, 48).
μου. Possessive genitive qualifying ὀφθαλμοὺς ("my eyes"). On the rhetorical effect of the separation of the genitive modifier from its head noun, see 9:6 on αὐτοῦ.
ἐπὶ τοὺς ὀφθαλμούς. Locative.
καί. Coordinating conjunction.
ἐνιψάμην. Aor mid ind 1st sg νίπτω.
καί. Coordinating conjunction.
βλέπω. Pres act ind 1st sg βλέπω.

9:16 ἔλεγον οὖν ἐκ τῶν Φαρισαίων τινές· οὐκ ἔστιν οὗτος παρὰ θεοῦ ὁ ἄνθρωπος, ὅτι τὸ σάββατον οὐ τηρεῖ. ἄλλοι [δὲ] ἔλεγον· πῶς δύναται ἄνθρωπος ἁμαρτωλὸς τοιαῦτα σημεῖα ποιεῖν; καὶ σχίσμα ἦν ἐν αὐτοῖς.

ἔλεγον. Impf act ind 3rd pl λέγω (see 9:8).

οὖν. Postpositive inferential conjunction and/or transitional particle (see 1:22 and 11:6).

ἐκ τῶν Φαρισαίων. Replaces the partitive genitive.

τινές. Nominative subject of ἔλεγον.

οὐκ. Negative particle normally used with indicative verbs.

ἔστιν. Pres act ind 3rd sg εἰμί. The enclitic ἐστιν is accented ἔστιν when it comes at the beginning of a sentence, when it expresses existence, or when it follows ἀλλ᾽, εἰ, καί, οὐκ, ὅτι, or τοῦτ᾽. The third condition is fulfilled here.

οὗτος . . . ὁ ἄνθρωπος. Nominative subject of ἔστιν. οὗτος and ὁ ἄνθρωπος belong together even though they are separated by the PP παρὰ θεοῦ. This unusual word order may indicate that the emphasis falls on οὗτος, which is "torn out of its natural context and made more independent" (BDF §473).

παρὰ θεοῦ. Source.

ὅτι. Introduces a causal clause.

τὸ σάββατον. Accusative direct object of τηρεῖ.

οὐ. Negative particle normally used with indicative verbs.

τηρεῖ. Pres act ind 3rd sg τηρέω.

ἄλλοι. Nominative subject of ἔλεγον.

[δὲ]. Marker of narrative development. It is printed within square brackets because the external evidence for (ℵ B D W 070 $f^{1.13}$ et al.) and against ($\mathfrak{P}^{66.75}$ A K L N Γ Δ Θ Ψ 𝔐 et al.) its presence in the text is evenly balanced.

ἔλεγον. Impf act ind 3rd pl λέγω (see 9:8).

πῶς. Interrogative particle.

δύναται. Pres mid ind 3rd sg δύναμαι.

ἄνθρωπος ἁμαρτωλὸς. Nominative subject of δύναται. The adjective ἁμαρτωλὸς ("sinful") stands in the fourth attributive position (see 3:15 on ζωὴν αἰώνιον).

τοιαῦτα σημεῖα. Accusative direct object of ποιεῖν. Fronted for emphasis. The correlative adjective τοιαῦτα ("of such a kind") stands in the first (anarthrous) attributive position (see 2:6 on λίθιναι ὑδρίαι). The use of the term σημεῖα for Jesus' miracles is one of the distinctive features of the FG (see 2:11, 23; 3:2; 4:48, 54; 6:2, 14, 26; 7:31; 11:47; 12:18, 37; 20:30; cf. Barrett, 75–78; Keener, 1:272–79; Thompson, 65–68).

ποιεῖν. Pres act inf ποιέω (complementary).
καί. Coordinating conjunction.
σχίσμα. Nominative subject of ἦν.
ἦν. Impf act ind 3rd sg εἰμί. On the function of the imperfect in the FG, see 1:39 on ἦν.
ἐν αὐτοῖς. Locative.

9:17 λέγουσιν οὖν τῷ τυφλῷ πάλιν· τί σὺ λέγεις περὶ αὐτοῦ, ὅτι ἠνέῳξέν σου τοὺς ὀφθαλμούς; ὁ δὲ εἶπεν ὅτι προφήτης ἐστίν.

λέγουσιν. Pres act ind 3rd pl λέγω. The historical present gives prominence to the Pharisees' question that follows (see 1:15 on μαρτυρεῖ).

οὖν. Postpositive inferential conjunction and/or transitional particle (see 1:22 and 11:6).

τῷ τυφλῷ. Dative indirect object of λέγουσιν.

πάλιν. Adverb "pert[aining] to repetition in the same (or similar) manner" (BDAG, 752.2).

τί. Interrogative pronoun functioning as the accusative direct object of λέγεις.

σύ. Nominative subject of λέγεις. The personal pronoun is emphatic, calling attention to the opinion of the formerly blind man vis-à-vis Jesus' identity.

λέγεις. Pres act ind 2nd sg λέγω.

περὶ αὐτοῦ. Reference. The personal pronoun refers to Jesus.

ὅτι. Introduces a causal clause.

ἠνέῳξέν. Aor act ind 3rd sg ἀνοίγω. ἠνέῳξέν, which has an acute accent on the antepenult, acquired an additional accent, the acute, on the ultima from the enclitic σου (Smyth §183; Carson 1985, 48).

σου. Possessive genitive modifying ὀφθαλμούς. Fronted for emphasis.

τοὺς ὀφθαλμούς. Accusative direct object of ἠνέῳξέν.

ὁ δέ. A construction used in narrative literature to indicate the change of the speaker in a dialogue. The nominative article stands in place of a third-person singular personal pronoun and functions as the subject of εἶπεν.

εἶπεν. Aor act ind 3rd sg λέγω.

ὅτι. ὅτι-*recitativum* that introduces the clausal complement (direct discourse) of εἶπεν.

προφήτης. Predicate nominative. Fronted for emphasis. Most English translations presume that the anarthrous προφήτης is indefinite, but this conclusion cannot be derived from a comparison with the articular προφήτης in 6:14 and 7:40 (*pace* Barrett, 360) because in these verses the predicate nominatives follow the verb, which is not the case here. A comparison with the preverbal anarthrous προφήτης in 4:19 may be more helpful because, even if according to Colwell's rule the definiteness of a preverbal anarthrous predicate nominative cannot be excluded a priori (see 1:1 on θεὸς), the context indicates that the understanding of Jesus' identity by the man who used to be blind is still inarticulate.

ἐστίν. Pres act ind 3rd sg εἰμί.

9:18 Οὐκ ἐπίστευσαν οὖν οἱ Ἰουδαῖοι περὶ αὐτοῦ ὅτι ἦν τυφλὸς καὶ ἀνέβλεψεν ἕως ὅτου ἐφώνησαν τοὺς γονεῖς αὐτοῦ τοῦ ἀναβλέψαντος

Οὐκ. Negative particle normally used with indicative verbs.

ἐπίστευσαν. Aor act ind 3rd pl πιστεύω.

οὖν. Postpositive inferential conjunction and/or transitional particle (see 1:22 and 11:6).

οἱ Ἰουδαῖοι. Nominative subject of ἐπίστευσαν.

περὶ αὐτοῦ. Reference. The personal pronoun refers to the man who was born blind.

ὅτι. Introduces the clausal complement (indirect discourse) of ἐπίστευσαν.

ἦν. Impf act ind 3rd sg εἰμί. The imperfect tense is retained from the corresponding direct discourse (see 1:39 on μένει).

τυφλὸς. Predicate adjective.

καὶ. Coordinating conjunction.

ἀνέβλεψεν. Aor act ind 3rd sg ἀναβλέπω. On the meaning of ἀναβλέπω in this context, see 9:11. The aorist tense is retained from the corresponding direct discourse (see 1:39 on μένει).

ἕως ὅτου. Temporal (BDAG, 423.1.b.ɔ). ἕως serves as an improper preposition (see 1:3 on χωρὶς αὐτοῦ). ὅτου is the neuter genitive of the indefinite relative pronoun ὅστις. ἕως ὅτου is an abbreviated version of the formulation ἕως τοῦ χρόνου ᾧτινι ("until the time at which"), in which the relative pronoun is attracted to the case of its omitted antecedent (Harris 2015, 188). This PP presumes that the situation changed afterward, i.e., that the Jews, after hearing from the man's parents, came to believe that he had been blind and received his sight from Jesus.

ἐφώνησαν. Aor act ind 3rd pl φωνέω.

τοὺς γονεῖς. Accusative direct object of ἐφώνησαν.

αὐτοῦ. Genitive of relationship qualifying γονεῖς. Moule considers the possibility that this could be an emphatic use of αὐτοῦ with τοῦ ἀναβλέψαντος ("the man himself who had gained his sight"), but he admits that "the αὐτοῦ is strange: the context seems to require *the parents themselves* . . . (τοὺς γονεῖς αὐτούς), not *the parents of the man himself*" (121–22).

τοῦ ἀναβλέψαντος. Aor act ptc masc gen sg ἀναβλέπω (substantival). Genitive in apposition to αὐτοῦ.

9:19 καὶ ἠρώτησαν αὐτοὺς λέγοντες· οὗτός ἐστιν ὁ υἱὸς ὑμῶν, ὃν ὑμεῖς λέγετε ὅτι τυφλὸς ἐγεννήθη; πῶς οὖν βλέπει ἄρτι;

καὶ. Coordinating conjunction.
ἠρώτησαν. Aor act ind 3rd pl ἐρωτάω.
αὐτοὺς. Accusative direct object of ἠρώτησαν.
λέγοντες. Pres act ptc masc nom pl λέγω (pleonastic).
οὗτός. Nominative subject of ἐστιν. Fronted for emphasis. οὗτός, which has a circumflex accent on the penult, acquired an additional accent, the acute, on the ultima from the enclitic ἐστιν (Smyth §183; Carson 1985, 48).
ἐστιν. Pres act ind 3rd sg εἰμί.
ὁ υἱὸς. Predicate nominative.
ὑμῶν. Genitive of relationship qualifying υἱός.
ὃν. Accusative of respect. λέγω + accusative is used to indicate the person about whom someone speaks (BDAG, 588.1.b.β). The antecedent of the relative pronoun is ὁ υἱός.
ὑμεῖς. Nominative subject of λέγετε. Fronted for emphasis.
λέγετε. Pres act ind 2nd pl λέγω.
ὅτι. Introduces the clausal complement (indirect discourse) of λέγετε.
τυφλὸς. Predicate adjective. Fronted for emphasis.
ἐγεννήθη. Aor pass ind 3rd sg γεννάω.
πῶς. Interrogative particle.
οὖν. Postpositive inferential conjunction and/or transitional particle (see 1:22 and 11:6).
βλέπει. Pres act ind 3rd sg βλέπω.
ἄρτι. Adverb of time.

9:20 ἀπεκρίθησαν οὖν οἱ γονεῖς αὐτοῦ καὶ εἶπαν· οἴδαμεν ὅτι οὗτός ἐστιν ὁ υἱὸς ἡμῶν καὶ ὅτι τυφλὸς ἐγεννήθη·

ἀπεκρίθησαν. Aor mid ind 3rd pl ἀποκρίνομαι. On the voice, see "Deponency" in the Series Introduction.
οὖν. Postpositive inferential conjunction and/or transitional particle (see 1:22 and 11:6).
οἱ γονεῖς. Nominative subject of ἀπεκρίθησαν.
αὐτοῦ. Genitive of relationship qualifying γονεῖς.
καὶ εἶπαν. Pleonastic clause under Semitic influence, which functions as a redundant quotative frame (see 1:25 on καὶ εἶπαν αὐτῷ).

καί. Coordinating conjunction.
εἶπαν. Aor act ind 3rd pl λέγω.
οἴδαμεν. Prf act ind 1st pl οἶδα (see 1:26 on οἴδατε).
ὅτι. Introduces the first clausal complement (indirect discourse) of οἴδαμεν.
οὗτός. Nominative subject of ἐστιν. Fronted for emphasis. οὗτός, which has a circumflex accent on the penult, acquired an additional accent, the acute, on the ultima from the enclitic ἐστιν (Smyth §183; Carson 1985, 48).
ἐστιν. Pres act ind 3rd sg εἰμί.
ὁ υἱὸς. Predicate nominative.
ἡμῶν. Genitive of relationship qualifying υἱός.
καί. Coordinating conjunction.
ὅτι. Introduces the second clausal complement (indirect discourse) of οἴδαμεν.
τυφλὸς. Predicate adjective. Fronted for emphasis.
ἐγεννήθη. Aor pass ind 3rd sg γεννάω.

9:21 πῶς δὲ νῦν βλέπει οὐκ οἴδαμεν, ἢ τίς ἤνοιξεν αὐτοῦ τοὺς ὀφθαλμοὺς ἡμεῖς οὐκ οἴδαμεν· αὐτὸν ἐρωτήσατε, ἡλικίαν ἔχει, αὐτὸς περὶ ἑαυτοῦ λαλήσει.

πῶς. Interrogative particle.
δέ. Marker of narrative development with a contrastive nuance.
νῦν. Adverb of time.
βλέπει. Pres act ind 3rd sg βλέπω.
οὐκ. Negative particle normally used with indicative verbs.
οἴδαμεν. Prf act ind 1st pl οἶδα (see 1:26 on οἴδατε). The verb stands in final, emphatic position.
ἤ. Marker of an alternative/disjunctive particle (BDAG, 432.1).
τίς. Nominative subject of ἤνοιξεν.
ἤνοιξεν. Aor act ind 3rd sg ἀνοίγω.
αὐτοῦ. Possessive genitive qualifying ὀφθαλμούς. The preposed pronoun is thematically salient (Levinsohn 2000, 64).
τοὺς ὀφθαλμοὺς. Accusative direct object of ἤνοιξεν.
ἡμεῖς. Nominative subject of οἴδαμεν. The personal pronoun is emphatic.
οὐκ. Negative particle normally used with indicative verbs.
οἴδαμεν. Prf act ind 1st pl οἶδα (see 1:26 on οἴδατε). The verb stands in final, emphatic position.
αὐτὸν. Accusative direct object of ἐρωτήσατε. Fronted for emphasis.
ἐρωτήσατε. Aor act impv 2nd pl ἐρωτάω.

ἡλικίαν. Accusative direct object of ἔχει. Lit. "he has mature age" = "he is of age" (BDAG, 436.2.b). Fronted for emphasis.

ἔχει. Pres act ind 3rd sg ἔχω.

αὐτός. Intensive pronoun that reinforces the implied subject of λαλήσει ("he himself"), pointing out a contrast between the man born blind and his parents (BDAG, 152.1.c). While the expression αὐτὸς περὶ ἑαυτοῦ may be an instance of "[t]he strengthening of the reflexive with αὐτός, frequent in Attic," in this formulation "αὐτός is emphasized, not περὶ ἑ[αυτοῦ]" (BDF §283.4).

περὶ ἑαυτοῦ. Reference.

λαλήσει. Fut act ind 3rd sg λαλέω.

9:22 ταῦτα εἶπαν οἱ γονεῖς αὐτοῦ ὅτι ἐφοβοῦντο τοὺς Ἰουδαίους· ἤδη γὰρ συνετέθειντο οἱ Ἰουδαῖοι ἵνα ἐάν τις αὐτὸν ὁμολογήσῃ χριστόν, ἀποσυνάγωγος γένηται.

ταῦτα. Accusative direct object of εἶπαν. This verse is connected to the previous one by asyndeton.

εἶπαν. Aor act ind 3rd pl λέγω.

οἱ γονεῖς. Nominative subject of εἶπαν.

αὐτοῦ. Genitive of relationship qualifying γονεῖς.

ὅτι. Introduces a causal clause.

ἐφοβοῦντο. Impf mid ind 3rd pl φοβέομαι. In this context, the verb is transitive ("fear someone"; cf. BDAG, 1061.1.b.α).

τοὺς Ἰουδαίους. Accusative direct object of ἐφοβοῦντο. Since the parents of the blind man are Jews themselves, the term "the Jews" could not refer to the Jewish people in general but only to Jewish religious authorities who are hostile to Jesus.

ἤδη. Temporal adverb ("already, now").

γάρ. Postpositive conjunction that introduces the clause explaining why the man's parents pleaded ignorance regarding the question of how and by whom he gained his sight.

συνετέθειντο. Plprf mid ind 3rd pl συντίθημι. Fanning emphasizes that "[t]he focus here is upon a *state* which existed in the past, with implication of prior occurrence which produced it" (306) and notes that this use typically occurs in explanatory clauses that provide background information of the events narrated in the main storyline (306–7).

οἱ Ἰουδαῖοι. Nominative subject of συνετέθειντο.

ἵνα. Introduces a complementary clause that completes the meaning of συνετέθειντο. In classical Greek, a complementary ἵνα clause is equivalent to a complementary infinitive (Wallace 1996, 476).

ἐάν. Introduces the protasis of a third-class condition.

τις. Nominative subject of ὁμολογήσῃ.

αὐτόν. Accusative direct object of ὁμολογήσῃ in a double accusative object-complement construction.

ὁμολογήσῃ. Aor act subj 3rd sg ὁμολογέω. Subjunctive with ἐάν.

χριστόν. Accusative complement to αὐτόν in a double accusative object-complement construction.

ἀποσυνάγωγος. Predicate adjective. Fronted for emphasis. ἀποσυνάγωγος ("expelled from the synagogue") occurs only in the FG (9:22; 12:42; 16:2). For a reconstruction of the historical background of this expression, see Martyn (35–66, 148–67; cf. Barrett, 137–44).

γένηται. Aor mid subj 3rd sg γίνομαι. Subjunctive with ἵνα.

9:23 διὰ τοῦτο οἱ γονεῖς αὐτοῦ εἶπαν ὅτι ἡλικίαν ἔχει, αὐτὸν ἐπερωτήσατε.

διὰ τοῦτο. Causal. The demonstrative pronoun is anaphoric, referring to the explanation in the previous verse. In this context, the PP διὰ τοῦτο functions as a connective; on this function of διὰ τοῦτο, see 1:31.

οἱ γονεῖς. Nominative subject of εἶπαν.

αὐτοῦ. Genitive of relationship qualifying γονεῖς.

εἶπαν. Aor act ind 3rd pl λέγω.

ὅτι. ὅτι-*recitativum* that introduces the clausal complement (direct discourse) of εἶπαν.

ἡλικίαν. Accusative direct object of ἔχει (see 9:21). Fronted for emphasis.

ἔχει. Pres act ind 3rd sg ἔχω.

αὐτόν. Accusative direct object of ἐπερωτήσατε. Fronted for emphasis.

ἐπερωτήσατε. Aor act impv 2nd pl ἐπερωτάω. There is no difference in meaning between ἐπερωτάω, used here, and ἐρωτάω, used in 9:21.

John 9:24-34

[24]So they called for the second time the man who had been blind and said to him, "Give glory to God! We know that this man is a sinner." [25]Then he answered, "Whether he is a sinner I do not know. One thing I do know, that though I was blind, now I see." [26]They said to him, "What did he do to you? How did he open your eyes?" [27]He answered them, "I have told you already and you did not listen. Why do you want to hear it again? You do not want to become his disciples too, do you?" [28]And they reviled him and said, "You are a disciple of that fellow, but we are disciples of Moses. [29]We know that God has spoken to Moses, but as for this one, we do not know where he is from." [30]The man answered and said to them, "Indeed, the remarkable thing about this is that you

do not know where he is from, and yet he opened my eyes. ³¹We know that God does not listen to sinners, but if someone is devout and does his will, he listens to this one. ³²From time immemorial it has not been heard that anyone opened the eyes of someone born blind. ³³If this man were not from God, he could do nothing." ³⁴They answered and said to him, "You were born wholly in sins, and are you lecturing us?" And they threw him out.

9:24 Ἐφώνησαν οὖν τὸν ἄνθρωπον ἐκ δευτέρου ὃς ἦν τυφλὸς καὶ εἶπαν αὐτῷ· δὸς δόξαν τῷ θεῷ· ἡμεῖς οἴδαμεν ὅτι οὗτος ὁ ἄνθρωπος ἁμαρτωλός ἐστιν.

Ἐφώνησαν. Aor act ind 3rd pl φωνέω.

οὖν. Postpositive inferential conjunction and/or transitional particle (see 1:22 and 11:6).

τὸν ἄνθρωπον. Accusative direct object of Ἐφώνησαν.

ἐκ δευτέρου. Temporal sequence ("for the second time"; cf. BDAG, 298.5.b.β).

ὅς. Nominative subject of ἦν. The antecedent of the relative pronoun is τὸν ἄνθρωπον.

ἦν. Impf act ind 3rd sg εἰμί.

τυφλὸς. Predicate adjective.

καὶ. Coordinating conjunction.

εἶπαν. Aor act ind 3rd pl λέγω.

αὐτῷ. Dative indirect object of εἶπαν.

δὸς. Aor act impv 2nd sg δίδωμι.

δόξαν. Accusative direct object of δὸς.

τῷ θεῷ. Dative indirect object of δὸς.

ἡμεῖς. Nominative subject of οἴδαμεν. The personal emphasizes the difference between the Jews and the formerly blind man.

οἴδαμεν. Prf act ind 1st pl οἶδα (see 1:26 on οἴδατε).

ὅτι. Introduces the clausal complement (indirect discourse) of οἴδαμεν.

οὗτος ὁ ἄνθρωπος. Nominative subject of ἐστιν. Harris suggests that οὗτος ὁ ἄνθρωπος "is a condescending if not contemptuous ref. to Jesus, as in v. 16" (2015, 189; cf. Robertson, 697). Runge, conversely, argues that this usage is "better explained as marking the participant as being thematically salient, as being in the spotlight" (2010, 373 n. 22).

ἁμαρτωλός. Predicate nominative. The adjective functions as a substantive ("a sinner"). Fronted for emphasis.

ἐστιν. Pres act ind 3rd sg εἰμί.

9:25 ἀπεκρίθη οὖν ἐκεῖνος· εἰ ἁμαρτωλός ἐστιν οὐκ οἶδα· ἓν οἶδα ὅτι τυφλὸς ὢν ἄρτι βλέπω.

ἀπεκρίθη. Aor mid ind 3rd sg ἀποκρίνομαι. On the voice, see "Deponency" in the Series Introduction.

οὖν. Postpositive inferential conjunction and/or transitional particle (see 1:22 and 11:6).

ἐκεῖνος. Nominative subject of ἀπεκρίθη. The demonstrative pronoun refers to the man who had been blind, serving as a third-person personal pronoun with a simple anaphoric force (Wallace 1996, 328–29; BDF §291.6).

εἰ. Interrogative particle in indirect questions ("if, whether"; cf. Zerwick §402).

ἁμαρτωλός. Predicate nominative. The adjective functions as a substantive ("a sinner").

ἐστιν. Pres act ind 3rd sg εἰμί.

οὐκ. Negative particle normally used with indicative verbs.

οἶδα. Prf act ind 1st sg οἶδα (see 1:26 on οἴδατε). The verb stands in final, emphatic position.

ἕν. Accusative direct object of οἶδα. It functions as a forward-pointing reference to the ὅτι clause that follows (see 8:41 on ἕνα πατέρα).

οἶδα. Prf act ind 1st sg οἶδα (see 1:26 on οἴδατε).

ὅτι. Introduces the clausal complement (indirect discourse) of οἶδα, which serves as a forward-pointing target of ἕν.

τυφλὸς. Predicate adjective.

ὤν. Pres act ptc masc nom sg εἰμί (concessive or temporal). On participles that precede the main verb, see ἐμβλέψας in 1:36.

ἄρτι. Adverb of time.

βλέπω. Pres act ind 1st sg βλέπω. The verb stands in final, emphatic position.

9:26 εἶπον οὖν αὐτῷ· τί ἐποίησέν σοι; πῶς ἤνοιξέν σου τοὺς ὀφθαλμούς;

εἶπον. Aor act ind 3rd pl λέγω.

οὖν. Postpositive inferential conjunction and/or transitional particle (see 1:22 and 11:6).

αὐτῷ. Dative indirect object of εἶπον

τί. Accusative direct object of ἐποίησέν.

ἐποίησέν. Aor act ind 3rd sg ποιέω. ἐποίησέν, which has an acute accent on the antepenult, acquired an additional accent, the acute, on the ultima from the enclitic σοι (Smyth §183; Carson 1985, 48).

σοι. Dative indirect object of ἐποίησέν.
πῶς. Interrogative particle.
ἤνοιξέν. Aor act ind 3rd sg ἀνοίγω. ἤνοιξέν, which has an acute accent on the antepenult, acquired an additional accent, the acute, on the ultima from the enclitic σου (Smyth §183; Carson 1985, 48).
σου. Possessive genitive qualifying ὀφθαλμούς. The preposed pronoun is thematically salient (Levinsohn 2000, 64).
τοὺς ὀφθαλμούς. Accusative direct object of ἤνοιξέν.

9:27 ἀπεκρίθη αὐτοῖς· εἶπον ὑμῖν ἤδη καὶ οὐκ ἠκούσατε· τί πάλιν θέλετε ἀκούειν; μὴ καὶ ὑμεῖς θέλετε αὐτοῦ μαθηταὶ γενέσθαι;

ἀπεκρίθη. Aor mid ind 3rd sg ἀποκρίνομαι. On the voice, see "Deponency" in the Series Introduction. This verse is connected to the previous one by asyndeton.
αὐτοῖς. Dative indirect object of ἀπεκρίθη.
εἶπον. Aor act ind 1st sg λέγω.
ὑμῖν. Dative indirect object of εἶπον.
ἤδη. Temporal adverb ("already, now").
καί. Coordinating conjunction.
οὐκ. Negative particle normally used with indicative verbs.
ἠκούσατε. Aor act ind 2nd pl ἀκούω. The meaning of the first ἀκούω in this verse is "listen."
τί. Adverbial use of the interrogative pronoun ("why?"). This clause is connected to the preceding one by asyndeton.
πάλιν. Adverb "pert[aining] to repetition in the same (or similar) manner" (BDAG, 752.2).
θέλετε. Pres act ind 2nd pl θέλω.
ἀκούειν. Pres act inf ἀκούω (complementary). The meaning of the second ἀκούω in this verse is "hear."
μή. Negative particle that introduces a question that expects a negative answer. The question is almost certainly ironic. This clause is connected to the preceding one by asyndeton.
καί. Adverbial use (adjunctive). The man does not compare the Jews ("you also") to himself but to Jesus' Galilean followers (Harris 2015, 189).
ὑμεῖς. Nominative subject of θέλετε. The personal pronoun is emphatic.
θέλετε. Pres act ind 2nd pl θέλω.
αὐτοῦ. Genitive of relationship qualifying μαθηταί. The preposed pronoun is thematically salient (Levinsohn 2000, 64).
μαθηταί. Predicate nominative.
γενέσθαι. Aor mid inf γίνομαι (complementary).

9:28 καὶ ἐλοιδόρησαν αὐτὸν καὶ εἶπον· σὺ μαθητὴς εἶ ἐκείνου, ἡμεῖς δὲ τοῦ Μωϋσέως ἐσμὲν μαθηταί·

καὶ. Coordinating conjunction.
ἐλοιδόρησαν. Aor act ind 3rd pl λοιδορέω. The verb means to "revile, abuse" someone (BDAG, 602).
αὐτὸν. Accusative direct object of ἐλοιδόρησαν.
καὶ. Coordinating conjunction.
εἶπον. Aor act ind 3rd pl λέγω.
σὺ. Nominative subject of εἶ. The personal pronoun is emphatic and contrastive, differentiating the formerly blind man ("you") from the Jews ("we").
μαθητὴς. Predicate nominative. Fronted for emphasis.
εἶ. Pres act ind 2nd sg εἰμί.
ἐκείνου. Genitive of relationship qualifying μαθητὴς. The demonstrative pronoun is used as a contemptuous reference to Jesus, who is absent (BDF §291.1; Robertson, 697). Contemptuous sense, however, is not a semantic value of ἐκεῖνος but a pragmatic effect that results from the use of the athematic demonstrative for a thematic participant (Runge 2010, 373).
ἡμεῖς. Nominative subject of ἐσμὲν. The personal pronoun is emphatic and contrastive (see σὺ above).
δὲ. Marker of narrative development with a contrastive nuance.
τοῦ Μωϋσέως. Genitive of relationship qualifying μαθηταί. Fronted for emphasis.
ἐσμὲν. Pres act ind 1st pl εἰμί.
μαθηταί. Predicate nominative.

9:29 ἡμεῖς οἴδαμεν ὅτι Μωϋσεῖ λελάληκεν ὁ θεός, τοῦτον δὲ οὐκ οἴδαμεν πόθεν ἐστίν.

ἡμεῖς. Nominative subject of οἴδαμεν. Fronted for emphasis. This verse is connected to the previous one by asyndeton.
οἴδαμεν. Prf act ind 1st pl οἶδα (see 1:26 on οἴδατε).
ὅτι. Introduces the clausal complement (indirect discourse) of οἴδαμεν.
Μωϋσεῖ. Dative indirect object of λελάληκεν. Fronted for emphasis.
λελάληκεν. Prf act ind 3rd sg λαλέω. The perfect tense, which is semantically marked for prominence, here primarily describes the past event, but, as Zerwick (§286) remarks, "the sense is . . . not that of the simple historical fact 'God spoke to Moses' but that of the resultant

dignity of Moses as commissioned by God and not, like 'this man,' without credentials."

ὁ θεός. Nominative subject of λελάληκεν.
τοῦτον. Accusative of respect. τοῦτον functions as a pronominal prolepsis because it anticipates the subject of the indirect question that follows (Zerwick §206; McKay 1994 §13.2.2); see 2:23 on αὐτοῦ.
δέ. Marker of narrative development with a contrastive nuance.
οὐκ. Negative particle normally used with indicative verbs.
οἴδαμεν. Prf act ind 1st pl οἶδα (see 1:26 on οἴδατε).
πόθεν. Interrogative adverb of place.
ἐστίν. Pres act ind 3rd sg εἰμί.

9:30 ἀπεκρίθη ὁ ἄνθρωπος καὶ εἶπεν αὐτοῖς· ἐν τούτῳ γὰρ τὸ θαυμαστόν ἐστιν, ὅτι ὑμεῖς οὐκ οἴδατε πόθεν ἐστίν, καὶ ἤνοιξέν μου τοὺς ὀφθαλμούς.

ἀπεκρίθη. Aor mid ind 3rd sg ἀποκρίνομαι. On the voice, see "Deponency" in the Series Introduction. This verse is connected to the previous one by asyndeton.
ὁ ἄνθρωπος. Nominative subject of ἀπεκρίθη.
καὶ εἶπεν αὐτοῖς. Pleonastic clause under Semitic influence, which functions as a redundant quotative frame (see 1:25 on καὶ εἶπαν αὐτῷ).
καί. Coordinating conjunction.
εἶπεν. Aor act ind 3rd sg λέγω.
αὐτοῖς. Dative indirect object of εἶπεν.
ἐν τούτῳ. Reference/respect. Fronted as a topical frame.
γάρ. When γάρ is used in replies, as here, "it affirms what was asked (giving the reason for a tacit 'yes'): 'to be sure, just so'" (BDF §452.2).
τὸ θαυμαστόν. Nominative subject of ἐστιν. Fronted for emphasis. τὸ θαυμαστόν functions as a forward-pointing reference to the ὅτι clause that follows (see 8:41 on ἕνα πατέρα).
ἐστιν. Pres act ind 3rd sg εἰμί.
ὅτι. Introduces a nominal clause that stands in apposition to ἐν τούτῳ (Wallace 1996, 458–59). In this context, it serves as a forward-pointing target of τὸ θαυμαστόν.
ὑμεῖς. Nominative subject of οἴδατε. Fronted for emphasis.
οὐκ. Negative particle normally used with indicative verbs.
οἴδατε. Prf act ind 2nd pl οἶδα (see 1:26 on οἴδατε).
πόθεν. Interrogative adverb of place.
ἐστίν. Pres act ind 3rd sg εἰμί.
καί. Coordinating conjunction.

ἤνοιξέν. Aor act ind 3rd sg ἀνοίγω. ἤνοιξέν, which has an acute accent on the antepenult, acquired an additional accent, the acute, on the ultima from the enclitic μου (Smyth §183; Carson 1985, 48).

μου. Possessive genitive qualifying ὀφθαλμούς. The preposed pronoun is thematically salient (Levinsohn 2000, 64).

τοὺς ὀφθαλμούς. Accusative direct object of ἤνοιξέν.

9:31 οἴδαμεν ὅτι ἁμαρτωλῶν ὁ θεὸς οὐκ ἀκούει, ἀλλ' ἐάν τις θεοσεβὴς ᾖ καὶ τὸ θέλημα αὐτοῦ ποιῇ τούτου ἀκούει.

οἴδαμεν. Prf act ind 1st pl οἶδα (see 1:26 on οἴδατε). This verse is connected to the previous one by asyndeton.

ὅτι. Introduces the clausal complement (indirect discourse) of οἴδαμεν.

ἁμαρτωλῶν. Genitive direct object of ἀκούει. The adjective functions as a substantive ("sinners").

ὁ θεὸς. Nominative subject of ἀκούει.

οὐκ. Negative particle normally used with indicative verbs.

ἀκούει. Pres act ind 3rd sg ἀκούω. The verb stands in final, emphatic position.

ἀλλ'. Marker of contrast.

ἐάν. Introduces the protasis of a third-class condition.

τις. Nominative subject of ᾖ.

θεοσεβὴς. Predicate adjective.

ᾖ. Pres act subj 3rd sg εἰμί. Subjunctive with ἐάν.

καὶ. Coordinating conjunction.

τὸ θέλημα. Accusative direct object of ποιῇ.

αὐτοῦ. Subjective genitive qualifying θέλημα. The personal pronoun refers to God.

ποιῇ. Pres act subj 3rd sg ποιέω. Subjunctive with ἐάν.

τούτου. Genitive direct object of ἀκούει. The demonstrative pronoun refers to τις. It marks the beginning of the apodosis of a third-class condition.

ἀκούει. Pres act ind 3rd sg ἀκούω.

9:32 ἐκ τοῦ αἰῶνος οὐκ ἠκούσθη ὅτι ἠνέῳξέν τις ὀφθαλμοὺς τυφλοῦ γεγεννημένου·

ἐκ τοῦ αἰῶνος. Temporal. Fronted for emphasis. "From eternity" is a Semitism for "from time immemorial, never" (Zerwick and Grosvenor, 316; cf. Moule, 73). This verse is connected to the previous one by asyndeton.

οὐκ. Negative particle normally used with indicative verbs.

ἠκούσθη. Aor pass ind 3rd sg ἀκούω.

ὅτι. Introduces a nominal clause that functions as the subject of ἠκούσθη: "[*That* anyone has opened the eyes of a person who was born blind] has not been heard from eternity" (Wallace 1996, 453).

ἠνέῳξέν. Aor act ind 3rd sg ἀνοίγω. ἠνέῳξέν, which has an acute accent on the antepenult, acquired an additional accent, the acute, on the ultima from the enclitic τις (Smyth §183; Carson 1985, 48).

τις. Nominative subject of ἠνέῳξέν.

ὀφθαλμοὺς. Accusative direct object of ἠνέῳξέν.

τυφλοῦ. The adjective modifies the substantival participle γεγεννημένου (lit. "of a having-been-born-blind man" [Harris 2015, 190]), standing in the first (anarthrous) attributive position (see 2:6 on λίθιναι ὑδρίαι).

γεγεννημένου. Prf pass ptc masc gen sg γεννάω (substantival). Possessive genitive qualifying ὀφθαλμοὺς.

9:33 εἰ μὴ ἦν οὗτος παρὰ θεοῦ, οὐκ ἠδύνατο ποιεῖν οὐδέν.

εἰ μὴ . . . οὐκ. A point/counterpoint set in which the exceptive/restrictive clause (the protasis of a of a second-class condition) precedes the negated clause (the apodosis of a second-class condition). In such arrangements, the exceptive clause establishes a "frame of reference" for the clause that follows (Runge 2010, 85–86). By introducing the excepted element first (the idea that Jesus is from God), the protasis restricts the application of the claim in the apodosis ("he could do nothing") only to the situations that do not include the exception (i.e., to the suggestions that Jesus is not from God). This verse is connected to the previous one by asyndeton.

ἦν. Impf act ind 3rd sg εἰμί.

οὗτος. Nominative subject of ἦν.

παρὰ θεοῦ. Source.

οὐκ. Negative particle normally used with indicative verbs. οὐκ marks the beginning of the apodosis of a second-class (contrary-to-fact) condition, which does not contain the contingency particle ἄν. This omission, which in classical Greek regularly occurred with verbs indicating obligation, propriety, or necessity, was extended in Hellenistic Greek to other verbs, such as those expressing possibility (Zerwick §319; Robertson, 920, 1014).

ἠδύνατο. Impf mid ind 3rd sg δύναμαι. In the NT, the imperfect verb forms of δύναμαι occur with either ἠ- or ἐ- augments (MHT 2:188). In the FG, the imperfect of δύναμαι is always augmented with ἠ- (here and in 12:39).

ποιεῖν. Pres act inf ποιέω (complementary).
οὐδέν. Accusative direct object of ποιεῖν. The two negatives οὐκ ... οὐδέν reinforce each other (see 3:27 on οὐδὲ).

9:34 ἀπεκρίθησαν καὶ εἶπαν αὐτῷ· ἐν ἁμαρτίαις σὺ ἐγεννήθης ὅλος καὶ σὺ διδάσκεις ἡμᾶς; καὶ ἐξέβαλον αὐτὸν ἔξω.

ἀπεκρίθησαν. Aor mid ind 3rd pl ἀποκρίνομαι. On the voice, see "Deponency" in the Series Introduction. This verse is connected to the previous one by asyndeton.
καὶ εἶπαν αὐτῷ. Pleonastic clause under Semitic influence, which functions as a redundant quotative frame (see 1:25 on καὶ εἶπαν αὐτῷ).
καὶ. Coordinating conjunction.
εἶπαν. Aor act ind 3rd pl λέγω.
αὐτῷ. Dative indirect object of εἶπαν.
ἐν ἁμαρτίαις. State or condition (BDAG, 327.2.b). Fronted for emphasis.
σύ. Nominative subject of ἐγεννήθης. σύ is emphatic.
ἐγεννήθης. Aor pass ind 2nd sg γεννάω.
ὅλος. Predicate adjective. In this context, ὅλος pertains "to a degree of completeness, *wholly, completely*" (BDAG, 704.2).
καὶ. Coordinating conjunction.
σύ. Nominative subject of διδάσκεις. Again, σύ is emphatic.
διδάσκεις. Pres act ind 2nd sg διδάσκω.
ἡμᾶς. Accusative direct object of διδάσκεις.
καὶ. Coordinating conjunction.
ἐξέβαλον. Aor act ind 3rd pl ἐκβάλλω.
αὐτόν. Accusative direct object of ἐξέβαλον.
ἔξω. Adverb of place ("out[side]").

John 9:35-41

[35]Jesus heard that they had thrown him out, and when he found him, he said, "Do you believe in the Son of Man?" [36]He answered and said, "And who is he, sir? Tell me, so that I may believe in him." [37]Jesus said to him, "You are not only looking at him, but also the one speaking with you is he." [38]He said, "I believe, Lord!" And he worshipped him. [39]And Jesus said, "I came into this world for judgment so that those who do not see may see, and those who see may become blind." [40]Some of the Pharisees who were near him heard these things and said to him, "We are not also blind, are we?" [41]Jesus said to them, "If you were blind, you would not have sin. But now you say, 'We see,' your sin remains."

9:35 Ἤκουσεν Ἰησοῦς ὅτι ἐξέβαλον αὐτὸν ἔξω καὶ εὑρὼν αὐτὸν εἶπεν· σὺ πιστεύεις εἰς τὸν υἱὸν τοῦ ἀνθρώπου;

Ἤκουσεν. Aor act ind 3rd sg ἀκούω. This verse is connected to the previous one by asyndeton.

Ἰησοῦς. Nominative subject of Ἤκουσεν.

ὅτι. Introduces the clausal complement (indirect discourse) of Ἤκουσεν.

ἐξέβαλον. Aor act ind 3rd pl ἐκβάλλω. The aorist tense is retained from the corresponding direct discourse (see 1:39 on μένει).

αὐτὸν. Accusative direct object of ἐξέβαλον.

ἔξω. Adverb of place.

καὶ. Coordinating conjunction.

εὑρὼν. Aor act ptc masc nom sg εὑρίσκω (temporal). On participles that precede the main verb, see ἐμβλέψας in 1:36.

αὐτὸν. Accusative direct object of εὑρὼν.

εἶπεν. Aor act ind 3rd sg λέγω.

σὺ. Nominative subject of πιστεύεις. Fronted as a topical frame.

πιστεύεις. Pres act ind 2nd sg πιστεύω.

εἰς τὸν υἱὸν. Goal of actions or feelings directed toward someone (BDAG, 290.4.c.β). For πιστεύειν εἰς + accusative ("trust or believe in someone"), see 1:12 on εἰς τὸ ὄνομα.

τοῦ ἀνθρώπου. Genitive of relationship qualifying υἱόν. The external support for the reading ἀνθρώπου ($\mathfrak{P}^{66.75}$ ℵ B D W sy^s co) outweighs the manuscript support for the variant θεοῦ (A K L Γ Δ Θ Ψ 070 $f^{1.13}$ 33 565 579 700 𝔐 lat sy$^{p.h}$ et al.). It is also highly improbable that a scribe would change θεοῦ to ἀνθρώπου if the former was the original text (Metzger, 194; Barrett, 364).

9:36 ἀπεκρίθη ἐκεῖνος καὶ εἶπεν· καὶ τίς ἐστιν, κύριε, ἵνα πιστεύσω εἰς αὐτόν;

ἀπεκρίθη. Aor mid ind 3rd sg ἀποκρίνομαι. On the voice, see "Deponency" in the Series Introduction. This verse is connected to the previous one by asyndeton.

ἐκεῖνος. Nominative subject of ἀπεκρίθη. The demonstrative pronoun refers to the man who had been blind, functioning as a third-person personal pronoun with a simple anaphoric force (Wallace 1996, 328–29; BDF §291.6).

καὶ εἶπεν. Pleonastic clause under Semitic influence, which functions as a redundant quotative frame (see 1:25 on καὶ εἶπαν αὐτῷ).

καὶ. Coordinating conjunction.

εἶπεν. Aor act ind 3rd sg λέγω.
καί. Coordinating conjunction.
τίς. Predicate nominative. Fronted for emphasis. "Interrogatives, by their nature, indicate the unknown component and hence cannot be the subject" (Wallace, 40 n. 12).
ἐστιν. Pres act ind 3rd sg εἰμί.
κύριε. Vocative of direct address.
ἵνα. Introduces a purpose clause. The construction is elliptical, requiring an introduction, such as the imperative εἰπέ ("[Tell me,] so that I may believe in him"). This is an example of brachylogy—"the omission, for the sake of brevity, of an element which is not necessary for the grammatical structure but for the thought" (BDF §483). For a similar construction, see 1:22.
πιστεύσω. Aor act subj 1st sg πιστεύω. Subjunctive with ἵνα.
εἰς αὐτόν. Goal of actions or feelings directed toward someone (BDAG, 290.4.c.β). For πιστεύειν εἰς + accusative ("trust or believe in someone"), see 1:12 on εἰς τὸ ὄνομα.

9:37 εἶπεν αὐτῷ ὁ Ἰησοῦς· καὶ ἑώρακας αὐτὸν καὶ ὁ λαλῶν μετὰ σοῦ ἐκεῖνός ἐστιν.

εἶπεν. Aor act ind 3rd sg λέγω. This verse is connected to the previous one by asyndeton.
αὐτῷ. Dative indirect object of εἶπεν.
ὁ Ἰησοῦς. Nominative subject of εἶπεν.
καί ... καί. "Both ... and, not only ... but also" (BDAG, 495.1.f).
ἑώρακας. Prf act ind 2nd sg ὁράω. This perfect tense could not be past-referring because the man born blind could not have seen Jesus in a literal sense before the scene described in vv. 35-37. Campbell argues that rendering ἑώρακας imperfectively, which is based on his view that the aspectual value of the perfect tense is imperfective, offers the most satisfactory interpretation of this verse: "You now see him, and the one speaking to you is he" (2007, 195). Porter's view, however, offers an equally satisfactory explanation because it presumes that only the stative aspect is grammaticalized in the perfect-tense form, not its temporal implicature. In the context of John 9, ἑώρακας is present-referring: "You are looking at him and the one who is speaking with you is that one" (1989, 265).
αὐτόν. Accusative direct object of ἑώρακας.
ὁ λαλῶν. Pres act ptc masc nom sg λαλέω (substantival). Nominative subject of ἐστιν.
μετὰ σοῦ. Association/accompaniment.

ἐκεῖνός. Predicate nominative. Fronted for emphasis. The demonstrative pronoun refers to the Son of Man. ἐκεῖνός, which has a circumflex accent on the penult, acquired an additional accent, the acute, on the ultima from the enclitic ἐστιν (Smyth §183; Carson 1985, 48).
ἐστιν. Pres act ind 3rd sg εἰμί.

9:38 ὁ δὲ ἔφη· πιστεύω, κύριε· καὶ προσεκύνησεν αὐτῷ.

ὁ δὲ ἔφη· πιστεύω, κύριε· καὶ προσεκύνησεν αὐτῷ. Καὶ εἶπεν ὁ Ἰησοῦς. The entire verse 38 and the first four words in v. 39 are omitted in 𝔓⁷⁵ ℵ* W b (1) sa^ms ly cw. Brown argues that the longer reading containing these words, attested in all other witnesses, represents "an addition stemming from the association of John ix with the baptismal liturgy and catechesis" (375). Metzger (195), however, rejoins by calling attention to the strong external attestation of the longer text and suggests that the omission could have been either accidental or editorial to connect Jesus' teaching in vv. 37 and 39.

ὁ δὲ. A construction used in narrative literature to indicate the change of the speaker in a dialogue. The nominative article stands in place of a third-person singular personal pronoun and functions as the subject of ἔφη.

ἔφη. Aor/impf act ind 3rd sg φημί.
πιστεύω. Pres act ind 1st sg πιστεύω.
κύριε. Vocative of direct address. Brown (375) suggests that "it seems appropriate to indicate a development from vs. 36 to vs. 38 in the use of the term" by translating this κύριε with "Lord."
καὶ. Coordinating conjunction.
προσεκύνησεν. Aor act ind 3rd sg προσκυνέω.
αὐτῷ. Dative direct object of προσεκύνησεν.

9:39 Καὶ εἶπεν ὁ Ἰησοῦς· εἰς κρίμα ἐγὼ εἰς τὸν κόσμον τοῦτον ἦλθον, ἵνα οἱ μὴ βλέποντες βλέπωσιν καὶ οἱ βλέποντες τυφλοὶ γένωνται.

Καὶ. Coordinating conjunction.
εἶπεν. Aor act ind 3rd sg λέγω.
ὁ Ἰησοῦς. Nominative subject of εἶπεν.
εἰς κρίμα. Purpose. Fronted for emphasis.
ἐγώ. Nominative subject of ἦλθον. Fronted for emphasis.
εἰς τὸν κόσμον τοῦτον. Locative.
ἦλθον. Aor act ind 1st sg ἔρχομαι.
ἵνα. Introduces either a purpose/result clause or an epexegetical clause that explains εἰς κρίμα (Harris 2015, 192–93).

οἱ ... βλέποντες. Pres act ptc masc nom pl βλέπω (substantival). Nominative subject of βλέπωσιν.

μὴ. Negative particle normally used with non-indicative verbs.

βλέπωσιν. Pres act subj 3rd pl βλέπω. Subjunctive with ἵνα. The verb stands in final, emphatic position.

καὶ. Coordinating conjunction.

οἱ βλέποντες. Pres act ptc masc nom pl βλέπω (substantival). Nominative subject of γένωνται.

τυφλοὶ. Predicate adjective. Fronted for emphasis.

γένωνται. Aor mid subj 3rd pl γίνομαι. Subjunctive with ἵνα.

9:40 ἤκουσαν ἐκ τῶν Φαρισαίων ταῦτα οἱ μετ' αὐτοῦ ὄντες καὶ εἶπον αὐτῷ· μὴ καὶ ἡμεῖς τυφλοί ἐσμεν;

ἤκουσαν. Aor act ind 3rd pl ἀκούω. This verse is connected to the previous one by asyndeton.

ἐκ τῶν Φαρισαίων. Replaces the partitive genitive (ἐκ τῶν Φαρισαίων = τινὲς ἐκ τῶν Φαρισαίων).

ταῦτα. Accusative direct object of ἤκουσαν. The demonstrative pronoun is anaphoric, referring to Jesus' words in v. 39.

οἱ ... ὄντες. Pres act ptc masc nom pl εἰμί (attributive). The participle modifies the implied τινές: "some of the Pharisees who were with him" (Haubeck and von Siebenthal, 563).

μετ' αὐτοῦ. Association/accompaniment, denoting spatial proximity (Harris 2015, 193).

καὶ. Coordinating conjunction.

εἶπον. Aor act ind 3rd pl λέγω.

αὐτῷ. Dative indirect object of εἶπον.

μὴ. Negative particle that introduces a question that expects a negative answer.

καὶ. Adverbial use (adjunctive).

ἡμεῖς. Nominative subject of ἐσμεν. Fronted for emphasis.

τυφλοί. Predicate adjective.

ἐσμεν. Pres act ind 1st pl εἰμί.

9:41 εἶπεν αὐτοῖς ὁ Ἰησοῦς· εἰ τυφλοὶ ἦτε, οὐκ ἂν εἴχετε ἁμαρτίαν· νῦν δὲ λέγετε ὅτι βλέπομεν, ἡ ἁμαρτία ὑμῶν μένει.

εἶπεν. Aor act ind 3rd sg λέγω. This verse is connected to the previous one by asyndeton.

αὐτοῖς. Dative indirect object of εἶπεν.

ὁ Ἰησοῦς. Nominative subject of εἶπεν.

εἰ. Introduces the protasis of a second-class (contrary-to-fact) condition. Typically, the present contrary-to-fact conditions have the imperfect in both the protasis and the apodosis, as here.

τυφλοὶ. Predicate adjective. Fronted for emphasis.

ἦτε. Impf act ind 2nd pl εἰμί.

οὐκ. Negative particle normally used with indicative verbs. It marks the beginning of the apodosis of a second-class (contrary-to-fact) condition.

ἄν. Marker of contingency in the apodosis of the second-class condition.

εἴχετε. Impf act ind 2nd pl ἔχω.

ἁμαρτίαν. Accusative direct object of εἴχετε. The phrase ἁμαρτίαν ἔχειν is found only in the Johannine literature (John 9:41; 15:22, 24; 19:11; 1 John 1:8).

νῦν. Adverb of time.

δὲ. Marker of narrative development with a contrastive nuance.

λέγετε. Pres act ind 2nd pl λέγω.

ὅτι. ὅτι-*recitativum* that introduces the clausal complement (direct discourse) of λέγετε.

βλέπομεν. Pres act ind 1st pl βλέπω.

ἡ ἁμαρτία ὑμῶν μένει. This clause is connected to νῦν δὲ λέγετε ὅτι βλέπομεν by asyndeton, which "indicates that the writer did not feel the need to specify any kind of relationship between the clauses" (Runge 2010, 20). Nevertheless, the contrary-to-fact conditional sentence in the first half of Jesus' statement functions as a parallel counterpart to his description of the real state of the affairs, suggesting a similar relationship between their clausal components. If so, the declaration ἡ ἁμαρτία ὑμῶν μένει represents a consequence of the claim of the Pharisees that they do see, i.e., that they possess perfect spiritual vision.

ἡ ἁμαρτία. Nominative subject of μένει.

ὑμῶν. Subjective genitive qualifying ἁμαρτία ("sin that you committed").

μένει. Pres act ind 3rd sg μένω. The verb stands in final, emphatic position.

John 10:1-6

¹"Truly, truly I say to you, the one who does not enter through the door into the fold for sheep but climbs in by another way—that one is a thief and a robber. ²The one who enters through the door is the shepherd of the sheep. ³The doorkeeper opens [the door] for him, and the sheep hear his voice. And he calls his own sheep by name and leads them out. ⁴When he has brought out all his own, he goes ahead of them, and the sheep follow him because they know his voice. ⁵They will never follow a

stranger, but they will flee from him because they do not know the voice of strangers." ⁶Jesus told them this figure of speech, but they did not understand what things they were that he was saying to them.

10:1 Ἀμὴν ἀμὴν λέγω ὑμῖν, ὁ μὴ εἰσερχόμενος διὰ τῆς θύρας εἰς τὴν αὐλὴν τῶν προβάτων ἀλλ' ἀναβαίνων ἀλλαχόθεν ἐκεῖνος κλέπτης ἐστὶν καὶ λῃστής·

Ἀμὴν ἀμὴν λέγω ὑμῖν. Metacomment (see 1:51).

Ἀμὴν ἀμὴν. Asseverative particles that mark the beginning of Jesus' solemn declaration (see 1:51). This verse is connected to the previous one by asyndeton.

λέγω. Pres act ind 1st sg λέγω.

ὑμῖν. Dative indirect object of λέγω.

ὁ μὴ εἰσερχόμενος ... ἀλλ' ἀναβαίνων. Nominative subject of ἐστίν. This formulation is comparable to a TSKS (article-substantive-καί-substantive) construction, in which, according to the Granville Sharp rule, the single article indicates that both participles have the same referent (see 5:24 on ὁ ... ἀκούων καὶ πιστεύων). In this formulation, the participles εἰσερχόμενος and ἀναβαίνων are joined not by καί but by a μὴ ... ἀλλ' point/counterpoint set, which negates the first participle and replaces it with the second participle. The whole participial construction is in a left-dislocation (see Runge 2010, 287–313), which is resumed by ἐκεῖνος.

εἰσερχόμενος. Pres mid ptc masc nom sg εἰσέρχομαι (substantival).

ἀναβαίνων. Pres act ptc masc nom sg ἀναβαίνω (substantival).

διὰ τῆς θύρας. Locative.

εἰς τὴν αὐλὴν. Locative. αὐλή denotes "a walled enclosure either to enclose human activity or to protect livestock" (LN 7.56).

τῶν προβάτων. Genitive of purpose qualifying αὐλήν ("fold for sheep").

ἀλλαχόθεν. Adverb of place ("from elsewhere, from some other way" [LN 84.8]). A NT *hapax legomenon*.

ἐκεῖνος. Nominative subject of ἐστίν, resuming ὁ μὴ εἰσερχόμενος ... ἀλλ' ἀναβαίνων. The anaphoric demonstrative reinforces what is already made prominent through the left-dislocation of the participial construction.

κλέπτης. Predicate nominative. κλέπτης means "thief" (BDAG, 547).

ἐστίν. Pres act ind 3rd sg εἰμί.

καὶ. Coordinating conjunction.

λῃστής. Predicate nominative. λῃστής means "robber, highwayman, bandit" (BDAG, 594.1).

10:2 ὁ δὲ εἰσερχόμενος διὰ τῆς θύρας ποιμήν ἐστιν τῶν προβάτων.

ὁ ... εἰσερχόμενος. Pres mid ptc masc nom sg εἰσέρχομαι (substantival). Nominative subject of ἐστιν. Fronted as a topical frame.

δὲ. Marker of narrative development.

διὰ τῆς θύρας. Locative.

ποιμήν. Predicate nominative. Fronted for emphasis. Although ποιμήν is anarthrous, it is probably definite because, according to Colwell's rule, the definiteness of a preverbal anarthrous predicate nominative cannot be excluded (Wallace 1996, 264; Haubeck and von Siebenthal, 563).

ἐστιν. Pres act ind 3rd sg εἰμί.

τῶν προβάτων. Genitive of subordination qualifying ποιμήν.

10:3 τούτῳ ὁ θυρωρὸς ἀνοίγει καὶ τὰ πρόβατα τῆς φωνῆς αὐτοῦ ἀκούει καὶ τὰ ἴδια πρόβατα φωνεῖ κατ' ὄνομα καὶ ἐξάγει αὐτά.

τούτῳ. Dative of advantage. Fronted for emphasis. The demonstrative pronoun refers to the shepherd of the sheep mentioned in v. 2. This verse is connected to the previous one by asyndeton.

ὁ θυρωρὸς. Nominative subject of ἀνοίγει.

ἀνοίγει. Pres act ind 3rd sg ἀνοίγω.

καὶ. Coordinating conjunction.

τὰ πρόβατα. Nominative subject of ἀκούει.

τῆς φωνῆς. Genitive direct object of ἀκούει. Fronted for emphasis.

αὐτοῦ. Possessive genitive qualifying φωνῆς.

ἀκούει. Pres act ind 3rd sg ἀκούω. Neuter plural subjects typically take singular verbs (see 1:28 on ἐγένετο).

καὶ. Coordinating conjunction.

τὰ ἴδια πρόβατα. Accusative direct object of φωνεῖ. Fronted for emphasis. The adjective ἴδια stands in the first attributive position (see 2:10 on τὸν καλὸν οἶνον).

φωνεῖ. Pres act ind 3rd sg φωνέω.

κατ' ὄνομα. Distributive (lit. "name by name").

καὶ. Coordinating conjunction.

ἐξάγει. Pres act ind 3rd sg ἐξάγω.

αὐτά. Accusative direct object of ἐξάγει.

10:4 ὅταν τὰ ἴδια πάντα ἐκβάλῃ, ἔμπροσθεν αὐτῶν πορεύεται καὶ τὰ πρόβατα αὐτῷ ἀκολουθεῖ, ὅτι οἴδασιν τὴν φωνὴν αὐτοῦ·

ὅταν. Introduces an indefinite temporal clause, which is fronted as a temporal frame. This verse is connected to the previous one by asyndeton.

τὰ ἴδια πάντα. Accusative direct object of ἐκβάλῃ. The pronominal adjective πάντα has attributive function although it stands in the second predicate position (see 5:36 on μείζω) because the pronominal adjectives such as πᾶς are exceptions to the rules about the relation of the adjective to the noun when the article is present (Wallace 1996, 308).

ἐκβάλῃ. Aor act subj 3rd sg ἐκβάλλω. Subjunctive with ὅταν. Here ἐκβάλλω means "to lead or bring out of a structure or area—'to lead out, to bring forth'" (LN 15.174).

ἔμπροσθεν αὐτῶν. Locative. Fronted for emphasis. ἔμπροσθέν is an adverb of place ("in front, ahead" [BDAG, 325.1.a]) that here functions as an improper preposition (see 1:3 on χωρὶς αὐτοῦ).

πορεύεται. Pres mid ind 3rd sg πορεύομαι.

καὶ. Coordinating conjunction.

τὰ πρόβατα. Nominative subject of ἀκολουθεῖ.

αὐτῷ. Dative direct object of ἀκολουθεῖ.

ἀκολουθεῖ. Pres act ind 3rd sg ἀκολουθέω. Neuter plural subjects typically take singular verbs (see 1:28 on ἐγένετο). The verb stands in final, emphatic position.

ὅτι. Introduces a causal clause.

οἴδασιν. Prf act ind 3rd pl οἶδα (see 1:26 on οἴδατε). While neuter plural subjects typically take singular verbs (see ἀκολουθεῖ above), this rule is not consistently applied in the NT, which is characterized by marked diversity, sometimes within the same passage or even the same sentence, as here. According to BDF, οἴδασιν is in the plural although its implied subject is τὰ πρόβατα because "οἶδε would have been ambiguous, and accordingly v. 5 also has pl." (§133.2).

τὴν φωνὴν. Accusative direct object of οἴδασιν.

αὐτοῦ. Possessive genitive qualifying φωνὴν.

10:5 ἀλλοτρίῳ δὲ οὐ μὴ ἀκολουθήσουσιν, ἀλλὰ φεύξονται ἀπ' αὐτοῦ, ὅτι οὐκ οἴδασιν τῶν ἀλλοτρίων τὴν φωνήν.

ἀλλοτρίῳ. Dative direct object of ἀκολουθήσουσιν. The adjective ἀλλότριος ("belonging to another, strange, foreign") is here used as a substantive.

δὲ. Marker of narrative development.

οὐ μὴ ... ἀλλά. A point/counterpoint set that emphatically negates the notion that the sheep will follow a stranger and replaces it with the claim that the sheep will run away from him. The emphatic negation οὐ μὴ is usually followed by the aorist subjunctive, but it could sometimes be followed by the future indicative, as here (see 4:14).

ἀκολουθήσουσιν. Fut act ind 3rd pl ἀκολουθέω. On the plural verb form, see 10:4 on οἴδασιν. The verb stands in final, emphatic position.

φεύξονται. Fut mid ind 3rd pl φεύγω. On the plural verb form, see 10:4 on οἴδασιν.

ἀπ' αὐτοῦ. Separation.

ὅτι. Introduces a causal clause.

οὐκ. Negative particle normally used with indicative verbs.

οἴδασιν. Prf act ind 3rd pl οἶδα (see 1:26 on οἴδατε). On the plural verb form, see 10:4 on οἴδασιν.

τῶν ἀλλοτρίων. Possessive genitive qualifying φωνήν. Fronted for emphasis (Robertson, 418).

τὴν φωνήν. Accusative direct object of οἴδασιν.

10:6 Ταύτην τὴν παροιμίαν εἶπεν αὐτοῖς ὁ Ἰησοῦς, ἐκεῖνοι δὲ οὐκ ἔγνωσαν τίνα ἦν ἃ ἐλάλει αὐτοῖς.

Ταύτην τὴν παροιμίαν. Accusative direct object of εἶπεν. Fronted as a topical frame. This is the first occurrence of the term παροιμία ("veiled saying, figure of speech, in which esp. lofty ideas are concealed" [BDAG, 780.2]) in the FG (10:6; 16:25, 29). In addition to the Johannine usage, this term occurs in the NT only in 2 Pet 2:22. The Fourth Evangelist never uses the synoptic term παραβολή (cf. Matt 13:3, 10, 13, 34, 34, 53; 21:45; 22:1; Mark 3:23; 4:2, 10, 11, 13, 30, 33; 12:1; Luke 8:9, 10, 11). This verse is connected to the previous one by asyndeton.

εἶπεν. Aor act ind 3rd sg λέγω.

αὐτοῖς. Dative indirect object of εἶπεν.

ὁ Ἰησοῦς. Nominative subject of εἶπεν.

ἐκεῖνοι. Nominative subject of ἔγνωσαν. The demonstrative pronoun refers to the Pharisees mentioned in 9:40, acting as a third-person personal pronoun with a simple anaphoric force (Wallace 1996, 328–29; BDF §291.6).

δέ. Marker of narrative development.

οὐκ. Negative particle normally used with indicative verbs.

ἔγνωσαν. Aor act ind 3rd pl γινώσκω.

τίνα. The neuter plural interrogative pronoun functions as the predicate nominative in an equative clause that, in its entirety (τίνα ἦν), serves as a direct object of ἔγνωσαν.

ἦν. Impf act ind 3rd sg εἰμί. The implied subject of the verb is neuter plural, agreeing with τίνα, because neuter plural subjects typically take singular verbs (see 1:28 on ἐγένετο).

ἅ. Accusative direct object of ἐλάλει. The relative pronoun refers to τίνα.

ἐλάλει. Impf act ind 3rd sg λαλέω. On the function of the imperfect in the FG, see 1:39 on ἦν.

αὐτοῖς. Dative indirect object of ἐλάλει.

John 10:7-10

⁷Then Jesus said again, "Truly, truly I say to you, I am the door for the sheep. ⁸All who came before me are thieves and robbers, but the sheep did not listen to them. ⁹I am the door. If anyone enters through me, he will be saved, and will come in and will go out and will find pasture. ¹⁰The thief does not come except that he may steal and kill and destroy. I have come that they may have life and have it abundantly."

10:7 Εἶπεν οὖν πάλιν ὁ Ἰησοῦς· ἀμὴν ἀμὴν λέγω ὑμῖν ὅτι ἐγώ εἰμι ἡ θύρα τῶν προβάτων.

Εἶπεν. Aor act ind 3rd sg λέγω.

οὖν. Postpositive inferential conjunction and/or transitional particle (see 1:22 and 11:6).

πάλιν. Adverb "pert[aining] to repetition in the same (or similar) manner" (BDAG, 752.2).

ὁ Ἰησοῦς. Nominative subject of Εἶπεν.

ἀμὴν ἀμὴν λέγω ὑμῖν. Metacomment (see 1:51).

ἀμὴν ἀμὴν. Asseverative particles that mark the beginning of Jesus' solemn declaration (see 1:51).

λέγω. Pres act ind 1st sg λέγω.

ὑμῖν. Dative indirect object of λέγω.

ὅτι. ὅτι-*recitativum* that introduces the clausal complement (direct discourse) of λέγω.

ἐγώ εἰμι ἡ θύρα τῶν προβάτων. This is one of Jesus' "I am" pronouncements in the FG with an explicit predicate; for other statements of this type, see 6:35, 48, 51; 8:12; 10:9, 11, 14; 11:25; 14:6; 15:1, 5.

ἐγώ. Nominative subject of εἰμι. Fronted for emphasis.

εἰμι. Pres act ind 1st sg εἰμί.

ἡ θύρα. Predicate nominative.

τῶν προβάτων. Genitive of purpose qualifying θύρα ("the door for the sheep"), which is supported by v. 9, or genitive of direction ("the door to the sheep") (BDF §166; Haubeck and von Siebenthal, 564). Wallace (1996, 100 n. 76) disagrees with the second classification because the genitive of direction "indicates where the head noun is going (or the direction it is 'moving' in)," which is not applicable to doors because they "don't move off their hinges." In his view, "[t]he idea is 'the door that opens for the sheep,' where the collocation of head noun and gen. noun implies a certain verbal notion."

10:8 πάντες ὅσοι ἦλθον [πρὸ ἐμοῦ] κλέπται εἰσὶν καὶ λῃσταί, ἀλλ' οὐκ ἤκουσαν αὐτῶν τὰ πρόβατα.

πάντες. Nominative subject of εἰσὶν. This verse is connected to the previous one by asyndeton.

ὅσοι. Nominative subject of ἦλθον. The antecedent of the correlative pronoun is πάντες. πάντες ὅσοι = "all who" (BDAG, 729.2).

ἦλθον. Aor act ind 3rd pl ἔρχομαι.

[πρὸ ἐμοῦ]. Temporal. This PP is missing in some manuscripts ($\mathfrak{P}^{45\text{vid.75}}$ ℵ*.2b Γ Δ 892^s 1424 pm lat sy^{s,p} sa ly pbo Aug), while in others it is placed before (Θ f^1 565 l 2211) or after ἦλθον ($\mathfrak{P}^{66}$ ℵ^{2a} A B D K L W Ψ f^{13} 33 579 700 1241 pm sy$^{h^{**}}$ Lcf). Internal considerations are not of much help here because the addition of this PP could have been motivated by a desire "to make more sense from a highly compressed statement," while its omission could have arisen from a desire "to lessen the possibility of taking the passage as a blanket condemnation of all Old Testament worthies" (Metzger, 195). Even though the external evidence for a shorter text is stronger, the fact that some copyists (D b) omitted πάντες could mean that their base text included this PP, whose scope and implications they wished to limit. The UBS editorial committee eventually decided to print πρὸ ἐμοῦ within square brackets to indicate that no satisfactory decision can be reached regarding the presence or absence of this PP in the text (Metzger, 195–96).

κλέπται. Predicate nominative (see 10:1).

εἰσὶν. Pres act ind 3rd pl εἰμί.

καὶ. Coordinating conjunction.

λῃσταί. Predicate nominative (see 10:1).

ἀλλ'. Marker of contrast.

οὐκ. Negative particle normally used with indicative verbs.

ἤκουσαν. Aor act ind 3rd pl ἀκούω.

αὐτῶν. Genitive direct object of ἤκουσαν.

τὰ πρόβατα. Nominative subject of ἤκουσαν. Unlike 10:3-4, which use the singular verb forms with πρόβατα, ἤκουσαν is in the plural because the term "sheep" no longer refers to livestock but to people, emphasizing their individuality (Wallace 1996, 400).

10:9 ἐγώ εἰμι ἡ θύρα· δι' ἐμοῦ ἐάν τις εἰσέλθῃ σωθήσεται καὶ εἰσελεύσεται καὶ ἐξελεύσεται καὶ νομὴν εὑρήσει.

ἐγώ εἰμι ἡ θύρα. This is one of Jesus' "I am" pronouncements in the FG with an explicit predicate; for other statements of this type, see 6:35, 48, 51; 8:12; 10:7, 11, 14; 11:25; 14:6; 15:1, 5.

ἐγώ. Nominative subject of εἰμί. Fronted for emphasis. This verse is connected to the previous one by asyndeton.

εἰμι. Pres act ind 1st sg εἰμί.

ἡ θύρα. Predicate nominative. The meaning of θύρα is here figuratively applied to Jesus, with "the emphasis . . . upon the door as a passageway and not as an object closing off an entrance" (LN 7.39).

δι' ἐμοῦ. Agency. The PP is placed before ἐάν for emphasis, because the elements that belong to a dependent clause normally come after the subordinating conjunction (BDF §475.1). This clause is connected to the preceding one by asyndeton.

ἐάν. Introduces the protasis of a third-class condition.

τις. Nominative subject of εἰσέλθῃ.

εἰσέλθῃ. Aor act subj 3rd sg εἰσέρχομαι. Subjunctive with ἐάν.

σωθήσεται. Fut pass ind 3rd sg σῴζω. It marks the beginning of the apodosis of a third-class condition.

καὶ. Coordinating conjunction.

εἰσελεύσεται. Fut mid ind 3rd sg εἰσέρχομαι.

καὶ. Coordinating conjunction.

ἐξελεύσεται. Fut mid ind 3rd sg ἐξέρχομαι.

καὶ. Coordinating conjunction.

νομὴν. Accusative direct object of εὑρήσει.

εὑρήσει. Fut act ind 3rd sg εὑρίσκω.

10:10 ὁ κλέπτης οὐκ ἔρχεται εἰ μὴ ἵνα κλέψῃ καὶ θύσῃ καὶ ἀπολέσῃ· ἐγὼ ἦλθον ἵνα ζωὴν ἔχωσιν καὶ περισσὸν ἔχωσιν.

ὁ κλέπτης. Nominative subject of ἔρχεται. Fronted as a topical frame. The article is generic. This verse is connected to the previous one by asyndeton.

οὐκ . . . εἰ μὴ. A point/counterpoint set that corrects the negated clause ("the thief does not come") by introducing an exception ("except to steal and kill and destroy"); on the function of the excepted element, see 3:13 on οὐδεὶς . . . εἰ μὴ.

ἔρχεται. Pres mid ind 3rd sg ἔρχομαι.
ἵνα. Introduces a purpose clause.
κλέψῃ. Aor act subj 3rd sg κλέπτω. Subjunctive with ἵνα.
καὶ. Coordinating conjunction.
θύσῃ. Aor act subj 3rd sg θύω. Subjunctive with ἵνα.
καὶ. Coordinating conjunction.
ἀπολέσῃ. Aor act subj 3rd sg ἀπόλλυμι. Subjunctive with ἵνα.
ἐγώ. Nominative subject of ἦλθον. Fronted for emphasis.
ἦλθον. Aor act ind 1st sg ἔρχομαι.
ἵνα. Introduces a purpose clause.
ζωὴν. Accusative direct object of ἔχωσιν. Fronted for emphasis.
ἔχωσιν. Pres act subj 3rd pl ἔχω. Subjunctive with ἵνα.
καὶ. Coordinating conjunction.
περισσὸν. Adverbial accusative ("in abundance, abundantly"; cf. Wallace 1996, 201, 293). The adjective περισσός ("going beyond what is necessary" [BDAG, 805.2.a]) is used here as a substantive.
ἔχωσιν. Pres act subj 3rd pl ἔχω. Subjunctive with ἵνα.

John 10:11-13

¹¹"I am the good shepherd. The good shepherd lays down his life for the sheep. ¹²The one who is a hireling and not a shepherd, whose sheep are not his own, sees the wolf coming and leaves the sheep and flees—and the wolf snatches them and scatters them— ¹³because he is a hireling, and he is not concerned about the sheep."

10:11 Ἐγώ εἰμι ὁ ποιμὴν ὁ καλός. ὁ ποιμὴν ὁ καλὸς τὴν ψυχὴν αὐτοῦ τίθησιν ὑπὲρ τῶν προβάτων·

Ἐγώ εἰμι ὁ ποιμὴν ὁ καλός. This is one of Jesus' "I am" pronouncements in the FG with an explicit predicate; for other statements of this type, see 6:35, 48, 51; 8:12; 10:7, 9, 14; 11:25; 14:6; 15:1, 5.
Ἐγώ. Nominative subject of εἰμι. Fronted for emphasis. This verse is connected to the previous one by asyndeton.
εἰμι. Pres act ind 1st sg εἰμί.
ὁ ποιμὴν ὁ καλός. Predicate nominative. The adjective καλός stands in the second attributive position (see 1:29 on ὁ αἴρων).
ὁ ποιμὴν ὁ καλὸς. Nominative subject of τίθησιν. Fronted as a topical frame. καλός is again in the second attributive position. This clause is connected to the previous one by asyndeton.
τὴν ψυχὴν. Accusative direct object of τίθησιν. Fronted for emphasis.
αὐτοῦ. Possessive genitive qualifying ψυχὴν.

John 10:11-13

τίθησιν. Pres act ind 3rd sg τίθημι. The phrase "to lay down one's life" is a characteristically Johannine expression; see John 10:15 (τὴν ψυχήν μου τίθημι), 10:17 (τίθημι τὴν ψυχήν μου), 13:37 (τὴν ψυχήν μου ὑπὲρ σοῦ θήσω), 13:38 (τὴν ψυχήν σου ὑπὲρ ἐμοῦ θήσεις), 15:13 (ἵνα τις τὴν ψυχὴν αὐτοῦ θῇ), 1 John 3:16 (ἐκεῖνος ὑπὲρ ἡμῶν τὴν ψυχὴν αὐτοῦ ἔθηκεν). The replacement of τίθησιν with δίδωσιν ("to give one's life") in some manuscripts ($\mathfrak{P}^{45}$ ℵ* D lat sy^s pbo bo) reflects the synoptic influence (see Matt 20:28; Mark 10:45; cf. Metzger, 196).

ὑπὲρ τῶν προβάτων. Representation ("on behalf of the sheep") and substitution ("in the place of the sheep"; cf. Harris 2015, 197). For the prepositional phrases with ὑπέρ in the FG, see 6:51; 10:15; 11:50, 51, 52; 13:37, 38; 15:13; 17:19; 18:15.

10:12 ὁ μισθωτὸς καὶ οὐκ ὢν ποιμήν, οὗ οὐκ ἔστιν τὰ πρόβατα ἴδια, θεωρεῖ τὸν λύκον ἐρχόμενον καὶ ἀφίησιν τὰ πρόβατα καὶ φεύγει – καὶ ὁ λύκος ἁρπάζει αὐτὰ καὶ σκορπίζει –

ὁ ... ὤν. Pres act ptc masc nom sg εἰμί (substantival). Nominative subject of θεωρεῖ. Fronted as a topical frame. This verse is connected to the previous one by asyndeton.

μισθωτὸς. Predicate nominative. In the NT, the adjective μισθωτὸς is used only as a substantive ("a person who has been hired to perform a particular service or work" [LN 57.174]; cf. BDAG, 654). The article ὁ in front of the noun does not belong to μισθωτὸς, as presumed in most English translations, but to the substantival participle ὤν; see the next verse, which also has an anarthrous μισθωτός.

καὶ. Coordinating conjunction.

οὐκ. The negative particle οὐ (οὐκ, οὐχ) is very rarely used with participles. Two possible explanations of its combination with ὤν here are (1) the Fourth Evangelist shows preference for καὶ οὐ/οὐκ/οὐχ (twenty-eight times) in comparison with καὶ μή (five times) (BDF §430.1); (2) οὐκ emphasizes facticity of the repudiated predicate nominative ("who is certainly no shepherd"; cf. Harris 2015, 197; Moulton, 231–32).

ποιμήν. Predicate nominative.

οὗ. Possessive genitive qualifying τὰ πρόβατα ("whose sheep"). The antecedent of the relative pronoun is the hired hand described with the preceding participial clause. This is a good illustration of the principle that the possessive genitive "need not imply the literal (and sometimes harsh) idea of possession of physical property" (Wallace 1996, 81) because the sheep of the hireling do not belong to him but are only entrusted to his care.

οὐκ. Negative particle normally used with indicative verbs.

ἔστιν. Pres act ind 3rd sg εἰμί. The enclitic ἐστιν is accented ἔστιν when it comes at the beginning of a sentence, when it expresses existence, or when it follows ἀλλ', εἰ, καί, οὐκ, ὅτι, or τοῦτ'. The third condition is fulfilled here.

τὰ πρόβατα. Nominative subject of ἔστιν. Since τὰ πρόβατα is used here as a collective noun, the verb is in the singular.

ἴδια. Predicate adjective. Lit. "whose sheep are not his own" = "who does not own the sheep" (cf. NRSV; NIV; HCSB; NET; ESV).

θεωρεῖ. Pres act ind 3rd sg θεωρέω.

τὸν λύκον. Accusative direct object of θεωρεῖ.

ἐρχόμενον. Pres mid ptc masc acc sg ἔρχομαι (predicative). The participle stands in the second predicate position (see 1:29 on ἐρχόμενον), functioning as the accusative complement to τὸν λύκον in a double accusative object-complement construction. For a similar construction, see 1:29, 47.

καὶ. Coordinating conjunction.

ἀφίησιν. Pres act ind 3rd sg ἀφίημι.

τὰ πρόβατα. Accusative direct object of ἀφίησιν.

καὶ. Coordinating conjunction.

φεύγει. Pres act ind 3rd sg φεύγω.

καὶ. Coordinating conjunction.

ὁ λύκος. Nominative subject of ἁρπάζει. Fronted as a topical frame.

ἁρπάζει. Pres act ind 3rd sg ἁρπάζω. The verb means "to attack, with the implication of seizing" (LN 39.49).

αὐτὰ. Accusative direct object of ἁρπάζει.

καὶ. Coordinating conjunction.

σκορπίζει. Pres act ind 3rd sg σκορπίζω. The verb means "to cause a group or a gathering to disperse or scatter" (LN 15.135).

10:13 ὅτι μισθωτός ἐστιν καὶ οὐ μέλει αὐτῷ περὶ τῶν προβάτων.

ὅτι. Introduces a causal clause.

μισθωτός. Predicate nominative (see 10:12). Fronted for emphasis.

ἐστιν. Pres act ind 3rd sg εἰμί.

καὶ. Coordinating conjunction.

οὐ. Negative particle normally used with indicative verbs.

μέλει. Pres act ind 3rd sg μέλω, used impersonally with the dative of person ("it is a care/concern, is of interest to someone" [BDAG, 626.1]), followed by περί τινος ("about someone or something"; cf. BDAG, 626.1.b).

αὐτῷ. Dative complement of μέλει.

περὶ τῶν προβάτων. Reference.

John 10:14-18

¹⁴"I am the good shepherd. I know my own and my own know me, ¹⁵just as the Father knows me and I know the Father. And I lay down my life for the sheep. ¹⁶And I have other sheep that are not of this fold. I must bring these also, and they will hear my voice, and they will become one flock, one shepherd. ¹⁷For this reason the Father loves me, because I lay down my life in order that I may take it up again. ¹⁸No one takes it away from me, but I lay it down on my own. I have authority to lay it down, and I have authority to take it up again. I have received this commandment from my Father."

10:14 Ἐγώ εἰμι ὁ ποιμὴν ὁ καλὸς καὶ γινώσκω τὰ ἐμὰ καὶ γινώσκουσίν με τὰ ἐμά,

Ἐγώ εἰμι ὁ ποιμὴν ὁ καλὸς. This is one of Jesus' "I am" pronouncements in the FG with an explicit predicate; for other statements of this type, see 6:35, 48, 51; 8:12; 10:7, 9, 11; 11:25; 14:6; 15:1, 5.

Ἐγώ. Nominative subject of εἰμι. Fronted for emphasis. This verse is connected to the previous one by asyndeton.

εἰμι. Pres act ind 1st sg εἰμί.

ὁ ποιμὴν ὁ καλὸς. Predicate nominative (see 1:11).

καὶ. Coordinating conjunction.

γινώσκω. Pres act ind 1st sg γινώσκω.

τὰ ἐμὰ. Accusative direct object of γινώσκω. The substantival adjective is in neuter plural because it refers to πρόβατα.

καὶ. Coordinating conjunction.

γινώσκουσίν. Pres act ind 3rd pl γινώσκω. γινώσκουσίν, which has an acute accent on the antepenult, acquired an additional accent, the acute, on the ultima from the enclitic με (Smyth §183; Carson 1985, 48).

με. Accusative direct object of γινώσκουσίν.

τὰ ἐμά. Nominative subject of γινώσκουσίν (see 10:8 on τὰ πρόβατα).

10:15 καθὼς γινώσκει με ὁ πατὴρ κἀγὼ γινώσκω τὸν πατέρα, καὶ τὴν ψυχήν μου τίθημι ὑπὲρ τῶν προβάτων.

καθὼς. Introduces a comparative clause that establishes an analogy between the previous verse, which describes the mutual knowledge between the good shepherd and his own sheep (γινώσκω τὰ ἐμὰ καὶ γινώσκουσίν με τὰ ἐμά), and this verse, which describes the mutual knowledge between the Father and the Son (καθὼς γινώσκει με ὁ πατὴρ κἀγὼ γινώσκω τὸν πατέρα). This verse is connected to the previous one by asyndeton.

John 10:14-16

γινώσκει. Pres act ind 3rd sg γινώσκω.
με. Accusative direct object of γινώσκει.
ὁ πατήρ. Nominative subject of γινώσκει.
κἀγώ. Formed by crasis from καὶ ἐγώ. καὶ is a coordinating conjunction; ἐγώ is the nominative subject of γινώσκω.
γινώσκω. Pres act ind 1st sg γινώσκω.
τὸν πατέρα. Accusative direct object of γινώσκω.
καὶ. Coordinating conjunction.
τὴν ψυχήν. Accusative direct object of τίθημι.
μου. Possessive genitive qualifying ψυχήν.
τίθημι. Pres act ind 1st sg τίθημι. Like in 10:11, the variant δίδωμι ($\mathfrak{P}^{45.66}$ ℵ* D W pbo) arose under the synoptic influence.
ὑπὲρ τῶν προβάτων. Representation and substitution (see 10:11).

10:16 καὶ ἄλλα πρόβατα ἔχω ἃ οὐκ ἔστιν ἐκ τῆς αὐλῆς ταύτης· κἀκεῖνα δεῖ με ἀγαγεῖν καὶ τῆς φωνῆς μου ἀκούσουσιν, καὶ γενήσονται μία ποίμνη, εἷς ποιμήν.

καὶ. Coordinating conjunction.
ἄλλα πρόβατα. Accusative direct object of ἔχω. Fronted for emphasis.
ἔχω. Pres act ind 1st sg ἔχω.
ἃ. Nominative subject of ἔστιν. The neuter plural relative pronoun refers to ἄλλα πρόβατα, which, as a collective noun, takes the verb in the singular (see 10:12 on τὰ πρόβατα).
οὐκ. Negative particle normally used with indicative verbs.
ἔστιν. Pres act ind 3rd sg εἰμί. The enclitic ἐστιν is accented ἔστιν when it comes at the beginning of a sentence, when it expresses existence, or when it follows ἀλλ', εἰ, καί, οὐκ, ὅτι, or τοῦτ'. The third condition is fulfilled here.
ἐκ τῆς αὐλῆς ταύτης. Source.
κἀκεῖνα. Formed by crasis from καὶ ἐκεῖνα. καὶ is adverbial (adjunctive); ἐκεῖνα is the accusative direct object of ἀγαγεῖν. Fronted as a topical frame.
δεῖ. Pres act ind 3rd sg δεῖ.
με. Accusative subject of the infinitive ἀγαγεῖν.
ἀγαγεῖν. Aor act inf ἄγω (complementary). On the function of the infinitive with δεῖ, see 3:7 on γεννηθῆναι.
καὶ. Coordinating conjunction.
τῆς φωνῆς. Genitive direct object of ἀκούσουσιν.
μου. Possessive genitive qualifying φωνῆς.
ἀκούσουσιν. Fut act ind 3rd pl ἀκούω. The verb is in the plural because the implied subject refers to individuals that compose the metaphorical flock (Harris 2015, 198).

καί. Coordinating conjunction.

γενήσονται. Fut mid ind 3rd pl γίνομαι. The external support for the plural γενήσονται ($\mathfrak{P}^{45}$ ℵ² B D L W Θ Ψ 1 33 565 1424 *l*2211 f vg^ms sy^hmg Cl [Did]) is slightly stronger than for the singular γενήσεται ($\mathfrak{P}^{66}$ ℵ* A K Γ Δ *f*¹³ 579 700 892ˢ 1241 𝔐 lat sy). The plural γενήσονται, though consistent with the plural ἀκούσουσιν that precedes it, is also the more difficult reading because it equates the people not only with "one flock" but also "with one shepherd," while the singular represents a stylistic correction (Metzger, 196). The use of the verb γίνομαι ("they will become") rather than the verb εἰμί ("they will be") indicates that, for the Fourth Evangelist, "the unity of the one flock is not a given unity naturally existing, but a unity created in and by Jesus" (Barrett, 376).

μία ποίμνη. Predicate nominative. The reading *unum ovile* ("one fold") in the Latin Vulgate is a mistranslation that has been adopted in a number of older English translations (Wycliffe's Bible, Cromwell's Great Bible, the Geneva Bible, the Bishops' Bible, the Rheims-Douay Bible, and the King James Bible [Metzger, 196]).

εἷς ποιμήν. Nominative in apposition to μία ποίμνη.

10:17 Διὰ τοῦτό με ὁ πατὴρ ἀγαπᾷ ὅτι ἐγὼ τίθημι τὴν ψυχήν μου, ἵνα πάλιν λάβω αὐτήν.

Διὰ τοῦτό. Causal. The demonstrative pronoun is cataphoric, referring to the ὅτι clause that follows. τοῦτό, which has a circumflex accent on the penult, acquired an additional accent, the acute, on the ultima from the enclitic με (Smyth §183; Carson 1985, 48).

με. Accusative direct object of ἀγαπᾷ.

ὁ πατὴρ. Nominative subject of ἀγαπᾷ.

ἀγαπᾷ. Pres act ind 3rd sg ἀγαπάω. The verb ἀγαπάω and its cognate noun ἀγάπη occur more often in the FG (forty-four times) than in all the Synoptics together (twenty-eight times).

ὅτι. Introduces a causal clause.

ἐγὼ. Nominative subject of τίθημι. Fronted for emphasis.

τίθημι. Pres act ind 1st sg τίθημι.

τὴν ψυχήν. Accusative direct object of τίθημι.

μου. Possessive genitive qualifying ψυχήν.

ἵνα. Introduces a purpose clause. Many commentators express discomfort with this classification because a telic ἵνα clause would mean, as Harris phrases it, "that Jesus' motivation ('in order that') in surrendering his life was to experience resurrection" (2015, 198). But Brown rightly points out that in the Johannine theology, Jesus' death, resurrection, and ascension constitute "the one, indissoluble salvific action of return to the Father" so that "resurrection is truly the purpose of his death" (399).

πάλιν. Adverb "pert[aining] to return to a position or state" (BDAG, 752.1).

λάβω. Aor act subj 1st sg λαμβάνω. Subjunctive with ἵνα.

αὐτήν. Accusative direct object of λάβω.

10:18 οὐδεὶς αἴρει αὐτὴν ἀπ' ἐμοῦ, ἀλλ' ἐγὼ τίθημι αὐτὴν ἀπ' ἐμαυτοῦ. ἐξουσίαν ἔχω θεῖναι αὐτήν, καὶ ἐξουσίαν ἔχω πάλιν λαβεῖν αὐτήν· ταύτην τὴν ἐντολὴν ἔλαβον παρὰ τοῦ πατρός μου.

οὐδεὶς. Nominative subject of αἴρει. Fronted for emphasis. This verse is connected to the previous one by asyndeton.

αἴρει. Pres act ind 3rd sg αἴρω. The aorist ἦρεν is well attested by the Egyptian textual family ($\mathfrak{P}^{45}$ ℵ* B), but the UBS committee preferred the present αἴρει because of its wider external support (Metzger, 196–97). Barrett, however, argues that the aorist ("no one has taken [my life] from me") is the more difficult and thus the more original reading because "it does not refer to earlier unsuccessful attempts upon the life of Jesus, but to the crucifixion viewed as an event in the past—viewed, that is, from John's own standpoint" (377; cf. Brown, 387). Schnackenburg, who also prefers the aorist because of its difficulty, calls ἦρεν a "proleptic" aorist "through which the speaker envisions the future in a lively manner" (2:509 n. 103).

αὐτὴν. Accusative direct object of αἴρει.

ἀπ' ἐμοῦ. Separation.

ἀλλ'. Marker of contrast.

ἐγώ. Nominative subject of τίθημι. Fronted for emphasis.

τίθημι. Pres act ind 1st sg τίθημι.

αὐτὴν. Accusative direct object of τίθημι.

ἀπ' ἐμαυτοῦ. Agency (see 5:19 on ἀφ' ἑαυτοῦ).

ἐξουσίαν. Accusative direct object of ἔχω. Fronted for emphasis.

ἔχω. Pres act ind 1st sg ἔχω.

θεῖναι. Aor act inf τίθημι (epexegetical to ἐξουσίαν).

αὐτήν. Accusative direct object of θεῖναι.

καὶ. Coordinating conjunction.

ἐξουσίαν. Accusative direct object of ἔχω.

ἔχω. Pres act ind 1st sg ἔχω.

πάλιν. Adverb "pert[aining] to return to a position or state" (BDAG, 752.1).

λαβεῖν. Aor act inf λαμβάνω (epexegetical to ἐξουσίαν).

αὐτήν. Accusative direct object of λαβεῖν.

ταύτην τὴν ἐντολήν. Accusative direct object of ἔλαβον.
ἔλαβον. Aor act ind 1st sg λαμβάνω.
παρὰ τοῦ πατρός. Source.
μου. Genitive of relationship qualifying πατρός.

John 10:19-21

[19]Again there was a division among the Jews because of these words. [20]Many of them were saying, "He has a demon and is out of his mind. Why do you listen to him?" [21]Others were saying, "These words are not those of one who is possessed by a demon. A demon cannot open the eyes of the blind, can he?"

10:19 Σχίσμα πάλιν ἐγένετο ἐν τοῖς Ἰουδαίοις διὰ τοὺς λόγους τούτους.

Σχίσμα. Nominative subject of ἐγένετο. Fronted for emphasis. This verse is connected to the previous one by asyndeton.

πάλιν. Adverb "pert[aining] to repetition in the same (or similar) manner" (BDAG, 752.2). In many manuscripts, πάλιν is preceded by a postpositive inferential conjunction οὖν ($\mathfrak{P}^{66}$ A [D] K Γ Δ Θ Ψ $f^{1.13}$ 565 700 892^s 1241 1424 $\mathfrak{M}$ sy^h pbo), but a scribal addition of this word to the text seems to be more likely than its omission (Metzger, 197).

ἐγένετο. Aor mid ind 3rd sg γίνομαι.
ἐν τοῖς Ἰουδαίοις. Locative.
διὰ τοὺς λόγους τούτους. Causal.

10:20 ἔλεγον δὲ πολλοὶ ἐξ αὐτῶν· δαιμόνιον ἔχει καὶ μαίνεται· τί αὐτοῦ ἀκούετε;

ἔλεγον. Impf act ind 3rd pl λέγω. On the function of the imperfect in the FG, see 1:39 on ἦν.
δέ. Marker of narrative development.
πολλοί. Nominative subject of ἔλεγον.
ἐξ αὐτῶν. Replaces the partitive genitive.
δαιμόνιον. Accusative direct object of ἔχει. Fronted for emphasis.
ἔχει. Pres act ind 3rd sg ἔχω.
καί. Coordinating conjunction.
μαίνεται. Pres mid/pass ind 3rd sg μαίνομαι. The verb means to "be mad, be out of one's mind" (BDAG, 610).
τί. Adverbial use of the interrogative pronoun ("why?").
αὐτοῦ. Genitive direct object of ἀκούετε.
ἀκούετε. Pres act ind 2nd pl ἀκούω.

10:21 ἄλλοι ἔλεγον· ταῦτα τὰ ῥήματα οὐκ ἔστιν δαιμονιζομένου· μὴ δαιμόνιον δύναται τυφλῶν ὀφθαλμοὺς ἀνοῖξαι;

ἄλλοι. Nominative subject of ἔλεγον. This verse is connected to the previous one by asyndeton.

ἔλεγον. Impf act ind 3rd pl λέγω. On the function of the imperfect in the FG, see 1:39 on ἦν.

ταῦτα τὰ ῥήματα. Nominative subject of ἔστιν. Fronted as a topical frame.

οὐκ. Negative particle normally used with indicative verbs.

ἔστιν. Pres act ind 3rd sg εἰμί. Neuter plural subjects typically take singular verbs (see 1:28 on ἐγένετο). The enclitic ἐστιν is accented ἔστιν when it comes at the beginning of a sentence, when it expresses existence, or when it follows ἀλλ', εἰ, καί, οὐκ, ὅτι, or τοῦτ'. The third condition is fulfilled here.

δαιμονιζομένου. Pres pass ptc masc gen sg δαιμονίζομαι (substantival). Subjective genitive qualifying ῥήματα ("the words spoken by one possessed by a demon").

μὴ. Negative particle that introduces a question that expects a negative answer.

δαιμόνιον. Nominative subject of δύναται.

δύναται. Pres mid ind 3rd sg δύναμαι.

τυφλῶν. Possessive genitive qualifying ὀφθαλμοὺς. Fronted for emphasis.

ὀφθαλμοὺς. Accusative direct object of ἀνοῖξαι.

ἀνοῖξαι. Aor act inf ἀνοίγω (complementary).

John 10:22-30

[22] At that time a Feast of Dedication took place in Jerusalem. It was winter. [23] And Jesus was walking in the temple, in the portico of Solomon. [24] So the Jews surrounded him and were saying to him, "How long are you going to keep us in suspense? If you are the Messiah, tell us plainly." [25] Jesus answered them, "I have told you, and you do not believe. The works that I do in the name of my Father—these testify about me. [26] But you do not believe because you do not belong to my sheep. [27] My sheep hear my voice, and I know them, and they follow me. [28] And I give them eternal life, and they will never perish, and no one will snatch them out of my hand. [29] What my Father has given me is greater than all, and no one can snatch (it) out of the Father's hand. [30] The Father and I are one."

10:22 Ἐγένετο τότε τὰ ἐγκαίνια ἐν τοῖς Ἱεροσολύμοις, χειμὼν ἦν,

Ἐγένετο. Aor mid ind 3rd sg γίνομαι. This verse is connected to the previous one by asyndeton.

τότε. Adverb of time.

τὰ ἐγκαίνια. Nominative subject of Ἐγένετο.

ἐν τοῖς Ἱεροσολύμοις. Locative.

χειμών. Nominative subject of ἦν.

ἦν. Impf act ind 3rd sg εἰμί. In this narrative unit, the imperfects ἦν (this verse) and περιεπάτει (next verse) set the scene for the main action that begins with the aorist ἐκύκλωσαν in v. 24. On this function of the imperfect in the FG, see 3:22 on διέτριβεν.

10:23 καὶ περιεπάτει ὁ Ἰησοῦς ἐν τῷ ἱερῷ ἐν τῇ στοᾷ τοῦ Σολομῶνος.

καί. Coordinating conjunction.

περιεπάτει. Impf act ind 3rd sg περιπατέω. On the function of the imperfect in the FG, see 1:39 on ἦν.

ὁ Ἰησοῦς. Nominative subject of περιεπάτει.

ἐν τῷ ἱερῷ. Locative. Elsewhere in the FG, this PP occurs in 2:14; 5:14; 7:28; 8:20; 11:56; 18:20.

ἐν τῇ στοᾷ. Locative.

τοῦ Σολομῶνος. Possessive genitive qualifying στοᾷ. The portico of Solomon was a covered colonnade named for Solomon, located on the east side of the outer court of the temple precincts.

10:24 ἐκύκλωσαν οὖν αὐτὸν οἱ Ἰουδαῖοι καὶ ἔλεγον αὐτῷ· ἕως πότε τὴν ψυχὴν ἡμῶν αἴρεις; εἰ σὺ εἶ ὁ χριστός, εἰπὲ ἡμῖν παρρησίᾳ.

ἐκύκλωσαν. Aor act ind 3rd pl κυκλόω. κυκλόω means "to move in such a way as to encircle an object—'to surround, to be around'" (LN 15.147).

οὖν. Postpositive inferential conjunction and/or transitional particle (see 1:22 and 11:6).

αὐτόν. Accusative direct object of ἐκύκλωσαν.

οἱ Ἰουδαῖοι. Nominative subject of ἐκύκλωσαν.

καί. Coordinating conjunction.

ἔλεγον. Impf act ind 3rd pl λέγω. The imperfective aspect of the verb form calls attention to the ongoing character of the conversation between Jesus and the Jews. On the function of the imperfect in the FG, see 1:39 on ἦν.

αὐτῷ. Dative indirect object of ἔλεγον.

ἕως πότε. Temporal ἕως serves as an improper preposition (see 1:3 on χωρὶς αὐτοῦ) with an adverb of time. ἕως πότε = "how long?" (BDAG, 423.1.b.γ).

τὴν ψυχὴν. Accusative direct object of αἴρεις.

ἡμῶν. Possessive genitive qualifying ψυχὴν.

αἴρεις. Pres act ind 2nd sg αἴρω. αἴρω τὴν ψυχήν τινος (lit. "to lift up the soul of someone") is an idiom for "to keep someone in suspense so that one cannot come to a conclusion in one's thinking" (LN 30.36). Moule (209) considers this a Semitism (נשׂא נפשׁ אל) that could mean "to set one's hopes on," but this meaning is not consistent with the request "Tell us plainly" that follows.

εἰ. Introduces the protasis of a first-class condition.

σὺ. Nominative subject of εἶ. Fronted for emphasis.

εἶ. Pres act ind 2nd sg εἰμί.

ὁ χριστός. Predicate nominative.

εἰπὲ. Aor act impv 2nd sg λέγω. It marks the beginning of the apodosis of a first-class condition.

ἡμῖν. Dative indirect object of εἰπὲ.

παρρησίᾳ. Dative of manner.

10:25 ἀπεκρίθη αὐτοῖς ὁ Ἰησοῦς· εἶπον ὑμῖν καὶ οὐ πιστεύετε· τὰ ἔργα ἃ ἐγὼ ποιῶ ἐν τῷ ὀνόματι τοῦ πατρός μου ταῦτα μαρτυρεῖ περὶ ἐμοῦ·

ἀπεκρίθη. Aor mid ind 3rd sg ἀποκρίνομαι. On the voice, see "Deponency" in the Series Introduction. This verse is connected to the previous one by asyndeton.

αὐτοῖς. Dative indirect object of ἀπεκρίθη.

ὁ Ἰησοῦς. Nominative subject of ἀπεκρίθη.

εἶπον. Aor act ind 1st sg λέγω.

ὑμῖν. Dative indirect object of εἶπον.

καὶ. Coordinating conjunction. This is not a special case of the so-called adversative καί (*pace* Haubeck and von Siebenthal, 567; Harris 2015, 201) but the standard use of καί joining two clauses that stand in tension with each other (see 1:5).

οὐ. Negative particle normally used with indicative verbs.

πιστεύετε. Pres act ind 2nd pl πιστεύω.

τὰ ἔργα. Nominative subject of μαρτυρεῖ in a left-dislocation, which is resumed by ταῦτα (see Runge 2010, 287–313). The left-dislocation of the subject of the clause marks it for prominence.

ἃ. Accusative direct object of ποιῶ.

ἐγὼ. Nominative subject of ποιῶ. Fronted for emphasis.

ποιῶ. Pres act ind 1st sg ποιέω.

ἐν τῷ ὀνόματι. Instrumental.

τοῦ πατρός. Possessive genitive qualifying ὀνόματι.

μου. Genitive of relationship qualifying πατρός.

ταῦτα. Nominative subject of μαρτυρεῖ, resuming τὰ ἔργα. The anaphoric demonstrative reinforces what is already made prominent through the left-dislocation of τὰ ἔργα.

μαρτυρεῖ. Pres act ind 3rd sg μαρτυρέω. The verb is in the singular because the subject (ταῦτα) is in the neuter plural.

περὶ ἐμοῦ. Reference.

10:26 ἀλλ' ὑμεῖς οὐ πιστεύετε, ὅτι οὐκ ἐστὲ ἐκ τῶν προβάτων τῶν ἐμῶν.

ἀλλ'. Marker of contrast.

ὑμεῖς. Nominative subject of πιστεύετε. The personal pronoun is emphatic and contrastive, highlighting the difference between the unbelieving Jews ("you") and Jesus' followers.

οὐ. Negative particle normally used with indicative verbs.

πιστεύετε. Pres act ind 2nd pl πιστεύω. The verb stands in final, emphatic position.

ὅτι. Introduces a causal clause.

οὐκ. Negative particle normally used with indicative verbs.

ἐστὲ. Pres act ind 2nd pl εἰμί.

ἐκ τῶν προβάτων τῶν ἐμῶν. Replaces the partitive genitive. When the PP with ἐκ is combined with εἶναι, it means to "belong to someone or someth[ing]" (BDAG, 297.4.a.δ). The possessive adjective ἐμῶν stands in the second attributive position (see 1:9 on τὸ φῶς τὸ ἀληθινόν). In a number of witnesses, this PP is followed by a clause καθὼς εἶπον ὑμῖν (𝔓⁶⁶* A D Γ Δ Ψ f¹·¹³ 565 579 700 892ˢ 1424 *l*2211 𝔐 it sy pbo boᵖᵗ). Given an equally strong support for the reading that does not include this clause (𝔓⁶⁶ᶜ·⁷⁵ ℵ B K L W Θ 33 1241 *l*844 aur c vg sa ac ly boᵖᵗ), a decision must be made on internal grounds. While the absence of καθὼς εἶπον ὑμῖν from the text could be explained as a deliberate deletion because the copyists could not find any declaration of Jesus that the Jews do not belong to his sheep, an expansion of an originally shorter text is probably more likely (Metzger, 197).

10:27 τὰ πρόβατα τὰ ἐμὰ τῆς φωνῆς μου ἀκούουσιν, κἀγὼ γινώσκω αὐτὰ καὶ ἀκολουθοῦσίν μοι,

τὰ πρόβατα τὰ ἐμὰ. Nominative subject of ἀκούουσιν. Fronted as a topical frame. This verse is connected to the previous one by asyndeton.

τῆς φωνῆς. Genitive direct object of ἀκούουσιν.

μου. Possessive genitive qualifying φωνῆς.

ἀκούουσιν. Pres act ind 3rd pl ἀκούω. The verb stands in final, emphatic position. Like in 10:8, the verb is in the plural although its subject is a neuter plural that usually takes the verb in the singular, because the term "sheep" no longer refers to livestock but to people, emphasizing their individuality. Wallace argues that "[t]he plural verb is no accident: v 27 contrasts with v 3 where real sheep hear the shepherd's voice as a group (τὰ πρόβατα τῆς φωνῆς αὐτοῦ ἀκούει), and v 4 where the sheep follow the shepherded collectively (τὰ πρόβατα αὐτῷ ἀκολουθεῖ)" (1996, 400).

κἀγώ. Formed by crasis from καὶ ἐγώ. καί is a coordinating conjunction; ἐγώ is the nominative subject of γινώσκω.

γινώσκω. Pres act ind 1st sg γινώσκω.

αὐτά. Accusative direct object of γινώσκω.

καί. Coordinating conjunction.

ἀκολουθοῦσίν. Pres act ind 3rd pl ἀκολουθέω. ἀκολουθοῦσίν, which has a circumflex accent on the penult, acquired an additional accent, the acute, on the ultima from the enclitic μοι (Smyth §183; Carson 1985, 48).

μοι. Dative direct object of ἀκολουθοῦσίν.

10:28 κἀγὼ δίδωμι αὐτοῖς ζωὴν αἰώνιον καὶ οὐ μὴ ἀπόλωνται εἰς τὸν αἰῶνα καὶ οὐχ ἁρπάσει τις αὐτὰ ἐκ τῆς χειρός μου.

κἀγώ. Formed by crasis from καὶ ἐγώ. καί is a coordinating conjunction; ἐγώ is the nominative subject of δίδωμι.

δίδωμι. Pres act ind 1st sg δίδωμι.

αὐτοῖς. Dative indirect object of δίδωμι.

ζωὴν αἰώνιον. Accusative direct object of δίδωμι. On the use of this phrase in the FG, see 3:15 on ζωὴν αἰώνιον.

καί. Coordinating conjunction.

οὐ μή. Emphatic negation, which is usually followed by the aorist subjunctive.

ἀπόλωνται. Aor mid subj 3rd pl ἀπόλλυμι. Used with οὐ μή to express emphatic negation.

εἰς τὸν αἰῶνα. Temporal.

καί. Coordinating conjunction.

οὐχ. Negative particle normally used with indicative verbs.

ἁρπάσει. Fut act ind 3rd sg ἁρπάζω. On the meaning, see 10:12.

τις. Nominative subject of ἁρπάσει.

αὐτά. Accusative direct object of ἁρπάσει.

ἐκ τῆς χειρός. Separation.

μου. Possessive genitive qualifying χειρός.

10:29 ὁ πατήρ μου ὃ δέδωκέν μοι πάντων μεῖζόν ἐστιν, καὶ οὐδεὶς δύναται ἁρπάζειν ἐκ τῆς χειρὸς τοῦ πατρός.

ὁ πατήρ. Nominative subject of δέδωκέν. ὁ πατήρ is placed before the relative pronoun for emphasis because the elements that belong to a dependent clause normally come after the subordinating conjunction (BDF §475.1). This is an example of hyperbaton (an alteration of the natural word order in a sentence). This verse is connected to the previous one by asyndeton.

μου. Genitive of relationship qualifying πατήρ.

ὃ δέδωκέν μοι πάντων μεῖζόν ἐστιν. This clause is attested in three major textual variants:

(1) ὃς δέδωκέν (ἔδωκέν 𝔓⁶⁶) μοι μείζων πάντων ἐστίν (𝔓⁶⁶ K Γ Δ ƒ¹·¹³ 33 565 579 700 892ˢ 1241 1424 *l*2211 𝔐)
(2) ὃ δέδωκέν (ὁ δεδωκώς D) μοι πάντων μείζων ἐστίν (ℵ D L W Ψ)
(3) ὃ δέδωκέν μοι πάντων μεῖζόν ἐστιν (B* [lat] bo)

If option (1) were original, it is difficult to explain why it would have been altered because it offers a smooth reading in which the masculine relative pronoun ὅς agrees with its antecedent ὁ πατήρ and the masculine comparative adjective μείζων serves as the predicate nominative ("the Father, who has given [them] to me, is greater than all others"). Option (2), which combines the neuter relative pronoun ὅ with the masculine comparative adjective μείζων, presents an awkward, if not impossible, Greek syntax (Barrett [382] proposes a tentative translation: "My Father in regard to what he has given me is greater than all"). Only option (3) offers a reading that can be construed in Greek, but its unusual sequence—i.e., the placement ὁ πατήρ, which functions as the subject of δέδωκέν within the relative clause, before the neuter singular relative pronoun ὅ—is certainly the more difficult reading that best explains the emergence of other readings (Metzger, 197–98; Barrett, 381–82).

ὅ. The relative pronoun introduces a headless relative clause that, in its entirety (ὁ πατήρ μου ὃ δέδωκέν μοι), serves as the subject of ἐστιν. Within its clause, ὅ is the accusative direct object of δέδωκέν.

δέδωκέν. Prf act ind 3rd sg δίδωμι. δέδωκέν, which has an acute accent on the antepenult, acquired an additional accent, the acute, on the ultima from the enclitic μοι (Smyth §183; Carson 1985, 48). The perfect tense, which is semantically marked, "expresses that what the Father 'has given' to the Son ... is definitely in his hand" (Frey 2018, 81).

μοι. Dative indirect object of δέδωκέν.

πάντων. Genitive of comparison.

μεῖζόν. Predicate adjective. μεῖζόν is a neuter singular comparative from μέγας, agreeing with the relative pronoun ὅ and thus referring to the unspecified content of the relative clause ("what my Father has given me"). μεῖζόν, which has a circumflex accent on the penult, acquired an additional accent, the acute, on the ultima from the enclitic ἐστιν (Smyth §183; Carson 1985, 48).

ἐστιν. Pres act ind 3rd sg εἰμί.

καὶ. Coordinating conjunction.

οὐδεὶς. Nominative subject of δύναται.

δύναται. Pres mid ind 3rd sg δύναμαι.

ἁρπάζειν. Pres act inf ἁρπάζω (complementary). The implied direct object of ἁρπάζειν is the unspecified content of the relative clause ("what my Father has given me").

ἐκ τῆς χειρὸς. Separation.

τοῦ πατρός. Possessive genitive qualifying χειρὸς.

10:30 ἐγὼ καὶ ὁ πατὴρ ἕν ἐσμεν.

ἐγὼ καὶ ὁ πατὴρ. Compound nominative subject of ἐσμεν. This formulation "reflects the normal order in Greek in which the so-called first person always occurred first in any listing of participants" (LN 92.1), unlike English in which the mention of the speaker first is considered impolite. This verse is connected to the previous one by asyndeton.

ἕν. Predicate adjective. Fronted for emphasis. The neuter singular form of the cardinal adjective refers to the functional unity between the Son and the Father and not to their personal identity, which would be expressed with εἷς (Talbert, 174; Haubeck and von Siebenthal, 566; Harris 2015, 202).

ἐσμεν. Pres act ind 1st pl εἰμί.

John 10:31-39

[31] The Jews picked up stones again so that they might stone him. [32] Jesus answered them, "I have shown you many good works from the Father. For which one of them are you going to stone me?" [33] The Jews answered him, "We are not going to stone you concerning a good work but concerning blasphemy, namely, because you, though you are a human being, make yourself God." [34] Jesus answered them, "Is it not written in

your law, 'I said, you are gods'? ³⁵If he called those to whom the word of God came 'gods' (and the Scripture cannot be abolished), ³⁶do you say to the one whom the Father sanctified and sent into the world, 'You are blaspheming,' because I said, 'I am the Son of God'? ³⁷If I am not doing the works of my Father, do not believe me. ³⁸But if I am doing them, even if you do not believe me, believe the works, so that you may come to know and continue to know that the Father is in me and I am in the Father." ³⁹Then they were seeking again to seize him, but he went forth out of their hands.

10:31 Ἐβάστασαν πάλιν λίθους οἱ Ἰουδαῖοι ἵνα λιθάσωσιν αὐτόν.

Ἐβάστασαν. Aor act ind 3rd pl βαστάζω. This verse is connected to the previous one by asyndeton.

πάλιν. Adverb "pert[aining] to repetition in the same (or similar) manner" (BDAG, 752.2) (referring to 8:59).

λίθους. Accusative direct object of Ἐβάστασαν.

οἱ Ἰουδαῖοι. Nominative subject of Ἐβάστασαν.

ἵνα. Introduces a purpose clause.

λιθάσωσιν. Aor act subj 3rd pl λιθάζω. Subjunctive with ἵνα. The perfective aspect of the verb form indicates that the intent of the Jewish leaders was to complete the task of stoning (James, 206).

αὐτόν. Accusative direct object of λιθάσωσιν.

10:32 ἀπεκρίθη αὐτοῖς ὁ Ἰησοῦς· πολλὰ ἔργα καλὰ ἔδειξα ὑμῖν ἐκ τοῦ πατρός· διὰ ποῖον αὐτῶν ἔργον ἐμὲ λιθάζετε;

ἀπεκρίθη. Aor mid ind 3rd sg ἀποκρίνομαι. On the voice, see "Deponency" in the Series Introduction. This verse is connected to the previous one by asyndeton.

αὐτοῖς. Dative indirect object of ἀπεκρίθη.

ὁ Ἰησοῦς. Nominative subject of ἀπεκρίθη.

πολλὰ ἔργα καλὰ. Accusative direct object of ἔδειξα. Fronted for emphasis. The adjective πολλὰ is in the first (anarthrous) attributive position (see 2:6 on λίθιναι ὑδρίαι), and καλὰ in the fourth attributive position (see 3:15 on ζωὴν αἰώνιον).

ἔδειξα. Aor act ind 1st sg δείκνυμι.

ὑμῖν. Dative indirect object of ἔδειξα.

ἐκ τοῦ πατρός. Source ("originating from the Father") or, perhaps, agency ("given me by the Father"; Zerwick and Grosvenor, 318; Harris 2015, 203); see 5:36; 10:37.

διὰ ποῖον... ἔργον. Causal. In this PP, the qualitative interrogative pronoun ποῖον ("what sort?") functions like the interrogative pronoun τί ("what?") asking an identifying question (Wallace 1996, 346).
αὐτῶν. Partitive genitive qualifying ἔργον.
ἐμὲ. Accusative direct object of λιθάζετε.
λιθάζετε. Pres act ind 2nd pl λιθάζω. In this context, the present tense is used for an action that is attempted but not yet accomplished (BDF §319; Fanning, 220; James, 206).

10:33 ἀπεκρίθησαν αὐτῷ οἱ Ἰουδαῖοι· περὶ καλοῦ ἔργου οὐ λιθάζομέν σε ἀλλὰ περὶ βλασφημίας, καὶ ὅτι σὺ ἄνθρωπος ὢν ποιεῖς σεαυτὸν θεόν.

ἀπεκρίθησαν. Aor mid ind 3rd pl ἀποκρίνομαι. On the voice, see "Deponency" in the Series Introduction. This verse is connected to the previous one by asyndeton.
αὐτῷ. Dative indirect object of ἀπεκρίθησαν.
οἱ Ἰουδαῖοι. Nominative subject of ἀπεκρίθησαν.
περὶ καλοῦ ἔργου. Reference.
οὐ... ἀλλὰ. A point/counterpoint set ("not this... but that") that negates the wrong reason for the attempt to stone Jesus ("for a good deed") and replaces it with the true reason ("for blasphemy"). On the function of ἀλλά in a point/counterpoint set, see 1:8.
λιθάζομέν. Pres act ind 1st pl λιθάζω. λιθάζομέν, which has an acute accent on the antepenult, acquired an additional accent, the acute, on the ultima from the enclitic σε (Smyth §183; Carson 1985, 48).
σε. Accusative direct object of λιθάζομέν.
περὶ βλασφημίας. Reference.
καὶ. Epexegetical conjunction ("that is, namely").
ὅτι. Introduces a causal clause that explains the charge of blasphemy that Jesus' Jewish opponents raise against him.
σὺ. Nominative subject of ποιεῖς. Fronted for emphasis.
ἄνθρωπος. Predicate nominative. This is an example of a qualitative preverbal predicate nominative because the idea is belonging to the human race rather than being a specific human being (Wallace 1996, 264–65).
ὢν. Pres act ptc masc nom sg εἰμί (concessive). On participles that precede the main verb, see ἐμβλέψας in 1:36.
ποιεῖς. Pres act ind 2nd sg ποιέω.
σεαυτὸν. Accusative direct object of ποιεῖς in a double accusative object-complement construction.
θεόν. Accusative complement to σεαυτὸν in a double accusative object-complement construction.

10:34 ἀπεκρίθη αὐτοῖς [ὁ] Ἰησοῦς· οὐκ ἔστιν γεγραμμένον ἐν τῷ νόμῳ ὑμῶν ὅτι ἐγὼ εἶπα· θεοί ἐστε;

ἀπεκρίθη. Aor mid ind 3rd sg ἀποκρίνομαι. On the voice, see "Deponency" in the Series Introduction. This verse is connected to the previous one by asyndeton.

αὐτοῖς. Dative indirect object of ἀπεκρίθη.

[ὁ] Ἰησοῦς. Nominative subject of ἀπεκρίθη. Although many manuscripts have the definite article ($\mathfrak{P}^{75}$ ℵ A K L Γ Δ Θ Ψ $f^{1.13}$ 33 565 𝔐 et al.), it is absent in $\mathfrak{P}^{45}$ B W.

οὐκ. Negative particle that introduces a question that expects an affirmative answer.

ἔστιν γεγραμμένον. The standard introductory formula for scriptural quotations in the FG (see 2:17; 6:31, 45; 12:14).

ἔστιν. Pres act ind 3rd sg εἰμί. The enclitic ἐστιν is accented ἔστιν when it comes at the beginning of a sentence, when it expresses existence, or when it follows ἀλλ', εἰ, καί, οὐκ, ὅτι, or τοῦτ'. The third condition is fulfilled here.

γεγραμμένον. Prf pass ptc neut nom sg γράφω (perfect periphrastic).

ἐν τῷ νόμῳ. Locative. Since the quotation that follows comes from the Psalms, "the reference of νόμος is not restricted to the first five books of the OT" (LN 33.56).

ὑμῶν. Possessive genitive qualifying νόμῳ (see 8:17).

ὅτι. ὅτι-*recitativum* that introduces the clausal complement (direct discourse) of γεγραμμένον.

ἐγὼ εἶπα θεοί ἐστε. A verbatim quotation of LXX Ps 81:6 (ἐγὼ εἶπα θεοί ἐστε).

ἐγώ. Nominative subject of εἶπα.

εἶπα. Aor act ind 1st sg λέγω. On the use of εἶπα for εἶπον, see Zerwick (§489).

θεοί. Predicate nominative. Fronted for emphasis.

ἐστε. Pres act ind 2nd pl εἰμί.

10:35 εἰ ἐκείνους εἶπεν θεοὺς πρὸς οὓς ὁ λόγος τοῦ θεοῦ ἐγένετο, καὶ οὐ δύναται λυθῆναι ἡ γραφή,

εἰ. Introduces the protasis of a first-class condition. This verse is connected to the previous one by asyndeton.

ἐκείνους. Accusative direct object of εἶπεν in a double accusative object-complement construction. The demonstrative pronoun refers to the addressees of God's utterance quoted in the previous verse.

εἶπεν. Aor act ind 3rd sg λέγω. The expression ὁ λόγος τοῦ θεοῦ in the relative clause that follows indicates that the implied subject of εἶπεν is God, but it could also be νόμος/γραφή (cf. CEB; NCV; Harris 2015, 203).

θεούς. Accusative complement to ἐκείνους in a double accusative object-complement construction.

πρὸς οὕς. Locative (motion toward). The relative pronoun οὕς refers to ἐκείνους.

ὁ λόγος. Nominative subject of ἐγένετο.

τοῦ θεοῦ. Subjective genitive qualifying λόγος ("the word that God spoke").

ἐγένετο. Aor mid ind 3rd sg γίνομαι.

καὶ οὐ δύναται λυθῆναι ἡ γραφή. Parenthetical comment inserted between the protasis and the apodosis to add rhetorical force to the condition stated in the protasis.

καί. Coordinating conjunction.

οὐ. Negative particle normally used with indicative verbs.

δύναται. Pres mid ind 3rd sg δύναμαι.

λυθῆναι. Aor pass inf λύω (complementary). Here λύω means to "bring to an end, abolish" (BDAG, 607.4). The verb has an implicit generic agent that is not specified (Wallace 1996, 436).

ἡ γραφή. Nominative subject of δύναται. In this context, νόμος and γραφή are used as virtual synonyms (see 10:34 on ἐν τῷ νόμῳ).

10:36 ὃν ὁ πατὴρ ἡγίασεν καὶ ἀπέστειλεν εἰς τὸν κόσμον ὑμεῖς λέγετε ὅτι βλασφημεῖς, ὅτι εἶπον· υἱὸς τοῦ θεοῦ εἰμι;

ὅν. The relative pronoun marks the beginning of the apodosis of a first-class condition and introduces a headless relative clause that, in its entirety (ὃν ὁ πατὴρ ἡγίασεν καὶ ἀπέστειλεν εἰς τὸν κόσμον), serves as the indirect object of λέγετε. Within its clause, ὅν is the accusative direct object of ἡγίασεν and ἀπέστειλεν. Harris (2015, 203) says that ὅν is the accusative of respect, but he does not distinguish the function that the relative pronoun has in its clause from the function that the entire headless relative clause has in the sentence in which it is embedded. It is certainly possible to regard the relative clause as serving as the accusative of respect vis-à-vis λέγετε (NET: "[D]o you say about the one whom the Father set apart and sent into the world, 'You are blaspheming,' because I said, 'I am the Son of God'?"; cf. ASV; ESV; KJV; LEB; NASB). Since, however, (1) the sentence ὃν ὁ πατὴρ ἡγίασεν καὶ ἀπέστειλεν εἰς τὸν κόσμον ὑμεῖς λέγετε introduces a direct speech (βλασφημεῖς), (2) the function of a headless relative clause is not determined by the case of the relative pronoun that introduces it, and (3) the forms of λέγω in the FG are regularly accompanied by the datives of indirect object (e.g., 1:38, 39, 41, 43, 45, 46, 48, 51; 2:4, 5, 7, 8, 20; 3:3, 11; 4:7, 9, 10, 11, 16, 17, 19, 21, 25, 26, 28, 34, 35, 50), it is better to regard the entire relative clause functioning as the indirect object of λέγετε (cf. HCSB: "[D]o you say, 'You are blaspheming' to the One the Father set apart and sent into the world, because I said: I am the Son of God?").

ὁ πατὴρ. Nominative subject of ἡγίασεν.

ἡγίασεν. Aor act ind 3rd sg ἁγιάζω.

καὶ. Coordinating conjunction.

ἀπέστειλεν. Aor act ind 3rd sg ἀποστέλλω.

εἰς τὸν κόσμον. Locative. See 3:17 and 17:18 for other examples of the combination ἀποστέλλω + εἰς τὸν κόσμον in the FG. On the portrayal of the world in the FG, see 1:10 on ἐν τῷ κόσμῳ.

ὑμεῖς. Nominative subject of λέγετε. Fronted for emphasis.

λέγετε. Pres act ind 2nd pl λέγω.

ὅτι. ὅτι-*recitativum* that introduces the clausal complement (direct discourse) of λέγετε.

βλασφημεῖς. Pres act ind 2nd sg βλασφημέω.

ὅτι. Introduces a causal clause.

εἶπον. Aor act ind 1st sg λέγω.

υἱός. Predicate nominative. Fronted for emphasis. In this context, the anarthrous preverbal υἱός is definite (Haubeck and von Siebenthal, 566; Harris 2015, 204). On anarthrous preverbal predicate nominatives, see 1:1 on θεὸς and 1:49 on βασιλεὺς.

τοῦ θεοῦ. Genitive of relationship qualifying υἱὸς.

εἰμι. Pres act ind 1st sg εἰμί.

10:37 εἰ οὐ ποιῶ τὰ ἔργα τοῦ πατρός μου, μὴ πιστεύετέ μοι·

εἰ. Introduces the protasis of a first-class condition. This conditional clause nicely illustrates the thesis that "[t]he protasis of the first class condition does not always, or even usually, *state* its hypothesis as a fact" (Wallace 1996, 708) because it depicts a hypothetical situation—that Jesus is not doing the works of his Father—whose truth is assumed only for the sake of the argument; εἰ cannot therefore be translated "since" (Wallace 1996, 690–91). This verse is connected to the previous one by asyndeton.

οὐ. Negative particle normally used with indicative verbs.

ποιῶ. Pres act ind 1st sg ποιέω.

τὰ ἔργα. Accusative direct object of ποιῶ.

τοῦ πατρός. Subjective genitive qualifying ἔργα ("the works that my Father demands"; cf. 9:4) or genitive of source/origin ("the works from my Father"; cf. 10:32).

μου. Genitive of relationship qualifying πατρός.

μή. Negative particle normally used with non-indicative verbs. It marks the beginning of the apodosis of a first-class condition, whose truthfulness is again assumed only for the sake of the argument (see εἰ above).

πιστεύετέ. Pres act impv 2nd pl πιστεύω. The imperfective aspect of the present-tense prohibition indicates that believing (or better: nonbelieving) is viewed as an ongoing process and not, as in the traditional view, as an action that has already begun and must now be stopped (e.g., "If I do not do the works of the Father, stop believing in me"; Wallace 1996, 717). πιστεύετέ, which has an acute accent on the antepenult, acquired an additional accent, the acute, on the ultima from the enclitic μοι (Smyth §183; Carson 1985, 48).

μοι. Dative complement of πιστεύετέ. The dative indicates the person "to whom one gives credence or whom one believes" (BDAG, 816.1.b).

10:38 εἰ δὲ ποιῶ, κἂν ἐμοὶ μὴ πιστεύητε, τοῖς ἔργοις πιστεύετε, ἵνα γνῶτε καὶ γινώσκητε ὅτι ἐν ἐμοὶ ὁ πατὴρ κἀγὼ ἐν τῷ πατρί.

εἰ. Introduces the protasis of a first-class condition.

δὲ. Marker of narrative development with a contrastive nuance.

ποιῶ. Pres act ind 1st sg ποιέω.

κἂν. Formed by crasis from καὶ ἐάν. καὶ is ascensive ("even"). ἐάν introduces the protasis of a third-class condition, which adds another, more narrowly defined provision to the protasis of the first-class condition.

ἐμοὶ. Dative complement of πιστεύητε. The dative indicates the person "to whom one gives credence or whom one believes" (BDAG, 816.1.b).

μὴ. Negative particle normally used with non-indicative verbs.

πιστεύητε. Pres act subj 2nd pl πιστεύω. Subjunctive with ἄν.

τοῖς ἔργοις. Dative complement of πιστεύετε. This dative indicates the thing to which one gives credence or the thing that one believes (BDAG, 816.1.a.δ). It marks the beginning of the apodosis of the combination of the first-class and third-class conditions.

πιστεύετε. Pres act impv 2nd pl πιστεύω.

ἵνα. Introduces a purpose clause.

γνῶτε. Aor act subj 2nd pl γινώσκω. Subjunctive with ἵνα. The perfective aspect of the aorist verb form portrays the acquisition of knowledge as a complete and undifferentiated process, regardless of how it occurred.

καί. Coordinating conjunction.

γινώσκητε. Pres act subj 2nd pl γινώσκω. Subjunctive with ἵνα. The imperfective aspect of the present verb form, which is marked for prominence, portrays the acquisition of knowledge as an ongoing process. It seems, however, that some scribes regarded γινώσκητε as redundant after γνῶτε and replaced it with πιστεύσητε (A K Γ Δ Ψ f¹³ 700 892ˢ 𝔐), πιστεύητε (ℵ), or πιστεύετε (579 1241 *l*2211) or deleted it completely (D 1424 [it] syˢ) (Metzger, 198).

ὅτι. Introduces the clausal complement (indirect discourse) of γινώσκητε.

ἐν ἐμοὶ ὁ πατὴρ κἀγὼ ἐν τῷ πατρί. The reciprocal formula of immanence that "tells of the closest conceivable fellowship, which exists after this fashion solely between the Father and Jesus, his Son" (Schnackenburg, 2:313). For other versions of this formula, see 14:10, 11 (ἐγὼ ἐν τῷ πατρὶ καὶ ὁ πατὴρ ἐν ἐμοί), and 17:21 (σύ, πάτερ, ἐν ἐμοὶ κἀγὼ ἐν σοί).

ἐν ἐμοί. State of being, describing a close personal relationship (BDAG, 327.4.c; LN 89.119).

ὁ πατήρ. Nominative subject of an implied ἐστίν.

κἀγώ. Formed by crasis from καὶ ἐγώ. καί is a coordinating conjunction; ἐγώ is the nominative subject of an implied εἰμί.

ἐν τῷ πατρί. State of being, describing a close personal relationship (BDAG, 327.4.c).

10:39 Ἐζήτουν [οὖν] αὐτὸν πάλιν πιάσαι, καὶ ἐξῆλθεν ἐκ τῆς χειρὸς αὐτῶν.

Ἐζήτουν. Impf act ind 3rd pl ζητέω. On the function of the imperfect in the FG, see 1:39 on ἦν.

[οὖν]. Postpositive inferential conjunction and/or transitional particle (see 1:22 and 11:6). The absence of οὖν in some witnesses (𝔓⁷⁵ᵛⁱᵈ B Γ Θ 700 *pm* vgᵐˢ pbo boᵐˢ) may have occurred through haplography because of the similarity with the ending of Ἐζήτουν, but the variants with δέ and καί allow for the possibility that this conjunction may not have been part of the original text (Metzger, 198).

αὐτόν. Accusative direct object of πιάσαι.

πάλιν. Adverb "pert[aining] to repetition in the same (or similar) manner" (BDAG, 752.2). For other attempts to arrest Jesus, see 7:30, 44; 8:20.

πιάσαι. Aor act inf πιάζω (complementary). On the meaning and the use of this verb in the FG, see 7:30 on πιάσαι.

καί. Coordinating conjunction linking two clauses that stand in adversative relationship (see 1:5).

ἐξῆλθεν. Aor act ind 3rd sg ἐξέρχομαι.
ἐκ τῆς χειρὸς. Separation. χειρὸς is a distributive singular (BDF §140).
αὐτῶν. Possessive genitive qualifying χειρὸς.

John 10:40-42

⁴⁰And he went away again across the Jordan, to the place where John had been baptizing the first time, and he stayed there. ⁴¹And many came to him, and they were saying, "John did no sign, but everything that John said about this man was true." ⁴²And many believed in him there.

10:40 Καὶ ἀπῆλθεν πάλιν πέραν τοῦ Ἰορδάνου εἰς τὸν τόπον ὅπου ἦν Ἰωάννης τὸ πρῶτον βαπτίζων καὶ ἔμεινεν ἐκεῖ.

Καὶ. Coordinating conjunction.
ἀπῆλθεν. Aor act ind 3rd sg ἀπέρχομαι.
πάλιν. Adverb "pert[aining] to repetition in the same (or similar) manner" (BDAG, 752.2).
πέραν τοῦ Ἰορδάνου. Locative (see 1:28). πέραν is an improper preposition (see 1:3 on χωρὶς αὐτοῦ) that specifies the location ("across the Jordan") where Jesus went after he left Jerusalem.
εἰς τὸν τόπον. Locative.
ὅπου. Particle denoting place.
ἦν. Impf act ind 3rd sg εἰμί.
Ἰωάννης. Nominative subject of ἦν.
τὸ πρῶτον. Adverbial accusative indicating time or sequence ("first, in the first place, before, earlier, to begin with" [BDAG, 893.1.a.β]). When used with the article, as here, τὸ πρῶτον means "the first time" (BDAG, 893.1.a.β).
βαπτίζων. Pres act ptc masc nom sg βαπτίζω (imperfect periphrastic).
καὶ. Coordinating conjunction.
ἔμεινεν. Aor act ind 3rd sg μένω.
ἐκεῖ. Adverb of place.

10:41 καὶ πολλοὶ ἦλθον πρὸς αὐτὸν καὶ ἔλεγον ὅτι Ἰωάννης μὲν σημεῖον ἐποίησεν οὐδέν, πάντα δὲ ὅσα εἶπεν Ἰωάννης περὶ τούτου ἀληθῆ ἦν.

καὶ. Coordinating conjunction.
πολλοὶ. Nominative subject of ἦλθον. Fronted for emphasis.
ἦλθον. Aor act ind 3rd pl ἔρχομαι.
πρὸς αὐτὸν. Locative (motion toward).

καὶ. Coordinating conjunction.

ἔλεγον. Impf act ind 3rd pl λέγω. On the function of the imperfect in the FG, see 1:39 on ἦν.

ὅτι. ὅτι-*recitativum* that introduces the clausal complement (direct discourse) of ἔλεγον.

Ἰωάννης. Nominative subject of ἐποίησεν.

μὲν ... δὲ. A point/counterpoint set that correlates a clause introduced by μέν with a clause introduced by δέ. Runge argues that "μέν simply creates anticipation of a related clause ... introduced by δέ" (2010, 75 n. 7) and adds that μέν is "always prospective, even in instances where δέ does not follow" (2010, 76). In this verse, the presence of the postpositive μέν in the assertion that John performed no sign creates the expectation that a corresponding clause with δέ will follow, which here carries more semantic weight because it redirects the focus from what John did not do to what John did do—i.e., that he spoke about Jesus and that everything he said about him was true.

σημεῖον ... οὐδέν. Accusative direct object of ἐποίησεν. In this formulation, οὐδέν functions as an adjective, standing in the fourth attributive position (see 3:15 on ζωὴν αἰώνιον).

ἐποίησεν. Aor act ind 3rd sg ποιέω.

πάντα. Nominative subject of ἦν.

ὅσα. Accusative direct object of εἶπεν. The antecedent of the correlative pronoun ("as many as") is πάντα. πάντα ὅσα = "all things that" (BDAG, 729.2).

εἶπεν. Aor act ind 3rd sg λέγω.

Ἰωάννης. Nominative subject of εἶπεν.

περὶ τούτου. Reference. The demonstrative pronoun refers to Jesus.

ἀληθῆ. Predicate adjective. Fronted for emphasis.

ἦν. Impf act ind 3rd sg εἰμί. Neuter plural subjects typically take singular verbs (see 1:28 on ἐγένετο).

10:42 καὶ πολλοὶ ἐπίστευσαν εἰς αὐτὸν ἐκεῖ.

καὶ. Coordinating conjunction.

πολλοὶ. Nominative subject of ἐπίστευσαν. Fronted for emphasis.

ἐπίστευσαν. Aor act ind 3rd pl πιστεύω.

εἰς αὐτὸν. Goal of actions or feelings directed toward someone (BDAG, 290.4.c.β). For πιστεύειν εἰς + accusative ("trust or believe in someone"), see 1:12 on εἰς τὸ ὄνομα.

ἐκεῖ. Adverb of place.

GLOSSARY

Adjectivizer—An article that transforms a nonadjective into an adjectival modifier. Thus, in the phrase τὴν παρὰ τοῦ μόνου θεοῦ (John 5:44), the article τὴν transforms the prepositional phrase παρὰ τοῦ μόνου θεοῦ into an attributive modifier of δόξαν.

Adjunctive—Providing something additional and supplemental. The term is used in relation to Greek conjunctions, especially καί when it signifies "also."

Anacoluthon—A logical and syntactical break in the flow of a sentence, in which a different idea and corresponding syntax begin without completing what came before.

Anaphoric—Referring back to a word or phrase that is coreferential. In the sentence "Ben went on a drive, and he liked it," the pronoun *he* refers, anaphorically, to *Ben*.

Anarthrous—Not modified by an article.

Antecedent—A word to which another word later in the discourse refers. A relative pronoun's antecedent is the preceding word about which the relative clause will provide further information.

Apodosis—The second element, providing the "then" clause after the protasis in a conditional sentence.

Articular—Modified by an article.

Ascensive—Rising or intensifying. The term is often applied to conjunctions, especially καί when it signifies "even."

Aspect—The depiction of an action, event, or state—either internally, as an unfolding process (e.g., "I am helping"), or externally, as a unified whole (e.g., "I helped").

Asyndeton—The absence of conjunctions connecting one clause to the next, effecting a faster sense of pace or intensity of tone. This is the default mode of connecting sentences in the FG.

Attraction—Rather than taking on the case required by its function within its clause, a relative pronoun occasionally reflects or "attracts" to the case of the antecedent.

Attendant circumstance—A dependent verbal participle that expresses an action that is closely connected to or prepares for the main verb. Although it is a dependent participle in that it does not occur independently of a main verb, it conveys its own verbal sense and may be translated as a finite verb connected to the main verb by *and*. An attendant circumstance participle is typically characterized by five key features: (1) it is aorist in tense, (2) it precedes the main verb in word order and in time of the action or event, (3) the main verb is aorist, (4) the mood of the main verb is indicative or imperative, and (5) it is common in narrative texts and infrequent elsewhere. In John 8:8, the participle κατακύψας in the sentence καὶ πάλιν κατακύψας ἔγραφεν εἰς τὴν γῆν is an attendant circumstance and may be translated "And again *he bent down* and continued writing on the ground."

Background—Information that does not advance the narrative or storyline but, rather, elaborates, supplements, or expands upon a feature of the narrative with supporting detail.

Cataphoric—Referring forward to a word or phrase that is coreferential. In the clauses "I saw her; Jane was running," the pronoun *her* refers, cataphorically, to *Jane*.

Causative—An action or circumstance is produced or initiated by the action of the verbal element.

Clausal complement—A clause that serves as direct object. Frequently this involves the use of ὅτι after verbs of speech; e.g., in the sentence καὶ ὑμεῖς λέγετε ὅτι ἐν Ἱεροσολύμοις ἐστὶν ὁ τόπος ὅπου προσκυνεῖν δεῖ ("you say that in Jerusalem is the place where it is necessary to worship"), the ὅτι clause serves as the clausal complement of λέγετε.

Complement—A clause, phrase, or word required to complete a given expression. This is especially common in double accusative constructions; e.g., in the sentence "Emmet calls turtles frogs," *turtles* is the object, and *frogs* is the complement. Without the complement, the expression is incomplete.

Concessive—An element introducing an idea, action, or circumstance that runs counter to the main clause. Concessive clauses are typically introduced with "although" or "even though."

Constructio ad sensum—A construction that does not correspond to the expected number or gender dictated by normal syntax, because it is responding to something inherent in the *sense* of that word rather than the word itself as a morphosyntactical entity; e.g., "The crowd is hungry and *are* getting restless." The plural *are* results from conceiving the singular crowd in terms of the multiple individuals making up the crowd.

Convertible/subset proposition—Specifies the relationship between subject and predicate in equative clauses. In a convertible proposition both subject and predicate have an identical referent and are interchangeable; e.g., "Christmas is the holiday on December 25." In a subset proposition, the predicate specifies the class of which the subject is an instance; e.g., "Matthew is a doctor."

Copula—The linking verb in an equative or copular clause, connecting a subject and predicate. In the copular clause αὕτη δέ ἐστιν ἡ κρίσις ("and the judgment is this"), the copula is ἐστιν.

Crasis—The formation of a single word from two words by contraction, e.g., κἀγώ for καὶ ἐγώ.

Development—The use of δέ that signals an advance in an argument or narrative but does not convey the overt continuity or discontinuity of a conjunction or adversative.

Deponency—When verbs with middle, passive, or middle/passive morphology were ascribed active meanings, they were labeled "deponent." This view has faced important challenges. Thus, the BHGNT acknowledge that middle morphology involves nuances associated with middle voice that should be taken into consideration. See Series Introduction for more.

Direct discourse—A record of the speech or thought of a character, introduced by an untranslated ὅτι and placed in quotation marks.

Double accusative construction—Some verbs can take two accusatives. In a person-thing double accusative, verbs of teaching, reminding, clothing, or asking can take an accusative direct object (the person) and an object-complement (the thing). Thus, in the sentence, "I taught Eliana the song," *Eliana* is the direct object and *song* is the complement. In an object-complement double accusative, verbs of making, sending, calling, and reckoning take both an object and the object's complement in the accusative. In the clause ἐποίησεν τὸ ὕδωρ οἶνον ("he had made the water wine") τὸ ὕδωρ is the direct object and οἶνον is the complement.

Double nominative subject-complement—Verbs that appear in double accusative object-complement constructions can, in the passive voice, have two nominative nouns functioning in the same manner as the object and complement of the object-complement double accusatives.

Elide/elision—The omission of a letter in a word or of an entire word. In the former case, the closing vowel in certain prepositions or conjunctions may be omitted, as in the α in ἀλλ' ἔγνωκα (John 5:42). In the latter case, an entire word is omitted and must be supplied by reference to context. In John 5:36, a second τῆς μαρτυρίας in the clause Ἐγὼ δὲ ἔχω τὴν μαρτυρίαν μείζω ("But I have a testimony greater than [the testimony] of John.") is elided, leaving only τοῦ Ἰωάννου.

Emphasis—Important information placed in a marked position for greater prominence.

Enclitic—A word that donates its accent to the word directly preceding it, as in πάντοτέ ἐστιν.

Epexegetical—An additional word or group of words that offer greater clarity. Infinitives can function in this way—clarifying or completing words like those relating to duty, ability, expectation, or necessity (e.g., "I hope *to eat*"). Similarly, an epexegetical use of clauses beginning with ἵνα or ὅτι function to clarify or complete an idea. When a head noun is ambiguous, an epexegetical genitive can be used to offer a particular example that clarifies the noun it modifies and may, therefore, be introduced in translation by "namely" or "which is."

Equative verb/clause—Equative clauses link subjects and predicates in constructions of the type "this is that." The verbs that do the linking (typically εἰμί, γίνομαι, or ὑπάρχω) are equative verbs. The sentence αὕτη ἐστὶν ἡ μαρτυρία τοῦ Ἰωάννου ("and the testimony of John is this") is an equative clause, and ἐστὶν is the equative verb.

External evidence—A term from textual criticism, referring to the evidence of manuscripts and versions (e.g., the text-type or antiquity of particular witnesses to a reading) rather than on considerations relating to the content of the text at hand (e.g., the author's style or theology).

Glossary

First-class conditional—Stipulates the truth of the protasis (by means of εἰ with an indicative verb) for the sake of argument. The apodosis takes any mood and any tense.

Focal/focus—The key piece of information in a clause, frequently highlighted by placement in a marked position.

Foreground—Events that are indispensable to or propel the storyline.

Fronting/fronted—When an element occurs earlier in the sentence than might be expected in standard word order. Typically, this refers to a preverbal location.

Genitive absolute—A dependent clause consisting of a genitive substantive and an anarthrous genitive participle, which is, most of the time, independent of the verb in the main clause. The participle is usually temporal but can perform any of the adverbial functions of participles.

Genitive of . . .—*agency* specifies the agent actually doing the action; *relationship* specifies a social or familial relation; *comparison* usually comes after a comparative adjective and is introduced with "than" (e.g., "greater *than cats*"); *content* specifies what something contains or is full of; *direction* indicates where the head noun is moving; *subordination* specifies what is subordinated under the head noun; *production/producer* specifies what produced the noun to which it relates; *price* specifies the value or price paid; *product* specifies what is produced by the head noun; *purpose* gives the purpose of the head noun; *separation* specifies the point of departure from which the verb or head noun separates; *source* specifies the origin of the head noun; *time* indicates the time within which something happens. Other genitive relationships include *appositional* (specifies or exemplifies an ambiguous or metaphorical head noun by providing a clarifying example), *partitive* (specifies the whole of which the head noun is a part), *attributive* (specifies an attribute of the head noun), *subjective* (the subject of the verbal idea contained in the head noun), *objective* (the direct object of the verbal idea contained in the head noun), *descriptive* (describes the head noun in a broad manner).

Gnomic—A grammatical feature that, when used in reference to tense, expresses timelessness or general truths.

Grammaticalize—Representing semantic features by means of grammatical markers (prefixes, case endings, etc.).

Hapax legomenon—The only instance of a word recorded in a designated body of literature (in this case, the New Testament).

Haplography—The unintentional omission of a segment of text.

Headless relative clause—A relative clause without an antecedent, e.g., "Among you stands [one] *whom you do not know*."

Hendiadys—Two words linked by καί and expressing one idea.

Historical present—The use of a present-tense verb when a past-tense verb would have been expected, thereby giving prominence to that element of the narrative.

Imperfective (aspect)—The function of present or imperfect tenses when used by a writer or speaker to frame an action or situation as habitual, ongoing, or viewed internally. See, by contrast, *perfective aspect* and *stative aspect*.

Indeclinable—Having no inflected forms; e.g., apart from a preceding article it is impossible to know whether Ναθαναὴλ is nominative, genitive, etc.

Indirect discourse—A record of the content of speech or thought introduced by ὅτι. If someone utters the sentence "I'd like to hold the baby," the indirect discourse would report the content of that utterance but not the utterance itself: "Someone said *he would like to hold the baby*."

Intermediate agent—The personal or impersonal agent by means of whom/which an action took place, though he/she/it is not the ultimate cause or initiator of the action. The intermediate agent is introduced with διά + the agent in genitive case.

Internally headed relative clause—The relative clause contains the "antecedent" it modifies. In John 6:14, the relative clause ὃ ἐποίησεν σημεῖον contains the "antecedent" (σημεῖον) in the larger construction Οἱ οὖν ἄνθρωποι ἰδόντες ὃ ἐποίησεν σημεῖον ("So when the people saw the sign that he had done").

Intransitive—A verb that does not take a direct object. (Some verbs allow but do not require a direct object and can, therefore, function transitively or intransitively.)

Lectio difficilior—A text-critical principle that states that the more difficult reading is more likely to be original.

Left-dislocation—A sentence-structuring device in which "the next primary topic of the discourse" (Runge 2010 §14.2) is put at the beginning of the sentence and then picked up again with a resumptive pronoun in the main clause; e.g., "*The parents with the new baby*, they need more sleep."

Litotes—Making a statement by negating the opposite idea: "no small feat" = "quite an accomplishment." This kind of understatement typically serves as a means of emphasis.

Marked—When a word departs from standard sentence structure, frequently to highlight or emphasize the element placed in the atypical position. If subjects usually follow verbs in a given language, a subject coming before a verb would be in a "marked" position.

Metacomment—A comment about another comment. A metacomment occurs when speakers "stop saying what they are saying in order to comment on what is going to be said, speaking abstractly about it" (Runge 2010, 101). The pragmatic effect can lend solemnity or slow the pace to emphasize the importance of the subsequent utterance.

Metonymy/metonym—Substituting a word or description closely associated with something for the name/term of the thing itself. "Lend me your *ear*" is metonymy for "Lend me your [auditory] attention." In the expression "For my flesh is true eating" (a wooden rendering of John 6:55), "eating" (βρῶσις) is a metonym for what is eaten; i.e., *food*.

Monadic—Use of the definite article signaling that something is one of a kind.

Nominal clause—A group of words containing a verb and functioning as a noun.

Nominalizer—An article that converts a word, phrase, or clause (frequently adjectives and participial constructions) into substantives.

Paranomasia—A play on words typically involving the use of two or more words with similar forms or sounds.

Parataxis—The juxtaposition of clauses or phrases, which are connected with coordinating rather than subordinating conjunctions.

Parenthesis—A distinct thought connected to but also interrupting the discourse in which it occurs. In John 7:22 the discourse is interrupted with the parenthesis "not that it is from Moses, but from the fathers."

Perfective (aspect)—The function of the aorist tense when used by a writer or speaker to depict an action or situation externally or summarily as a completed whole. See, for contrast, *imperfective aspect*.

Periphrastic construction—The combination of an anarthrous participle and a verb of being functioning together like a finite verb.

Pleonasm/pleonastic—The use of additional words beyond what is strictly necessary. In the FG, pleonasms are a function of Semitic influence; e.g., the addition of καὶ εἶπεν αὐτῷ after ἀπεκρίθη.

Point/counterpoint set—One statement is negated (usually by οὐ or μή) to reject a possible misconception or to establish a key point of contrast and is followed by a positive statement beginning with and emphasized by an introductory ἀλλά (Runge 2010, 92–100).

Predicate nominative/accusative/adjective—The anarthrous element in an equative clause sharing the same case as the subject that it identifies, renames, or describes. In the sentence "Teddie is tough," *tough* is the predicate adjective and would occur in the nominative case.

Prominence—The state of being more significant or highlighted than other elements. In Greek this is regularly achieved by means of word order or the inclusion of words that are not strictly necessary.

Pronominal prolepsis—A pronoun in the main clause that anticipates the subject in a relative clause.

Protasis—The "if" clause in a conditional sentence.

Qal wahomer—Like *a minore ad maius* rhetorical arguments, this rabbinic mode of inference holds that if something is true in a less important matter, it also is true for what is more important.

Redundant quotative frame—Additional verbs introducing direct discourse when a prior verb has already done so; e.g., "And he confessed and did not deny, but confessed, 'I am not the Messiah'" (John 1:20).

Right-dislocation—A structuring device in which grammatically dispensable information is placed outside of the main clause, thus providing post hoc elaboration of something within the main clause; e.g., "They went outside, Zoe and Lee."

Second-class conditional—The "contrary-to-fact conditional," in which the protasis assumes the falsity of a premise for the sake of argument (by means of εἰ and a secondary tense indicative, typically aorist or imperfect). The apodosis typically has ἄν and an indicative secondary tense.

Semitism—Semitic style, idiom, or sentence structure that is not normally found in composition by native speakers/writers of Greek.

Synecdoche—A figure of speech in which one term is used in place of another with which it is associated, specifically involving a part-whole relationship. In the sentence, "Do you have your own *wheels*?" the word "wheels" stands for the entire "vehicle" of which it is a part.

Stative (aspect)—The use of verbs in the perfect and pluperfect tense by a writer or speaker to depict a state of affairs or state of being without reference to unfolding action or process. See, by contrast, *imperfective aspect*.

Third-class conditional—Conveys a logical connection, a hypothetical, or a future eventuality. The protasis uses ἐάν and a subjunctive verb (any tense). The apodosis is in any tense and any mood. A "present general" condition is formed when the apodosis contains a present indicative verb.

Topical frame—A key thematic element is fronted to establish the frame of reference for the following clause. According to Runge, "The two primary uses of topical frames are: to highlight the introduction of a new participant or topic, or to draw attention to a change in topics" (2010, 210).

Ultimate agent—The person ultimately authorizing/initiating and, therefore, bearing final responsibility for an action without necessarily carrying out that action him- or herself. The ultimate agent is conveyed by means of the genitive with ὑπό, ἀπό, or παρά.

Unmarked—Reflects standard usage or word order and, therefore, is not highlighted by the writer or speaker for special prominence.

WORKS CITED

Aubrey, Michael. "Greek Prohibitions." Pages 486–538 in *The Greek Verb Revisited: A Fresh Approach for Biblical Exegesis*. Edited by Steven E. Runge and Christopher J. Fresch. Bellingham, WA: Lexham Press, 2016.

Bakker, Egbert J. "Voice, Aspect and Aktionsart: Middle and Passive in Ancient Greek." Pages 23–47 in *Voice: Form and Function*. Edited by B. A. Fox and P. J. Hopper. Typological Studies in Language 27. Philadelphia: John Benjamins, 1994.

Barackman, Paul F. "The Gospel according to John." *Interpretation* 6 (1952): 63–78.

Barrett, C. K. *The Gospel according to St. John: An Introduction with Commentary and Notes on the Greek Text*. 2nd ed. Philadelphia: Westminster Press, 1978.

Battle, John A. "The Present Indicative in New Testament Exegesis." Th.D. diss., Grace Theological Seminary, 1975.

Beasley-Murray, George R. *John*. WBC 36. Rev. ed. Grand Rapids: Zondervan, 2015.

Bieringer, Reimund. "'I Am Ascending to My Father and Your Father, to My God and Your God' (John 20:17): Resurrection and Ascension in the Gospel of John." Pages 209–35 in *The Resurrection of Jesus in the Gospel of John*. Edited by Craig R. Koester and Reimund Bieringer. WUNT 222. Tübingen: Mohr Siebeck, 2008.

Boring, M. Eugene. *An Introduction to the New Testament: History, Literature, Theology*. Louisville: Westminster John Knox, 2012.

Brown, Raymond E. *The Gospel according to John*. 2 vols. AB 29–29A. Garden City, NY: Doubleday, 1966–70.

Bultmann, Rudolf. *The Gospel of John: A Commentary*. Translated by G. R. Beasley-Murray. Louisville: Westminster John Knox, 1971.

Burkett, Delbert Royce. *The Son of the Man in the Gospel of John*. JSNTSup 56. Sheffield: JSOT Press, 1991.

Burney, Charles Fox. *The Aramaic Origin of the Fourth Gospel*. Oxford: Clarendon, 1922.

Buth, Randall. "Participles as Pragmatic Choice: Where Semantics Meets Pragmatics." Pages 273–306 in *The Greek Verb Revisited: A Fresh Approach for Biblical Exegesis*. Edited by Steven E. Runge and Christopher J. Fresch. Bellingham, WA: Lexham Press, 2016.

———. "Οὖν, Δέ, Καί, and Asyndeton in John's Gospel." Pages 144–61 in *Linguistics and New Testament Interpretation: Essays on Discourse Analysis*. Edited by David Alan Black with Katharine Barnwell and Stephen Levinsohn. Nashville: Broadman & Holman, 1992.

Callow, John C. "The Historic Present in Mark." Paper presented at a seminar at SIL. Horsleys Green, UK, 1996.

Campbell, Constantine R. *Basics of Verbal Aspect in Biblical Greek*. Grand Rapids: Zondervan, 2008.

———. *Verbal Aspect, the Indicative Mood, and Narrative: Soundings in the Greek of the New Testament*. SBG 13. New York: Peter Lang, 2007.

Caragounis, Chrys C. "'Abide in Me': The New Mode of Relationship between Jesus and His Followers as a Basis for Christian Ethics (John 15)." Pages 250–63 in *Rethinking the Ethics of John: "Implicit Ethics" in the Johannine Writings*. Edited by Jan G. van der Watt and Ruben Zimmermann. WUNT 291. Tübingen: Mohr Siebeck, 2012.

———. *The Development of Greek and the New Testament: Morphology, Syntax, Phonology, and Textual Transmission*. WUNT 167. Tübingen: Mohr Siebeck, 2004.

———. "What Did Jesus Mean by τὴν ἀρχήν in John 8:25?" *Novum Testamentum* 49 (2007): 129–47.

Carson, D. A. *The Gospel according to John*. PNTC. Grand Rapids: Eerdmans, 1991.

———. *Greek Accents: A Student Manual*. Grand Rapids: Baker Books, 1985.

———. "The Purpose of the Fourth Gospel: John 20:31 Reconsidered." *Journal of Biblical Literature* 106 (1987): 639–51.

———. "Syntactical and Text-Critical Observations on John 20:30-31: One More Round on the Purpose of the Fourth Gospel." *Journal of Biblical Literature* 124 (2005): 693–714.

Cassirer, H. W. *God's New Covenant: A New Testament Translation*. Grand Rapids: Eerdmans, 1989.

Colwell, Ernest Cadman. "A Definite Rule for the Use of the Article in the Greek New Testament." *Journal of Biblical Literature* 52 (1933): 12–21.

Conrad, Carl W. "New Observations on Voice in the Ancient Greek Verb. November 19, 2002." Online: https://pages.wustl.edu/files/pages/imce/cwconrad/newobsancgrkvc.pdf.

Cooper, Guy L., III. *Attic Greek Prose Syntax*. 2 vols. Ann Arbor: University of Michigan Press, 1998–2002.

Crellin, Robert. "The Semantics of the Perfect in the Greek of the New Testament." Pages 430–57 in *The Greek Verb Revisited: A Fresh Approach for Biblical Exegesis*. Edited by Steven E. Runge and Christopher J. Fresch. Bellingham, WA: Lexham Press, 2016.

Culpepper, R. Alan. *Anatomy of the Fourth Gospel: A Study in Literary Design*. Philadelphia: Fortress Press, 1983.

Culy, Martin M. "The Clue Is in the Case: Distinguishing Adjectival and Adverbial Participles." *Perspectives in Religious Studies* 30 (2003): 441–53.

⸻. "Double Case Constructions in Koine Greek." *Journal of Greco-Roman Christianity and Judaism* 6 (2009): 82–106.

⸻. *I, II, III John: A Handbook on the Greek Text*. BHGNT. Waco, TX: Baylor University Press, 2004.

Culy, Martin M., Mikeal C. Parsons, and Joshua J. Stigall. *Luke: A Handbook on the Greek Text*. BHGNT. Waco, TX: Baylor University Press, 2010.

Daise, Michael A. "Quotations with 'Remembrance' Formulae in the Fourth Gospel." Pages 75–91 in *Abiding Words: The Use of Scripture in the Gospel of John*. Edited by Alicia D. Myers and Bruce G. Schuchard. Atlanta: Society of Biblical Literature, 2015.

Daube, David. "Jesus and the Samaritan Woman: The Meaning of συγχράομαι (Jn 4:7ff)." *Journal of Biblical Literature* 69 (1950): 137–47.

Decker, Rodney J. *Temporal Deixis of the Greek Verb in the Gospel of Mark with Reference to Verbal Aspect*. SBG 10. New York: Peter Lang, 2001.

Dennis, John. "Seeking Jesus: Observations on John's Vocabulary of Death." Pages 157–69 in *Repetitions and Variations in the Fourth Gospel: Style, Text, Interpretation*. Edited by G. Van Belle, M. Labahn, and P. Maritz. BETL 223. Leuven: Peeters, 2009.

Dixon, Paul Stephen. "The Significance of the Anarthrous Predicate Nominative in John." Th.M. thesis, Dallas Theological Seminary, 1975.

du Toit, Herman C. "The Function of the Imperfect Tense-Form in the Narrative Discourse of John's Gospel: Some Remarks." *Neotestamentica* 51 (2017): 209–34.

Fanning, Buist M. *Verbal Aspect in New Testament Greek*. Oxford Theological Monographs. Oxford: Clarendon, 1990.

Fee, Gordon D. "On the Text and Meaning of John 20:30–31." Pages 2193–205 in vol. 3 of *The Four Gospels 1992*. 3 vols. Edited by F. van Segbroeck et al. BETL 100. Leuven: Peeters, 1992.

———. "The Use of the Definite Article with Personal Names in the Gospel of John." *New Testament Studies* 17 (1970): 168–83.

Fresch, Christopher J. "Typology, Polysemy, and Prototypes: Situating Nonpast Aorist Indicatives." Pages 379–415 in *The Greek Verb Revisited: A Fresh Approach for Biblical Exegesis*. Edited by Steven E. Runge and Christopher J. Fresch. Bellingham, WA: Lexham Press, 2016.

Frey, Jörg. *The Glory of the Crucified One: Christology and Theology in the Gospel of John*. Translated by Wayne Coppins and Christoph Heilig. BMSEC. Waco, TX: Baylor University Press, 2018.

———. "Love-Relations in the Fourth Gospel." Pages 171–98 in *Repetitions and Variations in the Fourth Gospel: Style, Text, Interpretation*. Edited by G. Van Belle, M. Labahn, and P. Maritz. BETL 223. Leuven: Peeters, 2009.

———. *Die johanneische Eschatologie*. 3 vols. WUNT 96, 110, 117. Tübingen: Mohr Siebeck, 1997–2000.

Goodspeed, Edgar J. *The New Testament: An American Translation*. Chicago: University of Chicago, 1923.

Gundry, Robert H., and Russell W. Howell. "The Sense and Syntax of John 3:14–17 with Special Reference to the Use of ΟΥΤΩΣ ... ΩΣΤΕ in John 3:16." *Novum Testamentum* 41 (1999): 24–39.

Hagner, Donald A. *The New Testament: A Historical and Theological Introduction*. Grand Rapids: Baker Academic, 2012.

Harner, Philip B. "Qualitative Anarthrous Predicate Nouns: Mark 15:39 and John 1:1." *Journal of Biblical Literature* 92 (1973): 75–87.

Harris, Murray J. *John*. EGGNT. Edited by Andreas J. Köstenberger and Robert Yarbrough. Nashville: B&H Academic, 2015.

———. *Prepositions and Theology in the Greek New Testament: An Essential Reference Resource for Exegesis*. Grand Rapids: Zondervan, 2012.

Haubeck, Wilfrid, and Heinrich von Siebenthal. *Neuer sprachlicher Schlüssel zum griechischen Neuen Testament*. 3rd ed. Giessen: Brunnen Verlag, 2015.

Heckert, Jacob K. *Discourse Function of Conjoiners in the Pastoral Epistles*. Dallas: SIL International, 1996.

James, Patrick. "Imperfects, Aorists, Historic Presents, and Perfects in John 11: A Narrative Test Case." Pages 184–230 in *The Greek Verb Revisited: A Fresh Approach for Biblical Exegesis*. Edited by Steven E. Runge and Christopher J. Fresch. Bellingham, WA: Lexham Press, 2016.

Jensen, Matthew D. "John Is No Exception: Identifying the Subject of εἰμί and Its Implications." *Journal of Biblical Literature* 135 (2016): 341–53.

Johnson, Luke Timothy. "Anti-Judaism and the New Testament." Pages 1609–38 in *Handbook for the Study of the Historical Jesus*. Edited by Tom Holmén and Stanley E. Porter. Leiden: Brill, 2011.

Keck, Leander E. "Derivation as Destiny: 'Of-ness' in Johannine Christology, Anthropology, and Soteriology." Pages 274–88 in *Exploring the Gospel of John: In Honor of D. Moody Smith*. Edited by R. Alan Culpepper and C. Clifton Black. Louisville: Westminster John Knox, 1996.

Keener, Craig S. *The Gospel of John: A Commentary*. 2 vols. Peabody, MA: Hendrickson, 2003.

Kerr, Alan R. *The Temple of Jesus' Body: The Temple Theme in the Gospel of John*. JSNTSup 220. London: Sheffield Academic Press, 2002.

Köstenberger, Andreas. *John*. BECNT. Grand Rapids: Baker Academic, 2004.

Kysar, Robert. *John, the Maverick Gospel*. 3rd ed. Louisville: Westminster John Knox, 2007.

Lappenga, Benjamin J. "Whose Zeal Is It Anyway? The Citation of Psalm 69:9 in John 2:17 as a Double Entendre." Pages 141–59 in *Abiding Words: The Use of Scripture in the Gospel of John*. Edited by Alicia D. Myers and Bruce G. Schuchard. Atlanta: Society of Biblical Literature, 2015.

Leung, Mavis M. "The Narrative Function and Verbal Aspect of the Historical Present in the Fourth Gospel." *Journal of the Evangelical Theological Society* 51 (2008): 703–20.

Levinsohn, Stephen H. *Discourse Features of New Testament Greek: A Coursebook on the Information Structure of New Testament Greek*. 2nd ed. Dallas: SIL International, 2000.

———. "Verb Forms and Grounding in Narrative." Pages 163–83 in *The Greek Verb Revisited: A Fresh Approach for Biblical Exegesis*. Edited by Steven E. Runge and Christopher J. Fresch. Bellingham, WA: Lexham Press, 2016.

Lincoln, Andrew T. *The Gospel according to St. John*. BNTC 4. Peabody, MA: Hendrickson, 2005.

Martyn, J. Louis. *History and Theology in the Fourth Gospel*. 3rd ed. Louisville: Westminster John Knox, 2003.

Mason, Steve. "Jews, Judaeans, Judaizing, Judaism: Problems of Categorization in Ancient History." *Journal for the Study of Judaism* 38 (2007): 457–512.

Matera, Frank J. "John 20:1–18." *Interpretation* 43 (1989): 402–6.

McGaughy, Lane C. *Toward a Descriptive Analysis of EINAI as a Linking Verb in New Testament Greek*. SBLDS 6. Missoula, MT: Society of Biblical Literature, 1972.

McGehee, Michael. "A Less Theological Reading of John 20:17." *Journal of Biblical Literature* 105 (1986): 299–302.

McHugh, John F. *A Critical and Exegetical Commentary on John 1–4*. ICC. London: T&T Clark International, 2009.

McKay, K. L. *A New Syntax of the Verb in New Testament Greek: An Aspectual Approach*. SBG 5. New York: Peter Lang, 1994.

———. "On the Perfect and Other Aspects in New Testament Greek." *Novum Testamentum* 23 (1981): 289–329.

———. "Time and Aspect in New Testament Greek." *Novum Testamentum* 34 (1992): 209–28.

Menken, Maarten J. J. "The Quotation from Isa 40,3 in John 1,23." *Biblica* 66 (1985): 190–205.

Metzger, Bruce M. *A Textual Commentary on the Greek New Testament*. 2nd ed. Stuttgart: German Bible Society, 1994.

Michaels, J. Ramsey. *The Gospel of John*. NICNT. Grand Rapids: Eerdmans, 2010.

Moffatt, James. *The Moffatt Translation of the Bible*. 2nd ed. London: Hodder, 1933.

Morris, Leon. *The Gospel according to John*. NICNT. Grand Rapids: Eerdmans, 1995.

Moule, C. F. D. *An Idiom Book of New Testament Greek*. 2nd ed. Cambridge: Cambridge University Press, 1959.

Moulton, James Hope. *A Grammar of New Testament Greek*. Vol. 1: *Prolegomena*. 3rd ed. Edinburgh: T&T Clark, 1957.

Moulton, James Hope, and Wilbert Francis Howard. *A Grammar of New Testament Greek*. Vol. 2: *Accidence and Word Formation*. Edinburgh: T&T Clark, 1963.

Newman, Barclay M., and Eugene A. Nida. *A Translator's Handbook on the Gospel of John*. Helps for Translators Series. London: United Bible Societies, 1980.

Novakovic, Lidija. *Raised from the Dead according to Scripture: The Role of Israel's Scripture in the Early Christian Interpretations of Jesus' Resurrection*. JCT 12. London: Bloomsbury T&T Clark, 2012.

O'Rourke, John J. "The Historic Present in the Gospel of John." *Journal of Biblical Literature* 93 (1974): 585–90.

Pennington, Jonathan T. "Deponency in Koine Greek: The Grammatical Question and the Lexicographical Dilemma." *Trinity Journal* 24 (2003): 55–76.

Pierce, Madison N., and Benjamin E. Reynolds. "The Perfect Tense-Form and the Son of Man in John 3.13: Developments in Greek Grammar as a Viable Solution to the Timing of the Ascent and Descent." *New Testament Studies* 60 (2014): 149–55.

Porter, Stanley E. *Idioms of the Greek New Testament*. BLG 2. 2nd ed. Sheffield: JSOT, 1994.

———. "In Defence of Verbal Aspect." Pages 26–45 in *Biblical Greek Language and Linguistics: Open Questions in Current Research*. Edited by Stanley E. Porter and D. A. Carson. JSNTSup 80. Sheffield: Sheffield Academic Press, 1993.

———. *Linguistic Analysis of the Greek New Testament: Studies in Tools, Methods, and Practice*. Grand Rapids: Baker Academic, 2015.

———. *Verbal Aspect in the Greek of the New Testament, with Reference to Tense and Mood*. SBG 1. New York: Peter Lang, 1989.

Poythress, Vern S. "The Use of the Intersentence Conjunctions *De, Oun, Kai,* and Asyndeton in the Gospel of John." *Novum Testamentum* 26 (1984): 312–40.

Ramelli, Ilaria. "'Simon Son of John, Do You Love *Me*?' Some Reflections on John 21:15." *Novum Testamentum* 50 (2008): 332–50.

Ridderbos, Herman N. *The Gospel according to John: A Theological Commentary*. Translated by John Vriend. Grand Rapids: Eerdmans, 1997.

Robar, Elizabeth. "The Historical Present in NT Greek: An Exercise in Interpreting Matthew." Pages 329–52 in *The Greek Verb Revisited: A Fresh Approach for Biblical Exegesis*. Edited by Steven E. Runge and Christopher J. Fresch. Bellingham, WA: Lexham Press, 2016.

Robertson, A. T. *A Grammar of the Greek New Testament in the Light of Historical Research*. 3rd ed. Nashville: Broadman, 1934.

Robinson, J. A. T. "The Destination and Purpose of St John's Gospel." *New Testament Studies* 6 (1960): 117–31.

Runge, Steven. "Contrastive Substitution and the Greek Verb: Reassessing Porter's Argument." *Novum Testamentum* 56 (2014): 154–73.

———. *Discourse Grammar of the Greek New Testament: A Practical Introduction for Teaching and Exegesis*. Lexham Bible Reference Series. Peabody, MA: Hendrickson, 2010.

———. "Functions of Copula-Participle Combinations ('Periphrastics')." Pages 307–26 in *The Greek Verb Revisited: A Fresh Approach for Biblical Exegesis*. Edited by Steven E. Runge and Christopher J. Fresch. Bellingham, WA: Lexham Press, 2016.

———. "The Verbal Aspect of the Historical Present Indicative in Narrative." Paper presented at the annual meeting of the Society of Biblical Literature, New Orleans, LA, November 21–24, 2009. Online: http://www.ntdiscourse.org/docs/ReconsideringHP.pdf.

Schnackenburg, Rudolf. *The Gospel according to St. John*. 3 vols. Translated by Kevin Smyth et al. New York: Crossroad, 1968, 1980, 1982.

Shepherd, David. "'Do You Love Me?': A Narrative-Critical Reappraisal of ἀγαπάω and φιλέω in John 21:15-17." *Journal of Biblical Literature* 129 (2010): 777–92.

Smith, D. Moody. *John*. ANTC. Nashville: Abingdon, 1999.

Smyth, H. W. *Greek Grammar*. Revised by G. M. Messing. Cambridge, MA: Harvard University Press, 1956.

Talbert, Charles H. *Reading John: A Literary and Theological Commentary on the Fourth Gospel and the Johannine Epistles*. Rev. ed. Macon: Smyth & Helwys, 2005.

Taylor, Bernard A. "Deponency and Greek Lexicography." Pages 167–76 in *Biblical Greek Language and Lexicography: Essays in Honor of Frederick W. Danker*. Edited by B. A. Taylor et al. Grand Rapids: Eerdmans, 2004.

Theobald, Michael. "Der johanneische Osterglaube und die Grenzen seiner narrative Vermittlung (Joh 20)." Pages 93–123 in *Von Jesus zum Christus: Christologische Studien*. Edited by Rudolf Hoppe and Ulrich Busse. BZNW 93. Berlin: de Gruyter, 1998.

Thomson, Christopher J. "What Is Aspect? Contrasting Definitions in General Linguistics and New Testament Studies." Pages 13–80 in *The Greek Verb Revisited: A Fresh Approach for Biblical Exegesis*. Edited by Steven E. Runge and Christopher J. Fresch. Bellingham, WA: Lexham Press, 2016.

Thompson, Marianne Meye. *John: A Commentary*. The New Testament Library. Louisville: Westminster John Knox, 2015.

Tolmie, D. Francois. "The Ἰουδαῖοι in the Fourth Gospel: A Narratological Perspective." Pages 377–97 in *Theology and Christology in the*

Fourth Gospel: Essays by the Members of the SNTS Johannine Writings Seminar. Leuven: Leuven University Press, 2005.

Torrey, Charles Culter. *Our Translated Gospels: Some of the Evidence*. New York: Harper & Brothers, 1936.

Turner, Nigel. *A Grammar of New Testament Greek*. Vol. 3: *Syntax*. Edited by J. H. Moulton. Edinburgh: T&T Clark, 1963.

———. *Grammatical Insights into the New Testament*. Edinburgh: T&T Clark, 1965.

Van Belle, Gilbert. "Theory of Repetitions and Variations in the Fourth Gospel: A Neglected Field of Research?" Pages 14–32 in *Repetitions and Variations in the Fourth Gospel: Style, Text, Interpretation*. Edited by G. Van Belle, M. Labahn, and P. Maritz. BETL 223. Leuven: Peeters, 2009.

van der Watt, Jan. "*Double Entendre* in the Gospel according to John." Pages 463–81 in *Theology and Christology in the Fourth Gospel: Essays by the Members of the SNTS Johannine Writings Seminar*. Leuven: Leuven University Press, 2005.

———. "Repetition and Functionality in the Gospel according to John: Some Initial Explorations." Pages 87–108 in *Repetitions and Variations in the Fourth Gospel: Style, Text, Interpretation*. Edited by G. Van Belle, M. Labahn, and P. Maritz. BETL 223. Leuven: Peeters, 2009.

von Soden, Hermann Freiherr. *Die Schriften des Neuen Testaments in ihrer ältesten erreichbaren Textgestalt, hergestellt auf Grund ihrer Textgeschichte*. Vol. 1, part 1. 2nd ed. Berlin: Verlag von Arthur Glaue, 1911.

von Wahlde, Urban C. "The Johannine 'Jews': A Critical Survey." *New Testament Studies* 28 (1982): 33–60.

Wallace, Daniel B. *Greek Grammar beyond the Basics: An Exegetical Syntax of the New Testament*. Grand Rapids: Zondervan, 1996.

———. "John 5,2 and the Date of the Fourth Gospel." *Biblica* 71 (1990): 177–205.

Young, Richard A. *Intermediate New Testament Greek: A Linguistic and Exegetical Approach*. Nashville: Broadman & Holman, 1994.

Zerwick, Maximilian. *Biblical Greek: Illustrated by Examples*. English ed. adapted from the Fourth Latin ed. by Joseph Smith. Rome: Pontifical Institute, 1963.

Zerwick, Maximilian, and Mary Grosvenor. *A Grammatical Analysis of the Greek New Testament*. Unabridged, 3rd rev. ed. Rome: Biblical Institute Press, 1988.

AUTHOR INDEX

Bold indicates the volume number.

Aubrey, Michael, **1**.63, 168

Bakker, Egbert J., **1**.xii; **2**.xii
Barackman, Paul F., **1**.xxi; **2**.xxi
Barrett, C. K., **1**.xxi, 13, 35, 60, 61,
    71, 74, 75, 85, 87, 96, 100, 122,
    124, 142, 146, 162, 168, 182, 189,
    198, 217, 230, 246, 253, 274, 279,
    285, 302, 317, 326, 327, 332, 341,
    358, 359, 366; **2**.xxi, 2, 4, 6, 10, 11,
    21, 22, 26, 32, 35, 36, 56, 58, 60,
    62, 63, 70, 71, 75, 80, 83, 88, 90,
    95, 97, 103, 108, 109, 114, 123,
    128, 131, 134, 137, 149, 155, 162,
    164, 165, 173, 182, 193, 199, 200,
    201, 202, 203, 206, 207, 212, 216,
    220, 221, 242, 250, 256, 275, 283,
    287, 294, 295, 308, 310, 311, 317,
    319, 321, 324, 326, 327, 334, 335,
    336, 349
Battle, John A., **1**.29, 110, 324, 387;
    2.28, 111, 234, 332
BDF (Blass, Debrunner, and Funk),
    1.1, 14, 16, 19, 23, 25, 27, 28, 34,
    36, 37, 39, 44, 45, 46, 52, 53, 54,
    56, 57, 59, 60, 66, 67, 68, 70, 72,
    77, 80, 90, 94, 96, 102, 105, 106,
    110, 114, 116, 117, 118, 120, 124,
    132, 133, 136, 141, 143, 146, 148,
    151, 169, 173, 174, 177, 182, 185,
    186, 187, 189, 191, 193, 194, 196,
    205, 206, 214, 225, 234, 236, 237,
    240, 246, 249, 250, 253, 265, 272,
    273, 278, 286, 287, 298, 302, 308,
    309, 312, 314, 315, 316, 318, 319,
    320, 321, 322, 326, 331, 334, 336,
    337, 341, 342, 348, 349, 351, 352,
    354, 366, 369, 375; **2**.3, 5, 7, 11,
    15, 21, 23, 24, 26, 35, 37, 38, 51,
    53, 56, 59, 60, 63, 64, 69, 70, 74,
    85, 93, 98, 103, 104, 105, 109, 115,
    120, 123, 137, 140, 145, 146, 148,
    149, 152, 160, 162, 165, 166, 173,
    176, 177, 179, 182, 187, 188, 191,
    192, 195, 196, 198, 207, 211, 215,
    216, 218, 220, 224, 237, 242, 244,
    246, 247, 253, 259, 260, 261, 264,
    267, 273, 275, 278, 282, 284, 288,
    290, 295, 299, 300, 302, 303, 314,
    321, 323, 327, 330, 333, 336
Beasley-Murray, George R., **2**.36, 90,
    109, 256
Bieringer, Reimund, **2**.296, 297
Boring, M. Eugene, **1**.205
Brown, Raymond E., **1**.2, 13, 16, 29,
    33, 69, 84, 86, 87, 101, 103, 112,

117, 123, 246, 258, 266, 268, 287, 297, 343, 358, 359; **2.**6, 44, 61, 63, 88, 90, 109, 110, 114, 115, 118, 127, 147, 149, 153, 159, 170, 171, 172, 173, 182, 189, 191, 205, 206, 212, 216, 219, 238, 241, 249, 255, 256, 259, 264, 268, 275, 286, 287, 288, 295, 302, 303, 307, 308, 311, 319, 322, 325, 326

Bultmann, Rudolf, **1.**14; **2.**52, 90, 114, 170, 171, 172, 208, 275, 284

Burkett, Delbert Royce, **1.**84

Burney, Charles Fox, **1.**xxiii; **2.**xxiii

Buth, Randall, **1.**17, 32, 37, 136

Callow, John C., **1.**14

Campbell, Constantine R., **1.**xi, xxiii, 26, 57, 59, 157, 229, 249, 253, 342; **2.**xi, xxiii, 9, 32, 42, 91, 203, 206, 217, 276, 311

Caragounis, Chrys C., **1.**xiii, 27, 28, 166, 287, 315; **2.**xxiii, 32, 36, 43, 47, 60, 107, 109, 116, 135, 139, 142, 146, 148, 166, 170, 182, 192, 203, 211, 219, 232, 302, 317

Carson, D. A., **1.**15, 16, 30, 34, 35, 49, 50, 65, 78, 79, 122, 128, 131, 132, 135, 137, 152, 153, 154, 157, 165, 170, 174, 176, 178, 189, 198, 200, 201, 206, 207, 208, 211, 214, 216, 220, 221, 222, 225, 226, 231, 235, 242, 248, 249, 251, 255, 257, 261, 265, 283, 290, 293, 295, 298, 301, 304, 306, 316, 320, 321, 322, 325, 327, 329, 330, 334, 335, 338, 339, 343, 356, 358, 365, 366, 367, 369, 373; **2.**7, 29, 30, 31, 55, 58, 64, 77, 79, 81, 93, 95, 98, 102, 108, 111, 112, 118, 121, 123, 125, 126, 130, 131, 135, 136, 139, 141, 147, 150, 155, 159, 163, 168, 171, 175, 176, 177, 178, 182, 183, 185, 191, 193, 194, 195, 196, 198, 200, 205, 209, 211, 212, 213, 220, 222, 239, 240, 252, 253, 267, 292, 297, 301, 305, 306, 307, 309, 312, 319, 323, 326, 328, 330, 335

Cassirer, H. W., **1.**2

Colwell, Ernest Cadman, **1.**2, 3, 12, 49, 167, 231, 317, 328, 347; **2.**264

Conrad, Carl W., **1.**xii, xiii, 312; **2.**xii, xiii

Cooper, Guy L., **1.**312

Crellin, Robert, **1.**179

Culpepper, R. Alan, **1.**40

Culy, Martin M., **1.**19, 20, 29, 37, 42, 48, 79, 80, 91, 109, 125, 189, 312; **2.**5, 12, 36, 148, 151, 192

Daise, Michael A., **2.**55

Daube, David, **1.**112

Dennis, John, **1.**238; **2.**41, 217

Dixon, Paul Stephen, **1.**3

du Toit, Herman C., **1.**xxv, 40, 44, 68, 94, 129; **2.**xxv, 15, 221, 270

Fanning, Buist M., **1.**xxiii, 39, 53, 56, 98, 134, 150, 191, 229, 236, 244, 252, 277, 281, 282, 284, 291, 308, 331, 369; **2.**xxiii, 10, 19, 32, 71, 83, 85, 87, 107, 121, 144, 146, 148, 162, 164, 190, 202, 262, 303, 315, 337

Fee, Gordon D., **1.**157; **2.**311, 312

Fresch, Christopher J., **1.**xxiv; **2.**xxiv

Frey, Jörg, **1.**xxv, 4, 15, 29, 64, 65, 84, 102, 104, 124, 162, 166, 168, 208, 226, 367; **2.**xxv, 62, 80, 107, 135, 167, 172, 174, 190, 200, 222, 301

Goodspeed, Edgar J., **1.**2

Grosvenor, Mary, **1.**81, 96, 124, 206, 228, 234, 267, 276, 288, 303, 338, 368; **2.**57, 115, 123, 132, 140, 142, 150, 151, 159, 160, 187, 213, 244, 262, 283, 290, 298, 333, 336

Gundry, Robert H., **1.**87

Hagner, Donald A., **1.**75

Harner, Philip B., **1.**3

Author Index

Harris, Murray J., **1.**2, 5, 9, 10, 13, 15, 17, 18, 22, 24, 27, 30, 37, 48, 54, 59, 63, 67, 70, 77, 78, 81, 87, 90, 102, 103, 108, 111, 120, 121, 124, 125, 127, 135, 141, 144, 158, 162, 167, 174, 188, 192, 200, 207, 220, 225, 226, 242, 279, 292, 296, 298, 299, 312, 318, 328, 333, 335, 339, 343, 344, 354, 357, 358, 363, 367, 368, 371, 372; **2.**5, 8, 11, 36, 44, 53, 62, 63, 64, 67, 84, 88, 95, 103, 110, 113, 117, 128, 132, 142, 148, 151, 152, 156, 157, 159, 167, 186, 193, 210, 221, 256, 268, 286, 299, 303, 306, 316, 333

Haubeck, Wilfrid, **1.**9, 24, 37, 48, 172, 173, 177, 200, 219, 250, 344, 347, 351, 363, 367, 372; **2.**41, 48, 65, 66, 116, 140, 148, 151, 193, 246, 277

Heckert, Jacob K., **1.**7

Howell, Russell W., **1.**87

James, Patrick, **1.**368, 369; **2.**3, 7, 9, 10, 15, 26, 27, 28, 35

Jensen, Matthew D., **2.**312

Johnson, Luke Timothy, **1.**66

Keck, Leander E., **2.**203

Keener, Craig S., **1.**17, 60, 71, 74, 142, 146, 182, 189, 198, 253, 326; **2.**35, 44, 56, 71, 310, 326

Kerr, Alan R., **1.**67

Köstenberger, Andreas, **1.**67

Kysar, Robert, **1.**66, 289

Lappenga, Benjamin J., **1.**65

Leung, Mavis M., **1.**14, 15

Levinsohn, Stephen H., **1.**xxv, xxvi, 17, 27, 36, 92, 93, 103, 120, 131, 141, 192, 219, 221, 239, 291, 322, 325, 330, 335, 338; **2.**xxv, xxvi, 24, 54, 64, 73, 78, 82, 87, 88, 93, 114, 138, 153, 169, 181, 191, 195, 243, 246, 271, 273, 274, 275, 305, 310

Martyn, J. Louis, **1.**332; **2.**75, 165

Mason, Steve, **1.**66

Matera, Frank J., **2.**296

McGaughy, Lane C., **1.**2

McGehee, Michael, **2.**296

McHugh, John F., **1.**18, 114, 117

McKay, K. L., **1.**xxiii, 64, 102, 308, 337; **2.**xxiii, 6, 7, 61, 110, 121, 124, 148, 180

Menken, Maarten J. J., **1.**23

Metzger, Bruce M., **1.**4, 5, 18, 20, 22, 26, 35, 41, 62, 85, 87, 96, 102, 104, 112, 114, 133, 144, 147, 148, 149, 171, 174, 199, 206, 215, 218, 222, 230, 232, 238, 260, 269, 273, 279, 296, 298, 302, 310, 313, 316, 341, 343, 351, 354, 358, 359, 360, 364, 366, 374; **2.**13, 23, 24, 37, 43, 46, 49, 55, 67, 74, 83, 84, 90, 97, 103, 107, 115, 117, 118, 119, 125, 126, 129, 137, 147, 149, 167, 173, 181, 182, 186, 191, 196, 200, 208, 211, 215, 231, 257, 263, 266, 276, 279, 301, 303, 335

MHT (Moulton, Howard, and Turner), **1.**10, 14, 22, 25, 27, 42, 52, 55, 90, 108, 144, 145, 219, 255, 339; **2.**36, 43, 48, 58, 73, 74, 85, 93, 104, 124, 147, 160, 169, 226, 228, 238, 249, 264, 267, 314, 317, 318

Michaels, J. Ramsey, **1.**32, 54, 84, 204; **2.**58, 206

Moffatt, James, **1.**2

Morris, Leon, **2.**327

Moule, C. F. D., **1.**5, 6, 23, 87, 90, 110, 286, 328, 338, 363; **2.**70, 140, 143, 146, 159, 201, 212, 299, 308, 310

Moulton, James Hope, **1.**90, 354; **2.**226, 247

Newman, Barclay M., **1.**32

Nida, Eugene A., **1.**3, 10, 32, 112, 118, 132, 277; **2.**14, 18, 52, 127, 154, 275
Novakovic, Lidija, **1.**69

O'Rourke, John J., **1.**14

Parsons, Mikeal C., **1.**19, 79, 189; **2.**5, 36,
Pennington, Jonathan T., **1.**xii, xiii; **2.**xii, xiii
Pierce, Madison N., **1.**85
Porter, Stanley E., **1.**xi, xxiii, xxiv, xxv, 1, 2, 4, 5, 8, 15, 39, 58, 59, 63, 79, 85, 88, 92, 102, 104, 116, 133, 193, 203, 211, 230, 313, 342; **2.**xi, xxiii, xxiv, xxv, 4, 6, 10, 19, 25, 60, 65, 83, 107, 110, 139, 146, 186, 196, 203, 206, 296, 297, 298, 307, 309, 326
Poythress, Vern S., **1.**17, 136

Ramelli, Ilaria, **1.**253; **2.**327
Reynolds, Benjamin E., **1.**85
Ridderbos, Herman N., **1.**84
Robar, Elizabeth, **1.**14
Robertson, A. T., **1.**xii, 1, 2, 3, 4, 11, 16, 36, 39, 55, 59, 66, 68, 70, 80, 85, 98, 123, 128, 148, 211, 273, 302, 317, 333, 336, 339, 349; **2.**xii, 4, 5, 32, 37, 45, 68, 104, 132, 160, 162, 209, 249, 261, 274, 295, 308, 314, 334
Robinson, J. A. T., **2.**58
Runge, Steven, **1.**xi, xxiv, xxvi, 1, 2, 5, 6, 7, 10, 11, 14, 17, 21, 25, 31, 33, 36, 46, 50, 54, 64, 72, 73, 74, 84, 86, 88, 91, 96, 102, 119, 132, 153, 155, 163, 167, 175, 208, 211, 221, 237, 239, 243, 249, 253, 273, 280, 288, 289, 300, 303, 333, 336, 339, 345, 346, 363, 376, 382, 383, 384, 385; **2.**xi, xxiv, xxv, xxvi, 1, 5, 28, 54, 68, 69, 79, 103, 117, 118, 120, 124, 130, 136, 143, 145, 170, 192, 211, 220, 221, 224, 264, 282, 311, 328, 329, 344, 345, 346, 347

Schnackenburg, Rudolf, **1.**85, 87, 148, 268, 359, 374; **2.**52, 88, 90, 114, 119, 155, 170, 182, 205, 250, 268, 295, 308
Shepherd, David, **2.**326
Smith, D. Moody, **2.**57, 311, 326
Smyth, H. W., **1.**15, 16, 26, 30, 34, 35, 49, 50, 54, 65, 78, 79, 98, 122, 128, 131, 132, 135, 137, 152, 153, 154, 157, 165, 170, 174, 176, 178, 189, 192, 198, 200, 201, 206, 207, 208, 211, 214, 216, 217, 220, 221, 222, 225, 226, 231, 235, 242, 248, 249, 251, 255, 257, 261, 265, 283, 290, 292, 293, 295, 298, 301, 304, 306, 316, 320, 321, 322, 325, 327, 329, 330, 334, 335, 338, 339, 343, 356, 358, 365, 366, 367, 369, 373; **2.**7, 29, 30, 31, 58, 64, 77, 79, 81, 93, 95, 98, 102, 108, 111, 112, 118, 121, 123, 125, 126, 130, 131, 135, 136, 139, 141, 147, 150, 152, 155, 159, 163, 168, 171, 175, 176, 177, 178, 182, 183, 185, 191, 193, 194, 195, 196, 198, 200, 205, 209, 211, 212, 213, 220, 222, 225, 239, 240, 252, 253, 254, 267, 292, 296, 301, 305, 306, 307, 309, 310, 319, 323, 328, 330, 335
Stigall, Joshua J., **1.**19, 79, 189; **2.**5, 36

Talbert, Charles H., **1.**84, 367; **2.**90, 295, 326, 327
Taylor, Bernard A., **1.**xii, xiii; **2.**xii, xiii
Theobald, Michael, **2.**296
Thompson, Marianne Meye, **1.**60, 71, 74, 75, 142, 146, 182, 189, 198, 253, 326; **2.**35, 56, 57, 71, 310
Thomson, Christopher J., **1.**230
Tolmie, D. Francois, **1.**55

Author Index

Torrey, Charles Culter, **1**.xxiii; **2**.xxiii
Turner, Nigel, **1**.42; **2**.96, 110, 238, 266

Van Belle, Gilbert, **1**.xii; **2**.xii
van der Watt, Jan, **1**.xxii, 260; **2**.xxii
von Siebenthal, Heinrich, **1**.9, 24, 37, 48, 172, 173, 177, 200, 219, 250, 344, 347, 351, 363, 367, 372; **2**.41, 48, 65, 66, 116, 140, 148, 151, 193, 246, 277
von Soden, Hermann Freiherr, **1**.269
von Wahlde, Urban C., **1**.66

Wallace, Daniel B., **1**.x, 2, 3, 5, 6, 8, 11, 12, 14, 18, 19, 22, 23, 27, 29, 34, 36, 39, 41, 45, 46, 51, 52, 53, 54, 55, 57, 58, 59, 63, 66, 67, 68, 72, 74, 75, 77, 78, 79, 81, 85, 87, 88, 91, 94, 100, 103, 106, 109, 110, 111, 113, 114, 115, 116, 117, 120, 121, 122, 123, 124, 126, 127, 131, 133, 135, 136, 140, 141, 146, 148, 150, 151, 152, 155, 162, 164, 165, 167, 168, 171, 173, 175, 176, 180, 181, 196, 200, 205, 214, 223, 227, 231, 237, 239, 251, 256, 264, 267, 272, 280, 281, 288, 293, 297, 299, 302, 312, 313, 315, 321, 322, 323, 331, 334, 337, 339, 341, 342, 347, 348, 349, 351, 352, 353, 354, 365, 369, 371, 372, 373; **2**.x, 3, 7, 8, 10, 14, 16, 21, 26, 28, 33, 37, 53, 56, 58, 60, 65, 66, 67, 68, 73, 74, 80, 82, 84, 86, 93, 102, 105, 106, 107, 109, 110, 113, 120, 129, 133, 136, 140, 142, 144, 147, 148, 151, 154, 159, 162, 163, 169, 170, 172, 174, 176, 178, 179, 185, 193, 194, 198, 204, 208, 210, 211, 213, 221, 224, 225, 226, 227, 229, 230, 232, 236, 239, 246, 247, 249, 250, 251, 255, 256, 258, 261, 262, 264, 273, 275, 280, 285, 291, 293, 295, 296, 297, 300, 303, 307, 308, 309, 312, 320, 332, 334

Young, Richard A., **1**.238; **2**.4, 16, 60, 67, 116, 164

Zerwick, Maximilian, **1**.10, 28, 34, 55, 67, 71, 77, 81, 96, 99, 108, 117, 124, 132, 137, 173, 177, 206, 219, 228, 234, 249, 256, 267, 276, 284, 285, 288, 298, 302, 303, 312, 319, 320, 324, 334, 336, 337, 338, 339, 368, 370; **2**.2, 23, 27, 28, 37, 43, 57, 60, 76, 84, 104, 109, 115, 120, 123, 132, 137, 139, 140, 142, 146, 150, 151, 157, 159, 160, 185, 187, 193, 194, 198, 203, 204, 207, 213, 216, 230, 243, 244, 255, 262, 282, 283, 284, 285, 287, 290, 291, 295, 296, 298, 320, 333, 336

GRAMMAR INDEX

Superscript is used to indicate the number of times a grammatical element appears within a verse.

accusative (adverbial), 1:41; 2:10; 3:4; 4:18, 27; 6:11; 7:51; 8:25; 10:10, 40; 11:29; 12:16; 13:33, 36; 14:19; 15:18, 25; 16:16^2, 17^2, 19^2; 18:13; 19:39; 21:14, 15, 16, 17^2

accusative complement in a double accusative construction, 1:29, 32, 33, 38, 41, 47, 48, 51^3; 2:11, 14, 16; 4:5, 18, 23, 46, 54; 5:6, 11, 15, 18^2, 19, 38; 6:14, 15, 19^2, 30, 62; 7:23; 8:29, 53; 9:22; 10:12, 33, 35; 11:16, 33^2, 54; 14:18; 15:15^2; 16:2, 32; 17:13; 19:7, 12, 13, 17, 18, 26, 33; 20:1, 5, 6, 7^2, 12, 14; 21:9^2, 11, 20

accusative direct object, 1:5, 9, 10, 11, 12^2, 14, 16, 18, 19^2, 21, 22^3, 23, 25, 26, 27, 29, 31, 32^2, 33^3, 36, 38^2, 41^3, 42, 43, 45, 47, 48^3, 50^2, 51^2; 2:3, 5, 7^2, 9^3, 10^3, 11^2, 14^3, 15^6, 16^3, 17, 18^2, 19^2, 20, 22^2, 23^2, 24^2, 25; 3:2^2, 3, 8, 10, 11^3, 12^2, 14, 15, 16^3, 17^2, 19^2, 20^2, 21, 27, 29, 32^2, 33, 34^2, 35^2, 36^2; 4:1, 3, 5, 7, 8, 10^3, 11^2, 12, 14, 15, 16, 17^2, 18^2, 21, 22^2, 23^2, 24, 25, 27^2, 28, 29^3, 31, 32^2, 34^3, 35^2, 36^2, 38, 39^2, 40, 44, 45^3, 46, 47, 48, 50, 52^2, 54; 5:2, 6, 7^2, 8, 9, 10, 11^2, 12, 14, 15, 16^2, 18^4, 19^5, 20^4, 21^2, 22^2, 23^5, 24^3, 26^2, 27^2, 28, 29^2, 30^4, 32, 34^2, 36^5, 37^3, 38^2, 39^2, 40, 41, 42^2, 43^2, 44^2; 6:2^2, 5^2, 6^3, 7, 9^2, 10, 11, 12, 13, 14^3, 15, 19, 21, 23, 24, 25, 26^2, 27^4, 28^2, 29, 30^2, 31^2, 32^2, 33, 34, 36, 37^2, 38^3, 39^3, 40^3, 42^2, 44^3, 46^2, 47, 49, 51, 52, 53^3, 54^4, 56^2, 57^2, 58^2, 59, 61, 62, 63^2, 64, 68, 70, 71; 7:1, 3^2, 4^3, 7^2, 9, 11, 12, 15, 16, 17, 18^3, 19^3, 20^2, 21, 22^2, 23^2, 25, 26, 27, 28^3, 29, 30^2, 31, 32^3, 33, 34^2, 35^2, 36^3, 39^2, 44^2, 45, 49, 51^2; 8:2, 3^2, 5^2, 6^2, 7^2, 10, 11, 12, 15, 16, 18, 19^4, 20^2, 21, 22, 25, 26^4, 28^4, 29^3, 30, 32^2, 34, 36, 37, 38^2, 39, 40^4, 41^2, 42^2, 43^2, 44^2, 45, 46, 47, 48, 49^3, 50, 51^2, 52^2, 53, 54^2, 55^5, 56, 57, 59; 9:1, 2, 4^2, 6^3, 8, 11^2, 13, 14^2, 15^2, 16^2, 17^2, 18, 19, 21^3, 22^3, 23^2, 24^2, 25, 26^2, 28, 30, 31, 32, 33, 34, 35^2, 37, 40, 41; 10:3^2, 4^2, 5, 6^2, 9, 10, 11, 12^3, 14^2, 15^3, 16^2, 17^3, 18^7, 20, 21, 24^2, 25, 27, 28^2, 29, 31^2, 32^2, 33^2, 35, 36, 37, 39, 41^2; 11:2^2, 3, 5^3, 8, 9, 11^2, 17, 19, 22^2, 26, 28^3, 31^2, 32, 33^3, 34, 36, 37, 39, 40, 41^2, 42, 43, 44^2, 45, 46, 47^3, 48^3, 49, 51, 52, 53, 55, 56, 57^2; 12:1, 2, 3^3, 4, 6^3,

7^2, 8^2, 9^2, 10, 13, 14, 16^2, 17^2, 18, 19, 21^2, 24, 25^4, 26, 27^2, 28, 32, 33, 35^2, 36^2, 37, 38, 40^3, 41^2, 43^2, 44, 45^3, 47^3, 48^6, 49^4, 50; $13:1^2$, 2, 3, 4^3, 5^2, 6, 7, 8^3, 9^3, 10^2, 11^2, 12^3, 13, 14^2, 15, 16, 17^2, 18^3, 20^5, 21^2, 23, 26^2, 28, 29^3, 30, 32^2, 33, 34^4, 35, 37, 38^2; 14:2, 3^2, 4, 5, 7^4, 8, 9^4, 10^3, 12^3, 13^2, 14^2, 15^2, 16^2, 17^3, 18, 19^2, 21^6, 22, 23^4, 24^4, 26^6, 27^2, 28, 30^2, 31; $15:2^7$, 3, 4, 5^2, 6, 7, 8, 9^2, 10^2, 11, 12^2, 13^2, 14, 15^5, 16^6, 17^2, 18^2, 19^3, 20^4, 21^3, 22^2, 23^2, 24^5, 25, 26; 16:1, 2^3, 3^3, 4^2, 5^2, 6^2, 7^2, 8, 10, 12, 13^2, 14, 15, 16^2, 17^3, 18^2, 19^3, 21^2, 22^3, 23^4, 24, 25, 26, 27^2, 28, 29, 30^3, 32, 33^4; $17:1^4$, 2^3, 3^2, 4^3, 5, 6^4, 7, 8^3, 11, 12, 13^2, 14^2, 15^2, 17, 18^2, 19, 21, 22^2, 23^3, 24^4, 25^3, 26^2; 18:1, 2^2, 3^2, 4^2, 5^2, 7^3, 8^2, 9^3, 10^4, 11^4, 12^2, 16, 18, 19, 20, 21^4, 22^2, 23, 24, 26^2, 28^2, 29, 30^2, 31^3, 32, 33, 34, 35^2, 38^2, 39^2, 40^2; 19:1, 2^3, 3, 4^2, 5^2, 6^4, 7^2, 8, 9, 10^4, 11^3, 12^3, 13, 15^4, 16^2, 17, 18^3, 19, 20, 22, 23^4, 24^4, 26^3, 27, 29, 30^3, 31, 32, 33^2, 34, 35, 38^3, 39, 40^2, 42; 20:1, 2^3, 5, 6, 7, 9, 12, 13^2, 14^2, 15^4, 18^2, 20^4, 21^2, 22^2, 23, 25^4, 27^3, 29, 30, 31^2; 21:1, 3, 5, 6^2, 7^3, 8, 9^3, 10, 11, 12, 13^2, 15^3, 16^3, 17^5, 18^3, 19^3, 20^3, 21, 24, 25^2
accusative in apposition, 1:14, 41, 45^2; 6:70; 8:40, 41; 9:13; 11:28; 14:17; $17:3^2$; 18:5, 6, 24; 19:13, 23, 39
accusative of reference/respect, 1:15, 45; 4:38; 6:10, 71; 8:25, 27, 54; 9:19, 29; 10:36; 11:44
accusative (predicate), 1:12; 2:9
accusative subject of the infinitive, 1:48; 2:24; 3:14, 30^2; 4:4, 24, 49; 5:39; 6:10; 8:58; 9:4; 10:16; 12:18, 29, 34; 17:5; 18:14; 20:9; 21:22, 23, 25
adjectivizer, 5:44; 12:21; 13:1; 18:16; 21:2
adverbial accusative: *see* accusative (adverbial)
a minore ad maius, 3:12; 13:14

anacoluthon, 6:24
anaphora/anaphoric, 1:2, 4, 21, 30, 33, 34, 37, 38, 41; 2:1, 2, 8, 11, 16, 21, 22^2, 23; 3:2, 8, 10, 16, 26, 30, 32; 4:9, 11, 25, 29, 32, 42, 43, 47, 49, 50; 5:6, 11, 14, 16, 19^2, 28^2, 37, 38, 39, 46, 47; 6:6, 9, 13, 14, 29, 39, 57, 65; 7:11, 17, 18, 22, 29, 40, 45, 51; 8:9, 44; 9:6, 9, 11, 12, 14, 23, 25, 36, 40; 10:1, 6, 25; 11:13, 28, 29, 51; $12:18^2$, 21, 27, 48; 13:11, 25, 26, 28, 30; 14:6, 12, 21, 25, 26; 15:8, 17, 19, 26; 16:1, 3, 4^2, 8, 13, 14, 15, 25, 30, 33; 17:1, 3, 20, 24; 18:1, 16, 17, 21, 25, 38; 19:7, 11, 15, 29, 35, 38; 20:13, 15, 16, 20, 22, 31; 21:19, 21
ἀντί (substitution), 1:16
ἀπό (agency), 5:19, 30; 7:17, 18, 28; 8:28, 42; 10:18; 11:51; 14:10; 15:4; 16:13; 18:34
ἀπό (causal), 21:6
ἀπό (distance), 21:8
ἀπό (locative), 1:33; 7:42; 12:21
ἀπό (partitive), 21:10
ἀπό (separation), 10:5, 18; 11:18; 12:36; 16:22; 18:28; 21:8
ἀπό (source), 1:44, 45; 3:2; 6:38; 11:1; 13:3; 16:30; 19:38; 21:2
ἀπό (starting point), 8:9
ἀπό (temporal), 8:11, 44; 11:53; 13:19; 14:7; 15:27; 19:27
asyndeton, 1:17, 23, 26^2, 28, 29, 35, 39^2, 40, 41, 42, 43, 45, 47, 48, 49, 50; 2:5, 7, 12, 17, 19; 3:2, 3, 4, 5, 6, 7, 8, 9, 10, 11, 12, 18, 22, 27, 28, 29, 30, 31, 32, 33, 35, 36; 4:7, 10, 11, 12, 13, 15, 16^2, 17, 19, 20, 21, 22^2; 24, 25, 26, 30, 31, 34, 35, 36, 38, 47, 49, 50; 5:1, 3, 6, 7, 8^2, 12, 14, 15, 23, 24, 25, 28, 30, 31, 32, 33, 35, 39, 41, 43, 44, 45; 6:1, 7, 8, 9, 10, 22, 26, 27, 29, 31, 35^2, 37, 43, 44, 45, 47, 48, 49, 50, 51^2, 54, 56, 57, 58, 59, 63, 66, 68, 70; 7:7, 8, 13, 17, 18, 19, 20, 21, 23, 24, 29, 32, 34, 36, 38, 41, 42, 46, 48, 50, 51, 52; 8:4, 12, 14, 15, 18, 20, 26, 27, 30, 33, 34, 37, 38, 39, 41, 42,

43, 44, 46, 47, 48, 49, 51, 53, 54, 56, 58; 9:3, 4², 5, 6, 7, 9, 11², 13, 22, 27⁴, 29, 30, 31, 32, 33, 34, 35, 36, 37, 40, 41²; 10:1, 3, 4, 6, 8, 9², 10, 11², 12, 14, 15, 18, 19, 21, 22, 25, 27, 29, 30, 31, 32, 33, 34, 35, 37; 11:8, 9, 11, 23, 24, 25², 27, 34, 35, 39², 40, 44², 48; 12:12, 16, 19, 22, 24, 25, 26², 27, 28, 30, 31, 35, 36, 41, 46, 48; 13:7, 8², 9, 10, 13, 16, 17, 18², 19, 20, 21, 22, 23, 26, 33², 34, 35, 36², 37², 38²; 14:1², 2, 5, 6³, 7, 8, 9³, 10², 11, 12, 14, 15, 17, 18, 19, 20, 21, 22, 23, 24, 25, 27², 28², 30, 31; 15:1, 2, 3, 4², 5², 6, 7, 8, 9², 10, 11, 12, 13, 14, 15, 16, 17, 18, 19, 20⁵, 22, 23, 24, 26; 16:1, 2, 12, 14, 15, 16, 19, 20², 21, 23, 24², 25², 26, 28², 29, 30², 31, 32, 33²; 17:1², 2, 4, 6², 7, 9, 14, 15, 16, 17², 18, 23, 24; 18:1, 5², 8, 11, 17, 20, 21³, 23, 25, 26, 30, 31, 34, 35³, 36², 37³, 38; 19:6, 7, 10, 11, 12, 15², 22, 28, 29; 20:13, 14, 15³, 16², 17, 18, 23, 26, 28, 29²; 21:1, 2, 3³, 5, 10, 12, 13, 14, 15², 16³, 17³, 18, 20, 22, 24

attraction (dative), 13:5; 17:5, 11, 12
attraction (genitive), 4:14; 7:31; 9:18; 13:38; 15:20; 17:9; 21:10
attributive genitive: *see* genitive (attributive)
αὐτός (intensive), 2:12, 24, 25; 3:28; 4:2, 12, 42, 44, 45, 53; 5:20, 36; 6:6, 15; 7:9; 12:24, 49; 14:11; 16:27; 18:28; 21:25

cataphora/cataphoric, 3:19; 4:37; 5:16, 18, 28; 6:29, 39, 40; 7:22; 8:47; 10:17; 12:18, 39; 15:8, 12, 17; 17:3, 26; 18:37; 21:23
cognate dative: *see* dative (cognate)
conditional sentence (first-class), 1:25; 3:12; 5:47; 7:4, 23; 8:39, 46; 10:24, 35, 37, 38; 11:12; 13:14, 17, 32; 14:7, 11; 15:18, 20²; 18:8, 23²; 20:15
conditional sentence (second-class), 4:10; 5:46; 8:19, 42; 9:41; 11:21, 32; 14:28; 15:19, 22, 24; 18:30, 36; 19:11
conditional sentence (third-class), 3:2, 3, 5, 12, 27; 4:48; 5:19, 31, 43; 6:44, 51, 53, 62, 65; 7:17, 37, 51; 8:14, 16, 24, 31, 36, 51, 52, 54, 55; 9:22, 31; 10:9, 38; 11:9, 10, 25, 40, 48, 57; 12:24², 26², 32, 47; 13:8, 17, 20, 35; 14:3, 14, 15, 23; 15:4², 6, 7, 10, 14; 16:7², 23; 19:12; 20:23², 25; 21:22, 23, 25
constructio ad sensum, 6:2, 9, 22; 7:49, 53; 8:33, 37; 12:12, 13, 18; 17:2
crasis, 1:31, 33, 34; 5:17; 6:44, 54, 56, 57²; 7:28, 29; 8:14, 26, 55; 10:15, 16, 27, 28, 38²; 11:25, 54; 12:32; 14:12, 16, 20, 21; 15:4, 5, 9; 16:32; 17:6, 11, 18, 21, 22, 24, 26; 20:15, 21

dative (cognate), 3:29
dative complement, 3:26, 28, 36; 4:21, 51; 5:10, 18, 24, 33, 38, 46²; 6:30; 7:23; 8:29, 31, 33, 45, 46, 55; 9:9; 10:13, 37, 38²; 11:20, 30, 33, 41, 56; 12:6, 13, 18; 14:11; 18:14, 15², 31, 37; 19:2, 12, 24, 29, 32, 40; 20:6, 22
dative direct object, 1:36, 37, 40, 42, 43; 2:22²; 4:21, 23, 50; 5:47²; 6:2; 8:12; 9:38; 10:4, 5, 27; 11:31; 12:26³, 38; 13:36, 37; 18:15; 21:19, 22
dative in apposition, 1:12; 4:5; 7:37; 20:19
dative indirect object, 1:12, 22², 25, 26, 31, 33, 38², 39, 41, 43, 45, 46², 48², 49, 50², 51²; 2:4, 5², 7, 8², 10, 16, 18², 19, 24; 3:2, 3², 5, 7, 9, 10, 11, 12², 26, 27; 4:5, 7², 9, 10⁴, 11, 12, 13, 14², 15, 16, 17², 19, 21, 25², 26², 28, 29, 32, 33, 34, 35, 42, 50², 52, 53; 5:6, 7, 8, 10, 11², 12, 14, 15, 17, 19², 20², 22, 24, 25, 26, 27, 36; 6:7, 8, 11, 12, 20, 25, 26², 27, 29, 30, 31, 32⁴, 33, 34, 35, 36, 37, 39, 43, 46, 53², 61, 63, 65², 67, 68, 70; 7:4, 6, 16, 19, 21, 22, 26, 45, 47,

52; 8:4, 5, 7, 10, 12, 13, 14, 19, 21, 23, 24, 25³, 27, 28, 34², 39², 40, 41, 42, 48, 51, 52, 58²; 9:7, 10, 11, 12, 15, 17, 24², 26², 27², 29, 30, 34, 37, 40, 41; 10:1, 6², 7, 24², 25², 28, 29, 32², 33, 34; 11:7, 8, 11, 12, 14, 16, 22, 23, 24, 25, 27, 32, 34, 39, 40², 44, 46, 49; 12:5, 22², 23, 24, 29, 34, 35, 38, 49; 13:3, 6, 7, 8², 9, 10, 12, 15, 16, 19, 20, 21, 24, 25, 26², 27, 28, 29², 33², 34, 36², 37, 38; 14:2, 5, 6, 8², 9², 10, 12, 16, 21, 22³, 23, 25, 26, 27³, 28, 29, 31; 15:3, 11, 14, 15, 16, 17, 20, 22, 26; 16:1, 2, 4³, 6, 7, 12, 13, 14, 15, 17, 19, 20, 23², 25³, 26, 31, 33; 17:2³, 4, 6³, 7, 8², 9, 11, 12, 14, 22², 24², 26; 18:4, 5², 6, 8, 9, 11², 16, 17, 20², 21, 22², 23, 25, 30², 31², 33, 34, 35, 36, 37, 38²; 19:3, 4², 5, 6, 7, 9², 10², 11³, 14, 15, 16, 21, 26, 27, 29; 20:2, 13², 15³, 16, 17², 18², 19, 20, 21, 22, 25², 27, 28, 29; 21:1, 3², 5², 6, 7, 10, 12, 13, 14, 15³, 16³, 17⁴, 18, 19, 21, 22, 23
dative (locative), 11:33; 21:8
dative of advantage, 10:3; 11:50; 12:2, 16; 13:12, 15, 26, 35; 14:2, 3, 8; 15:7, 8; 16:7; 18:39²; 19:17, 23; 20:19, 21, 23, 26
dative of agency, 6:13; 18:15; 19:17
dative of disadvantage, 5:14
dative of interest, 5:33; 6:7; 18:37
dative of manner, 3:29; 7:13, 26; 10:24; 11:14, 54; 12:33; 16:25; 18:20, 32; 21:19
dative of means/instrument, 8:6; 11:2, 43, 44²; 12:3, 40²; 13:5; 17:5; 19:34
dative of possession, 1:6; 3:1; 13:35; 15:8; 17:6, 9; 18:10, 39
dative of respect, 6:13; 11:33; 13:21
dative of sphere, 13:21
dative of time, 1:29, 35, 43; 2:1, 20; 6:22, 54; 12:12; 20:1, 19
διά (causal), 1:31; 3:29; 4:39, 41, 42; 5:16, 18; 6:57², 65; 7:13, 22, 43, 45; 8:43, 46, 47; 9:23; 10:17, 19, 32; 11:15, 42; 12:5, 9, 11, 18, 27, 39,

42; 13:11, 37; 14:11; 15:3, 19, 21; 16:15, 21; 19:11, 38, 42; 20:19
διά (instrumental), 15:3
διά (intermediate agency), 1:3, 7, 10, 17²; 3:17; 6:57²; 10:9; 11:4; 14:6
διά (locative/spatial), 4:4; 10:1, 2; 19:23
διά (means), 17:20
διά (purpose), 11:42; 12:30²
double entendre, 1:5; 2:17; 3:3, 31; 4:10; 6:33; 7:39; 8:21; 11:11, 23; 12:16, 23; 13:31, 32; 17:1

ἐγγύς (locative), 3:23; 6:19, 23; 11:18, 54; 19:20
εἰ μή ... οὐ (point/counterpoint), 9:33
εἰς (in place of ἐν), 9:7; 17:23; 20:7
εἰς (in place of the predicate nominative), 16:20; 17:23
εἰς (in place of πρός), 8:26; 11:31, 38; 20:1, 3, 4, 8
εἰς (goal), 1:12; 2:11, 23; 3:16, 18²; 4:14, 36, 39; 5:29², 45; 6:27, 29, 35, 40; 7:5, 31, 38, 39, 48; 8:30; 9:35, 36; 10:42; 11:25, 26, 45, 48; 12:11, 27, 36, 37, 42, 44³, 46; 14:1², 12; 16:9; 17:20, 23
εἰς (locative), 1:9, 11, 18, 43; 2:2, 12, 13; 3:4, 5, 13, 17, 19, 22, 24, 36; 4:3, 5, 8, 28, 38, 43, 45², 46, 47, 54; 5:1, 7, 24²; 6:3, 14, 15, 17², 21², 22, 24², 66; 7:3, 8², 10, 14, 35, 53; 8:1, 2, 6, 8; 9:7, 11, 39; 10:1, 36, 40; 11:7, 27, 30, 52, 54², 55, 56; 12:1, 12², 24, 46; 13:2, 3, 5, 22, 27; 15:6, 21; 16:21, 28, 32; 17:1, 18²; 18:1, 6, 11, 15, 28², 33, 37; 19:9, 13, 17, 27, 37; 20:6, 11, 14, 19, 25², 26, 27; 21:3, 4, 6, 7, 9, 11², 23
εἰς (purpose), 1:7; 9:39; 11:52; 12:13, 25; 13:1, 29; 18:37²
εἰς (reference), 6:9
εἰς (result), 4:14, 36; 6:27; 12:25; 13:1
εἰς (temporal), 4:14; 6:51, 58; 8:35², 51, 52; 10:28; 11:26; 12:7, 34; 13:8; 14:16
ἐκ (agency), 1:13; 6:65

ἐκ (causal), 1:13³; 4:6; 6:66; 12:3; 19:12

ἐκ (in place of ἀπό), 18:3²

ἐκ (in place of the partitive genitive), 1:24, 35, 40; 3:1; 6:8, 11, 13, 26, 39, 50, 51, 60, 64, 66, 70, 71; 7:19, 25, 31, 40, 44, 48², 50; 8:46; 9:16, 40; 10:20, 26; 11:19, 37, 45, 46, 49; 12:2, 4, 9, 20, 42; 13:21, 23; 16:5, 17; 17:12; 18:9, 17, 25, 26; 20:24; 21:2

ἐκ (instrumental/impersonal agency), 8:42; 12:3

ἐκ (locative), 1:32

ἐκ (means), 1:13³; 3:34; 9:6

ἐκ (partitive), 3:25

ἐκ (separation), 2:15, 22; 4:30, 47, 54; 5:24; 6:23; 8:59; 10:28, 29, 39; 12:1, 9, 17², 27, 32; 13:1, 4; 15:19; 16:14, 15; 17:6, 15²; 20:1, 2, 9; 21:14

ἐκ (source), 1:13⁴, 16, 19, 44, 46; 2:15; 3:5, 6², 8, 13, 25, 27, 31⁴; 4:7, 12, 13, 14, 22, 39; 6:31, 32², 33, 41, 42, 50, 51, 58; 7:17, 22², 38, 41, 42, 52²; 8:23⁴, 42, 44², 47²; 9:6; 10:16, 32; 11:1, 55; 12:28, 34, 49; 15:19²; 17:14², 16²; 18:36², 37; 19:2, 23

ἐκ (temporal), 9:1, 24, 32; 6:64; 16:4; 19:12

ellipsis/elliptical, 1:8, 21, 22, 32; 3:13; 4:1, 53; 5:2, 7; 6:22, 29, 46, 58, 62, 71; 7:22; 9:3, 36; 12:7; 13:2, 9, 18, 26; 14:2, 11, 31; 15:6, 13, 20, 25; 18:9, 32; 19:24, 37; 20:1; 21:2, 10, 15, 16, 17, 21, 22

ἔμπροσθεν (advantage), 1:15, 30

ἔμπροσθεν (locative), 3:28; 10:4; 12:37

ἐν (agency), 3:21

ἐν (association), 12:35

ἐν (causal), 3:15; 5:35; 8:21, 24²

ἐν (close personal relationship), 3:21

ἐν (instrumental/means), 1:26, 31, 33²; 5:43²; 10:25; 13:35; 14:13, 14, 26; 15:8, 16; 16:23, 24, 26, 30; 17:10, 12, 17; 20:31

ἐν (locative), 1:4, 5, 10, 14, 23, 26, 28, 31, 33, 45, 47; 2:1, 11, 14, 23², 25; 3:14, 21, 23, 35; 4:14, 20², 21², 44, 45², 46; 5:2, 3, 13, 14, 26², 28, 38, 39, 42; 6:10, 31, 45, 49, 53, 59², 61; 7:1², 9, 11, 12, 18, 28, 43; 8:3, 5, 9, 12, 17, 20², 35, 37, 44; 9:3, 5, 16; 10:19, 22, 23², 34; 11:6, 10, 17, 20, 24, 30, 31, 38, 54, 56; 12:20, 25, 35², 46; 13:1, 23, 31, 32², 35; 14:2, 13, 30; 15:4, 7, 11, 24, 25; 16:13, 33; 17:10, 11², 13², 17, 19, 26; 18:20², 26, 38; 19:4, 6, 41³; 20:25, 30

ἐν (manner), 7:4², 10; 12:13; 16:25², 29; 18:20; 20:12

ἐν (reference), 4:37; 9:30

ἐν (state of being), 6:56²; 10:38²; 14:10³, 11², 17, 20³; 15:2, 4³, 5², 6, 7; 16:33; 17:11, 12, 21³, 23², 26

ἐν (state or condition), 4:23, 24; 5:5; 8:21, 24², 31, 44; 9:34; 15:9, 10²

ἐν (temporal), 1:1, 2; 2:19, 20, 23²; 4:31, 45, 52, 53; 5:7, 9, 16, 28; 6:39, 44; 7:11, 22, 23², 37; 9:14; 11:9, 10, 24²; 12:20, 48; 14:20; 16:23, 26; 18:39; 19:31; 21:3, 20

ἐπάνω (advantage), 3:31²

epexegetical genitive: *see* genitive (epexegetical)

ἐπί (locative), 1:32, 33, 51; 3:36; 4:6; 5:2; 6:2, 16, 19, 21; 7:30, 44; 8:7, 59; 9:6, 15; 11:38; 12:14, 15; 13:25; 17:4; 18:4; 19:3, 19, 31, 33; 20:7; 21:1, 20

ἐπί (opposition), 13:18

ἐπί (reference), 12:16; 19:24

ἐπί (temporal), 4:27; 8:3, 4

ἕως (locative), 2:7

ἕως (temporal), 2:10; 5:17; 9:18; 10:24; 13:38; 16:24

first (anarthrous) attributive position, 1:18; 2:6; 6:55²; 8:55; 9:16, 32; 10:32; 12:24; 14:16; 15:13; 18:38; 19:4, 11, 37; 20:30

first attributive position, 2:10; 3:22; 4:23, 42, 44; 5:37, 44, 47; 6:12, 57; 7:8, 16, 37²; 8:16, 18, 31, 51; 10:3; 11:33; 12:49; 14:24; 17:3; 19:5²; 20:2, 25; 21:25

first predicate position, 5:28; 19:18

Grammar Index

fourth attributive position, 1:6; 2:6; 3:15, 23; 4:5, 9, 10, 14; 5:2, 5; 6:9; 7:38; 8:3; 9:16; 10:32, 41; 12:3²; 13:34; 15:2, 5, 8; 16:29; 19:11, 13, 29², 41; 20:22; 21:11

genitive absolute (causal), 2:3; 5:13; 6:18
genitive absolute (concessive), 12:37; 20:26; 21:11
genitive absolute (temporal), 2:3; 4:51; 5:13; 6:23; 7:14; 8:30; 13:2²; 18:22; 20:1; 20:19²; 21:4
genitive (attributive), 1:13; 2:6, 13; 5:1; 6:4; 7:2, 23; 12:24; 14:17; 15:26; 16:13; 19:42
genitive complement, 1:14, 27; 2:7; 5:45; 8:6, 52; 11:41, 42; 19:29²; 21:11
genitive (descriptive), 2:16; 6:35, 48, 68; 12:36; 17:12
genitive direct object, 1:37; 3:29; 4:14; 5:25, 28; 6:60; 7:32, 40; 9:31; 10:3, 8, 16, 20, 27; 12:47; 15:20; 16:4, 21; 18:37; 19:13; 20:17
genitive (epexegetical), 2:16, 21; 6:1; 8:1, 12, 44; 9:7; 11:13; 12:24; 13:1; 14:17; 18:1; 19:17, 31; 21:1
genitive in apposition, 4:12; 5:3³; 7:42; 8:44, 53; 9:18; 11:1; 12:38
genitive (objective), 1:4; 2:17; 3:10; 4:42; 5:42, 45; 7:13; 8:12, 34, 50, 54; 9:5; 11:9, 40; 12:7, 31; 14:17; 15:10, 26; 16:13; 17:2, 14, 24; 18:10, 12, 26; 19:14, 38; 20:19
genitive of agency, 6:45; 18:16
genitive of comparison, 1:15, 30, 50; 4:12; 5:20; 7:31; 8:53; 10:29; 13:16²; 14:12, 28; 15:13, 18, 20; 20:4; 21:15
genitive of content, 4:14; 6:13; 7:38; 21:8
genitive of direction, 7:35; 10:7
genitive of material, 12:3; 19:39
genitive of origin, 7:23; 10:37; 11:40
genitive of price, 6:7; 12:5
genitive of producer, 6:33
genitive of product, 4:14; 6:35, 48

genitive of purpose, 2:4; 5:29²; 6:68; 7:30; 8:12, 20; 10:1, 7; 13:1; 16:4, 21
genitive of reference, 7:35; 15:18
genitive of relationship, 1:12, 34, 35, 40, 42, 45, 49, 51; 2:1, 2, 3, 5, 11, 12, 16, 17, 22; 3:4, 13, 14, 18, 22, 25, 29; 4:2, 5, 8, 12², 16, 18, 20, 27, 46, 47, 49, 50, 51, 53; 5:17, 25, 27, 43; 6:3, 8², 12, 16, 22², 24, 27, 31, 32, 40, 42, 49, 53, 60, 61, 62, 66, 69, 71; 7:3², 5, 10, 42; 8:19³, 28, 31, 33, 37, 39², 41, 42, 44², 49, 53, 54, 56; 9:2², 3, 18, 19, 20, 22, 23, 27, 28², 35; 10:18, 25, 29, 36, 37; 11:1, 2, 4, 5, 11, 21, 23, 27, 28, 32, 39, 5; 12:4, 15², 16, 23, 34²; 13:2, 23, 26, 31; 14:2, 7, 20, 21, 23; 15:1, 8, 10, 13, 14, 15, 20, 23, 24; 16:17, 29; 17:1; 18:1², 2, 13, 16, 17, 19, 25, 26; 19:7, 12, 25⁴, 26, 27, 38; 20:17⁵, 26, 30, 31; 21:2², 15, 16, 17
genitive of result, 5:29²
genitive of separation, 5:13
genitive of source, 5:25, 28; 7:16, 42; 10:37; 11:9, 40; 12:3, 24, 43²
genitive of subordination, 1:49; 3:1; 8:54; 10:2; 12:13, 15, 31; 13:16; 14:30; 15:15; 16:11; 17:2; 18:33, 39; 19:3, 14, 15, 19, 21³; 20:13
genitive of time, 3:2; 8:2; 11:9, 49, 51; 12:7; 18:13; 19:39
genitive (partitive), 1:27; 2:1, 11²; 4:5, 39, 46; 5:3; 6:1; 7:37; 8:7; 10:32; 12:3, 11, 13, 21; 13:28; 18:22; 19:20, 21, 34; 20:1, 19; 21:2, 6, 12
genitive (possessive), 1:12, 14², 16, 18, 23², 27², 29², 36, 44, 51; 2:11, 15, 16, 17, 21, 23; 3:4, 8, 10, 18, 29, 35; 4:6, 12, 28, 34, 35, 51, 53; 5:5, 8, 9, 10, 11, 25, 28, 37², 43; 6:33, 51, 52, 53², 54², 55², 56²; 7:18, 38, 51, 53; 8:52; 9:6, 10, 11, 14, 15, 17, 21, 26, 30, 32; 10:3, 4, 5, 11, 12, 15, 16, 17, 21, 23, 24, 25, 27, 28, 29, 34, 39; 11:1, 2², 4, 32, 37, 44, 48; 12:3³, 13, 25², 27, 28, 38, 40², 41; 13:5, 6, 8, 9, 12², 14², 18², 23, 25, 37, 38; 14:1, 2, 13, 14, 24, 26, 27;

15:13, 16, 21, 25; 16:6, 22, 23, 24, 26; 17:1, 6, 11, 12, 26; 18:10², 15, 26², 31, 37; 19:2, 23, 24³, 25, 29, 31, 32², 33, 34, 36, 38², 40; 20:7, 12, 25³, 27⁴, 28², 31; 21:6, 15, 16, 17, 18, 20
genitive (predicate), 4:9
genitive subject, 2:3; 4:51; 5:13; 6:18, 23; 7:14; 8:30; 12:37; 13:2²; 18:22; 20:1, 19², 26; 21:4, 11
genitive (subjective), 1:13, 19, 29; 2:6, 13, 23; 3:3, 5, 11, 19, 20, 21, 32, 33, 34, 36; 4:10, 34², 38, 39, 41; 5:1, 24, 30, 31, 35, 36, 38, 42, 47; 6:4, 28, 29, 38, 39, 40, 51; 7:2, 3, 7, 17; 8:13, 14, 17, 21, 24², 39, 41, 44, 47, 52, 54, 55; 9:3, 4, 31, 41; 10:21, 35, 37; 11:13, 55; 12:38², 43², 47, 48, 50; 14:10, 21, 23, 24²; 15:7, 10⁴, 11, 16, 20, 22; 16:20, 22, 24; 17:6, 20; 18:19, 32; 19:35, 42; 20:23², 25²; 21:24
Granville-Sharp rule, 5:24; 6:33, 40, 45, 54; 8:50; 9:8; 10:1; 11:2, 26, 45; 12:48; 14:21; 20:17, 28, 29

headless relative clause, 1:3, 26, 33, 45; 3:11², 26², 32, 34; 4:18, 22², 38; 5:19, 21, 38; 6:14, 64; 7:25; 8:25, 26, 38²; 10:29, 36; 11:3, 22, 45, 46; 12:50; 13:7, 26, 27, 29; 15:7, 14, 15, 16; 16:13; 17:3, 24; 18:9, 21², 26; 19:22
hendiadys, 4:23
historical present, 1:15, 21, 29², 36, 38, 39, 41², 43², 45², 46, 47, 48, 51; 2:3, 4, 5, 7, 8, 9, 10; 3:4; 4:1, 5, 7², 9, 11, 15, 16, 17, 19, 21, 25, 26, 28, 34, 49, 50; 5:6, 14; 6:5, 8, 12, 19, 20; 7:6, 50; 8:3, 4, 39; 9:12, 13, 17; 11:7, 8, 11, 23, 24, 27, 34, 38, 39², 40, 44; 12:4, 22⁴, 23; 13:4², 5, 6², 8, 9, 10, 24, 25, 26³, 27, 31, 36, 37, 38; 14:5, 6, 8, 9, 22; 16:29; 18:3, 4, 5, 17², 26, 28, 29, 38²; 19:4, 5, 6, 9, 10, 14, 15, 26, 27, 28; 20:1², 2³, 5, 6², 12, 13², 14, 15², 16², 17, 18, 19, 22, 26, 27, 29; 21:3², 5, 7, 9, 10, 12, 13³, 15³, 16³, 17³, 19, 20, 21, 22

homoeoteleuton, 13:32
hortatory subjunctive: *see* subjunctive (hortatory)

ἵνα (appositional), 17:3
ἵνα (complementary), 8:56; 9:22; 17:4, 15², 21², 24
ἵνα (direct object), 4:47; 13:2; 19:31, 38
ἵνα (epexegetical), 1:27; 2:25; 5:7; 6:29, 39, 40; 9:39; 11:57; 12:23; 13:1, 34; 15:8, 12, 13, 17; 16:2, 30, 32; 17:2, 3; 18:37, 39
ἵνα (imperatival), 1:22; 13:19, 34; 18:9, 32
ἵνα (purpose), 1:7², 8, 19, 22, 31; 3:15, 17², 20, 21; 4:8, 15; 5:14, 23, 34, 36, 40; 6:5, 12, 15, 28, 30, 38, 50; 7:3, 23, 32; 8:6, 59; 9:3, 36; 10:10², 17, 31, 38; 11:4, 11, 15, 16, 19, 31, 42, 52, 53, 55; 12:7, 9, 10, 20, 35, 36, 38, 42, 46, 47²; 13:15, 18, 19; 14:3, 13, 16, 29, 31; 15:2, 11, 16², 17, 25; 16:1, 4, 24, 33; 17:1, 2, 4, 11, 12, 13, 19, 21, 22, 23², 24, 26; 18:9, 28, 32, 36, 37; 19:4, 16, 24, 28, 31, 35, 36; 20:31²
ἵνα (purpose-result), 3:16; 9:39; 12:40
ἵνα (result), 4:36; 5:20; 6:7, 50; 9:2; 11:37; 17:21
ἵνα (subject), 11:50; 16:7
ἵνα (temporal), 12:23; 16:2, 32
ἵνα (predicate), 4:34
infinitive (cause with διὰ τό), 2:24
infinitive (complementary), 1:43, 46; 3:2, 3, 4³, 5, 7, 9, 14, 27, 30²; 4:4, 20, 24, 33, 47; 5:6, 10, 18, 19, 30, 35, 39, 40, 44; 6:6, 10, 15², 21, 44, 52, 60, 65, 67, 71; 7:1², 4, 7, 17, 19, 20, 25, 30, 34, 35³, 36, 39, 44; 8:5, 21, 22, 26², 37, 40, 43, 44; 9:4², 16, 27², 33; 10:16, 21, 29, 35, 39; 11:8, 37, 44, 51; 12:4, 21, 33, 34, 39; 13:5², 14, 33, 36, 37; 14:5, 17, 22; 15:4, 5; 16:12², 19; 18:8, 31, 32; 19:7, 12, 40; 20:9; 21:6, 12, 22, 23
infinitive (direct object), 5:26; 8:6

infinitive (epexegetical), 1:12; 4:32; 5:27; 10:18²; 13:10; 19:10²
infinitive (indirect discourse), 4:40; 12:18, 29; 16:2; 21:25
infinitive (purpose), 1:33; 4:7², 9, 10, 15, 38; 6:31, 52; 13:24; 14:2; 21:3
infinitive (subject), 18:14
infinitive (temporal with πρίν), 4:49; 8:58; 14:29
infinitive (temporal with πρὸ τοῦ), 1:48; 13:19; 17:5
internally headed relative clause, 6:14; 11:6

καθώς (causal), 17:2
καθώς (comparative), 1:23; 3:14; 5:23, 30; 6:31, 57, 58; 7:38; 8:28; 10:15; 12:14, 50; 14:27; 15:10, 12; 17:11, 14, 16, 21, 22, 23; 19:40
καθώς ... καί (point/counterpoint), 13:5, 33, 34; 15:9; 17:18; 20:21
καθώς ... οὕτως (point/counterpoint), 14:31; 15:4
καί (adjunctive), 1:31, 32, 33, 34; 2:2; 3:23; 4:45; 5:17, 19, 21, 26, 37, 39; 6:11, 57², 67; 7:3, 10, 47, 52; 8:19, 53; 9:15, 27, 40; 10:16; 11:16, 37; 12:10, 18, 26, 42; 13:14, 32; 14:1, 3, 7, 12, 19; 15:9, 20², 23, 27; 16:22; 17:18, 19, 21, 24; 18:2, 5, 17, 18, 25; 19:19, 23, 35, 39; 20:6, 8, 21, 30; 21:3, 20
καί (ascensive), 1:31, 33, 34; 8:14, 16, 25, 38; 10:38; 11:22, 25; 12:42; 14:12
καί (epexegetical), 1:16; 10:33; 12:13; 14:6
κατά (distributive), 8:9; 10:3; 21:25
κατά (opposition), 18:29; 19:11
κατά (purpose), 2:6
κατά (standard), 7:24; 8:15; 18:31; 19:7

lectio difficilior, 1:24; 6:36; 16:13; 17:24; 20:18; 21:4
left-dislocation, 1:12, 18, 31, 33²; 3:14, 26, 32; 5:11, 19, 21, 26, 37, 38; 6:39², 57; 7:10, 18, 27, 31, 38; 8:26, 28, 45; 10:1, 25; 11:6; 12:16, 48; 13:27; 14:12, 13, 21, 26; 15:2², 5; 17:2², 24; 18:9, 11
litotes, 2:12; 3:34; 6:37

μέν ... δέ (point/counterpoint), 10:41; 16:9, 10, 11, 22
μετά (association/accompaniment), 3:2, 22, 25, 26; 4:27²; 6:3, 33, 66; 7:33; 8:29; 9:37, 40; 11:16, 31, 54, 56; 12:8, 17; 13:8, 33; 14:9, 16, 30; 15:27; 16:4, 19, 32; 17:12, 24; 18:2, 5, 18, 26; 19:18; 20:24; 20:26
μετά (manner), 18:3; 19:40; 20:7
μετά (temporal), 2:12; 3:22; 4:43; 5:1, 14; 6:1; 7:1; 11:7, 11; 13:7; 13:27; 19:28, 38; 20:26; 21:1
metacomment, 1:51; 3:3, 5, 11; 4:35; 5:19, 24, 25; 6:26, 32, 47, 53; 8:34, 51, 58; 10:1, 7; 12:24; 13:16, 20, 21, 38; 14:12; 16:20, 23; 21:18
metonymy, 6:55²
μή (introducing a question expecting a negative answer), 3:4; 4:12, 29, 33; 6:67; 7:31, 35, 41, 47, 48, 51, 52; 8:53; 9:27, 40; 10:21; 18:17, 25; 21:5
μή ... ἀλλά (point/counterpoint), 3:16; 6:27, 39; 7:24; 18:40; 19:21, 24; 20:27
μὴ μόνον ... ἀλλὰ καὶ (point/counterpoint), 13:9
μήποτε (introducing a question expecting a negative answer), 7:26
μήτι (introducing a question expecting a negative answer), 8:22; 18:35

neuter plural subject with singular verb, 1:28; 3:9, 19, 20, 21, 23; 5:36; 6:23, 63; 7:7; 9:3; 10:3, 4, 6, 21, 41; 12:16; 15:7; 16:15; 19:28, 31, 36; 20:30, 31; 21:25
nominalizer, 1:29, 35, 43, 45; 4:31; 5:28; 6:22, 62, 66; 7:50; 8:11, 23², 44; 9:8; 12:12; 18:6, 16; 19:23, 25, 38; 20:14; 21:2
nominative absolute, 19:19, 21

nominative complement in a double nominative construction, 1:41, 42²; 3:2; 4:25; 5:2; 8:4, 9; 9:7, 11; 11:16; 12:46; 19:17; 20:24; 21:2
nominative for vocative, 1:29; 12:15; 13:13²; 19:3; 20:28²
nominative in apposition, 1:18, 23, 27, 40, 42; 3:1, 13; 4:26; 5:29², 36; 6:4, 8², 15, 27, 42, 71; 7:2; 8:56; 10:16; 11:1, 2, 11, 27², 27, 39, 45, 49; 12:4², 13, 14²; 14:22, 26; 15:26; 16:13, 32; 18:2, 5, 16, 17; 19:19², 25², 38; 20:1, 18, 24, 31
nominative of exclamation, 1:29, 36, 47; 19:14, 26, 27
nominative (pendent), 6:39; 7:38; 8:45; 15:2; 17:2; 18:9, 11
nominative (predicate), 1:1², 4, 6, 8, 9, 14, 19², 20, 21², 22, 23, 25³, 33, 34, 40, 42, 49²; 3:1, 6², 10, 19, 28; 4:9, 10, 14, 18, 19, 24, 29, 34; 5:12, 13, 15, 27, 35, 39; 6:10, 14, 22, 29, 33, 35, 39, 40, 41, 42, 48, 50, 51², 55², 58; 6:63³, 64³, 69, 70; 7:18, 25, 26, 36, 40, 41, 49, 50; 8:12, 18, 25, 31, 33, 34, 37, 39², 42, 44³, 48, 54³, 55; 9:5, 8², 9², 14, 17, 19, 20, 24, 25, 27, 28², 36, 37; 10:1², 2, 6, 7, 8², 9, 11, 12², 13, 14, 16, 24, 33, 34, 36; 11:2, 25², 27, 38, 49, 51; 12:2, 6, 24, 34, 36, 42, 50; 13:10, 11, 25, 26, 35; 14:6³, 21; 15:1², 5², 8, 12, 14; 16:17, 18; 17:3, 6, 9, 10, 11, 17, 21, 22²; 18:10, 13², 14, 15, 26, 30, 33, 35, 37², 38, 40; 19:12, 21, 38; 20:14, 15, 31; 21:4, 7², 12², 20, 21, 24
nominative subject, 1:1³, 2, 3³, 4², 5², 6, 7², 8, 9², 10², 11, 12, 13, 14, 15³, 16, 17², 18³, 19⁴, 20, 21², 23², 25, 26³, 27, 28², 30⁴, 31², 32, 33⁴, 34², 35, 37, 38², 39, 40, 41², 42⁴, 43, 44, 45², 46³, 47², 48², 49³, 50; 2:1², 2, 3, 4³, 5, 6, 9³, 10², 11², 12, 13², 17², 18, 19, 20³, 21, 22², 23, 24, 25²; 3:1, 2⁴, 3², 4², 5², 6², 8², 9², 10², 13², 14, 15, 16², 17², 18², 19⁵, 20², 21², 22, 23², 24, 25, 26⁴, 27², 28², 29³, 31³, 32, 33², 34, 35, 36³; 4:1⁴, 2², 5, 6³, 7², 8, 9², 10³, 11², 12³, 13², 14³, 15, 17², 19², 20³, 21², 22³, 23³, 24, 25³, 26², 27², 28, 29², 31, 32², 33², 34², 35³, 36², 37³, 38⁴, 39, 40, 41, 42², 44², 45, 46², 47², 48, 49, 50⁴, 51², 52, 53⁴, 54; 5:1², 2, 3, 5, 6, 7⁴, 8, 9², 10², 11², 12, 13², 14², 15², 16, 17³, 18, 19⁴, 20², 21², 22, 23², 24, 25³, 26, 28², 30², 31², 32², 33, 34², 35², 36⁴, 37², 38², 39², 43², 44, 45³, 46; 6:1, 2, 3, 4, 5³, 7³, 8, 9³, 10³, 11, 12, 13, 14², 15, 16², 17², 18, 20, 21, 22⁵, 23, 24², 26, 27², 29³, 30, 31, 32³, 33, 35², 37², 39, 40³, 41², 42², 43, 44³, 45², 46³, 48, 49, 50², 51⁴, 52², 53, 54², 55², 56², 57⁴, 58³, 60³, 61³, 63⁴, 64⁵, 65, 66, 67², 68, 69², 70³, 71; 7:1², 2, 3², 4², 5, 6³, 7³, 8³, 10², 11², 12³, 13, 14, 15², 16², 17², 18⁴, 19², 20², 21, 22, 23², 25², 26², 27², 28³, 29³, 30², 31³, 32², 33, 34², 35³, 36³, 37², 38³, 39³, 40, 41³, 42³, 43, 44², 45², 46², 47², 48, 49, 50, 51, 52², 53; 8:1, 2, 3, 4², 5², 6, 7, 9, 10², 11³, 12³, 13³, 14⁴, 15², 16³, 17, 18², 19², 20², 21³, 22³, 23⁴, 24, 25², 26², 28³, 29², 30, 31², 32, 33, 34², 35², 36, 37, 38², 39², 40², 41² 42⁴, 44³, 45, 46², 47², 48³, 49³, 50², 51, 52⁴, 53³, 54⁵, 55, 56, 57, 58², 59; 9:2⁴, 3⁴, 4³, 7, 8², 9⁵, 10, 11³, 12, 14, 15, 16⁵, 17, 18, 19², 20², 21², 22³, 23, 24³, 25, 27, 28², 29², 30³, 31², 32, 33, 34², 35², 36, 37², 39⁴, 40, 41²; 10:1², 2, 3², 4, 6², 7², 8³, 9², 10², 11², 12³, 14², 15², 16, 17², 18², 19, 20, 21³, 22², 23, 24², 25⁴, 26, 27², 28², 29², 30, 31, 32, 33², 34², 35², 36², 38², 40, 41⁴, 42; 11:1, 2², 3², 4³, 5, 8², 9³, 10², 11, 12, 13², 14², 16², 17, 18, 19, 20³, 21², 22, 23², 24, 25³, 26, 27², 28, 29, 30², 31, 32³, 33, 35, 36, 37³, 38², 39², 40, 41, 42², 44², 45, 46², 47², 48², 49², 50², 51, 54, 55², 56, 57²; 12:1³, 2², 3², 4, 5, 7, 9, 10, 11, 12², 13, 14, 15, 16³, 17, 18, 19², 20, 21, 22², 23³, 24, 25², 26⁵, 27, 28, 29³, 30², 31², 32, 34⁵, 35⁴, 36, 38³, 39, 41, 42, 44², 45, 46², 47², 48³, 49², 50³; 13:1², 2, 3, 6, 7³, 8², 9, 10⁴, 11, 13, 14², 15², 16²,

18³, 19, 20², 21², 22, 23², 24², 25, 26³, 27², 28, 29³, 30², 31³, 32², 33², 34, 35, 36², 37, 38²; 14:1, 2, 3², 4, 5, 6³, 8, 9², 10⁴, 11², 12⁴, 13, 14, 16, 17², 19⁴, 20⁴, 21⁴, 22², 23³, 24², 26⁴, 27³, 28², 30, 31²; 15:1², 3, 4³, 5⁵, 6², 7, 8, 9², 10, 11², 12, 13², 14², 15², 16⁴, 18, 19³, 20², 23, 24, 25, 26⁴, 27; 16:2², 4², 5, 6, 7³, 8, 11, 13, 14, 15², 17, 18, 19, 20⁴, 21³, 22³, 24, 25, 26, 27³, 29, 30, 31, 32², 33; 17:1³, 3, 4, 5, 7, 8², 9, 10², 11³, 12⁴, 14³, 16, 17, 18, 19², 21⁶, 22², 23⁴, 24², 25⁴, 26²; 18:1³, 2², 3, 4, 5², 6, 8², 9, 10², 11², 12, 13, 14, 15², 16², 17³, 18², 19, 20⁴, 21², 22, 23, 24, 25³, 26³, 27², 29, 30, 31³, 32, 33², 34³, 35³, 36⁵, 37⁶, 38³, 39, 40; 19:1, 2, 4, 5², 6⁴, 7², 8, 9², 10, 11², 12³, 13, 14², 15³, 17, 19, 20³, 21², 22, 23², 24², 25, 26, 27, 28³, 29, 30, 31⁵, 32, 34², 35⁴, 36³, 37, 38², 39, 40, 41³, 42; 20:1, 2, 3, 4², 6, 7, 8, 10, 11, 12, 13, 15⁴, 16³, 17, 18, 19³, 20, 21⁴, 24³, 25, 26⁴, 28, 29², 30², 31; 21:1, 2², 3², 4², 5, 7³, 8, 10, 11², 12³, 13, 14², 15², 16, 17⁴, 18, 20⁴, 21², 22³, 23⁴, 24², 25³

objective genitive: *see* genitive (objective)
ὀπίσω (temporal), 1:15, 27, 30
ὀπίσω (locative), 12:19
ὅπως (purpose), 11:57
ὅταν (temporal), 2:10; 4:25; 5:7; 7:27, 31; 8:28, 44; 9:5; 10:4; 13:19; 14:29; 15:26; 16:4, 13, 21²; 21:18
ὅτε (temporal), 1:19; 2:22; 4:21, 23, 45; 5:25; 6:24; 9:4; 12:6, 17; 13:12, 31; 16:25; 17:12; 19:6, 8, 23, 30; 20:24; 21:15, 18
ὅτι (appositional), 3:21; 5:28; 9:30; 16:19; 21:23
ὅτι (causal), 1:15, 16, 17, 30, 50; 2:25; 3:18, 23; 4:22, 27; 5:16, 18, 27, 28, 30, 38, 39; 6:2, 26², 38, 41; 7:1, 7, 8, 23, 29, 30, 35, 39; 8:14, 16, 20, 22, 29, 37, 43, 44², 45, 47; 9:16, 17, 22; 10:4, 5, 13, 17, 26, 33, 36; 11:9, 10, 47; 12:6, 11, 18, 39, 41, 49; 14:2, 12, 17², 19, 22, 28²; 15:5, 15², 19, 21, 27; 16:3, 4, 6, 9, 10, 11, 14, 17, 21, 27, 32; 17:8, 9, 14, 24; 18:2, 18; 19:7, 20, 42; 20:13, 29; 21:17
ὅτι (clausal complement), 3:7; 4:35; 11:15; 14:28
ὅτι (clausal complement; direct discourse), 1:20, 32; 3:11, 28; 4:17, 35, 37, 39, 42, 52; 5:24, 25; 6:14, 42; 7:12; 8:33, 34, 54; 9:9², 11, 17, 23, 41; 10:7, 34, 36, 41; 11:56; 13:11, 21, 33; 14:2; 16:15, 20; 18:9; 19:21; 20:13, 18
ὅτι (clausal complement; indirect discourse), 1:34, 50; 2:17, 22; 3:2, 28; 4:1², 19, 20, 21, 25, 35, 42, 44, 47, 51, 53; 5:6, 15, 24, 25, 32, 36, 42, 45; 6:5, 15, 22², 24, 36, 46, 61, 65, 69; 7:7, 22, 26, 42, 52; 8:24², 27, 28, 34, 37, 48, 52, 55; 9:8, 18, 19, 20², 24, 25, 29, 31, 35; 10:38; 11:6, 13, 20, 22, 24, 27, 31², 40, 41, 42², 50, 51, 56; 12:9, 12, 16, 19, 34², 50; 13:1, 3², 19, 21, 29, 35; 14:2, 10, 11, 20, 28, 31; 15:18, 25; 16:4, 15, 19, 20, 26, 27, 30²; 17:7, 8², 21, 23, 25; 18:8, 14, 37; 19:4, 10, 28, 35; 20:9, 14, 15, 18, 31; 21:4, 7, 12, 15, 16, 17, 23, 24
ὅτι (consecutive), 14:22
ὅτι (direct object clause), 3:33
ὅτι (epexegetical), 2:18; 3:19; 14:22; 16:9, 10, 11, 21
ὅτι (subject clause), 8:17; 9:32
ὅτι-*recitativum*: *see* ὅτι (clausal complement; direct discourse)
οὐ (introducing a question expecting an affirmative answer), 4:35; 6:45, 70; 7:19, 25, 42; 8:48; 9:8; 10:34; 11:37, 40; 14:10; 18:26
οὐ . . . ἀλλά (point/counterpoint), 1:8, 13, 31, 33; 3:17, 28, 36; 4:2; 5:24, 30, 34; 6:22, 26, 32, 38; 7:10, 16, 22, 28; 8:16, 49; 10:33; 11:4, 51; 12:6, 16, 30, 44, 47, 49; 14:24; 15:16, 19; 16:13; 17:9, 15; 19:33, 34; 20:7; 21:23
οὐ . . . εἰ μή (point/counterpoint), 6:22, 46; 10:10; 13:10; 19:15

οὐ μή . . . ἀλλά (point/counterpoint), 4:14; 10:5
οὐ μόνον . . . ἀλλὰ καί (point/counterpoint), 5:18; 11:52; 12:9; 17:20
οὐδέ . . . ἀλλά (point/counterpoint), 5:22; 8:42
οὐδείς . . . εἰ μή (point/counterpoint), 3:13; 14:6; 17:12
οὐκέτι . . . ἀλλά (point/counterpoint), 11:54
οὔτε . . . οὔτε . . . ἀλλά (point/counterpoint), 9:3
οὐχί (introducing a question expecting an affirmative answer), 11:9

παρά (agency), 1:6; 4:9
παρά (association), 8:38; 17:5²
παρά (locative), 19:25
παρά (source), 1:14, 40; 5:34, 41, 44²; 6:45, 46; 8:38, 40; 9:16, 33; 10:18; 15:15, 26²; 16:27, 28; 17:7, 8
participle (attendant circumstance), 2:15; 8:2, 6, 8, 10; 9:11²; 12:14, 24; 13:25; 18:3²; 19:2, 29, 30; 20:7, 16
participle (attributive), 1:6, 9, 18, 29, 40²; 2:6, 9²; 3:29²; 4:5, 9², 10, 11, 14, 25; 5:2², 5, 12, 13, 23, 35², 37; 6:12, 14, 22, 27², 41, 44, 50, 51², 57, 58; 7:38, 49, 50; 8:3, 16, 18, 31; 9:7, 11, 40; 11:1, 16, 17, 31², 33, 42, 49, 52, 54; 12:4, 12, 17, 29², 49; 14:24; 15:2, 25; 18:22, 26; 19:13, 17, 24, 32, 39; 20:8, 24; 21:2, 24², 25
participle (causal), 1:9; 2:3, 23; 4:6, 45, 47; 5:6, 13, 44; 6:14, 15, 18, 61; 11:31, 38, 51; 12:6; 13:1², 3; 17:4; 18:4, 10; 19:28, 38; 20:15, 20; 21:12
participle (concessive), 4:9²; 7:15, 50; 9:25; 10:33; 12:37; 19:38; 20:26; 21:11
participle (conditional), 5:44; 15:2
participle (manner), 1:28, 31; 4:51; 7:15, 28²; 8:9²; 9:7; 11:3, 28, 32; 12:15; 13:22; 17:1; 18:18², 22, 24; 19:5, 17, 39; 20:6, 11; 21:8

participle (means), 17:4; 20:31
participle (imperfect periphrastic), 1:9, 28; 2:6; 3:23; 10:40; 11:1; 13:23; 18:18, 25, 30; 19:41
participle (perfect periphrastic), 2:17; 3:21, 27, 28; 6:31, 45, 65; 10:34, 40; 12:13, 14; 16:24; 17:19, 23; 20:30
participle (pleonastic), 1:15, 26, 32; 4:31; 6:52; 7:37; 8:12; 9:2, 19; 12:21, 23; 18:40; 19:6, 12
participle (pluperfect periphrastic), 1:24; 3:24; 12:16; 13:5; 18:18, 25²; 19:11, 19, 20
participle (predicative), 1:29, 32, 33², 36, 37, 38, 47, 48, 51³; 2:14; 5:6, 19, 38; 6:19², 62; 7:32; 8:4; 10:12; 11:33², 44; 17:13; 19:26, 33; 20:1, 5, 6, 7², 12, 14; 21:9², 20
participle (present periphrastic), 1:41
participle (purpose), 1:31; 6:6, 24; 8:6; 12:33; 18:32; 20:18; 21:19
participle (result), 5:18
participle (substantival), 1:12, 15, 22, 23, 27, 33²; 2:14, 16; 3:6², 8, 13, 15, 16, 18², 20, 21, 29, 31³, 33, 36²; 4:10, 13, 23, 24, 26, 34, 36³, 37²; 5:3, 7, 10, 11, 13, 15, 23, 24³, 25, 29², 30, 32, 39, 45; 6:2, 11, 13, 33², 35², 37, 38, 39, 40², 45², 46, 47, 54², 56², 57, 58, 63, 64²; 7:16, 18³, 28, 33, 38, 39; 8:12, 18, 26, 29, 34, 47, 50², 54; 9:4, 8³, 18, 32, 37, 39²; 10:1², 2, 12, 21; 11:2², 25, 26², 27, 37, 39, 44, 45²; 12:2, 4, 6, 13, 20, 25², 35, 44², 45², 46, 48³; 13:10, 11, 16, 18, 20³, 28; 14:9, 12, 21⁴, 24; 15:2, 5, 21, 23; 16:2, 5, 13; 17:20; 18:2, 4, 14, 21, 37; 19:11, 12, 35; 20:29²; 21:20
participle (temporal), 1:36, 38³, 42; 2:3, 15, 23; 3:4; 4:39, 47, 51, 54; 5:6², 13, 44; 6:5², 11, 14, 15, 17, 19, 23, 25, 59, 60, 61; 7:9, 14, 28², 40; 8:2, 3, 9, 10, 20, 30; 9:1, 6, 11², 25, 35; 11:4, 17, 28, 31, 32, 43, 56; 12:12, 14, 24, 36; 13:1, 2², 4, 21, 26, 30; 14:25; 16:8; 17:1; 18:1, 3,

18, 22, 32, 38; 19:2, 13, 26, 28, 33; 20:1, 5, 14, 16, 19², 20², 22, 31; 21:4, 7, 14, 19, 20, 21
partitive genitive: *see* genitive (partitive)
pendent nominative: *see* nominative (pendent)
πέραν (locative), 1:28; 3:26; 6:1, 17, 22, 25; 10:40; 18:1
περί (advantage/representation), 16:26; 17:9³, 20²
περί (reference), 1:7, 8, 15, 22, 47; 2:21, 25; 3:25; 5:31, 32², 36, 37, 39, 46; 6:41, 61; 7:7, 12, 13, 17, 32, 39; 8:13, 14, 18², 26, 46; 9:17, 18, 21; 10:13, 25, 33², 41; 11:13², 19; 12:6, 41; 13:18, 22, 24; 15:22, 26; 16:8³, 9, 10, 11, 19, 25; 18:19², 23, 34; 19:24; 21:24
periphrasis, 5:39
πλησίον (locative), 4:5
possessive genitive: *see* genitive (possessive)
predicate accusative: *see* accusative (predicate)
predicate adjective, 1:15, 27, 30, 39; 3:19, 33; 4:6, 11, 12, 35, 37³; 5:6, 9, 14², 30, 31, 32²; 6:45, 60; 7:6, 7, 12², 16, 28; 8:7, 13, 14, 16², 17, 26, 33, 36, 53; 9:2, 9, 18, 19, 20, 22, 24, 25, 31, 34, 39, 40, 41; 10:12, 29, 30, 41; 11:39; 13:10, 16², 17; 14:18, 24, 28; 15:3, 20; 16:15, 32; 17:10; 18:15, 18, 26; 19:14, 23², 31, 35; 20:4, 8, 27², 29; 21:7, 18, 24
predicate adverb, 2:1, 13; 3:8, 23; 4:6; 5:5; 6:4, 9, 22, 24, 25; 7:2; 11:55; 18:28; 19:42
predicate nominative: *see* nominative (predicate)
πρός (association), 1:1, 2
πρός (indirect object), 2:3; 3:4; 4:15, 33, 48, 49; 6:5, 28, 34; 7:3, 35, 50; 8:26, 31, 33, 57; 11:21; 12:19; 16:17; 19:24
πρός (motion toward), 1:19, 29, 42, 47; 3:2, 20, 21, 26²; 4:30, 40, 47; 5:33, 40, 45; 6:5, 17, 35, 37², 44, 45, 52, 65, 68; 7:33, 37, 45, 50; 8:2; 9:13; 10:35, 41; 11:3, 15, 19, 29, 32, 45, 46; 12:32; 13:1, 3, 6; 14:3, 6, 12, 18, 23, 28²; 16:5, 7², 10, 17, 28; 17:11, 13; 18:13, 24, 29, 38; 19:3, 39; 20:2², 10, 17³
πρός (purpose), 4:35; 13:28
πρός (reference), 21:22, 23
πρός (result), 11:4
πρός (spatial proximity), 18:16; 20:11, 12²
πρός (temporal), 5:35

redundant quotative frame, 1:20, 25, 48, 50; 2:18, 19; 3:3, 9, 10, 27; 4:7, 13, 17; 5:19; 6:26, 29, 43; 7:16, 21, 52; 8:14, 39, 48; 9:20, 30, 34, 36; 12:30, 44; 13:7, 21; 14:23; 18:25, 30; 20:28
right-dislocation, 1:12, 45; 3:1, 2, 13; 4:26; 6:8², 27; 8:40; 9:13

second (anarthrous) predicate position, 2:6; 9:1
second attributive position, 1:9, 29, 40, 41; 2:9; 3:16, 29²; 4:9, 11; 5:12, 23, 30², 35, 43; 6:13, 14, 22, 27², 32, 38, 41, 44, 50, 51², 58; 7:6², 18, 49; 8:16, 17, 31, 37, 43², 56; 9:11; 10:11², 26; 11:31², 42, 52; 12:12, 17, 26, 29²; 14:15, 26; 15:1, 9, 11, 12, 25; 17:13, 17, 24; 18:10, 16², 35, 36; 19:24, 32; 20:8; 21:24²
second predicate position, 1:29, 32, 33, 36, 47, 51³; 2:14; 5:19, 22, 36, 38; 6:10, 19², 62; 7:32; 8:4; 10:4, 12; 11:44; 12:9, 12; 17:10
subjective genitive: *see* genitive (subjective)
subjunctive (deliberative), 6:5, 28; 12:27, 49²; 18:11, 39; 19:15
subjunctive (hortatory), 11:7, 15, 16; 14:31; 19:24²
subjunctive with ἄν, 1:33; 2:5; 4:14; 5:19; 10:38; 11:22; 14:13
subjunctive with ἐάν, 3:2, 3, 5, 12, 27; 4:48; 5:19, 31, 43; 6:44, 51, 53², 62, 65; 7:17, 37, 51²; 8:14, 16, 24, 31, 36, 51, 54, 55; 9:22, 31²; 10:9; 11:9, 10, 40, 48; 12:24², 26, 32, 47;

13:8, 17, 35; 14:3², 14, 15; 15:4², 6, 7³, 10, 14; 16:7², 23; 19:12; 20:25³; 21:22, 23, 25
subjunctive with ἵνα, 1:7², 8, 19, 22, 27, 31; 2:25; 3:15, 16², 17², 20, 21; 4:8, 15², 34², 36, 47²; 5:7, 14, 20, 23, 34, 36, 40; 6:5, 7, 12, 15, 28, 29, 30², 38, 39², 40, 50²; 7:3, 23, 32; 8:6, 56, 59; 9:2, 3, 22, 36, 39²; 10:10⁵, 17, 31, 38²; 11:4, 11, 15, 16, 19, 31, 37, 42, 50², 52, 53, 55, 57²; 12:7, 9, 10, 20, 23, 35, 36, 38, 40³, 42, 46, 47²; 13:1, 2, 15, 18, 19, 29, 34²; 14:3, 13, 16, 29, 31; 15:2, 8², 11, 12, 13, 16⁴, 17, 25; 16:1, 2, 4, 7, 24, 30, 32², 33; 17:1, 2, 3, 4, 11, 12, 13, 15², 19, 21³, 22, 23², 24², 26; 18:9, 28², 32, 36, 37, 39; 19:4, 16, 24, 28, 31³, 35, 36, 38; 20:31²
subjunctive with ὅπως, 11:57
subjunctive with ὅταν, 2:10; 4:25; 5:7; 7:27, 31; 8:28, 44; 9:5; 10:4; 13:19; 14:29; 15:26; 16:4, 21²; 21:18
σύν (association/accompaniment), 12:2; 18:1; 21:3
synecdoche, 1:12; 2:23; 3:18; 15:21; 20:31

temporal frame, 1:1, 30, 35, 38, 43, 48; 2:1, 9, 10, 12, 22, 23; 3:2; 4:1, 31, 40, 43, 45; 5:1, 7, 14; 6:1, 12, 22; 7:1, 37; 8:7; 9:5; 10:4; 11:11, 20, 22, 29, 32, 33, 53; 12:1, 12, 16, 27, 31, 36; 13:1, 19, 31; 14:29; 16:5, 13; 17:5, 7, 12, 13; 19:1, 8, 30; 20:1
third attributive position, 1:18; 4:25; 5:2; 7:50; 11:16; 20:24; 21:2
topical frame, 1:1, 2, 3², 4², 5², 10², 11, 14, 15, 17², 18, 19, 21, 24, 25, 26, 28, 30, 31, 33, 34, 38, 39, 42², 45, 49; 2:5, 8, 9, 10, 15, 16, 17, 20, 23, 24; 3:2, 14, 15, 16, 18², 20, 21, 26², 30², 31³, 33, 35, 36²; 4:8, 12, 13, 18, 20, 23, 32, 38, 42², 44², 46; 5:20, 33, 34, 36, 39, 43, 45²; 6:6, 14², 18, 33, 35²; 7:6², 18, 40, 41; 8:7, 12, 21, 35², 38², 44, 47, 49², 50, 53; 9:30, 35; 10:2, 6, 10, 11, 12², 16, 21, 27; 11:4, 10, 11, 19, 20, 22, 25, 26, 27², 31, 32, 33, 37, 41, 42, 43, 45, 46, 49; 12:3, 8², 25², 26, 27, 29, 31, 34, 35, 44, 45, 46², 47, 48; 13:10, 13, 14, 15, 18, 20², 26, 38; 14:9, 10³, 12, 16, 20², 21, 24, 27, 28; 15:20, 23; 16:4, 7, 20, 21; 17:4, 9, 14; 18:20², 35, 36, 37², 38; 19:7, 20
TSKS construction, 5:24; 6:33, 40, 45, 54; 8:50; 9:8; 10:1; 11:2, 26; 12:48; 14:21; 20:17, 29

ὑπέρ (purpose), 11:4
ὑπέρ (reference/respect), 1:30
ὑπέρ (representation), 6:51; 10:11, 15; 15:13; 17:19
ὑπέρ (substitution), 11:50, 51, 52; 13:37, 38; 15:13; 17:19; 18:14
ὑπό (locative), 1:48
ὑπό (ultimate agency), 14:21
ὑποκάτω (locative), 1:50

vocative of direct address, 1:38², 49; 2:4; 3:2, 26; 4:11, 15, 19, 21, 31, 49; 5:7; 6:25, 34, 68; 8:4, 10, 11; 9:2, 36, 38; 11:3, 8, 12, 27, 32, 34, 39, 41, 43; 12:21, 27, 28, 38; 13:6, 9, 25, 33, 36, 37; 14:5, 8, 9, 22; 17:1, 5, 11, 21, 24, 25; 19:26; 20:13, 15², 16³; 21:5, 15², 16², 17², 20, 21

χωρίς (separation), 1:3; 15:5

ὡς (comparative), 1:14, 32; 15:6
ὡς (temporal), 2:9, 23; 4:1, 40; 6:12, 16; 7:10; 8:7; 11:6, 20, 29, 32, 33; 12:35, 36; 18:6; 19:33; 20:11; 21:9
ὥσπερ (comparative), 5:21, 26

www.ingramcontent.com/pod-product-compliance
Lightning Source LLC
Chambersburg PA
CBHW051241300426
44114CB00011B/838